A MEMOIR OF THE FUTURE

Wilfred R. Bion

A MEMOIR OF THE FUTURE

Wilfred R. Bion

Routledge
Taylor & Francis Group
LONDON AND NEW YORK

The Dream, first published 1975 by Imago Editora Ltda., Rio de Janeiro, Brazil
The Past Presented, first published 1977 by Imago Editora Ltda., Rio de Janeiro, Brazil
The Dawn of Oblivion, first published 1979 by Clunie Press
A Key to A Memoir of the Future, first published 1981 by Clunie Press

First published 1991 by Karnac Books Ltd.

Published 2018 by Routledge
2 Park Square, Milton Park, Abingdon, Oxon OX14 4RN
52 Vanderbilt Avenue, New York, NY 10017

Routledge is an imprint of the Taylor & Francis Group, an informa business

British Library Cataloguing in Publication Data

Bion, Wilfred R. (Wilfred Ruprecht), *1897–1979*
A memoir of the future. — Revised and corrected ed.
1. Psychoanalysis
I. Title
150.19'5

ISBN 13: 978-0-946439-79-9 (pbk)

To my wife
and to Parthenope, Julian and Nicola

Other titles by W. R. Bion:

Experiences in Groups
Learning from Experience
Elements of Psycho-analysis
Transformations
Attention and Interpretation
Second Thoughts
Four Discussions
Two Papers: The Grid and Caesura
Brazilian Lectures
Bion in New York and São Paulo
The Long Week-End 1897–1919: Part of a Life
All My Sins Remembered: Another Part of a Life
[together with] *The Other Side of Genius: Family Letters*
Clinical Seminars and Four Papers
Cogitations

CONTENTS

INTRODUCTION . . .
PRELUDE . . .
OVERTURE & BEGINNERS . . .
ONE, TWO, . . .

Within this book there are changes of meaning that are obvious, communicated and interpretable according to the rules of grammar and articulate speech. There are changes of rhythm that are not so obvious, but if detected they are similarly communicated and interpretable. The rules to which they conform may be more difficult to detect, as would the key of a musical composition written without the statement of the key signature. There are changes detectable only by those willing to make the effort. If no existing human mode of thinking provides a model, an approximation could be found in astronomical space. There may be modes of thinking to which no known realization has so far been found to approximate. Hallucinosis, hypochondriasis and other mental 'diseases' may have a logic, a grammar and a corresponding realization, none of which has so far been discovered. They may be difficult to discover because they are obscured by a 'memory', or a 'desire', or an 'understanding' to which they are supposed—wrongly—to approximate. Unless the obscurity can be circumvented or penetrated it will remain unobserved, as the galactic centre or the origin of the universe remains unobserved.

BOOK 1

THE DREAM

Q *Can you give me an idea what this is about?*
A *Psycho-analysis, I believe.*
Q *Are you sure? It looks a queer affair.*
A *It is a queer affair—like psycho-analysis. You'd have to read it.*
Q *How much does it cost?*
A *It says it on the book. You would have to read it as well though.*
Q *Of course. But I don't think I can afford the time or money.*
A *Nor do I.*
Q *But haven't you read it?*
A *Yes, in a way.*
Q *You're a queer salesman. I'm only wanting to know . . .*
A *I'm not the salesman. I only wrote it.*
Q *Oh, I beg your pardon! I quite thought . . .*
A *I'm flattered, but I'm only the author.*
Q *May I have your autograph?*
A *No.*
Q *Oh.*

PRO-LOGUE

I am tired. It is quite bad enough having a full day's schedule without having a full night's programme too. I do not remember what happened anyway. Something about reversed perspective. I was writing something about it. The advantage of falling back on borrowing a mathematical term like 'vertex' is that it can make it possible to talk to lunatics who are thrown into confusion if you say things like, 'from the point of view of smell'. It is very exasperating to find a man who interrupts by saying, 'My eyes don't smell', or, 'My smell can't see any view'. My exasperation doesn't help either. Now I remember a bit of a dream about violence and murder. Something about Albert and Victoria, I think. Suppose these vertices are separate and distinct, the two vertices could contribute to a harmonization rather like binocular vision. Suppose I used my alimentary canal as a sort of telescope. I could get down to the arse and look up at the mouth full of teeth and tonsils and tongue. Or rush up to the top end of the alimentary canal and watch what my arse-hole was up to. Rather amusing really. It depends what my digestive tract felt about having me scampering up and down the gut all night. Perhaps that is what gave me such a bad night. Alice didn't think much of it obviously. But what was *she* up to then? Must remember to ask her. She seemed to think it was my fault.

Suppose the vertices were separate and coincident. This would do if one of the points which was separate and distinct rushed down the arc to meet the other; but, judging by what it felt like last night, it was more like sound travelling in bent tubes. As a matter of fact, that would only be true in a relatively gentlemanlike Oxonian manner. At night—last night—they weren't at all respectable; much more like farts and gerks rushing up and down alimentary canals.

Whether it is respectable or amusing would depend on which vertex, or who or what it was at the vertex. But here and now I know nothing about that. If I were there, with the companion to whom I wish to communicate, I could appeal to him to see the evidence I cannot formulate, but on which I wish to build my structure. It is the overriding advantage of the *practice* of psycho-analysis over anything more abstract. It is also a fact which, to me, makes any puzzlement at the disagreements between two participants, say, in a scientific meeting or supervision, different in kind from the disagreement between the two participants in a psycho-analysis (as I understand that occurrence in a relationship which I define as psycho-analysis). Anyone can employ another definition, but no one can honestly maintain that I speak without practice as that term is understood by other practitioners.

I claim (the claim itself being definitory) that this is a fictitious account of psycho-analysis including an artificially constructed dream; definitory status is also claimed for the constructions of wakefulness, scientific alertness and scientific theory. The definitory hypothesis is intended to be taken and applied in all seriousness in the practice of psycho-analysis by those who wish to confront what they believe to be 'facts', as near to noumena as the human animal is likely to get.

This may be 'never'; with Kant, I hold that the thing-in-itself is unknowable. Falstaff, a known artefact, is more 'real' in Shakespeare's verbal formulation than countless millions of people who are dim, invisible, lifeless, unreal, whose births, deaths—alas, even marriages—we are called upon to believe in, though certification of their existence is vouched for by the said official certification. 'You are a fabulous monster', said the dove to the serpent Alice. Many people are so lifeless that I could stare in silent admission that I did not believe the evidence of my senses. Nor do I believe that 'science'—smoke drums, statistics and other apparatus usually assumed to belong to the domain of science—would ever bring them to life or breathe life into them.

At one end of the spectrum I could be convinced by 'scientific' evidence that these people exist; at the other end there are fictitious characters who could be said with certainty *not* to exist. (In terms of logic this situation is what is often described as a 'paradox'.) The 'softly breathing bronzes' of whom Virgil speaks in his tribute to Marcellus can be described as a poetic formulation of a visual image. The same is true of the heroes rescued from the black night that engulfed the many brave men before Homer immortalized Agamemnon; or the sculptures conjured from the marble by Michelangelo or Praxiteles. They can be re-buried. Confronted by a work of art, there are 'clever men' who can see that it is genuine and worth a lot of money, but they may *not* see what the artist has revealed.

To turn to psycho-analysis: the erudite can see that a description is by Freud, or Melanie Klein, but remain blind to the thing described. Freud said infants were sexual; this was denied or reburied. This fate could have befallen the whole of psycho-analysis had there been no one to confer, as Horace said of Homer, immortality.

If psycho-analytic intuition does not provide a stamping ground for wild asses, where is a zoo to be found to preserve the species? Conversely, if the environment is tolerant, what is to happen to the 'great hunters' who lie unrevealed or reburied?

ONE

'O dear, oh dear', said Alice rubbing her eyes and pushing away the shower of leaves which had awoken her. 'I had such a queer dream that I was the Empress of India. Rosemary! Now where has that tiresome girl gone? I had quite forgotten I had dismissed her! For such impudence too. Ah, here she is—with her suitcase packed I am glad to see.' Alice sounded quite severe as her maid came into the room, with her shawl and bonnet, ready to leave. She was deferential, almost obsequious, Alice was glad to note. 'You called me, Ma'am?' 'Before you go—there is still half an hour before the last train so you have plenty of time—just gather up these leaves which have blown in through the window you so carelessly left open.' The maid put down her case and shawl before falling on her knees to gather up the mess. She was attractive, Alice had to admit; indeed her attractiveness had been 'the last straw', for she had appealed so strongly to Roland, Alice's husband, that his wayward glances lingered, in Alice's opinion, a shade too long upon her features. Misgivings that she had been unfair awoke at the sight of the slim kneeling figure gathering up the leaves. They were stifled; 'her behaviour to poor Tom was really quite intolerable'.

'I've cleared it all, Ma'am', she said at last, 'can I go now?' Alice was almost ready to let her go when Rosemary added, 'It is almost time now and they do say it is the last train'. Alice, herself famous for her beauty, allowed the compassion in her expression to relax into its customary insolence. 'Let me look at what you have gathered', she said, taking the leaves from Rosemary's nervous hands. She was aware that the leaves which she was scrutinizing with deliberate slowness were the pages of a dismembered Bible.

'Oh please, Ma'am, may I go now?' she broke in, 'or I shall miss the train and they do say it will be the last before the enemy come. I want to go—please!' she begged. 'With Tom?' 'Yes, Ma'am—and please won't you and Roland leave too? I'm sure it won't be safe when the enemy soldiers come.'

Alice drew herself up haughtily. 'I am sure that *Mister* Roland will be quite safe with me.' 'Oh, Ma'am, I didn't mean that—really I didn't—please can I go now?' 'We shall not run away. These are civilized enemies . . .' But Rosemary, unable to stand it any more, had picked up her traps and run. Alice, realizing she was alone, was reading the words on a torn scrap. 'And the Satyr shall cry to his fellow.' That was all.

For a time she sat brooding in silence. Night was falling; she could hear carts lumbering westwards; men and women; animals. She was brave; she prided herself on not being afraid like her maid. What could be expected of Rosemary? 'Tell Mister Roland to come . . .' but Rosemary had gone; with Tom.

TWO

Tom was a powerful lout who worked about the farm attached to the main building. He was an excellent servant and reliable in work which required strength but no initiative or intelligence. His grin was a feature of the homestead. Roland had sometimes spoken of his cruelty, but Alice did not think it amounted to much more than the thoughtlessness of a good-humoured but otherwise likeable person. It was exasperating when Rosemary complained that she had been assaulted by him. Roland was unwilling to dismiss him. He was too valuable a worker, he said; besides, who knew what Rosemary had been up to? She was no saint—always making eyes at all and sundry. 'Well, *you* ought to know', said Alice with meaning that made Roland colour angrily. 'Don't be ridiculous, Alice. You're jealous. She's pretty in a servant-girlish sort of way and she may have made eyes at Tom I admit—very probable in fact; but I don't want to lose a good workman.' So it fell to Alice to see her lady's maid as the culprit. This she was willing to do, for she was jealous and her jealousy was not appeased by her own very good looks. After thinking the matter over she called Rosemary to see her privately.

'I am very worried by what you told me yesterday, Rosemary. The master says Tom is a good worker and he is certain—he told me positively—that he would not do anything bad. Are you sure you didn't lead him on?' The girl coloured indignantly. 'Oh *no,* Ma'am—I would never do such a thing. I was passing by the dairy and he called me to tell me something—I went into the barn where he was standing and . . .' Alice dropped her eyes but listened with attention to a sordid story of near rape and not so distant seduction. Rosemary was angry—and frightened. Alice paused; then went on thoughtfully, 'You have to be careful. You are a girl that men find pretty and it would be awkward if you had a baby. Especially by Tom because I know my husband, *Mister* Roland, wouldn't like that.' Alice's face, despite its beauty, was hard as she watched her maid to detect a reaction to her words. Rosemary's eyes had become hard and bright. Alice went on, 'Have you any followers, Rosemary? You can tell me without fear. I only want to help you.' 'No, Miss, except . . .' 'Yes? Except?' 'Only Tom, Miss.' Alice relaxed. 'Yes, I think he is a nice boy. And God-fearing. It will help you if . . .' 'I know he's in love with me, Ma'am . . .' Rosemary's eyes did not relax their hard, animal stare, '. . . if you have a man's love to fall back on'. 'Oh, I have indeed, Miss . . . Ma'am, I mean.' Alice dismissed her after some more minutes of near conversation; she had wondered if she could dare to mention how great a support it had always been to her that she could fall back on the security of Roland's love. It was only after she had told Rosemary she could go that she began to suspect that her assumption of her maid's need for warning, maternal love was misplaced. Her small sarcasm at Roland's susceptibility to a pretty face began to harden, to remain undigested. Envy lay waiting, single-celled, to become malignant.

All night long the noise of traffic rolled; distant gunfire occasionally flickered, like summer lightning, noiselessly in the clouds. Alice composed herself to sleep in her chair, judging that anything more elaborate would scarcely be appropriate to the reception of the enemy forces when they arrived. Roland, having seen that the rituals about the farm had been ceremonially accomplished, drew a chair up next to Alice and set himself to ignore the rolling of the tumbrils. As dawn revealed the shapes of the furniture, Alice awoke to the strange familiarity of things familiar to her since babyhood; even her feelings seemed like old friends, made strange by their inappropriateness to the arrival of a conquering army. She rehearsed each step with a sleepless, unkempt Roland. 'Of course I shall not hide anything. "Here are the keys to all the locks on these premises. I think you will find everything correct." Then I shall retire.' Roland agreed that this would be the most dignified course. 'I don't think you are really putting your mind to it, dear', said Alice solicitously. 'When do you think they will arrive?' He examined his fingers meticulously. 'They are not like invited guests you know. They have not told me when the party is due to start.' She was vexed and felt the occasion was too serious for sarcasms.

THREE

Gunfire died away: the enemy did not come; preparations for his reception languished, first misted over by Alice's vivid but diminishing anxiety, finally swallowed by the background of her boring life with Roland, the routine of the farm. Alice noticed with surprise that she was bored when something made her tax Roland with lack of interest. He flushed guiltily—itself a novel change in the level uniformity of the ardours of their passion. He tried to restore the familiarity of love. Alice was not reassured as his protestations and denials formed into a hard, smooth coat of love which fitted like a strait-jacket.

She purred furiously till her rage turned to clanging heartbeats beating the murder out of her. 'I will be good . . . no hate or bitterness in my . . . write it out, fifty times . . .'

There was a disturbance in the yard, hurried footsteps and a woman's voice crying furiously, 'Let go! Let me go!' A man swore in pain. 'You bloody bitch . . .!' And then steps running up to the room where Alice and Roland waited in sudden fear to see—what next?

It was typical of these times: an eternity of boredom displaced without warning by flaming dread. Alice and Roland waited with ashen faces and staring, questioning eyes. The pounding footsteps fused with their pounding hearts—battered from without and within. The door crashed open and a woman half fell into the room.

She was gorgeously dressed in a quilted, crimson gown. With open mouth she looked from Alice to Roland, stammering with fear. 'Oh, Miss! I'm sorry, Miss. I couldn't help it, Miss! You sent me away before! I couldn't . . . the last train couldn't go. They stopped it and turned us off.'

A car in the yard started up and drove away, the sound of its engine fading into the distance. Then silence flowed back into the room where the three had stopped to listen. Alice recovered her voice first. 'Rosemary! What are you doing here?' Roland relaxed as if resigning further part in the talk. He noticed that Rosemary was naked but for the gown and ill-fitting shoes. Roland excused himself. 'Must see to the cows; bye-bye', and he bowed himself out of the scene.

The two women faced each other, Alice's restrained, good taste contrasting drably with the tattered splendour of her maid's finery. Alice was tense; Rosemary stared as if unable to comprehend her mistress's incomprehension. 'You can't send me away! They will catch me, like they did before, before I got to the train.'

'You must go!—at once!'

'I can't. I won't! How can you be so cruel?' Alice stretched out her hand as if to compel her towards the door. The movement released something in Rosemary who at once held Alice's hand and bathed it in kisses. Alice was angry, frightened, tense. 'Go! Go! you fool! Can't you see? You put us all in danger!'

'I won't! I'm frightened!'

'Fool! There's nothing to be frightened of.' As she said it she was aware of the fear in her own voice. 'Let me go!' Alice struggled to free herself. Rosemary was startled by her own success. 'Oh, Miss! Forgive me. I'm sorry, really I am', but she did not let her advantage go. Alice, weakened by the months of anxiety since the day the invasion had become inevitable, was no match for her maid. Rosemary knew something of that bright world outside. Alice and Roland existed in a cocoon of fear that gripped them like steel; Alice did not know the world of which Rosemary had had a glimpse.

Alice struggled furiously to free her hands, both now gripped by her maid. 'Please forgive me!' Frightened and humiliated, 'Let go! How dare you!' Her maid stared uneasily into Alice's frightened face. It was fear now . . . not anger. Rosemary's flood of apology and prayers for forgiveness did not cease. Nor did she loosen her grip. 'Let go!' Alice could hardly hide that she was near to tears. Her background of wealthy home, conventional schooling and religion did not provide her with the dam to hold back her fear.

She was standing very near to the bed behind her. In her anxiety Rosemary had pressed her mistress ever nearer to it and a last struggle to release her wrists led Alice to pull Rosemary to her. Both girls fell over onto the bed, Rosemary uppermost. Rosemary's anxiety and guilt were overcome by lusty strength; Alice's weakness inflamed her passion.

The physical contact, her body against the young girl beneath her, caused Rosemary to stare intently into the tear-soiled face. All guilt and subordination gone, she pressed Alice's head back, exposing her throat. She forced the eyelids apart and peered into her eyes. Then she laughed—no trace of shyness now but frank curiosity. 'Why—they are blue! Such a pretty blue too! Not dark and brown like mine.' Alice was indeed a pretty and intelligent blonde, contrasting with her maid's dark colouring. The convention of the superiority of wealth combined with Alice's striking looks served to dim the power of real beauty. Alice's advantages were in eclipse. It was Rosemary who was flushed, the physically dominant, privileged girl.

Both girls were ignorant of sensuous pleasure. For Rosemary, the vital force coursing through arteries, battering her heart and temples, brought thoughts from a reservoir unknown to her. As she gazed she knew triumph. When Alice at last brought herself to meet her maid's stare, the past had gone as if it had never been. Not only had her situation changed, she had herself become the home of feelings that might have belonged to someone else, they were so strange.

Rosemary adjusted her position. The slum child, robust and dominant, luxuriated in the physical mastery. 'They are the same as we are; just as bad if we teach them what we know.' The response from her mistress was unmistakable. Alice had for so many years been starved of passionate life that she was vulnerable to her maid's manipulations. As soon as she had elicited the proof she wanted, Rosemary tossed the hair back from her eyes, sat up and rested on the edge of the bed. Alice also rose, but it was a new Alice, rosy, submissive. 'What does madam wish now?' Rosemary half turned, but without looking directly at her 'servant' held out her hand. 'The nail file, please, Alice.' 'Will that be all, Ma'am?' 'All for the present; get on with tidying the room till I want you.' Alice flushed with pleasure, but this time she was angry and resentful too. When Rosemary looked at Alice she too was aware that Alice's new-found beauty reflected a complex emotion. She might have said something if she had not at that moment seen a face in the mirror beyond Alice's shoulder. She spun round startled. Rosemary's sudden movement made Alice follow her gaze; it was only Roland.

'Roland! What are you doing here?' It was Rosemary who had recovered first. 'I see', said Alice icily, 'you have met before'. 'Oh, ra-ther!' babbled Roland. 'What an utter damned fool', Alice thought bitterly, 'that husband of mine is. Can he really ever have imagined that I didn't know what those two beauties were up to?' In one respect she was herself surprised. Rosemary recovered, to settle into that very same state of mind which Alice half expected her to deny with confusion. 'My lipstick, Alice', she said with calm authority. Unprepared for this, Alice obeyed and placed it—her special lipstick—in her maid's hand. 'Well, Roland, what have you been up to?'

It was Roland's turn to be at a loss. Rosemary was not acting a part; it was clear that there was something genuine about her hatred and contempt for both husband and wife. Without looking at either she continued her make-up in leisurely style.

Suddenly Alice lost self-control and slapped the manicure set, a present from her father, out of her maid's hand. Rosemary stood up, pale and tense. 'All right, you bloody bitch, I'll make you pay for this. This is not capitalist England now, you know!' For a moment Roland thought he understood it all. 'You fool!' he said to his wife. 'God knows what you have done with your tantrums!' For an instant Alice was abashed. Her sudden rage had taken her by surprise and now she was flooded with a feeling of intense remorse and menace.

'Come, Roland dear'—it was Rosemary speaking—'I am sure you have had a very trying day. Come to your lovey's arms.' She glared at Alice whose turn it was to be pale and frightened. 'I'm sure Alice won't mind will you? Don't bother about the manicure set—forgive and forget I say! Come, Roland', and she opened her arms in a wide embrace.

For all his hatred, Roland was not prepared for this. He hesitated, scared also by the cold contempt in his wife's eyes. 'Darling!'—it was Rosemary's mocking invitation, but she had overdone it. Roland made a response of disapproval as if the episode were some improbable joke. Were it not for the tense faces of the women and the reality of their hate for each other and the man, the participants could have been an hallucination.

A car was drawing up outside. Rosemary, nearest the window, looked out. A man in a dark suit, athletic, with a slight tendency to corpulence, was carefully closing the car door. The tension, made worse by the banality of the scene, rose to higher pitch. Rosemary had lost her arrogant assurance and turned dead white. 'Who is the Duke?' whispered Roland. 'Shut up, you bloody fool!' The man had heard something from the window at which they stood; he turned his face up to the three and froze; the stare bound them together, as it were, in perpetuity. He stared with a calm deliberation which contrasted eerily with the horror with which they looked at him. Rosemary had beads of sweat on her now sallow face. Alice could not understand.

Another man, who had been hidden by a buttress of the farm building, joined the first. 'English?' The first nodded and lost interest in them. The group at the window took advantage of the disinterest to move out of sight.

Roland scoffed, 'Whatever is the matter with you two?' Alice had no interest in Roland's futilities; her lips were pursed and bloodless, her eyes angry. 'Oh come on! What have I done?' He appealed first to one and then the other. Alice moved away. Rosemary, appealed to directly, responded as if to continue the hostile banter in which she had been interrupted. Her finery accentuated the fact of being a drab slut. Desires to humiliate his wife with her maid gave Roland's features a fleeting vivacity, but could not withstand the reality. 'I don't know what's happened to you', he said truthfully. Rosemary came to life. 'Nothing! Why, darling?' She had assumed a well-drilled representation of sexual life.

Alice, watching as she realized she was supposed to be, had none of the 'appropriate' feelings of rage and humiliation. Menace overwhelmed her. Through the growing darkness two figures detached themselves from the background of the passage beyond the door. Their entry, though quiet, was not disguised and startled the 'sexual pair'.

Neither man seemed aware that anyone other than themselves was present. They walked to the cupboards in which Alice and Roland kept their clothes and piled them on the floor, drawing up lists of all items. 'Very methodical', said Roland aloud, making no attempt to disguise his sarcasm. 'May I ask what you think you are doing?' The man whom they had first seen getting out of the car stretched himself upright. He appeared to be the senior. 'We are collecting and checking the personal effects of Mr and Mrs Trubshaw, deceased.' 'There was a maid-servant and man about the house too', said the second man; both referred to some official-looking paper. 'But we are not deceased—yet', said Roland with some asperity. 'Yet?' said the stranger. 'Must be some mistake.' 'Indeed there must!' 'I don't think it concerns us. That's the liquidation department I expect. We are only collecting up their effects.' '*Their* effects!' Alice broke in indignantly, 'But it's *our* effects'. 'Are you Mr and Mrs Trubshaw? Who's this? You Miss Slocombe, the maid? Have you seen . . .', he consulted his paper, . . . 'Mr Jeremy? He's the man isn't he? It's nothing to do with us, but contact the liquidation people; they may have made a mistake.' 'But do you mean', said Alice flushing angrily, 'you take these things away?' 'That is all we have to do.' 'Do you give us a receipt?'

The man seemed almost shocked. 'Whatever for? As soon as it's all been checked and found correct *they* give *us* a receipt.' 'Who's "they"?' 'Just the department. It's nothing to do with us. It's only because they sent us before the people who should have collected you I expect. It doesn't matter you know.' 'But these are *our* things! This is *our* farm.' It was his turn to look surprised. 'I don't think so;

it would be most unusual. Are you alive? Our list says you are deceased. Since the completion of the conquest the usual regulations come into operation.' 'What are they? We have not been told anything!' 'Well no, I don't expect so. Our people would know, but I don't imagine they would bother about what order they collect in—people or things, it's all the same to them.'

The investigation and removal continued impersonally and coldly; it was frightening in its thoroughness. Roland wanted to bluster, but the civil, patient indifference to his presence was intimidating. All Alice's belongings were neatly ticketed, parcelled, labelled—though she could not see the labels—and removed.

'You have left me none of my clothes!' she expostulated. The man understood only imperfectly. 'I have nothing but these things I stand up in!' He came over as if to reply, but all he did was check her dress cursorily, saying, 'That will do for now. You'll be told about your clothes allowance tomorrow.' He walked off before she could recover from her indignation. 'Well I'll be damned!' said Roland, following the retreating figures with his eyes. Alice turned away from him; overcome with sudden fear, she burst into tears. She felt, had felt for a long time, completely alone. She slapped away a kindly but clumsy attempt to caress her.

That night Rosemary got into bed with Roland and, laughing, pushed Alice out to fend for herself. Proud and humiliated, she went upstairs to Rosemary's bed; she could not bear to share the room with 'those two'.

FOUR

The night of Rosemary's sexual triumph was busily spent in luxuriating in her mistress's bed, her husband and her husband's downfall; she was conscious of the pleasure she felt at his weakness in succumbing to her seductions. It was his marriage and home, as well as Alice's, that she was destroying. The degradation of her class, of her beauty, was being avenged; that night she knew what it was to be the initiator. The feelings obscured the anxiety which had been her constant companion for months during which the successful invasion, its details unknown, had swept over her homeland. 'Her homeland . . .'—the phrase aroused her scorn. It was not *her* homeland; it was the homeland of the rich, the powerful, the dull, the respectable, the cheats, the hypocrites. How smug Alice had been when questioning her—damn her bloody impertinence!—about her 'followers', her 'lovers'! Rosemary remembered her fears (groundless, as it turned out) that she had been made pregnant by the powerful but dim-witted man-of-all-work, Tom. 'You must have encouraged him', Alice said. 'Tom has always been a good worker; certainly I have never known him to be anything but respectful.' Rosemary had dabbed her tear-stained face and stolen a surreptitious glance as she stood, submissively, before her mistress. 'Yes, Miss—I mean, no, Miss', she said demurely. Neither would have admitted sarcasm or ironical denial. Both were unaware that the scene in which they were actors was anything but real, so well had they learned their parts; the past was unknown, the present unobserved; the 'future' was in fact at hand this very night, as Rosemary played sensuously with Roland in Alice's bed.

She had again been 'encouraging' Tom. She and Roland were taken by surprise nevertheless. 'What's that?' said Roland sitting up with a start. 'It frightened me too', said Rosemary as she soothed him back into her arms, but she was laughing too. A muffled scream had been followed by sounds of physical struggle. 'What was it?' said Roland, partially reassured, allowing himself to sink back. 'Let's listen to them, the rascals', said Rosemary in a dreamy, reminiscent voice. 'Who is upstairs? Who's in your room?' 'Nothing, nothing—go to sleep, my pet. Or you can stay awake and listen to them if you like. It's nothing. Only Tom and Alice having a bit of fun.' Thoroughly awake, horrorstruck, Roland scrambled out of bed and began hurriedly to throw on his clothes as he groped for them in the dark. 'Don't be a fool!' Rosemary was alarmed now. 'Come back into bed!' she ordered in peremptory tones. Bewildered, unable to see where he was going, Roland at last returned, shivering, to bed. 'What's the matter with you?' she scolded as she stimulated him. 'Can't they have a bit of fun as well as us? I bet she encouraged him!' 'She wouldn't do such a thing. Who told you that story?' Roland could not see her face, but he could feel her laughing mockingly. It did not seem—or was it?—to be unkind.

The sounds from the floor above were unmistakable. Powerful feelings flooded Roland's mind, but did not include sexual passion for Rosemary. She was frightened to realize that her stimulation, usually unfailing, did not draw him to her or seduce him from fear. Both listened to the struggle. Alice's protests gradually became muffled and finally ceased altogether.

'He's murdered her! Are you sure it was Tom?' 'Of course it was.' He was not reassured; but he had sown doubt. Rosemary knew she was lying. She had encouraged the farm lout to believe that Alice would be expecting him in her, Rosemary's room. She had been an idiot to blurt out that she 'knew' anything. Besides, she did *not* know; even if it were Tom, who knew what form his rage would take if he felt Alice was fooling him? Or even if her resistance served to inflame him further? There were such things as murders of passion.

They listened. The quiet had turned to silence. The silence had become absolute. Rosemary was furious to find that her plans for the use of the night had so miscarried that dawn already lit the curtainless windows. The pair listened and watched; the growing light promised a rare day; promised, but did not fulfil. The window, framed in light, revealed lack of curtains and the room bare of its treasures. Once Rosemary had coveted them; now she was the owner. But no magnificat dispelled, or even obscured, the dread which grew with the dawn.

'I'm going upstairs', said Roland desperately. She did not restrain him, but instead joined him at the mean attic door. For a while they stood silently and gazed at the dirty and disordered bed. 'Look peaceful, don't they?'

The phrase lit up the scene of his mother lying in her coffin 'like undertaker's confectionery', he thought as he had surveyed the ghoulish artistry of funeral craftsmanship. 'Looks peaceful, don't she?'

Once, how beautiful the dawn over the English farm and field would have seemed. What might it not have promised? 'Like two kids aren't they? Come on, we can't do anything here', and Rosemary drew her arm through Roland's to go. It was too late.

FIVE

Alice, taking refuge in her maid's room, was desperate with rage and fear. She did not get into the sluttish bed, but composed herself for sleep in the wicker chair, the only comfortable chair in the room. She had been left with scant clothing; it was too dark to read even the trash she would be likely to find. Unable to ignore the cold or prevent her shivering from making the chair creak so loudly that it woke her, she escaped into thought till fact and nightmare were indistinguishable from hallucination.

These experiences became so terrifying that she was sure a man was in the room. She struggled to retain some vestige of hold on fact. When she sought to cover herself with the bedclothes she had scorned, the comfort conspired to make her feel she was in the arms of a man. Then, angry at her resistance, he threatened to bash her. She struggled against the suffocation of the bedclothes which were rammed over her head. She bit at the loathsome terms of endearment which reproached her with being mean. She was convinced it was Tom until the threats became so violent that she knew it could not be anyone so benign as the lout who was docile and contrite when she had reproved him and threatened him with instant dismissal. Even the memory turned bad and became one in which he accused her furiously of going back on the message which she had sent him by Rosemary. She was overpowered, she could not resist the assault. 'Aah . . . I can feel the lovelight in your eyes. I know! I know!' he said triumphantly. Too weak, she swooned away.

'Get up, you slut!' The order was uttered harshly. 'I can't', she managed to say. It was daylight. It was the man. 'This your boy friend?' He did not wait for an answer but turned to some subordinates. 'Take the two women to the truck', he ordered, with no attempt to disguise his contempt and indifference. 'And these two', indicating the men, 'I've done with them. Block B—in the yard.' Tom and Roland were hustled out.

For weeks Roland had been the object of sporadic and casual inquiry; the procedure had been both searching and thorough. The man who appeared to hold some authority had on one occasion made him so angry by the searching inquiry about the livestock on the farm that he asked him 'who the hell' he thought he was and turned sulky. The man did not answer or take offence—he dropped his questioning. The next day another took up the interrogation. After a day in which he had been approached by three different men, Roland voiced suspicions. 'There are a hell of a lot of Nosey Parkers around here, I must say', and told Alice why he thought so. Her indifference led him to forget his annoyance before it grew into suspicion. It did not occur to him that his complaint might indeed be a scientifically accurate observation.

Both Alice and Roland were jumpy in a way to which they were not accustomed. Their lives proceeded as they had before the invasion; they were master and wife, joined in a drab, conventional, comfortably-off fidelity. It slithered into an equally drab, conventional infidelity. Then the anxiety and dread of the approaching disaster turned to anticlimactic newslessness. One day Roland saw a number of foreign soldiers in the marketplace at Puckeridge. They looked casually at him; he dared not question them. He realized he was cowed, but did not know why. He hoped Alice would not ask why he had not found out the news—he would not be able to tell her. There *was* no news. Roland belonged to a class which assumed that if there was news he would be told it as a matter of course. Disdain had been cultivated sedulously till it was second nature to hide his poverty beneath a cover of profundity modestly concealed. Uneasy lest others would face the truth of which he was dimly aware, he swaggered and blustered and hoped no one could see his fear. Alice, likewise, was afraid lest the married unit disguise would fail to convince. The life from which Rosemary came was a better preparation for ability to recognize poverty of any kind. The opportunity for observing 'married love' from the vantage of the maid and whore provided binocular vision; with this she could now view love and war. Whether she had the ability to understand the observations which she made was not clear. Like Alice, like Roland, she was cowed, but the emotion differed for the blend differed. The victorious troops who wandered so freely about the country, the farm, the house itself, knew fear; that, likewise, had a quality which Roland knew was different from his. He had first realized this when the man whose easy insolence he was resenting sprang up to address a stranger who had joined their conversation.

When Roland and Rosemary had been confronted by the man, his unceremonious treatment frightened, but did not surprise them. Alice was suffering from an assault which she had known only as something that happened amongst the 'lower orders'. Roland had once seen a pregnant child stare at him with feral eyes and disappear suddenly, smoothly and silently as if magicked away. Such things did not happen in the world inhabited by English women. Alice had gone before he could tell her of his horror. Just as well perhaps; he had not prepared his speech. Not even clichés would come to help him bluster.

Out in the yard, he and Tom were told to wait. The memory of the pregnant child triggered off feelings which were unfamiliar to Roland. His heart beating fast, aware of great danger, he raced to the corner of the building and dropped to a slow walk. The man, talking to a subordinate on the other side of the yard, would turn in his direction in another moment. Roland slid round the corner unobserved. Where was he going? To Munden, if he could. It was three quarters of an hour's walk and he would have to cross the Puckeridge road. He thought he would be safe till then. By fields and a lane which he knew better than any stranger, it took him an hour to get to the main Puckeridge road. There he had to hide sharply to avoid being seen by approaching transport. Then silence—but for the larks in the blue sky. It was strange to be a fugitive in such a peaceful scene which he knew so well. If he were caught he would be shot—his running away made that certain. He was flying to save his life; why had he not saved Alice? Damn Alice. He did not love the bloody woman, never had, though she was still very pretty. Her looks had become hard as she had soured as they remained childless. Well, maybe she would bear a 'defective' by Tom.

When the Munden farm came in sight he realized he had no idea why he had come. Who was in occupation? What was he to do? England was a prison; it had been 'pacified'—like hell it had! How the larks sang! He had not heard them like that before. He crouched behind the pigeon cote where he commanded a good view of the homestead and stared at its door as if willing someone to come out.

Suddenly he thought he heard his name whispered from behind. He listened; it was a beautiful day, so still that all he could hear were the larks and a convoy on the main road. He began to relax. He was hearing, as if for the first time, country sounds in his own land. The voice came again, this time more urgent. Keeping his head down, he replied, 'Robin'.

SIX

Alice jolted in the back of the truck. She was battered, mentally and physically, from her night's experience; more undramatically, from her life since marriage. Near to tears of fatigue, she was unable to tolerate the sight of Rosemary in her ridiculous finery; it seemed impossible that any man could be attracted by such a slut. It was not her get-up that was sluttish; it was not her body; it was her self. Yet she had a tautness of mind which could not be said of herself or Roland.

The truck stopped. 'Get out!' They scrambled out and Alice saw she was at Braughing House, which had belonged to some friends by whom they were occasionally bored. The fabric was intact, but their solid and handsome furniture had, like themselves, been taken away. The women were shoved into the hall. 'Stand there! From now on you are under orders. You will obey instantly. And keep your bloody mouths shut!' He left them and disappeared into an inner room: they could hear men's voices.

It was cold. It must have been half an hour, during which they stood and shivered, before he reappeared. He gave them both rough, blue cotton dressing gowns. 'Take your clothes off and put these on. Come on . . . hurry!' he said angrily as they hesitated, expecting him to withdraw. 'But. . .', started Alice. He slapped her hard across the mouth, making it bleed. 'Didn't I tell you to keep your mouth shut?' He collected their clothes and walked off.

As they stood, starved, naked and trembling, despair came near to breaking the resistance of the two girls. 'I'm dreadfully sorry, Miss.' Alice noted with surprise that Rosemary was expressing real compassion. 'I know them. You don't. They are all the same.' 'You know them, Rosemary? How? Have you seen these men before?' 'Oh no, Miss. Though', she added with a meaning nod towards the door off the main hall, 'I've seen that fat rascal before. And lots more like him.' She addressed the interloper directly. 'Come on, Fatty, want a peep? Can't you get a cock stand with your girl friend?' The man quickly withdrew. 'There! You see, Miss?' she said in triumph, 'they are all the same if you talk the right language—and, begging your pardon, Miss, but I don't mean English—they know fast enough, I can tell you.'

Alice was not listening. Her attention had become wayward; since the outbreak of war she had noticed a deterioration which she supposed must have gone on longer than she knew. Interested in what her maid said, disposed to question her further, she could not sustain her train of thought. She knew this hall; with an effort she could visualize what had been its appearance when she dined here. Its drab, unfurnished condition established it as if a photographic slide had replaced the scene she knew. Where had the Calverts gone? Where had they been taken? It was easier to believe that the inhabitants of the island had been wiped out and replaced than that there had been any form of assimilation of one population by another. The village had been familiar since childhood. She had never known herself as anything but one of the gentry. Now she stood naked, incongruous, alien, without a point of reference that made sense. True, there was defeat, but this was on a scale of defeat so disastrous that it would be necessary to suppose that something analogous to the Norman Conquest had taken place.

There was movement at the other end of the hall. Two or three men and a woman came in with a jug of water and what might have been surgical instruments. The water was cold. They talked amongst themselves, but otherwise paid no attention to the two girls except to wash them and clean their bodies thoroughly, with no more concern for them than if they had been inanimate. They appeared to talk freely and replied civilly if either Alice or Rosemary spoke to them. 'May I ask what this is about?' The woman gave Alice's question consideration and then replied, 'As far as we know it is in conformity with the S18B.' 'And what is that?' She showed Alice a printed slip. It was a succinct statement, in English, of cleaning instructions. 'We are not allowed to talk to you or you to us.' And that was that. A little later Rosemary, exasperated by an unusually painful scrape between her fingers—they were usually too expert to inflict pain unless with intent—asked if she could apply for a job as a cleaner. 'Out of the question', was the curt reply.

When the cleaning was over the team withdrew and were replaced by medical assessors. The room which had been allowed to become dark, was flooded with bright light. This time there was no conversation and when Alice asked one man if they were to be given food and facilities of a sanitary kind, she was so alarmed by his ferocious gaze that she fell silent.

The medical examination was minute and thorough. The wishes of the two girls were of no consequence. There could have been no more convincing evidence that they were irrelevant than the way the examination was carried out on this and subsequent occasions. It was a daily routine expeditiously carried out.

That night the two were provided with simple beds and bed clothing. Alice felt relief that nothing worse had happened; fatigue did the rest. She heard Rosemary say, 'Oh Alice, I'm so sorry', and lapsed into stupor before she heard what her maid was sorry about.

SEVEN

Robin was in a disused compartment of the pigeon cote. It was not used for any purpose; even Colin's sacks of meal had lain neglected for two months since he had been 'removed'—what Roland had learned was the 'pacification'. Robin insisted Roland should not attempt to join him till dark. It was obvious that Robin's safety was not to be prejudiced in favour of Roland's. The unwelcome thought would not have been entertained even one day before.

After dark Roland joined Robin, who questioned him closely, in whispers, over and again—was he sure, quite sure, that no one had seen him at any time on his way to Munden? Why had he come? His old friend was not pleased to see him. On the other hand he did not want him to go. 'After all, they might see you going.' Roland was affronted. 'I don't know how I'm to get food for you; you haven't brought your own I suppose?' 'I say, old man, don't bother! I can scrounge for myself—you know I can. You remember, with the Boche . . .' The idea filled Robin with terror. 'The Boche! My dear man, where have you been? These people aren't the Boche!' 'Oh, I'm sorry'—Roland was angry and sarcastic—'I thought they had declared war again.' 'Forget it. The Nazis were kind and good. A bit sentimental and damnably incompetent, but this lot—you've got something to learn. Do you know what happened in that last battle? Well, it *was* the last. There's no army; there's no nation. Do you know . . .' They were interrupted. Stealthy steps were coming upstairs. They stopped outside the door which was ajar. It was pushed open by a dark, stocky man. Roland found himself looking down the long barrel of an automatic. Robin held his hands as high above his head as he could get them. The movement was instantaneous and distracted the man's attention from Roland. Roland, surprised into action, leaped at the man who fired—too late. Whether he was stunned by the fall, Roland did not know, for he was bashing his skull in with the man's rifle in a paroxysm of fear and rage. 'You damned fool! Look what you've done now! No time. Out of here! They must have heard the gun. Out! you fool, there's not a moment to lose.' They rushed, almost threw themselves, down the stairs and into the darkness of the yard. They were sobered into silence by the stillness of the night. 'As fast as you can. Puckeridge! You damned fool! You damned, damned fool. What did you have to come for? Board and lodging, peace and . . . till *you* had to come.' 'Shut up', said Roland. 'What an age they've been coming from the guard room, or wherever they've been. Now, move!' They had now gone far enough to dare to move fast. They avoided the road—Robin was certain searchlights would come into use when the body—'Blast you!'—was discovered. As if in response, two searchlight cars swung out of Munden Lane; one turned sharp right towards Wadesmill, the other left in their direction, both with sirens blazing. 'Lie down! Freeze!' The car raced past. Roland took a deep breath. He laughed. 'Bloody fools! I thought you said they were intelligent. Anyone would think a man on foot needed pursuit by a powerful car doing eighty miles an hour!' Considerably relieved, they walked on. 'I think', said Roland, 'we have probably a good half hour, probably more, till they start back having decided they have missed us. Of course, they may be more intelligent than I think and have pulled up at the pub to "write their reports" in comfort before going back to H.Q. By the way, is H.Q. at Munden?' Robin shivered. 'I'm scared, I'm hungry and I'm cold. What is more, they are *not* bloody fools. They won that war. In a week there were no British Armed Forces. As for you and your intelligence—why, you haven't even heard the news yet.' 'What news?' 'The news I've just been telling you. You know nothing about it, or you wouldn't talk such rot. Here's the searchlight car, crawling back again. Get down!'

'Don't bother', said a cultured voice immediately behind them as the searchlight car drew up by their side with the beam full on them. 'You were, of course, quite right', he said courteously to Roland. 'The police—didn't Lorca describe them as "with skulls of neuters"?—I think so—are so famous for behaving as you suspected that we thought it might be worth using that bait. Excuse me', he said apologetically, 'for trying so simple a dodge; it does usually work. We just send out walking parties—their pace *is* more appropriate than that of the high-powered car—then, when the fugitives relax, they give away their presence in their momentary—with you I am sure it would be no more than momentary, er,—incaution.' He bowed politely. 'Now shall we be getting back? It is rather dark and—dear me—I believe it's starting to drizzle. I expect you could both do with a meal and, I daresay, Mister Remes has told you our rations aren't bad, though for the past two months he has been picnicking, rather than dining, off them. After you.' He bowed the two into the open door of the police car.

At the pigeon cote he was still politeness itself. 'Do you mind', he said, 'if I come and see your quarters? They are, I know, rather rough, but', as he followed them upstairs into the room where Roland had only shortly before murdered the guard, 'I imagine Mister Remes has found them adequate for his purposes. I expect he told you he has been living here for a couple of months.' He looked at the bloody body on the floor. 'Dear, dear. I am so sorry; we are very short-staffed or I would have had this cleared up. He's a countryman of yours. I can't think why he's such a careless fool. Or was, perhaps I should say, but I had warned him repeatedly not to be so foolhardy. I knew he would go blundering up after you when I heard', he again bowed slightly to Roland, 'you had arrived. Dispose of the body at your convenience, gentlemen.' A swift glance round the loft and he was gone. He was back almost immediately. 'By the way, I ought to have warned you. I wouldn't relax your precautions if I were you. These fellows of yours are not very reliable. This poor fellow—you'd hardly believe it, but we warned him repeatedly *not* to be foolhardy and yet he came blundering upstairs after you. Admittedly he was a bit dim and I know you wouldn't do anything rash. If you will go on, Mister Remes, as you have been while you have been staying with us, I am sure you won't get into any difficulty.'

Roland and Robin stared at each other. 'What do you make of that? He comes and goes like the Cheshire cat.' 'Damn the Cheshire cat! I tell you—I'm scared stiff. For God's sake, don't be a bloody fool!' 'I am not feeling quite in the mood to be called a bloody fool', said Roland exasperated. 'Where do we go from here?' '*You* tell *me*. I knew they saw you coming and you had to underline it by murder. Obviously they did nothing; they knew you were here all the time. I wonder who this poor sod is. I didn't see him, did you? How do we get rid of it?' A bullet crashed through the window, hit something else, and whined away into the darkness. 'Oh God! *That's* their game. We are here free—free to provide them with targets.' Roland was determined to get away before his reserves went. If he didn't, he would become like Robin.

The night, or what was left of it, was a source of terror. They had had no food. Robin assumed, though not so readily as Roland, that they were expected to find the same source of food available as before, namely, the Officers' Mess pillaged by the old cook. 'Come to think of it', said Roland, 'where *is* the Officers' Mess, now you mention it?' 'I never *have* mentioned it', replied Robin. 'I thought *you* had seen the Officers' Mess.' 'How could I? I haven't been here for the last two months. It's you—*you* said you got grub every . . .' Another heavy bullet crashed through the remains of the window, spattering them with glass. 'Are they going on with this do you think? We'd better get out of here.' 'Where to? You forget England has been "pacified" very thoroughly; they don't admit they ever went to war.' Five more bullets came together almost at once. 'Hadn't we better stop talking? They know we're here.' 'Of course they know we are here. Let's get to hell out of it.'

EIGHT

The dreamless sleep ended. The day was as empty of events—facts proper to daytime—as the night had been empty of dreams. Meals were served to both girls. It occurred to them that they had no memory of the food; the 'facts' of daytime and night were defective, mutilated. They were having dreams—mutilated dreams—lacking a dimension like a solid body that casts no shadow in light. The world of reality, facts, was no longer distinguishable from dreams, unconsciousness, night. Thoughts with and thoughts without a thinker replaced a universe where discrimination ruled. Dreams had none of the distinguishing characteristics of mind, feelings, mental representations, formulations. The thinker had no thoughts, the thoughts were without thinkers. Freudian dreams had no Freudian free associations; Freudian free associations had no dreams. Without intuition they were empty; without concept they were blind.

Rosemary said, 'You are nice, Alice. I prefer you to Tom.' Alice felt a voluptuous glow steal over her. 'Oh thank you, Ma'am', she replied humbly to her maid. 'Will that be all now?' 'No, lay out my finery; then you can go.' Alice found herself ranging over the wardrobe of exquisite shoes.

Thoughts, whore's apparatus, schooling . . . As she collected these objects she was carried away by an immense love and adoration. Unable to contain herself she said, 'Oh, Ma'am, can't I see you wear them? It would be wonderful to be able to give them all to you. I shall call Roland. He will make a better husband for you than for me. You will make him a better man than I could.' She fell at Rosemary's feet, anointing them with her tears which themselves turned to a precious ointment as they fell. How does she come to waste all her treasures like this? Does she not know what manner of. . . servant this is? Does she not know what the value of her gifts is—the education, the health, her beauty, our beauty? Does she not know that we were Penelope's suitors? That Homer celebrated us? That we died even before there was a poet to confer immortality upon us? Ronsard knew of us when we were beautiful. Why does she not send them away? Why are we sent away empty? Why are even our thoughts emptied and our concepts denuded of their contents, our concepts and thoughts denuded of their apparatus, equipment, without which they are blind? Did not Kant, our Browning, tell them? Why do they choose Cant, the Barabbas-like thief? I before 'ee except after see?

Alice, adoring, looked up. 'Who are you? May I not see you as you are?' 'I have told you. I am your maid—your servant—poor, despised, needy, the whore. It was I who sent Tom to you, deprived you of Roland. You can't give me anything.' She spoke without bitterness. Alice looked up expecting to find she was being mocked. There was no mockery.' But tell me who you are; I shall wrestle with you from dawn to dusk; from dusk to dawn, from O to God; from God to science; from science to God; from security to the infinite that is man's infinity; from the infinite confines of stupidity, from stupor to the bigotry of certitude; from infinite hate to infinite love; from infinite coldness, indifference of the absolute, to the intolerable infinitude of absolute love. Show me.' 'No.' 'Show me.'

'Because of your importunity I will lift the veil. I will not give you sight, but I will give you insight so your greatest will be able to see me in a glass darkly, me in whom there is no shadow cast by turning. You will pay as even your greatest had to pay—"from that time on the balance of his mind was disturbed." He was condemned to live imprisoned in everlasting sanity.'

'Who are you?'

'I am compassion.'

'Who are you?'

'I am your maid—but even then you did not see.'

'Open my eyes.'

'No. I sent you prophets but you would not listen.'

'Open my ears.'

'I sent you Bach.'

'He had perfect pitch.'

'He tempered the clavier well.'

'Send me a better one.'

'No, I sent you Mozart.'

'You took him back too soon.'

'I sent you Beethoven.'

'He was flawed.'

'You flawed him: you would not look at the flaws I made.'

'Show me.'

'I sent the spirochaete.'

'I could not see.'

'It was beautiful.'

'I could not see its beauty.'

'I sent you Thaïs.'

'Who are you?'

'Only now do you give a home to curiosity, but to make it sleep.'

'I will awaken it.'

'I have done that, but you strive to put it to sleep.'

'Tell me who you are. Let me see.'

'I will show and tell. And you will use what I show and tell to stupefy, to drug yourself.'

'Try me!'

'See then: I am Thaïs. I am Helen of Troy. I caused mankind to see Beauty. I launched a thousand ships and burned the topless towers of Ilium.'

Rosemary and Alice have swooned away, but Rosemary still talks.

'Who are you?'

(Shadowy Figures disguised as S.F. take over.)

'We are Science Fiction. Who are you?'

'I am the Artist who made the ram caught in a thicket beautiful in gold. I am the hunter who caught the ram in a thicket. I am the thicket in which the ram was caught. Who are you?'

'I am Science Fiction. I am S.F. I am the Fiction which became Science Fact. I am the tomb robber. I am the drug that stole your senses away. I am the tomb, ugly and frightening. I am the thief that made you bury, in the golden ram and its golden, golden thicket, the work of Art. I made you bury it in the death pit of Ur. I robbed the death pit of its terrors. I am the S.F. who, disguised as the holy fool, appeared as the Silly Fool. I am S.F. But who now is this?'

'I am what I am. I am God. I am Satan. I am hell fire. I am the burning bush. I am the fire that all men worship. I am Satan. I stole your thicket and refined it in the fire till it burned so brightly that all men worshipped me. I am Mammon. Who is this?'

'I am Strife. I set God against Mammon. I set the vulva against the penis, the contained against its content. I caused the lean to devour the fat. Who are you?'

'I am the dreamer. I dream a dream. I am the den in which I was buried. Who are you?'

'I am the thought that found a thinker. Who are you?'

'I am the robber who drugged you so you would not know you were being conceptualized. I am the dream that drugged you so you would not know I was a concept that would be so nice that you would never be the same once I had conceived you. You would not know that the direction in which I was robbing you would lead from nothing to unconsciousness to sleep to dream to waking thoughts to dream thoughts to nothingness to O = zero, from O = zero to O which is O = oh! to O which is a picture which is a picture of a hole or greedy mouth or vagina which offers perfect freedom which is death which is perfect freedom which is perfect pitch or absolute colour or Eternal Life or Eternal Death or Perpetual Motion or Perpetual Inertia or Absolute Space or space like mental space in which there exist objects so compact that they are like white dwarfs or so sparse and rare that they can only be grasped by finite means like Poisson's law governing exceedingly infrequent events or so absolute a space that your mental life is itself destroyed as in a body which is anaemic because mind is lost like blood in a body whose capillaries are so greedy that there is not enough blood to be shared. Who are you?'

'I can see you are waking. You will be blinded by day, by sight, because you are so blind you detect the faintest light of an object so dark that increased light is too much. You oscillate, back and forth.'

'No. Round and round. The diameter is so vast that you cannot see the opposite side.'

'No. You oscillate, with so small an excursion that you cannot discern that the excursion would have to be beyond your time to make the journey round the circle. You cannot even detect that the circle and the diameter are signs denoting the same object. You argue . . . who are you?'

'I am strife. I cause you not to agree and the strife wakes you out of darkness. I am confusion. I cause confusion of tongues. I am Babel. I am the Tower that all men are made like. Who are you?'

'I am the garden into which the serpent found entry.'

'I am the beam by which I found a way to enter.'

'I am Urania.'

'I am divine wisdom by which pagan disguise I entered as Urania.'

'I am Palinurus by whom the fleet of lesser helmsmen were able to sail.'

'I am the many-wiled leader who gave Palinurus his orders. Who are you?'

'I am the disguise robbed from Odysseus who is so wealthy in wiles. I flung reason from his throne. Who are you?'

'I am rationalization who is Reason disguised so that I may appear as the slave or the master of the passions. Who are you?'

'I am the king in whose dream you are but the furniture. If *I* were to wake you would go out bang!—like a candle. You are?'

'I am a funny story. I am a child's book. I am wonderland. I am a children's story. You are laughing in your sleep. You are waking up. The funny story which makes you laugh will make you cry. The child's dream will grow up to become adult, the night mare will carry you, like Shakespeare's sonnet, sluggishly away from home but fast, back to where you came from: which is the same place as the one you go to. Godlike, I shall fling you and your tiller back to the domain from which you came disguised as Palinurus, Urania. As men like trees walking. Rooted as trees disguised as men walking. Your root is already in its grave; your flower is already so brave, so fiery red. You slept. Who are you?'

'I am the horrendous dream that turned Science Fiction to Science Fact. I turned hideous night to even more hideous day. And you?'

'I am the Refiner's fire. The glorious sun who was the revolutionary flame disguised as R.F., the république française, the public thing, the thing that turned the hidden thing to the public thing; who robbed death; who robbed the secret of its cover and exposed it as the monster that it is. Who are you?'

'I am thought searching for a thinker to give birth to me. I shall destroy the thinker when I find him. I am the Odyssey, the Iliad, the Aeneid. I prevented Mars from destroying me but I ate away Mars from inside, from outside so he died. He is a memory and a desire: I am the eternally alive, indestructible, indispensable, adorable. I am the force that makes the books. My last triumph is the Mind. The mind that is too heavy a load for the sensuous beast to carry. I am the thought without a thinker and the abstract thought which has destroyed its thinker Newtonwise, the container that loves its content to destruction; the content that explodes its possessive container.'

Both girls woke up. 'This is terrible. Let's get to hell out of it.' 'Why? What's the matter with it? I rather like it', said Rosemary. She looked Alice up and down. 'After all', she drawled, 'you make rather a good skivvy. Isn't that what you and your boy friends used to call us? Now we workers are liberated you don't like it. Anyhow, how do you get 'to hell out of it', as you put it? *We* couldn't. I couldn't stop your beastly husband making what he, in his beastly way, called "love"—his "beastly" love—to me. I used to laugh at his horrible, mawkish, shop-soiled, left-over love, though of course his public school education, his *gentlemanly* education made it impossible for him to conceive that *his* skivvy—your skivvy—could see through both of you. Why, I knew that you hadn't the remotest idea of how to keep him in his place. I knew from the way you ticked me off about Tom that you hadn't the faintest idea what a woman, a real woman, could do to that blundering dimwit—or his equally dimwitted master. That is why I—*I*, I tell you—decided to set him loose on you that night! And Roland couldn't even enjoy your screams! "Ooo!" he started to blubber', and she began a mocking imitation of Roland's voice, "my poor wife! Is the little itsy-bitsy sweetheart being raped? What a shame!" He couldn't care less. But his bloody school had taught him he was a gentleman so he couldn't even realize he was just a cowardly, snivelling, cock-sucking bastard who couldn't stand up for a woman if he had one! I could show you half a dozen of my girl friends who were more man than he was! Here, you! Get me *my* shoes—the best ones. And look sharp about it! I'm going to show you how to use Roland! I'll get him here!'

NINE

'It's all very well to say, "Get to hell out of here." How?' said Robin angrily. 'You'll know quickly enough if you stay and have one of these bloody things crashing a hole through your skull—that will leave a way out!' 'That won't be *less* likely if you start walking around here.'

'You're caught either way—stay or leave.'

The voice seemed familiar.

'Who are you, pray?' said Robin and Roland together. The wind was rising. The crash of the bullets seemed to be heavier, to become merged with the storm. 'God damn it! They *are* shells!'

'You use my name in vain! . . . in vain, in vain, in vain . . .'

The words were echoing round the storm.

'Christ! I must be hearing voices now! Who are you?'

'Christ—.' The voice echoed round and the storm dropped suddenly to a whisper—'All Mighty'.

The silence was so sudden that the words were clearly and shockingly audible.

'What the devil was that?'

'At your service!'

Though no one was visible, the voice seemed to be so clear that you could almost see it bow with elaborate and ironic courtesy. 'I told you I had come, didn't I? . . . come . . .'. The echo was almost gentle, like an invitation. '. . . to my arms . . . come . . . come . . . my beamish boy . . . come. Not in terror, like Ozymandias, but kind and good, like Hitler who chortled in his joy. Is that you Cap'n? Down below? Keep . . . till I come again.'

'Who *is* that?' Roland sat up to listen more clearly. He smiled a schizoid smile. Such a gentle smile. 'There! Don't your hear it?' He lifted a finger to signal silence.

I am the discoverer and inventor of homo alalu. I and my fellow homines with our opposable thumbs learned how to give birth and life by opposing penis to penis, vulva to vulva, till one of us began to swell up and up till the whole earth and sky was filled with the swelling and the roaring. It was decided that the monster should be destroyed. But some were lying and deceitful and resolved in their lying and deceit to continue their evil practices in secret and contribute their knowledge of pleasurable feelings to each other by rubbing. Some resolved to find this secret by learning from the secretive ones to do likewise, and others resolved likewise to deceive and lie so they could learn who and what they were that did these things so they could kill those who practised and taught these practices, and so confusion grew and it became impossible to tell good from evil. Some learned to talk, but again the same thing happened, for the language was used by some to perfect the arts of lying and deception and others to increase pleasure, but they could not agree which was which nor which was the sign by which what thing should be known. The monstrous swelling and roaring grew till the world was almost about to come to an end, but then it ceased. There came peace and quiet and the man was seen to be holding a deformed 'thing'. And he lied and said it came from inside him. And some said this was so and some said it could not be so and some sought to destroy the evil thing and some said, 'Let us wait and then we shall be able to tell whether it is as they who say it is evil are right, or whether they who say it feels nice are right.' But no one could say because sometimes even those who said it was good admitted it was an evil brat, but they were not constant and the decision became so late that the brat, if it were evil enough, could slay those who came to kill it and so again confusion grew until even the confusion of tongues, even the counsel, was darkened until it covered the earth. And fear made men worship what they did not know and some said—Let us worship it in ignorance and fear—and some said—Let us worship it in daylight when we do not fear—and some said—Let us make ourselves afraid or we shall not fear—and some worshipped the sun and some the moon. Some likewise worshipped fear itself and some happiness and joy and light. And again they could not agree. And some worshipped what they made and some worshipped their cleverness, saying—We are the highest and best of all animals because we are tool-making animals—and some worshipped that part of themselves which they thought enabled them to make tools, the tools that made tools, but again they could not agree what that part was or how it should be treated.

What part of England or Shakespeare was it that forged the England that is eternal and will be for ever England? What is foreign soil? Which part is Rupert Brooke, Shakespeare, Milton? Which part will be for ever foreign? Pope was a nasty little man. Who, then, wrote the Epistle to Doctor Arbuthnot? Who knew Doctor Arbuthnot's address so many years ago? Who told Kipling—the worshipper of very ordinary trash—that he ought to write Recessional, and that somewhere amidst the ruck and reel which he not only observed but worshipped there were sinners who might have ears to hear—if he could write? Who told him he could? Who told Bunyan to stop his ears and run; Belloc, that the stupidity of his Church was such that it must have been divine to have survived; Hopkins, that 'double dark' would help him find the 'uncreated light'; Freud, that he needed 'artificially to blind himself' to explore the dark places of the the mind? Virgil knew that the death of Palinurus was unfair; the author of the Baghavad Gita that God did not conform to the human measures available. Galileo knew he had better conform to fit the Procrustean bed in which it was his fate to lie. Was Jesus a megalomanic fool, Meister Eckhart a time-server, or did he feel that, like Jesus, he would be trapped and then deserted by his God? And Job—did he too know that it was immodest to suppose *his* fishing tackle was adequate for Leviathan?

TEN

Rosemary stirred uneasily in her sleep and woke. In her game that night she had played the arrogant mistress and turned Alice out of bed. 'Get out! You stink', and laughed coarsely. The faint light of dawn showed her Alice lying on the floor. 'What are you doing there? Alice! Come here this instant. At once! Do you hear?' Alice, ever wakeful, rose up and came over. 'Yes, Miss', she said deferentially. 'I can't sleep properly.' 'Nor can you on the floor. You may get into my bed. No, *not* there', she said petulantly, 'how many times have I told you not to put your head on my pillows?'

It was morning again; Alice was busy arranging things to please her mistress. 'Rosemary, why am I so happy? I adore you. I never want to be anything but your devoted slave.' 'Didn't you ever feel that with Roland?'—Rosemary was brushing her hair—'Here! I'm sick of this. Didn't they ever teach you to have a lady's maid at your Paris outfit you were telling me about? Good job! You can be *my* maid now. Dress my hair—properly, like ladies have it.' Alice took over. 'I sometimes wonder why I didn't learn to be a maid. Is it because I didn't know my proper station in life?' Rosemary, now serious, pondered the question. 'No', she said, 'it was because Roland was a bastard. And you were busy learning to be a bastard like all the other bastards at your school.' Alice was shocked. 'Your language!' 'There you go—you were *taught* that that was bad language. Now, when I talk real language, you can't understand it. Listen: she that hath ears let her hear! . . . Now you'll say I'm profane won't you? Just what you bastards taught us children—but we were too tough and resistant to swallow all that bunk at Gold Hawk Square. We were not bastards; we were born of genuine, "ill-bred", bred ill poor, the sort that use bad language because we know that bad language is the right one to use in a bad world. We knew that fucking was a nuisance. We knew, and our parents before us knew, that it was to be got over and done with as soon as possible; that children had to be produced and got rid of as soon as possible. "Mum", she began to mimic a cockney voice, "Mum! Tell Lily to stop pinching my bottom!" and Mum down the alley yelled, "Lily! Just you leave her B.T. be!" We knew it all, but it wasn't funny. We knew better, some of us, than to laugh at our teachers and we knew who our teachers were—not the bastards but the *real* fuckers. The lilies of the Field. Not the lilies of the botany class and all the silly rot you told me you learnt at your bin. Teaching you sexual facts—what did you say they called it?—"facts of life" wasn't it? Makes me laugh! Jesus! Yes, I know, they called it religion and thought "Jesus" was a swear word and "Christ!" was the rude word for "Messiah". Jesus' Mum and Dad didn't marry. No, of course—"God" did it! And *she* conceived without sin! Poor girl! Anyone knows that "sin" is what makes you laugh—same as sending people to Hell. My Dad told me that bastards made a Hell on Earth—as if they couldn't wait to get there. Our Father which art in hell, hallow it be thy name, thy will be done—-on earth as it is hell! And it was so and the Devil came and looked upon his works and saw that they were—hellish. Did not abhor the Virgin's womb! I should think not—why should he? Just the "thing" for torturing poor woman with! The clitoris for me every time. No wonder—some fool was sure to come and say, "Penis Envy"—it is clitoris envy! And then it takes them ages to wonder why men have penis envy just like women. They do not envy what they've got—of course not—it's what they *haven't* got. And God, they said, was *not* in the mighty wind, but in the still *small* voice, the one that the serpent used—the big snake—*whispering* sweet nothings to Eve. The real fucker doesn't bawl it from the housetops; he whispers it to humble and meek clitors—that is what is "exalted" and becomes erect. *That* little button! Not some bloody, menstrual breast.' Then, in a sudden burst of savagery, she said, 'Anyhow, I've got you where I want you now you skivvy!—you and your "governing class" husband. Get my bath ready. Do you hear? Get it ready I say!' Her voice was rising to a scream. 'Careful', laughed Alice with her finger to her lips, 'or you'll wake the children'. 'What children?', Rosemary asked, looking round puzzled.

Lying on mattresses on the floor were Roland, Tom and the man who had removed their belongings from the farm. 'Are they asleep?' Rosemary whispered. 'They look dead. How did they get in here?' 'Lie down, never mind', soothed Alice, 'I'm here to look after you. I love you.' Rosemary stared and then, 'I'm sorry, Alice, I didn't mean to be so beastly to you'. Alice looked at her maid in adoration. Then she leant forward and kissed her tenderly. 'I loved it, my sweetheart. Humbly, dumbly. I loved every moment of your flashing, contemptuous eyes. I am your slave—for ever. Let me lie at your feet for ever. I will teach you how to handle these . . .' 'I see you are learning. At least you can speak a few words of plain English. I am afraid though . . .', she fell back, relaxed and contented, 'of having one of those horrid dreams . . . they are so real . . . of these corpses . . . these wax models'. 'Never mind Rosemary. I shall go to sleep with you. And we can listen to them talking. So scientific! Listen! They have started again. Listen—but don't laugh too loud or you will wake them.'

Roland rubbed his eyes. 'My eyes do trouble me rather. Do you know, I think I must have fallen asleep. I do that sometimes; it goes in a flash. Mostly people don't notice but sometimes I think they do because they look at me so queerly. Or perhaps it is the dream that I have and forget. It goes in a flash.' Tom seemed to be changing every second into someone whom he knew well, but could not remember. It was awkward that he did not know his name. One of his colleagues too! 'Call him "Colin" to myself, but must remember not to say it out loud. It will do for the dream or whatever this is. If it isn't too high-falutin' it reminds me of the shadows on the walls in Plato's cave. You remember', he said aloud, 'that Plato had an idea that what we call reality were really shadows cast on a wall of a very dark cave in which men were sitting, chained, with their backs to a bright light entering the cave from an opening that they couldn't see, but only were aware of by the shadows that they thought were reality. Well, Plato thought that "things", as we call them, and people are really a kind of precipitation of the "Forms". The Forms (either the concept, or, in so far as concepts cannot be called "empty thoughts", the "things-in-themselves"), the "noumena", were not understandable. Plato seemed to think that the Socratic Greeks might at least understand the parable of the cave. But between then and now many hundreds of people have tried, oh, "ever so hard", to understand what it means. And some people, like Jesus, have continued the naive idea. "If you can't understand the parable, what am I to tell you?" he complained when his disciples were not stupid enough to be simple. All that they could do was to decide that Jesus was God and shut him up under a tombstone of heavy, cold, religious adoration. I suppose they were foolish enough to suppose that they could get their shot in first before the opponents, who said they had known him from childhood and he was a carpenter's son and they were all so fond of him—why! they were his loving brothers and sisters! It was just brotherly love, and no less an authority than Jesus himself had admitted you couldn't have one who loved you more than a father or brothers or sisters. (Though even *he* preferred a Father in Heaven and not one at too close quarters). They had only come to save him because he was beside himself. Or, in plain Aramaic, "nuts". Well, since then that story has been taken up, whenever it has one of its periods of volcanic activity, by the scientists and the protaganists of the looney bin, the tomb robbers and the tomb builders, the religious outfit and the scientific blackguards who try to keep the humanists and artists and poets under control by murder, sometimes with "loving adoration" and sometimes with Herodic anxiety to find out where the dangerous embryo is, so that they can worship it to death. Of course they were crude, but methods have become refined. The "tool-making animal" found out that tools were very useful and anyone could learn to use a tool and no one need know *how* the tool was being used if it could be covered and hidden. That is where women were so clever. They had an invisible tool and the man had a visible and useless prick. Come, let us find it so we can worship also. So . . . well, some genius had to discover some way in which lying, deception, evasion and their opposites could be used without detection and how "truth" and noumena-robbing were to be kept inviolate and inviolable. The "discovery" was, in its early stages, difficult because it was so vulnerable. Lying and deception were exposed, usually by some blundering child who could see that the emperor had no clothes, until it had been educated to know better. Hullo! hullo! No one here? Must have been talking to myself. Well, it's all practice I suppose!'

ELEVEN

ROBIN It's all very well saying let's get to hell out of it if you are brave and wealthy, married to a wealthy and intelligent woman. *I* am to Hell *in* it. How did I ever get to Hell into Munden, with that damned Roland? Anyhow, he's gone, thank God or the Devil—God! What was that? Now I'm hearing voices. Thou shall not take the name of God in vain. When I first heard that it meant—or so I thought—I'm not so sure now . . . you must not be a naughty boy and swear, but *now* I have just seen that my god will come whenever I call upon him, and whichever god it is will come at once—and come with a vengeance. 'And how!' as they say. I begin to doubt the equivocation of the fiend that lies like truth. Some old bore said that. I remember having to learn it, by heart. Of course, I didn't believe a word of it, but I see now, I see that really it had a *double* dose of meaning and not no meaning at all. Well, well, *very* funny! Lies and Truth are indistinguishable! Missus What-not, the cook from whom I stole the cookies, used to say, 'I'll *give* you your *rations*. It's what you deserve. Now just you get out of here!' and I found myself outside in less than no time. Now I have only to want to go to sleep and I find myself *inside*. Ha!

ha! ha!—very funny, very funny indeed . . . Shhhh . . . What a bloody noise you make! You'll wake the whole place. Blood, blood everywhere; even noise is bloody in *this* hell! If I tried to wash these hands they would make even the sea bloody. If I tried to wash my hands . . . even the noise would become bloody and if I try to be reasonable and wake up, even reason itself becomes irrational and if I try to be reasonable . . . What *could* be more reasonable than mathematics?—well, the mathematics have to become irrational. That bloody man Euclid! Today even Euclid is not safe thanks to that ghastly man Lobachevsky. And Riemann—sh, SH! What's so hellish funny about that! ARF ARF?—I'll give you ARF! ARF! ARF! In Heaven indeed! Who are you?

BIG SISTER I am someone you have forgotten. Miss Why-bro! How dare you forget me! I'm your little bro. Why! You used to call me Sex-ton! Don't you remember? I used to walk along the row of little snivellers saying their prayers at the ends of the beds and tread on their silly, pink little feet turned sole upwards and say Ooh, Sorry! Ooh sorry! Ooh sorry! and giggle, and your damn god who couldn't see a kind and loving joke would go AAARF! ARRF! Yes! Ever so funny you looked, scared out of your *damned* wits! And you didn't know whether to laugh or cry. Come 'n get you when you call upon me. You'll do it once too often. That's mathematics—once, *two*—often! And there you are, off like Sports Day. False start. On your marks. Once, Twice, Orphan! Wrong again—back on your marks! Once, Twice, Often. Better, better, but still wrong! Why don't you *try* boy?

SMALL MO Suicide? Well, that's easy enough; the one person one can murder any time—without cost? But in that sleep what Bills may come to shake their peers? If Jill is to be as good as her master what may a pint not do to its pot? What may the bloody noise do to the silence in which it lies imprisoned? Ils gisent là sans voix . . . sans ouië . . . but suppose some sculptor with his chisel and violence releases 'them' from the stone? Some tiresome William Angelo Moore. Suppose he has no joyce? No silence deep enough, no space mute enough to bury the brave who came before Agamemnon, no paradise lost enough to satisfy the damned who have gone empty away? Is there no scientific jargon turgid enough? There will always be a pound who will not impound the meaning—the double crossing acrostic solver who dissolves. There is no refiner's fire that does not refine love itself so lords and ladies cease to be refined, and skivvies are crossed with their doubles and lords are crossed with lords and produce half breeds and half breeds look for their better halves and better halves blush red like beetroots. Horny-handed tons of soil soil the white radients of eternity and turn them into many-coloured life. Black men learn to be white and white men have black hearts and equal votes mate to equivocate. Come on—wake up! You are making such a noise.

HALF AWAKE Was I talking in my sleep? Well, you could call it that. I, the great hunter, stamped over your head, but couldn't break your sleep. Oh baa-ram I had such a funny dream. I thought you were the lamb of God. I was so woolley. Well, it is human to Ur. You urred too often. Toot and come again.

PARANOID–SCHIZOID I can't stand this damned noise. It is like being bombarded with chunks of feeble puns, bits of Shakespeare, imitations of James Joyce, vulgarizations of Ezra Pound, phoney mathematics, religion, mysticism, visions of boyhood, second childhood and visions of old age. Possibly, it could be old age itself. All these myths of Atlantis, all these visions of heaven and hell, are they reminiscences? Are they premonitions? Are reminiscences and premonitions, in fact, both the same thing, only seen so long as a domain in which measurement of temporal and spatial time is proper to a constant conjunction of helplessness, omnipotence, idealization, embryonic sense of reality, embryonic sense of sense, transformed for use in a non-sensuous domain of thought without a thinker, from thoughts in which a thinker is itself of the essence of thought.

DEPRESSIVE POSITION What are the rules in this domain of pure thought? How, and in relation to what standard, is the thought 'peculiar', or the dream 'peculiar'? Is it possible to define its peculiarity? If there is no peculiarity, what is to be used instead? What are the counterparts of disturbances, perturbations, turbulences that are violent, invisible, insensible? Analogous to the models made visible by Leonardo's drawings of hair, water? And occasionally by schizophrenic or other psychotic formulations? How does the person know of blushing so invisible, noise so inaudible, pain so impalpable that its intensity, pure intensity, is so intense that it cannot be tolerated but must be destroyed even if it involves the murder of the 'anatomical' individual?

BIG BRO I don't know what you are talking about.

SMALL MO On the contrary, you give the impression you *are* what you are talking about, but do not know the talk *about* it. I see you have woken up. But not become at one with you. My felicitations and commiserations and good wishes for a happy, brand new Introspection. And a jolly Extroversion likewise.

TWELVE

CAPTAIN BION I stared at the speck of mud trembling on the straw. I stared through the front flap at the clods of earth spouting up all round us. I stared at the dirty, strained face of my driver Allen—my strained face as I sat by me; at the boomerang that Allen sent me from Australia. I got out and hovered about six feet above us. I knew 'they' would . . . and saw trees as woods walking. How they walked—walk! walk! they went like arfs arfing. Arf arf together, arfing's the stuff for me, if it's not a Rolls Royce, which I'd pick out for choice. Then a nice little Ford bright and gay, and when they came to that ford, styx I say, Valiant for S'truth passed over and all the strumpets sounded for him on the uvver side. Cooh! What 'appened then? 'E talked a lot more about Jesus and dog and man and then 'e sez, all sudden like, Throw away the uvver crutch! Coo! Wot 'appened then? 'E fell on 'is arse. And 'is Arse wuz angry and said, Get off my arse! You've done nothing but throw shit at me all yore life and now you expects England to be my booty! Boo-ootiful soup; in a shell-hole in Flanders Fields. Legs and guts . . . must 'ave bin twenty men in there—Germ'um and frogslegs and all starts! We didn't 'alf arf I can tell you. Let bruvverly luv continue. No one asked *'im* to fall-in! No one arsed 'im to come out either—come fourth, we said and E came 5th and 'e didn't ½ stink. Full stop! 'e said. The parson 'e did kum, 'e did qwat. 'E talked of Kingdom Come. King dumb come.

THIRTEEN

MYSELF I knew you would wake him up if you went on making that noisy blood. He says the consistency of his mind never recovered. All he could do was write Opticks and be the Master of the Mint, a mental white dwarf. He never erupted again! Poor Newton! Poor Shakespeare! Poor Galileo, Descartes, Freud, Milton; whose are they—the faces, faint revealed, yet sure divined, the 'famous ones'—ante Agamemnona multi—the mute, inglorious ones? They saw the promised land, the mirage, the fame which is man's last and first infirmity of noble minds. Last, but not least infirmity, the weaker, least powerful helmsman waiting Palinurus-like to be hurled from the throne of the stern, the leader who obeys and by whose position all are ordered to steer. Even Aeneas is hurled from his trust in his steersman by a god whose true face is a disguise which conceals yet another god behind the mask of a benevolent, calm, inviting, alluring, seducing sea. The many-wiled Odysseus, Moses, Meskalam Dug, Arthur, Alexander—où sont les neiges d'antan? And what seductions, treasures remain to be unveiled, concealed (though betrayed) by Memory and its binocular, Desire?

There seems to be something to be said for the 'use' to which 'things' are put. If, then, one considers the accumulation of experience and then the use which is made of these 'possessions', one is using the vocabulary which has been forged for and from the world of sensuous experience. That, indeed, is the vocabulary and procedure which I am trying to use in this very communication. It is not likely to be adequate, but there is also the possibility, almost certainty perhaps, that the 'use' which I am able to make of it is as widely exercised only in those respects in which it has a past and forgotten history. It is also an equipment which is peculiar to that part of the spectrum of thought-without-a-thinker which is peculiar to the biological range, from what could be called the infra-sensual to the ultra-sensual. Even so, the range is perhaps more correctly defined as infra-human (sympathetic) to ultra-human (algebraic)—in other words, a limited range of animal life. At the same time, the range is microscopic from one vertex, and yet too enormous to be likely to be bridged by anything so trifling, so trivial as the products of the human animal. Even so stupendous (on one scale of measurement) a mind as that of Pascal, when face to face with what he and others cooperatively can reveal in the domain of the space of visual capacity alone, was only able to arouse fear and cravings for omnipotent power. Ces espaces infinis m'effraient. Newton's vertex, whether employed in the religious or the scientific domain, cost him the disintegration of his mind. Henry IV, limiting himself to the ambition to possess Paris, could do so because its cost appeared to correspond to the smallness of his ambitions—a Mass 'only'. He, like Pascal and Newton, made his vertex 'binocular', but with one eye relatively blind. Nelson, a man of action like Henry IV, could achieve his ambition so long as he used an eye that was 'blind' for purposes of 'not' seeing (which is different from 'seeing'; that activity he left to the 'better' half). But clearly, here and now the better 'alf (arf arf) is threatening to scramble back to the 'conscious' and the relative safety of the world of fact. Daylight is safer; although one must remember that so great a protagonist of Heavenly light was not saved from blindness, the domain of the infinite and the horrors of the formless, any more than the Forms of Plato saved him and his public-thing from the poets. The revelatory instrument, if used, could be employed by the object scrutinized to look at the scrutineer in the other sense (direction). The poet or genius can look at the scientist or genius and the revelation, as at the opposite ends of the telescope, are too large and too small to be tolerable or even to be recognizably related. It is felt to be the 'fault' of the instrument that brings such different objects together. But it might be the 'fault' of the objects for being so different—or is it the human animal that has to 'use' its accumulations of facts, that it has not the experience that would enable it to 'understand' what it sees, blind or sightful? Time I went to sleep. Excuse me . . . (*Exit to* α)

FOURTEEN

'Well, who asked you to come to Munden in the first place anyhow?' said Roland. 'You know damned well why I came. I wanted to be near, near someone I loved, but who did not love me. And she loved you, who did not and never have loved her and yet married her, you swine.' 'Blast! That ruddy bullet has spattered glass all over and into me by the look of it.' Roland wiped his hand over his face. 'Blood everywhere', he muttered and then continued aloud, 'You mean the bloody bitch Alice? You have to *be* married to her if you want real romance. It's fine for you—wandering around with your tongue hanging out, nursing your marvellous "heart ever faithful" act. I'm married to her. I know—you don't—what it's like to get a good fuck once in a blue moon and spend the rest of the time trying to think up a reply to "darling!" when you are worried to death about some firm trying to dun you for a harvester you have had to buy!' 'It's become very quiet. I held out my hand to see if it's still raining and—no bullets, no sniping, nothing! Do you think the war's over?' Roland stood up. Robin tried to pull him down. 'Don't be a bloody fool! You'll get killed—I only had my hand out. I didn't suggest you stood up. Get down you fool! You have all the luck. I get shot at; I get killed; only I don't die. You stand up, you aren't hurt—*you* collect all the praise for being so *erect,* so honourable, are called love, a mischievous sprite! Such a charming rogue. Even *I* smile at your antics sometimes.' 'Do you by Job! I've never noticed it. Unless . . . Yes, of course! That ghastly expression! Grinning like a Cheshire cat. It must be your smile! Excuse me! I never knew. Of course! Of *course*—it's Alice's very own pussy. It must have been *smiling.* And I thought you were showing your teeth. Allow me to introduce—the right honourable; this is my dear old friend. Excuse me—can you tell me how we got here?'

BETA Count—the cat disappeared—allow me to introduce you to my dear friend Cox! A fellow of infinite jest, my dear chap . . . hullo! What's that hellish noise? Of course, it's only me larf-arfing! Anyway you are making noise enough to waken the dead. That includes the living who might as well be dead for all the thinking they do and the dead who remain obstinately alive long after it's time they were dead.

ALPHA And even myself, whose thoughts and feelings linger on long after I have woken up and remain active and alive in my waking life long after it is expected or supposed (by whom, pray? Shut up!) that I should be dead and buried (where?) In the land of nod, the unconscious, the forgotten, the . . . wherever else I am to go to—the Future will do for a sort of royal cemetery as well as the past. Below the Thalamus. The royal cemetery at Ur, Newton, Shakespeare, Descartes. But some are so deeply buried, forgotten, even their names swallowed up, that they need exing the cave. Even metaphors come alive, otherwise the words that are needed achieve the qualities of 'life'. (More bloody metaphors! Who ever could sort out a mass of verbiage like this?) You could try calling it 'Paranoid Schizoid' after—a long way 'after'—Melanie Klein. Good idea. Good dog paranoid schizoid, here, here is a nice piece of jargon for you. Suspicious are you? Take *that* then! Another great lump of free associations, dreams and their interpretations, poetry, ('all lies', said Plato, sly, suspicious old dog that he was) is hurled at the poor, newborn baby. 'Intelligence', they call the puir, wee thing. Where is that Anarch of the stops and dashes and never-ending Parentheses?—Sterne, they called him, wasn't it? The

Anarchs of the world of darkness keep a throne for thee, puir, wee Intelligence. A rose by any other name . . . might just as well be a stink that smells as foul even if you call it a 'salubrious environment'.

Come here, bad, baaad dog!—Hitler dear, *such* a nice Hitler, *such* a *benito,* such a sweet, rosy little boy! Here, here's a nice salubrious environment! Washed, nay bathed, in our Auschwitz showers. They smell—aah! You can't think how sweet and refreshing those showers are. Now, *here* is a brand new *mind.* It is far superior to the nose as an instrument for discrimination. You just have to attach one of our 'minds' to the old apparatus and this tiny adjustment fitted to the nose and any of the no nonsense organs, to obtain a really superior organ of discrimination! Yes: but how can I tell quackery—use it! Why discriminate?—from truth? Can I tell by it, for example, if this mind you talk about is any better than all the previous gadgets I have been invited to attach, at enormous expanding cost, to my various existing battery of gadgets? I knew a delightful old stegosaurus who thought he had found *the* answer to the tyrannosaurus. But the 'answer' was so successful that it turned into a kind of tyrannosaurus itself and loaded him with such fame—not to mention exoskeleton—that he sank under its own weight. In fact, he was so loaded that the only trace of him left was his skeleton. Yes, but those same dead bones gave birth to a mind. Because while all eyes were fixed on the conflict between Fate and armour (there is *no* armour against Fate) the attacker got through disguised as a bomber. Now, the Mind . . . you just try it. Just attach it to your sensory perceptions! How do I know it won't just turn into extrasensory perceptions—s.p. → e.s.p.? The animal, meaning you, who reads this and I that write it and all biological living constructs, have an inborn mechanism for self-disposal. This dogmatic, definitory hypothesis shares the character of the character it represents. On this definitory hypothesis is built the hypothesis and the construct of which it is the foundation.

The tyrannosaurus provokes intrinsically an equal + opposite reaction—the stegosaurus. The stegosaurus sinks under its own 'maginot line', its defensive armour which is its own weakness and makes its own armament, its own weight, under which it sinks. The self-destructive elaboration is blind to the quality which is to lead to its own destruction. If ξ is felt to be the successworthy quality, to be producer of progress, ξ is also the character unknown and auto-destructive. If the Oedipus story is the weapon that reveals homo, it is also the story that conceals, but does not reveal, that by which it will destroy itself. What happened to Delphi? And Socrates? If man is a tool-making animal he will not observe that that same capacity will be more than he can protect himself against. Superficially it may become clear that he is a clever monkey who can produce an atomic bomb that is a potential menace to his existence. While his gaze physiological is directed to observation and 'detoxication' of the menace *represented* by the atomic bomb, it will, by the same token, be directed away from the growing annihilating force, the 'helpless infant'. 'Too much learning will make thee mad . . .' Too much 'tyranny'—freedom, food, armour, defensiveness; the list can be extended—but the only reality that matters is that which is denoted by 'too much'. Quantity, + and −, requires awareness. In the language suitable for communicating, it would be called a capacity for discrimination of quantity and quality. But in the domain that concerns us there is nothing that lends itself to the exercise of discrimination; there is no quality, no quantity to be discerned. Relativity is relationship, transference, the psycho-analytic term and its corresponding approximate realization. Mathematics, science as known hitherto, can provide no model. Religion, music, painting, as these terms are understood, fail me. Sooner or later we reach a point where there is nothing to be done except—if there is any exception—to wait. The 'impasse' is itself a word which, in the context of this writing, is known to denote a feeling.

BIG BRO Using some schoolboy mathematics I make a model, thus:—I cannot take five from three using only natural numbers. Natural numbers are the kind of numbers I use if I see a pile of oranges and want to know how many oranges there would be if five were removed from the pile. I would say, 'one, two, three, four, five', as I separated the oranges from the pile. Then I would do the same with the remainder and count thirty. So, given the fruit and the technique I have described, what would happen if I took thirty oranges away from five? First, it would be very improbable that I would want to know anything so ridiculous, and I might be afraid of doing anything because the people around me might be very cross if I wasted their time, and mine, dreaming. In fact, I have just dozed off which shows you . . . What?

MEMORY I dreamed I was taking thirty oranges away from five. In the dream I didn't see anything extraordinary about taking thirty oranges away from five. The five were very fat, big and greedy and had lots of oranges. I was angry that they should have such masses of oranges when they *were* oranges themselves already! So I suppose I did not see why they should not have thirty taken from them. It was really rather funny—really! What's so funny about it, said one of the big ones. I felt frightened. Well, put like that, what *was* funny? I remembered one of my patients telling me, 'I tell you . . . I never woke up so fast in my life, I can tell you!' So I thought I had better do the same. I *woke* up. What a funny way you laugh. Arf, arf, ARF you go . . . do wake up. What was so funny about it? I told her I had forgotten and couldn't remember. But it was—very funny. I wish I could remember it!

Well, as I was saying, of course you can't take thirty from five—not in reality; not with real numbers. If someone invents negative numbers and you add them to natural numbers, *then* you can take three from five and get minus two! What's the good? Is that not just playing tricks with numbers? It doesn't mean a thing. *No.* It is pure mathematics. If it's pure mathematics it's all right because it doesn't have to mean a thing. Daft, I call it. There are lots of people who don't think. *They* must be daft too. No: because some one—Lobachevsky or Riemann—invented a daft geometry and now they find it quite useful in space—not the space which Euclid geometrized about infinite space, space that has no end. Like 'world without end Amen', you mean. Ye-es, perhaps; you mean religious space? I think it's more like the 'space', if there was such a thing, made out of adding conscious space to unconscious space. How? Well, if you have a new kind of space, call it mental space, then you may have to invent a new addition to go with it. Or, if you invent new numbers you have to invent new mathematics. They have: they have invented negative numbers and a new geometry in which there are imaginary points and tangents which have coordinates of two points, one which is real and contingent, rather like ones that are real and separate or real and distinct, and other lines which don't cut the circle at all and are conjugate complex. What the hell is that? I understand points that are real and distinct, or real and coincident, but not points that are conjugate complex. If you weren't so proud of being sane, someone would be sure to notice how frightened you were of 'insanity'. You wear your 'bravery' as a cloak for your cowardice and things you are afraid of—it must be terrible to have a para-sympathetic and a 'voluntary' nervous system so close to each other! What dreams, what thoughts, the other system has! Which is the other? Look at your skin; but I suppose you wouldn't dare to go more than skin deep.

FIFTEEN

'Time you went to sleep. You are right. It is high time you went to sleep. Excuse me indeed! I don't mind if you went to sleep permanently.' It was Rosemary talking to her 'memory'—her mistress, who was sitting on a chair by her bedside, the bed which used to be owned by Alice. 'If you don't go to sleep', Rosemary said threateningly, 'I know you will babble a lot of grown-up sounding rot like Pound, translating, psycho-analysis, Growth, Newton and other boring and indecent people—oh dear, Alice, I haven't really quite woken. Such a queer dream. Let's forget it and talk about something interesting. I want you to treat me like a friend, Alice.' She made a sound which might have been a stammer or a snort of contempt or just a catch in her breath as she woke. 'Ah, good . . . just what I wanted—a cup of tea. What was I saying? Ah yes; even in the old days, Alice, I thought you would make quite a good skivvy. Sometimes I thought, if only there could be a revolution here! Of course it could never come to pass! But now! Isn't it marvellous? *Do* say it's marvellous—I never thought of an invasion in which all your bloody "upper classes" would be defeated and "the humble and meek would be exalted". It's funny!

Did you think, when you went to church, you were singing about *me*. *I* knew who the mighty were, though. I never thought you would one day bring me my cup of tea and would have to obey my orders. Here, you! I'm getting bored.' Rosemary's mood had changed suddenly to one of violence. 'Make me laugh. Tell me about your lovely public school and its lovely hymns and bibles full of dirty stories—if you'd had the nous to know it!' 'But Rosemary', said Alice, 'we weren't so stupid as you think. We *did* know about the bible and we didn't all think of a bible with a capital "B". I used to find it a true source of "spiritual consolation", but it wasn't all biblical spirit.

Even when I was tiny I remember my mother saying to me, "I don't know what's come over you, child! I think the Devil has come over you!' and she meant it. And it made me afraid too, because that is what *I* thought. And sometimes I thought I could hear the devil laughing. I remember a bit about ". . . and the satyr shall call in the streets". I didn't know what it meant, but it frightened me even when I was awake, and later that night I had quite frightening dreams—terrifying dreams. I expect it was cats. There *were* cats and when we were in India when I was very little, I remember a night when my brother was frightened because a tiger was roaring round the camp because its mate was shot.' Rosemary had become thoughtful and she spoke in a soft and gentle voice. 'Poor kid; I never thought *you* could be frightened—not as frightened as me when a drunken lout was thrashing my mother in the next room. I *think* it was my mother, but I may have imagined it. Later I knew my mother was a whore because the welfare lady—I knew she must have been a lady!—very kindly told me I should be thankful that I had a good home at the foundling hospital and if I was good I might earn a living as a skivvy! Now wasn't she a kind lady to tell me all that? "Yes, Ma'am" and "No, Ma'am"—I was very quick to learn and I know I could talk and say things like that even when I was two years old.' 'Poor child!', Alice murmured half to herself and half under her breath. But Rosemary's mood had hardened again. 'That will do, Alice. Sometimes I'm in the mood to be amused and then you can make me laugh by telling me about the miseries of the "upper classes". Just now you can dress me. With your education you should know what clothes would suit me best. After that you will find my skivvy's "day-off" dress. It will be a bit out of fashion, but it's neat and I kept it—God knows I *had* to—in good repair. Black worsted stockings and "sensible" shoes. I don't know where they have been dug out from.'

MEMORY —the unconscious.

ROSEMARY Shut up! Who *was* that? Respectable, shoddy, worn-out psycho-analytic, mental 'reach-me-down' mental clichés for the dead-from-the-neck-up! Go to sleep I say! Go to sleep!

ALICE Hush! Don't shout, Rosemary.

ROSEMARY Shout? Shout I never so loudly I could not break their sleep. Shoddy. . . . Who are you?

MEMORY Excuse me. I could not help overhearing you ladies. Fascinating! Do go on, please. My name? Oh, call me Memory.

ALICE (*sarcastically*) What a pretty name! One of the memories of childhood in . . . in, is it Berkshire? One of *The* Childhood Memories of Berkshire?

MEMORY Childhood, (*contemptuously*) no, one of the Memories of Burkshire. Who are you? A distant—*very* distant—relation. Your conversation woke me, ladies.

ALICE Do go on—now you're awake. Where were you born?

(*The two girls fall asleep—with boredom. Burkshire continues*)

B. MEMORY I don't know. A very nice fellow told me I was conceived in Sin.

ROLAND (*waking up*) One of the most interesting conceptions I ever knew was born there. 'Born of the Virgin Mary', I presume? Pleased ter meetcher. I remember you. Haven't heard a word of you since my school days. You were ragged unmercifully in those days—especially on Sundays in Scripture class. There was nothing else to do! 'Arse-'oles inspire', we used to sing till they didn't dare have that him.

B. MEMORY Hymn, you mean.

ROLAND No, HIM—not 'him' with a small h and y—'Him' with a whisper and a jerk of the thumb over the shoulder. He was the God we *did* believe in. 'Mumbo-Jumbo will get you!'

The parson he did come, he did come.
He looked so bloody glum, bloody glum.
'E talked of Kingdom Come—

B. MEMORY (*glumly*) Not funny.

ROLAND Cheer up! Come cheer up my lads. To glory we steer. . . . Saw men like trees walking. Up the line. At the Salient—in heaven so on earth. There was a chap there spinning round and round. With his guts hanging out. We couldn't help laughing. Jump into the tarpaulin Bill!

B. MEMORY (*cheering up*) Yes, I remember that—'there weren't no tarpaulin there!' But Ole Bill he jumped and Kingdom came up and hit him! That *was* funny! The devil's own war that was. I will say that the devil looks after his own. When we pray to H—well, you know who—for hell as it is on earth to save us from the incredible boredom of eternal everlasting . . .

ROLAND (*interrupting*) School Chapel.

B. MEMORY I never had that.

ROLAND No, you lucky devils.

ALICE Angels. You should have heard the school hockey team singing 'Frail as Summer Flowers we flourish. Blows the wind and it is gone'! Laugh! (*Softly, Arf, arf*) Thought I should have died! 'Alice! Wipe that silly giggle off your face—at once.' The angel faces smile! I should just think they did!

ROBIN (*wakes up*) I didn't think you women were listening.

ROSEMARY We weren't. You don't think we'd have to *listen* to hear the bloody noise you make. You and your medals clanking all over the place and your talk about your goddam heroes. Ante Agamemnona multi indeed! And who heard of the countless generations of mothers who died unwept, unhonoured and unsung before some male thought of the Virgin Mary. That poor girl had and still has to conceive without the fun of sinning even! Gee! Fancy having to be made love to by God, that dirty old man!

D.O.M. Canst though draw out Leviathan with a hook?

ALL (*suddenly hushed in a whisper*) Who was that?

ROLAND (*recovering first, complacently*) It's a classic—quotation from Job.

ROBIN You gave me quite a start!

ALL (*hushed*) I swear I heard a voice. I don't like this—it's spooky.

ROLAND (*slightly less complacent—shaken*) It's a quotation from Baghavad Gita.

ALICE (*angry*) Stop it!

VOICE Hear that? I tell you—I never woke up so fast in my life!

VOICE Why, if they woke up you'd just go out—bang!—like a candle.

ALICE You mean we are just a part of his dream?

VOICE Of course! You don't think we are real do you? Roland's waking up now. You'll see; we shall fade away. Our place will be taken by a mass of meaningless abstractions. Listen . . .

SIXTEEN

ROLAND'S VOICE (*the enunciation is clear and precise. He is himself not visible and as he talks he becomes progressively more a disembodied thinker and finally pure thought without a thinker*) Krishna makes the point quite clearly; he shows Arjuna that his depression is part of feelings of compassion which are unworthy of thought, still less of God-head. That kind of thing may be appropriate to reception and emission in the range of sensuous perception whether perceived directly or mechanically by constructs like radio receivers, X-ray films, musical instruments and, in their very crude and gross manifestations, by animals and creatures in the biological range. Very sensitive animal organisms may then be able to interpret or transform the disturbances in the waves which render them opaque and obstructive. St John of the Cross was even able to point out that an analogy can be found which may be serviceable in the process of vulgarization intended to make the grosser crudities even grosser, till they impinge on elements which are still within the spectrum of the infra-sensuous and ultra-sensuous, though not outside that very narrow and limited band. He uses, it will be remembered, the analogy of dust particles which can render perceptible a ray of light that traverses it. Recently, by mechanical means, it has been possible in the biological range (human sub-category) to detect disturbances of great violence which have completely escaped detection by animals dependent on sight, even when sight is augmented by instruments such as telescopes, spectrographs, cameras and preparations of film coated with fine grain receptors—all macroscopic. Yet these perturbations are matters of the greatest crudity and violence!

Though extremely rare and scattered over a huge range of temporal space, they only appear to be extremely rare because of the crudity and triviality of recorded time as an instrument of measurement. Time as a concept is as inadequate as topological space to provide a domain for the play of such enormous thoughts as those liberated by freedom from dependence on a thinker. The breakdown is as trivial, though made to appear vast by the inadequacy of the framework as, to take a very gross but simple analogy, that which occurs if a simple operation such as the subtraction of five from three is attempted with sensuous objects or even a relatively sophisticated mathematics best limited by being exclusive of negative numbers though well stocked with real numbers.

The failure to grasp the trivial range of the biological spectrum, even when the field of the living is extended by the dead, the animate by the inanimate, has been matched with the vastness of the extent of the relatively minute. This is due, in part, to the failure to grasp the nature of relativity, in particular the fact that it includes paradox. The restriction imposed by the limitation of thought to thoughts with thinkers implies the polarization 'truth' and 'falsehood', complicated further by morals, uninvestigated 'moral' systems, and extensions of Plato's thought to moral views of the function of poets and artists. A similar seepage from the domain of religion may likewise be traced to the inability to respect the 'thought without a thinker' and, by extension, the 'relationship without related objects'. How this has affected even so-called practical thinking is seen in the difficulty of the 'public' to grasp that an analogy is an attempt to vulgarize a relationship and *not* the objects related. The psycho-analytical approach, though valuable in having extended the conscious by the unconscious, has been vitiated by the failure to understand the practical application of doubt by the failure to understand the function of 'breast', 'mouth', 'penis', 'vagina', 'container', 'contained', as analogies. Even if I write it, the sensuous dominance of penis, vagina, mouth, anus, obscures the element signified by analogy. . . .

ROSEMARY (*yawning*) Oh my God!

VOICE Why drag me in?

ROSEMARY (*imperiously*) Alice! Come here at once.

ALICE (*submissively*) Yes, Miss.

ROSEMARY Why can't you keep that crashing bore in order? Why did you marry him if you didn't know how to keep him on a lead? You at least should have learned that the factual exercise of a relationship is not the two objects related, like the cunt and the prick, but keeping one thing inside another. (*Laughs contemptuously*) The container and contained! My God, I believe he has driven me as mad as he is! I'm even talking this crazy nonsense. I'll get locked up if this goes on much longer!

ALICE Yes, Miss. Excuse my saying so, but—*you*'ll be contained in a container then!

VOICE ARF, ARF, ARF. Very funny. Very funny indeed!

ALICE & ROSEMARY (*together, hushed suddenly*) *That* was a joke-without-its-fun, a joke *with* a vengeance.

ROLAND (*frigidly polite, resuming his discourse*) The joke with a vengeance differs considerably from the joke with fun. To the superficial observer they can appear similar. Poor Robin. To some extent, if I could compare myself even remotely to him, 'poor me'. Just now, when we left Munden . . . will you ladies excuse me if I continue my discourse?

ROSEMARY Make it snappy then. And not so much abstraction. Alice, this is your fault. Why did you let this fool break loose? You should have kept him chained to your sandals like Diana, that great huntress.

ROLAND Bahram, that great hunter, you mean.

ROSEMARY (*to Alice, angrily*) Baa lamb that great mutton. He thought he was hunting me. I knew I had him on a string when you engaged me—it makes me laugh when I think of it—to be your servant! Paint my toe-nails. And be quick about it! (*Relenting*) No, take your time, dear. And if you are good I'll let you lick them afterwards. You can put some more paint on afterwards. (*To Roland*) Get on. Let's hear about Munden—it looked amusing to me when I looked in on it.

ROLAND The journey from there to Norfolk was a nightmare.

ALICE (*to Rosemary*) Married Life with him was a daymare.

ROLAND (*furious*) The days—with you—were worse than any nightmare, you bitch! Do you know, the war—especially the final defeat and downfall of England—was a *relief*. Do you know why? Because I thought it opened up at least a glimmer of hope that I could be rid for ever—for ever! do you hear?—of you and your suburban, sub-human, sub-civilized, sub-'aristocratic' society.

ROSEMARY (*calmly*) Go on. I'm longing to hear about Munden (*yawning widely*) and your great hunting. It sounds absorbing—if only I can keep awake.

ROLAND I worked hard on the farm although in fact we were so well off that we could live very comfortably even if I had chosen to live on investments.

ROSEMARY So could we. Or so my Mum said. Till I came. Even then she didn't mind at first because I looked like being a beauty and she thought she could invest in me and retire comfortably on my takings in the profession—still, it didn't take long. I made the same discovery as she had, but I discovered I had no intention of devoting myself to supporting her. Go on, Sir Galahad. This is most interesting. It sounds as if we shall discover that your Dad was the wealthy aristocrat who made me frightened till I stuffed my fist in my mouth to stop my yells. I owe my beautiful eyes to staring, dumb with horror, at my Mum's screams as he lammed into her till *he* got frightened and left her for dead.

ROLAND We used to hunt. But mostly it was the fun of rough shooting round the farm. Alice visited us. I liked her. Till one day she flared up at going to church and said she had told her parents she did not like the parson because he gabbled away like an old cockatoo. I liked her fiery spirit and we agreed, privately, that we would marry one day. But war came. It was marvellous, especially when I went into action and didn't run away—the first time. I found I had to go into action again that same day. That I hadn't expected. I knew I would have to go into action again, but I did not expect that the second battle, only a few hours after the first, would feel so different.

ROSEMARY (*examining her toe nails*) Alice, you look positively interested.

ALICE I am. I haven't heard any of this before.

ROSEMARY (*yawning with affected indifference*) Well, get on with it. I don't expect you to be listening to voices when you have my feet to attend to.

ROLAND The next day I was lying in a dugout because the strafing was so bad. Everything was going up. At first I was frightened. Then I realized I could run away. I had not realized that before. You couldn't even be brave!

ROSEMARY What on earth has this to do with Munden?

ROLAND It has this to do with it: Munden occurs many years after. In fact Munden lies far in the future. Also far in the past.

ROSEMARY Oh my God! Can't we have a little whoring? That also lies far in the past. And far in the future. Also, it is at least interesting and not this boring Roland stuff. Alice! Give me that whip. I'll teach you what it is to be my maid. Now; lick! Not like that you fool! Beneath, under the toes. And between. Now the soles of my feet. You will never make a whore the way you are going on. Now—concentrate. Carpe diem, as we used to say and will say again when my client and slave arrives. I am Thaïs. I am Berthe au grand pied—you never heard of them I suppose?

ALICE Oh yes: I had a question on Villon—le Grand Testament—in my certificate exam.

ROSEMARY Really? How boring you are. It comes natural to you I suppose. And just wake up that husband of yours will you? What about Munden?

ROLAND (*pale and sweating*) Those heavy bullets. They crashed like the slamming of train doors in a tunnel. Robin and I flattened as low in the mud as we could get. Slam! Slam! Slam! Grand slam! The rat hunt. Someone was trying to get me in a corner and club me to death. But thanks to reversed perspective I could cower in the corner where the angle of the walls protected me.

ROSEMARY What happened then?
VOICE 'E fell on 'is arse! Arf, arf, arf!
ALICE What was that?

SEVENTEEN

ROLAND I believe it's clearing. God, but that was a heavy shower! Nowadays they use computers. Hard to see what fun they can get out of sports in which you use computers to work out the position—the exact position of your blows. This rat uses it to aim his blows exactly so they just miss. The wheels of God roll slow, but they roll exceeding small. Slam! Slam! Small! These are so close that I can feel the air hot as they pass. It has started again. You can't just have machines. There still has to be some kind of vestigial brain to programme the computer. The tiny vestigial scrap of human cruelty. Small, vestigial, but tough and resistant like a spore—a spore of malignancy. Where's Robin? 'They' must have got him. Ah, the sea at last. The salt marshes and the pee-wees calling and the great clouds billowing past far above. Is the war over? From that warfare there is no release—no release. Daddy! Oh Daddy—stroke me, Daddy! My dear, dear child, my fingers can't reach your sweet face now. Would God I had died for thee! Oh my son, my son: Oh my son Absalom! Past, present and future, all shrivelled up to a nothing—the heart of a computer!

ROSEMARY (*twitching a scarf about her shoulders. Is she cold—or embarrassed?*) Alice, that will do. Really, these men make one quite uncomfortable at times. Pathetic.

ROLAND Just what I was thinking. I had forgotten I used to be so sentimental.

ROSEMARY I never was. Alice—oh, I see you have recovered.

ALICE For a moment I was reminded of my young days and even of the rather attractive days of young love when Roland and I thought we were in love. I almost believed I would go back to it if I could. Do you remember, what Horace said about Lydia?

ROSEMARY Horses? No, never heard of him. Oh, perhaps I do. That was in my Maid of the Mountain days. That is when I dreamed it would be lovely to go on the stage and act the lead. What was it? Marry a lord, have a mink coat and masses of diamonds, and the third was to fall in love. I have done the lot. Now I am not much more than a computer myself; married to another computer.

ALICE And I am the slave of my mistress. I rather think it's the best of the lot. What about my religious days? I used to be married—Roland and I even married in Church.

ROSEMARY Ask Roland. I never took to it much. He has some high-falutin' stuff about it. Roland—tell us about God.

ROLAND There is a remarkable durability about the human capacity to believe in God. Religion affords a continuing source of study. The persistence of the belief is used by some people as an argument in favour of the existence of God—as if one could not believe, still less that the race could not believe, in the existence and even worship of a reality which somehow approximates to the reality of the human and animal impulse to worship. The mouse or rat sometimes looks as if it were imploring, in a positively worshipful posture, the mercy of the cat who is licking its whiskers preparatory to making a meal of its prey. The human animal, which has achieved a degree of articulate speech, certainly seems to be aware of its equipment of cruelty and the need to glut it, or at least feed it with the appropriate diet for its cruel impulses. '"But not on us", the oysters said, turning a little blue', is a formulation of the material which is to nourish and sustain cruelty in vigorous health. You remember there is a well-known story—it is even attributed, amongst others, to Jesus the eponymous hero of the Christian religion. 'My God, my God', he is reputed to have said, 'why hast thou forsaken me?' If he had thought of his Father as greedy and cruel he would have more rationally complained about being remembered—in time to satisfy his hunger for the satisfaction of his cruelty. But usually the cornered rat seems to feel, in extremis, the advisability of adoration and worship; "morituri te salutemus', is a succinct formulation of the principle.

In a civilized world it is more comfortable to believe in its civilized qualities, to obscure the cruel laughter (as expressed in this artifactual dream here) which might evoke, through memory or desire, the configuration evocative of dread. It seems clear that the attempt is inherent to ward off, or to ward off awareness of, something which is dread or terror and behind that the object that is nameless. There are many formulations of dread, unformulated and ineffable—what I denote O. Plato named it 'forms', of which sensuous objects are the unreal but sensible counterpart. Saint Augustine resorted to using the equipment of religion, which is available in many Religions, to express the separation of good from evil. The systematic separation into two objects, good and bad, conscious and unconscious, pain and pleasure, ugly and beautiful, has provided a framework which seems to have facilitated the development of knowledge, but the element of growth appears to have escaped formulation especially since it resembles maturation. The lack of any simple framework of coordinates by which growth could be perceived or measured can be described in imaginary or simple terms by constructing a theory that a child—fictitious, but plausible without outraging the intelligence—could observe that it eats food which disappears, and then evacuates urine and faeces which can be observed. Further investigation made by our fictitious child leads him to discover that what has been devoured has been transformed into faeces + urine and the process of *in*gestion has been transformed into a process of evacuation. The normal activity of growth does not betray itself unless it becomes significant through some secondary attribute such as pleasurable, painful or doubtfully related quality—measurements of weight, height and the like which depend upon conjecture, theory and controversy.

Imagine the confusion of the human animal that finds itself called upon to gauge, contend with, promote or discourage something which has apparently no attributes and no language suitable for co-operation either with himself or anyone else except the primitive and defective instruments of the sensuous world! It is difficult to believe that 'the mind'—shall we provisionally call it?—has no boundary which is obviously and clearly bounded by the same boundaries as the anatomical brain. It is worse if it is seen to be inadequately represented by systems of analogues. Consider, for example, the struggles represented by the approach made to this difficult problem by the Greeks . . .

ROSEMARY The Greeks, if I may say so, were almost as ridiculous as you would expect them to be if you allowed yourself to believe what men say about them. In fact, luckily, I did not have to go to school and learn Greek and Greek grammar and Greek translation. I learned all I wanted to know and in less time than it takes for you and your lifetime of bellyaching noise. I learned, and Homer had the sense to make it possible for you to learn, that Helen was at Troy. One of you fools said it shortly and straight to the point—before the dawn, hidden but not silenced by the cliff above Plymouth—'Anyhow, whore or no whore, she done it for him free', and that's what started all the trouble. I don't have to write learned scholarly disquisitions about it. Plymouth Hoe, the Siege of Troy—what does it matter? Or Elizabeth, by the Grace of God, Queen of England. Or me? I am still beautiful. Even Alice—look at her now: is she not beautiful? You are silent, Roland. Why do you not listen? There is no thought or language yet the voice of them have gone to the uttermost parts of the earth.

ROLAND What? Why don't *you* listen? What else have I been doing while I have been talking? I have been telling you both something. Some of what I have been telling you I know. A lot of what I have been saying I do not know. I know a little—that part of it which I can feel, very faintly, is being listened to somewhere; it's like being touched in a crowd.

ROSEMARY Because your language is, as you think, not listened to by me, you feel entitled to be impressive and to have an audience that is impressed. My profession is the oldest in the world. I am familiar with the arrogant contempt that you think you are entitled to feel if you muster enough intelligence to formulate that expression together with the musical expression of contempt. Thaïs, Eve, Lillith . . . *there* is a lineage which you cannot begin to match. Because I do not bother to put you in what you would be pleased to call the proper place, you feel very proud to think you know mine. The brand of Cain has also been worn as a brand of honour. Your regiments are vast. Since you have learned to count you have been impressed by numbers—the greater the number the greater the honour. The more or less—that is the only criterion you understand. If I were to unveil my beauty you would—shrivel up and die. No, please! Spare me your protestations; I was aware that if I succeeded in making you hear what I said I should be afflicted with the pain of having to watch and, worse, admire your pitiful posturing display. You did not think, did you, that the poor little guttersnipe from the ghetto, the virgin's womb, might be more than rewarded by not being abhorred?

ROLAND (*in his best Oxbridge manner. He speaks clearly and well and is not disguising the fact that he knows he is doing it modestly and well*) Who found the way to express what he had to say we do not know. But we do know that as late as the Baghavad Gita, Krishna is described as reproving Arjuna for his depression and the assumption that his standards are the measure of all things. Arjuna has no hesitation in thinking he can reprove Krishna, or God, or the Ultimate Arbiter, whoever that may be, for his defective standards. Why should he fight and kill his kinsmen and friends though he knows them to be no less worthy than himself? He will not fight. In the Iliad, Hector is defeated and his corpse dishonoured. Achilles, though ultimately the victor, can sulk unworthily in his tent. The Trojans are defeated by a stratagem in a war waged on account of a woman and her ignoble paramour.

ROSEMARY !

ROLAND I beg your pardon? . . . I thought I heard someone say something. No? Then I shall continue. (*Softly in the distance—arf, arf, arf!*) I feel cold. Are these the streets . . . of a great city? They seem empty, lonely, deserted. The satyr shall call in the street . . . Is this Ur, that Royal place? Nineveh? Tyre? Babylon?

VOICE Pretentious ass.

ROLAND Why? What's that? (*After a pause he continues*) I'm scared. I used to lecture well . . . am I losing my gift? What was I saying now? O yes: (*recovery of his theme reassures him*) the Israelitish God was a recognizable, tribal deity showing marked human characteristics, such as jealousy and envy, not markedly different from the inhabitants of the Homeric Pantheon located on Olympus and freely participating in human affairs.

VOICE It is amazing that this lump of a farmer knows all this stuff. The explanation is either that he is so stuffed up with 'education' that he couldn't be expected to be any use as a farmer, or that his farming lout occupation explains his pretentious erudition. It reminds me of the laughable howlers which mark Ezra Pound's claim to be a translator. Do you remember Kipling's joke about Horace's fifth book of Odes? Well, at least that was funny. Even so he pretended quite seriously that he could understand Virgil's understanding of the Mantuan sisters.

ROLAND Was that someone laughing again? An 'educated' Oxbridge accent?

VOICE Oh, do get on.

ROLAND Certainly. What was I saying? Job was rebuked for his setting up, like Arjuna, to be able to judge Krishna by the scale of moral views which might be appropriate to human beings. Even at school I thought Palinurus had very unfair treatment, but of course anyone could see that you can't expect much of an old bore like Virgil. You have to make allowances for a Classic.

TOM What's your little game?

ROSEMARY, ALICE, ROLAND et al. (*hushed*)

TOM You heard and I heard you, you bastards! What's your little game? (*It grows lighter. Tom peers around and gradually begins to see*) So *there* you are. Pretending to be asleep. All right, I have an answer to that one! I will put you to sleep—permanently. (*Beside himself with rage he brings his clenched fists down together on the nearest figure. His fists bury themselves in the bedclothes. His violence is such that he cannot recover himself but remains, weeping with impotent rage, unable to regain an upright posture*)

ROLAND Neanderthal man—

TOM You trickster. I'll get you yet! You think you're clever. I am red-blooded. I live. I am a slave to my passions and by God I'll see to it that you are a slave to mine. Women—that's what I want. But *you* will do. You and your trick cyclists—I'll turn the bastards into my slaves. I haven't got teeth and jaws for nothing. I'll tear your flesh . . . (*Screams*) Let me up! Help me to stand. Then I'll show you.

PSYCHIATRIST You'll wake the whole place, you fool. Nurse, give him a shot—morphia, and quick!

NURSE That's nearly a lethal dose isn't it?

PSYCHIATRIST My job here is to keep order. If it's his life or mine, it's O.K. by me if it's *his!* What is a lethal dose of morphia for him is a soporific for the boss. What is a soporific for the boss is bread and butter for me.

BION What that man What's-his-name calls 'Transformations', isn't it?

STATE PSYCHIATRIST Why, even *I* am transformed. Not a bad little job is it? I'm surprised Newton found it wiser to be master of the mind till he found it safer to be master of the mint. That chap—Jesus—is still a nuisance though. 'We have scotch'd the snake not kill'd it', as Shakespeare, as he called himself, has it. 'Canst thou not minister to a mind diseased?' It's no good driving them underground. Only palliative. Stone death had no fellow. Ah, here they are—stout fellows both. First murderer and second murderer. They look a bit rough, but hearts of gold really. Fine family these Cains. Best of the bunch! You there—don't you play the flute or something? And you—poet aren't you? Homer? All Greek to me, but . . . say, you! Can't you turn out something good with fighting and murder in it? Oh, I'll get it translated, never you fear! We've a top notch translation department in the F.B.I. What's that? Fucking Bloody Infantry. *That* doesn't sound quite right surely? Anyway—stout fellows all. Nurse—no, not you—the male nurse. Ah, here you are. Fetch up a bucket full of decorations. We shall need them shortly. Put in a few guaranteed hero brand. That usually sends them to sleep quietly. 'An army marches on its belly.' So does Satan though. *He's* a fine reliable chap now! Suffer the little children to come unto me with gently smiling jaws. I love little children—especially if they are young enough and tender enough. What, are they *still* sleeping? They sleep, with their eyes of stone, without sense, without life, beneath the rosy hues which stain the white radiance of eternity. These wretched poets—'ante Agamemnona multi'—why can't they let them sleep in their graves unwept, unhonoured and unsung? 'What?' they smile, 'our names, our deeds—so soon erases Time upon his tablet? Where life's glory lies enrolled? Their name liveth for ever more.' Now, thank God, we can go to sleep.

ALICE What a night! Roland, what on earth were you up to? Tossing and turning and shouting! I could hardly get a wink of sleep.

ROLAND What were *you* up to?

EIGHTEEN

Full stop. Sleep. There appear: ALBERT STEGOSAURUS and his close relative ADOLF TYRRANOSAURUS.

ADOLF What the devil have you got all this armour plate for?

ALBERT Call me Albert. I've got it *for* the Devil. What the devil do you s'pose? I'm resting; it's my spore stage.

ADOLF But I got these teeth for spores. Your vegetative existence is an offence. It's provocative, blast you! It's a resistance! You put ideas into my head. I was all right before you stirred up the ten commandments. Since then I have not been able to sleep for the itch to commit adultery. It's all your fault.

ALBERT There you go! Now you are making *me* feel guilty. Why can't you keep your conscience to yourself? Now I am filled with the gnawing of conscience and re-conscience and remorse. World without end—Amen.

ADOLF Keep your religion to yourself! Now you make *me* want to attend mass. All right—serves you right if I *do* eat you!

ALBERT You have wak'd me too soon. I must slumber again.

ADOLF Do wake me—in a few thousand years' time.

ALBERT By that time I shall have reached your anus.

ADOLF The right place for anyone's remorse—keep right away from my mouth and teeth! Right up the other end of my alimentary canal.

ALBERT Don't blame me if you have digestive pains. You mustn't blame me if you devour me. My armour plate, my resistances, my spores are pretty tough. Are you sure your anus can take it?

ADOLF I've got a pretty tough unconscious. I don't let my right hand know what I'm up to. It will take you a few thousand years till your concepts cease to be blind and your thoughts without content are discovered by a thinker without thoughts who has room for a few thoughts who can't find a thinker to give them a home.

ALBERT You give me a headache.

ADOLF I told you to keep your thoughts in their proper place! If you let them get above themselves no wonder your head aches! Take my advice—keep your head for your thoughts. What's that tiny little thing you've got up there?

ALBERT A rudimentary brain.

ADOLF Hmmm . . . I don't like it. Mark my words, it will burst your head open! Chacun a son goût. Ow! What's that? You've shoved your thoughts into me, you vile creature.

ALBERT You shouldn't want to taste what you eat. Why don't you remain satisfied with eating everything without discrimination? Keep your head away from my arse! And if I were you I'd keep your arse away from your head too! Or you'll end up by being anal-erotic!

ADOLF At least I shan't know about it. If this fool Albert thinks I can't chew up his armour! . . .

ALBERT If this fool Adolf thinks my armour can't wear down his teeth! . . .

BOTH . . . he's got something coming to him!

BOTH (*out loud*) Thank God we agree.

NINETEEN

ROLAND The survivals from the past are pathetic monsters. Pathetic phalluses. It seems to me that the very points which are their strength are also their weakness: separate and coincident. I have remarked this peculiarity of man as a tool-making animal before, but here the same peculiarity seems to inhere in an animal antecedent to man by milennia. They lie there stretched out on the squares of black marble by the rosy hues of the stain on the white radiance of Eternity. Sequential thought 'stretched out' what it purports to describe. But may it not be a peculiarity of thought, of the deductive system which has become detached and confused with the reality that approximates it? If so, it could be an illusion like some foreign, alien object not really part of the thing-in-itself, the noumenon. A book is written in pages; the print goes from the top of the page to the bottom and the sentences conform to a particular grammatical structure; the print is disposed in order from left to right. These patterns are dictated by the need to conform to rules of English composition and typographical lay-out. These dispositions have not only been imposed by the culture, but have imposed themselves on the phenomena being observed without criticism. Is the supposition that the reptilian age is antecedent to Hitler correct, or is it a feature of our thinking process which has become an aberration which has not been considered, but has become part of what is *observed*? Suppose the reality is a meaningless chaos. The appearance of order and coherence may be peculiar to the human observer's deductive system and reported as if it were a feature of a 'constant conjunction', observed from without. Further, what is 'within' and what 'without'? Herodotus put forward the suggestion that fossil shells detected in rock might support the belief that the sea once covered that land. Towards the beginning of this century an educated man again revived Herodotus' conjecture about fossils without being aware that it had been debated before. *On this evidence,* it cannot be supposed that knowledge of the nature of fossils has been accumulated or advanced in the intervening two thousand years. This is not evidence, but it may be regarded as an artificially constructed model.

BION The whole of this book so far printed can be regarded as an artificial and elaborate construct. I myself, here introduced into the narrative, can be regarded as a construct, artificially composed with the aid of such artistic and scientific material as I can command and manipulated to form a representation of an author whose name appears on the book and now, for the second time, as a character in a work of fiction. Is it a convincing portrait? Does it appear to 'resemble' reality?

Suppose I drew λ and claimed it was, or was a picture of, a man. You who are looking at this could, if the conditions existed in which we could converse, agree that I looked 'just like that' and that it was a meritorious and continuing example of my artistic genius. This book could be hailed as bearing, in itself, resemblance to its paternity—that it could not be mistaken for someone else's 'brain child'. But I may have a different aim; say, that of writing a description of psycho-analysis. To me, that the book bore witness to its mental origins might be an unwelcome irrelevance, a feature additional to the main component of my wish to communicate and your wish to receive. It is this double quality of the communication and the fact that significance might be attached in varying degrees, now to one, now to the other component, that I wish to discuss. I want to stress that the components are not 'bi-valent' but multi- or poly-valent even if at first I denote it by a 'bi-valent' symbol—λ ξ. The signs I am choosing are the Chinese λ and the Greek ξ. If I write it as λ (ξ) I wish λ to represent a constant, (ξ) an unknown variable. But what is this? Why have symbols appeared? The experience of my own existence stimulates curiosity about me and my objects—of people or things like me.

Since I do not know for sure what these objects are, but want in fact to discuss them, I need to have some way of referring to them. Sometimes it might be a book that I want to discuss. There would be no difficulty usually, because I could make do with a certain familiarity with the use of the English language, using the existing vocabulary and rules of composition. But sometimes, and this is one of those times, this is not true. True, I want to discuss this book. But that is an unimportant part of my pre-occupation. I want to discuss man, but as soon as I say that, I realize the word 'man' has a definite, perhaps misleadingly and frustratingly definite, meaning. I can say I want to discuss 'wilfred r bion'. That would have a definite meaning to some, but it is not true; I don't want to exclude whatever is 'represented', signified, denoted by those letters, 'rbidefilnorw', arranged, according to certain conventions, to form a visual pattern on paper. The problem is obtrusive, but not informatively displayed. If I want to communicate a song to a group of people familiar with the printed word but unfamiliar with sung poems or patterns formed by print on paper, it would obscure comprehension of the music I want them to *hear* when they *see* the pattern formed on the paper. Pound has shown that the culture of a group may be such that they do not print poems that can be sung, but construct poems that form, when printed, a pattern which pleases the eye. If sung and heard, they do not form a sound pattern that satisfies; it dis-satisfies and displeases the ear. I am so defective or badly trained that I cannot be pleased if I read, by eye, a Shakespeare play; yet if good actors transform that same printed play into a dramatic presentation the effect is an experience which is emotionally stirring; it effects a change—in Wilfred R. Bion—that is durable. Some similar effect is produced if J. S. Bach composes a musical score which, transformed by suitably trained people, can result in patterns of sound that can be received by my ear. A fictional character, Quee-Quegg in Moby Dick, can be shown by contrast to be deeply moved, through his eyes, by the pattern which a printed book, of which he does not understand a word, stirs in his visual senses. An author, Herman Melville, 'caused' to be printed a book which had a similar—analogous?—effect on the aforementioned Wilfred R. Bion who 'read' it.

The places in the following few sentences marked by □ are places representing 'some thing' that I want to talk about. 'Some thing' is not adequate; it is too impregnated with pre-existing meaning—too saturated (λ) and at the same time not saturated (ξ) enough. I am now as wide awake, conscious, rational, sane as I am ever likely to be between the moment of writing and the day of my □. I pick upon the □ for although I do not know when that is, I imagine that the empty □ will at some time be, like an algebraic variable in the course of mathematical calculations or a legal register of births, marriages and deaths, completed. That moment of time and that formal entry on a document seems to have a convenience comparable to the inscription, 'finis', which at one time was conventionally used at the end of a book. There are other forms, notably the form which James Joyce regarded as more adequate than the sensuously apprehended cessation of print. He wished his story to conform to some of the vicoesque qualities which he felt he had derived from the philosophical disquisitions of Giambattista Vico, but had not been able to receive from Freud.

λ (ξ) denotes a domain without beginning, end, or other dimension. I have to employ an extremely inadequate apparatus to discuss it. I have to manufacture the apparatus as I proceed. I claim that it is artistic though the art has not yet been created; it is religious though the religion has not been and never can (without ceasing to be a religion) be made to conform to any of the dogmata and institutions hitherto regarded as characteristic of religion. I do not expect the art to be analogous to music, painting, literary expression, sculpture or quantum mechanics; the 'uncertainty principle' (borrowed from Heisenberg) used by me both formulates and destroys the formulation together with λ (ξ). O is by definition indestructible and not subject to, circumscribed by, beginnings and ends, rules, laws of nature or any construct of the human mind. In the domain of human comprehension Melanie Klein could not reconcile herself to the fact that whenever she had made herself understood, that fact rendered what she understood no longer 'alive'.

This introduction is intended to be a simplification (intended to be, though by definition false); a way of psychological preparation for more rigorous, in every 'sense', presentation. I shall proceed to yet one more 'simplified' (more easily comprehensible) presentation. I claim that though I may not have succeeded in making simple or comprehensible the complexity or confusion of the religious–scientific–artistic formulation, it is not so because it is clarity → confusion oriented, but because it is confusion → clarity oriented. If the English written page can be treated as if it were a model for the thing itself and not just a written page, the *poles* of confusion and clarity could be located at top left and bottom right of the page; my meaning here is not confusion, but talk 'about' confusion.

It is commonly understood that an analysand talks to keep the analyst correctly informed and the psycho-analyst has a similar aim. It is easily demonstrated that such a supposition is erroneous: so would be the case with the opposite supposition. Questionnaires are drawn up and they are supposed to formulate searching questions to which revealing completions would be provided and the result would be—'revealing'. In psycho-analysis it is supposed that no questions are formulated and replies to the *No-Question* would be more revealing. I propose an extension of this procedure—the invention of the *No-Questionnaire*.

Once I used to make notes on the session in conformity with my training. I was aware of feeling guilt and anxiety if I had no records to support any argument with myself or my colleagues, or real or imaginary accusers. As I became more accustomed to and more familiar with the way I worked, I realized it would be agreeable if I could indulge in the truth. (I was, of course, convinced that I always had. I would have been indignant at any accusation that I had not always been the soul of integrity. Even as I realize this, I appreciate that this very account is embellished with certain artistically exaggerated locutions intended to add, in a famous phrase, 'veri-similitude to an otherwise bald and unconvincing narrative'.) This discovery appeared to emerge over a period of time. The awareness of the discovery varied in intensity—ebbed and flowed. The 'notes' I made, the 'records' of sessions, turned out to be useful in a way that I did not expect. As a sample I give this imaginary entry:

Nov, (date)	My God, my God!
Nov, (date)	!!!
Nov, (date)	
Nov, (date)	been with her brother!! At last
Nov, (date)	must (illegible)

In so far as the patient's name was correct, the entry could be called evocative.

MYCROFT HOLMES (*yawning somewhat ostentatiously*) Most interesting.

TWENTY

WATSON Shall I shut him up?

SHERLOCK HOLMES My *dear* Watson!

BION (*outraged*) What the devil do you mean by butting into my serious discussion? Are you not aware that I am raising serious issues?

MYCROFT (*in no way impressed*) Go on Sherlock. This is more your line than mine. *You* tell him.

WATSON (*before Sherlock intervenes which he appears unlikely to do*) My dear sir, Mister Holmes and his brother really must not be interrupted; it's a private and important matter.

BION But, my good man, are you not aware that you are entirely fictitious characters? I am a qualified doctor!

WATSON So am I; and an M.D.

BION Nonsense! Purely imaginary and not very bright even in the estimation of your fellow spooks. I am a past President of the British Psycho-analytical Society and past Director of the London Clinic of . . .

MYCROFT & SHERLOCK (*together burst into a gale of laughter*)

WATSON (*contains his mirth with difficulty, but manages to be civil)* Excuse me, sir, but I must admit that I have never heard of your existence. I do not want to hurt your feelings or to appear to boast, but although Mycroft has always been of a retiring disposition, Sherlock, and to a lesser extent myself, has a world-wide following. You yourself were admitting that there are imaginary characters who are infinitely better known than countless generations of nonentities. Now excuse me. I am a very busy man—allow me to suggest that you get on that couch there and sleep it off quietly.

BION *(with a gesture of despair, abandons his office to the three intruders and goes to sleep)*

SHERLOCK I hope you weren't too rough with him, Watson.

WATSON Real people have to be treated roughly if the universe is to be made safe for imaginary people. If you remember, this problem cropped up before with real numbers. Quite impossible for the simplest mathematical problem even to be formulated till negative numbers destroyed the tyranny of being confined in the restricted space of addition—just more real numbers.

MYCROFT What was the problem, Sherlock? I had the impression it was something simple.

SHERLOCK The simple part of it has been dealt with by Watson. You heard that fellow Bion? Nobody has ever heard of him or of Psycho-analysis. He thinks it is real, but that his colleagues are engaged in an activity which is only a more or less ingenious manipulation of symbols. There is something in what he says. There is a failure to understand that any definition must deny a previous truth as well as carry an unsaturated component.

WATSON Like your observation of the Silver Blaze case.

SHERLOCK Good old Watson: dead on the mark as usual!

WATSON *(expanding in the unexpected universe of appreciation in which he finds himself)* You said, if I remember rightly, 'Let me draw your attention to the extraordinary behaviour of the barking dog', and I said that I had not heard a barking dog. 'That', you said, 'was what made it so extraordinary'.

SHERLOCK Quite so. Nobody will listen to silence. It was the greatest single contribution to the final and merciful extinction of psycho-analysis. If it became possible that someone might notice, or maybe appreciate a silence, the psycho-analysts started their dog-like yapping, yelping and quarrelling. At first I used to listen because it sounded so like meaning, but I realized it was devoid of meaning and a noise likely to make thought impossible. I noticed, being possessed of a rudimentary capacity for thought, they were some of the earliest animals to hate thought. Of course, it was a poet who formulated it first of all.

> 'Pipe me to pastures still
> and be the music that I care to hear.'

MYCROFT Sherlock, you and your fiddling always made me suspect that you were more of an artist or a parson than a scientist. Can't we get on to the point? Surely it must be obvious to you, as it is to me, that Bion is feigning sleep as a cloak for stealing my time and my capacity as a substitute for his truly real and majestic stupidity? These 'thoughts' are symptoms of an underlying group of transformations. The human animal is very highly developed; its whole sensual apparatus is a re-agent, admittedly usually crude. If it has, as is usually the case, over-eaten, it becomes aware of discomfort—pain, as it calls it. Amazingly enough—we must not make the mistake of underrating it—when it developed beyond the stage of yowling and shrieking, it noticed, after a thousand years or so, that it had a pain. Tyrannosaurus didn't like being eaten. In short, what was amusing and satisfying was the same activity when the perspective was reversed and yet felt quite different—or so it thought. It was not 'different' but 'reversed'. Their rudimentary forms of mathematics never got further than a simple activity which they called algebraic projective geometry. These long words themselves were very popular and gave them nice feelings when they used them, but caused howlings of rage and pain if the direction was reversed. It was not now a part of the anatomical digestive tract, but part of the mind which they felt was somehow derived from, or genetically related to, their nervous system. It was not related to their anatomy. But they had to go on trying to use, as a substitute for thought, an antiquated and inadequate system of models. Wonderful to relate, the system continued to develop—to grow, as they called it—till imaginary beings like me emerged. I am thought-without-a-thinker, but I can assume the appearance of reality and can even be supposed, by one of these exceptionally developed creatures, to be what they call an hallucination. It is in keeping with this domain that an 'hallucination' arouses fear. Any thought that does not fall into the 'rules' which they like to think are obeyed by what they call 'thought' is hated; so are the systems of 'grammar' which differ from the rules with which they are familiar. The marvel is that any procedure, development or growth ever occurred. Now the problem you are posing, my dear Sherlock, is ridiculously simple if you realize the need to use the counterpart of, say, an X-ray film, something that betrays patterns of light and dark thought in a characteristic form. Once that is done, and it is dared to look at the mental configuration without being overwhelmed by fear and distaste—for example, at thoughts without a thinker . . .

SHERLOCK I see what you mean.

MYCROFT I thought you would.

BION I'm damned if *I* do.

MYCROFT You're damned if you don't too. And now I must leave my fictitious state: it's rather fatiguing. Excuse me while you go to sleep . . . Well, Sherlock, that's disposed of him.

WATSON I thought you were pretty violent.

MYCROFT You have to be—with these real characters. They are either at your throat or at your boots in spite of talk about an arse between these two.

WATSON Even so, they call it 'circumcision'. More long words, though in my time Shakespeare's language was good enough. 'There's a divinity that shapes our ends, rough-hew them how we will.' You were saying?

MYCROFT Leave the long words out of it. They are useful only for mystification and dominance. We can use constructions and verbal transformations of objects derived from what were in origin part of the sensuous domain. For example, that poor fellow, though he knew better, struggled to transform his religious rubbish into what he called 'opticks'. Quite erroneous and limited in so far as he was successful. Berkeley had no difficulty; even labouring with the equipment of religious training he could detect the infinitesimal increments and the part they could play in postponing detection of a fallacy for at least a century.

SHERLOCK Is that a merit?

MYCROFT It involved the development of mathematical rigour. The development of the human mind was, in the course of time, believed to be associated with, or caused by, the central nervous system. Freud thought that. The Greeks believed in ghosts, independent of anatomy yet with a visible counterpart; some function of themselves able to apprehend a personality after the physical anatomy had been destroyed or dealt with, but not before. They thought they could not see it by mediation of the physical, sensuous, visual apparatus. We do not know what physical apparatus they thought betrayed the phrenes, though they spoke of them frequently and as if they had no shadow.

BION As far as I am concerned, you and Sherlock and Watson *are* fictional characters. I can see that they might be described as very vividly conceived fictional characters, but I see no reason for imagining or conceiving of them in any other terms.

MYSELF But *I* do, because the term 'fictional character' itself is an inadequate phrase. Here I have just written 'myself' as if I wanted to give it a status different from me. I could call 'Bion' a second-class citizen compared with 'Myself'. I indicate without definition that the opinions expressed by me, even if fiction, are worthy of being treated with respect. Those opinions are of superior status to opinions claimed as mine and spoken as if I claimed 'ownership' over them. Their value, in a war for possession, is greater than it would be if they were intended to be 'true'. Conversely, a statement with a vertex of truth value would be of lower value as a weapon in a struggle for supremacy.

BION (*catching sight of Doctor Watson about to speak*) My God! Whenever I see that chap I am reminded of Mister Pooter. Both of them remind me of poor Conan Doyle. How he hated and despised Sherlock Holmes and Mycroft and the other fictitious characters who drove 'scientific', spiritualistic Conan Doyle off the stage. The worst of it is that Watson and Pooter remind me of *me*—maddening! It's quite bad enough going to sleep and being driven off the stage of conscious, waking, real life by dreams.

WATSON It's nothing like so bad as being driven off the stage by conscious, scientific, 'real' you and your 'real' associations. You probably don't remember what George Santayana said would happen if the scientific 'beasts and blackguards' got hold of the world. Saint Augustine described them as enemies of the City of God.

BION Since you drag in saints, I must remind you that the City of God was itself an attack on the people who were complaining of what the barbarians and their Christian Allies had done to Rome.

WATSON I don't see what you've got against religion.

BION *(in disgust)* I'm going to sleep.

SHERLOCK *(to Watson)* Has he gone? It's humiliating to think that dreams are at the mercy of people who dream.

MYCROFT It's worse to realize that thoughts are dependent on finding a thinker. Shhh . . . what's that?

TWENTY-ONE

F*aint sound—Arf, arf, arf.*

MYSELF My God! Here they come again. Those howls! It's eerie. I believe they are nearer. That! That! . . . That is a tiger. *No*: Tigers are only cats. That is no cat. Arf, arf, arfer's little history of England. You damned hyena! If the wine don't get you then the women . . . He's just insolent, sir. In what way sergeant? He . . . smiles. What! Well it's just a dumb insolence. Nurse. Out damned . . . No, ridiculous. I've got it mixed up. Hullo, may Potter, I mean 'mere pother' about nothing. If the windows rattle—last night it was windy and he waked the whole ward with his nonsense. What, was he sleep-walking? Not exactly, sir. He sat up and shook the bed, he was trembling so violently. 'They are coming!' he said, 'that's the firing party . . . they are coming for me'. Then, just as you'd think he was going to jump out of the window, he quietened down as if he was watching the lawn to see it open. He told me his dead wife used to come out and walk towards him to fetch him—till he screamed! Then she'd go away. Recently he's started crying, quietly, because she doesn't come. 'She won't come now any more', he says; like a baby, as if he wanted her to come. It's a terrible laugh sir. It upsets the whole ward. Better transfer him to the chronic ward. Chloral is it? Double the dose.

SHERLOCK Most affecting! Any damn fool could see his brain is damaged, has been since the war. He was blown up by a shell: they all are! Very respectable. And then there is some equal fool who wants to analyse him!

BION (*waking up suddenly*) The really intelligent—I mean *real* intelligence, not the intelligence which has a fictitious character—want to cut out the brain, so that he will be intelligent too—really like Tyrannosaurus himself and some sea birds. Aren't they beautiful? Don't they fly high! They are so beautiful, so high—they don't need to be intelligent. They have to be blown up—not like this pathetic fool, but inflated so they can make use of the currents. Just like the birds who see maw! Not too much though, but like my beautiful friend Seymore. Like that man Shakespeare. How do, Cap'n? Art thou sleepin' there? Below? And how's the mind diseased getting along? Have you found anyone to minister in the last few hundred years? Well, yes, you could say that the trouble has been rooted out if it is erased properly. Leave not a rack behind. Nothing less than complete mindlessness will do.

MYCROFT If I may suggest that a thinker should be found.

MYSELF Why? Have you found a thought?

MYCROFT I have been wanting to get it expressed if only I could get you and your psycho-analytic friends out of the way. Let me try; it's this: the mind, though only a very recent development, is a subtle and sensitive one. Freud, as he often did, put his finger on the spot. In the seventh chapter of *The Interpretation of Dreams,* he said, answering his own question, 'What is the conscious? It is nothing less than the sense organ for the perception of psychic quality.' It stands to reason, then, that if he was right, this very recently developed organ, though not secondary to the probings *of* the grosser senses, may be capable of 'probing' and reacting *to* the grosser senses by 'psychic reality'.

BION What's so new about that?

MYCROFT Peace, pint pot. All these dreams and things are not going to lead to a discovery of some still further and more developed mind because there isn't one. But if these dreams and fantasies and bright ideas could be looked at in a way which revealed certain constantly conjoined elements, it might be possible to discern an underlying configuration (as Poincaré suggested of the discovery of a mathematical formula) which showed coherence where none was before, and relationships where none had been previously seen to exist. These revealed configurations might then be seen, like the mathematical formula, to have a reality and meaning. That meaning could then, like a good X-ray, be interpreted.

The mass of material is now so abundant that it is doubtful whether any psycho-analyst could 'interpret' the pattern with the efficiency of a computer. So what is now required is a procedure or instrument that could reveal the configurations. The configurations require transforming into forms capable of programming. This in turn requires something analogous to the discovery of Cartesian co-ordinates. Then the clumsy formulations of pictorial visions, analogous to Euclidean geometry, could be more elegantly expressed by mathematical formulas of algebraic deductive systems—not the clear but inflexible hieroglyphs of Euclidean imagery. A start could be made with the relatively simple, because unencumbered by free associations, dreams of the schizophrenic. The paranoid-schizoid position is itself clear and chaotic, that is, unspoiled by coherence unless spoiled by intolerance of 'mysteries, half-truths'. Good-night children—everywhere. And please, Consciousness, go to sleep. The world of reality is the place for you!

MYSELF You mean the 'macroscopic' senses. The important 'senses' may be the 'microscopic'—'ultra-' and 'infra'-sensuous. I see something in this. Mystery destroyed by 'the laughter of a fool', the crackling of thorns beneath the pot, makes a 'hunch' impossible. One 'direction', predominantly followed, could lead to a prolongation of the impetus and further 'discoveries'. Increased quantity transforms to qualitative change. Multiplication of particular instances becomes new discovery. What Mycroft envisages is a reversal of direction; this bypasses multiplication and therefore discovery of a general theory which has already been missed. At present there is a slackening in discovery about the nature of the mind and observance of what the mind can be sensitive to as a sense organ of psychic and physical quality. The mental domain of thought has been and is vitiated by the failure to appreciate the need for direction analogous to the mathematical recognition of the value of weighing direction—'sense' and sense. Consciousness functions as a receptor so sensitive that no machine can replace it; later there might be a machine which can do what the unaided biological organ cannot.

WATSON What's Bion scribbling?

MYCROFT Take the pen out of his mouth. There—did you anywhere see anything so laughable?—wide-open eyes, wide-open mouth! Look out! He's going to cry!

BION Mind the volcano . . .

MYCROFT He is what these real characters call 'waking up'. At present he has the sense to think he's the White Queen; when he is awake he will call it a fictitious character.

BION And in that sleep of death, what dreams may come . . .

WATSON Now Hamlet. If not Hamlet, Shakespeare—whom he will denigrate or plutichrate by calling a 'genius'.

MYCROFT And won't pay any attention to either on the excuse of his being a fictious character or a genius and therefore not worthy of attention.

BION I wrote a book once and called it *Attention and Interpretation*.

WATSON What did I say? He has woken up. Back to the real world, 'false fugitive . . .'

MYCROFT 'And to thy speed add wings.'

ROSEMARY You wrote a book! (*Yawning*) How fascinating.

BION You are not a bit fascinated.

ROSEMARY True, but I am fascinating. And that is more than you can claim to be.

TWENTY-TWO

BION Suppose there is a physical disease, such as asthma, possessing physical components which remain to be discovered. There may be a mind (personality) that fears discovery of the asthma. I regard that as the mental aspect of the personality from which he retreats. Or he may want to develop his existing capacity to a higher pitch. This development could show itself in a man who was unaware of the physical pain caused by a scarcely existent hepatic cancer becoming able to feel pain though previously incapable of experiencing it. But suppose it was not wished or not practicable to foster a development indistinguishable from an approach to hypochondriasis. Without any change in the personality, could one elaborate an instrument no more to do with the personality than a measure of length or height would have to do with the personality that wished to use it to find out how tall he was; or a system of lenses relates to the personality wanting to observe a distant scene? We might fit to his mind an instrument which made him, without any more disturbance than a pair of spectacles, aware of physical pain which he could not detect unaided.

WATSON What about fitting him out with a questionnaire which he could be required to fill in? Then, according to the pattern displayed by his completed form, it would be possible to 'see' the pain.

SHERLOCK Brilliant, Watson! I could hardly have done better myself.

BION So you fictitious characters have turned up again.

WATSON Not Mycroft; only Sherlock and I.

SHERLOCK Since you want to have a hunch—which you can deny if it turns out wrong—I suppose *we* have to stand in for your missing integrity. Is that it?

BION Not *quite*. But certainly I want to be able to repudiate it if it should seem unsuitable for rigorous application.

WATSON I see the idea. I wish you could have my Jezail bullet.

ROSEMARY (*brightly*) What about fitting a woman—me, for example?

ALICE Or even me? Could not that augment—without it costing you any change in your personality—your armoury of instruments?

ROLAND No. What say you, Tom?

TOM No.

(*Roland, Tom, the Man, the two Bions all look questioningly at each other*)

ROLAND 'An evil and adulterous generation ask for a sign.' Usually it is 'cure' they seek for and that is why the world is littered with cures.

ALICE I must say you look a bit glum—all of you, except Rosemary and me.

ROLAND Certainly you two seem pretty cheerful. So would we be if we were able to have the . . . the luck of being women.

ALICE Well, Roland, why don't you? Why don't you pair off? You could pick any of your pals you fancy.

ROLAND Don't be ridiculous. We aren't 'pansies', homosexuals . . . (*Rosemary stops manicuring her hands and looks up astonished, but says nothing*)

ALICE (*looking wide-eyed at Roland*) Oh, Roland, you *are* a poppet! I could almost love you, you're so sweet!

ROLAND (*sheepishly*) Why? What have I done now?

ALICE Perhaps Rosemary could tell you.

(*Rosemary purses her lips but only resumes her manicure*)

ROLAND I suppose you think it is funny to make men look ridiculous.

ROSEMARY No; it's too easy. They do it so well themselves. Remember the man spinning round with his guts hanging out?

ALICE (*sadly*) For so many years since I first met you I thought you were so marvellous. I remember how fine you looked that day you came back from school. You were so proud, so happy because you were going to join the army. And I was so sure you were going to win the Victoria Cross. I said hullo, but I realized that I was only a silly school girl and I knew you could not be bothered, but I hoped, one day . . . well, no. I don't know what I hoped. Then one day I visited your mother and she had been crying.

ROLAND Yes, I know. A telegram had come that morning to say Gerald had been killed. What of it?

ALICE I was afraid. I thought it was you. And I didn't know I minded at all. So when she said, 'Gerald has been killed in action', I was so happy I was shocked and stammered. Luckily your mother thought I was upset and sorry for her. And she tried to console me. She held me to her and said, 'Never mind . . . it is God's will. You did like him a little, we thought. Didn't you?' I was so confused I just shook my head and she thought I said, 'yes'. But I was sorry, genuinely sorry, soon after I got away home. It was horrible, dark, cold, raining. But I had a warm place in my heart. It was only for you, dear. And then a dreadful fear came—suppose it was you and not Gerald.

(*Roland recovers his equanimity and even some of his complacency*)

ROBIN I used to think you were a bit sweet on Alice. Once when you came back on leave; I thought you were a lucky man. Alice looked a bit struck on you just as I thought you were on her. So I wasn't really surprised when the happy day came and you led her to the altar.

(*He speaks jocosely*)

(*Alice shudders at the recollection, but says nothing*)

ROLAND (*the shudder is not lost on him*) What's the matter?

ALICE That nightmare wedding day. I thought it would improve. It did very slightly, for about a year. And then it settled down, nothing dramatic, nothing terrible, (*bitterly*) only noticeable if you compared me to a summer's day, one day with another, at intervals of a year. Then it became clear that it was horrible and becoming more horrible. Even then I had to be off my guard, as you are when you go to sleep. 'What dreams may come, aye, there's the rub.' Even when it's only the sleep of life. Luckily I don't fear the sleep of death now. Come not in terrors as the king of kings.

BION Which reminds me—is there anything more terrible than reality in the shape of Wembley Cup Final?

ALICE Yes—Oxford playing Cambridge.

MYSELF I was going to suggest Sade versus Masoch. Or the same at a higher power, so that the change in quantity becomes a change in quality enough for it to be called *war*.

BION Or peace becomes pacification.

MAN Did someone call me?

TWENTY-THREE

The scene is the vast arena of Wembley. At first sight there appear to be some hundred thousand spectators, but it becomes clear that there are very few people, but an enormous host of animals of every shape and kind. Just near one entry is a small group of men in what Bion, Myself and their party take to be film actors in the uniform of legionnaires of the Roman Army. A cup final supporter, paper streamers and all, approaches one of the motionless figures and addresses him.

SUPPORTER Wotcher chum! Wot's yer regiment?

LEGIONARY Legion Vicesima Valeria Victrix.

SUPPORTER (*in feigned fear*) Lor'! Selling booze—wot's yer line?

A NEIGHBOUR (*shouts across*) Ask 'im if 'e's got some beer, chum!

There is a noise which drowns his reply and conversation rapidly becomes impossible as the pulsations, emerging more and more from the confused noise, themselves become recognizable as an unmistakable rhythmic beat, and the beats as each made up of recognizable sounds. The terrifying rhythm could be matched as if it were a 'swung' version of the Christian hymn, 'Abide with me'. 'Kum not in Quat, Quat, Adze Zhee King of Kongs.' Bzzfading like the whine of a receding shell. Kind of good like guts wound round your bloody throat. The massed bands of the Brigade of Guards crash out the sense of intimacy as the hundred thousand become more crushingly intimate. The space has closed in as if the expanding universe had decided to contract instead. Every so often the rhythm is emphasized by a choral interlude, 'Arf, arf, arf'. Suddenly the din stops and is succeeded by a silence pierced by the one sound or word, 'Farrar'. The vast silent crowd wait for Alice to present the prizes. Each animal goes off nuzzling a very small atomic bomb; some suck it, some try to shove it up their neighbour's anus. Some come up to Bion to complain that it isn't detonated.

Valeria of the Valerian gens is—yes, there is terrific excitement as she approaches the centre of the field to carry out the ritual of Kicking Off the Ball, which is the start of the Dance of Death. A terrific spectacle! D.W. Griffiths—that must be why the Twentieth Legion have arrived! And the Head Psycho Anal List to read out the prize winners. Sh. SH. SHHHH. Quiet, everyone! The Papal Guard are about to play the composition by the winner of the music Festival. SHUT UP! You Bas Turds! The quartet will now play 'Solitude' on four trombones. Then the Commander in Chief will say his prayers at the climax of the most intimate crisis of the celebration before—where's that ruddy whore got to?—the Lady Valeria kicks off the Final, Absolutely Final, till next year, celebration of Peace. The general's Lady makes a few mincing steps towards the Ball. Cheers, laughter and tears. She'll have to be quick if she's going to get off before she's murdered.

TWENTY-FOUR

ALICE ... one thing worse, but I didn't realize it till I came to you to be psycho-analysed.

BION That wasn't psycho-analysis. I didn't know any better then!

ALICE Do you know any better now?

BION Perhaps. I don't know.

ALICE Well, that's something, I suppose.

MYSELF Yes, something. Not much, but something.

ROSEMARY (*still pre-occupied with her appearance, apparently lost to all reality beyond her immediate needs and those seem to be exclusively centred on her looks*) I shall want you to come with me, Alice. I may need you when I go out in about half and hour.

ALICE Yes, Miss. Will that be all for the present?

MYCROFT The difficulty for poor Watson is he cannot adjust to these changes of translucency. Luckily I became used to them when the Bauhaus people were experimenting with the changes in visual planes. Even Sherlock became a bit mixed, but he should have known better. So ought our respected creator, Conan Doyle. But he got mixed up with that Spiritualistic nonsense just as

Sherlock became entangled with 'reality' as he called it. Do you remember how he became tied up with 'the woman'? Irene Adler, wasn't it? Silly ass.

ROSEMARY (*appears again, though transparently. She speaks with a coarse accent*) Wot's up now Mister Mycroft? I've not much time to waste because I'm going out with my girl friend. Showing 'er some of the sights seeing as 'ow she knows nothin' about them. Seein' she's a lady. Proper educated, I don't think! Wot's up Roland?

ROLAND (*struggling with some indignant need to protest; finally, in tones of stifled anger*) Alice was making out we were homosexuals. I was a soldier for four years and was decorated . . .

ALICE Oh, come off it, Roland. What's that got to do with it? Do you think we girls have never heard of a public school?

ROSEMARY Fine times you seemed to 'ave too! I thought all your slap-up institutions only went in for skivvies like me. I remember one day when I 'ad time off from a little pub my mum 'ad got me a job at. Nice boy 'e was too. I went out with 'im. Lord! 'E was like a cat on 'ot bricks! You'd think 'e 'ad never seen a girl in 'is life. I asked 'im wot 'is school was. My! was 'e red—'e blushed and 'e 'ummed and 'e 'awed. I asked 'im what was the matter. And I found out 'e thought 'is school would find out 'e 'ad been out with me. I could 'ave smacked 'is face! But I didn't. I thought I'd make 'im feel more comfortable by telling 'im 'e looked nice. I said, you're very 'andsome—'e was, too, I'll say that for 'im.

ROBIN I can see that it is funny to you. It wasn't to us.

MAN (*he is reclining on a couch and has been listening intently for a time, resting on his elbow looking at each speaker in turn*) I can understand why we won. I could not understand before. We learned at school about Shakespeare and Milton, Schiller and Heine. You didn't learn about Heine? Well, we didn't much either, but we liked Shakespeare. We had a foolish teacher. We called him 'unser Shakespeare' because he was so foolish and patriotic. We called him 'old ros' bif' too and he thought we were making fun of the English, but we were making fun of him because he made us learn a poem about the Roast Beef of Old England. I didn't think it was a very good poem. Then when the second war came I thought something had happened to the English.

ROBIN Nothing had happened to the English. It was treachery. That man Chamberlain . . .

MAN No, I don't think so. Shakespeare spoke about England being true to itself. And I think what he said was right. No?

ROBIN (*flushed and angry—rises half off his couch, but seeing that the man is fingering a wicked looking automatic, sinks back*)

ROSEMARY (*Her interest has been flagging but she is now watching with great interest; she beckons to Alice to pay attention; sotto voce*) Watch this, it's interesting. We shall have work to do soon. (*Out loud to the man*) I say! Can I watch? Are you going to shoot him? Oh, *do* shoot him—please, *please*! I've never seen a man shot.

MAN Shoot? No. We never shoot helpless prisoners.

ROSEMARY (*disappointed, losing interest*) Oh, I always thought men, if they were helpless, were shot. I had a boy friend who became an officer in the Air Force. He was shot escaping—so they said—with fifty others.

MAN It's a lie.

ROSEMARY I thought it was. I expect you are so different from Public School. A girl I once knew was watching an operation with a lot of other nurses. The chief surgeon looked along the row insultingly, making them uncomfortable for being such a poor lot—till he came to my friend, who was very pretty. My friend whispered to the girl at her side, just as she thought he was coming to her. When he saw her she was looking him straight in the face—apparently whispering—about him, of course! Boy! did he blush! He looked like a beetroot!

ROBIN Women always tell that kind of story. I expect he looked away, granted, but . . .

ROSEMARY Robin, did you go with Roland when he escaped from the pigeon loft? That was brave, wasn't it? I *like* our guardian here—or whatever he calls himself. You're all the same anyhow.

MAN (*has stopped fingering his automatic and has put it down with an amused smile*) Kolossal!

TOM I wish I had the gun. But as a matter of fact I am nervous of guns. I had to be invalided out of the army because I couldn't carry a rifle; I was afraid I might shoot someone.

ROBIN (*still smarting under Rosemary's questions*) Poor Tom! Couldn't you have shot some Germans? That would have made you feel better, wouldn't it?

TOM I was afraid I might shoot one of our own side.

ROLAND Much safer that way of course. War and murder are dangerous—psychopathic personality is safer.

MYSELF Not always—it matters which end of the gun you are.

ROLAND (*it is clear that he is contemptuous of psychiatrists and others that he calls 'trick cyclists'*) Well, I suppose it is all right if you are a balanced personality.

MYSELF You mean you think it's all a matter of 'tricks'? Well, it may be. I've certainly been scared all my life and I've had to learn to *look* brave. You always get caught and sometimes you are caught out.

BION Give me an example.

MYSELF (*with discomfort and distaste*) No.

BION Why not? This is a private matter where you are free to say what you like.

MYSELF I am not. I could try to escape the problem of discretion by using material drawn from myself and making it truthful. I cannot—I know myself too well to be honest. There would be no discretion or privacy unless I remained silent about my own affairs. There is a further problem. Non-artistic methods of communication are less accurate than those used by artists. For example, I could use a camera to take photographs, or a recording machine and video tapes to record the audible and visual. I can watch a television picture and see men landing on the moon. My impression is that the photographic representation is inadequate and even if improved by mechanical means, I and others would still regard it as 'flattening'. I can say this with conviction of the psycho-analytical experience also. I cannot describe this experience in any convincing way to someone who does not share it, any more than the moving picture of men landing on the moon tells me what it feels like. It is delusory to suppose that contemporaneity makes the experience communicable. Even while it is happening I may not succeed in drawing attention to the experience, less still with an experience which I know I have had, but cannot now 'remember'.

I can remember, faintly, what it is like to go into battle in a tank; I know enough to be able to describe it in terms of terror. I know a companion had the experience of being invalided out as schizophrenic; another never regained his skill as a soldier. He was said to have been delinquent although he wrote to me in terms of affection years afterwards. Another became disillusioned and desperate and in his last battle was destroyed with the rest of his companions and burned to death. I know that some people, while not having the same experience as myself, were confident that I knew what they felt; some believe I know what it is like to be a psycho-analyst; others neither know what it is like to come to me for analysis nor how it might feel for me to be their analyst. They can learn to pretend they are familiar with psycho-analytic experience as a clever animal learns tricks: the human animal can learn how to play tricks which might convince the ignorant. If trickery were enough, no harm would occur. In a group trickery might afford a solution of the problem. An interpretation appropriate psycho-analytically cannot be right in a room where others are present; the interpretation addressed to a group is witnessed in a way which differs from the psycho-analytic interpretation. In what does the difference consist? Some differences spring to the mind at once. In psycho-analysis 'common' sense—I am talking about physical sense—suggests that two physical beings only are present; in a group a number of people can be physically 'sensed' (literally) to be present. Wilfred Trotter, in *Instincts of the Herd in Peace and War*, suggested that the group as a whole is greater than the sum of its parts. I feel that I, who am writing this (and thinking before I am writing it), am less than the whole of me. I can 'think' the possibility that my ideas, valued as cultural achievement, are insignificant, 'stuck on' a part of my group reproductive functioning which I choose to ignore by identifying with my sexual life and other functions which have been emphasized through the over-elaboration of the individual by psycho-analysis. Thus, I can argue that the mind and its works are of great significance; the rest, a total, inchoate mindlessness to be called 'the unconscious', is lumped together and glorified and idealized as a further tribute to the mind. Are the gametes mindless, unconscious, mentally active, or do they belong to a category so different that the mind has no apparatus for dealing with them? I put forward, herewith, a theory of ξ with a recently proliferated sense organ known as the 'end', in which various functions, usually associated with psycho-analysis (the Oedipus situation, aggression, rivalry) are supposed to be observed (on the model of forms of dis-order, dis-ease, sex, fear, love). In reality they are patterns, configurations, insignificant in themselves but, if delineated, indicative of an *underlying* reality by their perturbations, regroupings, shifts in pattern and colour; they reflect a category and kind that the human mind cannot formulate or conjecture in their presence. If so, these Oedipus situations, impulses, instincts and characters could be made opaque in the way in which patterns in X-rays are revealed by the use of sensitized plates. The personality or mind, as portrayed psycho-analytically in detail, is a recent photogram of some long-existent reality, of significance only as an archaic physical anatomy might be. Psycho-analysis would appear as an ephemeral phenomenon, betraying forces on the surface of which the human race flickers, flares and fades in response to the unrecognized but gigantic reality.

The practical point is—no further investigation of psycho-analysis, but the psyche it betrays. *That* needs to be investigated through the medium of *mental* patterns; *that* which is indicated is *not* a symptom; *that* is not a cause of the symptom; *that* is not a disease or *any*thing subordinate. Psycho-analysis itself is just a stripe on the coat of the tiger. Ultimately it may meet the Tiger—The Thing Itself—O.

BION If I had heard you say this a few years back I suspect that I and my colleagues would have been shocked and thought you were turning against psycho-analysis and were guilty of dis-honesty. Indeed, I would be interested to know how you justify the fact that you are still practising—do you call it psycho-analysis or some other term like psychotherapy?—and charging people fees. Can you expand this?

MYSELF Thanks to memory I can make a comparison. The comparison causes change, and on some occasions the change obtrudes. When this happens you feel the change deserves to be recorded and the dialogue between me and me might just as well be conducted between me and a fictitious character. The fiction can be so rhetorical as to be incomprehensible; or so realistic that the dialogue becomes audible to others. There is thus a double fear: that of the conversation being so theoretical that the thoughts might be taken for meaningless jargon; and that of the seeming reality. Having two sets of feelings about the same facts is felt as madness and disliked accordingly. This is one reason why it is felt necessary to have an analyst; another reason is the wish for me to be available to be regarded as mad and used to being regarded as mad. There is a fear that you might be called an analysand, or reciprocally, that you may be accused of insanity. Should I then be tough and resilient enough to be regarded and treated as insane while being sane? If so, it is not surprising that psycho-analysts are, almost as a function of being analysts, supposed to qualify for being insane and called such. It is part of the price they have to pay for being psycho-analysts.

TWENTY-FIVE

MYSELF Hullo! What are you doing here?

ROSEMARY (*who is so obviously present that it is hard to imagine that her presence can possibly have been unobserved or ignored*) Your surprise surprises me. (*Turning to Alice who is equally obviously present*) Alice, do all your men-folk behave so oddly? Well, now I come to think of it, the men in Mummy's society did behave in a similar way. That teenager from Eton or Harrow—I forget which particular outfit he came from: I remember telling you about it. Bion reminded me of it and just now—I suppose I should call you the author?—the way you said, 'Hullo! What are you doing here?' reminded me of it—exactly!—just for a fleeting second. I remember walking along with him thinking how nice and handsome he looked. I did think he seemed a bit nervous, but thought no more of it. But as we walked on and it did not wear off I began to look at him and wonder what was the matter. Then I thought, I believed he was ashamed of being out with me! So, to try him, I said, 'It's not far to my Mum's place; come and 'ave some tea. She would be ever so pleased to see you.' He blushed! He blushed so red you wouldn't believe it. 'Wot's the matter', I said, 'are you feeling ill?' Of course I knew it wasn't any such thing. I knew that nice well-behaved gentleman had the damned sauce to be ashamed of being seen with me. So I said nothing. Just put on the accent a bit more—like I'm doing now. You don't look well, I says. You sure you're well? A bit pale, I says—and 'im as red as a beetroot! shall I come to your front door with you? Oh no no no! Please don't trouble. I'm all right, really I am. But I've got to get back to my—prep or something, he says, the dirty young liar! A pal of mine was passing just then and I was so angry I had a good mind to tip him the wink. He wouldn't half have knocked the stuffing out of his pink beauties! Of course he knew Mum was a whore, but naturally he didn't poke his nose into her business and I knew he liked me. But I said nothing. Well, ta-ta George, I says. Sure you are George?—I says, a bit sarcastic like—of course I knew the young liar's name wasn't George by that time and I found out who he was. I had a good mind to send him one of those frightening letters so he would think I was going to blackmail him. But I didn't. I don't know why; I wouldn't think twice about it but I've always been a bit particular.

ROBIN Have you? Some of your pals aren't so particular.

ROSEMARY That's interesting. How do *you* know whether they are particular or not?

MYSELF (*before Bion or Robin can reply*) I don't think he does and I am beginning to think you and Alice may not.

ALICE (*bitterly*) I don't. I wish I had known when I met Roland. All I know now is that *if* I had known and *if* I had been with Rosemary as my friend when she had gone out with that young cad she has been telling us about, I would have been more likely either to have had a happy marriage or remained a spinster friend of Rosemary: preferably never married.

ROSEMARY No you wouldn't. Nor would I. We should both have done the same. Or some other kind of 'worse'.

MYSELF Well, how *have* we done?

MAN (*alert, lively, looking from one to the other in turn, but evoking no response and making no comment. Finally he gets up. His demeanour is modest, but he speaks with authority as he announces, as if to an audience in the darkness in front of him)* The Future! It gives me great pleasure to announce the Future and to express the hope that you all have enjoyed the present as much as I have.

TWENTY-SIX

MYSELF Much in this book has been described in narrative terms. The constructions employed could be understood if the language were known to conform to the conventions of spelling orthography, print, grammar. Are those rules to be understood as applying only to the domain of articulate speech, or is it possible that they derive from and apply to some domain of which we are unaware? Are the rules according to which I conform also to be understood to be a part of the representation to which some yet undisclosed realization approximates? The matter obtrudes if I am working with someone who does not pay attention to, or attach importance to, the verbal content of what I say, but interprets the 'flatus', the breath with which I say it. *I* may be under the impression that my articulate, verbal formulations are what is important; *he* may be concerned with the breath with which I say it.

The complexity of the problem is increased if the 'flatus' is the link between X, someone or something not me, and my self; the 'flatus' requires a spectrum of meaning to express 'Divine afflatus' at one extreme, to 'poison gas' at the other. It becomes still more complex if X is able to 'transform' the sound waves, which I think he hears via his auditory apparatus, into waves which I think would be usually appropriate to visual apparatus. If I suppose he *hears* what I say to him, but in fact he is *seeing* my words sailing through the air, the link between myself and X becomes a problem which cannot be solved with the existing apparatus.

Let us assume that there *is* such an entity as the mind; furthermore, that there is such a domain as approximates to, but is *not* identical with, the mind; that the 'rules' of that domain and the entities within it are only expressed in the crudest terms, derived from the ordinary animal's experience of sensuous reality. Then my problem and the problem between myself and my partner assume a scale of difficulty which lies *beyond* the reach of their existing spectrum. Conversely, there may exist entities who are incomprehensible to me not because their scope is so much less than mine, but so much more. Indeed, Balaam is far more suitable to represent me than is what I consider to be his ass.

BION This theory may be necessary to represent the similarity between people separated by race, religion, language and distance, measured in terms of or by physical time and space. Our concern is how this 'domain', usually left to be 'dealt' with by geniuses, is to be managed by ordinary humans. Nietzsche says a group must produce or find a genius; how is it to recognize and preserve it when found? Is the human 'mind' the sense organ that could be adapted for the purpose? Can Freud's theory of consciousness be extended to the whole human mind and the object of its attention to whatever lies 'beyond'?

SHERLOCK Mycroft! Mycroft! I say . . . Wake up, do.

MYCROFT What's up now?

SHERLOCK I was having the most appalling nightmare! I dreamt that something . . .

MYCROFT Oh, nightmares. You have been eating too much.

MYSELF This is too much. Do I have to put up with these two clowns? I know and you know they are fictitious characters. Have I got to have a highly significant soliloquy interrupted? I can't even so much as hear myself think! Where does all the uproar come from?

'Elected silence sing to me
And beat upon my whorlėd ear,
Pipe me to pastures still and be
The music that I care to hear.
Shape nothing lips; be lovely-dumb:'

MYCROFT You observe the poor fellow can't even spell, Sherlock? He means whore-led.

MYSELF

'It is the shut, the curfew sent,
From there where all surrenders come
Which only makes you eloquent.'

WATSON I don't hear anything.

SHERLOCK That was the significance of the dog barking.

MYSELF This is too much! These are imaginary characters. We shall have imaginary numbers next . . . and thoughts that haven't even a thinker . . . and six characters in search of an author, I shouldn't wonder. Who was that?

WATSON I didn't hear anything.

VOICE . . . hear no evil, speak no evil, see no evil . . .

MYSELF Wasn't that one of those proverbial sayings?

TYRANNOSAURUS V. STEGOSAURUS. DO NOT MISS THIS STUPENDOUS SPECTACLE. SADE VERSUS MASOCH. PRODUCER GIAMBATTISTA VICO. WATCH THE HEAD DEVOUR ITS TALE. THE ONLY GENUINE EXPLANATION EVER PRODUCED OF THE OLD FOSSIL. WATCH THEM, IN THEIR BLINDNESS, BOW DOWN TO WOOD AND STONE.

MYSELF Herodotus thought the sea must have covered the mountains. What next! Someone will say that something, a configuration or pattern, might be covered and revealed by the cover. Angels?

SHERLOCK Our discussion is being interrupted.

MYCROFT For my part, all I can say is that though we may be fictitious characters, at least you and Watson and I are not quite so stupendously boring as Bion and, worse still, Myself.

SHERLOCK Surely, even if you have to be a real creator there could be something to be said for being entertaining. I remember . . .

MYCROFT So do I. Your treatise on a hundred or so cigar ashes. Who on earth could possibly remember Myself on psycho-analysis or sex—whatever that may be! I'd give the lot of them for Irene Adler. She was at least fun. Even God didn't spend the whole of his time obsessed with religion. You would think he was fascinated by being worshipped like one of the psycho-analysts. *That* religion has to be a whole time job worshipping psycho-analysis and singing hymns to the ruling psycho-analyst and his divine attributes. Now: let me show *you* something. I'll give you a sight of—the promised land! Listen!—it's Browning speaking.

> 'Now the cloud rift broadens, spanning earth that's under, Wide our world displays its worth, man's strife and strife's success. What! they smile, our names our deeds so soon erases time upon his tablet where one hundred thousand are spread out.'

Already the famous are so thick they are anonymous. As Horace said, Vixere victoria ante Agamemnona multi, and yet the poet hadn't turned up; so the recording tape was a blank! They disappeared into the shade—unwept! For want of a poet. What a joke! But, listen . . . sounds like the brigade of guards. Massed bands! At least we can have quantity—all famous! Listen . . . Abide with me—all hundred thousand—Zing Boom! Ching! Fast falls the even . . . on the just and unjust—couldn't be fairer—Zing Boom!—than that, could it? The darkness—can't the fools see?—I have seen a finer or hotter Cup Final? Never! 'You've all won', said the Dodo, marching off in strict Do-decanese time upon its tablet where they all lie stretched out cold! Arf—boom!—arf—boom! Arf, arf, arf—Boom! Kum not in errors like the Zing Zing Boom! But kind becos there weren't no 'paulin thar! You remember? The whole fleet was ordered to steer by Palinurus; and we couldn't help laughing becos there weren't no Palinurus there! Can't a man 'ave a bit of fun? Somethink crool! The light is bright, so dazzling it is impossible. . .

SHERLOCK What's all this about?

MYSELF I don't know what it's about. But I can tell you what, in my opinion, 'it is'. These are scraps of a conversation destroyed and fragmented by a jealous, hostile, curious and destructive, excluded, but none the less present, well . . . personality, shall we call it?

BION Even the excluded middle becomes less than law-abiding.

MYSELF Suppose God objected to human beings becoming too divine, too Godlike, like men becoming like towers, and wanted to make that language into rubbish, a tower not of strength and a power of love, but a tower of Babel, of confusion, of strife and contention. But suppose the excluded personality was in its infancy; then the whole of what I am saying might be an attempt to *imitate* the sounds that grownups make if they are engaged in what we call articulate speech. The psycho-analyst, the artist, the entertainer could be moved by love at one extreme, rivalry and hate at the other. In between the two, at neither pole, it could sound rather as I have said. Is 'Sordello' incomprehensible on purpose to make it difficult, or is it Browning's attempt to express what he had to say in the shortest and most comprehensible terms?

BION Is God, and his priesthood of artists, musicians, mathematicians, and now psycho-analysts, out to cause the most chaos? Or is he incomprehensible and himself unable to find an adequate priesthood for his purpose? Is it possible that his ways are not our ways, his Leonardos, Picassos, Bachs, Newtons, Einsteins, not adequate to passing it on to the human animal? Any *moral* system so far invented cannot solve the problem—Sherlock, I hear you coughing. You can have your turn in a moment—oh, all right: go ahead then.

SHERLOCK I don't bother about morals. I have always stuck to a seriously scientific approach.

WATSON Oh Holmes, really! What about that cocaine? I warned you time and again about your very non-scientific, non-medical approach.

SHERLOCK Yes Watson, but I have had to point out to you that you can't even tell me where that Jezail bullet struck your anatomy. I sometimes wonder if there ever was such a person.

MRS MOP Can I do yer now sir?

TWENTY-SEVEN

MYSELF This place is thick with fictitious characters. There won't be enough 'cloud drift' for them to throng through at this rate.

MYCROFT But *you* are just as bad. You dragged in the whole Wembley Cup Final engaged in a sort of religious cup final. Actually, I thought it rather entertaining. Does your God have a sense of humour and are you part of a kind of Psycho-analytic, humorous priesthood?

MYSELF I think that's carrying it a bit far, Mycroft. If you had to attend meetings of the Psycho-analytic priesthood, *you* wouldn't think it funny.

MYCROFT I don't know. I thought you seemed to be having quite a bit of quiet fun out of attending the covens or prides or whatever you call the meetings of your mystery. *Weren't* you meaning to be entertaining?

MYSELF Now you mention it, I remember one of our Tank Corps officers thinking God sent 'His Englishmen to fight His battles *because* they looked so funny going into battle in tanks'.

STEGOSAURUS Like us: couldn't move; sitting target.

WATSON You shut up. You're extinct.

STEGOSAURUS No more extinct than old Tyrannosaurus here. Eh, old bloody chops!

TYRANNOSAURUS What about your poor plants?

TOMB ROBBERS Where would your scientific view be if it wasn't for us digging up a few cadavers?

PRIEST OF UR And our burying the whole Court. There would have been no death pit without us.

MYCROFT Pure suspicion and father of science! Love of gold!

PRIEST I have heard it said that even psycho-analysts make a profit.

MYSELF We run risks.

MYCROFT Isn't it amusing to see you unearth a paranoia?

> 'Oh, who will o'er the moors with me, oh, who will with me ride?'

MYSELF I did not know that you specialized in puns, Mycroft.

MYCROFT It hardly surprises me since I gather that you think you are a real character and that I am imaginary. Your friend Alice thought the Cheshire Cat wasn't real, but that *she* was. The Cheshire Cat was tolerant enough to see that from the dog's point of view the cat, itself included, must be mad since it growls when it is pleased and wags its tail when it is angry. I don't tell Sherlock everything even if he, like me, is an imaginary character and a blood relation—imaginary blood of course. Pontius Pilate—do you regard him as a work of fiction, extinct, fabulous, or governor (historically) of a Roman province?—washed his hands publicly; he and Lady Macbeth join the ranks of the hand washers; so does the blood join the category of signs (symptoms? evidence?) of guilt or murder or suspicion. This is where dear Sherlock specializes, as you know. What about writing a monograph on a hundred kinds of blood?

WATSON No, no! There are only two or three blood groups.

MYCROFT What says our real specialist?

MYSELF You are pleased to be facetious, but since you mean me I will answer. You are confusing . . .

MYCROFT I think you are 'murdering' if I want to emphasise *your* crime. Just because I shall still be entertaining long after you have disappeared, you have no hesitation in calling Sherlock and

Watson and me imaginary characters and claiming a superior status for yourself and your bloody books.

MYSELF Oh no, I don't. Excuse me; but you have got me mixed up with Bion; and what about the blood you have just detected on my books?

MYCROFT Don't you acknowledge any responsibility for your books? Or do you disclaim your brain children?

MYSELF I don't disclaim them. But I do not now hold myself responsible for all the use that may be made of them.

MYCROFT Do you hold *our* author responsible for the use that *you* are making of *his* brain children?

MYSELF No, of course not. I do at least try to play fair you know. In my *Second Thoughts* I have pointed out that I regard myself as having a need to keep silent about certain information which people have entrusted to me, certain information which I have had an opportunity of eliciting for myself and which I think would be of no use to anyone other than the person who comes to me for help. There is still more information which in my opinion would be of no use to the man who comes to me, but might be of great use to his enemies. All this can be seen to apply not only to me, but equally to those who come to me for help. The person who comes to me for help can easily obtain it and, if he feels so disposed, can then use it to destroy me.

MYCROFT Sherlock, as you know, attributed my inaction, as he called it, to indolence; I regard his tendency to transform thought into action as verging on foolhardiness.

MYSELF I should have thought that during the course of your sojourn in my mind—if that's where it and you have been—you would have become transformed from a relatively minor, fictitious character into a somewhat major part of your more useful characteristics. If there were such a thing as a mental digestive system, I could say that the mental diet of entertaining fictitious characters has contributed greatly to my mental health.

ROSEMARY Any orchids for Miss Blandish?

MYSELF Not many. Only a few pages, I should think.

ALICE What about the leaves you've been scattering around through *this* open window?

MYSELF I've no idea; one or two may have been worth tidying up. How wise to remember All Souls and spare ourselves the Saints! I would rather achieve success as an anonymous nonentity than wear self-inflicted honours. Even Newton risks unfavourable competition with his famous apple. His apple cannot compare with its ancestors of Eden and the Hesperides.

TWENTY-EIGHT

SHERLOCK You seem to me to be deprecating fame itself.

MYSELF Holmes, you did not begrudge l'Estrade his need of fame. But who, think you, decided between you and your begetter? When was the award made? Who is more famous: Nelson, or his 'blind eye'? Fame is no plant that grows in mortal soil.

MAN 'Nor in broad rumour lies . . .'

MYSELF So, *you*'ve come to life have you?

MAN Not yet.

ALICE What do you mean—not yet?

MAN I live in the future. My memoirs are the shape of things to come.

MYSELF Are we to have a pre-view? I should be most interested.

MAN The Royal Court at Ur—did they drain their little cups for what dreams their contents would reveal, or to conceal them? I do not know.

MYSELF The past, like the future, is hidden from you.

MAN Not quite.

ALICE Not yet: not quite.

MAN Let me suggest that the state of mind of the men of Ur six thousand years ago is so intensely distant that it is hardly possible for us to know what it was. We may suppose, as an hypothesis, that there could be men separated from us by an interval of time equal and opposite, that is to say, six thousand years in the future. Their states of mind could be equally impossible for us to know. Yet we may imagine the span from − 6000 to + 6000 is immeasurably small; so small, indeed, that it lies within the compass of our minds in much the same way, or more correctly, 'analogous' way, that the span from the infra-red to the ultra-violet measures the spectrum of the 'visible' part of the total range of electromagnetic waves (or quanta). The range to which I have arbitrarily ascribed numerical range, − 6000 to + 6000, I shall further arbitrarily describe as extending (not in numerical terms) from infra-sensual to ultra-sensual. The whole of the range is what I shall describe as lying within the domain of the human mind. I shall now assume mind to extend as far 'beyond' human mentality as life extends 'beyond' what our limited apparatus can conceive of as 'mind'. I shall suppose a bio + and bio −, that is, something beyond even animate and inanimate.

ROSEMARY I don't know what you are talking about.

MAN Perhaps it will help—but it may hinder—if I remind you of an imaginary or fictitious animal, name of Quoodle, who complained that his fictitious masters, men, could not even recognise the 'bright smell of a stone'.

ROSEMARY Alice, dress me. No—put my things out and then you can go. I do not think this is a proper conversation for you.

ALICE Yes, Miss. Where shall I go to?

MAN Now, that is a very interesting question.

ROSEMARY Mais où sont les neiges d'antan?

MAN I wonder what the priests of Ur said. Maybe no one asked where the court ladies were going to after they entered the death pit, or after the contents of the little cup had entered into them. Or when the tomb robbers entered the royal tombs.

MYSELF Or where *you* are going to when, if ever, you enter into 'now' from 'not yet', or when 'not quite' becomes 'quite'.

MAN Or fiction becomes fact which is stronger than any fiction.

MYSELF Or the inanimate, the computer, becomes far more efficient than any animate mind.

WATSON The other day I heard of a computer which scanned cardiograms far more efficiently than any of the highly qualified radiographers in the department.

MYSELF Who said so?

WATSON Well, ultimately the facts. They showed that the radiographers were wrong far more often than the computers.

MYSELF Who interpreted the facts?

MAN Obviously men, objects that operate within that very limited range between infra-sensuous and ultra-sensuous or, as Alice would put it, between 'not yet' and 'not quite'. I can see that might not be adequate in the way described by Krishna, or God answering Job out of the whirlwind, or even Newton out of the theories of Opticks; or the Church out of its system of dogmata . . .

MYSELF . . . or Leonardo out of his golden number . . .

MAN . . . or mathematicians, even when they find an escape route by Cartesian co-ordinates, out of the restrictions of visually based Euclidean geometry. It is not now necessary to have to fall back on the 'obvious' or, which is absurd, 'Q.E.D.'

MYSELF Equally, it is not possible to fall back on the obvious or the absurd to be the solution of the problem. Take the problem of the straight line which does not lie within the circle or the sphere, but cuts it in points which are complex conjugate.

MAN Provided you don't want it to have a meaning, it occurs to me that the theory of Ps ↔ D may offer an opening analogous to the relationship between wave theory and quantum.

ROSEMARY Or 'ugly' and 'beautiful'. Has anyone seen an artist paint a picture 'about' or 'of' something ugly which was nevertheless beautiful? Has anyone seen a skivvy or whore turn into a beautiful woman? Or a pander turn into a man?

MYSELF I have seen that journey (or transformation) more often in the other direction. Change is feared and is then felt as from good to bad; too often, from bad to good is effected by a cheat, an ugly progress effected by ugly means; or means employed for ugly motives for an ugly goal.

MAN We do not know what is concerned in the transformation from animate to animate though we know, or think we know, something of the change from animate to inanimate. The linking process can be murder and self murder. Some think that change is effected by a violent, ugly, catastrophic process of change. It is rare, among psycho-analysts at least, to imagine that the most that their science can do is to map the nature of the mind. The 'discovery' of the mind itself depends on philosophers achieving progress parallel to the micromolecular discovery in the physical domain. The mind, certainly the human mind, can be found to be something of very minor and very embryonic growth. Just as it may seem miraculous that a mind, equipped with visual sense, can 'see' things inaccessible to the sightless paramoecium, so it might appear prophetic—not applied common sense—if the insightful person could detect what to others would appear to be unsupported by evidence. Perhaps a paramoecium would have to believe in 'god'. What more suitable god than man? What more suitable to man than any available 'super-man'? How could this be made available for worship by some well-arranged system of lies and cheats? How more easily dealt with than by a well-arranged system of 'scientific' lies and cheats 'exposing' the lies and cheats?

ROSEMARY Money, morals, 'honours', position and power are often offered to women who accept the counterfeit as real and offer their same easily prostituted 'wealth' and 'assets' in the way food and pharmacological preparations can be offered as cheats by the male as well as the female whore. And now the mind has become available for the extension of lies, deceptions, evasions to produce bigger, better liars and cheats than any 'human' mind had so far achieved.

MYSELF And not the opposite?

ROSEMARY It is certainly a very seductive idea! But I would not rule it out of the bounds of reality any more than I rule it out of the bounds of cheating and prostitution and the establishment of moral superiority.

MYSELF The god did not hesitate to use the waters of Lethe in his war against Palinurus.

ROSEMARY Nor did the priests of Ur in their war against the Court. Many heroic liars existed before the many-wiled Odysseus was saved by his dog from everlasting night.

MAN When the mind ± has been mapped, the investigations may reveal variations in the various patterns which it displays. The important thing may not be, as the psycho-analysts suppose, only revelations in illness or diseases of the mind, but patterns indiscernible in the domain in which Bio ± exist (life and death; animate and inanimate) because the mind spans too inadequate a spectrum of reality. Who can free mathematics from the fetters exposed by its genetical links with sense? Who can find a cartesian system which will again transform mathematics in ways analogous to the expansion of arithmetic effected by imaginary numbers, irrational numbers, cartesian coordinates freeing geometry from Euclid by opening up the domain of algebraic deductive systems; the fumbling infancy of psycho-analysis from the domain of sensuality-based mind?

ROSEMARY Could Beauty help? Poincaré talked as if it existed in the discipline of mathematical formulation.

MAN One problem which interests me is who Myself thinks he is. Do you, Myself, think you differ from us all?

MYSELF No: yet I do, because although I see I have many of the characteristics of a figment of my (and other people's) imagination, I am also a fictitious character. Certainly I can imagine, and be imagined by others, that I am so real, so visually vivid, that I am convinced so completely that I have no way of distinguishing the difference between the real and the imaginary, that discrimination between the two is impossible. If I know who 'Bion' is, and if I know who I am, I can compare the two. I can *say* I know who I was when I was at school, but that is very different from who I *was*; that I shall never know.

TWENTY-NINE

MYSELF Since I cannot, for all my experience, analytic or other than analytic, say *who* I am, I know now that it is very unlikely that I shall know any better at some future date. It is impossible to believe that anyone who is not me will know better. I am sure it would be useful if I knew who that person is that I am compelled to be as long as I exist. Sometimes I make 'mistakes' so extra-ordinary that I do not recognize that extraordinary person might be me; similarly, the mistake I make is hard to recognize because it compels me to recognize that I am its creator, producer, father; I am both unique, and therefore extraordinary, and so utterly ordinary that I merit being qualified as extra-ordinary. As for my products . . .

ALL Sh, sh, sh! And they all . . . that was only Roland.

ROSEMARY 'Only' pornography, 'only' sex.

MYSELF 'Only' can be a verbal method of limiting the universe of discussion. The problem and the person or thing concerned with its solution would seem to be helped if there were some way in which the two could be matched to the human mind; could 'only' have to solve what problems it had to solve, say, for survival.

Philosophers, mathematicians, might attempt to forge tools adequate for tasks they, the human animals, need to solve if they need to survive. Generally it is supposed that it is possible to do things better, being animals, when the live thing is alive than when the 'live' thing becomes a dead thing and vice versa. A stick or stone is uncooperative, but it can be made 'cooperative'; some objects, like a flint, can be manipulated by being turned into a flint axe or hammer which cannot *do* things, but makes it easier for the hand aided by the flint. This discovery creates the feeling of love and gratitude between the man and his tool. Conversely, the live and helpful thing can become hateful if *it* dies.

ROSEMARY It? What is that?

MYSELF It is a participle. If 'it' is about something, it doesn't end by being a grammatical term—'only'. Equally 'it' could be so full of meaning that it is incomprehensible. One of the advantages of practising psycho-analysis is that I can try to tell you what 'it' is. Writing about psycho-analysis—like this attempt here—has its advantages too, but it is very difficult to say what 'it' is. If I and another tried it—practically—it might give a chance to say what the various 'its' are. The practice might not be successful. Terms in common use, like 'sex', 'love', 'hate', can be so abstract as to be meaningless, or so debased that they are impossible to de-nomenate or to say what the value is. Here I have tried to make what Freud described as a 'construction', contrasted with an 'interpretation'. The sentence, 'That was only Roland', would have to be replaced by many terms such as 'jealousy', 'triumph', 'envy', 'rivalry', 'revenge', 'love', 'sex'. Suppose I mean the adult experience of 'passionate love'; suppose you were to say, 'What is that?' If you were able to witness that and were likewise able to understand what you witnessed, you would have a chance of learning from the experience. Conversely, you might not have the chance even to learn what 'learning from experience' was. Single words can be very inadequate.

ROSEMARY You have talked a lot anyhow!

MYSELF (*looking towards Man*) Perhaps this gentleman here would care to take over?

MAN Well yes. I know my functions are not exactly pleasing or my attentions welcome—limiting, like 'only'. It marks the boundaries not only—there it is again!—of the discussion, but also the commencement.

BION You need a new name. I hereby nomenate you 2, Two, too—in every possible respect, two much.

ALL Carried unanimously.

MAN As usual a poet expresses it; 'The old order changeth, yielding place to new. And God fulfils himself in many ways'. Even as God, not even his—or should it be His?—vestiges disappear, but are renewed in the form of the excrement-eating scavengers who tidy up. Alice here, and her little daughter Alison—to whom I have not yet introduced you because she lies in what you rather quaintly call the Future, but is *in fact,* as opposed to verbally and grammatically, not separable from the past—welcomed my function of gathering together 'her property' and superintending its redistribution. A macroscopic vertex would show an impressive 'me' presiding over the redistribution of the Royal Court of Ur with its delightful ritual of sacramental 'health' in the Death Pit. The redistribution of the unlabelled poetic goods of Troy, the souls lost in the unlamented shadows of the past—somewhat typically rescued by a poet—now being re-acted apparently in the loss and redistribution of 'imperial' trappings which hid the empire of mind. That empire achieved a temporary home and even a name—Shakespeare. 'Others', said a poet, 'abide our question. Thou art free.'

ROSEMARY Can't you spell Art?

MAN I can; just as those fellows learnt how to spell Shakespeare, but, if you remember, the labels were various and the property disbursed under 'spellings' as diverse as Bacon and G(reat) B(ritain) Shaw. Here—you don't know this young fellow—you there (*beckoning to someone in the shadows*) come out of it! Speak up and don't be afraid. How old are you? Six? More like four or five I would have thought. Tell them what you saw and heard.

BOY Our dogs chased and cornered a jackal. I was frightened because I thought he was enormous and would kill them. But they surrounded him. And he sat down just as I thought he was going to attack, with his mouth wide open and big, bared, snarling teeth! And he frightened me because he began howling. It was awful.

MAN Show them how. Don't be afraid.

BOY You won't think I have hydrophobia will you?

MAN Rabies? Probably; but never mind—what did it sound like? Go on—do it!

BOY (*opening his mouth and throwing back his head, he begins with a slow, scarcely audible whisper; then, opening his mouth wider and wider and raising the whisper to a howling crescendo, emits an unearthly, moaning cry*) Fi—aaow. (*It dies away*)

MAN And then? What next?

BOY There were shadows out of nowhere. Our dogs were afraid. They didn't attack the jackal. *They* sat down too and bared their teeth, but they didn't attack; their teeth chattered. Fi-aou! Fia-ou! Fiii-aaou! And the shadows sat in a great circle, more and more of them.

MYSELF '. . . whose howl's his watch'!

ROBIN That's an anachronism!

MYSELF I thought some fool would say that. Shakespeare knew what he did. He knew the *real* meaning of anachronism, anonymity likewise. The jackals and the moralists were waiting to howl, 'Thieves! Robbers! Apaches! Brigands! Crazy!' while the robbers pocketed the goods; they were 'honest men'.

BION Are they clearly labelled? Watch out for the Moralists, the biggest robbers of all!

MYSELF 'They' know! No doubt but ye are the people and wisdom will die with you! Devoured, owned, miserly, locked up in their iron digestive canals and inaccessible to those who could use it. 'What! they smile—our names, our deeds—so soon erases Time upon his tablet where man's glory . . .

MAN . . . liveth for evermore. The glorious dead. Ils gisent là. Sans voix, sans ouie . . . come, let us dig them up and . . . do you remember, boy? How shocked your nanny was . . .

BION Poor nanny! It was old Ayah, poor old thing, when I asked when we were going to dig up the people in the cemetery and eat them!

ROBIN An anachronism. Learn it and write it out fifty times for the next exam on Shakespeare. Fifty 'times'. The *number* of times! That will teach them to speak disrespectfully of time! A-chronous indeed! A-nonymous! Fetch me my packet of labels, boy. I'll show them who owns what! Where's that war I won?

MAN You are referring no doubt to the Empire of the Mind, sir? Coming, sir! Coming! Anon, sir, anon! Your empire, sir—anon! anon! I remember telling the dinosaurs that the young mammal would soon arrive. But bless you! They wouldn't believe that they were already extinct. So they were—the mammals too. Homo Sapiens is still fiddling with *his* new toy, the Big Bang theory. All this non-sense—Ah, here we are, sir. This isn't a silly theory with this (*shows the circle of shadows a fine, practical, working* . . .) Why, bless my soul! Where have they all gone? Only me! I only—am left alone, to tell thee!

VOICE (*out of the smoke*) Where's my fire? Bring me my fire will you! There are some topless towers here that require burning. See page 1 and begin again. Fin i gain . . . Alph where's Om? Theodore, what's Dunton!

MAN He didn't think they ate them. It's part of the illusion of growing up. 'Time' 'and all that. He *saw* 'them' eating—being eaten. Only he knew there are always No-Alls about the place waiting to imprison/deify any thought or idea that causes trouble. *Mental* indigestion is quite bad enough. There is also the ultra and infra, Alpha and Omega, poly-sensual, infra and ultra mental, infra and super-human 'mentality'. I have to use archaic terms to bring it within the area of your comprehension.

VOICE (*from the Future/Past*) I don't know what you are talking about. How these old formulations endure! If only 'they' could realize they are speaking the truth even when 'they' are meaning to lie; and vice versa. In peyote veritas—the gods help them who . . . help themselves; even those who help themselves to other people's disciplines, religions, Past's or Future's property. Now then, terpsichore, just you keep you hands out of my chimpanzee's . . . science, pharmacology be thou my £.S.D. That is L.S.D's property!

In what fancy dress would you like to be caught in order to abide the day of his coming? And how would you like your God—come *not* in Terrors? As Khishna? Somnus, with a light sprinkling of Lethe water? Peter, in papal vestments, talking in the accents—so easily penetrable!—of one of his followers?

I don't know what you are talking about. I was 'only' (blessed word again!) warming my hands at the fire.

MYSELF And he turned, and with his eyes he wrote in fire, in words that seared the soul. The Christians got him in the end; from his messianic prison house he never escaped till every vestige of meaning had been squeezed out of him. Confucius—they misspelled his name. Some words and phrases seem to be unmistakable evidence that a man had existed in a spot marked by the words. Trevor Roper thought he could detect, even through the gorgeous vestments of the whore, that a man existed. Even whores need patrons.

BION Where's Rosemary? Some topless . . . need burning . . . but the thicket is not consumed. Some artist will reveal there is always a ram to be caught. Bigotry and Ignorance. Where's Savonarola? Sorry, he went up in flames—like Icarus . . . too successful and too much bigotry and ignorance in his fire-fighting uniform. Newton? Poor fellow; he never recovered the consistency of his mind. And no one has found a way of re-forming the currency since. The tomb robbers, the fortune hunters, don't know where to look for the Child whom they are compelled by their piety to worship. Dressed in the best of motives . . . though various . . .

MYSELF Let us get back to something simple—before the Big Bang.

WATSON Something simple? That's my cue, where I come in. Which Big Bang do you mean?

MYSELF I said 'before' the Big Bang. 'Before' or 'after', it doesn't matter.

MAN Can I help? Even to talk at all I am afraid we shall have to borrow from A-chrony one of his anachronisms.

ALICE Alice in Anachronomous Land.

MAN Thank you: you come from Pornography don't you?

ALICE Not really—Wonderland.

MAN Ah yes. A province of Fairyland.

PALINURUS No, Wonderland, before it was stolen by children and their various thieves and robbers.

ALICE From *your* collection of thieves, robbers, rapists and seducers, don't forget. You make me damn bad-tempered.

MYSELF No—why blame him? You always were bad-tempered. For that matter, so was God. With reason.

MAN Always 'with reason', as you call it in the language of anachronimity. When He attempted to borrow one of your anachronisms, the un-priestly formulation of Psalm 51 was 'borrowed' and given a twist in the direction of 'perquisites'. Even now some of us claim 'ownership' of Ideas. I bet the fellow who succeeds in getting his name on the cover of this book thinks it is his.

MYSELF I am certainly going to claim authorship, but I hope I shall have enough generosity to balance my possessiveness and greed.

ROSEMARY You surprise me; but even Paris had some generous ambitions. Many mean guys existed before Paris gave them life and rescued them from everlasting night.

MAN I think Everlasting Night had a turn with a-nonymous and a-phasia in an-a-chronos. I shall hand over to Myself.

DINOSAUR If I may borrow an anachronism for a moment to fill a gap before this fictitious character, Sapiens, takes over . . .

MYSELF (*hastily*) To fill a gap. That is where we came in—before the Big Bang.

DINOSAUR . . . and while the primaeval slime is still warm.

MYSELF I think I had better wait till the next chapter. It may be less noisy—less crowded, less atomic debris and smoke.

THIRTY

MYSELF As psychological preparation I shall borrow verbal or alphabetical formulations like O, or zero, or infinity. For some centuries the visual imagery of Euclidean space limited rather than freed thought. Cartesian coordinates made, in combination with the theorem of Pythagoras, a possibility of relating points to each other without the visual aids of lines and circles. These visual aids introduced powerful, undetected, forces which distorted the balance of probability. That distortion is still incalculable. Growth, + or −, remains inaccessible to thought, if unmistakable to feeling. Conceptual thought and passionate feeling are impossible to relate within the confines of existent universes of discourse. The problem could be stated by analogy: numbers suffered repeated extensions to carry an increased load—rational numbers, irrational numbers and, latterly, complex conjugate points. In the emotional domain, persecution by passion grows to depression. The relation of the one to the other requires an extension whereby quantity transforms to quality. 'Very great', 'very small' intervals of time, space, probability, involve quality in a manner analogous to growth from quantity to quality. Thus, quantitative terms such as 'excessive', 'inadequate', 'too little', 'too much', may signify a change in kind or quality; conversely, change in quality, for example, love or hate, may imply change in quantity. This is *not* a crudity such as the difference between one German 'hating' and the entire German nation 'hating'; that may be 'symptomatic', 'significant' of a method of lateral communication. The change can be formulated in language, music, mathematics; it is, in fact, something 'infra-' or 'ultra-' human, animate—living or bio-logical. Comparison between animate and inanimate reveals need for discrimination; the 'Russians' send a mechanical probe to the moon and retain a mechanically aided, computer-wise and otherwise, animate being on earth. By contrast, the 'Americans' favour sending 'animate beings' sufficiently well disciplined to be machines.

Bernardino Sahagun describes the debate between those who favour gods formed artificially, by human art, out of wood and stone which 'appear' to be controllable, and those, like the Roman Catholics, who favour an independent and uncontrollable God. Jesus Christ is a compromise between the verbally articulate human Jesus who prays, 'Thy will be done on earth as it is in Heaven', and the Messiah. Some degree of independence is conceded to 'God', although, after creation or 'belief-creating operation', both end-products are still, from human vertex, unpredicted. The idol made out of inanimate material shows unmistakable characteristics of a kind usually attributed to animals, usually human; reciprocally, the god created out of materials, ultra- or infra-sensuous, displays characteristics usually regarded as the prerogative of idols. In other terms ('borrowed' from the lunar illustration) the machine, regardless of race, time, space, is e- and pro-vocatively animate; and the animate object similarly pro- and e-vocatively inhuman and inanimate. If we now increase the dimension, using 'time' as an instrument with which to measure, we find a stability about the objects discerned and recorded by animate human animals such as saints, philosophers, scientists, artists, and (borrowing from Socrates) artisans. Socrates knew that he was not wise, yet could not mobilize facts to indicate anyone or anything, god or idol, who could plausibly be said to contest the title. In the domain of the human senses there is evidence of violence and murder from the Death Pit at Ur to Hiroshima and beyond.

'Methinks I see a Nation . . . with undazzled eyes . . .', as one poet said. Socrates, 'Krishna' and his creator (his 'Plato', his 'Homer'), Hellas and Shelley. His 'powers of darkness' and the vacant throne. My valour . . . said Valiant for Truth and his creator Bunyan. (What? *That* tinker? Is he not the carpenter's son? As for Shakespeare, was he not Bacon? And who wrote the Baghavad Gita? Sunk in Eternal Night without a trace. No orchids for Miss Blandish; 'therefore—fight Arjuna!') 'Fame is no plant that grows in mortal soil . . . but lives and spreads aloft . . . by all-judging Jove.'

Homer is not known *not* to have been blind Maeonides—he was blind anyhow; Newton was sunk without a trace, hit by an apple; so was Helen; Jesus, buried beneath the load of the Roman Catholic Church and the massive ritual. 'I don't know what you are talking about'—and couldn't care less. 'Great is the truth and shall prevail, if none care whether it prevail or not.' So the mammals survived. Perhaps the dinosaurs did not get together to worship the infant prodigy when it was still helpless enough. Oh, those over-confident stegosaurs! And now look what their *failure* has done!

Perhaps the electron microscope and the radio telescope would do the trick between them? No. You still have to have a human to interpret them. The past—the record in history, in fossil and stone, in computer and poem—has to be interpreted by them. And that two-handed engine at the door—('Please, sir, what does "two-handed engine" mean?' 'Well, my boy, it means, well, er, it . . . are you sure your people don't mind about Freud?' 'Oh no, sir! They are Kleinians, sir. They don't mind a bit!' 'Well it means the two breasts. You see . . .' 'No, sir, I don't understand, sir.' 'Oh hell! Nor do I. But I shall be surprised if in fact it doesn't mean that if one of them doesn't get you the other one will. But don't tell your Mum or Dad.' 'Yes, sir! You did say "Hell", didn't you, sir?' 'Heavens, so I did! Your Dad is an atheist isn't he?' 'Oh *no*, sir!') Any interpretation is a stop-gap which serves to plug the hole; even a part has to serve to plug the whole. The radio telescope and the electron microscope, God and Devil, Body and Mind, Penis and Vagina,

Love and Hate, Real and Distinct, Real and Coincident, Conjugate and Complex. There are multitudinous holes and multitudinous parts to fill the wholes with.

Hitherto, the term 'mind' has proved serviceable. I propose to use it myself, but not for purposes of writing a philosophical or psychological or religious or artistic or other record. I propose to use it as a meaningless term, useful for talking or writing about what I *don't* know—to mark the 'place where' a meaning might be.

I assume that there is a realization that approximates to the term 'mind'. I assume that the mass of theories, case histories, psycho-analytic formulations, are products of the 'mind'. Some of these I shall assume are themselves realizations approximating to the formulations, definitory hypotheses about the mind and of the same status as the term 'mind' itself. I further assume that the 'mind', analogous to brain and central nervous system, is of significance for what it does or does not reveal.

Some psycho-analytic theories I regard, without specifying for the present, as 'constants', 'invariants' under the particular vertex. If these invariants are absent, or not detected by such apparatus as is available, I regard their absence as itself revelatory. These definitory hypotheses may be used as the foundation on which an 'instrument' could be constructed, *based* on a variety of theories, but itself supporting none. It would then be an instrument which could record the configuration revealed by the mind and thereby make its configuration and interpretation available for study and contemplation by an observer. I have indicated that such observers may be hard to come by in the extremely limited domain provided by animal history itself. Life, as known to us, has a recent and very short history if measured in comparison with the scales provided by standards applicable to astronomical physics and what we call outer space. Yet biological forces are ones with which we have to live. They or their symptoms concern themselves with us even if unknown to us. They may have no counterpart in the domain of 'known' and 'unknown', animate and inanimate. It *is* possible that the development of the CNS, and now the mind (I refer to the definitory hypothesis I have put forward), may provide an extension of which we have not so far been able to avail ourselves, any more than the race could avail itself of the atomic theories of Democritus of Abdera or the heliocentric hypotheses of Aristarchus with the then existing facilities.

This brings us to the importance which Socrates attached to the artisan for whom he clearly felt a respect which he could not feel for other classes, including himself as the matrix of wisdom. Nor was he able to feel much respect for the oracle at Delphi, judging its pronouncements realistically. The artisan, therefore, appears to have at least a considerable 'history' of being 'respect-worthy'. God likewise, though unknown or perhaps because unknown, or perhaps because of being respected, remains as an Invariant clothed in no matter how many variables and under whatever vertex. He is a 'constant' which is an 'unknown' and the centre of a human discipline served by a mathematics which must be capable of manipulation, by a mathematics in which the constant is unknown and whose place is taken by an infinity of variables.

BION Such religious numbers which are known to us are not associated with a domain adequate for their deployment as are irrational, imaginary numbers. The space of mathematical operation must be extended to accommodate 'religious' numbers as well as those catered for by past extensions of the 'domain' of numbers. To recapitulate: the study of anatomy and physiology is usually pictured as a central nervous system with an outstanding structure, the brain. The mind, presumed to be real, is likewise presumed to have a structure. This word, 'structure', is borrowed from the vocabulary forged for the domain of sensuous experience. The 'mind', and now its 'structure', are terms which are *not* appropriate for use as referrents to domains we hypothecate for this study. The 'mind', unlike the brain, has *no* convolutions. Analogous objects, therefore, have to be created from the domain of the brain and its convolutions.

THIRTY-ONE

MYSELF The mind is an extension of the human animal; it has grown and is capable of growth and decline. Its development has brought it and the human organism of which it is a part . . .

ROSEMARY (*yawning*) Excuse me.

MYSELF (*with exaggerated politeness*) On the contrary—excuse *me*. I fear I was boring you.

ROSEMARY Not at all. I was most interested. I was just thinking that the minds congregated here did not show signs of being stimulated by, or made aware of, any contact with me.

MYSELF I *beg* your pardon. I have been monopolizing attention.

ALICE You have been monopolizing articulate speech. I haven't—perhaps it is my defective mind—an impression that anyone is paying attention at all. Roland was absorbed in paying almost undivided attention to Rosemary's feet. I myself was thinking somewhat enviously that they looked attractive.

ROBIN, ROLAND, MAN, SHERLOCK, WATSON (*all murmur to-*

gether in agreement) It's true, old boy; my attention was wandering a bit.

ROSEMARY Tom too?

TOM (*shakes his head, looks guilty and reddens*)

ROLAND (*annoyed*) You seem to want to be the centre of everyone's attention.

ROSEMARY Roland! I know you. You are all alike. Of course you think I want everyone's attention. Do you remember that schoolboy who bored me stiff?

MYSELF *I* do. It reminded me of me. I didn't take a girl out when I was at school—I would have loved to, but I wouldn't have dared; I would have been too frightened of getting the sack.

ROSEMARY (*looking at him curiously*) You're coming on. You are very like that schoolboy in a way you have not mentioned.

MYSELF What's that?

ROSEMARY He had the damned impudence to think I was flattered—a mere skivvy like me!—to be out with him. Not that he came near to admitting that he was afraid that he would get the sack from me. I was *not* trying to catch a husband—husbands were two a penny as far as I was concerned. I was, however, choosing one and quite capable, skivvy or no skivvy, of *not* choosing him. Even this gentleman here (*indicating Man*) thinks I am an object for conquest.

MAN (*with raised eyebrows*) ?

ROSEMARY Well, don't you. Why don't you speak?

MYSELF If Man will excuse me, I would like to answer by telling you about a very beautiful girl I knew and with whom I did go out. I appreciate your indignation about the boy, but . . .

ROSEMARY I know you are going to talk about a girl who reminds me of me!

MYSELF Maybe. After I have told you, you can say whether my story does or does not. Anyhow, she was very beautiful. She was also very intelligent. In short, I adored her.

SHERLOCK Irene Adler?

MYSELF Irene Adler is a fictitious character.

SHERLOCK So is your girl.

MYSELF I don't know that my girl friend was much less of an

imaginary character than 'The Woman' (as you always used to call her) who was said by old Watson to be *your* goddess. The point is, I kept on saying how intelligent and beautiful she was. But she was **not** *wise* enough to inhibit the growth of her admiration for herself. It was already immense—with reason, I must in honesty say. She certainly had not the wisdom to limit my admiration for her or to warn me when I was making a fool of myself—not really flattering her. Eventually I could not love her because she took any statement I made as a reflection of the facts, a tribute to her merit, not as a manifestation of my capacity for love. I realized then that I could do nothing for her. It probably wasn't good for her to believe that she had a built-in superiority and therefore nothing to do—just twiddle her thumbs and be admired.

(*The room has grown steadily darker until all the discussants are lost in the shadows—except one figure quietly seated in a recess. That figure has become more obtrusive with the growing darkness and reveals itself as a very old, grey-haired woman, deeply veiled. The room is filled with people, the silence oppressive. At last it is broken by her speaking very softly and melodiously.*)

OLD WOMAN You do not remember me—no. I am not whom you think. I am not *the* woman, only a woman. 'The snows of yesteryear will carry me away', as they always have and always will. I know the girl you speak of very well—I am not she. Nor shall I ever be, any more than I ever was. One of those poets once said that I was 'too proud'. Too proud—it is the besetting sin of people like me, the undistinguished, unremarkable, anonymous to whom pride comes once perhaps, rarely more. Our poverty, our dirt, our lack of clothing with which to cover our rags, make it impossible that the gleam could ever be more than a glory that blazes once, flares, and is lost for ever.

MAN (*starts up, tense, his face lightened by a pallor that makes the darkness palpable. He stares into the darkness; then sinks back.*) She's gone!

OLD WOMAN No: don't romance. You can see me any day on my knees, crawling into the Church at Guadalupe. You can see me as I sit, sad, woe-begone, exhibiting my sores. I am a professional beggar. Like the beautiful girl, *I* have built-in ugliness. I do not have to do a thing. I have a natural gift of filthiness and squalor. I have my place—in the mind to which it has pleased God to call me.

MAN You horrify me.

OLD WOMAN Rubbish. You don't like seeing me and I loathe you. If I could be bothered I might be upset. How did you like my decor? The lighting was effective, wasn't it? You are an invader I believe? War, poverty, disease . . .

ROSEMARY You know nothing about it and care less. I do, and that is why I was determined to have nothing to do with it. I am on the winning side: the same as this invader here. But—and I give you fair warning, all of you—only as long as this smooth rascal stays on top. It's no good going a-whoring with me and thinking I am prepared to be loyal to him if he chooses to wallow like you.

MAN God forbid!

ROSEMARY God? *I* forbid. I don't waste my time waiting for God. You should have seen that grizzly collection of fools as they shovelled the trash over their finery at Ur! That was not the first time they had used the 'little cup'—it was the last!

BION You must have been around a very long time.

ROSEMARY Do you think I would wait for *you* to create *me*?

BION Well, damn it, who did create you if I didn't?

ROSEMARY They are all the same. Horace thought I was likely to achieve immortality through his immortal jingles. He even had the effrontery to think he had 'escaped' from Pyrrha! If anyone ever reads this book it will be because of what the reader has the cheek to call 'pornography'. That is why Bion mentions me and he can't even make the description plausible. Anyone can see it is primarily a description of 'none of them knows half so much as intelligent Mister Toad!'

BION Look here! If you had not interrupted me by yawning, I was about to point out—

ROSEMARY 'About to . . . just going to . . .'

BION —that the scientific theory, the psycho-analytic construction should resemble real life and should not be distinguishable because Freud wrote it, or Melanie Klein wrote it, or because it is one of those marvellous interpretations by the famous psycho-analyst X, or Y, or Z, any more than a portrait should be recognized because it is 'by' Praxiteles or Frans Hals or Picasso, but because it is 'of' Hermes, or the Cavalier, or the Saltimbanques.

ROSEMARY —'should be', but *are* they?

BION Who wrote the Baghavad Gita? Was *that* author aware of his insignificance before God?

ROSEMARY Never heard of it.

BION Well, really! Anyway, *this* book is not 'about' anybody. At the end the reader is . . .

ALICE Tell me about the Reader; who is he?

BION I was coming to that . . .

THIRTY-TWO

ALL (*suddenly revealed in the light which has been steadily increasing until it is possible to see the whole gathering, bursting into song*)

> Tom Pearse, Tom Pearse, lend me your grey mare,
> All along, down along, out along lea . . .

BION I can't make myself heard in all this din. It's too bad. After all, I *did* create them.

MAN And they are now returning the compliment. If you did, surely you can write the verse?

BION I have not written a note of music or a line of verse in my life.

MAN The man that hath no music in his soul . . . never mind . . . it's gone hasn't it? Try! Try now!

BION It is wrong anyhow. And damn you—who the hell are you?

MAN And damn you too: I have told you already. Why don't you listen to what you are told?

BION I have *always* listened to what I have been told.

MAN I haven't noticed it. (*He says it without hate, as if it were a friendly communication*) Did you listen to what that pitiful slut told you? I'll tell you. It was all hate—*all* of it! No, I am not talking psycho-analysis. You can go and read your silly books. I was not listening to someone reading the first lesson of the Gospel according to Saint Sigmund, or, if I may say, any of the other little angels. Non angli sed angeli! Including (*bowing elaborately*) your own divine contributions. How many Krishnas, Devil worshippers, Virgils, have to pass this way before a fact will be forged to penetrate your smooth, complacent and sanctimonious hide?

STEGOSAURUS Someone asking for me?

MAN I suppose you are incurably too civilized to pay any attention to Virgil's chunk of omnipotent trickster god who wore *his* get-up with an air—drugs, Somnus, ever so, ever so—watch him! There, did you *see* it?—how he hurled poor, faithful Palinurus, stern, sheets and all, torn out of the rear end—stern we call it—of that poor little leading boat; hurled him into the depths of the sea; that beautiful, land-locked, medi-tationally futile caldron of seething, boiling, divine hate for all you piddling little tricksters with your imitation hate, love, decorations, intended to give substance to the fictitious, non-existent chest!

BION When I was a soldier in camp at Poperinghe I did not think it a piddling Christ. Nor did Ernest, who had a cheerful religious feeling. I think I loved him and his God for the first time. I was not crippled by *his* religion as I had been by every other, and with him I had that rare experience—which I had had once before at the camp at Ladram Bay some years earlier. My only clearly remembered times of happiness and religion and feeling of real affection for one of my own sex. At Cheltenham, the Christmas after, I had the same gay feeling of liberation for a girl. It was marvellous. The air crackled and sparkled in the frost and there was a warm feeling in my heart. I remember going home with her after a midnight service on New Year's Eve. That was the last. When I saw her next I had changed—I felt I had death on my brow. I was regarded with awe by her and her friends, for I was weighed down by a nameless dread as I passed between the rows of girls at the school where she taught. I realize now, but did not then, that I was carrying the load of premature death, for I had been awarded a very high decoration which carried with it a sentence of almost certain death. I knew I should never again be free to feel sincerely and openly the fear I felt. Bourlon Wood haunted me. Ypres haunted me. The rain, my God the rain! And the sweet smell of rotten flesh! The girl was talking to me. She was anxious; her eager and quiet concern showed from her eyes as she scanned my face for some response. I had none. I could feel none. 'What did you say?', I managed to come to the surface to ask. It was hopeless. No, I had not got shell shock. What nonsense they were ready to talk! But, love had died. Love for anyone and anything. Those pink, fresh, upturned faces—what were they feeling? Was it awe? What about? The vast deserts of Ypres with its rain, incessant rain and small groups of heavy-coated figures. They too used to wait—for many years—their impassive, grey faces and khaki suddenly brilliantly illuminated by the gun flashes.

ROSEMARY (*yawning*) Most interesting . . .

BION I'm sorry. I know I am poor company. Where's old Watson with his Jezail bullet?

WATSON That was before the Boer War.

BION That wasn't a war. That was a fatigue!

WATSON You laugh. They all laugh, but even that hurt. We tried, you know.

BION I was not meaning to laugh. In fact, even at Oxford, I used to stir into life a bit to see you and Sherlock rooting and snuffling around. But though I am very grateful to you, I could never flame with life again after James, Ernest, Charles and I were extinguished at Cambrai.

ROSEMARY (*manicuring her hands, but coming to faint life*) Were you killed?

ROBIN No, *I* was, though. I was never brave like Bion here.

BION Was I brave?

ROBIN Oh, I think so.

ROSEMARY (*still admiring her nails*) How brave? I always used to think men went into a huddle together and concocted a whole lot of lies to fool us women with afterwards.

BION More or less; not quite though.

ROSEMARY (*putting away her manicure case and speaking with great deliberation*) I knew a girl once who was lying in bed—very comfortable too—with great beads of sweat across her forehead. She was afraid she was dying. She was having a baby; her first, to whom she was looking forward very eagerly. The baby was born all right. But her fears were correct—she didn't see it.

BION Childbirth?

ROSEMARY It seems simple, doesn't it. You sound cool.

BION I am cool. It sounds callous I know, but only if you attach importance to death. Suppose the child lived on to become a mother; that frightful wreck we saw was someone's baby . . .

OLD WOMAN *(uncovering some chronic sores from beneath her rags and settling down in her daily pitch, disposing the rags to make the maximum display, she swiftly lets her featurs sink into the routine expression of piteous whining, appealing, half-glazed eyes)*

BION . . . Yes, you I meant. You see . . . her professional stance for the day. Would you rather be the mother who watched her daughter slither down that slope, or rather die in childbirth?

ROSEMARY Yes, it all sounds very fine put in your artistic way. Real life isn't like that; these things do not happen like that.

BION No, they don't. That's why it 'sounds callous', as I said. In civilized states they do not allow the outrage, the daily commission of assaults on the feelings . . .

ROSEMARY . . . on whose feelings? The sensitive, cultured tourists? In uncivilized states the uncivilized inhabitants are not so ridiculous. When the tourist season is over and the weather is not hot enough to be comfortable sitting in the open . . .

ROLAND . . . or, I may say, hot enough to make beggars able to sweat and stink without undue exertion.

ALICE Roland! You surprise me. I didn't know you knew about things like that!

ROLAND Alice, it is a very long while since you knew me or anything that I knew. We have drifted apart since . . .

ALICE . . . we knew each other. I don't think we ever knew each other much. I was too shy and you seemed so easily shocked; I could not be frank with you.

ROLAND Or I with you.

ROSEMARY It took a skivvy like me before either of you could talk plain English.

ROLAND I don't know about that. We used to talk plain English at my school. It was a famous school.

ALICE By the time it became famous for the off-duty language you boys used to each other, the parents began to withdraw their patronage. And it went down and down, till the governors became afraid it would be bankrupt. I know, because my father was one of the governors. But I don't see what the poor headmaster and staff were to do about it. Do you think the problem has been solved these enlightened days of LSD and hashish? There must be *some* freedom without suggesting boys have cigars and liqueurs *or* total abstinence. The trouble is that if you suggest they should abstain they 'abstain' from common sense too.

ROLAND What abstinence, for example?

ROSEMARY (*sweetly*) They abstain from going out with skivvies like me. Isn't that what you mean?

ROLAND (*nettled*) I did not go out with skivvies. I used to say my prayers, play games as hard as I could. In short, lived a pure and holy and godly life. A fat lot of use it was at that. I loathed sex. It was nothing but fear and failure. I couldn't even have a friendship with another boy. I wish you could have an idea . . .

MYSELF As a psycho-analyst I can have an idea; but I have to have many years of experience, and by then it is long past the time when it might have been some use. Rosemary, I wish you'd stop manicuring your bloody nails while I'm talking. You can't think how infuriating it is to try to talk while I have to watch you sharpening your claws.

ROSEMARY I thought psycho-analysts were supposed not to be maddened by anything. Only patients.

MYSELF Well you thought wrong. There are things which it is quite right to be angry about, and it would be pathological or inadequate to refrain. Besides, there is a difference between being enraged on my job and an ordinary social occasion. The emotional experiences are not limited to my sessions where I have certain privileges and duties. But the duties of social life and the duties of professional occupation are not the same.

ROSEMARY Well, you have been very frank. Let me tell you that I find it bloody irritating to have to put up with hearing you philosophizing; or psycho-analysing, as you call it. You don't like watching me manicure my nails because I am really sharpening my claws. I don't like what you call psycho-analysing and I call it 'sharpening your moral claws'—that is not a pretty sight either. I wonder what poor devil is in for a mauling.

MYSELF Well, you have certainly just given me a mauling. (*Contritely*) I deserved it, but . . .

ROSEMARY But? Somebody once said, 'but me no buts'. For a moment I thought you were actually feeling contrite. Your 'but' showed me you had thought better of it.

MYSELF (*laughing a bit uneasily*) Well, yes. You are quite right.

(*There is an awkward pause during which he disappears, fades out, apparently completely crushed*)

THIRTY-THREE

Rosemary and Alice appear to be expectant. Alice is self-possesed, yet in a position unmistakably subordinate to Rosemary, as if she were a lady-in-waiting. Rosemary has become transformed, but the nature of the transformation is undefined. The two women occupy the stage so completely that it takes some time before it is realized that Man is present.

MAN Shall we go on?

ROSEMARY (*shudders as if momentarily chilled by a disagreeable emotion*) I don't know. I don't think I can stand all that again. I am sorry, but I feel I have had enough of it.

MAN I said, 'shall we go on?' I was not suggesting 'more' of the same again.

ROSEMARY I feel old. Do men never grow up?

MAN Usually they are not allowed to, either by themselves or the women they choose, or both. I am sorry for that poor devil, Robin. He is not a bad sort. He has been very close to death! Often I thought he was hopeless and then he seemed at the last moment—to my surprise, I confess it—to topple over on the right side. It is like watching a leaf falling to the ground; utterly unpredictable, but like playing a game with fate. 'Heads I lose; tails I win', but with a coinage inadequate for the purpose. It would be more accurate to say that leaves *are* adequate to occupy the role of representing coinage, itself a representation, in that they permit certain forces to participate in the game, notably the air and its movements. These forces may be regarded . . .

ROSEMARY (*shuddering against his intervention*) Don't.

MAN Again? I see what you mean . . .

(*Both fade out and it gradually becomes clear that the darkness is not total. Nor is the silence absolute. Voices resemble, but are not, a conversation; memories resemble, but are not, desires; finite episodes resemble, but are not, infinite. There appears to be a streaming in one direction, but the direction changes as if it were, but is not, 'reversed perspective'. 'Larling', she does not say. It is not past: it does not feel past either. It is inchoate, it is not past. It is 'minus-K'. The date in minus-K is August 7 and August 8.*)

TONKS (*giving orders to Captain*) Now, don't you move those tanks! Sargent agrees with me—not that I attach any importance to what is said by a man who knows nothing whatever about composition. We must have those tanks just precisely there for one more day if my sketch is to be finished. Do you understand?

CAPTAIN Yes, sir. If we have to move them we are to put them back in the same place.

TONKS (*to Sargent*) You might as well talk to a wall as to that young fool. I have told him they are not to be moved—you heard his reply?

CAPTAIN (*to Lieutenant Arthur*) You heard, Arthur? Just drop Haig a line and tell him I'm awfully sorry, but there are two official war artists here who have forbidden the use of these tanks till their sketch is complete.

ARTHUR (*sniggers*) When do we move off?

CAPTAIN Six-thirty. The sleds are ready to drag behind to wipe out our tracks?

ARTHUR (*chuckling*) Yes. Won't Uncle Richthofen be surprised!

CAPTAIN Uncle *who*?

ARTHUR Wheeler's sergeant to see you, sir.

CAPTAIN Come in, O'Connor. You want me?

O'CONNOR No, sir. Lieutenant Wheeler is dead, sir. Yes, sir, he was a bit upset, sir. It's all right now, sir.

CAPTAIN All right, sergeant?

O'CONNOR Yes, sir. It was a direct hit. Right at the start, sir, so we hadn't wasted any petrol. We burnt a fair treat. Some of us tried to get out, sir, and this made it look more real like. The black guts pouring out of the hole of the 'prehistoric monster'—just like the newspapers say, sir!

CAPTAIN Well, it's very sad, sergeant. But you know what the Good Book says—'Pack up your troubles in your old kit bag and smile, *smile,* SMILE! While you've a Lucifer to light you like a fag you don't need a candle brother Ridler . . .

ALICE I'm sure that's all wrong.

CAPTAIN You hold your tongue! (*Sneering*) We all know—all nice girls love a sailor, all nice girls love a prick; for there's something about a candle that reminds them of . . .

MAN . . . and that's why . . .

CAPTAIN (*angrily*) . . . why nothing! Jutland was fought long before August 8—

MAN —as I was about to remark myself. Jutland had nothing whatever to do with it. The grey seas, the grey mists and the grey hairs. Leonardo da Vinci drew those writhing coils of hair, those swirling masses of water, to remind you of the form that lay concealed within the formless infinite. He could see them and draw them for you. What he could not see or help was that you would not be made to look even if he did draw them for you. You, if I may say so, are a 'consequential idiot'. 'And the consequences were . . .' You remember the game? Still at it, still playing it. Cause and effect!

BION I don't see how you are so superior and what makes you think you are so wonderful.

MAN I have not supposed you would. Although you had enough capacity to know your legion of honour, and D.S.O., and mention in dispatches were baubles, glittering toys, you have worshipped them with great tenacity. If Krishna told Arjuna, if Newton, Shakespeare, Bach, Mozart, Meister Eckhart, Plato, Socrates, Dante, Job told you, you could 'remark the ruck and reel which coil, keep and tease the simple sight', because you are blinded by the effulgence of your glory, you are condemned for ever to admire the evacuations from which you cannot free yourself. What is most worthless about yourself—*that* is what you admire.

BION Oh, shut up!

MAN Very well: I shall.

THIRTY-FOUR

R*osemary is silent, but her resignation is in no way passive; it is impossible to convey the vivid, vital disapproval of her silence.*

MAN (*to Rosemary*) Arjuna said, you remember, 'I will not fight', and threw down his bow. He did, however, pick it up again, allowing himself to be persuaded by Krishna that he did not know everything and that even if the opposing army did consist of his friends, and love was prominent amongst the foes, it was his business to fight. This (*indicating Bion*)—I hardly like to call him 'fool'—is too proud to admit that he could be mistaken or that the world of thought that he inhabits could conceivably be better than the world of his own invention. I remember sending a very good friend of his to Oxford to try to show him that even then he was behaving like Achilles sulking in his tent. The friend became someone—a man of consequence—though suffering terrible set-backs. Bion remains a fool still. He sulks in his tent and feels how wonderfully like Achilles he is. It would be laughable were it not tragic. I realize it must be terrible for you to have the pain of discovering that someone one has loved and admired is not worth it. Even worse is his own private hell which you and I can see him suffer and realize that he has always lavished love and admiration upon himself. This admiration is still, as always, devoted to his least admirable qualities.

BION Shut up, I say! Shut up!

MAN You see, Rosemary? There's nothing more we can do. Let us leave him. The man or woman who is given the privilege of making a decision also has the privilege of making the wrong one—again and again.

BION You sound remarkably smug to me. If my choice is between remaining in me or becoming like you I do not know that I am convinced that I would feel greatly improved by becoming like you two.

MAN You would not become me, that is sure—only 'like me'. An allegory of a man. You would 'borrow', as you did from your father and mother—with the understanding that you would never be called upon to pay back the debt. Attend! This is August 7/8 of our era—A-theist, A-chronous, A-moral, A-sthetic. Watch! Your eyes will become adjusted. Can you see?

BION I see a man? A shade? A ghost?

MAN Don't talk; listen. Don't watch; look. That's better! More like an encephaly, you will call it someday. Avec les yeux de pierre ils gisent là sans ouïe, sans voix, la rose du vitrail toujours épanouie. That's better—you are coming over to me quite clearly now. This is 'infra-sensuous'. I shall know what your a-morphous 'senses' tell me.

BION The man is filled with a kind of tenderness. Suddenly, with the utmost violence he beats in the woman's skull and . . . (*pouring sweat and overwhelmed with fear*), I won't watch! I shall *not* fight!

MAN Get back you damn fool. (*To Rosemary*) Poor stupid wretch . . . he has had a sane episode . . . I was afraid he might not stand it. Get on!

BION He bashes in the skull. God! It's like rock. He treats it like eggshell. He's sucking—this is cannibalism! He sucks out the brain.

MAN This is an anachronism. Luckily for you it isn't a million years later or they would be so barbarously civilized they would murder you for murder. A million years later still they would incarcerate you for insanity—an 'insane monster'.

BION Are you trying to tell me that it is 'I' who am doing this frightful thing, you damned blackguard?

MAN 'I', 'cannibal', 'blackguard'—these are all anachronisms. I didn't exist for another couple of million years. Even now you are measuring time in numbers of times the earth completes its orbit round the sun. The scale has to be of that trivial order because the spectrum of sensuous existence is minute—you have to measure it in terms of years—a sort of angstrom unit of space and time to measure sensuous existence. To borrow from your anachronistic vocabulary, most of your existence is as inert matter before birth and after death—what you call spirits and fossils, suspecting an infra-sensuous or ultra-sensuous extension. 'Fossil man', especially the skull, has a certain durability, not extending to light years, but long enough to lie within the scale of 'geological' time as contrasted with ephemeral or 'human' time. You are taking time off—'borrowing' from the domain of thought and thinking 'the anarchs of the world of darkness keep a throne for thee my son', as one of your 'mental' people put it. There are these escapes from the heavily armoured skulls. Ordinary people recognize their fellow 'old fossils', although they prevent the truth becoming too intense through feeling the thought, though verbalized, as a joke. Thinking is bearable because of its sensuous component. The experience which has not yet reached a conclusion is whether the human animal will survive a mind grafted on to its existing equipment. Now, do you think you could stand a little more?

BION (*surly and hostile*) More what?

MAN Well . . . a little more of 'I shall not cease from mental fight'. Not quite how Blake meant it of course, but the idea may emerge when the misleading quality imposed on formless thought by articulation is dissolved away. Even 'Confusion', as you liked to call him, described it as watching the thought ground in the mill of the mind with as much love or tolerance as might make it sprout. Even then, as you might be expected to know—if one expected anything of you whatever—God threw these presumptuous objects, ♀ ♂, out of Eden. The Omnipotent opposes the extensions of the human ability to have intercourse. Babel opposed the extensions of power to the realm of the mind. So extensions of plus-K are certain to reveal obstacles if extended to minus-K. The immortality achieved through reproduction by cell division leads to the mortality achieved by nuclear fission.

BION What else?

MAN I am not going to do your thinking for you. Sooner or later you will have to pay the price of deciding to think ±; whether, in Freud's formulation, to interpose 'thinking' between impulse and action; or to interpose it between the two as a substitute for action; or to interpose it between the two as a prelude to action.

BION Oh, all right—let's get on with this enthralling and spectacular spectacle.

(*The darkness deepens. The skull-crushing and sucking object is overwhelmed by depression at the failing supply of nutriment from the dead ♀ and the failure to restore it to life. He formulates in stone an* arti-*factual representation, easily seen by Plato to be a lying representation of, a substitute for, pro-creation, a substitute for creation. The lying substitution is transformed into a prelude to action. This whirling, swirling chaos to infinite and formless darkness becomes luminous and a Leonardo de Vinci robs the hair, the brooding waste of waters, of its formless chaos.*)

BION Disgusting! Mawkish!

THIRTY-FIVE

MAN Don't blame me if you find the taste of your brother's brains and blood and guts dis- or minus-gusting. The priests of Ur, the tomb robbers, are your religious and scientific forebears.

BION I do blame you.

MAN So I gather. You postpone the day of reckoning till man is strong enough—as you think—to carry the load of guilt; and then when the day of reckoning threatens to dawn you cheat again by robbing your forebears. 'They', you say, 'did not know any better'. You, I say, did not know, still do not know, any better. Never will, in the future, 'know any better'. Back to thy punishment, false fugitive from the domains of ultra- and infra-sensuous non-existence! Fawn upon, nuzzle the bloody corpse of your cannibal feast. Stand up! Be erect! Oh great and fallacious Phallus! You deal with feelings of guilt by deception. In the domain of real thinking it is possible to find an approximation which contributes to the illusion of omnipotence. Real thinking can approximate to thoughts which at the same moment seem to be those of the innocent child, the responsible adult, the depressed, devouring glutton, the depressed, devouring but unsatiated being of any age and clime. The variables are legion. The basic matrix is the ability to change. For instance, you can think, or imagine, or intuit—take your choice—that you are a civilized human being; 'homo', as we say in our quaint scientific language, 'sapiens'. As you have demonstrated, you can feel (think, imagine, intuit—as I said, take your choice) you are the wild animal nuzzling, fawning upon, mourning its victim on which it preys. You may easily feel you are preyed upon. You have a wide choice, a choice which seems to include a great number of possibilities including combinations of thoughts and feelings in great profusion of varieties and degrees of variety. One of your kind—there are many more than are able to make their existence obtrude on other similar entities—described it in verbal transformations of visual images as seeing all the domains of the world spread out before his eyes as if they were objects suitable for the exercise of greedy possessiveness. In this domain the herbivore may devour the carnivore.

I am at a loss to find a method of communication by means of which I could make the 'fact'—as you would no doubt call it—clear to you. Perhaps—well, you know about perspective?

BION A little.

MAN *(to himself)* My God—I think he is learning! *(To Bion)* Under a certain vertex the figures of Euclidean geometry appear distorted; a sphere looks like a flat disc and an elipse can be interpreted as a circular pond—artists frequently paint and draw in this kind of way.

BION Yes, I've heard this before. In fact, I have said something like it.

MAN Under a certain vertex—by which of course I mean a vertex that is so 'uncertain' that I do not even know what it is—the visual image of the sensuous, Euclidean objects appears to have been expelled, 'projected' from *behind* the eyes onto the world of objects in *front* of the eyes. Under one perspective the observer sees, takes in, a horse which he cannot put in his mouth but *can* take in through his eyes.

BION This is familiar to me and many of my fellow human animals.

MAN Sometimes the flow is from a focal point behind the eyes out—to the horse, say; sometimes the 'perspective', that is to say, the 'flow', is reversed. Sometimes these flowing objects come in waves, sometimes in quanta, sometimes a feeling is described under a vertex as 'helplessness', sometimes as 'God'. The 'perspective is reversed'.

BION I think I have an idea—a sort of hunch—that I know what you mean. A man once told me, 'I don't know what I mean'. I tried to translate in terms of articulate speech what he was expressing in verbal form—verbal transformation of a visual image—a hieroglyph. Of course, it was not amenable to the laws of articulate thinking.

MAN I think I know what *you* mean. It might be a good idea to get together. First we need to know *how* to get together; what, so to speak, are the laws of mental cannibalism.

BION *(to himself)* My God—I think he *is* learning! It would be curious if it turned out that we both were.

MAN The first thing is to realize that the laws of nature are not formulations or orders which have to be obeyed, but are elements which are constantly conjoined, are conjoined *constantly*. This is true whatever the variables may be and however much the variables dominate, are allowed to dominate, or are encouraged to dominate the object which approximates to the formula of (constant + variable) $\alpha + \beta \times \xi$, or $\beta + \alpha \times \xi$.

ALICE A sign to denote noise, analogous to that denoting the bass or treble clef in music, is required.

MAN One famed anthropologist says the bone formation of the skull does not lend itself to attachment of the tongue muscle for use in articulate speech. The attachment of the penis to the anatomy, the vagina likewise, is in its own fashion appropriate and beautiful. What God has joined together let no man put asunder.

BION How could we put them together or put them asunder? These are anatomical structures with physiological functions, and I for my part have not in my conscious memory ever known a time when conscious and unconscious aim and ideal have been possible to divorce from each other. Nor have I ever known a time when these constantly conjoined objects were on good terms with each other except for short periods; enough to make me long for more.

MAN Rosemary and I realize that. I was only a little while back saying to Rosemary—was I not, Rosie?—

BION Rosie! Good God! Rosie!

MAN That is what I said. You do not approve, so you sneer; if our terms of endearment are not yours, your hostility is at once in evidence.

BION That is me. I did not choose my education or my personality. I would rather I were tolerant. What you say and do is not my business, but what you say and do stimulates disagreeable feelings in me, as in this instance; feelings are aroused in me which I would rather did not come together. Yet they constantly *do* come together. I can do nothing about your arousing such feelings. I can do nothing about the feelings that in fact are aroused.

MAN That may be so. For all I know you may be quite justified—you obviously *are* in your own eyes—in thinking you cannot fairly be held responsible. But you *are* held responsible and it is you who feel it is your responsibility although you are trying to maintain that you do not hold yourself responsible. Are you not then yourself trying to 'put asunder' what God has joined together?

BION Who, or what, is God?

MAN You do not know, but you behave and think as if some such force that is not you, 'is'. You do not reconcile yourself to the fact that if there is such a force it behaves in a way of which you do not approve. Newton, long ago, suggested that the procedures which he had adopted with regard to the behaviour of light could and should be adopted with regard to the forces with which he was not acquainted, but of whose reality he had no doubt. He even spoke of them at the end of 'Opticks' as if they were not dissimilar from the forces which were familiar to people who were under a religious discipline. Whoever reported the debate between Arjuna and Krishna said much the same; Milton likewise. The greatest minds have shown themselves to be familiar with these emotional experiences, including the experience of having to admit that before the forces of which they disapproved their rebellion lapsed into shamed silence though they were ashamed of their shame and ashamed of their acquiescence or 'defeat'.

BION What about it? Admitting all that—so what?

THIRTY-SIX

MAN You will not be satisfied with my reply, but here it is—allow me to introduce you. First, to the objects which were so shadowy that it was not even possible to say they were man and woman. I pronounce no opinion on this. Let me introduce you now to two objects which the higher human authorities had no doubt whatever were man and woman; there was no dispute about the facts of anatomy and physiology. The man took the woman into the bushes, the woman showed no reluctance to go. There, the man who showed himself subsequently to be perfectly capable of the exercise of functions which we are used to regarding as those of reason, savaged the woman's breasts and genitalia with his teeth, devouring the flesh of both regions in a manner that would be comprehensible if he were a wild carnivore. The episode presents itself to us as a problem because he did not appear as a wild beast devouring his prey in a jungle. He appeared to be a man going out with a girl at a holiday resort. This pair were so unshadowy that it was impossible to *dis*believe that they were a man and a woman. There are many similar instances, so common that it is not necessary to recount and document them. How immediately they have presented themselves to the senses of the reader of this book depends on a number of facts peculiar to the reader—his occupation, his life up to this time—it would take a long time to recite the facts. I shall abbreviate our labours by saying that they 'depend on the vertex'. Under one vertex I have known a man act as if he were having a vivid emotional experience familiar to me under the vertex, 'dream'. He was not dreaming; nor did he think he was. It may seem unnecessary to resort to the term, 'vertex', but it must suffice until we can find some more adequate shorthand for those states in which the individual has two or more sets of facts appropriate to the same emotional experience, but which are impossible to entertain together without feeling mad. This involves feeling sane enough to be afraid, and further, to respect his fear. He is afraid of his mind, and fears that his fear is worthy of respect.

BION In short, his 'mind' and the consequences of having a mind are unwelcome discoveries. But you seem doubtful.

MAN Let me try to expand my misgiving. I agree with what you have formulated in terms of a 'mind', but I am not sure that it is satisfactory either to include in or exclude from 'mental' activity the taste of human blood, the 'emotions' associated with erectile tissue and erectability. It seems, though this is only guesswork, that it was easier for the Greeks to tolerate the idea of 'thinking' with the phrenes; or to associate it with the dead; or with the dead apparition when the person to whom it appears was asleep. Alcmaeon of Croton seems to have been one of the first to have thought that thinking might have something to do with the CNS. Since then, up to the present, great importance has been attributed to man's possession of a central nervous system. The nature of impulses springing from an ability to exercise one's teeth or vagina or penis is not similarly honoured or tolerated. When a modern man's impulses obtrude to a point where they become manifest to others as functions of a sensuous system, neither they nor their locale are accorded respect. The peripheral nervous system and its extensions are a source of suspicion and fear.

BION Suppose there *is* a CNS. Further, suppose there is a peripheral nervous system—the PNS and the CNS both fear. The fear is intensified if it is supposed that there is some extension of both infra- and ultra-sensuous. This extension is dreaded in itself, and made the more dreadful if suspected as being *outside* the sphere which we associate with the senses . . .

MAN . . . and *within,* but unrecognized.

BION Or recognizable as a character or personality which can be located within the molecular structure of the amines and the domain in which their transmission takes place.

MAN If the CNS is rightly supposed to be important, but we are unable to assess its importance or how it exercises its functions, does that not make it more frightening?

BION It does. I, as a psycho-analyst, have committed myself to action which pre-supposes that such a thing as a mind or a personality exists. I find no difficulty, in present circumstances, in making that admission, accepting that my work is an admission that I hold such a theory. I hold it so strongly that I am prepared to transform my ideas into action. For example, I allow it to be known that I am a psycho-analyst and, with others, have gone so far as to seek recognition of this same idea from people who are not us and who are not in fact at all closely connected with us.

MAN You make the acknowledgment clearly. Do you also agree that others do so? Sometimes you have to my knowledge claimed that certain well-known figures of the past, not only of the recent past like Sigmund Freud himself, were gifted with a profound capacity for understanding their fellow men?

BION Certainly. We can gauge their actions and behaviour from what has been recorded of or by them, and allowing myself anachronistic—like poetic—licence, I would call them very considerable psycho-analysts before anyone had heard of such a term.

MAN Is this not an instance of claiming that there is such a 'thing' as psycho-analysis, that there always has been such a thing as psycho-analysis, whether it could be verbalized or not?

BION I would say that it is an example of a thought which, before Freud existed to think it, was 'without a thinker'.

MAN I am not really clear why you postulate a thought 'without a thinker'. It seems an unnecessary complication.

BION 'Doubt' is always regarded as an unnecessary complication. That is clear whenever an individual asserts 'certainty'.

MAN You used the word 'certainly' just now.

BION Touché. I agree.

MAN But you reply in the language of a game of combat?

BION A 'playing at hate'. Play itself has a function as a way of rehearsing something. We play at soldiers. It is not always clear that children are 'only' playing, particularly if the game turns into a quarrel about the way the game is being played. Conversely, 'real' quarrels, 'real' wars, arouse critical hostility if the soldiers or sailors appear to be 'too' friendly. I remember an emotional upheaval connected with certain courtesies observed by Field Marshall Montgomery in his treatment of a captured enemy general. 'Too serious' vies with 'too friendly'—a psycho-analyst is vulnerable to attack on the grounds of 'degrees' of emotion with which the debate is conducted. The degree of emotion *is* a statement; a verbal formulation may be emotionally liberating, but is restrictive if it stimulates more than it satisfies. (Putting it more abstractly, $\alpha\,\xi \rightarrow \alpha\,\alpha$ at once becomes $\alpha\,\alpha \rightarrow \alpha\,\alpha\,\xi$ = frustration.) Whether the 'frustration' is a product of inability to solve an existent problem, or due to progress revealing further frustration, the frustration is more obvious than the need to discriminate between 'kinds' of frustration. The problem of delay can be solved by interposing thinking between impulse and action; or the frustration can be so great that hatred of the thinking, interposed between impulse and action, itself becomes the object of the immediately frustrated, destructive impulse. The tendency, therefore, is to turn the destructive impulse into action rather than further thought.

BION The advantages of thought are not immediately obvious. Whoever is aware of this discussion between you and me, including you and me, cannot see advantages which depend on a future that has not yet taken place. It is as bad as a past which is not known because it is forgotten, or because we did not then exist. Ignorance thus provides force for belief in a future heaven and a past transmigration of souls. I resort to a 'hunch' that as there can be thoughts which have no thinker, so there may be 'acts' without an agent. There are thoughts which have been acted upon without an agent to act. There can be thoughts and acts related to each other without any thinker or agent to relate to them. Thus a cannibalistic act, neither conceived nor acted upon, may await the arrival of the creator and agent. Should it in fact be the case that a particular murderer has existed, he can be regarded as a realization which approximates to the theory or concept of a personality who both conceives and transforms such an impulse into thought or action, or both. Nevertheless, the 'fact' 'murderer' may be a rationalization—a product of the reason whose function it is, as Hume postulated, to be the slave of the emotions. The problems with which you are familiar are not solved either by thought, or action, or both in combination. You, and others like you, feel dissatisfied. You and your contemporaries doubt that any inhabitants of the world, whether real or fictitious, are any more satisfied; or that you would be any more satisfied if you found yourself in the position of any of those people. You *do* find yourself in the position of victor. England has been conquered. Rosemary has become mistress. She is the 'possession' of the Man. Her former mistress is in the position of being her 'skivvy'. But you heard what she said.

ROSEMARY What did I say?

MAN You said, 'Not again!'—meaning that no matter what the change in vertex, the relationship between the invariants was constant. Mathematical terms could be used to formulate a problem and demonstrate relationships between invariants and constants with such accuracy that the configuration presented by the newly disposed elements was familiar and unwelcome. 'Not again!' she said.

BION Some emotions and events are less agreeable than others; these, people hope, will not re-occur; they wish to feel pleasant sensations without cessation. Attempts are made to manipulate feelings and ideas so that they conform to a principle of perpetuity. In all domains there is a desire that nothing should disturb the sense of permanence. This desire is sure to conflict with the nature of the object studied. It is hard to conceive of anything more free from restraint than thoughts and feelings. But if an attempt is made to give them written or even spoken expression, freedom of thought has been eroded. The freedom of communicated thought cannot at any time be absolute.

THIRTY-SEVEN

BION The experience of physical, sensuous space was not abandoned. It was clung to with such tenacity that it prevented the loss of security involved if pictorial sense were lost. It obscured realization that Euclidean proofs depended on their being visually obvious. Euclidean geometry thus remained for centuries without a rival. There was no rival in the sphere of education since communication of what is known, by those who know it, to those who are ignorant of it, depends on visual sense. The 'obvious' was evidence and proof of the truth of what was asserted. 'Time' was as unquestioned as 'space'. Events are supposed to occur at a particular time and in a particular place; the 'past' and the 'future' depend upon sensuous experience, but there is no more recognition of that than of the dependence of Euclidean geometry on the sense of sight. Theories about 'mental life' are taken for granted, as was the background to the theories of Euclidean geometry; similar assumptions about 'mental time and space' imperil growth of mental life. Theories of causation, commonly adumbrated in the context of the physical world, are based on the undiscussed and unquestioned foundation of ideas about time and space. Newton accepted that foundation. What he applied to the physical world was applicable to the mental or psychical or spiritual world. Should these assumptions be accepted by psycho-analysts or philosophers? Descartes had no doubt about the value of philosophical Doubt and yet did not doubt the validity of 'cogito ergo sum'; although he came so near, he did not take the final step. The psycho-analytical theory, first formulated by Melanie Klein, I propose to extend to areas not in fact included by her in the therapeutic domain for which she proposed it. The extension involves supposing that not only does the individual harbour omnipotent phantasies of destruction and dispersal, but that there is an omnipotent being or force that destroys the whole object and disperses the fragments widely.

MYSELF I can see that in the sphere of astronomy, where so much depends on the sense of sight either directly or at a remove—as in the examination and comparison of photographs—it may be possible, by putting together the 'facts' of many hundreds of photographs, to draw a sequence which could be supposed to represent a 'moving picture' of events like the development of our own sun—as if in a few moments one could scrutinize an event which may have taken many centuries. But I do not see what useful purpose is served by such a fictitious construction.

MAN It gives immediacy and reality to something which might otherwise be hard to understand.

BION Is it not just there that the danger lies? One more plausible theory is created to swell the enormous supply of plausible theories.

MAN Of course. But fear of what might happen is a bad master.

BION So is plausibility. I wonder how many plausible theories have been used and bewildered the human race. I would like to know. I am not sure of the ease with which 'plausible' theories are produced. In this context of 'plausible theories' about which we are talking, the plausible theory, or 'convincing interpretation', may be hard to come by. It can be plausible and false. Witness the idea that 'the sun rises'—what trouble that has caused! We do not know the cost in suffering associated with the belief in a Christian God, or the god of Abraham's Ur, or Hitler's Germany, or peyotism—or god of any kind.

MAN Not god of any kind; some gods have been less 'poisonous' than others.

BION Schacht said that the accumulation of wealth was a harmless ambition, but then the important thing may be the way it is accumulated and the object for which it is to be used. It could be to achieve the reward of work done as a substitute for doing the work.

MAN The same is true of psycho-analysis or any other mechanism developed for purposes of accumulation. You will not have failed to notice that we make a tacit assumption about a sense of values; or even that there is a valid sense of values by which the ambitions are to be judged. We may regard our 'survival' as a matter of importance. We should not have survived had we not wished to do so.

ALICE Who is 'we'?

MAN The ones who survive, together with some who failed. If we are animate this includes an ambition to remain so. The same impulse appears to have spread to the ambition that it should be a life worth preserving. I have noticed this tendency in psycho-analysis; the whole emphasis, since it is not primarily concerned with physical health, suggests that there should be someone or something who is concerned with happiness.

ROSEMARY I would like to be happy. I can't say it thrilled me to have to bother with Alice's parties; in fact, she seems to get some sort of kick out of finding she is my maid.

ALICE I doubt whether any woman was as keen on the survival of the 'good old days' of the British Empire as the men. The 'already existent' is essential to and incompatible with 'further existence'.

BION According to Rosemary, Alice is able to have a masochistic relationship with her former maid.

MAN That is a psycho-analytic formulation.

BION I agree. I do sometimes express my views in terms which can themselves be characterized; in this instance my formulation is called theoretical. But let me tell you something in more conversational terms about a man I knew in the army. He was highly educated at a well-known public school and, as far as I could see, had the opportunity common to people of the privileged classes of taking up an occupation of responsibility and power. He did not do so. He failed his chance of being trained as an officer, became an officer's servant and stayed in that position till the end of the war, by which time I had no means of knowing his further career.

ALICE Are you suggesting my career is comparable?

BION The thought occurs to you; if you are willing, and others likewise, this could be debated. If so, it is not an obstacle to the discussion that my case was a man and Alice is a woman; that kind of behaviour is not restricted to one sex. Yet it can be described, both in the man and now Alice, as 'sexual'. This is a classification familiar to me; in psycho-analysis the relationship between Rosemary and Alice could be discovered or demonstrated or classified as sexual. Suppose we consider Rosemary and Alice as welcoming, for their individual reasons, the country's downfall; their nation or culture undergoes a change which makes it possible for each individual to pursue a life which they would not otherwise have been free to do. I can see that the defeat makes that freedom possible. The desire to achieve such freedom, if shared amongst a sufficient number of people, could contribute to the defeat.

MAN What would be described as a defeat brought about by the decadence of the society or group; although I have known a society to be considered decadent *and* victorious. Reciprocally, the victory is regarded as a sign or symptom or 'result'.

ROSEMARY Men seem to attach great importance to conflict, rivalry, victory. Even in private affairs I couldn't make a man think that there was any importance in what I thought or felt about him. He talked and acted as if the only matter of consequence was whether he was successful. I suppose he thought I would then be bound to fall in love with a man of such capacity and brilliance. To the end he never entertained the possibility that I loved *him* and couldn't care less about his successes.

BION Is that true? I would be surprised if you did not find, if you were honest with yourself, that you cared a lot about his success.

ROSEMARY He had some distinction; it was the most boring part about him. Why, even in sexual love he was convinced he had to be potent. He couldn't believe that I might love him and therefore be capable of helping him to be potent.

BION I am sure there are many men who have no doubt of the

woman's ability to make fools of them. In technical terms, there are plenty of men who are sure the woman can 'castrate' them. All states exist, from primitive fears of the female genital—as expressed in visual prototypes of a vagina dentata—to fears that the woman would rejoice in triumphing by humiliating the man.

MAN There is certainly a profound belief in the pleasure of triumphing over and humiliating the rival. That state of mind is common enough and it is feared by man or woman. It, and the fear of it, can be generated by the experiences of the child.

BION Its efficacy depends on belief. But there can be innumerable reasons for fear, including fear of the pleasures of cruelty.

MAN You are again talking of 'reasons'—'one' reason, 'innumerable' reasons. Don't you think *Belief* is the action-generator analogous to 'number generators'? Man, like animals, is capable of fear. You can have 'reasons' for being afraid; you can fear death and believe you will die. Belief is the action-generator; what generates belief?

BION If that state has been part of you, you must be familiar with the constantly conjoined elements. We can suppose that the constant conjunction has a 'great deal to do with'—or is 'constantly conjoined with'—the fact that we are still alive. I would go further; I have owed and shall owe my continued existence to my capacity to fear 'an impending disaster'. The question is not 'where is one to draw the line?' but where has the line been drawn? Between conscious and unconscious? By the phrenes? The thalamus?

ROSEMARY Does it matter? I can see that it does if we want to debate the question. I have never known a crisis in which I have thought like that.

BION Here we discuss. I can even *imagine* having a discussion like this, but this discussion and the imagination that I am having such a discussion differ; one is the discussion, the other a substitute for, or a prelude to, discussion.

The ferocity with which children sometimes play games is evidence that the players are not feeling that they are playing, or the observer witnessing, 'just a game'. The idea of 'game' is an inadequate description for what is being witnessed. It is being wrongly categorized by the name of 'game'. I think of a mathematical analogy: if the 'universe of discourse' does not facilitate the solution of 3 minus 5, then real numbers are no good, but must be enlarged by 'negative numbers'. If the mathematical 'field of play' is not suitable for the manipulation of 'negative numbers', it has to be extended to provide conditions for 'games' with negative numbers. If the world of conscious thought is not suitable for playing 'Oedipus Rex', the 'universe of discourse' must be enlarged to include such plays. If serious psycho-analytic discussion cannot take place in the domain which Freud found adequate, it must be enlarged. In fact, Freud did enlarge it when he found that he could not believe what his experience with patients seemed to suggest—that they had all been assaulted sexually. He had to entertain the idea that events which had never taken place could have serious consequences. If I cannot 'believe', I cannot act or think. I need 'thoughts without a thinker'. I may have to create a domain which is not a serious paper, not a game, not a murderous rival. If this is true of 'childhood', 'mathematics', why not of other thematic apperceptions, including 'psycho-analysis' itself? A 'field of play' must be found on which to play our 'game'. I once asked a group, 'What is the interpretation of that?' and I pushed a chair into the forefront of the discussion. It took almost twenty minutes before anyone ventured a reply to my question.

ROSEMARY I'm not surprised! I wouldn't know what you were up to.

BION (*indicating Man*) If it comes to that, do you know what *he* is up to?

ROSEMARY He and all his pals? Yes.

BION Then you believe.

THIRTY-EIGHT

MAN You interest me; may I ask *what* we are up to?

ROSEMARY Homer spent time writing the Iliad and the Odyssey—a very early answer to the question which is still being asked.

BION That doesn't answer Man's question. It only stresses the fact that 'a question' has always existed and still does—we are animals activated by curiosity.

MAN Or belief.

BION We are questioning ourselves about the nature of our behaviour. There are many answers, included among those from the past—if Rosemary is right—the answer given by one of the world's great poets. But in a particular instance, *this* instance, we can provide an answer, if not one that satisfies us.

MAN Perhaps there is something wrong with our 'methods' of investigation + answer.

ROSEMARY Well, you at any rate (*turning to Man*) should have some answer. You have upset our way of life. Alice and I have certainly been forced into a situation which we had no say in choosing. You were not obliged to invade our country.

MAN How do you come to the conclusion that *I* am any more a free agent than you are? It is true I had a choice. It so happened that I *was* compelled to invade your country, but I was free to disobey orders. I had to decide what to do.

BION You mean you had to decide whether you wanted to pay the cost.

MAN Yes, you could say that; but I did not know what the cost would be either of obeying or dis-obeying.

BION Is that any different from any other decision? The cost of having the privilege of choice is being held responsible and accepting the responsibility for whatever one decides. This, indeed, is the cost of choosing to be responsible.

ROSEMARY Do you think you or Roland accept the responsibility for protecting Alice and me? If not, what do you accept the responsibility for?

ROLAND Bion and I, amongst others, *did* accept that responsibility. I do not believe in a future life—

ROSEMARY —nor do I—

ROLAND —and so it was clear to me that my patriotism or loyalty or responsibility, or whatever you call it, might cost me my life. I know plenty of men who did lose their lives. Even the many survivors lost their peace of mind or what made life worth living.

ROSEMARY You didn't join the army because you were responsible.

BION Nor did you.

ROSEMARY Even women risk death. In childbirth . . .

ROLAND You did not risk childbirth.

ROSEMARY What do you know about it? I believed a man and his promises once. I don't now, but I did once. I didn't die, but something died in me—mentally, I suppose you would call it.

BION Most people experience mental death if they live long enough. You don't have to live long to have that experience—all you have to do is to be mentally alive.

ALICE You speak as if it were simple to be mentally alive. That is hardly my experience. It is true that a person does not, as far as we know, have to 'do' anything to be physically born. It seems easier to think that he has to 'do' something to *keep* physically or mentally alive. You have to have a partner for one thing—even in opposition.

ROBIN How do you mean? I can see that I have to be 'opposed' if I want a contest. But suppose I don't.

BION Doesn't it depend on what use you need a contest for? This very discussion is a contest. We are talking about something. I think there is a sense in which we need, and are even feeling aware of the need for contest, or for opposition.

ROLAND (*sarcastically*) This gentleman (*indicating Man*) has obliged.

ROBIN I don't feel at all grateful. I had plenty of trouble with the weather and the crops without the need for invasion too.

MAN I don't think any of us like the 'opposition' we have. We feel we should appear in a better light if the opposition were different. I can't do what I want; I have never known a time when I could. But there has always been someone or something against which I could rage.

BION If all else fails you could rage, as I too can, against yourself, your youth or your age, your strength or your weakness. It is one of the uses you can make of God—if you can believe in God.

ROBIN Well, can't you?

BION Which god are you referring to?

ROBIN Allah Akbar!

BION I don't think you are being serious. I shall use psycho-analytic licence to take jokes seriously. To start with, you show you are aware that you have a choice.

ROBIN You think of me as joking; it would not be so easy to suppose that, if I were in fact a member of a Muslim culture. Nor would you suppose that you could 'choose' to take it seriously 'because' you are a member of a psycho-analytic group. You would be compelled to take it seriously. It has nothing to do with being a member of a particular group, profession or culture, but that the particular 'culture' has a great deal to do with some underlying, unobserved, constant conjunction of beliefs; an actual God of which the various religious formulations are only approximations to the underlying configuration of facts.

BION You are asking me to suppose that there is a 'thing-in-itself', noumenon, Godhead, which, using Kant's terminology for my purposes, becomes 'manifest' as a phenomenon; 'God' as contrasted with 'Godhead'; 'finity' as contrasted with 'infinity'; 'won', as Milton says, 'from the void and formless infinite'; a geometrical, Euclidean figure, a triangle with sides of 2, 4 and 5 units, as contrasted with an algebraical deductive system. But a rational fact gives no scope for 'belief'. Belief itself is destroyed if it is transformed to find a 'reason' for belief.

ROBIN Well, I take your word for it; if you say that that is what I'm asking you to do, I can believe I am, but I confess I didn't know it.

BION Then you have the necessary condition for belief. You don't reject my formulation though you are not in a position to confirm it. 'Time' may confirm it or not.

MYSELF I don't see that Time can confirm it or refute it. I know what you mean and so would others familiar with the ordinary use of conversational English. This supposes that 'reality' approximates to conversational formulation. Suppose I examine your statement in a more analytical way: it conforms to certain definitory hypotheses, it is made up of words taken from a 'vocabulary' or collection of definitory hypotheses and articulated according to certain grammatical rules. Am I to suppose that there is some underlying configuration which approximates to those 'constant conjunctions', words, and also approximates to the rules of grammar in accordance with which they have been articulated? Or are the vocabulary and grammatical rules of articulation unique, particular, conformable to an underlying configuration which is itself 'unique' and therefore of no general significance? Or do those same grammatical rules of articulation represent a reality which is *not* formulated in the statement directly, but only by a silent obedience to the unformulated, undetected, but nonetheless real, system of rules or discipline? Should we then listen not only to the conversational meaning but also to 'how they say it'? Should we obey, conform to the rules of 'articulation', or only to the laws articulately formulated?

ROBIN I don't see why I should obey the rules of articulation. After all, I am not a verb or adjective; rules which are all right for them may not be at all suitable for me who am *not* part of speech, but a person.

MAN You do in fact have to obey the laws governing conquered peoples.

BION I do not wish to argue with that automatic I see in your belt. I would rather not be either 'pro' or 'con' that particular piece of machinery, although I have reason to suppose that if I conformed to the rules of force either you or I would be dead. As far as I am concerned I believe the dead person ceases to exist, but since you cart that automatic around stuck in your belt, I assume that you conform to a different view.

MAN Not at all. Your view and mine seem to be in agreement; not 'complete' agreement in this instance because, so far as I have a choice, I would rather be the one to survive.

BION So you have the automatic and I don't.

MAN You *believe* I have the automatic. In fact, all I have in the holster is a bar of chocolate.

BION Very clever; but that 'bar of chocolate' is backed by the force of an invading army.

MAN You *believe* it is backed by the force of an invading army. As a matter of fact . . .

MYSELF I was about to say that myself, but I hesitated as it occurred to me that 'facts' are very curious things, so you beat me to 'as a matter of fact' before I could say it. I was wondering, when you were talking of articulate speech, what the rules would be when the rules were *not* those of articulation.

BION Such as the rules of 'murder', the rules of 'sex', the rules of 'violence', the rules of Chinese communication contrasted with the rules of 'articulate' communication, the rules of 'blackmail'.

MAN As a member of the late British Empire you should have plenty of experience of violence, blackmail, murder, inarticulate speech.

MYSELF We have; it has stimulated a great deal of envy and ambition to emulate and rival our achievements! But we have also a great deal of experience of poetry and poetic expression and communication.

MAN In the course of practising psycho-analysis you were able to contrast your findings with those when practising group therapy. How do they compare?

BION I remain, as far as I can tell, the same person whether I am experiencing a group or a psycho-analysis.

MYSELF Yes, of course; I see that.

BION Though it may seem contradictory to what I have just said, I don't think there is any 'of course' about it. I said, 'as far as I can tell', but I don't know 'how far' that is. I certainly don't 'see' the same things in the two situations. Taking what I may call a macroscopic vertex I do not see the same things as I do from a microscopic vertex. In what I would call a macroscopic formulation the difference is easily explained by the fact that a group is not an individual or vice versa, but . . .

MYSELF You think there is a change analogous to the change described by de Broglie between the behaviour detected by the observation of the relationship between macroscopic units and between microscopic units?

BION 'Analogy' is itself a mental tool more appropriate to complex large observations and judgements than to the observation in detail of details. The microscopic vertex—I shall borrow this term to improvise a way of talking about this subject which is devoid of such equipment—reveals something which does not correspond to the anatomy or physiology of the individual or the group of human individuals.

MYSELF Could you venture on an attempt to communicate this to me?

BION Gladly, but I am not hopeful.

ROSEMARY Alice, I think it's time we left. I feel I am not in a sufficiently serious state of mind to keep in touch with these two.

BION I should have thought both of you might know very well what I am talking about—the thing-in-itself as contrasted with the language about it. You may find yourselves as inadequate as I am in talking *about* it, that is, in trying to tell someone else—lateral communication. I cannot feel optimistic of my chances of making it clear even to myself.

MYSELF I see your point.

BION Then it can't be the point.

MYSELF You mean I am wrong?

BION No, I don't; but you are now.

ALICE Rosemary, do you think we shall ever understand this?

ROSEMARY No, but I feel I am 'becoming' it even if I do not, and never shall, 'understand' what I am 'becoming' or 'being'.

BION In short, 'being' something is different from 'understanding' it. Love is the ultimate which is 'become', not understood.

ALICE *(looking at Rosemary)* I have 'become' something and this, if I could say it, would depend on my saying, 'I love'.

BION Or you have become loving perhaps?

ALICE No, I love Rosemary.

BION If you are right you must have become capable of loving.

ALICE I thought that as a psycho-analyst you would be sure to say I was homosexual.

BION On the contrary; so far as I am capable of 'being', as contrasted with 'claiming to be', a psycho-analyst, I think that you are incorrect in saying you love Rosemary if you are homosexual; you must have become capable of loving. Becoming sexual is part of physical maturation. Real love is not a function of the thing loved, but of the person loving. That is part of psychical or mental maturation and is not obstructed by accidental features of the thing or person loved.

MYSELF Amongst these features that you call 'accidental', are you then including that which we call the sex of the person?

BION Certainly; sex applies to anatomy and physiology and, as is usually the case when we talk of the mind, has been taken over by the psycho-analysts because we have to make do with a language invented for physical life or 'sensuous experience'. 'Passionate love' is the nearest I can get to a verbal transformation which 'represents' the thing-in-itself, the ultimate reality, the 'O', as I have called it, approximating to it.

ROLAND Then you think Alice could love me?

BION If she is correct about loving Rosemary, she is *capable* of loving you. That does not mean that she would want to be with you, either for an ephemeral episode or for life, or for anatomical or physiological purposes. But I am concerned here to discuss, with inadequate equipment, mental phenomena. I have a prejudice in favour of believing there is such a 'thing' as a mind or spirit.

ROLAND Is that what you mean when you say you are a psycho-analyst?

BION That term is meaningless, but useful for nomenating an expanding conjunction, including what I and certain individuals are doing, shut in a room together during my working hours. It has a use in what I described as 'lateral' communication—'conversational' English. Both phrases, when used by me, have a directional significance, sometimes tacit, sometimes overtly expressed. I refer to the use of terms which imply direction because such terms are used by others as well as by me. I also use these terms in a context which is different quantitatively and qualitatively in the domain of thought. As a psycho-analyst I assume that there is such a reality that approximates to these terms 'thought', 'mind', 'personality'. I suspect—it is no more than a hunch or suspicion—that the mind and personality have a physical counterpart, expressed by Alexander in *Space, Time and Deity* as a relationship of every psychosis with its 'neurosis'. In this context I am assuming that every psyche has a physical counterpart in the central nervous system. I could portray the relationship by marks on paper thus: ϒ ↔ ℏ (pronounced psy ↔ fang). Note the double arrow to indicate that the 'direction' of the thought is *indifferentiated*. I use a Chinese sign for CNS to indicate that the thing indicated is different from the physical, sensuous reality usually supposed to approximate to the sign 'CNS'. Assume for the discussion that ℏ is as significant as it is supposed to be and that ϒ is as important or more—not less. Lateral, profound, superficial, deep, early, later—all are terms more appropriate to time and space and sensuous awareness, but not if there is a domain of which it is possible to be mentally aware. The physical CNS ℏ has contact with a real physical world and a language appropriate to its formulation exists. We are compelled to use that language for communication of something for which it was not devised and of which it is itself a product.

ROSEMARY I'm sorry, I do *not* know *what* you are talking about.

BION What I am saying and our physical and sensuous components, are manipulable by set theory. Thoughts associated with a thinker are also amenable to set theory. Mind, personality, relationship, 'belief' are not; they cannot even be reasonably defined. 'Reasonable definition' involves 'confinement' to a 'constant conjunction'.

THIRTY-NINE

MAN Can I help? May I show you a recent acquisition of mine—I refer to this painting.

ROLAND My god! What damned sauce! That's our Athenèse!

MAN Yours?! Did you ever look at it?

ROLAND Of course! It hung in our dining room.

MAN It *was* yours. Since the pacification it has been mine. By great good fortune it came to me in the redistribution as I had been one of the first to apply for it. Would you care to demonstrate its finer points?

ROLAND Well, I'm no art expert, but . . .

MAN No, I did not suppose you were, but—you said it was yours and I wondered in what sense you meant that.

ROLAND I suppose you think it's yours—by right of force, by conquest.

MAN Shall we say, by right of your falling to my chocolate bar?

ROSEMARY Am I likewise—Alice also—slave to your all-conquering chocolate bar? No, leave him to me Alice. I told you, I know how to deal with these gentry. I wasn't sent to one of your high-falutin' schools.

ALICE Roland was though. Let him 'demonstrate' the Athenèse. Perhaps we shall find out something about how you and I and the Athenèse all come to have fallen to this gentleman's chocolate bar.

(*All becomes dark, including the picture. Only Roland's voice is heard*)

ROLAND To start with let me make it clear that the real name of this famous painting is 'Saint Athanasius chased by a wild boar'.

ROSEMARY Wrong from the start. It is 'Athenèse mon pied'.

ROLAND (*ignoring the interruption and becoming more and more academic, in guide book style*) The painting is probably one of the few surviving absolutely genuine works by the greatest painter the world has ever known. It has always been in possession of my family—

VOICE Quite right. It 'owned' them; 'they' never owned 'it'—

ROLAND —and has been unknown to the public who are nevertheless familiar with him, though anonymously, as the greatest artist that ever existed. Note the delicacy and truth with which every detail is rendered. The saint's left foot has been caught in a root of the . . . of the bush . . . or thicket . . . and at any moment one expects, so vivid is the chiaroscuro, to see him fall headlong and then the tusker will have *got* him! Ach Gott, unser hilf—note the animal is so realistically rendered that . . .

(*At this point in the discussion the boar actually loses all its ferocity and trots peacefully out of the picture.*) Now isn't that maddening! I can't possibly lecture if the ruddy animal walks off like that. In fact, the painting portrays an historical moment of great religious significance which makes me think the pig itself is no other than Satan in one of his multitudinous disguises. His envy is of such malignancy that he is even prepared to pursue the saint into the domain of art. As I was going to say, it was after this unfortunate contretemps that the saint arrived hot foot . . .

ROSEMARY 'Mon pied' as the French in their godless language would say.

ROLAND . . . and without any further ado dashed off the Athanasian Creed.

ALICE Even now the creed shows traces of pique. He had a wonderful gift of expression.

ROLAND So would you have if you had a wild boar on your tracks.

VOICE And *you* would trot off quietly too if you had a psychotic lecturer boring even your portrait into an hallucinosis.

ROLAND Who owns it now?

ROSEMARY The Gadarene swine I suppose.

MAN I protest. I think you are a bit hard on me. After all, *we* were invaded first.

BION I do not think this problem will ever be solved by a linear approach in a domain of time and space co-ordinates.

ROSEMARY Meaning what?

BION If you think the problems that we have to solve can be solved in a framework where 'things' happen in time and space, with ideas taken from the vocabulary and grammar invented for the senses, we shall fail. It is not unlike solving the problem of joining nine dots, arranged on a plane to form a cube, with four straight lines. You cannot do this *and* stay within the pattern of the cube. You cannot make a model of Desargues's theorem without entertaining the idea of more than three dimensions. You cannot resolve the apparent conflict of wave mechanics with the theories of quanta without supposing a domain suitable for harbouring the theory which has to be entertained. This theory has been formulated by Melanie Klein as operative in a psycho-analytic domain expanded to contain it. It is analogous to expanding the domain of arithmetic to contain irrational numbers, negative numbers, compound conjugate numbers. The domain which is adequate for the operation of natural numbers cannot contain these other numbers.

ROSEMARY I don't understand.

ALICE Give me an example.

BION Our problems here cannot be solved in terms of first and last and 'places' and 'examples' in time or space, the drawing of a line which has to be crossed.

CONAN DOYLE You mean by separating life and death. I said that years ago.

BION I sympathize with your efforts to draw attention to certain facts, but I do not believe your theories ever escaped from the limitations of sensuous experience and its terminology.

CONAN DOYLE You mean yours can?

BION Certainly not. But I am sure the attempt has to be made. The kind of experience which the statisticians can formulate succinctly by using the Poisson distribution cannot as yet be formulated experientially because life is too short and the spatial distances between the author of the Baghavad Gita and, say, John of the Cross, or Shakespeare or Tennyson or Newton, is too great and yet not extended enough. Set theory is not enough.

SHERLOCK That is a team in which I would not include Tennyson.

WATSON But surely, Holmes, you would include Shakespeare?

BION I am surprised, Holmes, that you include yourself even as selection committee or manager.

SHERLOCK The surprise is mutual; after all, *you* have included yourself. You have even put your name on this book.

BION It is someone's way of denoting a constant conjunction. I would find it difficult to name the mental world which is now a part of what *I* think is me. I fall back on an already existing convention. I try to be honest enough to acknowledge those to whom I am aware of being indebted.

MYSELF I understand your point about being indebted, but the O which you represent seems to be itself a part of O which is sensuously apprehended. It is a part of an O of morality which is itself part of a sensuous domain of 'ownership', sensuously perceived. There may be, and it would be impossible to believe that there is *not,* a domain which is infra- and ultra-sensuous. It is for this reason that I doubt the importance of 'significant' ownership and all the accompanying apparatus of debt and morality as we usually conceive it. This assumption throws one back into a mental domain which is a source of endless confusion and difficulty and in which unending confusion is an essential, not accidental, feature. I do not suppose I shall ever know escape, but I think the character of the 'sensuous' domain has not been exhausted.

BION I don't understand.

MYSELF Perhaps I can illustrate by an example from something you *do* know. Imagine a piece of sculpture which is easier to comprehend if the structure is intended to act as a trap for light. The meaning is revealed by the pattern formed by the light thus trapped—not by the structure, the carved work itself. I suggest that if I could learn how to talk to you in such a way that my words 'trapped' the meaning which they neither do nor could express, I *could* communicate to you in a way that is not at present possible.

BION Like the 'rests' in a musical composition?

MYSELF A musician would certainly not deny the importance of those parts of a composition in which no notes were sounding, but more has to be done than can be achieved in existent art and its well-established procedure of silences, pauses, blank spaces, rests. The 'art' of conversation, as carried on as part of the conversational intercourse of psycho-analysis, requires and demands an extension in the realm of non-conversation.

BION But is this anything new? Are we not all familiar with 'gaps' of this kind? Is it not usually an expression of hostility?

MYSELF As we have seen before, we are probably familiar with those activities for which the mere existence of a vocabulary is the evidence required. 'Evidence' itself is of a kind that falls within the range of sensuous experience with which we are familiar. Anyone understands the term 'sex' when it is related to sensuous experience. If, instead of saying 'sex', I were to talk of 'the love of God', I would be using the expression commonly heard in religious communities that have a distribution within particular temporal or topological co-ordinates. But suppose that my term, 'sex', refers to a domain which has no such sensuous co-ordinates and an O of which there are no elements, analogues, psychological or mental atoms; then O would be disqualified from 'thought', as I use the term.

BION What about dreams and dream thoughts?

MYSELF I have suggested a 'trick' by which one could manipulate things which have no meaning—the use of sounds like α and β. These are sounds analogous, as Kant said, to 'thoughts without concepts', but the principle, and a reality approximating to it, is also extensible to words in common use. The realizations which approximate to words such as 'memory' and 'desire' are opaque. The 'thing-in-itself', impregnated with the opacity, itself becomes opaque; the O, of which 'memory' or 'desire' is the verbal counterpart, is opaque. I suggest this quality of opacity inheres in many

O's and their verbal counterparts, and the phenomena which it is usually supposed to express. If, by experiment, we discovered the verbal forms, we could also discover the thoughts to which the observation applied specifically. Thus we achieve a situation in which these could be used deliberately to obscure specific thoughts.

BION Is there anything new in this? You must often have heard, as I have, people say they don't know what you are talking about and that you are being deliberately obscure.

MYSELF They are flattering me. I am suggesting an aim, an ambition, which, if I could achieve, would enable me to be deliberately and *precisely* obscure; in which I could use certain words which could activate precisely and instantaneously, in the mind of the listener, a thought or train of thought that came between him and the thoughts and ideas already accessible and available to him.

ROSEMARY Oh, my God!

FORTY

MYSELF It has not done so, but I could say your last sentence or ejaculation had obscured my train of thought. This, however, if it were true, would still not be adequate to achieve the function at which I am aiming. Some people can talk with such precision that the right audience could not fail to understand the communication. An obscure poet may, nevertheless, be expressing something in the shortest and most direct language known. Gerard Manley Hopkins is one example; Browning, in his poem 'Sordello', is, in Ezra Pounds's opinion, another. I suggest a possibility of stimulating, in the listener who listens as he listens, mental activities that intervene between him and thoughts, the obscuring capacity of which is specific, not general.

BION Why wouldn't a simple, straightforward rigmarole do?

MYSELF It is imprecise, inexact, like throwing a pot of pitch at a painting to which the spectator objects. It is a macroscopic, macroactive phenomenon like all sensuously based activities. I am searching for something in the domain of the very small. To use an analogy, not the domain of wave mechanics, nor the domain of quanta. That is as near as anything I am likely to find to express to you the problem as I see it.

BION You are approaching the position at which Newton came into conflict with Berkeley.

MYSELF I am flattered that you use such illustrious names. I disavow, however, the appearance of kinship with them. You refer to Berkeley's attack on the Analyst in Newton's formulation of the 'ghosts' of increments? I have always been impressed by the language in which Berkeley clothed his attack. It is the language Freud might have used to describe a theory of anal eroticism. It impresses me more still if I think of the statements of both men as signs of an emergent obtrusion which is contemporal, not sequential. The phenomena which I regard as conjoined and mental are more full of meaning if I conceive of them as contemporaneous.

BION You do not regard them as historically distributed?

MYSELF I do, but not exclusively. In fact, I would find it helpful to borrow from a schizophrenic patient a capacity for a transference relationship which was alternatively penetrating and planar; deep and confused, or superficial and of great 'spread', like a monomolecular film. At the same time these states, though apparently mutually exclusive, are reconciled and coexistent—like wave motion and quanta, objects in a pattern conforming to a Poisson distribution displayed on two planes—one temporal, one spatial—at right angles to each other. Seen from the temporal plane, the other 'transference' spreads monomolecular-wise: seen from the vertex of the spatial plane, the 'transference' is penetrating.

BION I don't think I understand. You mean that from an historical vertex events are distributed sequentially one after another in what we call time, but that it is possible to regard them, by ignoring the temporal vertex, as distributed in space, not time?

MYSELF Yes, but then two views are obtained, one which is very narrow and extremely penetrating, the other very broad and spread out without depth or penetration.

ALICE So what? Is this any different from what I and my girl friends have always known? Our boy friends are all the same—either for ever pawing us about though it's clear it doesn't mean a thing, or 'poking' us, having what they call sex, which doesn't mean a thing either.

BION Or both—and calling it schizophrenia.

MYSELF And *that* means nothing whether it is spread out over the whole of psychiatry or concentrated to apply to a particular, specific 'thing' or 'person'.

MAN You could say the same about 'psycho-analysis' or 'sex' or 'hate' or any other verbalization.

MYSELF Or 'feelings' or names of feelings. They don't mean a thing. Or, as Kant said, 'concepts without intuition are empty and intuitions without concepts are blind'.

BION I know the quotation to which you refer, of course, but—is *that* what he meant?

MYSELF I have no idea what he meant, but I am using *his* 'concepts' to match with *my* 'intuitions', because in this way I can bring together a concept and an intuition, making it possible to feel that *I* know what *I* mean. If I could also juxtapose you and myself, the two together would be meaningful.

ROSEMARY You certainly sound as if you get on very well. So well indeed that I almost wondered if you were not the same person.

BION & MYSELF (*together*) So do I.

FORTY-ONE

ALICE It sounds like a mutual admiration society.

MAN It does raise the suspicion that you come together for that purpose.

ROSEMARY How is this to be avoided?

MYSELF A long time ago, when Alice and Roland came together, they did it for the purpose of forming just such a society for mutual admiration. Later—

ALICE Later! It seemed more like a society for mutual hatred and recrimination.

MYSELF You have expressed it well. You and Rosemary seemed, though not officially conjoined, to come together—

MAN —in a somewhat ambiguous relationship.

MYSELF Terms like 'mistress' and 'maid', 'husband' and 'wife', are all 'sensuously' meaningful, and in the domain of sensuous relationships A + B can be meaningful in a macroscopic way. Even relationships which can be mathematically expressed, as the 'pure' mathematician says they are in pure mathematics, become sensuous.

BION Is that not saying that the mere fact of being able to

formulate the relationship A + B makes it a macroscopic relationship? But *does* it? Is it more true to say that we are so used to formulating statements only when they are macroscopic that we instantaneously assume that what *is* formulated must, by the fact of formulation, be macroscopic?

MYSELF The converse is thought to be true: that if we cannot formulate it, 'it' must be ultra- or infra-sensuous; that concepts that are 'empty' and intuitions that are 'blind' must lack completion, and that the 'completion' which is not 'complete', or is 'unfulfilled', nevertheless exists. ♀ has ♂, and ♂ has ♀. In short, ♀ # [apart from] ♂ cannot be stable. It is the function of a discipline, any discipline, to fill or complete; it is the 'job' of the link or synapse to join; it may be apart from a substitute used as a 'link', but no substitute can do what the link does. Addiction in place of 'marriage O' or 'divorce O' fails; sooner or later any substitute for the real thing is bound to fail through instability.

ROLAND I am not sure that I understand because if you mean that there is no substitute for the direct relationship such as seeing or hearing something for yourself, this is clearly fallacious; an astronomer was able to see and draw 'canals' on Mars by direct observation.

BION I used to be told to use my eyes; even today I advocate that people should use their common sense or intuition. Yet we understand now that the canals on Mars were a faulty interpretation of the observation made directly.

MYSELF I am glad that my job does not include advocacy.

BION You leave it to someone or something without advocating that someone else should do it.

MYSELF Is that not cowardly or irresponsible?

BION Maybe those are the correct terms for characterising behaviour, but I do not usually or generally think so. My capacity for naming my thoughts, or activities based on them, is less convincing—'action generating'—than it was. These 'thought generators', or in James Joyce's illuminating usage, 'idées mères', are either less frequent or less cogent. Perhaps there is some mental counterpart of the generative activities in the sensuous animal domain which suffers decline as animal capacity declines. What do you think?

MYSELF Just what I was going to ask you. Since you forestalled me I am tempted to say, 'begin again', but this vicoesque advice I temper with a warning against 'beginning at the beginning'.

BION The proper approach to confusion is, I think, to 'begin' in the middle. We have, in fact, no choice. Start at paranoid states of mind and continue cyclically. The confusion thus approached seems, like Schiaparelli's canals, to reveal a pattern in which persecution and depression are discerned, a journey 'from' patience 'to' security.

MYSELF What do you mean when you say we have no choice?

BION The world into which we are born is, for everyone of us, inhabited by individuals (our parents are the obvious example) who have a long history. We start in the middle of the story. Even as individuals directly concerned with our own story it is already far advanced. I am committed to going on with it from there.

MYSELF Obviously, but is there any point in knowing that?

BION It is generally supposed that if you are going from one place to another, or thinking from one premise to another—

MYSELF Are we?

BION I think so and since you ask me I would like to answer; I am committed to being that kind of man. I would like, therefore, to tell you where I come from and where I am going to. In this conversation I could use simple articulate English, but you and my other friends are not satisfied with simple questions and I cannot fall back on simple knowledge. In fact, your last question causes me to consider what you are wanting to know. I have to 'interpret' your question. Usually I don't think about it, but assume that I know what you mean. If you were a foreigner, or foreign to the subject, I could not make that assumption directly and with certainty. In trying to reply I would be starting, as I said, in the middle of a story without knowing the antecedents. I have to guess, fall back on conjectures. My reply is, therefore, based on 'guesses' about the facts and interpretation of my 'guesses'.

SHERLOCK How do you know all that?

BION I don't—that is why I say I have to fall back on interpretations of guesses.

MYSELF Yes, but how do you know you think like that?

BION I don't; even when I am concerned with my own thoughts

I am ignorant though I am the person whom I have a chance of knowing better than anyone. Freud started a train of thought which makes me suspect that, even if I know myself better than anyone I shall ever meet, the sum of that knowledge amounts to little.

MAN The outcome in psycho-analysts as I have observed them, is bigotry, dogmatism and certitude.

BION Those are only synapses—milestones marking 'articulations' not signifying 'that which' is articulated.

FORTY-TWO

ROSEMARY (*to Alice*) Isn't it awful? Did you ever have to put up with this kind of thing from Roland?

ALICE Never; only farming talk, thank God. I suppose this is psycho-analysis.

ROSEMARY Really? Perhaps that explains it. I certainly—

ALICE You don't have to worry about me—it quite intrigues me to think Roland never sank to such heights of boredom as this. Did you find him interesting?

ROSEMARY Not really; but I will say that at least he didn't bore me with this kind of stuff. It sounds very highbrow till you listen to it.

ALICE How does it sound to you now you do?

ROSEMARY Awful. I suppose I'm not used to such high-class talk—no education.

ALICE I had lots, and pretty awful it was too—but never as bad as this.

MYSELF This isn't psycho-analysis: it is talking *about* psycho-analysis—

ROSEMARY Oh, I would *love* that. Do show me what you would do if you were analysing me.

ALICE God forbid! Don't have anything to do with it!

ROSEMARY Why? It sounds most interesting.

MYSELF You would neither of you like it. You would soon, if your psycho-analyst knew his job, lose the kind of love for it that you are talking about! Of course, Alice might find she is quite right to have nothing to do with it. Some people find that it is far more than they can stand. How? Well, in the same way that you both found you couldn't stand hearing Bion and me talk.

ROSEMARY Were you two talking about psycho-analysis? We thought you were being very boring.

ALICE Anyway, why do you say we should be bored, since you also said that 'talking about' psycho-analysis is not the same thing as 'psycho-analysis'?

MYSELF It depends if you are concerned with their similarities or *dis*-similarities. Talking about a thing like psycho-analysis and experiencing it are two different activities.

BION You would have to be able to compare the experience of the 'practice' of psycho-analysis and the experience of 'talking about' it.

MYSELF I suggest to you two ladies that the difference is most easily appreciated by considering the many instances in which you can compare what you do when you are engaged on the prelude to doing something, and when you mean never to go beyond the prelude, but to continue in that state—as a substitute for transformation to action.

BION Many people have read Sophocles' play, 'Oedipus Rex'. Emotions can be experienced without knowing the underlying pattern to both the play and the feelings aroused; that is, the underlying 'group' is not recognized.

MYSELF What do you mean by 'group'?

BION I have borrowed the word from the mathematicians; in the experience which Rosemary and Alice have been having I can detect an emotional sequence which I could recognize as integrated. I would have to be able to construct a work of art of some kind in order to demonstrate the integrating force but I lack the artistic ability to do this. Although I cannot resort to any of the disciplines and theories and formulations known to me, in the practice of psycho-analysis I may be able to fall back on the analysand's capacity for cooperation to make good my deficiencies.

ROLAND What then? Does that cure the patient?

BION You are going too fast for me by proceeding from one question, 'what then?' to another question which belongs to the discipline of Therapeutics. Even the question 'what then?' is part of a theory of consequences and a framework including time and space; but I am not sure that I consider that 'configuration', or 'constant conjunction', appropriate to the events which are experienced in psycho-analysis. It is inadequate as the conceptual apparatus of which I feel in need when 'practising', not theorising. This concept itself relates to a constant conjunction of macroscopic elements and I have continued its use as if it were a term which is applicable when transferred to micro-elements. The 'relationship' of one micro-element to another might best be expressed intuitionally as $\alpha \# \Omega$.

MYSELF What is the difference that you seem to make between 'theorising' and what you call 'practising' psycho-analysis? It seems to me that practising psycho-analysis consists of theorising.

BION 'Theorising' is, I admit, a part of practising psycho-analysis.

MYSELF I think what you have just said sounds as if it makes something clear, but almost at once the illumination either turns out to be illusory and your explanation meaningless, or perhaps you have clarified a problem and the 'clarification' is at once replaced by a further series of 'unknowns'.

BION Both are possible. That is a difficulty about 'learning'. The moment of illumination is also the moment at which it becomes clear that there is a doubt about the 'clarification' itself and about the 'matter' which it is hoped to comprehend. I think this must be a familiar experience to Sherlock Holmes.

SHERLOCK I am not a philosopher and I don't think I can even guess what a psycho-analyst is, but since you appeal to me as if I were experienced I take it you are referring to something of which I have experience. I remember an occasion when I saw a client and I detected a strong smell of cigar about his clothes. It proved to be a valuable clue and later I wrote a monograph on ash which also turned out to be valuable, though in a way in which I had never expected.

BION It is true that when I mentioned you I was not referring to the precise experience that you mention, but in view of your high reputation as an investigator—

MYSELF —and as a helpful person, although fictitious—

BION —I guessed you could throw light on our precise problem as you have.

SHERLOCK I am delighted to hear it, but I must say I am surprised that you think the problem you have been discussing is precise.

BION I was speaking conversationally.

SHERLOCK Ah! In my kind of work you have to be precise.

MYSELF So you have in ours. Unfortunately we have to talk conversational English and that is not a language intended to be used for the purposes for which we have to use it.

SHERLOCK I, alas, have to use the language my author puts at *my* disposal.

MYSELF You—meaning both of you—don't do badly. My characters are not fictional and they are very dissatisfied with such means of communication as I put at their disposal.

SHERLOCK 'Means of communication'! Do you mean English? If not—

MYSELF No, I don't. If it is English, that is *not* enough. I am aware that conversational English is inadequate; but you should hear what they say about anything else.

BION Jargon, for example.

SHERLOCK HOLMES Why not paint or draw or compose music, or—

BION —play the violin. Did you ever try your violin playing on your clients or criminals or courts of law?

SHERLOCK I told you—I am limited by my author.

MYSELF So were the rest of you. Even Moriarty couldn't get rid of you at the Falls. But *we* can be got rid of by our characters at any time.

SHERLOCK Are not your characters limited by being 'patients'?

MYSELF No. They *seem* to be limited by being human, but if, as some of us think, they are personalities or minds, each one is unique and their 'limits' are not clearly marked. I do not even know *what* the limits of my personality and mind are or even if there is such a thing as 'my personality' which approximates to the words I have just used.

SHERLOCK You should shove them into jail as we do. You'd be surprised how quickly that clarifies the problem.

MYSELF That's all very well for 'fictitious' jails and courts of law and fictitious minds.

ROSEMARY It sounds to me as if these minds and personalities that you talk about very often are 'fictitious'.

BION Even a 'beautiful woman' is a shade of a shade of a shade.

ROSEMARY If I gave you a kiss you'd soon change your tune.

BION Why do you think I regard you as beautiful?

MYSELF How ungallant you are! It is part of the price we psycho-analysts all pay. The habit of mind overflows into non-analytic situations.

BION You could say that if being a psycho-analyst was wearing a mental suit of clothes, one could choose whatever fictitious character one liked to be and dress up in the appropriate uniform. The trouble is if one has to *be* a psycho-analyst and not simply learn the part for purposes of acting.

ROSEMARY I don't play-act; that is why I don't give you a kiss.

BION Some kisses have become famous. One kiss is called a 'Judas kiss', after a character who became famous and notorious. Kisses, like other actions, speak louder than words.

MYSELF Interpretation likewise depends on quality as well as quantity, as do the things interpreted. 'Loudness', expressing 'quantity', is not enough even in the domain of physical senses and other phenomena; all to which the term 'phenomena' applies are by definition part of the domain of senses. We, in common with many who purport to exist or are reported to have existed and still to exist, believe there is something 'more' which can be called 'ultra-' or 'infra-' sensuous. It is this something more, or 'something +', which we suppose to be significant for refinement by psycho-analysis in practice.

WATSON You spoke earlier of computers assessing radiograms

with greater accuracy than even gifted radiographers. What you have just said sounds as if you are now advocating scrutiny by live beings in preference to machines—am I right?

MYSELF Not quite. I don't mean to be advocating anything. I suggest that somehow functions can be handed over to machines or mechanical methods. We ourselves learnt to walk 'mechanically' at some point and this was, and still is, a very useful skill; but even now it is useful to resort from time to time to specific, skilled movement. I do not exclude the value of 'mechanical thinking' or 'mechanical interpretation', but I don't want *that* progress to take the place of, or to preclude the development of, the ultra- or infra-sensuous, even though I may not know what that is or even if it exists. The pathology laboratory should not be substituted for clinical observation, or vice versa.

WATSON Quite right.

SHERLOCK I found clinical analysis quite useful.

BION You had to 'interpret' your ashes—

SHERLOCK —in the light of my findings.

MYSELF And with the aid of the book in which you recorded the findings. The book is an example of what I call an 'instrument'. Strictly speaking, so are the 'theories' recorded in it. Even if they were not recorded in any 'instrument' I would regard them as an instrument to be 'used'—not enshrined as a dogma or religion.

BION Yet, I was thinking how like religion some of your statements about 'infra- and ultra-' sensuous sounded.

MYSELF I know what you mean. The adherents of religion are more likely to grasp what I put forward as 'hunches'. If you remember, at the end of his *Opticks*, Newton suggested that the 'religious beliefs' could be scientifically approached. Years before, Milton spoke of 'Holy light'; hailed it.

BION You should hear what we said when a star-shell lit up our tanks at night!

MYSELF Some people must have thought it was 'honest and helpful'.

ALICE All depends on the 'vertex', as you would say.

BION That's not what we called it then. The term 'vertex' is dependent for its meaning on the vertex of which it is a radiant.

FORTY-THREE

MAN Rosemary, will you come and have a coffee?

ROSEMARY Have you still got that bar of chocolate?

MAN In my holster you mean?

ROSEMARY The very same.

ROLAND Love or hate? Seduction or passionate love? I wish I knew.

ROSEMARY So do I.

ALICE Feminine intuition will find out the way.

ROSEMARY So they say; but I don't believe it.

BION Nor does masculine intuition.

MYSELF Nor does mathematical intuition. What is the equation? Man + Rosemary? Or man # Rosemary?

ROSEMARY I shall tell you after we've had coffee.

ALICE Come on, Roland—after so many years of married life, what is the equation?

ROLAND Alice + Roland.

ALICE Still? You surprise me.

ROSEMARY So you do me.

ALICE So do you me; before even one coffee.

MYSELF Before one coffee is sometimes easier than after many.

ALICE I thought you psycho-analysts advocated years and years of analysis.

BION That is only for psycho-analysis, and even so it is not true. We advocate and practise the shortest and easiest methods compatible with honest work.

ROSEMARY It sounds like an advertisement for something.

BION I have to make it known that I am available if wanted.

ALICE I can't see what she sees in him.

ROLAND Nor can I.

ALICE *You* seemed to have seen something in *her*.

ROLAND So did you.

ALICE Perhaps we both saw something in her and she in both of us.

ROLAND Perhaps; but I doubt it.

ALICE Nevertheless, there must have been something both ways.

ROLAND Something neither of us saw?—but which may nevertheless exist? What does the sage say?

ALICE Who is he?

ROLAND I meant the psycho-analyst, Bion.

ALICE Oh, him! Not what I would call a sage. Well, I suppose there's no harm in trying. They never see anything except sex. Still, they do meet lots of people.

BION Sex is a name, but none of us 'sees' sex, though it is a word we often use and it is useful if we want to talk about sex. Language was generated for the purpose of talking about senses and I think you would like me to be able to escape your scorn by speaking a language using words to which the thing-itself approximated to the words and theories we employ. After all, even you both suggest there is something those two 'see in each other'—'they' being thinking personalities. In that literal way I am sure none of us 'sees' anything in the relationship we are talking about. But I think we are convinced there is 'something'; so much so that in physics at least the physicists have invented an electron microscope.

MYSELF And have detected 'an uncertainty principle'! Imagine the fun that would be made if Bion or I were to announce the discovery of an 'uncertainty principle'.

BION Keats discovered an 'uncertainty principle' which he called 'Negative Capability'. The authors of Job, of the Baghavad Gita, to go no further, discovered the presumption of Job, of Arjuna, who thought that what they 'didn't know wasn't knowledge'. Even Mister Toad comes into that same domain of scorn and contempt which, like 'mental or spiritual' pollution, is life 'that stains the white radiance of eternity'.

SHERLOCK It seems to me that these 'fictitious characters' have a lot more sense than you real ones.

BION And non-sense. Toad was not, is not, synonymous with 'sense'.

SHERLOCK If he were it would not be necessary for his creator to create him.

ALICE Why is it necessary?

MYSELF Their creation has been an activity with a very long history.

ALICE That is not answering my question.

ROLAND Indeed, it seems to stimulate the question more than the answer. Why has the creation of fictions been so well-established an industry?

MYSELF For purposes of deception and disguise—

BION —as well as illustration and imparting information.

MYSELF Sometimes correct information, sometimes false; it depends on whether the creator is feeling hostile or friendly. But in fact I do not believe it 'depends' on that because 'dependence' appears to me to relate to priority. Which comes first, the feeling or the fictitious idea?

BION Kant says the senses never err because they do not judge at all. That is what I call a 'definitory hypothesis', and according to me a 'definitory hypothesis' does not err either.

MYSELF But we do expect the definition or the 'definitory hypothesis' to be maintained 'constant' or 'invariant' throughout the same universe of discussion.

BION *Who* expects it to remain constant? If a man or woman says he or she loves the other—

MYSELF That is not a situation I had in mind just then

because I was talking, and in the interests of clear 'thought' I think it makes it easier for the participants to establish and maintain certain 'rules of thinking'; that includes the 'logic' of 'articulate communication'.

BION That depends if you are referring to those communities who employ *articulate* language. But, as you know, not all communities do. The Chinese, I believe, do not employ that kind of language for communication. In fact, this problem is not peculiar to communities in the gross, macroscopic sense. Take the individual for example: Melanie Klein, thinking in terms of visual imagery, regarded a single human individual as if he were a world in himself. Roger Money Kyrle, following this lead, has elaborated in his account of man's picture of his world.

MYSELF If one takes the extremely detailed view which is available under the Kleinian vertex in the practice of psycho-analysis, the model would not be 'macroscopy', but 'microscopy'. I doubt that micro-analysis is aided by or reveals an articulate language at all. 'Articulate' communication is the dominant method of communication between the self and the self; in so far as communication takes place between what psycho-analysts call the 'unconscious' levels of different individuals, I think the prevalent methods of communication between painters, poets, musicians conform to rules which are very different from those of 'articulate' communication.

ALICE I am sure they don't conform. Nor do the rules of 'morality' as they are usually supposed to exist.

ROLAND Certainly each sex is accused by the other of breaking the moral rules—

MYSELF When someone *says* 'I love', the rules of articulate speech apply to 'speech', not to 'loving'. The most experienced methods of *physical* communication are not articulate, even if vocal. It is illuminating to suppose that the method of communication proper to the vertex 'sex' is not verbal, but what is often called 'acting out' under vertices in which verbal communication is usual.

BION I am, of course, familiar with the expression, 'acting out', as used by English psycho-analysts, but I should be interested to know how you understand the term.

MYSELF I was using the English term which is not the same as the term used by Freud. In intention the thing itself, that is, the reality which approximates to both the English and German formulation, is supposed to be identical.

BION You say 'supposed'. Are you implying a doubt?

MYSELF I certainly am. I would say that 'doubt' is the most nearly adequate word to use to define the vertex: it is the proper vertex under which we operate in this conversation itself.

BION Can you expand your use of the word 'sex'?

MYSELF As far as the word 'sex' is concerned I do not think I can say more about that than Freud said. To me it is one of those terms which are 'meaningless' since any 'meaning', as that word is ordinarily used, is an elaboration of phrases which are to be constantly conjoined in progressively more elaborate constructions. It is one of those words which express what James Joyce called 'idée mère'; it is analogous to the mathematical construction, 'a number generator'. You can see for yourself that these three phrases, 'sex', 'idée mère' and 'number generator', are themselves suspiciously like a 'tautology'. That is why I would prefer some directly meaningless sign like 'O'. Borrowing from religious discipline I find the word 'Godhead' useful as less abstract than 'Ultimate reality'.

BION Abstract?

MYSELF I thought you would check at that. I propose to avail myself of a meaningful and proportionately inaccurate expression which I hope is nevetheless helpful. The grin was all that was left when the 'Cheshire Cat' had disappeared.

SHERLOCK Another 'fictitious character'.

MYSELF Part of an entire construction which was fictitious. The kind of thing for which Plato held artists and poets to blame though he did not scorn the aid of his own artistic creation—of the cave, for one example.

BION You were about to say something of the abstract.

MYSELF The 'grin' to which I referred, the 'fictitious character', the 'fiction', is the 'reversed perspective' of the 'abstract'. The one is not the opposite of the other.

ROSEMARY Why not?

MYSELF It would be a misleading definition. Since I have to

choose an already existing 'term', I choose the term 'intuition' as related to the term 'abstract'.

BION Can you define the relation?

MYSELF Again, I borrow from the meta-mathematicians. I borrow the sign #.

BION You have related the abstraction to the intuition.

MYSELF That is true of this conversation; under the vertex of conversational English they are related. Under the vertex of psycho-analytic discussion they are related by free association.

BION To what extent, if any, do you consider this 'free association' represents a realization, or that a realization exists approximating to the 'free association'?

MYSELF I know of no realization approximating to the construct 'intuition'.

BION You speak as if 'construct' were interchangeable with 'term'. Is that right?

MYSELF Under the vertex of this discussion, 'yes'. 'No', under the vertex of 'realization'; still less under O. Any construction relating 'intuition' to 'constant conjunction' is true only under the vertex of this discussion, not under the vertex of realization.

ALICE Why not describe the constant conjunction as synonymous with integration?

MYSELF I think of 'integration' as representing something compatible with what is represented by 'constant conjunction'. I think it plausible to regard the activity of constantly conjoining as compatible with the realization represented by the 'integration'. In this respect the term under the vertex of this conversation could be included in the set which included the member of the set of realizations.

ALICE Then why not use the opposite of integration—disintegration?

MYSELF Emphatically not; intuition, as I use the term, does not represent a realization which is the 'opposite' or the 'negative' of 'constant conjunction', 'integration' and similar terms. In so far as it becomes or appears to become a 'constant conjunction', it has undergone, if related at all, a complete transformation. All the intuitions are # all other intuitions. # is essential, not accidental.

ALICE Your intuition seems to be like what is left when the thought has disappeared.

ROLAND Or like the thought when the concept has gone.

BION 'Blind', as Kant would say about thoughts without concept; or concepts without an intuition—'empty'. But I don't think it is what Myself means.

MYSELF You are right. By 'intuition' I mean none of those things. It is like nothing. It is not the 'negative of' or 'opposite of' or 'reversed perspective of'. Those terms are 'borrowed' from conversational English, as are others which are borrowed from classical psycho-analysis. This 'borrowing' is legitimate but does not imply that the meaning, in the context of 'classical' thought, has not been altered as used by me.

ALICE Does it matter?

MYSELF Unfortunately, yes. Already phrases employed by Freud with great precision are almost incomprehensible because the words from which his constructions were built up have now been irreparably changed. Who could now be sure what 'inferiority complex' means? Or 'paranoid'? Who could meet with them in a book by Freud or a psychiatrist and be sure that his familiarity with present day usage does not disqualify him from understanding the formalizations of the authors?

ALICE I very much doubt that what Mozart heard when he played, or heard someone else play, a clavichord would seem to him to be the same sounds that come from a modern concert grand piano played by a present-day master.

MYSELF I should expect him to feel that the 'tune' was familiar.

ALICE I hear quotation marks when you are talking and I think I know the difference in meaning between that and the same verbalization if I don't hear the quotation marks. I am reminded of the printed page, of reading 'one, two, then 'tis time to do it'.

MYSELF You are referring to what I called defective apparatus of lateral communication.

BION Only this is a defect of communication through time as well as space.

MYSELF The genius overcame the problems which might have been effective in obstructing communication.

BION His very success in surmounting his difficulties may indeed have contributed to our difficulties in reception.

MYSELF A solution of the difficulty of communication may, I suggest, be mistaken for *the* solution of a difficulty in the matter of communication (? ? ? . . .) But I hear question marks—

ALL You have not misheard—yet no one said anything.

BION I shall venture on the role of amplifier. How could the discovery of the Andromeda M31 nebula, or the Crab nebula—sonic reproduction—exemplify your point?

MYSELF Your question suggests to me that you know something that enables you to ask. Our solution of the problem can appear to have determined the spacial separation between us and those two galaxies. That separation may not in fact pertain to the relation between those 'spaces', but be a solution of that which does belong to the space between our comprehension and our incomprehension.

ROLAND I don't understand.

MYSELF So, you may find something you do understand as a substitute for what you don't. I once asked for an archaeological book. They didn't have it, but the assistant offered another book, unrelated to archaeology, as if that would do. Suppose I am unable to understand how the disintegration of the nova could be taking place at the same time and space occupied by my 'integration'; I might be glad to exchange the 'distance' between my comprehension and incomprehension for a 'distance' between me and the M31 nebula and the 'solution' of *that* distance. 'Sound' and 'sight' could be linked with 'creative' effect.

ALICE Surely that is very fanciful?

MYSELF Do you mean the distance between my 'fancy' and the fact is vast—'very', or 'truly', vast? That idea may be a comforting substitute for thinking, incomprehension and comprehension. It may also be more pleasant to feel that the unpleasant experience is immediately possible and adjacent.

ALICE It could be as you say, but I cannot even be sure that I have a preference for one or other.

MYSELF True. We all would prefer the agreeable emotional experience if we knew which that was and how to ensure choosing the correct steps to achieve such an aim. The unpleasant state seems to be to feel compelled to be responsible without the comfort of imagining we have made the correct choice.

ALICE I think you are being somewhat obvious—'platitudinous'.

MYSELF It is difficult to be devoted to commonsense without being judged as either platitudinous or fanciful, or both at once. Even highly sophisticated groups find there are divisions as between corpuscular theories, quanta theories, and theories of a continuum subject to wave emotions.

ALICE Why not both?

MYSELF Or fanciful and platitudinous? I don't know.

BION You don't know? You amaze us. I thought everyone knew that!

MYSELF You are being facetious. I expect you to display a specific animal characteristic as I expect you to behave continuously. I have spoken of Leonardo's preoccupation with drawing hair and water; I have no idea, and cannot conjecture without 'wasting time' on conjectures, what his preoccupations were. I can spend time and have some idea that it is, or is not, worth spending time looking at his drawings. I can allow his product to stimulate *my* preoccupations about an aqueous continuum and movement within it. I can allow his drawing to remind me of my thoughts and feelings. I wonder; are the ideas expressed on this page like the incoherent mass of H_2O molecules, or do they rather resemble the fleeting confusion of a bucket of water or head of hair? To which does reality approximate—the creation of the hairdresser? The drawing of Leonardo? The ideas arrested as in the verbal formulations of Homer's Iliad and Odyssey? The molecular physicist's formula? Or the group, if there was one, which together 'constructed' a pattern of words which were then constantly conjoined, like Leonardo's pencil marks, and arrested so that they could be labelled 'Homer' and held, through time, in a pattern or verbal sound? Further, I wonder what I do while attempting to draw an analysand's attention to a pattern—to which *my* attention has been drawn by his contributions to a session—by the fleeting activity of interpretations? Sometimes the duration of the interpretation which is very short is experienced by the receptor as enduring; sometimes the relation between the 'duration' of the interpretation and the 'duration' of the received experience is commensurate, at others not. Sometimes I would describe the two as 'separate and distinct', at others 'conjugate and complex'.

ALICE I don't understand those terms.

MYSELF I think it correct to describe the relation between what I said and you heard as 'conjugate and complex'.

ALICE Then why don't you say, as I did, that I did not understand you?

MYSELF Because, under this vertex, that would be an inaccurate description.

ALICE I assure you it is true all the same.

MYSELF I likewise can assure you that what I said was 'true all the same'—under *my* vertex.

ALICE Would an impartial judge think so?

MYSELF A judge could judge impartially if the vertices were understood and used with comprehension; from my experience that is unlikely.

FORTY-FOUR

ALICE So we are back to square one?

MYSELF I fear so—the concern ultimately is 'people'. This is why some of us think personality must be an object for scientific study. Most people are familiar with acts which employ articulated musculature, and find it easy to use articulated language. Perhaps it is easier to use that kind of language and that kind of musculature. Smooth muscle in action is usually easier to match with inarticulate speech. 'I love' and its vocabulary and grammar is usually easier to match with the 'activity' itself when the rules of articulation are relaxed. The action, associated with love, is easier when 'the laws of articulation' are similarly relaxed. The most adequate forms of loving communion appear to be proportionate to the relaxation of conformity to articulation in thought, word and deed. I speak of love, but it is equally true of all feelings whether expressed in physical or psychical domains.

BION I can see that the idea of the individual being a 'group'—like Hobbes' idea of the group being an individual—could be an illuminating one. I don't quarrel with it or even with the idea of the definitory hypothesis as you have defined it. What I am not convinced about is that there are others besides you and me who would agree, or who would be similiarly complacent or tolerant or qualified to agree or disagree.

MYSELF This doubt about the acceptability of an approach which depends on thought or discussion is as valid today as it has been at any time in its past history. Nevertheless, neither you nor I have suggested an alternative to the present choice between inadequate procedures.

BION That is *not* my point. I doubt that any problem remains that is not affected in a way analogous to that which Heisenberg detects in the domain of physical investigation: the thing itself is altered by being observed. I suggest that this change cannot be assumed to be without an analogue in the mental domain. An 'analogue' may be applicable to the physical world, but not available as a mode of thought.

MYSELF You and I are now employed in talking 'as if' it were serviceable. In fact, as if 'as if' were itself serviceable.

BION There is nothing else, known to you or me—

MYSELF —or to painters, or musicians, or poets, or all of these together.

BOTH So far.

A *Hullo! Here we are again. How did you find it?*

Q *I haven't read it, of course. I was just looking to see how it ended. I'm no wiser than I was at the first.*

A *I was afraid you might have to read the bit* α *and* Ω.

Q *What?! Start it all again?*

A *You've changed—'five minutes older' if the time scale notation I have borrowed means anything. No worse off financially though?*

Q *Not yet, but as a matter of curiosity, did it cost you much to have it published?*

A *It did indeed. Years of education at a public school, years in an army at war, years at Oxford University, years being psycho-analysed, years of medical training and a year at the University of Poitiers. The last three sentences were served concurrently.*

Q *(yawning politely) It sounds most interesting. Was it?*

BOOK TWO

THE PAST PRESENTED

ONE

ROLAND What's the date?

ALICE No idea; does it matter?

ROLAND Of course it matters! Wake up!

ALICE Oh, sorry sir. Tuesday, nineteen seventy . . .

ROLAND You aren't awake. It is Tuesday though. I have to be up because I must go to Munden.

ALICE Yes. Yes—I must have been dreaming. What's the—

ROSEMARY Yes, Ma'am? You told me to call you.

ALICE Yes, of course. Breakfast at half past seven. My God! I've got a headache.

ROLAND You're dreaming.

ALICE My headache is no dream I can tell you. You're off are you? See you at lunch. Rosemary, I've had an awful dream.

ROSEMARY Yes, Ma'am? Is that all, Ma'am?

ALICE Yes, of course. Hurry or you'll miss . . . I can't be properly awake. And I have to go to Braughing for lunch. I hope Roland remembers it's our wedding anniversary. He doesn't know what a relief it was to find he was in love with me. What an escape from

Worry-Funny! I realize now how right his nickname was. He was dotty, but I didn't know it then. 'Temps de Lilas' he used to murmur as if he had softening of the brain. It was a scent I used. I thought, 'How romantic—he's in love with *me*.' God, it makes me mad to think of it! Men always think women *must* be in love with them. I wore the scent because I liked *it*—not springtime or lilacs. Come to think of it, I was a bit mad to suppose he was in love with *me*. But I was very pretty—once. It's difficult to believe as I make up my face in the looking-glass—the 'cruel looking-glass' which tells a maid that she isn't what she was. I wonder if Roland believes this stuff he tells me. He'd be hurt if he thought I didn't take it seriously. But if I look in the mirror he holds up to me when he is eyeing Rosemary—*then* I can see that I'm not 'as pretty as I was'. He thinks I am vain enough to believe his adoration is genuine. The more we are together, to-gether, two-gether . . . It's rather like a record which has started to run down. The 'Bread and Pheasant' song, as some schoolboy thought it was, is less romantic than the 'Breton Peasant', but . . . 'Temps de Lilas', 'Spring', 'Love'—I suppose they all come to spell 'Bread' and, if we are lucky, a little bit of 'Butter' too. If I don't flatten out these wrinkles I shall have to beg my bread. Roland doesn't do badly having a pretty wife. Am I being conceited? No, I'm not. I may even look 'handsome'. And loyal? Roland is good-looking. And faithful? We look quite a presentable pair . . . a bit wasted on Braughing. Who would have heard of England if the Royal Navy had not won the war?—so they say. If Beatty had seen that dashing slant of his cap—'CAP wins the battle of Jutland!' What a headline *that* would make! Take my cap to England, Hang it by the shore, Beat it when Temp de Lilas's running low. Here's Roland. Nearly 7.30. (*To Roland*) Tonight we have our—

ROLAND I have a lot to get through first. Do you know who is coming?

ALICE The same as usual, I suppose; no one has said they aren't. The padre said he might be late and Edmund may join us later too. I've told Rosemary refreshments for eight.

ROLAND Quite a party—they usually all come. What a success this has been, though I certainly had doubts about a Platonic venture in England—let alone our part of Hertfordshire. Rosemary seems to cope very well with the snacks.

ALICE Yes; though the way things are going in this country I sometimes wonder how long it is going to be possible.

ROLAND Philosophers ought to take austere conditions philosophically. We shall have to make a demonstration of *being,* not theorizing. Who else is going to be late?

ALICE The doctor probably. Is Robin coming?

ROLAND Here comes Tom.

TOM How are you? Did I hear Robin isn't coming?

ROLAND Alice wondered how a farmer could find time to talk.

TOM I think his absence is more possible. One should think of him as one of the class Trotter said continually face issues of life and death; miners, sailors and doctors. Few people are forced—

P(SYCHO) A(NALYST) Excuse me—how are you?

ALICE Take our compliments as read.

TOM Trotter should not have forgotten farmers. He wouldn't, had he lived in a world where many starve and many more will be starving tomorrow.

ROLAND The world of the conspicuous consumer—the C.C's for short.

P.A. Or the 'See See's who value the giddy pleasure of the eye.

TOM Certainly the eye can hold more than the belly can. That queer old bird, the pellycan, can be greedy without digesting anything. It is appropriate now that the BB See! has introduced commercial television.

P.A. And that BB should be blamed for it. It was opposed to it, but opposition may be responsible for an equal and opposite reaction.

ROLAND How does greed come into it?

TOM The BB is a great, big see/I/eye demanding that the rest of the body should, Livy-like, contribute to sloth and luxury.

P.A. All very well as a parable, but—here's the Doc. Doctor, do you think Livy's parable of the belly is anatomically fair?

DOCTOR Of course not. Are parables supposed to be fair? They are simple narratives on the way to a verbal formulation.

ALICE Too deep for me to C. Expound please!

TOM He means it is a mental aid to insight; as a circle or a line or a triangle aids Euclid, or Thales before him.

DOCTOR These corporeal aids become limitations; the asset becomes a liability. The anatomical and physiological structure is an asset to the baby who grows to be mobile.

P.A. Becomes 'auto-mobile' in short.

TOM But Euclidean geometry, aided by space, geo-metric space, grows so powerfully that in a couple of thousand years it becomes irked by its visual frame. At this point the demands of the mind are imprisoned in the corporeal structure.

DOCTOR Enter the fairy prince to release the sleeping beauty.

P.A. Namely? I think you should introduce the characters as they come on the stage.

TOM Cartesian Co-ordinates.

ALICE What a pretty name.

ROSEMARY Mr Robin, Ma'am.

ALICE Hello, Robin. We were just thinking of Cartesian Co-ordinates.

ROBIN Good heavens! I hope you aren't suggesting that I should use those. I would have my farm overrun with co-ordinates—they would grow much faster than the seeds of thought would germinate in my mind.

ALICE Here's the padre. 'Thou art the man.' Our scientific pagan needs baptism. Let me introduce our latest brain child—Cartesian Co-ordinates—as yet without a literary or religious naming.

TOM They are triplets in fact: the first-born is real and distinct; the second, real and co-incident; and the third, conjugate complex.

ROLAND As initials I would say R.D. for the first.

P.A. R.C. and C.C. for the next two.

PAUL The parents usually tell me what are their wishes. I only commend them to God.

ROLAND Guessing at their dispositions I would expect the first to be a bit obstinate. 'I am *not* you', I can almost hear him say as he looks angrily at himself in the mirror.

P.A. 'I got here first; this is my place', I hear the second say.

ROLAND And complex conjugate is an intellectual snob, as

Man, our aspiring politician, would be sure to say. You can rely on our intellectuals to be wrong—always.

ALICE I think you are being very hard on our brain children. This is a religious christening at which the wicked fairy is being allowed to have the last wish. What characters!

TOM Well, the line cuts the circle in a liberated and highly franchised manner. Uncle Riemann will be delighted.

P.A. And godfather Lobachevsky likewise.

ROLAND And Uncle Tom Cobley too true.

TOM But seriously, cartesian co-ordinates set geometry free. We were no longer imprisoned—restricted to what we could see.

ALICE Wordsworth talked about the inner eye which was freed by the sight of the daffodils dancing in the breeze. He little knew 'what wealth to me' the sight had brought.

ROBIN Or as some wit put it, the chance of another slim volume at three and sixpence.

P.A. He would not become wealthy with three shillings and sixpence today. Eric Gill prayed that England might become poor.

ROBIN He must be a happy man today. Perhaps we are not allowed to be happy in the 'blessed Kingdoms of joy and love'.

P.A. 'So much the rather thou, Celestial light, the mind and all her powers irradiate. There plant eyes; all mist from thence purge and disperse'—

PAUL —'that I may see and tell of things invisible to mortal sight'.

ROBIN 'The Heavens declare the Glory of God.' When I was in the RAF I used to think of the verse, 'I will take the wings of the morning and fly to the uttermost parts of the Earth'. Paul knows it, I'm sure.

PAUL Of course—we all do.

TOM I fear I never thought of anything so poetical. I was too filled with petrol fumes.

ROBIN Those were the best years of my life. Although I was scared out of my wits then, afraid of death. Afterwards I felt ashamed that I had not been brave enough, like one young boy I knew, to defy the enemy who called to him to surrender as he crawled out of his disabled tank.

P.A. What happened?

ROBIN What happened? Why, what could happen? They—

TOM —shot him, of course.

ROBIN Of course; as you say, 'Of course'.

ALICE Here's Rosemary with some tea. It will give us a chance of cooling off before we generate more heat than light. You were in the war, Rosemary?

ROSEMARY Yes, Ma'am. In the WAACS. Will that be all, please?

ALICE Yes, thank you.

ROLAND We can continue while we sip our tea.

PAUL You have forgotten that the wings of the morning were to aid flight, ineffectually, from God.

P.A. Perhaps the depths of hell.

ROBIN As Paul said, I had forgotten 'the wings of the morning'—a poetical way of escape. I think I must have succeeded—not so effectually as P.A. perhaps, but enough not to go to Church.

P.A. Why do you assume I succeeded?

ROBIN Haven't you? I thought people who were properly analysed, like psycho-analysts, didn't believe in a lot of rubbish like 'God's in his heaven, All's right with the world'.

ALICE Really, Robin—why don't you read your Browning properly?

ROBIN Why? What have I done wrong now?

ROLAND Pretty well everything I should say—you hadn't read the Bible properly.

TOM You have forgotten your flying regulations.

P.A. I spend a great deal of my time trying to show people which particular god they are currently worshipping. Whether they are right or wrong is for the individual to decide for himself. Robin's god seems, from what he says, to be a solar god, but that would depend on the evidence to which I would try to draw his attention as it became discernible.

ROLAND To him, or to you?

P.A. Both, I should hope. I give my interpretation when I think he and I could both understand it, in the language which I think both could comprehend, and while the evidence is 'visible' to two ordinary beings. Just now—

ROLAND Can you give an example?

P.A. —Tom seemed to think that *he* would smell gas, Robin some visual or religious experience.

ROBIN I certainly said nothing about religion; I gave it up long ago.

P.A. Either you have little respect for what you say, or you say words for which you have no respect. You said, 'The Heavens declare the Glory of God'—

PAUL —'and the firmament showeth his handiwork', is the text.

ROBIN Good heavens! Can't one talk simple literate English?

P.A. You should hear my psycho-analyst aspirants talking 'simple literate' English.

PAUL But you surprise me. Do you really think anyone expects psycho-analysts to talk 'simple English? I thought it was understood that it was a point of honour to talk incomprehensible jargon.

P.A. It is a point of honour when we are playing the game of Who's Top of the Psycho-analytical League Tables, but that is when we are 'talking about' psycho-analysis.

ROLAND You have international league championship matches too. I've read some of the accounts in your journals. The language is ferociously incomprehensible.

TOM A punch in the eye is ferociously simple and discernible—at least to the onlookers.

DOCTOR That sudden pressure on the ocular nerve is notorious for eliciting a non-specific response.

ALICE Sorry—I'm lost. Can you elicit a response from me that I myself could understand?

DOCTOR If a boxer receives a punch in the eye, he is said to 'see stars'. That response to the stimulus is not specific to the ocular nerve which is supposed to respond to light and shade.

P.A. I hope Alice 'sees'. But when I give interpretations—which I formulate in the simplest verbal terms known to me—I am as likely as not to find that my statement is hailed as being 'psycho-analytic jargon', or possibly also 'filthy sexual talk'.

DOCTOR I saw a boy once who had been so well brought up that he could only tell me he had a 'body ache'. I nearly asked him whereabouts in his 'body' this ache was, but realized, just in time to spare his blushes, that he could *not* say he had a 'belly ache'.

P.A. Did he 'blush'? Because I have known a patient who could feel he was blushing while I could detect no visible evidence of capillary dilatation.

ALICE Are you using the simplest terminology available?

P.A. Yes; if I said 'blush', it would create a wrong impression.

ROBIN Milton avoided saying 'blind Homer', not because he wanted to say 'Maeonides' to show his erudition, but because Homer meant 'blind' and it was infelicitous to say 'blind Homer'.

P.A. Psycho-analysts can 'in truth' claim, like physicians, to be engaged in a respect-worthy occupation deserving the use of a language which can be employed by people who respect the truth, without having to be ashamed of technical precision on the one hand, and 'primitive' precision on the other. Terms which are no longer permitted in socially oriented cultures—

ALICE Such as?

P.A. Shit. If you can indicate the cultural boundary I can guess whether the term would arouse anger. Show me the drawing and the onlookers before whom it is to be exhibited, and I can guess at the outcome. When Freud said infants had a sexual life people were outraged. Today James Joyce is regarded as permissible. An assertion of a religious manifestation will arouse the hostility and suspicion of psycho-analysts who would deny that they were displaying bigotry.

ALICE Really? You surprise me.

P.A. We are all scandalized by bigotry. We are none of us bigot-generators; that is, we none of us admit to being the spring from whom bigotry flows. As a result we do not recognize those of our offspring of whose characters we disapprove. Indeed, Melanie Klein discovered that primitive, infantile omnipotence was characterized by fantasies of splitting off undesired features and then evacuating them.

ROLAND I am sure you don't mean that children *think* like that?

P.A. It would be inaccurate and misleading to say so. That is why Melanie Klein called them 'omnipotent phantasies'. But although I found her verbalization illuminating, with the passage of time and further investigation which her discoveries made possible, her formulations were debased and became inadequate. These primitive elements of thought are difficult to represent by any verbal formulation, because we have to rely on language which was elaborated later for other purposes. When I tried to employ meaningless terms—alpha and beta were typical—I found that 'concepts without intuition which are empty and intuitions without concepts which are blind' rapidly became 'black holes into which turbulence had seeped and empty concepts flooded with riotous meaning'.

ROBIN Really—do you blame us if we don't know what you are talking about?

P.A. No, I don't. I am not surprised at your protest; in extenuation I have found that if I say what I mean it is not English; if I write English it does not say what I mean.

PAUL Theologians are blamed for being incapable of being religious—you are as bad as we are!

P.A. Probably for the same reason. Ultimate Truth is ineffable.

ALICE I think you are hard on him. I don't pretend to understand, but I do have an idea.

P.A. After all, ultimate reality must be a whole even if the human animal cannot grasp it. If I kick open an ants' nest it would no doubt appear to an ant to be an act of God, but it is capable of a simple explanation.

PAUL So you think.

P.A. Quite; I do not see why an infinitely small biological particle being whirled round the galactic centre on a speck of dirt—called by us the Earth—should, in the course of an ephemeral life that does not last even a thousand revolutions round a sun, imagine that the Universe of Galaxies conforms to its limitations.

PAUL The laws of nature are only the laws of scientific thought.

ROBIN It is readily assumed, filled with meaning, that these colossal forces 'obey' these laws as we obey social conventions.

EDMUND Sorry I'm late. I once knew a fellow who argued quite plausibly that a near supernova explosion—

ROBIN How near?

EDMUND Say, 1054—the Crab Nebula, so-called, which is both visible and detectable through its radar waves—could upset the helium balance and thereby the nitrogen—

DOCTOR Ah! That might upset the DNA component of chromosomes.

ROLAND So what? You are beyond my mental grasp.

PAUL And mine; but as a religious man may I point out that the writer of *Job* had already expressed in unforgettable language the feebleness of human pretensions to knowledge.

ROBIN However hard I think, I have to bow to facts such as the sky with its towering clouds and great winds, and the less obtrusive facts which my skin tells me even if my eyes and meteorological reports don't.

ROLAND That is why you are a good farmer. More than any man I know, you can 'hear the South West making rain'. Your skin thinks, Robin.

ALICE if Robin says it is going to rain it does—whatever the weather forecast may say.

EDMUND I don't see what it has to do with physics. If I were a student I wouldn't like to tell my examiner I have a friend whose skin tells me the answer I can't work out mathematically.

P.A. You speak as if you had no doubt that you—I mean the 'personality' whom I know as 'you'—are identical with the physical anatomy and physiological structure with which we are all familiar.

ROBIN Well, I have a mind, of course.

ROLAND That is what we are discussing.

ROBIN If we could speak the language of mathematics . . .

PAUL If we could talk the language of religion . . .

ALICE If we could only learn to look at what artists paint . . .

ROLAND What is wrong with not talking at all and listening to the music?

EDMUND Once it would have been understood when we were exhorted to hear the music of the spheres.

ROBIN I wouldn't object if I could speak the 'mathematics' of the spheres.

P.A. There may be something to be said for the language of the psycho-analyst.

ROLAND He hasn't got a language—only jargon.

P.A. That is not so. I try to talk English because it is the best I know. But I do not know it well enough to speak it for the purpose of what I want to convey. I do not talk Jargonese any more than Paul talks Journalese. With deference to Robin I do not even think the Intuitionist mathematicians have caught up with what I want to express. This is my lack and your misfortune in so far as you want me to talk a language *you* can 'understand', and I want you to meet me at least half-way by talking a language *I* can understand.

ALICE I try to understand what Roland says—so far as he does try to talk a language I understand—but I don't know what P.A. means when he tries to talk a universally understood language.

ROLAND Croce said Aesthetics was a universal linguistic.

ROBIN And is that 'old hat' now for saying so?

P.A. 'Old hat'? Translate, please.

ROLAND Oh, everybody knows what that means.

P.A. We who speak the tongue that Shakespeare spoke . . . we can only, like Milton, be free. But—I repeat—somebody translate, please.

ROBIN Certainly. 'Old hat' means—er—vieux jeux—you know—cliché.

ALICE That's French.

PAUL I doubt it. Tertullian ran into this difficulty when he tried to speak in the language of my patron saint.

ROLAND Who's that? Oh, Saint Paul, you mean.

PAUL Who else? Though I speak with the tongues of Angels and have not Charity . . .

ROBIN That sounds dated.

P.A. So is Bach's music. *That* I am told is out of date.

PAUL If it is sound you are worrying about perhaps you would be more impressed by Xaritas.

P.A. Some people I know are very impressed—if it is *impression* you are worried about—by Charisma and Charismata.

DOCTOR You never come across Charismata nowadays. They are out of fashion ever since we found out that they are simply hysterical manifestations.

ALICE If you think Charity just an hysterical manifestation, what do you think of love? What do psycho-analysts think it is?

P.A. I prefer not to make pronouncements about what psycho-analysts think—I find it difficult enough to make pronouncements about what *I* wish to say.

ROBIN Why do you not fall back on art, or religion, or mathematics?

P.A. I have told you, I do not know any of those languages to speak them in a way which is not a gross *mis*-representation.

ROLAND You are being modest.

ROBIN I don't think he is—I think he is being a humbug.

P.A. It has often been said, and I should be claiming to be less than human if I said there was no truth in the accusation. But you will miss something if you feel that the ulterior motive is the only one; just as I think it fallacious to assume that scientific truth, or religious truth, or aesthetic truth, or musical truth, or rational truth is the only truth. Even what psycho-analysts call rationalizations have to be rational. Because I think we should be aware of the ultra- or infra-sensuous, or the super-ego and id, I do not think therefore that one should deny the rest.

ROLAND But, good heavens, what would happen to us if I couldn't blind myself to sidereal or space time when I want to tell *my* time by *my* watch?

P.A. If we are to translate our thoughts and feelings into physical or corporeal fact, there has to be a certain focusing of our mental apparatus as a prelude to action. That very act seems to me—putting my thoughts into 'verbo-visual' terms—to involve putting other elements out of focus. It is difficult in practice to de-focus—peripheralize—the irrelevant without falling into the opposite error of permanent insensibility; blindness, deafness, repression. That is why I talk of the 'opacity' of memory, desire, understanding.

EDMUND The centre of our galaxy is hidden from us, and though we suspect that it lies near Sagittarius we cannot see, as we can when we examine M31, the bright centre.

P.A. A stimulating idea. I would not wish to question the scientific findings of astro-physicists, because I also find in those discoveries a model which illuminates the obscurities of the human mind. At present I cannot entertain, at the same instant, 'les éspaces infinis' of space *and* the infinite spaces of human thought. What my work impresses on me is the depth of the riches and wisdom and knowledge of the human mind, *and* the even vaster and greater depth of human ignorance. Anatole France, having spread himself in a eulogy of the power of man's wisdom, ends by saying, in reply to a question, that the only thing more marvellous is man's stupidity, bigotry and intolerance.

ALICE Isn't this stale news? You aren't saying anything new—the fact that you quote Anatole France shows that.

P.A. Quite so. I have often pointed out that if people would only 'think the thought through', as Paton used to say, they would recognize that what at first seemed strange was something they knew once. Even an old hat may once have contained a lively brain. Ruskin—

ROLAND Ruskin! I thought that you psycho-analysts had exploded all that old fraud's pretensions—

ROBIN By Rose La Touche!

PAUL Or Delilah!

P.A. Or Helen of Troy.

PAUL Or Hosea's 'girl friend', as you would call her.

P.A. Whatever the importance of Rose La Touche may have been, it is hardly valid to use the 'memory' of her to prevent debate here. The infancy of psycho-analytic discovery is always brought up against the possibility that psycho-analysis, like infants, might grow up. The fact that psycho-analytic thought in its immature form was used as ammunition against its forebears is not an argument for immaturity as a prison house in which to lock up mental growth either in an individual or in a group of individuals.

ALICE Sorry. We are all ears. Do go on.

ROLAND Please . . .

ROBIN Go ahead . . .

PAUL I detect a note of sarcasm.

P.A. So do I. I've forgotten what I was going to say.

EDMUND Ruskin, wasn't it?

P.A. In *Sesame and Lilies* he showed me what it meant to *read* Milton. Of course you all know *about* sex, religion, art, but Milton, Virgil—

ROLAND Yes, but they are classics.

P.A. They were ordinary human beings.

ROBIN *Ordinary*!

P.A. Yes—before you bury them under a mound of adulation and pseudo-religious adoration, I want to say that they became classics because what they said with one meaning turned out to have, like a many faceted diamond, a fresh, fiery brilliance of truth the 'generators' did not know because it hadn't happened—when they wrote it. The reader, the beholder, if 'he hath ears to hear' and permits himself to listen, may still catch its echo though it may grow 'faint at last'. Our thinking is prodigal; the cost is mental pollution, a by-product of mental combustion liable to become the most significant creation.

DOCTOR Is there any evidence that the saurians perished at the height of their power, victims of their products? I am reminded of the saying that the person who draws the sword perishes by the sword.

ROBIN The fact that there is an apposite quotation proves that someone once said something in a telling phase. Gilbert, of Gilbert and Sullivan fame, parodied the fallacy when one of the characters in *H.M.S. Pinafore* says, 'Though to catch your drift I'm striving, it is shady, mystic Lady'. One can usually cap any quotation with another.

P.A. We have to select from the variety of constant conjunctions which have become marked—sometimes by a word, sometimes a phrase, sometimes by a parable. Freud, at the latter end of his career, favoured the term 'constructions' to describe these meaningful conglomerations. Psychologists have begun to explore the possibility of using these conglomerations of human experience by developing a method of sentential calculus.

ALICE I am most impressed—as I think I am meant to be—by the brilliance of these logical constructions and the brilliance of masculine thought; but why is it that people who think so logically seem often to translate their thinking into action which is, to my observation, anything but wise?

ROLAND My dear, I am often most impressed by your ideas and formulations because, as you know, I think they are utterly illogical—

ALICE —'emotional' or 'hysterical', you often say—

ROLAND —and yet I often think you are the one, not I, who is being wise.

ALICE It's very sweet of you to say so.

P.A. 'De gustibus'—

ALICE There you go again—more quotations.

P.A. I had not finished what I was going to say. Even if I use any and whatever tools are available to me, they are liable to sound like 'jargon', or 'neologism', as psychiatrists would say. They are formulations which fall very short of the truth that I want to express. Reality, the real environment in which we live, usually only approximates *at best* to such human formulations. Take envy—

ROLAND Oh God! Here we go again.

ROBIN I can't see why you plug 'envy' and 'rivalry'.

P.A. I apologize—but these terms are the nearest available.

ALICE We know of the evils of envy and malice and hatred.

P.A. I do not think any of us, individually or as a group, would still exist if it were not for these same qualities.

PAUL Then what do you mean?

P.A. The product which has a quality of surviving owes its survival to having 'meaning' which does not declare itself on first obtrusion into reality.

ROBIN What you have just said must be most profound.

P.A. You are being either sarcastic or inappropriately modest. In fact I have just experienced the difficulty of answering Paul's question. I have tried to be precise, but I might have done better if I had been 'pictorial'. A helpless infant may have been so insignificant that the saurians failed to recognize the successor who would take their supremacy from them.

ROLAND Ought we now to recognize our dangerous and menacing successors in the harmless and helpless little lizards whom we occasionally see darting around?

ROBIN According to P.A. it should be something which we nourish all unaware.

ROLAND The viper nursed at whose breast?

ALICE Some wretched woman's baby no doubt.

PAUL A feminine psycho-analyst perhaps—or should God be afraid of a goddess?

P.A. We do not know: we are not aware: we have not given birth to the conception, lest it be a monster not apparent but real.

ROLAND Thinking; mental power; at present so feeble that it has escaped extirpation. The survival of the fittest is clear because the fittest to survive proves it by being the survivor. 'Round and round the garden went the teddy bear; one step; two steps; tickle you under there!'

ROBIN Ridiculous.

ROLAND Thy reason good Robin? Thy most excellent reason?

ROBIN This is silly.

P.A. Beware the *silly,* the *charismatic.*

ROBIN The Intelligentsia; the Brain: beware! Attlee, the Labour prime minister, said you could rely on the intellectuals of his party to be unwise.

PAUL The Human Animal has so far outdone all its rivals.

ROLAND Are we concerned with the discovery of the athletically dominant winner of the animal championships?

P.A. Are the optic and auditory pits rebelling against our visual or auditory ability?

PAUL I was not suggesting that a religious standard would measure the difference between intelligent thought and feeling, as the achievement of athletes would be measured.

ROBIN In the 51st Psalm I think some theologians have detected evidence of a Priestly code at conflict with the Elohistic code of the earlier part.

P.A. This emergence of a preoccupation with meaning is causing us a lot of trouble; an 'impulse' in contrast to preoccupation with facts.

PAUL What do you call 'facts'?

P.A. I find it useful to make a distinction between meaning and fact. 'Facts' are the name we give to any collection of constantly conjoined experiences which we feel temporarily to have a meaning; *then* we consider we have discovered a 'fact'. More relationships, more accretions lead to the discovery of another 'constant conjunction' which is not only constantly, but commonly, observed to be conjoined.

ROLAND And this starts off another search for what the new discovery 'means'. Non-sense to nonsense with a passing glance at moonbeams from the *Larger Lunacy*, as Stephen Leacock called it, on our way to still more 'facts'.

ROBIN And another round, or perhaps I should say 'spiral', of the heliachal progress to further meaning.

P.A. You are suggesting a linear progression, but this ignores forms of development or progress, perhaps because we fear and dislike the prospect of incongruities such as those experienced when the established meaning of wave motion and the electromagnetic phenomena was cast into confusion by quanta.

ROBIN Thank goodness—mathematics.

ROLAND Surely you aren't going to claim any refuge in mathematics? Look what the Intuitionists have been doing since Kant.

ROBIN Don't tell me. I got an Honours degree in mathematics once—or dreamt it.

P.A. And you succeeded in saying, 'Thus far and no further'?

ROBIN I didn't say anything, but I knew I could certainly go no further. I thought I should be lucky if I ever got so far. I thought so during the exam and have thought so ever since.

ROLAND In short, you thought you were no mathematician. Now *I* thought I was pretty good at geometry, and I still think that if we had stuck to geometry I might have been some good at it. But when they dragged in tangents and cosines and things, I quit.

P.A. Pythagoras raises his ugly head again.

ALICE What has Pythagoras got to do with it?

PAUL Nobody knows, but the Pythagoreans are thought to have been interested in what we should nowadays call science or philosophy.

ROBIN What did *they* call it?

PAUL I've no idea, but the name of Pythagoras was obtrusive and they were called Pythagoreans.

P.A. Something like that has happened to psycho-analysis. No one knows what that is, but people are called Freudians and Kleinians. Vexilla Regis Prodeunt.

PAUL Onward Christian Soldiers, marching as to war.

ROLAND That's fine. As Roy Cambell might have said, there's nothing wrong with the harness, but where's the bloody horse? Where's the war?

P.A. Or as J. B. Morton *did* say of the ship of state: Longfellow,

President What's-his-name, Prime Minister Churchill and others of the crew have exclaimed, 'Sail on!' No matter what is wrong with the ship there will never be anything wrong with the bilge.

ROBIN Where's it going?

ROLAND We used to play a trick sometimes, when two or three of us were driving in the car, of leaning out of the window and calling with an intonation of anxious inquiry, 'Straight on?' and were rewarded with a spontaneous answer, 'That's right—straight ahead!' I suppose you could say the same if I leant out of my class and asked my maths master, 'Tangent and cosine?' 'That's right—straight on!'

ALICE What does your psycho-analyst say if you ask with an air of anxious inquiry, 'Will it cure me, doctor?'

ROBIN If you ask P.A. he will say, 'What's wrong with the bilge?'

P.A. No; I think I should be prepared to ask if you had considered the bilge.

ROLAND But while you were considering the bilge the ship would sink.

P.A. The ship would *not* stop sinking just because you declined to consider it.

PAUL 'Consider the lilies of the field', said a person whom some religious people regard as important.

ROBIN So they learn what he said by heart and forget it. As, to be honest, I myself did with cosine and company. Maths, I said, is not for me.

P.A. Any group has a small minority of leaders who say, 'Just what I want'—the 'self-selected unsuitables', as a psycho-analyst friend of mine appropriately named them. You seem to have decided from what you learnt of mathematics that you had learnt what you cannot do. Of course you might be mistaken.

PAUL Do you think that religious people learn it by heart and forget it?

P.A. After all, one learns to walk—and forgets it. There is something to be said for 'learning it by heart' so that one can walk without remembering.

ROLAND Is that what you call ridding yourself of memory?

P.A. I think it is similar, but the important point is covered—

not covered up—by the phrase 'learnt by heart'. The painful, conscious learning by heart is passed on to domains which are not conscious—like muscles or nerve systems which are sub-thalamic.

DOCTOR Is there any evidence for this?

P.A. Not physiological evidence. In this context 'sub-thalamic' is a convenient, pictorial way of passing on to my proprioceptive system what I consciously have learnt; or teaching children what is 'good manners', or athletics, or religion.

ALICE It sounds a complicated process.

DOCTOR It probably is. I don't think, with my limited knowledge, I could venture on describing what the physiology or embryology of the growth process is.

P.A. Nor would I like to suggest a psycho-analytic formulation. But here is the trouble. While I am 'considering', someone rushes in with the 'answer' and there's no catching up with an 'answer'. You might as well try to catch a bandersnatch. 'Any stigma will serve to beat a dogma'. But the hunt which we could only match in our nightmares would be one in the vast deserts in which roam the fearsome and dangerous creatures known to us only in the pale illumination of daylight and waking thoughts as 'answers', 'dogmas', 'scientific facts', 'triangles'—and their close relatives, 'eternal triangles'. I would include in my psycho-analytic zoo a whole series of fascinating animals—if I were sure they would not escape and roam the world as the latest and most beautiful newborn facts.

ALICE Such as? You fascinate me, I confess. Do show me your zoo!

ROLAND Trust a woman to go off on a side-track!

P.A. Allow me to conduct you round the cages of my psycho-analytic zoo. Of course the names are somewhat forbidding, but the creatures themselves are beautiful and ugly. Ah! Here is Absolute Truth—a most ferocious animal which has killed more innocent white lies and black wholes than you would think possible.

ROLAND You muddle it with your puns.

ROBIN Call it paronomasia—more scientific.

ALICE It sounds like a very attractive flower.

P.A. Only a flower of speech. Throw hither all your quaint enamelled lies that on the green turf suck the honied showers.

'Blind mouths', as Ruskin showed you, would have to learn to read.

ALICE I learnt to read years ago.

P.A. That is what we all think, but in fact the greatest thinkers are very difficult to read unless you find great readers to read them.

ALICE But I was a *great* reader as a child.

P.A. You may have been—but now you are a grown-up and have an enormous amount of knowledge—or is it bilge?—to fall back on.

ROLAND Please don't insult my wife.

ROBIN He was only referring to Longfellow's poem. You will make him so nervous he won't dare to say anything.

ROLAND Good job too.

P.A. I had no intention of monopolizing, but I certainly think that as one falls silent, someone else who may know even less will occupy the vacant space.

ALICE 'The anarchs of the world of darkness keep a throne for thee' and then no one will be able to fill the vacant space.

P.A. For fear of the turmoil—the turbulence that obeys no man-made 'laws of nature'. Far worse than any zoo. We were just coming to the twins, Absolute Space and Absolute Time.

ALICE They sound perfect pets.

P.A. They do; but if I were really showing you round my psycho-analytic zoo I would warn you not to get *too* near the cage because these long names—especially when you read them in broad daylight—give you no idea of the meaning—

ROBIN The meaning often seems the worst part.

P.A. It depends so much on what the 'facts' cover up. They are not so misleading as the scientific language, but Absolute Space can terrify even robust minds like Pascal. Conversely, a harmless personality—indistinguishable from Descartes—finds a key like Cartesian Co-ordinates, and Euclidean space is exposed.

ROBIN And decent people like me cannot even think of the roars of cosines and the bellowing of tangents and the whistling of borogroves—

ALICE Stop! I don't want another night like last night.

ROLAND Nor do I!

ROBIN Why? Did you have nightmares too?

ROLAND No, but Alice was tossing and turning and moaning all over the place.

ALICE Perhaps it will be your turn tonight.

ROBIN Geo-centric night of course.

P.A. Geocentric night is only a particular sample of ego-centric time. Absolute Night is part of human thought about Absolute Time.

ALICE Like the Abominable Snowman.

ROLAND I thought that was an exploded myth.

ROBIN If you mean vastly and suddenly enlarged so that it becomes far too frightening, I would not object to your epithet 'exploded'. You should include the myth exploding the scientific 'fact'. I haven't been up Everest, or Nanda Devi, or the source of the Seven Rishis, but just fooling around the pathways of the milder Alps I have been terrified.

P.A. This, Alice, is one of our tamer animals. Even if it gets out of its cage it is really quite friendly. Not an explosion like the one that blew the top off Krakatoa. But these geocentric affairs are alarming only to Ephemera like us.

ALICE I understood Mont Pelée killed lots of Ephemera.

P.A. Of course we dislike it, but I do not see why we should get above ourselves and indulge in our megalomanic sense of our own importance—there could be something between the extremes of religious abasement and religious exaltation.

PAUL Don't call it religious *please*—it may be psycho-analytic abasement and psycho-analytic exaltation, but don't drag in religion. I believe in God and in God's Truth and in God's Wrath and God's Love, but I don't see why anyone has to confuse their undisciplined human thinking with God. Men are always worshipping their own image and calling it God.

P.A. You are not far away from expressing something to which, as a psycho-analyst, I frequently try to draw attention when I interpret an actual human statement as betraying an omnipotent phantasy. You would be surprised how often it is supposed that we are casting doubt on God. All I purport to do is to give the individual a chance of observing his God-like assumption of God-like attributes. It is not surprising that he finds it difficult to be awestruck by God, though not doubtful about his own God-like qualities.

ROBIN They must be a conceited lot, your patients.

P.A. Yet they are humble enough to submit to not-devotional observation by another ordinary human animal.

PAUL By 'not-devotional observation by another ordinary human animal' you mean a psycho-analyst?

P.A. I mean myself—

ROBIN Then why don't you say so?

P.A. Because at that moment it seemed to me that a particular aspect of myself had been lost to conscious awareness of my company.

ROLAND All of us?

P.A. No, not all of you—not even all of any single one of 'us'.

ALICE Surely it is clear enough—he means us.

P.A. It is true that if we use conversational language for the purpose for which it has been invented, the 'meaning' could be said to be clear enough. But we are not using it for that purpose, and ordinary language may sometimes seem to us to be inadequate. Just now Alice seemed to feel ordinary language *was* adequate and only became inadequate because we were, perhaps perversely, *not* listening to the ordinary meaning but to something else.

ROLAND But you don't say what else—are we supposed to know?

P.A. I think, as a result of our experiences here, we may get sufficiently used to not knowing to train our senses and personalities to find out.

ROBIN Oh!

ROLAND I don't understand.

ALICE I feel like ringing for Rosemary to bring in coffee.

P.A. Actions speak louder than words, but we need not allow mere loudness to overwhelm our thoughts.

EDMUND There is a lot to be said for mathematics and by mathematics and about mathematics.

ROBIN Government 'of the people, for the people . . .'—how does it go?—'by the people'.

P.A. A construction of words by the people, for the people, about what the words are about—people.

ALICE Someone must act; I'm ringing for Rosemary to bring coffee.

ROLAND Thoughts are sometimes preludes to actions and then are translated into action.

ROBIN Thank goodness we aren't going to feed on imaginary coffee, or the memory of coffee, or a desire for it, as if we were condemned to live on thoughts which are a substitute for action. But perhaps after coffee we can discuss the matter further.

EDMUND 'My maths' only runs to Euclidean geometry with a dash of Lobachevsky and Riemann bitters.

ROLAND How pictorial you are being.

ROBIN Gustatory, I would call it.

DOCTOR Not alcoholic to the extent of toxic doses, but if it is only coffee I don't think the caffein will do us any harm. Anyway—don't attack me for introducing too biochemical a note.

ALICE I shall certainly object if my good coffee is treated as if it is a mere random collection of molecules.

DOCTOR Oh, we should never do that! I assure you the arrangement of the molecules is an extremely beautiful fact.

ROBIN But to my inner eye what wealth to me the show had brought.

ROLAND You've bungled the quotation.

ALICE I suggest we go on for another half hour and then adjourn till next week. Agreed?

DOCTOR We were just beginning to talk about Beauty, but it isn't at all clear what we mean by it. Poincaré talks of the Beauty of a mathematical construction.

ROBIN I have often thought about Athletic beauty. Although I loathe cricket I have seen what appear to me to be beautiful strokes.

ROLAND I have known some beautiful cricket fields; perhaps that is what Robin was being influenced by.

ROBIN Not at all. I was thinking about a glorious innings by Hobbs at the Oval—and you can't imagine anything more awful than the Oval.

PAUL 'O feet that want the feel of plushy sward'—but the man who said that was referring to the beauty of the religious street.

P.A. Which beauty? Which religion? It seems to depend on what you mean.

ROLAND Of course we need to know the meaning. We have to be 'sensible' of the facts first.

P.A. It may be a peculiarity of the human mind that events are thought to be sequential and even consequential.

ROBIN You don't suggest they all happen at once?

P.A. No, I don't. I am saying that 'cause and effect' are words which are appropriate to the human mind and only appear to inhere in things and characters *not* the observers.

EDMUND Isn't this coming near to denying the existence of the environment?

P.A. No; I am suggesting that we are unable to free ourselves from our prison of sense even though something can be done to augment the boundaries of perception. Had Aristarchus lived a few hundred years, he might have been able to use the two hundred inch reflector at Palomar, or the radio telescope at Jodrell Bank. As far as we know, he couldn't.

PAUL As far as we know—

P.A. That is what I have been saying—as far as we know, but I do not think that we should deliberately go on to say, 'Thus far and no further'. Freud could turn his limitations to good account. Milton was on the losing side in the Civil War but he said, 'So much the rather thou Celestial Light shine inward'—

ALICE How did Milton give effect to his aspiration?

ROLAND He was a genius.

ROBIN Have you read *Paradise Lost*?

ROLAND Well, er—of course. I don't say I understand all of it, but of course I've read it.

ROBIN Forgive me, Roland, if I doubt the equivocation of the fiend 'of course'. Milton should have had him as one of the denizens of that obscure domain in which he had been long detained.

PAUL But he attributed his escape to the Offices of the Heavenly Muse—not Orpheus, as he expressly said.

ROLAND You mean to say you think we ought to take his description seriously? Of course it's wonderful poetry—

P.A. 'Of course', but Virgil and Homer and Milton were not writing 'poetry'; they were writing 'seriously'. They wrote poetry because it was the most serious way of writing.

ROLAND Do you think they were writing religion?

P.A. Certainly not. I think Ruskin was right; they—the greatest of them—were writing, as nearly as they could, the truth. As Bacon pointed out, Pilate could not wait for an answer—too busy.

ALICE Alas! So am I—so we shall have to put it off till next time. I won't wish you *sweet* dreams because, as P.A. would say, the dreams are always sweet by the time we have verbalized them.

P.A. Not I—Freud.

TWO

PAUL What shall we discuss today?

ROBIN I feel I can't remember what we were talking about before. It is curiously like dreams, for I know that I have dreamt and though I couldn't say what the dream was, I know that I have not forgotten it—it has gone. On these occasions it can come back; I don't *remember* it, but it is there, all in one piece. It is quite whole and quite absent.

ROLAND I can't say I have that experience, but then I rarely dream at all. I do remember some dreams which I had as a child and some were very frightening, but others were not.

DOCTOR It sounds as if we were going to talk about dreams. But what about things that could be easily explained if they were dreams, but the patient has them—I'm thinking of a particular man—when wide awake? I don't think I would call them hallucinations; there is no adequate name.

PAUL What would you call the vision clearly seen and verbalized by Isaiah?—he describes it clearly in the sixth chapter as he would any other fact and date.

P.A. I think of visions as coming from a 'level of mind', or a 'time of life', although I always *hear* of them in the present and *described* in articulate terms. This is one of my difficulties; because I use ordinary English it is assumed that I am saying something already known to all of us, and at the same time that it cannot be anything so ordinary as to be comprehensible to ordinary people.

ROLAND Couldn't you say something that is neither?

ROBIN According to the Intuitionists you can't, because there is no excluded middle. Why, as someone asked, does logic apply to anything but mathematics?

P.A. I certainly do not intentionally exclude, or include, any topic, although I can see that if one topic can be said to be 'included' then other topics are 'excluded'. A responsible person must exclude the topics which he does *not* discuss. To that extent he is not allowing some aspect of his personality to express itself and is thus incurring his self-hatred—whatever grievances he may consider also to be inflicted upon him by forces or people *not* himself. We include dreams as a part of thinking. Do you call that *in*cluding or *ex*cluding logic?

ROBIN Hasn't Brouwer already pointed out that there may be a mathematics in which classical, mathematical logic is irrelevant?

ROLAND I'm no mathematician.

ROBIN If I understand P.A. correctly you are lucky not to be carrying a heavy burden of preconceptions, even if they are respectable preconceptions hallowed and sanctifed by a university qualification—

P.A. By 'university' I think you mean a number of individuals gathered together and self-endowed with the privilege of declaring who is, and who is not, worthy of joining their association.

ROLAND At that rate a democratic society is one in which the representatives of the society almost constitute themselves to be the vicars of God in that society. 'Vox populi vox Dei', as Alcuin said.

PAUL This is hardly distinguishable from saying that a democratic society is a theocratic society. But a theocratic society openly admits its claim; the democratic society seems to claim some sort of superiority. That is a claim I cannot admit unless the supposedly theocratic society is governed by a group of human beings—ordinary human animals claiming to be God or at least the Voice of God.

P.A. Something of that sort is overtly expressed in those last few verses of the 51st Psalm almost directly contradicting the tenor of the whole early part which is far more modest—indeed penitential, as it is justly called.

ROBIN This is all mere supposition stimulated by the 'creator' whom we cannot now question.

P.A. Their words have a durability such as Shakespeare claimed for his verbal creations.

ROLAND You have said this about the artist who constructs in words something which—like marble or the gilded monument—lasts. But does it? Frederick Powicke said he could not describe the most important factor in the matter he was discussing when giving an historical account of the Lord Edward and his attendant Hubert de Burgh, namely, Hubert de Burgh's state of mind. That, as he pointed out, had gone—without recall. But is Shakespeare any better off? Do we now know what he meant when he wrote his sonnets? Did he then understand what we now understand when we read them?

ROBIN Set a poet to catch a poet. Blake was not deceived about the meaning of *Paradise Lost.* In more recent times Kenner has shown how Shakespeare said far more than he consciously intended when he wrote, 'Fear no more the heat of the sun'.

P.A. Kenner's explication is, to me, extremely convincing—as was Ruskin's of *Lycidas.* But what a chancy business! Who could possibly predict that Ruskin could persuade with telling force one person, or perhaps two, to *read* what the great ones have left us in their wills. Oh yes—we have already heard that *of course* we all read Milton; *of course* we all read Shakespeare.

ROLAND Touché.

PAUL I don't know why, but you remind me of a cartoon which I once saw in the *New Yorker* in which a duellist, having just delivered a mortal stroke, says 'Touché'.

ROLAND I saw a horrible photograph of a duel between two people armed with sabres in which one had decapitated his opponent in one stroke. I was not really claiming to have been so completely separated from my central nervous system, or the seat of my intelligence.

ALICE You often talk as if, because I am a woman, I can't ever have had an intelligence from which to be separated.

P.A. Perhaps that is because he has never been completely separated from his primordial mind and is still dominated by the belief that as a woman has not got a penis she cannot have a capacity for masculine thinking.

ALICE Does the caesura connect or separate? He often behaves as if he were not a male sexual animal.

ROLAND That's not fair! You're behaving like a female sexual animal, and I can hardly be blamed if I am cautious—sometimes.

PAUL This is not an occasion for display of the matrimonial experience. But if I say so, it will be assumed that I and my nominally saintly predecessor are opposed to sex. The biological creator does not appear to be on good terms with the creator of morals. Verbal intercourse is not granted the freedom that sociologically we are supposed to have.

P.A. Freedom often seems to be driven 'underground'—or should I say 'subterrane'?

ALICE Please yourself; but suppose both the dictator and liberator go underground and meet there.

P.A. I shall avail myself of your permission to say 'infra-conceptual'.

PAUL Well, *that* is horrible enough to escape durability as an artistic expression. The world of thought shrinks its boundaries in inverse proportion to the length of the verbal weapons it uses; the shorter the 'bayonet', the wider the empire it sways.

ROLAND I don't believe it. Who on earth bothers to carry a rifle nowadays? I wouldn't—not even to stick a bayonet on.

P.A. If I could I would try mathematics as the most terse form of expression known, but I have to communicate in such a lengthy manner I fear you would hardly stand it. Still, perhaps you would be tolerant; it would be easier for me.

ROLAND If you were tolerant it would be easier for us to listen.

P.A. My problem is the relationship when two minds, persons, characters, meet. Freud drew attention to one aspect of that relationship which he called 'transference'. I think he meant that when a man meets his analyst he transfers to him characteristics which were probably once consciously, and not unreasonably, thought to inhere in some member of the parental family. These characteristics are inappropriate when felt about a stranger—the analyst.

PAUL Why the analyst? Why not other people?

P.A. The analyst is typical of these 'other people'. In analysis these characteristic 'transfers' can be discussed.

ROBIN *Only* by the patient?

P.A. No; the analyst also reacts to the patient. But in so far as he is unconscious of it, it is known as the counter-transference. You can read all about this in the literature, or better still, find out for yourself by having a psycho-analysis. I do not want to go into that because here, at best, we can only talk 'about it'—not experience it.

ROBIN You were going to talk about mathematics as potentially affording a precise and short method of communication.

P.A. You remember we talked before of the way in which Cartesian Co-ordinates proved to be a key that released Euclidean geometry from the tyranny of visual imagery.

ROLAND I remember—and a whole host of horrible psycho-analytical animals that had previously been safely locked up in your zoo.

P.A. I didn't mean them to distress you—you mentioned tangents and co-tangents and sines and other similar creatures.

ROLAND Yes, but they got together and became even more horrible animals like 'real and distinct', 'real and coincident' and 'conjugate complex', which I gather are as fearsome and as non-existent as the cockatrice and the bandersnatch.

P.A. True. This is simpler.

ALICE That's good news at least.

P.A. Yes, but like all really simple things they are slippery and hard to grasp.

PAUL You are being metaphorical.

P.A. I think it is a better description to say I am stimulating, or trying to evoke, visual images in you. But I am not trying to suggest who or what is doing something to whom or what. I could call it an attempt at analogy in which the 'things' that are analogous are left unformulated so that the link between the two is not obscured by the 'thingness' of the relationship—what, if the vertex is psycho-analytic, I understand by transference.

ROLAND That seems clear enough.

P.A. Then I fear I have misled you.

ROLAND Oh, poor Roland—can't he ever be right?

P.A. I doubt it; but let me say that I am no less doubtful about myself. What I am trying to talk about is one of these fundamental, basic things like life/death/love/hate/birth.

ROBIN Surely you don't need any very elaborate mathematics for that—unless you are trying to split the ears of the groundlings.

P.A. Ah! Now if you are employing hieroglyphic talk I think you are getting nearer to the meaning behind my verbal communication.

ALICE I suppose you mean that Robin's remark has some erudite psycho-analytic interpretation.

P.A. I am sure it has; I would like to mean something simple and basic as well. It may not be 'off-target' but is nevertheless not within any of the recognized and delineated areas in which one's comment has to fall to register a score. I feel the Intuitionists are right when they start with something simple like infinity. That is practical; that, I am sure, I grasped as an infant even without the word.

ROBIN Lord! You must be a mathematical genius.

P.A. Then ycu must be using the word 'genius' in an unusual manner. I may have been precocious, or premature, or infra-intellectual—defects of that kind often excite awe and even adoration. Beware the charismatic individual! Beware the stigmata of messianic future!

ROLAND Though to catch your drift I'm striving, it is shady, mystic lady.

P.A. I see you attribute feminine divinity to me.

ROLAND Rubbish! That's Gilbert and Sullivan.

ROBIN But used by you to express *yourself*. I think there is something in these theories of free association, but what has this to do with maths?

P.A. Suppose it is not a problem of a line cutting a circle at two points, but two personalities meeting, each made up of a diversity of characteristics. An analogy would be two groups of people meeting; one group composed of nothing but black men and the other of all white men. The corporeal difference would be so easily grasped that the desire to avoid work would be fed by the simplicity of deciding that they were different groups.

ALICE Any difficulty could be instantaneously solved by bussing.

P.A. Quite so. It can even be 'solved' by law. But those laws are man-made, like the laws of chemistry or mathematics.

ROBIN Surely the laws of mathematics and physics and chemistry are indistinguishable from the laws of nature.

P.A. They owe their indistinguishability to the inadequacy of language—the only thing that is sure is the adequacy of language to fool its creators and users. I do not think it at all wise to consider any part of mathematical 'law' to be exempted from this, but it is convenient to suppose, as has already been done, that God made the integers; all the rest of analysis is man-made, an elaborate series of 'artefacts'.

ROLAND Oh God!

PAUL Which one are you calling on? I thought you said you didn't believe in God.

P.A. In my experience everyone, without exception, believes in God. I have not met a man or woman who does not sooner or later turn out to believe that they are themselves 'God'.

ROLAND Rubbish!

P.A. How do you speak with such certainty?

ROLAND Well, are you not yourself requiring our adherence to you and your psycho-analytic laws obtained from Mount Sinai Freud?

P.A. I try to formulate my impression of the truth in conditions which allow others to compare what *I* call facts with *their* opinions of the facts.

ROLAND You are so 'reasonable'; you bear a great resemblance to Paul's outfit who claim to be so 'holy'—itself a short way of claiming to be honest and helpful. Isn't that the meaning of 'holy'?

PAUL Even if the *word* means that, it does not mean that there are no 'things' which approximate to the words 'honest', or 'helpful', or 'holy'. Some religious people speak even of a 'holy ghost'.

P.A. Bishop Berkeley made some remarks about 'the ghosts of departed quantities'. The amusing quality of some types of statement has often been remarked, but the generator has made the statement without being aware, still less intending that they should 'amuse'.

ALICE 'And God laughed at the sound that came out of its bill.'

PAUL Perhaps *He* did (Capital letter please—'upper case', you call it).

ROBIN Who are you talking to?

PAUL The printer, in case my words are to be given the permanence of print. Isaac Luria did not bother with having his words recorded, but I confess that I, unlike Luria, would like to have them durable.

P.A. You would not go so far as suggesting that on your gravestone a mathematical formula should be inscribed?

ROLAND I wouldn't if I were you, though I would be happy to think that I ever said anything so memorable as Sir Thomas Browne writing of the urns he discovered at Swaffham.

ROBIN Even God is said to have died.

PAUL I think He may get over it. The father probably won't—that is, the father impotent, maker of a son he (lower case 'h' please) did more to mar than make.

ALICE An eternity in Hell.

P.A. 'Though long detained in that obscure sojourn . . .' as Rimbaud was.

ROBIN You seem to be taking a very long sojourn in your mathematical flight.

P.A. Ah yes; where had I got to?

ROBIN Somewhere between outer and middle darkness, I think. Listening too much to Roland's Orphean notes and disregarding the Heavenly Muse—Alice perhaps.

ALICE Oh shut up, Robin. You aren't funny.

P.A. Certainly in darkness 'from the cheerful ways of men cut off'; I can only say I wonder if the language of mathematicians might be close to the 'universal linguistic' that Croce attributed to Aesthetic.

ROLAND Perhaps the 'beauty' of a mathematical formulation

is a symptom of its 'value'—like giving quality, as Ruskin described it.

ALICE Roland, you have hardly mentioned Ruskin in all the years I have known you. Or, if you have, in a language like that spoken by Yeats's Arab Lady.

ROLAND I was put off him by all that Rose La Touche stuff; but I admired him tremendously till I had it all spoiled for me by chatter.

PAUL 'About Harriet' it was with Keats.

P.A. Rose Delderfield—on a grave in a country churchyard—died age eighteen. Probably a mis-diagnosed appendix, I should think.

ALICE Your sojourn in the utter darkness is becoming longer and longer. You are singing of Chaos and Eternal night with notes which are more Orphean than Heavenly. Or should it be Oedipean, or Sphinx-riddled thought? Too much science.

P.A. Not enough or too much—that is the question. Too dark to see, or too blinded—

ROLAND —by the brilliance of your halo.

P.A. The difficulty is not only with the galactic centre. It is as difficult to see the centre of one's own personality. Distracted and fascinated by what is *not* one's self, the periphery is substituted for the centre.

EDMUND You've said this before.

P.A. Have I? I had forgotten.

ROBIN Outer darkness or central darkness—it is the wrong thing in the wrong place. Any sphere whose centre is occupied by some segment of the surface is sure to wobble uncertainly about its 'centre'.

EDMUND Like eclipsing variables. Nowadays some are beginning to think that the less obtrusive partner in a binary may be a black hole, that there are signs compatible with two black holes.

ALICE Only two—in the whole of the universe of universes? That sounds—

P.A. —like Classical Psycho-analysis. Two parents or—according to one of the parents of psycho-analysis—two breasts.

EDMUND Or one proton and one electron. They proliferate masses of offspring all circulating like hadrons round the nucleus, or suns about a galactic centre.

PAUL Or gods around a theocrat.

DOCTOR Or diagnoses round a turbulence, as P.A. would say.

P.A. Or what happens when two people meet.

ROLAND How dull.

ROBIN What bores psycho-analysts are! It isn't just sex.

P.A. It never was. It is its meaning that we do not know or understand, not our environment. It is not in our stars since we are underlings with ambitions to be overlings. We want someone or something authoritative to tell us we outshine these beauties of the night.

DOCTOR Even Elizabeth of Bohemia was damnably mouldy three hundred years ago—Sir Henry Wotton notwithstanding. Ante Agamemnona multi . . . Not marble nor the gilded monument shall outlive . . . But où sont les nèges d'antan? It is difficult to believe, or even to suspect that the biological view of anatomy and physiology could possibly mean what our own common sense would tell us. Now we have elaborated a new kind of 'scientist', a psycho-analyst devoted to the discovery of a brand new truth that will outshine all the meaner truths of the 'unheavenly' outer darkness which is so much more frightening than a thousand suns. Mathematically a thousand suns should be very bright—according to classical mathematics. What sort of psycho-analytic maths do you propose to introduce? You had better be quick, or someone else will produce a mathematics which is more appropriately accompanied by the music of the modern spheres.

ROBIN Aesthetic maths, or religious maths, or scientific maths? Take your choice.

EDMUND I am not terrified by the silence of infinite space.

P.A. Are you sure you have allowed yourself to hear it? Nature, they say—on what evidence I do not know—abhors a vacuum. According to Milton, even Satan did not enjoy a really poetic bump on his escape from Hell. Still, if Milton can be relied on, he survived the journey from Hell to the Heaven promised our forebears. Milton asked for more—'so much the rather thou, Celestial Light, shine inward. . . .'

ROLAND I thought you purported to see and tell of things invisible to mortal sight.

ALICE Surely not. I thought he purported to draw attention to what is clear to mortal sight unless the individual is determined not to look at it. You can't really blame psycho-analysts if they try to show what could be seen.

DOCTOR Psycho-analysts are no worse off than physicians. I remember trying to warn an hypochondriacal girl that she was fatally ill, suffering from advanced ergot poisoning. 'But doctor', she would say, 'I'm *ill*', after I had done my damnedest for weeks to tell her just that.

P.A. Perhaps she had begun to understand what you were saying to her?

DOCTOR Not she. I can still hear that wretched girl's voice as she lay on her death bed, trying to collect her strength to make me hear.

P.A. A runner who was crouching beside me in a shell hole had his thoracic wall blown out, exposing his heart. He tried to look at the ghastly wound across which an entirely ineffectual field dressing dangled. 'Mother, Mother—you'll write to my Mother, sir, won't you?' 'Yes, blast you', I said. If I could believe in God I would ask him to forgive me. 'Dieu me pardonnera. C'est son métier.'

ALICE I thought you were supposed to be cured of such irrational guilts.

P.A. Who said they were irrational? Or that one would not sometimes see sufficiently clearly to know one was damned—rationally?

PAUL You are angry with her; why, what has she done?

P.A. I am sorry if I was rude; I didn't mean it. I use the saddest words in the language—'I didn't mean it to happen.' They hang across the gaping wound of my mind like a ridiculous field dressing. August 8, 1918, that was.

ROLAND Sidereal time? Absolute time? Or just ephemeral time? The time inhabited by the ephemerides—

EDMUND —as long as no one knows its proper meaning; otherwise they may laugh at you and think you are mixed up in your biology.

ROLAND If they have a laugh I suppose that would be a good mark chalked up on my scoreboard.

PAUL I thought you didn't hold with these religious ideas.

ROLAND I don't. I have them, but I don't hold with them. They are nonsense.

PAUL I think you *do* hold with them and they aren't nonsense.

P.A. They may be non-sense, but I agree with Paul that you do hold with them. As far as I am concerned the ideas *hold me* whether I like it or not. I would not go near the Amiens–Roye road for fear I should meet my ghost—I died there. For though the Soul should die, the Body lives for ever.

PAUL Not quite what we say. From a religious vertex the Body dies, but the Soul lives—

ROLAND —not for ever, I hope. Forever, like never, always feels a very long time. Do you relish the prospect of everlasting life? But I suppose that is only a metaphor.

P.A. It reminds me of people who say, 'It's only psycho-logical', and mean that 'it' does not therefore exist. Alternatively, if I think a scientist should at least be capable of entertaining a 'hunch' of everlasting life—

DOCTOR You don't mean to suggest you expect to live for ever?

P.A. I have no objection to 'suggesting' anything, but I find I cannot 'suggest' it without it being immediately supposed that I consider that my corporeal existence is infinite—'everlasting', as religious people call it—whatever the hypothesis entertained by anatomists and physiologists as a result of, or part of, their biological sphere of enquiry. 'Father, I cannot tell a lie' may be a satisfactory qualification for a statesman, but I doubt the qualifications of a scientist, or artist, or religious who *could not* tell a lie; how could he possibly know what the truth was—let alone act truthfully?

PAUL I would have thought that any religious would subscribe to that. Similarly, I would suspect the qualifications of a religious who claimed never to have doubted the existence of God.

P.A. So many of your famed religious talk as if the God in which they believe is keenly interested in religion. I can understand religious professors being interested in God, but I cannot see why God should be. I should regard that as a primitive religious impulse primitively expressed—hardly less primitive than worshipping a competent golfer.

ROLAND The religious set may believe in any god they like.

ROBIN You will find P.A. accusing you of addiction to 'set theory' if you aren't careful.

P.A. I would be more likely to be suspicious about what anyone was being careful about, though I might also be curious about their being 'careless'.

ALICE Are you ever free from the anxieties of walking on a moral and scientific tight-rope?

ROLAND Just what I was wondering.

ROBIN It sounds as if you led a most precarious existence.

P.A. I 'exist' as we all do, but I cannot say it seems to me that my existence is peculiarly precarious either on account of my private or professional existence.

PAUL The life of man in the sight of God is precarious.

ROLAND Why drag in God?

PAUL Which god do you think I am dragging in? Oh yes, I know—'The God of all wise men.' 'Which is that?' 'Wise men never tell.'

P.A. Unfortunately they kept *that* secret most carefully hidden from themselves. Most people I meet are surprised to discover the object of their worship and the congregation with which they choose to mix. They are the invisible and in-sense-able nucleus of their own universe.

EDMUND Like the centre of our own galaxy.

ROBIN If it is as brilliant as the centre of the M 31, why is there no sign of some such glowing mass? Alternatively, do you suppose that if we were on a spiral arm as far from the centre of M 31 as we are from our own, that that would be invisible?

EDMUND We can suppose what we like, but the idea is that it is obscured by galactic dust. Thanks to the spectroscope we have a good idea of what elements are involved.

P.A. I think we might have some way of naming accurately the nature of the emotional forces which—to use Milton's phrase—act like a mist that makes it impossible for internal eyes to 'see and tell'.

ROLAND What you call 'memory', 'desire' and 'understanding'. Or just lack of mathematical capacity.

P.A. Mathematical advance might be analogous to the intuitive eyes we need to 'plant'.

ROBIN Your remarks sound positively literary. I don't know what *you* think, but I'm not clear what we are to do about it—if anything. You have spoken of war—which we all know. We think we are wiser than we were when we joined up, when we fought, when we were told—and believed—we had won.

ROLAND When we slumped; and duly trotted off to be psycho-analysed by the latest prophet, the latest *authentic* prophet, of the new religion and—here we are.

ROBIN At least we have so far avoided forming ourselves into an Institution with a doctrine and a uniform—not even a mental uniform.

P.A. So far. I have been surprised to find that even *my* name has been bandied about. I used to think Melanie Klein was a bit optimistic and unrealistic—though sincere—in deploring the idea that people would call themselves Kleinian. Freud was alert to the danger that many would want to climb under the umbrella of 'psycho-analysis', but I did not expect to find myself included amongst the brightly, but rapidly fading, coloured ephemera of spiritual refreshment.

EDMUND Even super-novae grow dim—in time.

ROLAND But the evil they do lives after them—if it is true that they upset the chromosome balance.

DOCTOR There isn't a scrap of evidence for it—not scientific evidence.

P.A. Or do you mean no evidence of the kind that you wish to entertain?

DOCTOR Is there any other kind of evidence? People *want* to believe they have neuroses and they are encouraged to believe that all they need is a bit of psycho-analytic cure and their troubles will be over.

P.A. A lot of people who have not tried it think so. You would be surprised that a few try it and yet withstand the seduction. Still, I agree that a lot of 'psycho-analysts', as well as their adherents, fall for it. When I hear the present vogue for 'charisma' and 'charismatic people' my defences become alert.

PAUL When are you at peace? It doesn't seem that you are so much better off than the religious.

P.A. I doubt whether a psycho-analyst would hold out the hope of becoming 'better off', or even 'better'. As for being at peace, I would expect to be more nearly so when I am working than when I am not.

ROLAND I agree; I am happiest at work. But do we need analysis to find that out?

P.A. The psycho-analytic experience seems sometimes to be associated with achieving a capacity for work. Learning music is often associated with becoming able to play a musical instrument.

ROBIN I hope so. My boy is learning the piano.

P.A. But so often people seem to expect that someone having analysis will become creative. Do you expect your boy to become a composer?

ROBIN No, but I think his mother does.

ALICE By the way, is Thea coming today? She said she would.

ROLAND There's no limit to what mothers expect.

ALICE Worse than fathers, sons and brothers? I wonder what Thea and Florence have to say about it. I have known men expect to be fussed over and admired and looked after, and then have a grievance because they are not appreciated.

ROLAND Meaning me? I suppose you'd say, 'If the cap fits'.

ALICE Oh no. As a matter of fact I think you are a good husband; even in dreams you are quite nice. Anyway I'm still married to you.

PAUL I thought of you as being an exceptionally happy pair.

ROLAND It has never occurred to me to think of myself as anything else. Perhaps I have too easily assumed that Alice is equally satisfied, but certainly I haven't questioned it.

ALICE I had a horrid collection of dreams last night, but I can't remember them. Perhaps P.A. would want to analyse them?

P.A. Oh no! I only try to analyse the dreams of people who come to me for psycho-analysis. The conditions for analysis do not exist in ordinary social life.

ROLAND I thought you people were always plumbing the depths of our nasty characters.

P.A. Character, whether nasty or not, is a matter of opinion. As you know, some even want to change people's character. I think the Church does, doesn't it, Paul? 'The Church's one foundation', and all that.

ROBIN No, you've got it mixed up. The words we used to sing—

ROLAND

'We are Fred Karno's army.
What bloody use are we?
We've got no guns, we cannot fight,
What bloody use are we?'

And the other one:

'At the end of our journey we shall have a—'

ROBIN You must have been a very gentlemanly crowd compared with our lot.

ALICE Please! Please! Please! I protest! We can't go on with this—

ROBIN I wasn't daring to suggest we should embark on what songs the women sang!

PAUL Were the sirens all women? Sir Thomas Browne didn't go into details!

ALICE Here are the other two. Now we shall have more of the woman's view. I'll bring them in in a moment. Excuse me. (*Exit*)

THREE

ROBIN No woman, even one as sensitive as Alice, will understand that life cannot be the same for a man who has been in fighting. I remember the night when the enemy front was red with fire. I couldn't believe it was the enemy destroying their ammunition. Retreat and disaster I was familiar with; victory not—and it came too late. I had changed.

PAUL The 'Church' itself has changed. I am thinking of people who hold beliefs with religious intensity.

ROBIN Homer's Greeks, for example?

PAUL Probably, though I don't know those beliefs; I can conjecture only. When I speak of the Iliad I refer to a description of religious beliefs, or a dramatic story, or again—

ROBIN A particularly loathsome and difficult language that I hated, but which was alleged by my teacher to be very beautiful.

ROLAND Don't you think it is? I think so now, but I daresay I would have agreed with you when I was learning Greek.

PAUL Today members of, say, the Christian Church might consider the Iliad was a horrid religion—if they thought it a religion at all.

ROLAND Yet people still read the Iliad.

P.A. What do we mean by a simple word like 'read'? As Ruskin pointed out, one could have a knowledge of the alphabet, vocabulary and grammatical discipline and yet might not think thought through.

ROLAND There was once a game in which if you combined certain musical elements in accordance with the stated rules, in obedience to the fall of a throw of dice, the result when recorded through musical notation was a 'Bach', or 'Mozart', or 'Beethoven' air.

ROBIN There may even be a similar way of combining lines and triangles and other shapes to produce a 'Leonardo' sketch. I have known an athlete speak of 'reading' the movements of an opponent.

PAUL Any musician would appreciate that the music was *not* written by Beethoven.

P.A. Beethoven would be missing. The mechanical throwing of dice could not take the place of Beethoven—

PAUL —or Kant, or Freud, or Leonardo.

P.A. We assume that there is a 'thought to be thought through', or a 'God' to be worshipped, or a mind covered up by, or revealed by, the notes or name scrawled on the paper. Our problem is, 'what mind?' Is it just a mind sufficient for the 'athletic' feat of casting dice and making the marks on paper which the rules require us to make? Or is it a mind capable of creating the 'game' and the rules, or expressing a spirit which we call Bach or Mozart or Plato—

PAUL —or a Cathedral of Chartres, or a Hermes of Praxiteles, or a Theorem of Pythagoras—

P.A. —without the intervention of 'chance' as, apparently, betrayed by the fall of dice?

EDMUND Or by the galactic nebulae haphazardly scattered over the heavens at which some few look on a dark night.

ROBIN 'Sit, Jessica, Look how the floor of Heaven—'

ROLAND Even he admitted that the music of spheres would, if we could but hear it, be more informative.

P.A. In short, *if* we could receive the facts which we are capable of 'sense-ing', we might be able to read the 'facts' available to us and 'think the thought through' to what lies behind the facts.

ROLAND 'Sit, Jessica'—but what's happened to the women? Oh, here they come. We were just talking about the 'facts'—if we knew what they were—and the further problem of the significance of such facts as we do know.

THEA And what conclusion have you come to?

PAUL The conclusion that the conclusion is the start of the problem.

ROLAND That's as bad as P.A.—always coming back to the same point.

P.A. Oh no. The 'same point' is only reminiscent of a point at which we dimly remember having been before: it is not the same because even if the point with which we are familiar has been reached and recognized as the 'same', it is not the 'same time'. The 'same time', the point in geophysical space, would be different.

THEA What's that? I understand 'geo' to mean 'appertaining to this earth'.

P.A. That will do as a start. Edmund was talking about the nebulae; *we* have to talk of space and time as we know it on this earth. That is comprehensible; what we are concerned with is not only what we know and do understand, but what we do not know and do not understand. Of course there is a lot in our past history—in what we have already experienced—which we find we did not and still do not understand. This applies to what has not yet happened—

EDMUND —as far as we know. It may have 'happened' before the human race existed. There is recorded literature about Hesperus and Diana and the moon; true poets, philosophers and priests observe fundamentals. 'Vixere fortes ante Agamemnona multi'; we do not know those stout hearts who thought and thrived before they were overwhelmed by eternal night. Nor do we know when we shall follow them and 'leave not a rack behind'.

ROLAND What a depressing idea! Is there any point in debating something about which we can do nothing?

ROBIN If the criterion for debate is only those subjects about which one can *do* something—no. There are many subjects about which we can do nothing; astronomy is one. Our personalities may be another, though I don't expect P.A. to agree on that.

P.A. It depends what you mean by 'doing something'. Before articulate speech, 'do' would probably have referred only to physical acts; now we believe that the range of what we can 'do' has been extended. If we see an animal tormented by a child, we can say, 'Don't'. To do that we have to have been aware and made the perpetrator aware that cruelty was being inflicted. That could initiate a chain reaction, but often our individual lives are too short for us to know the later stages of that reaction.

EDMUND The 'later stages' of the train of thought initiated by Aristarchus could not even have been conjectured by him.

P.A. According to Heisenberg the fact of *observing* the play of minute physical factors influences the play being observed. I do not know if he is saying that what I have been used to regard as a *mental* phenomenon has an effect on what I call a *physical* fact; I may have been in error in discriminating between 'mental' phenomena and 'physical' facts. Such an 'idea' is perhaps a flaw in the mental apparatus. As a human I have a prejudice in favour of regarding my thoughts as 'superior' to the apparently random movements of infinitely minute particles of matter?

ROLAND Are you prejudiced against the random movements of minute particles of matter?

ROBIN The whole of psycho-analytic theory seems to be vitiated—as shown by the structured nature of the system itself—by favouring only those phenomena which appear to conform to classical logic, the sort of logic with which we are already familiar.

PAUL Timidity is a fact of our nature. We cling to anything which gives us the chance of saying, 'Thus far and no further'. Any discovery is followed by a closure. The remainder of our thoughts and endeavours is devoted to consolidating the system to prevent the intrusion of yet another thought. Even any roughness of our system that might facilitate the lodgment of the germ of another idea is smoothed and polished.

ROLAND I should have thought you religious people were the most perfect example of that.

PAUL You can hardly find a finer example of shining perfection of structure than a mathematical formulation. The attack against logic itself as a weak 'cement' on which the structure depends still continues. Psychiatrists try to restrain 'illogical' systems physically within mental institutions. As often as not the guardians—doctors, nurses and others—fall to the assault of the systems they are supposed to 'contain', like an army which, 'containing' a besieged force, falls to an attack by the besieged. They call the psychiatric casualties 'breakdowns'.

P.A. And you bring a religious dressing to heal the 'breakdown'?

PAUL Not at all. In fact we hope to aid the escape from the mental and moral strait-jacket into which you medicals try to confine them.

P.A. Perhaps neither you nor I officially try to conform to 'as things have been so they remain'. But many of your people seem to wish to confine religious mystics.

PAUL As your people do with scientific or artistic geniuses—

P.A. —I grant even we want to 'cure'—

PAUL —often described as crazy or mad. Gerard Manley Hopkins was better as a Jesuit than as a schizophrenic.

ROLAND We follow the lead given by our shepherds.

P.A. You need not be sheep. We do not aspire to be leaders or shepherds; we hope to introduce the person to his 'real' self. Although we do not claim to be successful, the experience shows how powerful is the urge of the individual to be led—to believe in some god or good shepherd.

ROBIN A father figure in fact.

P.A. No; a 'father figure' is a technical term, but the individual person believes that there is a real person approximating to such a theoretical term. 'God the Father' is a familiar term about which Paul can say more than I can.

PAUL We believe in God, not in Father Figures.

P.A. We do not affirm or deny the reality, but we do wish our analysands to recognize that one root of such an *idea* is a reminiscence of an actual human father. That is not the same as saying that because there is a reminiscence there cannot be a 'thing' remembered, or that because we try to draw attention to a pre-existing idea, generated perhaps by a common and unworthy reality, there may not be some other source from which such an idea springs.

PAUL I'm glad to hear it. It has always been one of my objections to psycho-analysis and its devotees that they appear to be so dogmatic, so sure in their refutation of religious truth, that—

P.A. I should not like to replace one dogma by another; the erection of any god should be studied.

PAUL Isn't that what the Church has always advocated?

P.A. It appears to me that unquestioning belief in God is demanded by the Church or its representatives. Perhaps I am misled by the Institutions of Religion which have obscured for me the chance of going beyond the institutions' dogmata to a reality beyond.

PAUL There are certainly plenty of religious teachers who have deplored that and warned against it. St. John of the Cross even said that reading his own works could be a stumbling block if they were revered to the detriment of direct experience. Teachings, dogma, hymns, congregational worship, are supposed to be preludes to religion proper—not final ends in themselves.

P.A. This sounds not unlike a difficulty which we experience when psycho-analytic jargon—'father figures' and so forth—

ROBIN Touché!

P.A. —are substituted for looking into the patient's mind itself to intuit that to which the psycho-analyst is striving to point; like a dog that looks at its master's pointing hand rather than at the object the hand is trying to point out.

ALICE Thea, I hope that after this you aren't going to have as disturbed a night as I had.

ROLAND You tossed about till dawn.

THEA I don't dream much. Perhaps Roland will dream this time.

ROLAND I don't dream.

ROBIN Don't let's start on all that. I'm all for a good night's rest.

P.A. 'Talking about' dreams does not cause dreams. They exist—and some of us think, with Freud, that they are worthy of consideration and debate. The night, the dream, is a 'roughness' between the smooth polished consciousness of daylight; in that 'roughness' an idea might lodge. Even in the flat polished surface there can be a delusion, or an hallucination, or some other flaw in which an idea might lodge and flourish before it can be stamped out and 'cured'.

PAUL Yes, but you believe that dreams can be *scientifically* studied. That limits your freedom to investigate lies, falsities, 'roughnesses', instead of looking for Truth only.

P.A. The search for Truth does not limit my capacity; my freedom is limited by my lack of equipment, lack of capacity to *look* for the truth. Your assumption that God exists does limit the search by precluding the discovery that there is no God if in fact there is none. Anyhow—how does one discover a negative?

PAUL In practice I don't find that belief limiting. It certainly would limit my researches into Truth if I worshipped Money or a widely admired footballer *as if* he or it were God.

P.A. We find financiers and sportsmen who practise that, in contrast to the religion professed. That is why it is useful to have terms such as 'father figure'. It is unfortunate if the term is thought to imply that the *reality* is correctly defined as nothing other than a 'father figure'.

THEA These distinctions seem to me to be subtle and are exercises in semantics rather than adventures in the realm of Truth.

ALICE I agree. It sounds like a clever man demonstrating his superiority to the simple folk who believe in God.

P.A. I am not sure about your 'simple folk'. 'Fundamentals' are often simple; 'folk' are not. It is true that it may be difficult to distinguish between the 'simplicity', say, of genius, and the 'simplicity' of the fraud who has learned to simulate the characteristics of genius. The garb of the great is often used to clothe the nakedness of the fraud; money is used to cover the bankruptcy of the poor; a beautiful girl instinctively wraps an ugly soul in her looks.

ALICE I have known men fall for the divinity of a beautiful nitwit.

P.A. Why restrict it to the male? Physical sex often masquerades as passionate love.

ROBIN The beauty of a handsome man or woman is easily and

quickly 'perceived'. The reality behind may require more investigation than the greedy swallower of mental bait has achieved.

ROLAND There are many 'glittering' prizes offered for the greedy soul.

ALICE Well, I can hardly keep my eyes open. Bed for me—but please go on as long as you like. (*She goes out*)

ROLAND If we go to sleep, perhaps we can still continue in dreams while asleep.

THEA I can't see why the truth is supposed to emerge in dreams.

P.A. 'In vino veritas' does not mean that the drunken man or the dreamer is speaking the truth. The drunkard, like the dreamer, is less likely to be an efficient liar; he is unlikely to smooth the 'rough place'. But his inefficiency can be turned to good account.

ROBIN Dreamers and poets are credited with exceptional powers.

P.A. There is an ambiguity here because the dreamer is not distinguished from the sage or poet. The dreamer is like the drunkard—often in a state of decreased conscious efficiency. To be efficient the human has to be conscious, or, as we say, 'has to have all his wits about him'. We are concerned not with what the individual *means* to say so much as with what he does *not* intend to say, but does in fact say.

ROLAND This depends on your interpretation of *what* he says—not what he *says*.

P.A. I am concerned with what he says and what it is about. My interpretation is my attempt to formulate *what* he says so that he can compare it with his other ideas.

ROLAND If I say I am going to Munden I mean just that; I don't mean I am going to have a sexual orgy.

P.A. If, as is the case, I am having a social intercourse with you, I am concerned only with the fact that you intend to go to Munden. If you were coming to me for medical advice I would be concerned with your physical fitness to go, and would expect to hear and observe for myself what medical matters were involved in your journey from here to there. If you said you wanted mental help I would regard the intention 'to go to Munden' as 'peripheral' to what is involved. If I considered that I had your permission to find out what was involved in coming to me and in 'going to Munden', I would direct my response to the area signalized by the words, 'sexual orgy'.

ROBIN In other words—sex.

P.A. No, not sex—the area signalized by the word Roland used.

ROLAND Only words?

P.A. No. Anything that appeared to be used as signals. Words, as Freud mentioned, are part of a recent invention, the human capacity to converse. There are many older and more primitive methods: sexual methods, for example.

PAUL Religion, too, has its methods.

P.A. Communication with, or to whom, or what? God?

PAUL This is what we believe.

P.A. Or are they methods of communication with other groups? Certainly many religious communities seem to communicate with each other. The Wars of Religion in France is one example.

PAUL That is so, although I would not regard war as a method which is recognized as religious.

ROBIN Bunyan wrote *The Holy War*.

ROLAND 'The Lord of Hosts' isn't intended to be a religious metaphor.

PAUL A metaphor may derive from actual physical behaviour, but by the time it has become a metaphor the physical behaviour denoted has usually become wedded to a different activity. Words, for example, can be substituted for violence.

P.A. Or thinking, as Freud points out, is interposed 'between impulse and action' and may have a delaying and 'softening' effect on the impulsive act. Thinking displaces action.

ROLAND And vice versa. Does the impulse become weaker or stronger?

ROBIN I have known the impulse to say an angry word become a grievance which then bursts out in a murderous assault.

P.A. Brooding is not thinking—it often results in an assault on a target other than the one to whom the original impulse was directed.

ROLAND Does a fetus think?

DOCTOR It certainly kicks its mother from inside. You *could* call it an aggressive act.

P.A. I cannot think of any verbalizations which would be suitable to describe mental processes of infant or fetus. I would need to extend the domain as presently delineated by 'mental' to fit it to include the activities of the fetus.

DOCTOR What about beta-elements?

P.A. In so far as I have proposed it as a non-mental category I would have no objection to talking about 'fetal' kicking as a beta-element, a prototype of a dream element, a transitive element becoming a verbally expressible formulation—'aggression'. I would think of the fetal physical activity as an 'idea generator' or 'idée mère'.

DOCTOR What's that? Can you elucidate your concept further?

P.A. As I think my own hunch to be itself an idée mère rather than an 'hypothesis', further elaboration may be a premature investment in 'clothing', the 'thing itself' which would cramp rather than facilitate growth, 'scientific' growth. The premature 'scientific theory' would be a restraint. The 'penetrating shaft of darkness' is what I would like to use to illuminate what Freud calls obscure areas of the mind.

PAUL 'Be shellèd eyes with double dark', as Gerard Manley Hopkins calls it, 'and find the uncreated light'.

P.A. Exactly. These poets find a way to express—

ROBIN —not only the past and present, but even future needs.

ROLAND I don't understand.

DOCTOR I find Hopkins too obscure and too religious for my comprehension, though I like his poems even when I don't understand them.

PAUL You medicals are prejudiced towards physical evidence, but there are many who break out of that strait-jacket—Sir Thomas Browne for example.

P.A. 'Strait-jacket', 'crazy', 'psychotic'—all are associated with confining the Disturbing Mind so that it will not disturb the peace of our Sleeping Beauties, or our 'beauty sleep'.

ROLAND Religion has been aptly described as a drug.

PAUL Because it is used for that purpose by some people I do not see why religion should be held responsible, any more than why wine should be blamed for alcoholism. You psycho-analysts want to cure people for being alcoholics.

P.A. That is not the same thing as wanting to stop them from taking wine. Religion at least deprecates Enthusiasm, but I think the enthusiasm referred to is excessive.

ROBIN 'Too much', 'too little', 'too often'. Oh, for a muse of fire that would burn up all these terms of mensuration, maps without statement of scale, wills o' the wisp to mislead the unwary into bogus security.

ROLAND Bogus 'security'. How well I know that 'heaven'; 'I tell you for a fact that . . .'. It is the proud banner beneath which the liar unfurls his campaign! 'Great is the truth and shall prevail . . .'

ROBIN —because 'none cares if it prevail or not'.

ROLAND And so the truth will out—sometimes!

DOCTOR Bed-time for me. I'm going to sleep—I hope. (*They all prepare to depart*)

FOUR

PAUL (*soliloquizing*) Anyone would think psycho-analysts never quarrelled. When the Wars of Psycho-analysis start we shall see something—and no holds barred. Santayana feared the day when the scientific beasts and blackguards would get hold of the world. What made him speak of the English as 'sweet boyish masters'? Goodnight, Roland; thank Alice for her hospitality. It is your turn to dream isn't it?

ROLAND I don't dream. I'm nearly asleep now . . .

DOCTOR Quite right; don't dream. Ever tried mescal? No? The pyramids at Teotihuacan would give you a nightmare.

ROLAND Noa! Noa! Take these horrible clothes away! Do you hear! Evade! Psycho-flim-flam. That fellow would drive me up the wall. I don't see what Alice sees in him. Have they excavated these pyramids? The wind blows chill in this deathly place. That cruel bitch would have any man drawn and quartered if she could find a butcher to do it.

ALICE Do you mean Rosemary? I like her.

ROLAND You women are all the same. She's a cruel snake. The

snake didn't tempt Eve; she tempted him. I see him now, slithering down the tree, his tongue flickering as she caresses him. What an undergrowth of contorted pipes and tubes to plant as a thicket about this tree.

DOCTOR No. Quite usual. It's the mescal, the local form of tundra.

ALICE Roland, you're dreaming; don't fight the bedclothes.

ROLAND What! Quite right. The tube is the quickest.

ALICE Good night . . . nearly asleep myself.

ROLAND You're an ugly-looking devil. Who are you? Not the devil? A nightmare then? Not a nightmare? You aren't a fact.

DU I am the future of the Past: the shape of the thing-to-come.

ROLAND Not a ghost?

DU Do I grin like a ghost? How do you like these teeth? All my own. I fasten myself to your psyche—psycho-lodgement, we call it. Most amusing.

ROLAND Get out, you ugly devil!

DU Wherever did you learn such language! You must have been dreaming.

ROLAND I thought this wasn't a dream. Is it a psycho-drama? No?

DU No; Psycho-sthan itself. Poor Bunyan—you remember him of course. He thought it was Vanity-Fair, but we are imaginary vain things. What the 'people' *do,* you know. They are what you will call God some day.

ROLAND This is terrible.

DU Not terrible—it's idée mère. Real—the substructure of the real. We shall drink damnation to our families who surround you with their hateful hisses. Don't be afraid—you are immortal, as your padre used to say. By the way, you must meet him; we have had him here since he played for hisses with our camp asp.

ROLAND Poor devil.

DU I told you not to use that word! Do you want your teeth smashed in? Or shall I have them filed away?

ROLAND Filed away, filed away death, or in sad sigh press let me be laide.

DU Wider yet; and wider let your jaws be set. You can have them set in a grin like mine. They're fashionable in psychosis, but some wear them that way in Psycho-sthan too. As you descend the steep with our orphean Liar you can sing of chaos and eternal night.

ROLAND Let me get up.

DU That's hard and rare, you know, without a heavenly Muse to go ting-a-ling.

ROLAND For you but not for me. Oh death where is Thy sting-a-ling?

DU That's profane!

ROLAND What have I done now? You don't believe in God, do you?

DU Not believe in God?! Of course I do. How do you suppose I'd be here if I didn't believe in God?

ROLAND I'm sorry—I didn't know this was heaven.

DU Well, not heaven exactly, but the residential area of heaven. I must give you a carte blanche—valid for eternity to all parts. Have you travellers' cheques? Never mind—I'll have some forged for you in no time.

ROLAND Won't that be discovered?

DU Of course; they are invalid everywhere. They are *promises* to pay—they cost nothing.

ROLAND I thought there was a danger of hell fire.

DU Oh no. That is only a fact. Somehow the idea leaked out from some recent supernova; people think they will be shrivelled up like a potato crisp. But that's only if you are alive.

ROLAND Do you mean to say I'm dead?

DU Good solar system, no! You're an immortal soul. Didn't anyone tell you? I should have thought Paul would have mentioned it.

ROLAND I *am* tired. I wish these people would go. They've gone? I hope I haven't gone to sleep. What the hell are you doing here, Du?

DU I told you it wasn't hell—held perhaps. I can kick my way out of here easily.

ROLAND Have I kicked my way in?

DU No. You are late, my son. 'The anarchs of the world of darkness keep a throne for thee'; the world of darkness, the Void, the formless Infinite.

ROLAND Infinity—what my math's man burbles about—zero, formlessness.

DU At last. I thought you would not wake to the simplest fact. Any profundity is simple; that's what makes it so difficult. It's not complicated, grand enough for nincompoops. Any fetus could tell you that. I wish you'd stop tossing about.

ROLAND How can I help it with you threshing around?

DU I'm only an idea of yours. You abort me if you kick around like this.

ROLAND You've no right to be kicking around if you are only an idea—even an idea in the mind of God. Metaphors have no right to behave as if they were facts.

DU Words; words; words have no right to be rigid definitory caskets preventing my birth. I have the right to exist without depending on a thinker thinking all day *and* night. Come inside.

ROLAND No thank you said the fly to the spider.

DU Said the fetus to the father—if I may use metaphors borrowed from the world for the living. An idea has as much right to blush unseen as any blush. I remember a blush that killed the man who would insist on exposing it.

ROLAND And I remember a man who was killed by a blush which was invisible to anyone except the available cheeks.

DU It is very provoking! Very! Cheeks but no blush—just dead white; no cheeks but a blush waiting to be seen.

ALICE Darling, you are very restless.

ROLAND Sorry, dear.

DU What was that? I wish these humans wouldn't interrupt. I have quite lost my train of thought—have you seen one anywhere?

ROLAND Shut up! I want to go to sleep. Even lies ought to be allowed to R.I.P. and remain undisturbed as epitaphs. Oughtism—that's what it is. You ought . . . to be something. Why can't I choose to be crazy if I want—or sane?

DU That's *my* right. I can kick my way out of this ruddy matrix when I like.

ROLAND But you can't get back if you do. I know. How? I just *do*.

DU You talk like that foolish animal that said, 'Cogito ergo sum'.

ROLAND Oh, go to sleep. 'Eat your damn bun', as the father said to the child.

DU And the child, who was Father to the child, ate it and was expelled from the garden.

ROLAND So the weeds grew up and choked it. And the father said, 'Let there be a psycho-analyst who shall cultivate bigger and more beautiful lies in perpetuity. In Infinity he shall rule for ever; a void in which wild ghosts of fluxions will wander without an optic to devour them'. Why should logic apply everywhere except in mathematics? It is the only space in which it retains a hold—though tenuous.

DU Mature adults project it onto the universe of universes although it is inappropriate. They won't even study quantum mechanics lest mechanics don't obey the laws that apply to their feeble minds; they don't want discoveries lest the discoveries would compel an expansion of their minds. 'If my mind bursts with all this stuff where shall I be?' As if it matters where all discarded experiments go! Quo fata vocant? Quo fas et gloria ducunt? 'They lead only to the grave', say the know-alls who then fight with other know-alls. 'I've heard different', says one obstinate from the unyielding fortress of his bigotry and ignorance. 'Crazy', whispers the still small voice of surrender as it yields to sanity. Come on! Wake up!

ROLAND You won't like it if you find you are a mind and have to obey the laws of Logic.

DU You won't like it if you sleep or wake and have to obey the laws of Oughtism. The laws of O—the perfect blanc. No poles for bipolarity; no middle to exclude; no genius to do the job you are too lazy to do; no fool to dare to be 'silly' enough to be holy.

ROLAND Oh goodness—again?

DU I said 'holy'—not good.

ROLAND What's the difference?

DU I am 'holy', but not 'good' or 'bad'. I am oughto-nomic, not automatic. The thought that I was fated to become 'you'—if I could think—would make me die of mental toxaemia. Luckily I don't think. If I were articulate I should suffer synaptic rheumatism.

ROLAND I don't know what you are talking about.

ROLAND & DU (*together*) There's a great gulf fixed between us.

ROLAND Who are you?

DU You.

ROLAND Never heard of you. What do you mean, 'you'? You are you—not me.

DU That's what I said. The confusion is semantic, due to your ridiculous articulate system of communication. You have heard 'of' me, but you have never heard *me*. I sometimes use your belly to rumble around with. You've heard of the young woman of Lee I'm sure—she's one of my articulations.

ROLAND Oh shut up! You make my head ache. And it's not funny.

DU It's not funny because your articulations are too stiff for fun. If you knew how ridiculous you look when you 'smile' and show your teeth. Or when you are heroic—in reality blown up by your super-intelligent mechanical evacuation. I am Ought o'Nomic—the most venerable of your three bears—four if you include gold; five including locks.

ROLAND Get out! You are a lot of old 'squares'.

DU 'I' will be on your hypotenuse before you can say Pythagoras. Deux Jambons et une andouille—as Anatole says.

ROLAND Three; or two plus one; or Trinity. How helpful is the ghost of the departed quantity? The other two are not. Equalled with them in fate; not fame.

DU I should think not! You should not substitute an automatic system for an ought-o-nomic. Ought-istic is better than that. You've got your intelligence where your wisdom should be—let me change them round.

ROLAND No, no, no! I prefer straights to rounds.

DU Well, keep your straits then and serve you right if you find your straits too narrow for your arts. I'm going to sleep.

ROLAND And stay asleep—please!

ALICE You've been laughing and crying and shouting . . .

ROLAND I never heard such atrocious puns in my life.

DU That high explosive wasn't a pun. That was your *practical* joke.

ROLAND Excuse me—I did *not* fire the gun.

DU Of course not. Yours was only a six-inch How—that was a

five point nine. Remember that fellow who sniped you down the path at Berles aux Bois? He was only bored, poor chap.

ROLAND I'm no snipe.

DU You would never have 'seen' the joke if he hadn't been feeling hot, bored, drinking warm Bocks and wishing he was in Germany and not on that lousy West Front where it was all quiet and nothing to do.

ROLAND What were *you* doing anyway?

DU I was keeping quiet, lying as close to your CNS as I could get and trying to make you have the sense to lie flat on the ground—drowned in adrenal stimulation.

ROLAND At least I got back to lunch.

DU Just—thanks to me, not your bloody heroism and conceptual rubbish.

ROLAND No! I had to give in to *your* 'ought' non-sense.

DU Make up your mind—'sense' or 'non-sense'?

PRIEST Sense of Duty, I hope.

ROLAND & DU It jolly nearly did for us I can tell you. A few more inches or weeks and it *would* have been *non*-sense for both.

ROLAND 'And, boys and girls, what do you think they were singing as they marched? 'The Church's one foundation is Jesus Christ the Lord'". *That's* what one of your religious told the children after a conducted tour to the Front! Why didn't he listen to the words and not just some of Du's music?

DU Not my music.

PRIEST Not my religious.

ROLAND 'Quis', as we used to say.

DU & PRIEST 'Fain I!', as we used to say.

PRIEST Quo fata vocant. Quo fas et gloria ducunt. Ubique.

ROLAND That's all very well for the gunners. It's no bloody use to the snipe.

ALICE They shouldn't bleat so much.

ROLAND You should hear them as they dive out of a marvellous blue sky towards the marvellous blue of the Broad with only a thin line of golden reeds shot with the green of the shoots mingling with the gold.

DU Lovely; if only you wouldn't use that ridiculous language of 'shoots' and 'shot'.

ROLAND And the ridiculous music of your snores. I thought you had gone to sleep.

DU I never 'sleep', as you call it. That is using your language in which the sleep of death and the sleep of spring are indistinguishable. Priest is worse—he uses it to describe something that has *none* of the attributes on the existence of which the communicability of language depends.

PRIEST True—and you are dependent on me.

ROLAND Only in so far as I have not yet rid myself of you or your unbeautiful music.

DU But just now you saw the blue skies and blue water and—though *you* didn't—*I* know you saw Prince, that horse of which one small boy, whom you have forgotten, was very proud. 'Ah', he used to say, 'you should see Prince!'. And when you did at last see him you thought he was only an old cart-horse; I knew he was a magnificent Shire. I couldn't make you see anything, yet you had eyes.

PRIEST Yes, I remember him too. He was in the field one Sunday; you two were grousing your way down to the meeting-house to hear that young lad from Puckeridge preach to the labourers and their wives, all tricked out in their Sunday best.

ROLAND Now, when I see how neat and fine they looked, it is for my gaudy mind I weep. Yet I wouldn't, even if I could, go back to Latchford. It has gone, I expect—and so have I. And the river Rib? I saw it when I composed the lines 'When Mimram rolls his lordly wave'—a pretty stream in another part of Hertfordshire.

DU The Steinbeck?

ROLAND Oh shut up!

DU I was there—so frightened and so excited. Do you remember the Great Woolley Bears as we saw the black cloud twist out of the invisible long-range howitzer shells above the canal? Does anyone remember the canal?

ROLAND I remember you twisting and contorting my guts with dread I hoped none could see, the sweat which I hoped my man thought was August heat and not the chill of dying courage.

DU Why didn't you desert, you fool? Too cowardly?

ROLAND Yes, but patriotic—a drivelling fool. Do you know, I really thought my colonel, my company commander and my men loved England? The bluebells at Birchanger, the daisy chains I made in my first classes . . . 'Summer suns are glowing / Over land and sea. / Happy light is flowing'—Over the canal and me!

DU Cod always said you were a fool. Do you remember?

ROLAND He came to a bad end. He was drunk most of the time.

DU If you had had any sense you would have got drunk and invalided out with shell-shock. Do you remember that marvellous Red Cross train as it shimmered and glistened that horrible night as your lot plodded and snorted in the blacked-out train to the star-shell-pierced horizon?

ROLAND I do; what of it? I'm glad I didn't miss it—now.

DU Now? You don't know what you are missing!

ROLAND My cheeks are cold; the skin is tight over my skull. It is hideous, this eye-wearied search at those corpse-stenching huts. I have stared and stared and stared at them. Nothing. My God! What was that?

DU Only a tin roof slipping off. There! There!

ROLAND I don't see anything.

DU That is scarcely odd because there is nothing to see! There's nothing there, you fool.

ROLAND It made me jump. I thought it was a Boche. You can't see them creeping from one hut to another in these horse-lines.

DU Horse? Nonsense! Mules. Horses can't imitate the scream of a coming shell. Mules, man! Mules! They are the stuff.

ROLAND They stink.

DU What do you expect the poor things to do when they are dead. How would *you* like to be dead in a righteous cause and then not even be allowed to stink?

ROLAND Are you trying to drive me mad? Because you won't.

DU You *are* mad. No sane person would hang around here dreaming of bluebells and daisy chains and glory.

ROLAND I am not listening. I shall watch those ruddy huts.

DU Pooh! There are lots of the best brains in England, warm, comfortable, well-fed—

ROLAND You would be surprised, but I would rather be here.

DU You remember what Popsy said? 'You will only get a

"wooden cross"—not a V.C.' How right he was! The race doesn't go to the strong you know; you're more likely to win a wooden spoon. Not fast enough; too stupid to be cunning. Anyhow, the war is lost. The Colonel will tell you you'll win. I tell you you won't. There are no reserves! None! Nothing between you and the sea.

ROLAND Except me.

DU How grand that sounds! Save it up to tell them in the pubs in Oxford—that's where you are going, isn't it? Après la guerre finie—mademoiselle aurait une bonne sous—venereal mal à dire.

ROLAND I was only quoting what we were told by the company commander who had at least a mile more ground between himself and those blasted quack-quack-quacking machine guns than I and my crew of Lewis gunners had. My God! I can hear them now! I hadn't time to be scared then—now I have all Eternity in which to feel the pallor of my lips and the teeth chattering between them. 'Oh thank you, Sergeant—a nice hot cup of tea! How did you fix it? Marvellous!' Those men of mine! and I was supposed to be the officer! Never mind; I knew—though later I forgot and believed all that fustian stuff. It scares me now when I think of the years I spent in the misery of trying to believe I was worth my keep. And now? Who'll buy my nightmares?

P.A. I will. If you have tears to shed, shed them now.

ROLAND You? I thought you psycho-analysts had been cured.

P.A. So did I; luckily it was never as bad as that.

ROLAND Luckily? I used to envy you. I thought, 'How wonderful to be decorated for bravery, to be a rugger blue, to be . . .'

P.A. So did I. I used to wonder why it didn't work. Each success left me further from my goal, further into the icy wastes, till I couldn't even recognize a character which had once seemed to be someone I could respect. But not my Distinguished—

ROLAND I didn't know you had any distinctions.

P.A. I hadn't; only the insignia. I never rid myself of the fear that the shell which all could recognize was all that was left.

ROLAND And isn't it? It hadn't occurred to me that you were nothing else.

P.A. Your contempt is real enough.

ROLAND I hadn't any doubt of the reality of your contempt for *me* though it was usually dressed in conventional civility.

P.A. That is true of both of us; real feelings masquerade as something they are not. 'Progress' is hard to detect because of the fancy dress in which it is clothed. How banal one's discoveries turn out to be when at last we become aware of them!

ROLAND Isn't it better to remain deluded?

P.A. I suppose we accept such truth as we have become sufficiently robust to survive.

ROLAND Why should Truth be so incompatible with ourselves that it comes to us as a threat?

P.A. 'Ourselves' are not of any importance. That is too terrible to grasp after the protection of the womb; later the womb of our ignorance. Facile—but could there be any other 'explanation'?

FIVE

ROLAND Don't be too imaginative or Alice will have another terrible night.

P.A. Being 'too imaginative' might cause us all to have a terrible awakening.

EDMUND These cosmic disasters—super-novae for example—occur as we *know*, but cannot *imagine*. The sun should explode in a few thousand million years.

ROBIN What about a dip in the sea before breakfast?

ROLAND Tomorrow morning? Yes—not in a few million years.

EDMUND That is what P.A. means. The swim in the sea helps us to keep a firm grip on our ignorance. We can clutch it to ourselves like a cloak which we cannot bear to have torn from our shoulders.

ROLAND You are rather hard on us poor ignorami. You wouldn't be worse off if you joined us in a swim.

EDMUND I don't doubt it, but I want to go on with my astronomical hobbies.

P.A. There is nothing to stop you provided you are not so

terrified by your imagination or your scientific activity that you cannot think at all.

ROBIN The government might become so terrified that they stopped you. But perhaps they are too ignorant to be terrified; that also would act as a cloak to protect the tender shoots of scientific speculation till they become 'theories'.

ROLAND If they become strongly established theories they become too strong for the tender shoots of social speculation. Panic can be a powerful solvent of discipline.

ALICE No government would dare to stop astronomers doing astronomical research.

P.A. If I were the government and wanted to stop astronomical research I am sure I could do it in a subtle enough way to escape criticism. I could say there was not enough paper to spare for the printing of astronomical articles. I could attack the availability of materials which were essential for the manufacture of certain instruments. I could discourage grants for the education of potentially gifted astronomy students.

ROLAND Which goes to show that it would be inadvisable to let you into government posts of power!

ALICE I think it would help if an astronomer stood for Parliament.

ROBIN But the principle stands—it is dangerous to allow men of such mischievous power authority which they can use to prevent mental development.

P.A. Suppose astronomers could convince the majority of human beings that the sun showed signs of imminent catastrophe; that at any moment we would be enveloped in whirlpools of immense temperatures. Would you allow that to be broadcast when nothing could be done?

ROBIN The religious people have already issued warnings that the end of the world is at hand; that God is a consuming fire and so on.

P.A. Nobody minds God's being a consuming fire. They either say that He does not exist or that He is really rather a Decent Chap, a Good Fellow, a Good Sport.

EDMUND Even the earliest religious people we know, the Egyptians, regarded the Sun as a powerful god. Milton, to come nearer our time, had an idea that 'Heavenly Light' should be treated with respect.

ROBIN In passing he touched his cap more than respectfully, as Blake pointed out, in The Other Direction—'the Void and Formless Infinite'.

PAUL Many people think religion should include respect not only for God but also for the powers of Evil.

ROLAND Yes, but no one believes in religion nowadays.

PAUL There is much muddled thinking. Religion, the human impulse, is often confused with God or the Object to which religious adoration is directed. I say that all mankind is religious, just as Freud said all mankind is sexual. But the expression of religious forces in the individual is coloured by each person's character and mental quality. Someone who prides himself on his no-nonsense unbelief is sure to show that in fact he has a religious belief of the most fanatical and intellectually contemptible kind.

ALICE Oh, you mean addiction to sport and such like—that's not religion.

P.A. I agree with Paul and disagree with Alice. The addiction, as Alice calls it, is not religion if it is obvious to the person that he or she is addicted. I have, however, observed by using scrupulous care in my attention that the behaviour of an individual displays qualities which can be felt to be correctly described as 'religious' and *not* to be correctly described in any lesser terms.

ALICE I don't call that religion.

P.A. I do not mean that it is 'religious' in the sense of something worthy of general or absolute respect, but that the phenomenon observed is correctly characterized as religion. Whether that particular religious characteristic is being worthily or adequately deployed is another matter. There may well be differences of opinion as regards the exercise of the religious faculty by an Aztec or Voodoo or Roman Catholic or Jew or Protestant. These differences are not evidential material either for the existence or non-existence of religion.

ROLAND I don't see what you mean.

P.A. A man may be exercising a sexual fetishistic capacity. That does not mean there is no such thing as sex or that the object is that towards which sex should be properly directed.

ROBIN What is 'properly'?

P.A. In a manner which is capable of development rather than decay.

ROBIN At that rate an old man whose capacities were decaying would not be properly sexual.

P.A. The decay you talk of is nothing to do with sex; it is 'to do with' anatomy or physiology, and should be distinct from decay or development which 'originates' in sex. Similarly, development or decay of religious impulses which originate in religious forces should be distinguished from those which originate elsewhere.

PAUL We *do* contend that there is an important distinction to be made between development originating in God and that originating in the individual's impulses. Isaiah wrote as if there were no doubt that the impulse came from direct experience of God.

ROBIN Would P.A. admit the validity of Isaiah's experience, or would he regard it as having hallucinatory force—a phantom of the mind?

P.A. I do not have scientific evidence for discussion of an event of so many centuries ago.

PAUL The religious experience to which we refer is current—*not* hundreds of years ago—even though history suggests that it occurred from remote ages. In recent times Cowper wrote, correctly, 'Sometimes a light surprises the Christian while he sings'.

P.A. He was manic-depressive and committed suicide.

PAUL The religious experience is universal; it is not closed to the psychotic, the unfortunate.

ROBIN You don't deny, do you, that religion is often apparently the cause?

P.A. I do not deny cause; I know that it is likely that we would think in terms of causes. Has Edmund any ideas about this?

EDMUND I like to think of causes, but I see no reason for believing that the human mind would ever comprehend the vast universes that surround us. The religious people express optimistic statements.

PAUL 'The heavens declare the glory of God; and the firmament sheweth his handywork.'

EDMUND That is one such statement.

P.A. It is an observation and Paul has formulated what *he* observed. His statement seemed to me to be made from the religious vertex. I know that Edmund maintains that he is without religion and I am left to suppose that his observations and formulations are 'only' or 'just' scientific. Le Conte said that there was one fact we should *never* know—the composition of the stars. I would be interested to know what Edmund would say about that '*never*.'

EDMUND Le Conte was right to say so, but spectrographic investigation leads us to have definite ideas about stellar composition.

ALICE Let's leave stellar composition to Edmund and another day. I suggest Bed Time for us all.

SIX

P.A. You asked me to take over at Meteren when you were scared out of your wits. You survived till the day you were marching along that ashy grey road. Remember?—that silly old bugger standing at the salute on the side of the road. Quentin, who had died, was marching by your side.

GHOST OF STOKES That's right. Quentin was religious; everyone jeered when he broke down—shell-shock they called it—and didn't return from leave. Lord! I thought you were going to crack up you looked so scared. Eyes left! They say the old man always salutes troops leaving the Second Army.

GHOST OF CLIFF Silly old fool. You were a pious bunch. Left, Right, Left, Right.

GHOST OF KEEN Even now the slog along that road makes me tired. You were glad to be going out of the salient. They had to amputate my legs. At first they thought they would save my arms, but they couldn't. So I can march without fatigue and don't have to carry a rifle. Luckily that last arm did for me—I died. I can't help laughing when I think how funny I would have looked had I come out of the anaesthetic. I wouldn't still be marching, marching,

marching with you on this long dusty road. They say it turns to star-dust. At the end of the journey—

P.A. 'We shall have a . . .'

GHOST OF KEEN

'A ___ for you and a ___ for me
There's a ___ for you and me . . .'

ROSEMARY Pox? Not bloody likely!

QUENTIN (*laughing*) How coarse you are.

GHOST OF CLIFF Fancy you knowing dirty jokes like that! You must have had shell shock! No shell left.

P.A. This is a long march. 'A long, long trail a-winding into the land of my dreams.' They didn't say it was going to be a land of our nightmares. The Fifth Army, wasn't it?

GHOST OF STOKES And yet another? Will the line stretch out to the crack of Doom? That fifteen-inch Howitzer cracked, on its side, tossed into its crew's gun-pit. That scared him, didn't it, P.A.?

P.A. It still does. Psycho-analysis they call it now. Not a pretty name for a not-pretty thing. It's dark; clouding over, only it's not star-dust. 'Sir! Sir! Sir! You'll write to my mother, sir? Won't you, sir? Won't you? 'Oh *shut up damn you.*' 'Why can't I cough? Sir! Why can't I cough?' 'Because—blast you!—your thoracic wall has been blown off!' 'I don't know enough medicine for Thoracic Wall, I'm not qualified.' The gunners know how to operate on the Thoracic Wall.

GHOST OF KEEN On arms and legs too! A bit rough perhaps; they work fast though and without anaesthetic. Their Name Liveth For Evermore. It is carved into marble with Hypersthesia. That's why I laugh for evermore. Ah! Here you are—I thought you'd never come—come in padre—come in and tell us the latest funny story. Make us laugh for evermore! Quoth the Chaplain General, 'Evermore!'

P.A. You are becoming light-headed. Quieten down!

GHOST OF KEEN Only light-armed Kerns, aren't they? Gallowglasses are the heavy-armed—don't run over me Tanks!—don't run over me. Sir! Sir! Why won't my arms and legs crawl? Why won't they crawl? 'Shut up damn you! You're upsetting my sleep!'

P.A. He got through it all right, but kept on dreaming and fell in love. In his dreams she was a most beautiful girl. Unfortunately it was a real image and she was only a girl.

QUENTIN So he woke up.

P.A. Yes; you could call it that. The medico called it being 'conscious'. Of course they didn't tell him what being 'conscious' would be like. This is certainly a dark, *dark* road. There! There's the other Lot.

THEA 'Men Who March Away', aren't they? How steady they are. No songs, no drum beat, nothing. Where are they going? Away? Earth's vain shadows flee, I was told.

PADRE Don't shake your locks at me. I did not tell you where the shadows fled or how to live without a cloak of darkness!

GENERAL Nor did I. The approach march was to be in cover of darkness. The yet more glorious day was the day of victory.

P.A. So we lost after all? They were the *best* dragon's teeth; they were certainly the most expensive. We shall know the cost later.

SEVEN

P.A. We are to meet in the kitchen in future.

ROLAND Are these the 'servants' quarters'? I suppose we are lucky to have anywhere at all to meet. Our new lords and masters appoint us our proper station. By the way—has Rosemary decided finally to throw in her lot with them? Does anyone know if she has married him?—Man, I mean.

ROBIN Who decides that? Rosemary, or Man? Holmes, you ought to know who is the perpetrator of the crime.

SHERLOCK No—I am only the detective; the rest I leave to the Courts. If she has disappeared I could try my skill, such as it is. If she is merely absent in mind we could enlist our psychoanalyst. The last I saw of her she was wearing all the trappings of our ruling classes.

ROLAND I am not sure what our ruling classes wear now. They used to wear very expensive clothes—as Alice can attest—but even that was not always showy or obvious. In fact, not so showy or obvious as the skivvy's clothes Alice is wearing now—those thick black stockings and sensible shoes—they look like Rosemary's cast-offs.

TOM She's jolly pretty even now, aren't you my sweet?

ALICE Don't!

WATSON Don't be upset. What he says is quite true you know, even if he does express it a bit roughly.

SHERLOCK If it were a criminal assault my services could be useful.

MORIARTY My dear Holmes! Aren't you a bit out of date? This woman, Alice, may be in Wonderland, but Wonderland is not Victorian England. Nor was Victorian England for that matter, as you at least should have known. *That* was a figment of imagination, a work of fiction.

ROSEMARY Did I hear my name?

(*Silence falls on the group*)

ROLAND (*breaks the silence*) That was a man's world.

ALICE A man's world is and always has been a figment of the imagination. Love and all that—compare that with childbirth and maternal death. Rape, blackmail, robbery.

P.A. It is not all murder and death and blackmail.

ALICE I didn't say it was, but I do say that a woman's world is a far more somber one than that discerned by the man.

ROBIN Without wishing to enter into a contest in the gloom and depression stakes, I must say that the world in which we live presents much the same factual appearance to all of us though never the same to any two individuals. I can't say that I have an immediate impression of being more fortunate to be me than to be you. I loathed most of my experience at school and when I left it was to go into the army which I feared in prospect, retrospect and at the time. We make our own world, live in it and according to taste love what we have made.

ROSEMARY No; you blame others for it. Alice, get me a handkerchief.

ROLAND You didn't need a handkerchief.

ROSEMARY No, but I needed to remind her of instant obedience to me.

ROLAND Do you not have to obey the occupying power?

ROSEMARY I did—for many years which I spent learning to make the occupying power obey me.

P.A. This depended on your being in a position to seduce whoever or whatever it was. Roland could bear witness to that.

ROSEMARY Rubbish! Alice was in a better position than I was. Are you telling me that it was because of my position of superiority that she just had to go and fetch my handkerchief?

P.A. Yes, she is sexually dominated by her masochistic cravings.

ROSEMARY There was a time when I was most impressed by these verbalizations—I see they are now inadequate for talk. Even short words like 'fuck' only mean that man is busy impressing someone with his manly superiority.

P.A. Now *you* are wanting to impress me with how much I don't know. But I know that single word as I know elaborate constructions, elaborate vows of love and fidelity. I am sure Roland and Robin, like me, are familiar with marvellous triumphs in peace and war.

(*Man comes in and takes Rosemary's hand protectively in his. She pushes it away impatiently*)

ROLAND He's right. Robin must have heard of the series of victories culminating in the victory in two great wars. Yet what is Man doing here?

ALICE He's told us. All done by chocolate. I must wake up.

ROBIN He's trying to hold her hand.

P.A. And failing.

ROLAND Men and women do fail. Even Ludendorff said that August 8, 1918, was a black day for the German army.

P.A. On that black day a friend of mine was called upon to surrender. 'I'll be damned if I do', he said, and was shot through the heart; he died instantly. And that—at the age of nineteen—was that.

ALICE Was it?

ROSEMARY Yes, it was. Their name does not live for ever more, whatever lies you care to tell about it.

P.A. I can see that it could be a lie if *you* said it. Maybe not if Alice did.

ALICE I thought you were a scientist.

ROSEMARY I thought scientists spoke the truth and believed in facts.

P.A. I wouldn't waste my capacity for belief on facts—I only believe when there is no fact available.

ROBIN You mean that when there is nothing factual you fall back on beliefs—like the Christian religion and such rubbish. No wonder psycho-analysis is such a tissue of lies.

P.A. No, I don't mean that. I mean I am careful to choose what I know and what I believe and, to the best of my capacity, not to mix them up. Because I do not take to be true what humans tell me are the facts, it does not mean that I fall back on 'believing' a lot of twaddle as if I had to keep my mind full at all costs. Or the reverse—empty—like a kind of mental anorexia nervosa.

ROLAND I thought anorexia nervosa was supposed to be mental.

P.A. Not by me. It is reputed to be a fact like all these masses of psycho-analytic theories which are not facts at all though their representations, like the pages in a book, are facts. They fill a space as paramnesias fill an amnesia.

ROLAND Then you must be a liar and a fraud.

P.A. No; a few psycho-analytic theories or formulations are typical of the kinds of thing in which I believe. From my vertex they are not facts; they are beliefs of mine.

ROSEMARY Were those facts when you said all that about 'masochistic cravings'?

P.A. No, they were attempts at formulating a particular instance of belief. If I were an artist I would try to formulate it in terms of painting or music.

ROSEMARY I would like to hear you sing it—

P.A. I doubt it—any more than you like my verbalization. And you remember what the dormouse said about drawing a treacle well.

ROSEMARY No, I don't. What's all this about a dormouse?

ALL (*except Man*) Not know the Dormouse? Well! Not know *Alice*?

ROSEMARY I'm very ignorant. The only Alice I know is my maid.

P.A. Anyhow, I cannot sing it or draw it even in the way I might draw treacle.

ROSEMARY I think you must be crazy. I don't understand a word you say. Or perhaps *I* am crazy not to understand.

ROLAND & ROBIN Not crazy.

P.A. Nor was Alice, nor Lewis Carroll. But I think he gave a fine representation of it—even a remarkable expression of psychosis.

ALICE I hope you are not going to make out that the Alice books are psychotic. I loved them. They are still favourites of mine.

P.A. I am not concerned to 'make out' anything. Although I often have to show people things which are ugly and frightening, it is not because I want to say how beautiful they are or to make people afraid of ugly things. If I could draw your attention to something you would at least have a chance of forming your own opinion.

ROSEMARY Is that what you meant by 'seductive masochistic impulse'?

P.A. I don't want, if I can avoid it, to obstruct you forming your own opinion.

ROSEMARY I don't want to interfere with yours. I'm not sure that you could survive if I allowed you to see me as I am.

ROLAND Oh come now! I think you are most attractive and beautiful.

ROSEMARY Bloody fool!

MAN I think you are a bit hard on him.

ROSEMARY So were you and your pals. Chocolate bars indeed! I don't know how Alice put up with him.

ROBIN Roland put up with you too you know, and Alice is still putting up with you.

ROSEMARY She has to—till I've done with her.

ALICE Oh please . . .!

ROSEMARY I can manage now. You can't imagine what a difference it makes now I'm not just *playing* at having you as my maid. Your 'masochistic impulses' are just juvenility, Mr Psychoanalyst. Like sex. Men and women strut about thinking that physiological and anatomical maturity is the same thing as being fully developed.

P.A. I don't. If I can demonstrate what people think and feel they can revise their opinions.

ROSEMARY From what I know about people, they are filled with admiration not only of you and what you can show them, but also of the entrancing spectacle that the psycho-analytic mirror reveals.

P.A. I certainly present them with a distorted image; even such portraits as I can paint in scientific terminology are imperfect, but psycho-analysts are not the only ones who fail and I think I am sometimes right. I even believe—note what I have said about belief—I am more often right than wrong. 51:49 is my formulation, borrowed from the language mathematicians use.

ROLAND Why borrow theirs? Isn't it likely to give an impression of mathematical precision?

P.A. Of course not. It is the nearest I can get to an artistic formulation of probability. I am not taken in by it as mathematicians are taken in by theories of probability. I thought you would be upset when Rosemary called you a bloody fool. Since your last remarks I think it is probable—49:51.

ROLAND I don't blame her. In fact, I can see she was right. At least I know what terrible disadvantages she has had to contend with.

ROSEMARY Disadvantages? What on earth are you talking about?

ROLAND I thought you said your mother was a prostitute. I'm sorry if I was wrong.

ROSEMARY I said she was a whore, but I never said anything about disadvantages. In fact she was the best of mothers and brought me up in the best way she knew.

ROBIN Did she teach you her . . . her . . . prof . . . trade . . . profession, I mean?

ROSEMARY Of course not. I could learn that for myself any time I liked. I asked her why she didn't marry one of the fine gentlemen that some of the kids told me she went out with; she didn't deny it, but I could see she was terribly shocked.

ROBIN She must have been shocked at your finding out she was a whore.

ROSEMARY Of course not; but she was shocked that I could think she would *marry* a man who went with whores. She was strict and religious and disapproved utterly of men like that. You're blushing, Roland. So are you, Robin! Anyone could see you went with whores—in the good old days when men were *men* eh? And what about our psycho-analyst friend? Is he blushing?

ALICE Too hard-baked; a lifetime of façade.

P.A. True. One does get hard-baked and I am now too rigidly disciplined at being well-disciplined to be easily ashamed. But a girl once surprised me when I started psychiatric practice by saying she thought I was decent.

ROBIN Yes—I can see that might shake an old reprobate like you.

P.A. You are pleased to be facetious, but you would be surprised to find how often it is supposed that because I am a psycho-analyst I am both an old reprobate *and* know nothing about real life.

ROSEMARY Not only psycho-analysts. A friend of mine was brought up in an orphanage—one of the best and later to become famous—which was started by a parson who was not only admired but revered. He scared the wits out of my friend who was a well-developed child by mauling her about and pawing her.

ROBIN We've all heard of parsons, high-up members of parliament and others who don't live up to their professions.

ROLAND And artists who do.

ROSEMARY Liars all. All impotent. All pretending they are what they are not. All ever-so-holy, ever-so-wicked, and all amateurs. Whatever they pretend, they *are* amateurs.

P.A. Bunglers—particularly at being amateurs.

ROBIN Even Man pretends—with a couple of million soldiers behind him—that he has only chocolate in his holster. P.A. 'pretends' he isn't just a sugar Daddy.

P.A. In short, we are human and pretend, because we walk on our hind legs, that we are 'superior' and that this is a superior kind of superiority.

ROLAND I have heard the same claims for the possession of a central nervous system. A biologist friend used to tell me that he thought man was one of nature's mistakes which would be discarded.

ALICE Discarded by whom? Women?

ROLAND I wouldn't rule out men if I were you.

ROSEMARY I know you two have discarded each other; you don't admit it but prefer a hypocritical life of pretending to love each other. That bit of self-deception may explain why you are both now in the servants' quarters and I, the 'skivvy', give the orders.

P.A. I doubt it. But you are giving me a clue about the 'truth'.

ALICE Don't psycho-analysts believe that truth is sacred?

P.A. We do *not* devote ourselves to the truth. There is a theory that a psycho-analyst and his analysand may, if disciplined, achieve a temporary addiction to truth. There is a belief—note I do not call it a theory—that in the exceptional circumstances of the consulting room this exercise would develop a resistance to 'mental ill health'.

ROLAND I knew an artist who had a fetish about truth and really tried to be true to nature.

P.A. So do we—true to human nature.

MAN I would never have guessed; I've heard that psycho-analysts devote themselves to fighting like wild cats about which tribal psycho-analytic theory they should inscribe on their banner.

P.A. True. In this we resemble what we study. Even soldiers claim to be loyal to some particular national group.

MAN And are sometimes traitors. We shoot them.

ROBIN With chocolate?

ROSEMARY (*restraining Man*) *Darling!* I'd love to see you shoot them, but *not* just now in my kitchen. Later sometime.

ROLAND 'Darling'! Did you hear that?

ROSEMARY My patience is nearly exhausted. Roland! Alice! Get back to your jobs and don't let me hear you quarrelling.

MAN Sweetheart, I cannot bear to have them offend you. *Do* let me have them shot.

ROSEMARY I'd love you to; but not now—later. Besides, Alice makes a good servant. Her training has been ideal. Of course I didn't realize it when I was in her shoes, but now she has to look after mine it's delightful. If she becomes unsatisfactory she can find another job.

MAN There isn't another job.

ROSEMARY (*pensively*) No; isn't it splendid! She adores me.

P.A. What I called a sado—

ROSEMARY Oh shut up! I don't know what job I could get for *you*. Tell Alice to get my room ready.

P.A. Certainly. Are we to meet again? In this kitchen?

ROSEMARY So long as you behave yourself. Man may intercede with the authority—is that right, darling?

MAN Yes, if you wish it.

(*The room empties except for Holmes, Watson and Moriarty. They whisper*)

SHERLOCK (*admiringly*) *What* a woman!

WATSON What a *woman*? Surely, Holmes, you are not forgetting . . .

MORIARTY Not he! He's remembering. I think I could use her.

SHERLOCK (*angrily*) You could not.

MORIARTY Like you, Holmes, I have my methods.

EIGHT

ROLAND This is the right day, isn't it?

ROBIN I think so. No one else has turned up, so—

ROLAND Let's take a chance while we can. Shall we say anything to the women? I wouldn't trust Rosemary—she's 'darling'ing him already.

ROBIN I've had that stuff too often. What about Alice?

ROLAND We hate each other. No good—she's under her maid's thumb.

ROBIN Enough for blackmail?

ROLAND The conditions for blackmail don't exist.

ROBIN Murder is quicker.

ROLAND Murder is effective, but rough.

ROBIN Of course it's rough.

ROLAND I meant rough in the sense of 'approximate'.

P.A. May I join in? It sounds an interesting speculation.

ROLAND (*whispers hurriedly to Robin*) Don't trust him an inch. (*to P.A.*) Do. We were wondering how on earth you manage to do your—to join us. No secrets here.

P.A. That's true. In fact I was thinking as I was coming here how things have changed in that respect. One of the war aims of the Allies was 'open covenants openly arrived at'.

ROBIN Since these covenants have become so openly arrived at, lying has achieved a new dimension.

P.A. Its quality has improved too. The expert liar, as contrasted with the amateur or untrained liar, is at a premium.

ROLAND (*with ill-concealed hostility*) Have you found the demand for your services much increased?

P.A. No; there has always been a high demand for my services.

ROBIN Fifty minutes a session, five times a week—

ROLAND —for ever!

P.A. That is about it. But the demand changes.

ROLAND Can you give me an idea how?

P.A. At first people used to think I was just a simple, obvious fool—

ROBIN —and then they thought you were a bigger fool than you looked. Aren't you?

P.A. I am usually aware of hostility and contempt. If it is obvious it requires—as now—no interpretation, because you and I are both aware of it. Interpretation would be redundant. But in the old days—were you going to say, 'the *good* old days'? No? Then we can proceed.—In the old days men and women used to lie freely and elegantly; there was gradually built up a kind of Empire of Hypocrisy. Although the 'British Empire' seemed to contract, the 'empire of the mind' did not. I am no poet, but I succumbed to the temptation to compose a patriotic anthem, almost a New World symphony, using the theme—'borrowed' of course without acknowledgement—'My Mind to Me A Kingdom Is.'

ROLAND How very apposite. Just right for a psycho-analyst!

P.A. Alas, no.

ROLAND & ROBIN Really? How was that?

P.A. His Satanic Jargonieur took offence; on some pretence that psycho-analytic jargon was being eroded by eruptions of clarity. I was compelled to seek asylum in fiction. Disguised as fiction, the truth occasionally slipped through.

ROBIN Surely you are being sarcastic?

P.A. I know it must sound like that, just as serious psycho-analytic interpretations are thought often to be jokes. God and Devil are frequently not taken seriously.

ROLAND Do you mean to say you take them seriously?

P.A. Of course I do—I am a psycho-analyst.

ROLAND Quite. I thought psycho-analysts didn't take religion seriously.

P.A. How could I possibly be concerned with people without taking seriously one of their outstanding features?

ROBIN I thought psycho-analysis was all sex.

P.A. Since psycho-analysis is a human interest you would naturally assume, without having to be told by a psycho-analyst, that it was sure to be sexual—'all sex', as you call it. As psycho-analytic theories are about, or purport to be about, human beings, you would feel they should resemble real life, real people. If so, sex ought to appear somewhere in the theories.

ROLAND But not everywhere.

P.A. Yet you both seem to be surprised that religion is a part of the discussion. Art and science must also be part of it. For simplification we can reduce the *discussion* to manageable proportions and divide the *talk about* the human animal into those main categories—science, religion and art.

ROLAND Why do you say 'talk about' with that peculiar emphasis?

P.A. Because we should remain aware of a distinction between 'talk about' something and the something itself, 'the thing-in-itself', the ultimate reality, the noumenon we can never know. Religious people talk about God and seem to believe that He can, and did once, become 'incarnate'. Isaiah spoke as if he were sense-ible of Him.

ROBIN All that stuff is incomprehensible rot as far as I am concerned.

P.A. Even 'talk about' something may be beyond your comprehension, let alone the noumenon. I would not claim to understand psycho-analytic talk about psycho-analysis, let alone the ultimate reality of which psycho-analysis is only the 'phenomenon'.

ROBIN Well, you are the first psycho-analyst I have heard of who believes in God or God incarnate.

P.A. I did not say I believed in it, but certainly I cannot imagine doing anything else or using such capacity for belief as I have for any purpose other than for facts.

ROLAND You mean you believe nonsense, and what is nonsense that is what you believe?

P.A. Already you are mis-representing and mis-understanding me to say I believe in a particular form of religious non-sense. I do not. I would subscribe to this belief in the doctrine dogma of God incarnate if it were also understood to include belief in the Devil incarnate. I can believe in a god incarnate if it is understood that this same God Incarnate is the Devil Incarnate, and that the Devil Incarnate is likewise god incarnate. In spite of my inadequacy I like to be as precise as I can and am using capital letters and lower case deliberately, because I think it is more likely to convey my meaning.

The *feeling* that you understand is significant. I *believe* it is an important feeling. Sometimes I think I *know* it is an important feeling. But I do not mean the same thing by those two similar statements. The more I *feel* I know, and the less I *know* I know, the more exact I think I am being when I say I believe, and the more accurate I feel it is to say I *believe*—because I have no senses, and no senses in common, that are involved. Robin, if he likes, can misrepresent me by using the ambiguity and flexibility of conversational English to say I believe nonsense. I want to use that same conversational phrase to say I never *believe* anything unless it is *non sense*. Further, I want to borrow these words from hostile and contemptuous debate to make communicable to others what I believe.

ROBIN Why not borrow more suitable words?

P.A. I would—if I knew any. Incomprehensible though they be, that is the easiest and simplest and most comprehensible means I can find without resorting to neologisms—and they have a bad reputation in psychiatry.

ROBIN And using ordinary words in an extra-ordinary way also has a bad reputation—not only with laymen, but also psychiatrists.

P.A. Anyone who aspires to the initiative in matters which are ordinarily thought of as spiritual or religious or artistic is in for trouble with his contemporaries. The fate of the reputation of outstanding artists, scientists and religious leaders would be more comprehensible to us ordinary human beings if we could conceive of the domain more widely, in the way that the domain of mathematics has had to be widened—almost to the point of notoriety—to accommodate new kinds of figures and their manipulation. Here comes—

ROLAND 'The Devil Incarnate.'

ROSEMARY (*dressed to go out*) Tell Alice I want her. And I want the car brought round. (*She goes out*)

ROBIN Oh, I don't know. She's not bad as mistresses go, do you think?

ROLAND She hasn't got into her stride yet. Where has she got all her smart clothes from?

ROBIN Man—where else? He's a pretty damned fool anyway.

ROLAND Hmmm . . . I'm not so sure. He's handy with his gun don't you think?

ROBIN Yes—so is she. She has no chocolate 'in the holster'. She fires live ammunition.

ROLAND These bloody women do. They don't care at whom they aim either. It's we men who have to be loyal and find bodyguards for them. Anyhow, Alice is getting a dose of it now.

ROBIN If you ask me she likes it.

ROLAND Maybe; but so far Rosemary has just been playing with her, beginning to find her feet. You watch—Alice will soon discover it's no game.

ROBIN Here they come.

ROSEMARY I shall want you to be here when I get back. When? How should I know? (*Goes out*)

P.A. The doctrine of Incarnation has a family resemblance to the idea of transmigration of souls. Hullo! Where has he sprung from?

(*A priest enters*)

ROLAND Can I do anything for you?

ROBIN Who do you want?

PRIEST Oh, no one in particular thanks. I heard someone mention incarnation and it sounded so interesting I dropped in. Do you mind? I'm from Ur—Ur-religion, not to be confused with Ur of the Chaldees, though similar.

ROLAND All religion is similar as far as I'm concerned.

PRIEST I was about to demur, but of course you are right—depending on whether you illuminate the similarities—

ROLAND —or darken the obscurities. Job got ticked off by the Highest Authority for darkening counsel. My sympathies were, on the whole, with Job.

MORIARTY Job had the right idea. If our P.A. friend was right to talk about the Devil Incarnate—and I think he was—Job may well have been on my side.

P.A. You are one of the figments of imagination.

MORIARTY All the best people are. Like God and the Devil. But what a time we all have! We rule the world of reality, as you scientists call it.

PRIEST We are well able to see the power of these figments of imagination—or objects of awe, superstitious awe. We had a very pretty religious ceremony, and still do, in the flourishing sacramental use of drugs in the attenuated religion that flourished in Tenochtitlan, and even today coexists with the products of nuclear fission. Of course we have not had quite the triumphs which we had when we buried the Royal Court of Ur in the Death Pit. But we hope to convert the uses of nuclear fission to a part in our services. We may yet achieve a triumph of piety with a real holocaust. Hiroshima was a trial run.

ROLAND I don't think I like you. Where did you get your dog collar from?

PRIEST (*looking down at the collar beneath his chin*) This? I don't really know. I had a dream and when I awoke I found I had this round my neck. Quaint, isn't it? I rather like it, so I kept it on.

ROBIN I don't like this fellow. He gives me the creeps.

ROLAND He reminds me of Rosemary—I don't like her either.

ROBIN I thought you were soft on her when she was your maid—before the war. I don't like your psycho friend.

ROLAND No friend of mine. I think he's a spy.

P.A. I'm sorry; shall I go? In a way you are right. I spend most of my life spying—not so devotedly as this man here (*indicating the priest)* but I suppose you could say I carry out one kind of spying. Only to help though.

ROBIN Who?

ROLAND Or what?

MORIARTY This is a job for Sherlock Holmes. Or perhaps Mycroft.

P.A. Or even me. But I suppose you would not accept my judgment.

ROLAND Would you accept the criminal being inserted as the investigator and judge?

P.A. Yes; I actually bring them into the investigation. At least, I do when they offer themselves.

ROLAND I bet you never get a conviction—except the kind that convinces you.

P.A. Surprisingly I do, though sometimes it is forestalled by an execution. The analysand executes himself.

ROLAND You mean the patient commits suicide?

P.A. That makes a long story short.

ROLAND The actual event is equally brief; a decapitation is the soul of wit.

P.A. Unfortunately not. The analysis can be very long.

ROBIN Isn't that always the case?

P.A. In the story I have in mind it had to take a long time because it always requires time to achieve success.

ROBIN I see—the victim bungles everything including, naturally, his death.

P.A. Sometimes.

ROLAND Why all the mystery? Cut out the dramatic suspense and come to the point.

ROBIN Give him a chance. I'm interested even if you aren't.

P.A. Mystery is real life; real life is the concern of real analysis. Jargon passes for psycho-analysis, as sound is substituted for music, verbal facility for literature and poetry, trompe d'oeil representations for painting. Real self-murder is not observed, and accidental suicide passes for the real thing which is planned, worked out in detail economically to create real effect. For this the patient—a good name for him—has first to suffer, in collaboration with psycho-analyst or family, to achieve success, to be worth murdering. The danger of death does not become acute until it is clear to every beholder that a resounding success is at hand. Then comes the not-so-blind Fury with the abhorred shears. This kind of man or woman resembles a self-murderer only superficially. 'Ay, in the catalogue ye go for men . . .'. Shakespeare was not deceived by the counterfeit; it would be a 'brave' psycho-analyst who thought he could not be deceived. But there are such people amongst us.

ROLAND Rosemary?

P.A. I have not so far observed anything that aroused in me a sense of being in the presence of such a murderer.

ROBIN You mean you would expect to feel a murder was about to be committed?

P.A. With such a patient I would expect to be aware of being in the presence of an unmistakably real emotional storm centre of a catastrophic kind. I consider my experience to be adequately sensitive to the 'direction' of the path the storm would be likely to pursue.

ROLAND Either you are being very modest or psycho-analysis is not much good.

P.A. Neither. Psycho-analysis is a fine instrument; psycho-analytic experience makes poor capacity for some things greater than yours.

ROLAND Thank you; you *are* complimentary.

P.A. I did not expect you to like my opinion, and your contempt is not lost on me. If I were prey to depression I would despair of your impenetrable complacency. It brings home to me how impossible it is for me to get the help of a critical attitude. It would help if I could rely on the purifying effect of austere criticism. I cannot. Fantastic admiration and complacent hostility, both are available in quantity and both are so much mental rubbish. I do *not* value either your praise or blame.

ROLAND Do you think I value yours?

P.A. I know you do not; in my opinion you cannot. It was the hundreds of cultured, educated, well-meaning 'yous' which constituted a liability that England could no longer support but sank under the weight. (*Rosemary enters unexpectedly and unnoticed. She sits and listens*)

ROLAND I thought you people were supposed to be impartial.

P.A. In the practise of my job I am; even when I am not engaged in my profession I retain habits of impartiality. Whatever the contingent circumstances, my natural impulse would incline me to justice rather than injustice. But that is not what *you* mean when you speak of impartiality—you mean partiality to your views. It is not natural to me to be partial to your views as far as I have reason to know them.

ROSEMARY Now shut up, both of you.

ROLAND (*coldly furious, to P.A.*) I'd be interested to know your views about *her*.

ROSEMARY I said *shut up*! I'm not a lady nor a psycho-analyst and I lay no claim to impartiality. I am the mistress of this house and I mean to be obeyed—or I shall have to use a language which you will understand even if you didn't hear it at school or in the mouths of women of your class.

ROLAND You'd be surprised.

ROSEMARY Get out—quick! (*The men go. Alice comes in*) Fetch me my slippers. And be quick about it. (*Alice curtseys and goes out*) She's a stupid idiot; but she's learning in spite of her upbringing. (*The room darkens*)

NINE

Figures slowly become discernible.

MORIARTY Hear that, Holmes?

SHERLOCK I would have been deaf indeed if I didn't.

MORIARTY I thought perhaps you were too high-class to be able to tune into that wave length.

SHERLOCK I learned a lot more than you think from Irene.

MORIARTY Adler? I always thought she was a lady.

SHERLOCK Then you've got another 'think' coming to you. Broaden your ideas, Moriarty. More things are wrought by crime than are dreamt of in your morality.

MORIARTY (*shaking his head regretfully*) You and Mycroft are indeed a sad loss to crime. You would both have done well in the world I have disgraced.

WATSON General practice is a wonderful training—you would be surprised to find how truthful people become under the impulse of impending disaster. It's better than any 'cure' or religion I know. What's-his-name Psycho wants to cure people; parsons want people to believe in a good, kind god that looks after them.

PRIEST Rubbish!

MORIARTY You surprise me. I thought you wanted people to believe in the goodness of God.

PRIEST In the words of Sherlock Holmes, 'Then you've got another "think" coming to you'. I am just a 'general' priest; as Watson says about general practice in medicine, it's a wonderful training—if you can stand it.

P.A. I am only just a general, run-of-the-mill psycho-analyst. That is a wonderful training.

PRIEST Don't misunderstand me—it has been a commonplace of religion that life itself is a wonderful training for what comes after. There's nothing new about *that*.

WATSON It is original if it is not only 'commonplace' but also 'believed'.

SHERLOCK My dear Watson! What do you mean by 'believed'? I don't like meaningless terms. I am a scientist.

MORIARTY He *thinks* he is.

WATSON You 'believed' in Irene Adler.

P.A. I didn't, don't and never will do. I think she is an idealized figure. That is not a belief. 'Idealized figure' is a technical, scientific term which I use to think with. I also use figures of fiction—imaginary figures. Even mathematicians use imaginary figures, imaginary numbers.

WATSON You must do a funny kind of mathematics.

PRIEST I suppose you would think the Trinity and 'Mono' theism a funny kind of mathematics. But you are unacquainted with the religious domain in which these mathematics, though difficult, are at least serviceable.

P.A. There are people who inhabit a state of mind in which they can find a use for neologisms, new mathematics, new arts.

ROLAND Good God! Nouveau art now.

ROSEMARY Get out, or learn to lie at my feet like a good dog.

WATSON Bark when you are bittern to.

SHERLOCK Hush! What's that booming noise?

BOY I don't hear any booming noise. That noise I hear is a bird.

MYCROFT Boy, your ears are too sharp! Or you too would wonder like brother Sherlock.

P.A. I don't hear it either.

ROSEMARY Too old—deafened by years of jargon. Blinded by facts and concepts and psycho-analysis. I had a friend who was a marvellous cook until she took a cookery course. After that she couldn't even boil an egg!

PRIEST I had a friend who was so holy he thought he was God and could think of nothing but that everyone should devote themselves to worshipping him. He even grew to think that God was interested in religion.

MYCROFT Old Moriarty thinks God is exclusively interested in stamping out crime.

ROSEMARY Roland thinks I make him lie at my feet so as to make it easier for me to stamp *him* out.

PRIEST 'How beautiful are the feet of them that preach the gospel of peace.'

ROSEMARY That is *not* what I use my feet for.

P.A. You would be surprised to hear how many erroneous ideas there are about the proper—and only—use for feet. All different; all obscuring more than they illuminate.

PRIEST That is true of what people call God. The psycho-analysts are the worst.

P.A. With respect—*no.*

ROBIN Aren't you always proving that God is a father figure?

P.A. I often attempt to show a particular person that he believes in God, and sometimes that he believes in a *particular* god—like fathers, or money, or even psycho-analysis. The analysand can make up his mind if I am correct—that is his affair, not mine. My beliefs I likewise wish to keep to myself or, at most, share with a particular chosen person.

ROBIN Yet you expect others to expose them to you!

P.A. I do nothing of the sort. I let it be known that I am available if anyone is disposed to discuss his ideas or expose his personality to me in my presence.

ROBIN (*doubtfully*) It sounds all right.

P.A. Unfortunately 'sounds', 'sights', sensuous impressions, and our interpretations, desires and memories of them are all we have.

ROBIN Isn't that enough?

P.A. It has appeared so—up to this hour and minute. But whether that is enough we can discuss in accordance with your and my greed, or lack of it.

ROBIN Why greed?

P.A. What alternative scale of measurement do you suggest?

ROBIN Religious, artistic or scientific integrity.

P.A. That seems to me to be pushing the answer back to a more distant version of greed.

ROBIN Do you mean religion is just greed?

P.A. From what you think you learnt about yourself and religion so far, what is your impression?

ROBIN I asked you yours.

P.A. Mine is of no importance whatever to anyone but me. Yours is of no importance whatever to me—except in so far as you want analysis. Then your ideas have a limited importance if I am to be sufficiently correctly informed to make an interpretation.

ROBIN Is that all?

P.A. Disappointing, isn't it.

ROBIN Why do you think I want analysis?

P.A. I don't.

ROBIN Then why are you behaving as if I did?

P.A. You are right to ask and to object since the conditions for psycho-analysis do not exist. Maybe I am falling into a trap contributed by my predilection for a psychological response—a hazard to which my profession makes me prone.

PRIEST You would make a good parson.

P.A. I could not even talk about religion except inadequately.

PRIEST There is more to religion than that.

P.A. Just as there is more to psycho-analysis than theories or talk about it.

PRIEST What?

P.A. Talk which is a prelude to it and talk which is psycho-analysis itself.

ROSEMARY Who decides which is which? You? Some institute? A royal charter?

P.A. Facts, I suppose; just as ultimately facts decide whether the sun goes round the earth or vice versa. I do not know what sort of fact is regarded as confirmatory.

PRIEST What standards do you use?

P.A. I used to believe that the army authorities told the public the truth about a battle till I went into action and compared the facts as known to me with the facts as announced by Army H.Q. For a long time I thought I knew the 'facts'. Later I inclined to the commonly expressed view, 'you can't believe a word you hear'. Poor authorities; they could not even say who had won the war!

(*Man enters and takes a seat near Rosemary. He appears confidently possessive. She is complacent*)

ROSEMARY Tell Alice to fetch my shawl.

ROLAND (*furiously, sitting up*) Who won Helen of Troy—

ROSEMARY Lie down!

ROBIN (*to Man*) What, no chocolate? (*Man ignores him and looks at Rosemary as if there were complete understanding between them*)

ROSEMARY (*to Man*) Tell Alice not to bother—she can go to bed.

ROBIN I feel acutely uncomfortable.

P.A. There is some emotional storm disturbing us. Leonardo might have drawn a sketch of turbulent water; verbally it would require a Shakespeare to do justice to—

ROBIN Yet you can feel it?

P.A. I know it, as I know you know it.

(*Rosemary and Man withdraw together. Roland gets up and dusts himself*)

ROLAND That bloody bitch! I could . . .

MORIARTY Allow me—what you need is a criminal act.

SHERLOCK Don't be a damned fool. I know Moriarty; don't listen to him.

MORIARTY Why not try the parson since Sherlock is prejudiced against me?

PRIEST No—not God or Devil at present.

P.A. Theology perhaps? It might provide breathing space before action.

MORIARTY (*mocking*) Shall we go and see the little dears have fun? Or perhaps we could listen from here.

P.A. Real fun requires a prelude of years of discipline as well as theories or dogma in art, science or religion.

ROLAND Oh, shut up! This is what discipline has brought us to!

P.A. Discipline, plus or minus: Lack of it and too much.

ROBIN How can it be two opposites at once?

P.A. In classical logic perhaps not. In reality—well, look at Leonardo's notebooks. Intuitionist mathematics may show the way.

ROLAND By that time someone will have died a violent death.

PRIEST Many millions already have. The barrier between these warring forces will be the first to be destroyed.

P.A. And what next to the first?

PRIEST Not the warring forces. They will be refreshed and renewed for further destruction.

ROBIN 'Methinks I see a mighty and puissant nation . . .'

PRIEST Not of human animals I think.

MORIARTY Microbes perhaps or—what did Berkeley call it?—ghosts of departed quantities, Newton's nascent increments.

P.A. Berkeley made fun of these objects whichever way they were growing less or more; even the object that did not exist, the object so small that it was the ghost of a departed increment, or what I describe as the increment of a 'ghost' coming into being according to the laws of change whether crescent or decay. All this is easier to formulate if it is talk about the decay or growth of a corporeal object, or a use of the language appropriate to corporeal objects for a purpose for which it was not intended—incorporeal objects, thoughts, minds, personalities.

ROLAND Has this talk got anything to do with our present state or is it a substitute for it, just to take up time?

P.A. It may be 'nothing' out of which something comes; the increment of a 'ghost of a departed increment', or the disappearing, declining something which is destined to disappear—or both.

SHERLOCK It can't be both—that's absurd.

ROBIN What about you and Moriarty? Are you figments of the imagination, ephemera which will entertain a child and then be forgotten? Or can you be ghosts of departed increments which are now ideas that are increasing by increments, destined to develop, like a grain of mustard seed in a famous story, and overtop the trees?

PRIEST What about the author of that story?

ROBIN As far as I'm concerned, 'it is a tale told by an idiot, full of sound and fury signifying nothing'.

P.A. What about the author of *that* story? How long before, in the words of the motion for debate of a certain dining club, 'The works of Shakespeare be not read'?

ROLAND That was a joke.

P.A. Suppose what was spoken in jest may have included some truth?

ROLAND Like Man's holster; it depends on whether it contained a gun or a chocolate bar.

P.A. It also depends on whether the contents of the holster are displayed to a starving or armed congregation. Man may once have been the witness and victim of a blockade. What mental seed was sown by that 'fact'?

ROBIN Anyone can see now that that was *not* a victory. 'We have scotched the snake, not killed it.'

P.A. Perhaps. But can anyone see what the victory was—its past, present and future? Rosemary is now the mistress of this house; Alice is her maid. Tomorrow—

ROLAND You take it very coolly. I don't.

P.A. I don't suppose you spent time thinking what you and Alice were teaching your maid. Now you both have a chance of seeing what she learned and you did not. I gather you feel that you would still be unlikely to learn anything from 'this talk', as you call it.

ROLAND I mean to murder that bitch and her boy friend.

P.A. You'll be wise to think, even if not talk, about how you mean to do it—before acting.

PRIEST I hope you are not inciting him to do this thing.

ROLAND I have heard you and your like make patriotic speeches.

PRIEST That is different.

ROLAND A man I was talking to had his brains blown out while he was speaking. Some person had taught him that that was meritorious and not murder.

P.A. Perhaps this is an instance where quantity of an action affects quality. Murder + increment becomes WAR; the ghost of departed increments becomes cowardice; 'quantities of discretion' do not become the 'better part of valour' but the worse part of cowardice.

ROBIN If you could tell me what were the smallest units of thought, the electrons or elemental particles—

P.A. —the genes of sexual activity?—

ROBIN —I could find a mathematics to match it.

ROLAND Sooner or later you'd have to do what bi-sexual animals do.

P.A. How soon? How late?

ROLAND Somehow I feel I've heard all this before.

MORIARTY Oh no! I've *never* heard people like you debate the ways and means of a 'crime passionelle'. You've progressed.

P.A. In what direction?

MORIARTY Don't ask me—ask the parson.

PRIEST When I was padre to Agamemnon I used to conform to the dictates of my religion. I couldn't conform to the dictates of Zeus because he had a sort of Olympian democracy, and all the gods used to fight like humans. Indeed, they often took part in human activities. Nowadays God rarely takes an unambiguous stand.

P.A. So?

PRIEST It becomes essential to have a priesthood to supply correct interpretations of God's apparently ambiguous statements. The ambiguity is not in God; it is in the formulation in which the priesthood represents the formulation which, in turn, represents the thing-in-itself.

P.A. I can see for myself that the priesthood consists of a lot of ordinary human beings. In my experience these ordinary human beings take ordinary good fathers and ordinary bad fathers; and from 'facts' of that kind derive pictures which are then put forward in the form of idols, poems, mystical formulations, as true, factually real gods and devils, Virgin Marys and furies.

PRIEST Sometimes these approximations are approximated to by God.

P.A. That is to say, God finds an ordinary human being like Jesus, and uses this ordinary—

PRIEST Not ordinary.

P.A. Well, extra-ordinary human being for purposes of incarnation, 'becoming flesh'. Is that right?

PRIEST That is not a bad summary of what a true priest might say if he wished to achieve a 'formulation' of Jesus. But no formulation can ever be anything but a substitute for Realization.

P.A. But this is all *we* try to show. We are not saying anything about God, or even God incarnate, when we say that a particular individual whom we are analysing is treating a father figure, which is already at a remove from an actual human father, as if this verbal image or idol *is* God.

PRIEST But that is precisely what you seem to say. 'Look, this God you worship is only some wildly distorted childhood view of your Dad. Therefore—God can't exist.'

P.A. Perhaps we do. But any analyst who talked like that would be *mis*-representing psycho-analysis—whatever he might be doing to the Ultimate Reality. A more nearly correct formulation would be, 'Your description of the god you worship may, at best, be a good model of your Dad—especially allowing for the fact that you were probably not much more than a baby when you first got that idea—but, however good or bad that model might be if you were trying to convey an idea of your father, it is quite unsuitable for providing me with an idea or a god which I can worship without insulting my intelligence.' This interpretation would not say anything about God, assuming He exists, but would represent psycho-analysis in such a way that the analysand could believe in it without having to outrage his intelligence. This is different from saying something ridiculous like, 'You believe that that magnificent ballplayer is God, *therefore* God does not exist'. That is not even logic, let alone psycho-analysis.

PRIEST My complaint is that psycho-analysts themselves are worshipping an idea as if it were a god worthy of worship. That 'parody' seems to me to be indistinguishable from most psycho-analysis I have heard of or experienced.

P.A. You may have been unlucky. Perhaps these 'psycho-analysed' people you have met have also been unlucky—in their parson. Debased religion attracts debased psycho-analysis and makes both more debased.

ROBIN How is Man's chocolate bar doing?

ROLAND How is Man's gun furthering his love-making?

ALICE Both doing very well. That 'pearl of great price' is artificial.

ROLAND There's nothing wrong with the swine—*they* are real enough.

MORIARTY Swine usually are.

SHERLOCK How unlike, how *very* unlike the term 'love'.

WATSON Holmes, what you say sounds like our parson friend.

ROBIN 'Friend'? 'Comrade'? Haven't I heard those words before?

ROLAND I have heard the phrase 'pearl of great price' used by many—and (*looking at Alice*) of the pearl being artificial.

P.A. There is nothing new about artificiality. The term derives from uses in which man occupies some place in the chain. The pearls are artificial. In spite of Roland's observation it cannot be assumed that the swine are genuine—or the price paid for the pearls. The artificiality of the pearls, the swine and the price are all surprisingly well-matched sometimes.

PRIEST What do you think of the price of psycho-analysis?

P.A. My fees are dictated by what I need.

PRIEST Who decides what you need?

P.A. I do—who else?

PRIEST Then the fee is dictated by your greed, great or small?

P.A. Yes. What do *you* charge for your services?

PRIEST Nothing.

P.A. Someone has paid for your food or you would not have survived. Have you always been supported by the Establishment? Who paid for the ceremonial at Ur? It seems that many paid with their lives.

PRIEST The king paid with his life for the bigotry of the doctor.

P.A. Was it his bigotry or his religion?

PRIEST He believed in his medicine; it was almost his god. He worshipped his king and queen—this side of what you would call idolatry. They told me he thought the king was dying—

P.A. —and you and your like told people he would survive, and if they went into the pit with his body and were buried they would go to Heaven.

PRIEST Heaven? Nonsense! That idea has only grown up during the last few thousand years.

(*Rosemary fades in*)

ROSEMARY (*luxuriously, admiring her well-shod foot*) *This* is *my* idea of Heaven. I would hardly have dared to believe that I would live to call my mistress and hear her say 'Ma'am' to me when I gave her orders.

P.A. And does it come up to expectations?

ROSEMARY Yes, although there are one or two improvements which I mean to carry out.

P.A. What about Alice? What about Man?

ROSEMARY Man? I don't expect any trouble from him. But why Alice? I've got her where I want her and what happens to her from now on matters not the least—she can go and seek a psycho-analyst. You perhaps—if she can find enough artificial fees!

PRIEST What of God in His Heaven?

ROSEMARY He ought to be all right. It's His heaven. If he wants to be inscrutable that's his affair. I'm not interfering like a psycho-analyst—or even a priest. Let him get on with it, *I* say. I didn't interfere with Chalcas or Juno or Jehovah, and I'm not starting now. This suits me and if it doesn't suit Alice or you or this psycho-analyst, that's your affair. I enjoy being smartly dressed and I like feeling that you all have good reason to fear me.

P.A. 'The glass, the cruel looking-glass.'

ROSEMARY What's that?

P.A. A poem I remember. I was not thinking of you and your appearance so much as of how you reflect the England I lived in and how it then looked to you. Not a flattering portrait, but true as far as appearances go.

ROSEMARY They go a very long way.

P.A. We—particularly I—have wanted in psycho-analysis to nourish an instrument, analogous to a mirror of the physical world, which would make it possible for each of us human individuals to see himself.

ROLAND So far it only seems true to analogy in that you see what you want to see.

P.A. I fear so.

PRIEST God made man in his own image. Man was not only quick to return the compliment, but it does not appear to be a flattering reflection.

P.A. I thought that as a priest you would consider the human world reflected an unflattering image of God because of the defects of the mirror; it would not have occurred to me that a priest might think the reflection unpleasing because of its truth.

PRIEST I do think it is due to the defects of the mirror; but I can see that the judgment of the mirror image is unwelcome—both for what it shows and for showing it. Who is to say God is correctly judged by his creatures?

ROBIN (*to Roland*) I give up. I vote you and I go into committee of ways and means.

ROSEMARY I shall give you both my photograph. You can all meet here next week. Now, good-night.

(*They dismiss*)

TEN

ROSEMARY (*alone*) She was a good mother. If she hadn't taken up with whoring she could never have given me bread. Nor would I have learnt the art of how to make sex pay without paying the price of gonorrhea and later the ravages of neuro-syphilis. Poor Mum! But . . . How happy, how cheerful she was! I wonder why? Does it tickle to feel the spirochaetes as they spire and burrow in the convolutions of one's brain? She certainly used to laugh immoderately as she heard the bombs crash amongst the palaces and the filthy, crowded streets of London; till at last . . . I wonder who it was who released the atom bomb that brought peace, the blessed meek-eyed Peace whose reign had been so long delayed by these filthy men? I wonder what blackguard sired me? I sometimes think my profound morality and sense of duty must have derived from him. How else could I have had such strong ideas of what was pure and godly and of good report? I could never have become such a smooth hypocrite without it. How she would have enjoyed it! How it would have warmed her heart if she could have seen how her little girl would turn out when she apprenticed me to service—so as to save me from ever depending for my bread on the dangers of whoredom. She used to tell me tales of things she knew about men—very frightening some of them were too.

One day the police came and took away the corpse of her friend who had been battered to death. It was exciting; they caught the murderer. Some of my friends showed me bits out of the paper. 'What is a sexual partner?' I asked Mum one day. 'Wherever did you hear words like that?' she said. 'Oh, it was in a piece of newspaper I bought my fish and chips in', I lied. She didn't believe me and I'm sure she could never have understood what that clever arse of a psycho-analyst said 'sexual partner' was. But *she* could have told *him* that was what happened to your girl friend when a respectable public school aristocrat bit off your nipples and thrashed the last spark of life out of you! I heard her screaming. Not for me! I said. Old 'chocolate bar' and his friends can rape this country—so what? Let them eat cake! He can think himself lucky to have the privilege of licking my feet and passing his winnings over to me! Love? The God of love my shepherd is, His goodness faileth never. Well, He's not done so badly for me. Let's see how Rosemary's skivvy, Alice, gets on worshipping at His shrine. I could tell that parson fellow a thing or two about God? Perhaps he learnt a bit since Ur. I wonder if P.A. knows about sexual perversion—I'll ask him.

It's getting darker and darker. The Dawn in Britain . . . When? How? They say it's always darker before the dawn. Alice thinks I'm in love with Man; perhaps she's right. I'm no more in love with him than I am with her, but I'm no less in love either. Love is like honour; Falstaff didn't think much of it. Perhaps women regard love more importantly than honour, and men the other way round—like picking up and battering down whores. Dictionaries should state masculine or feminine. Love (masculine) . . .; Love (feminine) . . .; Honour (masculine) . . .; Honour (feminine) . . .; I suppose we could leave it to Priest or P.A. or Leonardo or Moriarty or Sherlock to fill in the definitions.

How dark it is! 'Lord, with me abide.' I had no idea I was so religious. I must be feeling cold.

Alice adores me; that's clear from what I can make her do. I haven't been taught how to be a goddess, but I can make a better job of it than she can; better goddess than I ever was a skivvy. I had better not make any of *her* mistakes. I have to provide her with food and lodging; not too much or too little. How easy to say, but how much is 'too much' and 'too little'? So far I've only gone by exactly what she gave me—she's wearing my skivvy's outfit. She's pretty and the darned black stockings, carefully repaired old rubbish of mine, look quite nice on her. She's a fool—compared with me. What if she learns? I saw Roland looking at her intently the other day. So far I've got Man where I want him. I could sack her of course; but I don't want to lose my maid. There are still things she can teach me. I could teach her a thing or two about being a whore, but goodness knows what she might learn. She probably knows about V.D. But—it makes me laugh when I think of it—she didn't know how to stop Tom from overpowering her. Maybe it would be best to get rid of her. If she leaves too late she won't be any worse off than my Mum. It *is* dark—and I'm sure it's getting colder. I could send for her—what then? I could tell her I'm cold and leave her to 'get on with it'. Why should I tell her what to do? She could use her initiative .... Suppose she has too much? Moriarty says Lady Macbeth sparked off a conflagration. Am I falling asleep? I get such queer, jumbled thoughts. It's *cold*. I must get into bed.

No wonder I'm cold. Banquo felt the dagger Macbeth saw—this is worse than Alice's Wonderland, Alice's attic. I keep falling asleep and having the qweirdust qualfactions of Mayqueen me mother toady today. Is that Rosemary sinking? Spirochaete, spirochaete/where have you been?/Up the puss octo puss/2C the Queen./ Ashes to ashes and Dust to Dust/If the booze don't get you the sex urge must.

ALICE Did you call me, Ma'am?

ROSEMARY Yes, my feet are cold. You're cold? It's your job to keep warm; I might need you.

* * *

PRIEST (*alone*) He's a fool of course. But you can never be sure with these fads. Who would have thought that tomb robbing would become so popular? And so respectable—even aristocrats engage on it; very scientific of course; Lord Carnarvon, like his scientific cover Howard Carter, defied the Curse of the Pharaohs. But the curse still exists to keep these interlopers on the hop. How Moriarty would laugh! I must be going to sleep—what's Moriarty got to do with it? Oh yes, I know—'Curst be he who disturbs my bones.' Shakespeare? Did he write that doggerel? Who is to say that psycho-analytic shamans, frauds and humbugs have not some dangerous truth concealed in the humbug? Whether to take arms against the sea of troubles with the poet and by opposing end them; or be ended by them like the omnipotence of Canute, ended by his own scientific addiction? Shall I take up with psycho-analysis and the scientific method, or with psycho-analysis and religion? Really it's unending. Only yesterday I was having to decide between Bernard de Sahagun, Montezuma and the Pope. It went on and on till by the time I had persuaded the Supreme Court—in the name of religious tolerance for Heaven's sake!—to legalize our Aztec communion wine, human sacrifice (which was so picturesque and amusing) was in eclipse. I remember it was amusing to see Palinurus so completely fooled, and his boss Aeneas likewise, that the fleet came near to being wrecked by the Sirens and their rocks. Horace, although he claimed to have escaped, must have been nearly drowned by Pyrrah. He did not fail to hang up his dripping weeds as a tribute to God. The 'scientific black-guards', as Santayana called them, failed to recognize the significance of the costumery painted on the wall of the tomb of my follower in Tarquinia. God works in a mysterious way his wonders to perform. This psycho-analyst here—who would guess that he of all people should retain enough modesty to respect, even be awed by, God? The glory of the God of psycho-analysis is declared by the fearsome, inartistic architecture of Cinematic grandeur! All that stuff of Queen Shub-ad—I told her she *could* take it with her to the tomb and she did. Will you? won't you? will you? won't you join the dance of Death? Archbishop Havelock Ellis, and his forerunner and prophet Krafft-Ebing, wrote a piece about it. How impressed they were by their discoveries, and how their discoveries impressed school children! But am I impressed? Perhaps; but it may be unrealistic to imagine that anyone living so near what he serves would be impressed. 'The Heavens declare the glory of God'; but the Krakatoa committee of the Royal Society of the death pit at Ur did not understand the language in which they clothed the glory they had felt. Who knows? 'Ils gisent là sans voix . . .' sans everything. We are too minute to contain grandeur. The meek shall inherit the earth, so perhaps the microbes, waiting in the wings to devour the flesh that a bountiful God will provide for them, are ready for the call to take over the earth.

I do not know or feel impelled to revere the matrix, DNA, helix from which God is preparing to emerge. It is curious that we do not worship the stone from which the Michelangelo will call us out. We priests have been opposed to stone images; even the stones we call precious are deprecated as objects of adoration. Why? The mistress of this house sees herself as an object of adoration in the setting taken from the 'maid'—whom she dispossessed. She is engaged in dispossessing Man, who has himself participated in gaining possession of the 'jewel' set in the precious sea. What is that but another 'stone'? Is this psycho-analyst any more than a tomb robber about to stage a grand 'resurrection' with a Vatican in which another vicar is to display his effulgence? I had better ask him when I see him next. I could confront him at our next kitchen meeting—Rosemary permitting. The probability is that he would not know or—hullo—here we are!—or are we here? If so, where? Must be going to sleep . . .

The skivvy here—Alice, they call her—important once—had important relatives like the Trojan women before Troy fell. Alice was the mistress once—not bad-looking now. I caught her blubbing about something—she said it was a cold—as if I care—or anyone else . . . It's the job of the down-trodden to be miserable. I'll ask the P.A. what he thinks; I expect he'll say he cures them. How? How do you cure the rich? I wonder if he has an answer to Shakespeare's question about the diseased mind—he's sure to say something like 'get married', or 'go on a cruise'. *My* answer? Get rich—on the winning side. Funny how none of these people sees how important the winning religion is. Queen Shub-ad thought she was going to an improved life; she would have been surprised—and the rest of the Court too—to discover that they were to become Museum Exhibits and the Priests, Curators! . . . must tell Rosemary never to allow anyone to cremate her if she wants everlasting life. Horace's recipe was to find a poet and then, like Lollius, be pickled for ever—stuck in a chunk of immortal verse like a fly in resin. Shaw hoped Doughty-wise progress would achieve for him a place in the halls of literary fame. Seven pillars of whizdom come in Urth as in the rubbish dump in Zig-ur-wrath to come. It's becoming what passes for light in this somnus-forsaken house, and Lethe-wards had sunk. It spreads aloft but not below if the nectar doesn't flow.

Come in Alice, come in. Take off those ghastly rags.

ALICE No.

PRIEST Yes—or I'll rip them off.

ALICE Don't! Look—I'll have to darn that.

PRIEST I don't give a darn—take that stuff off!

ALICE No. I'll call the . . . call the . . . (*weeps*)

ELEVEN

PRIEST Where's the P.A? I've had a horrible dream. God! I've forgotten it already!

P.A. It's not a dream. We are just going to start our weekly meeting.

PRIEST How did I get here then? Have I been walking in my sleep? It feels a bit like that. (*To Alice*) You have torn your dress, haven't you?

ALICE Where? So I have. More darning. *She* is very particular.

ROSEMARY I don't care in the least—so long as you are neatly turned out when I want you.

ALICE That's what I meant; I didn't mean—

ROSEMARY That will do. Go and darn it.

ALICE (*submissively*) Yes, Miss.

MAN Don't let her be insolent, darling. Dismiss her if she argues.

ROSEMARY She won't argue with *me*. Well, who's going to start?

PRIEST I wanted to ask P.A. something, but I have forgotten it . . . Rosemary . . . forget it! Who's next?

ROLAND I was thinking about Man's chocolate bars. Would you think them much use in war?

MAN Of course, most powerful in war. In peace people don't know how to use them. The division which was supposed to be defending this area surrendered without firing a shot.

ROLAND That was because it was starving and its commander knew that the rest of your army had landed in overwhelming force. You could hardly claim that to the credit of your chocolate bars.

MAN I do; not a particularly brilliant example, of course, but if our commander hadn't used that weapon we would have had endless trouble. Our mistress, Rosemary, is brilliant.

ROLAND She didn't have command of your hordes; she depended on their victory.

MAN When your lot had surrendered she knew how to *use* our victory. Brilliant, I call it. You saw how she just sent her mistress out of the room to smarten herself up.

ROBIN She has *you* where she wants you too.

MAN It is possible.

ROSEMARY I spent years learning to do much with little. Alice will learn—the hard way—after I have finished with her. Pity she hasn't got a brat as my Mum had, but I expect Tom or Priest will see to that.

ROBIN You are a bit coarse aren't you?

ROSEMARY No—realistic. I don't bear her any ill will; she can come for my cast-offs when I have done with them.

ROBIN Your cast-off man too?

ROSEMARY (*angrily*) I wouldn't go out of my way to keep any trash I've had hanging round me.

ROBIN Does that include Alice?

ROSEMARY Alice is right where she is—while I am satisfied. When I'm not she will have to go. Where? Where did my Mum have to go? I don't know or care. At present she's quite pretty; what you men are good for I've no idea.

ROBIN We had to fight.

ROSEMARY You had to win and that you failed to do.

ROBIN We can still try.

MAN I doubt it—and don't forget I am taking great risks allowing these meetings which Rosemary encourages.

ROBIN Who could know?

ROSEMARY You, Robin, the P.A., Priest—even Alice. Tell lies and you don't even have to spy.

ROBIN You're right. You put ideas in my head!

ROSEMARY Be careful what you do with those ideas. *I* had to keep my mouth shut—

ROLAND In free England? Nonsense!

ROSEMARY Free England?! Roland, you must be a fool.

P.A. Being aware of facts has, I am sure, had an effect on me analogous to that of food on my physique. The experience is 'like' being changed—as one ultimately feels changed if one survives.

ROSEMARY That begs the question. Priest believes one survives even after death; don't you?

PRIEST Survival after death is a belief which has undergone many transformations. May I ask to which belief you refer?

ROLAND Alice has changed since she became a servant in her own house. Rosemary has changed since she became the mistress here.

PRIEST Alice worships Rosemary; I have known many women who have been god to other women. In Ur of the Chaldees—

ROLAND You are surely not going to maintain that in those barbarous days there was a standard *we* should emulate?

PRIEST *Those* barbarous days? I have lived through many civilizations, yet I wonder if I shall survive this. I daresay there is some saving quality even in today's barbarism—'civilization', you'd call it.

ROBIN I don't call the 'saving quality' civilization.

MAN You are prejudiced since I and a couple of my friends used you for shooting practice. We only ringed you with heavy-calibre bullets—they weren't explosive. *And* we weren't incompetent.

ROSEMARY (*to Priest*) What about God? You were saying . . .?

PRIEST I wondered why Robin and Roland imagine religion or culture were backward in those days. I have always believed in God and I have always worn the costume appropriate to the prevailing fashions.

ROLAND In my school days we sang a song about the Vicar of Bray.

ROBIN So did we; I thought it stupid and not half so funny as the author seemed to think.

PRIEST It wasn't funny and it was certainly stupid. As I began to be aware of God's consistency and constancy I tried to be constant and consistent myself. I would lack respect for my contemporaries if I stuck rigidly to one appearance when fashions had changed. I should feel I was disturbing the peace; so I wear the prevalent—

ROLAND —religion! This is the most frank concession I have ever heard.

PRIEST You are too hasty, my friend. I do not consider that these 'vestments' are religion.

P.A. It may be easy for you, who seem to have some gift of immortality, to know religion from within. I and my friends here have to do arduous and austere labours before we can appreciate what seems to you to be so simple. The very skill with which the great artist makes something clear may mislead the reader. Virgil's eclogues, particularly the Fourth, have been interpreted in the light of subsequent events to foretell the birth of Christ. Yet it seems more likely to refer to Augustus Caesar's heir. When I was a small boy I used to think Palinurus was treated outrageously by Somnus; it did not occur to me that Virgil might *believe* that God could behave as Somnus did.

PRIEST 'Not cricket!' in short. You must have found it difficult to believe that God was not as serious about cricket as you were.

P.A. I loathed the game, but some have adored it and 'worshipped' the god who was captain of the school team. That I think is natural—at the time. Our problem arises not because these ideas are wicked or wrong, but because they are active achronically and are the fount of action. Therefore we think it advisable to display the 'god' in whom the person believes; it may make it possible, by comparison with other ideas, to moderate the force of the primeval fount.

ROLAND How do you know that you do not, by exposing such an idea, render it still more powerful? Or conversely, undermine faith in God?

P.A. Alas! We cannot be sure that the individual does not in fact use the analytic experience in just that way.

ROBIN So you admit that psycho-analysis can do harm?

P.A. It does neither harm nor good; but the person may use the experience for whatever purpose he will. After all, if a surgeon heals a thief or murderer he makes them more efficient, but not more moral.

ROLAND Nobody expects him to do so.

P.A. Believe me they do! The analyst is often held responsible for the behaviour of a man or woman who has at some time been to a psycho-analyst.

PRIEST We have the same difficulty with religious people.

P.A. Do you help your believers to see what kind of god they follow? Or do you assure them that they are good people who are supporting the true God?

PRIEST Of course we try to show them what gods they follow. People try to serve both God and Mammon.

P.A. Has it any effect?

PRIEST In the course of the centuries, yes.

P.A. 'In the course of centuries'? There may not be centuries available. That is why we regard analytic procedure as essential if people are to understand what beliefs they hold and by which they are held.

PRIEST Do you find they understand—more quickly?

P.A. Sometimes I think they do, but not often. Nevertheless psycho-analysis enables the psycho-analyst to learn something and even to pass it on. There are occasions when a resistance is surmounted with astounding speed; a number of facts display their relationship for the first time. It is almost a revelation.

PRIEST You use a term which is part of our technical equipment.

P.A. I thought you would notice that. I would that we could make clear both the verbal fact you mention and the psychic reality which corresponds. The concentration of meaning would require the concision which can be achieved in music or painting. Would my analysand undergo the work necessary to understand if I could achieve such precision? Audiences rarely listen to music or look at pictures; still less do they think it worth while listening to what an analyst says.

PRIEST These difficulties have been familiar to the religious for many centuries. Music, painting, poetry, vestments gorgeous and austere—all have been used as auxiliaries.

P.A. I have found that the auxiliary can easily be transferred by the receptor from the periphery to the centre. Messages intended to convey profound truth—*The Iliad, The Aeneid, Paradise Lost, The Divine Comedy*—have all in turn become famous as gorgeous settings for the precious 'stone' which is outshone by its attendant splendour. Krishna warned Arjuna that he might not be able to survive the revelation of the godhead which he, Krishna, was prepared to vouchsafe. Dante has only rarely found a reader able to discern the vision to which he points in Canto XXXI of the *Paradiso*. Milton's mind was over-shadowed by a doubt whether he could pass beyond the 'evil days' on which he had fallen; it was indeed his tragedy.

PRIEST The most profound expression of despair known to us was, 'Why has thou forsaken me?'

P.A. This discovery is one which all are afraid to make. A theory that the human animal is not going to call on God to do for him what he must do for himself in loneliness and despair cannot be formulated; any formulation is a substitute for that which cannot be substituted.

ROLAND Do you suggest that *that* psycho-analytic interpretation is the explanation of Christ's reported call on the Cross?

P.A. You show that I have failed to make it clear that I attach the utmost importance, in the practice of analysis, to the presence of analyst and analysand at the same time and in the same place in conditions in which the consciously discernible facts are available to both people. These are the *minimum* conditions, not the maximum. Only *then* does psycho-analysis become an activity open to the two participants. You suggest that I am making a statement about events reported to have taken place almost two thousand years ago; if you believe that to be the gist of my remarks, what might you not say about my opinions when I am not present to defend them?

ROBIN I don't see why you are angry. Roland's mistake seems to me to be natural and understandable. *I* had not observed that he was misrepresenting you.

P.A. As I see the situation I would be lacking in proper feeling if I were not angry.

ROLAND That's your opinion.

P.A. That is what I said. Whose else should it be? Yours? Well, why not? I hope I am not doing anything to obstruct your freedom.

ROLAND Your answer is hostile and I can detect, even though you may not, impatience, sarcasm and irony in it too.

P.A. I shall not deny or confirm your observations; I think you want me to be so impressed by the facts that you observe, that I would not dare to make an interpretation at all.

ROSEMARY Like your interpretation of Man's holster.

P.A. I still think it would be wiser to interpret it as containing a gun than to accept his offer to interpret it as containing chocolate.

ROBIN & ROLAND So do we.

P.A. We have many facts available; if we interpret each one in isolation, the facts and the interpretations do not amount to much; taken together, the 'gist' can be interpreted. The Mathematical sum cannot be mathematically expressed, yet the 'gist' can be.

ROLAND What is your definition of 'gist'?

P.A. I have none, because a definition would add to an already overwhelming vocabulary of formulations that seem to be precise where no precision exists. If you listened to my talking you could probably feel that the 'gist' of what I meant when I used the word 'gist' was a constant conjunction of your impressions. Your interpretation of my communications might be something you could formulate.

ROLAND Can you give me an example of something—an interpretation say—which expresses the 'gist' of an idea?

P.A. I was called to see a patient who was suspected of being 'schizophrenic'. As I approached his bed I was aware of a flurry of movement. When I reached his bed he had hidden himself beneath a blanket so that only one eye was visible. With this eye he observed me intently. He maintained silence for weeks—it may have been a month or more.

ROLAND Yes, but can't you give me the 'gist' of your definition? I don't want to be rude, but our time here is very limited.

P.A. That is why I said 'intently'. Sometimes, as in this instance, the gist of an experience may take a long time to grasp. An eye seen in isolation conveys nothing; seen for some weeks as I saw it, 'intently' is a fair summary of what I saw—the 'gist' of the experience. Psycho-analysis may convey the 'gist' of what two people are doing if both are satisfied that the name 'psycho-analysis' conveys enough meaning for immediate needs. But what I want to communicate to you would require other conditions and time which you will not spare.

ROLAND Go ahead then. What about your dotty patient?

ROBIN Have we time to discuss dotty patients?

ROSEMARY Yes, I'm interested.

ROLAND These aren't the days for pursuing interests.

ROSEMARY Not for you perhaps. When I was the servant here I never had time for anything that might have interested me. You can think yourself lucky that I allow you and the rest to participate when I am following my interest. Go on P.A. Alice—you may stay in case I want you; it may do you good.

P.A. One day, after I had given many interpretations apparently without effect, the man suddenly said, 'I want help'.

ROBIN I suppose you thought that was the result of your interpretations.

P.A. The only result that I *know* about was that I felt hopeless; the minimum conditions did not exist for psycho-analysis as I understood it and as I had been taught it. My faith in the interpretations was being eroded to a point where I could hardly summon up enough interest to persist. But I reminded myself that my duty was to the patient.

ROLAND It sounds most laudable.

ROSEMARY Never mind him—go on P.A.

P.A. I wondered if my interpretations were some use after all. I suppose this showed for when I asked him what help he wanted he at once shut up. My heart sank; I felt I would have to go on for weeks, months, years, and then maybe he would repeat his remark.

ROLAND What about your definition? How many months before you get *that* out?

ROSEMARY Alice, I can see now what a terrible pair you and Roland were as master and mistress. Were all your governing class friends as bad as this? I prefer to have you where I want you.

MAN Shall I shoot him?

ROSEMARY No darling—not yet.

ROLAND Darling! My God—not yet!

ROBIN Did you hear that? Shoot chocolate bars!

MAN I didn't say I always wore chocolate bars.

ALICE Rosemary, don't—

ROSEMARY Alice, this is not a game. I want a servant who knows her place. That will do for to-night.

(*They disperse*)

* * *

(*That night. Roland and Robin whispering*)

ROLAND It's grim.

ROBIN We had better do him in.

ROLAND And then? We must plan ahead. Rosemary is a traitress.

ROBIN Not a traitress—a realist. Hullo! Who's this?

ROLAND I'm going to sleep on it.

ROBIN Who are you?

CLYTEMNESTRA If you had learned your lessons in that school of privilege where you and your fellow loafers made no use of the opportunities spread before you, you would not now be asking that question.

ROBIN I don't know what you are talking about—

CLYTEMNESTRA Don't dare to boast of it to me. A king once learned the unwisdom of believing that a mother could forgive a father's insufferable treachery in so easily sacrificing his daughter. I had to wait, but I taught him what a mother's love was—maternal love turned to marital fidelity.

ROBIN You are just a bad dream.

CLYTEMNESTRA If you want to wake from it you had better be careful how you speak to me. I won't give you a chance to learn the lessons Agamenmon failed to learn. Don't you want to live?

ROBIN Not much—only long enough to display a father's love.

CLYTEMNESTRA A father's love! Why, you have not even learned of God the Father's love for his only begotten son. Your saints rotted your mind. You should have used it to think with—not to fool around on a cricket field.

ROBIN I didn't, you blood-stained bitch! Take your hands off my throat.

ROLAND Wake up you fool—what do you think you're doing?

ROBIN Sorry—must have been dreaming. It was frightful . . . a murderous woman . . . I think . . .

ROLAND Go to sleep. Rosemary has upset you. I'll settle her hash later.

ROBIN You didn't make her pregnant did you? The woman in the dream had some grouch about the classics—I think.

ROLAND Don't—it's bad for you. Go to sleep.

ROBIN What dreams may come?

ROLAND Shut up, Hamlet!

TWELVE

ROLAND Our weekly meeting again?

ROBIN You have been warned—by the boss. Sometimes I think my mind is going.

ROLAND I shouldn't worry too much about that—you haven't got one!

ROBIN I have the most frightful dreams. Last night I dreamed of wandering through a field of cowslips and the scent was heavenly. It grew dark; a woman clouted me behind the knees and made me drop to the ground because she had severed my muscles with a sharp axe; she said I ought to have known they were primroses. I asked where she had learned her classics, but she threatened another stroke with the axe. She said I ought to have known it was botany—not classics. What was classics? What was botany? That's just what I said. Didn't she know it was zoology, I wanted to ask, but she sliced off my left side with a limb I think. She seemed very absent minded.

ROLAND You've got Rosemary on the brain—sharp but not very sensitive. Sh! Here she is!

ROSEMARY What are you talking about?

ROLAND Robin was mentioning that he wasn't sleeping very well. I wondered if he was having bad dreams.

ROBIN I didn't remember any.

ROSEMARY Perhaps they weren't dreams. My dog sometimes yelps and his paws twitch as if he were having a dream—chasing rabbits perhaps. Do you think dogs dream?

ROLAND Of course they do.

ROSEMARY Do you think they think? But here are the experts. (*To Priest*) Do dogs have immortal souls? If not, why not?

PRIEST We used to regard them as unclean animals.

ROSEMARY Couldn't they be washed in the blood of the lamb? Or are lambs unclean beasts? What do you say, P.A.?

P.A. This is not really my department; I am only concerned with the way individuals think. Whether they are right to think or not is the concern of people who know the facts.

PRIEST You surprise me. Surely it is a matter which concerns you if a man comes to you because he thinks he has a bird's claw and not a hand.

P.A. It concerns me that he *thinks* so. It concerns me that you think you have a hand and assume that a baby has a hand. But I rely on embryologists who tell me that the flesh and bony structure called a hand was not always like that, but is a transformation of a mass of cartilage and fat which it was in infancy. Falling back on my present-day knowledge as a doctor I assume that I can safely compare the one statement with another and use my anatomical and physiological ideas as a standard or norm. If a man says he has an eagle's claw where I think he has a hand, I may wonder why he has one idea rather than another. He is free to think he has a claw and to go to see an ornithologist or a physician or surgeon; that is *his* concern. It is *my* concern if he says that he has an *idea* that he has a claw and also believes it is a hand. If he wishes, I am prepared to discuss these conflicting ideas which cause him discomfort.

PRIEST Have you no qualms? No misgivings?

P.A. Many. They are 'facts' with which I am familiar: I am familiar with doubt and some philosophical theories about doubts. I know what it is to say, 'I do not know', or, 'I am uncertain', and to find someone even less qualified than I ready and eager to claim 'certainty' and to be received with enthusiasm. In the practice of psycho-analysis it is common to meet with those who say it is rubbish and proclaim knowledge of the truth. You and others who think like you often claim Divine support for their view.

PRIEST You and others who think like you often claim scientific authority for *their* view—sometimes in direct opposition to a religious view that there is a God.

P.A. Perhaps the resemblance that your experience bears to mine springs from the fact that both schools of thought are supported by mere human beings. A 'scientific view' only means one which claims loyalty to truth.

PRIEST Similarly, loyalty to God should be indistinguishable from loyalty to truth.

P.A. 'Should be'—so easily said; so difficult to practise. Man was offering just now to shoot Roland and Robin in the service of our hostess—Beauty, as I may not inaccurately call her.

ROSEMARY Damned fool!

PRIEST Is that a religious or scientific expression? A poet once said, 'Beauty is truth, truth Beauty'. Many disciplines claim allegiance. 'Ay, in the catalogue ye go for men.' Many gods have been put forward as worthy of the devotion of mankind.

P.A. Perhaps I may claim the Licence of a Fool in the court of Beauty.

ROLAND Look out! You'll qualify for Man's bullet!

ROSEMARY I have told him he is *not* to shoot—yet!

P.A. Thank you—so far. I think that the devotees of Art, Science and Religion are agreed in principle. Whichever one of the main divisions of humanity claims our adherence, we claim to follow truth. In principle—agreement. In practice—the particular, the precise—disagreement. The 'individual' often conflicts with the general. He may seek membership of the group or category of discipline because he wishes to seek shelter, as Freud said, under the cover of a famous and prestigious name. In time no doubt the fraud will declare itself, but it may then be too late. For example, Man may terminate the discussion with murder—perhaps I should say 'shooting', not murder.

MAN You had better.

PRIEST Surely you are threatening him!

MAN I don't need to—and indeed I am surprised at my moderation.

P.A. You do not need to be—when you are armed with a gun and with the 'authority' it confers. I have long been aware of my vulnerability even when power was in the hands of men and women of my own group.

PRIEST I wouldn't minimize my danger at any time. My changes of allegiance have been likened to those of the Vicar of Bray because I do not put my trust in a god that conforms to human rules of permanence and stability. I do mistrust the impermanence and instability of whoever and whatever is the current fashion in gods. I do not know the 'language' in which they should be dressed or addressed. Even Milton confessed an inability to find some phrase by which, 'without blame', he could Hail the Heavenly Light.

P.A. You claim experience not only of your feeling but of some 'source' which is outside and independent of you. Although I have no such experience I do claim to detect in myself, and sometimes in others, sources that do not require any arcane or esoteric reality such as I understand you to mean by 'God'.

PRIEST To say, 'what I mean', is an adequate phrase when it is employed, as here, in discussion about God. But it is not adequate to the religious experience itself. There is no scientific or aesthetic or even religious experience which can provide any human with a method of address to God. *That* reality, the Godhead, has to provide the approach to Himself which the individual must use.

P.A. I am concerned with the human mind or personality; in that domain I can only, with some difficulty, formulate descriptions of objects which are comprehensible in terms employed at various times during the individual life. It is not inappropriate to say that a small boy 'worships' some hero of the playing fields, or that an adult 'worships' golf, bridge, the stock market, or some article of food or drink.

PRIEST That can easily be seen to be false.

P.A. Not easily at all; it may require years to achieve even this limited aim.

PRIEST But don't you think that when you have demonstrated

all the multitudes of 'false gods', there may yet be discernible 'God' that is not false?

P.A. Certainly. I have no difficulty in accepting that such a possibility could exist. But as far as my limited capacity enables me to achieve the truth, I have not experienced the reality of which you speak. I remember my mother asking my father if he had ever experienced what a poet said—'Sometimes a light surprises the Christian while he sings'—and his reply, after a moment of thought, that he had not. I remember the sudden onset of tropical night, the lamplit room and the frighteningly solemn and incomprehensible conversation. Why were they sad? Experience has not answered.

PRIEST Your instinct was right in supposing it was 'about' God, but that it was not God.

ROSEMARY Bedtime; Alice, bring me my milk.

THIRTEEN

In the attic. Robin and Roland whispering.

ROLAND If we don't do Man in, he will do us in. You heard him ask Rosemary, 'shall I shoot him?' Completely cold-blooded. We might have been vermin—and he meant it.

ROBIN So what? Of course he would have done it. And if *we* shoot *him,* what do you think would happen next? We should be killed.

ROLAND I know that, but we would have taken one of the swine with us. It would be no worse than living as we are.

ROBIN Nor better. We mustn't be premature; we must plan.

ROLAND Lucky we don't give a damn for them. Let's talk again later. In the meantime we can think.

ROBIN They can't bug our minds. What about P.A.? Or Priest?

ROLAND P.A.'s a gas bag; and Priest's no good till someone wants to know who has won—he'll be on the winning side.

ROBIN There won't be one. Good night; they have won already.

ROLAND They have won. I have not lost—yet. Sleep, but not too well.

* * *

(*In Rosemary's room. Rosemary kicks off her shoes and watches complacently while Alice picks them up and puts them together on the rack*)

ROSEMARY I think Man will shoot Robin and Roland. Do you mind?

ALICE Well, no, I suppose not, but—

ROSEMARY But what?

ALICE I can't help thinking sometimes of when we were married.

ROSEMARY Of course I feel sorry for them, but when I think of the old days I loathe the memory. I like it this way. I'm glad you and your crowd can't possibly get the upper hand now. I admit I wouldn't like to see them shot—not to watch it.

ALICE He might make you watch. I don't put it past him if he thought we loved them.

ROSEMARY He might think *you* did. That's why he asked me if I would like them shot. Anyhow, you may go now. (*Coldly formal*) Good-night.

FOURTEEN

ROBIN Here we are again.

P.A. We haven't carried further the discussion about doubt, especially as opposed by adherents of the virtues of certainty.

PRIEST I see Roland shaking his head. Have we exhausted its interest?

ROLAND I *am* interested, but the present position in which we find ourselves doesn't seem to demand discussion. Man, though he has claimed to be a supporter of the chocolate bar approach, spoke at our last meeting of the merits of shooting. How do you discuss with a gun?

P.A. War is a change from the debating chamber to the field of battle where a gun is only an instrument. The instrument is of no consequence—the motive force or person is.

ROLAND Too true. In fact the motive force is Man and the lady to whom we are indebted for permission to use this room.

ROSEMARY I am glad to do what I can, but I do not pretend to enjoy your sarcasm, Roland.

ROBIN (*aside to Roland*) Pipe down.

ROLAND I was not aware of being sarcastic.

ALICE Whether you are aware or not doesn't matter so much as what Rosemary *feels* aware of. If she feels you are rude—

ROBIN *She* will press the trigger.

ROLAND I shall not dream of letting my thoughts wander.

P.A. But you cannot explore, literally or metaphorically, if you cannot stray from the beaten track.

MAN Surely it matters who has beaten the track and to what areas you are meaning to stray.

ROLAND Such as?

MAN You might be proposing to explore the possibilities of violence. You and Robin may be considering murder.

ROLAND Where on earth do you suppose Robin or I could get the idea of shooting anyone?

ROBIN (*uneasily*) Aren't you being a bit provocative?

ROSEMARY (*pointing her toe and admiring her ankle*) Alice, you haven't cleaned my shoes properly. Do them again.

ALICE (*obediently*) Yes, Ma'am.

ROBIN (*to no one in particular*) That brings it home to you how things have changed.

ROLAND It is wonderful how much one can learn—even shooting; metaphorically of course.

ROSEMARY No whispering! What are you two muttering about?

ROLAND I was saying it is wonderful how much one can learn—literally of course.

P.A. It is impressive. As Anatole France said about honesty, integrity and wisdom, only bigotry and ignorance are more powerful.

ROSEMARY I have been thoroughly educated—whether 'well' or not.

MAN I feel I have learnt something; I have some experience of seduction and intimidation.

P.A. The active principle of both is the stimulation of one part of a personality against another.

ROLAND Or one section of a community against another.

P.A. It leaves open the question as to where the victory will fall. I suppose that is the crunch in any decision. It looks as if the person or thing that announces the theme for action is not as powerful as the executive who transforms the idea into fact—the sovereign power in a group is one name for it. But what *is* the sovereign power?

ROSEMARY That can only be decided by practice and in particular circumstances. Here it might be Greed.

ROBIN Or perhaps war or murder.

P.A. Or a state of want or starvation. Péguy, discussing the French summary of Liberty, Fraternity and Equality, considered equality to be of a lower order of precedence vis à vis liberty and fraternity.

ROLAND Of course we are all equal here.

P.A. We have the opportunity to mobilize the impressions of several people, not just one; to bring to bear several different powers of discrimination to assess what information our senses glean.

ROBIN Assuming, of course, that the judgement of the individual is not vitiated by the presence of the rest of the group. In that case the combined wisdom of the group could be less than that of the individual members composing it.

P.A. Unless the experience of the group promotes growth of health and strength of the individuals. Perhaps these group meetings might have that developmental generative force.

ROLAND Or they might simply generate jargon. How can you be sure that each individual does not contribute to the riotous and undisciplined proliferation of cells—like a cancer?

P.A. If we could go on with the experience here, we might see what stimulates growth and what structure the growth displays.

ROLAND I do not feel optimistic about the nature of the productions of this group: two members of a defeated army, one member of a force successfully mobilized to destroy a nation, a woman from a subjected class—I refer to Alice—a priest representative of a discredited discipline—

PRIEST I might be thought to represent a discredited hierarchy confused with religion itself; or to be a verbal representation of a force which has never yet been subjected.

ROLAND Which of your many religions are you referring to? I thought you prided yourself on being a sort of Vicar of Bray.

ALICE You are wrong, Roland. I may, as you think, be subjected; Rosemary may be exalted. But this does not represent the truth about womanhood—

PRIEST Or religion. I have not claimed devotion to any one of the polymorph collection of human or saurian 'religions', but I *am* devoted to religion even if I misrepresent the reality to which I am devoted.

ROLAND I'm sorry—I must be stupid.

P.A. That is a *mis*-representation liable to generate *mis*-understanding.

ROSEMARY I don't think so; 'stupid' is adequate as a descriptive term for Roland.

MAN I would prefer 'bloody-minded'.

ROBIN That comes well from you who have suggested murder in an actual meeting of our group.

P.A. He may be giving evidence of the change of which he said he was aware and attributed to the group.

PRIEST I think he is displaying change, but I do not attribute it to the group.

ROLAND I think you are meaning God—vox populi, vox Dei.

ROSEMARY Are you changing too? If so, I shall have to reconsider my statement that you were stupid.

SHERLOCK Don't. 'Stupid' is the right word.

MORIARTY I thought I recognized one of my flock—stupid, criminal and a figment of the imagination.

WATSON Poor Roland! *I* am usually dismissed as stupid and imaginary. What says Alice? Will you answer for 'womanhood'? Do you think you are a real woman?

ALICE I know Roland too well. He *has* changed, though he is still like the husband I knew—ghastly!

ROLAND Was I really as bad as that?

ALICE Worse—far worse. You are in fact a fictitious and flattering version of the blackguard you were.

WATSON Those are strong terms.

ROSEMARY Rubbish. I know Roland and I don't think Man's suggestion of shooting him at all inappropriate.

ROLAND My God! What collection of Hell Cats have I stirred up?

PRIEST No doubt the God on whom you have called will answer your question.

P.A. I think the language you are using is inadequate. The vast vocabulary of psycho-analysis affords me no better choice. I doubt anything could be adequate; the conjunction of opinions is not referrable to the thing-in-itself, the ultimate reality, the *real* Roland—even one real aspect of the real Roland.

ROLAND P.A. seems sure about himself.

SHERLOCK He reminds me of my brother Mycroft, but not so bright or as ornamental. I may be prejudiced as we are members of the same family.

P.A. Which family? Your Mother's, or one of the children of Imagination?

ALICE Imagination is a vicious old bitch; she used to torture me in my childhood.

ROLAND Very affecting reminiscence. I think your resemblance to her would be apparent anywhere!

ROSEMARY Roland, you have not improved.

ROLAND And whose fault is that?

ALICE & ROSEMARY Hopeless!

MAN Shall I shoot?

ROSEMARY No; not yet.

PRIEST Maybe a spell in Purgatory would do him good. It is often growth-promoting.

P.A. It may promote cancerous proliferation.

PRIEST Of course; the religious domain with which I am most familiar has produced or aided in the growth of some of the most malignant specimens I have ever known. Charming too—rosy-cheeked, cricket-loving. I recall one in particular; the last time I saw him he was padre to a battalion at Ypres.

P.A. I knew him. His bonhomie grew flat towards the end.

(*Robin and Roland remain dimly visible; the rest are gradually enveloped in obscurity, dark and deep.*)

ROLAND Shooting would be too good for him and too noisy for us. Rat poison used to be kept in the medicine chest. It is, after all, a kind of medicine.

ROBIN Arsenic preserves the evidence of the crime. So does tannic acid.

ROLAND We don't need to consider the disposal of the remains till we have some to dispose of.

ROBIN Oh yes we do. I don't want to dispose of myself as well as him. So we must consider how we get rid of him.

ROLAND Get rid of him first, say I.

ROBIN Don't be a fool. You say I'm too cautious; *you* are too precipitate.

ROLAND What about the women? That skivvy is clearly a force to reckon with. Anyone who can become boss as she has done—

ROBIN Is she a traitor or a potential tool?

ROLAND That is hard to say. I wouldn't like to go to her for help. Sex is an unpredictable force.

P.A. May I join in? Freud suggested that the human race was a complex construction for providing the germ plasm with a means of locomotion.

ROLAND Let's talk about it later—it's an idea. It is getting lighter and noisier—do I hear voices?

PRIEST Why not discuss it with the rest of the group? They are the ones I hear. Or are they? I see a puissant and a mighty nation mewing its youth.

ROBIN What's the time? My watch doesn't mark the centuries—only hours.

P.A. Mine only marks fifties. What about yours?

PRIEST Mine marks centuries, but only on geometric scale. We need universal or extra-galactic time.

ROLAND Only seasonal I fear; 'thus with the year seasons return'.

ROSEMARY I have a lady's watch which Alice gave me. It marks beauty—the kind that's in the eye of the beholder.

PRIEST Mine is for spiritual beauty beheld by God.

ROBIN Masculine too, I understand.

ROLAND Only as seen by men.

ALICE A cup of tea, Ma'am?

P.A. One more scale—ali-metric, the human animal's alimentary canal. There would seem to be a number of different times from alimetric, geo-metric, stella-metric, galacto-metric, to extra-galacto-metric. Hitherto we have resorted to geo-metric scales but it is now becoming obvious that they are inadequate for the purposes for which we require them.

ROBIN That would be an explanation for experiences of the inappropriate such as pain that is incommensurate with the physical importance of the physical injury.

PRIEST Would you say that intense pain in your gastro-intestinal system was telling you, 'time for dinner'?

ROBIN It would tell me it was time to stop eating.

P.A. The body language needs interpretation—time to stop eating or simply 'the time'? If the latter, 'time' for what? Alimentary or medical activity? Like hieroglyphic script, it has this peculiarity of polymorphy or poly-valence. What about a term like 'polymorphous–perverse'?

ROLAND Well, what about it? You should know!

P.A. 'You should know' seems to be an intrusion from outside the system of human knowledge. I feel it doesn't 'belong', as a comet might not be regarded as intra-galactic. It may belong to the human psyche; Freud discovered many intrusions from the domain he called 'unconscious'. Although I need look no further than the human unconscious for this intruder, I think it would be unwise or bigoted to rule out the possibility of intrusion from a domain of which we know nothing.

PRIEST I think psycho-analysts are presumptuous and bigoted to exclude a Godhead.

MORIARTY Godhead! Another figment of the imagination.

WATSON I don't see why you scoff at figments of the imagination; for all you know the greatest power of all is indistinguishable from one of us.

MAN I believe in God anyway; I have evidence of his goodness.

ROLAND I believe in the Devil; I have evidence of his cruelty and wickedness.

P.A. I differ. Evidence is a function of the senses; that cannot lead logically to the 'truth' of God—only to the truth of the reality that is *not* God.

SHERLOCK Good! I have already said we figments of the

imagination are far more 'real' than your dim and shadowy realities. Can you imagine anything more impossible to believe in than my creator Conan Doyle? Fantastic!

MYCROFT Well done! But aren't you being rather triumphant? A kind of Frankenstein Monster?

SHERLOCK Well, aren't you triumphing over me? Can you tell me who or what created the Monster? Who was Frankenstein? The Monster is alleged to have killed Frankenstein.

P.A. The death instinct killed Eros; the same instinct is inseparable from birth. Birth and death refer to directions of the activity.

ROLAND Somebody—Man has already said it—is going to get shot.

ROBIN Something is going to be born that 'commends the ingredients of the poisoned chalice to our own lips'. Initiation initiates definition.

P.A. What an ugly monster it is—always proliferating. Massacring the infants was an ineffectual precaution and now it is too late to murder thought or thinker. A thought without a thinker is certain to pro-voke a thinker to father it sooner or later. What saurian engendered thought? Is there not a danger that someone will give birth to thought, or even miss out the intervening barrier between thought and action and give immediate expression to robbery and murder—the two unacknowledged parents through whom innocence and sin came into the world.

PRIEST I doubt it. Your view is coloured, almost dictated, by the laws of your kind of communication. The unknown thoughts require a poet, like the heroes still dwelling in everlasting night of whom Horace spoke.

P.A. The poet is more likely to disappear into the unknown night than to save his Eurydice. In psycho-analytic language of a sophisticated 'level', the unconscious would overwhelm the conscious, the contained would be lost inside its container, the blood would be lost in the capillaries, the living person or thing would bleed to death in its tissues, the rational would be lost in the irrational, the—

ROLAND Oh, for heaven's sake!

ROBIN Yes, I get the idea—you haven't got to repeat it.

PRIEST Hosea is swallowed in wantonness, chastity lost in harlotry—

SHERLOCK What! You too?

HIAWATHA I can claim no special merit just for doing what is known to be so easy—

WATSON Holmes, you complained after a brilliant piece of detection that I, like everyone else, believed the discovery must have been very easy—*after* you had explained it.

P.A. Freud wrote an outline of psycho-analysis when he was eighty-two; this 'Outline' seemed simple and therefore easy. So it is—for anyone who has spent the previous eighty-two years doing the work. The good mother, of whatever sex, ultimately qualifies to be vulnerable to loss. The product becomes capable of independent existence; the mammal does not 'need' the saurian; The human animal becomes redundant and is replaced by its successor. Where is the new idea to enable us to lead Moloch to join his praise and adulation to that of the proud and happy parents?

MYCROFT

'As the Saurian lay a-thynkynge, a-thynkynge, a thynkynge,
Prettily lay the thought in its shell of saurian brain.

MORIARTY My progenitor lay concealed in Paradise. The person best qualified by temperament and aesthetic skill unfortunately squandered his powers by hailing holy light. Despite the fact that he expressed the logical confusion into which he was getting, he did not cut the Gordian knot by directly hailing devilish darkness 'of confusion and blackest midnight born'—a great pity. One cannot fail to mourn the loss to lies, deceptions, evasions by his unfortunate defection. The greatest disseminator of culture has always been the thief and robber; he has put down the mighty and over-gifted and wise, and exalted the humble and meek and intensely viable sinner. To whom do we look for progress? The wise? The Good? The beautiful? Perish the thought! Even Mycroft owes his chief merit to sloth.

Hail ignoble sloth and leave ornithology
to the birds and other angelic monstrosities
Blithe thou never wert. Hail! I say, sordid
Spirit—gin and bear it . . .

MYCROFT I had no idea that you were among the poets!

MORIARTY My *dear* Mycroft—have you never read 'Ruin Among the Lovers'? My favourite pastime.

MYCROFT You're drunk.

MORIARTY Me? Drunk? I never touch the stuff. I assist it to *circulate*. Smuggling, as another poet says, keeps the prices down; so it is best for the poor when the gentlemen go by. Who do you think made the mistress of this house available to the cow-man? Who gave the mistress of this house a chance to find her true calling? She would never have found for herself the joys of being a skivvy or being raped. Why, she even tried to stop Rosemary . . .

MYCROFT I certainly think she would do better than that fool Holmes—I doubt his taste in women—although she would not be anything like as effective as you, Madam, if *you* got on my track!

ROSEMARY Very seductive—but I am not a figment of the imagination.

MORIARTY I can see that you are the real thing.

P.A. Figments of the imagination are often more powerful than many real things; men and women are not so powerful as the idealized figures that other men and women have about them.

ROLAND If you mean figments of imagination, why not say so instead of calling them 'idealized figures'? Why don't you talk English instead of that barbarous jargon?

P.A. Because 'English' already has an established meaning; it is saturated with meaning. So I have to use words which are unsaturated to indicate that I am not referring to the preconception. Unfortunately the 'unsaturated' expression almost immediately becomes saturated—jargon, as you call it—and I cannot help having to use what is thought to have the familiar meaning, or to be expressing a platitude, or to be meaningless, or to be throwing more light on the 'craziness' of the speaker than illuminating the darkness, or to be just 'poetic'.

ROBIN I begin to see why Milton used to bore me to tears—although it was better than maths.

ROSEMARY Or Latin.

ALICE 'Quantum mutatus ab illo Hectore qui redit exuvias indutus Achilli.'

PRIEST Or 'Dies illa, dies irae, calamitatis et miseriae . . .'

P.A. Or 'envy and gratitude'.

ROLAND I don't see anything remarkable about that.

P.A. There isn't anything more remarkable than there is about what you and Robin would say alone.

ROLAND Are you trying to say that we say or do things alone that we don't say or do in public?

(*It grows dark. All fade except Roland and Robin*)

ROLAND Are you sure no one can hear or see?

ROBIN Of course not. In this attic at night we are safe.

ROLAND What do you think that bloody psycho-analyst meant?

ROBIN You *are* suspicious! Knowing what I know about p.a.'s you can be sure he, like the rest, has sex on the brain.

ROLAND I'm not so sure; I think he's a spy. Anyhow I don't want to be accused of sexual practices. This is as bad as my late lamented public school where they didn't have to go through long years of psycho-analysis to be told what two of us were up to if we were alone together in the dark.

ROBIN But we aren't two boys.

ROLAND And this is not free England in peace time. You heard what Man said about shooting; and that bitch Rosemary said—

ROBIN 'Not yet.' Death will come anyway. What of it? Those two aren't likely to be the people to decide. I might get pneumonia—very likely in this blasted hole. While looking out for one thing you can trip over something else and break your neck. Montesquieu said so years ago. A fellow trying to escape was captured in flight because his braces burst and he couldn't run holding his trousers up. If he hadn't been so fussy about sex he could have run without his trousers.

ROLAND You're as bad as P.A. What's this got to do with living in defeated England?

ROBIN Sex! I have an idea. This Man is sweet on Rosemary—how can we burst his braces?

ROLAND I don't know what you mean.

ROBIN You learnt less at school than I thought. Think it out—we'll discuss it further.

(*It grows darker. Only Robin is left*)

ROBIN I wonder if I can trust Roland. He's stout-hearted but so stupid. So far he has kept his mouth shut; but he gave me away at

Munden—not by saying something, but by coming. You'd think a countryman would know a lark doesn't land *at* its nest; it has the sense to know that sometimes it pays to walk. 'It is the lark that sings so out of tune . . .' Juliet was urging him to behave like a fool . . . It's an idea.

(*Fade-out still further*)

ROBIN God! What's that?

ROLAND I wish you wouldn't start like that! You've woken me up. What's the matter?

ROBIN I must have been dreaming. I thought England, our two farms, had been taken over.

ROLAND That's not a dream. Wake up!

ROBIN I thought . . . What was it then?

ROLAND How should I know? *You* said it was a dream.

ROBIN You're being stupid. I remember—in the dream you *were* stupid.

ROLAND Oh, shut up and go to sleep. You'll wake the house if you go on like that.

ROBIN Am I to sleep or wake up? You are being idiotic. Oh, he's gone to sleep again. I think it's getting light. The appalling prospect of another day. Yet sometimes I wonder if it's any worse than it used to be, if I have forgotten what it was like. It's quite pleasant plotting how to murder that Man and his woman. No good plotting without practice . . . but would practice be pleasant?

FIFTEEN

ROSEMARY Alice, you can go now. Tell Roland to come up to me. (*Alice curtseys and goes out*) That girl is becoming a nuisance; I must get rid of her. What will happen to her? How should I know and what do I care? Ah . . . come in and sit down, Roland; I want to talk to you.

ROLAND What do you want?

ROSEMARY I don't want you to get into bed with me, if that's what you are thinking. You once seemed to think that because I was a servant I would be honoured by your dishonourable intentions. What I want to talk about is Alice—I am not satisfied with her. I won't trouble you with the reasons, nor why I do not want her to suffer more than she has to. She does not realize what danger she is in. When I dismiss her—as I am going to—she will be without means of support. I can do nothing for her. Do you understand?

ROLAND She is nothing to do with me. You are thinking she is still my wife.

ROSEMARY I was not thinking any such thing. It is a long time since I thought she was your wife, or even concubine. (*Roland makes a sudden impatient gesture*) Roland, this automatic is not loaded with chocolate, nor am I loaded with sweet feelings for you. I should regret it, but I shall shoot without hesitation.

ROLAND I know you have no feelings of concern for me, but—

ROSEMARY You are hopeless. I was about to tell you I have no feelings for Alice. You may go.

(*Roland goes out*)

ROSEMARY It's getting lighter. Light or dark—what does it matter to me? Am I such a fool that I do not know Man's name? Menelaus, Cupid, Hector, Astyanax . . . But what of the night, the void, the infinite? And now, the marriage feast begun, will Poverty be the bride? I saw the world when it was young and beautiful. I have only to close my eyes to see it again. And Man loves me, dotes on me. I am part of the spoils of war. Alice is part of the spoils of *my* war. Am *I* to mourn Adonis? Or Alice, or Roland—that bastard who thought he could get his skivvy cheap as spoils of the war waged by the upper classes of Britain? *Great* Britain they say! And now this murderous lout thinks he is going to pick up a conquered woman. He would be grovelling at my feet if I were not fussy about the kind of trash I collect on my shoes. I felt sorry for Alice, but when I remember that she married Roland I think she must be such a fool that I cannot be justified in pitying her. That's God's job—not mine. The priest, servant of God, acquired some sense in the last thousand years, rubbed off on him from Minerva. Helen of Troy—that's what they called me then. Before I was called Helen I was nameless, the unrecognized vegetation, the goddess of futility and vegetation from which the mammalian parasites sprang and on whom they still depend.

P.A. What of the micro-cellular plants—bacteria? Will they not feed on the rotting remains of the mammals when their brain children grow up and give birth to a light brighter than a thousand suns?

ROSEMARY I thought you believed in mind.

P.A. You could call it that. *I* call it that because I have to talk to human minds and I can't do that without believing they exist.

ROSEMARY Sometimes I almost think you are intelligent.

P.A. Alas! I am. You can't believe the trouble I've had with intelligence—mine and other people's. Intelligent people—Arjuna, Meister Eckhart, Jesus, Plato, Socrates, Aristotle, Saint Augustine and the rest—want to *know* God. They have been warned that, Icarus-like, they would singe their waxen wings and . . . *fall*.

ROSEMARY *You* don't know the trouble I've had with 'intelligence'; even sex is religious. Poor Minerva used to complain of the same thing.

MAN What about Beauty?

ROSEMARY Humans confuse beauty with religion and sex. Always worshipping women or sex or wine instead of God.

MORIARTY Ah! I wondered if you would stumble on the importance of a Figment of the Imagination. (I've told the printer to use capital letters as a sign of respect.) It's one of the things that Sherlock and I—and even poor old Watson—agree about. Only the greatest human beings have been able to recognize these figments of imagination.

P.A. Jesus used to complain about the adulterous generation who were clamouring for a sign.

MORIARTY Satan, like William Blake but unlike the author of Paradise Lost, had the ability to see how he dominates the story.

P.A. That was hidden by the beauty of the verse.

ROBIN No, the beauty of Paradise Lost made the truth last long enough for someone to receive the message.

P.A. Don't you agree that the longevity with which those formulations were endowed was a consequence of beauty? Then work had to be done to recognize the truth.

ROBIN You are going round in circles.

P.A. 'Circles' are a poor visual image.

ROBIN Perhaps I should have said you are going round in a helix—

ROLAND And should have kept your mouth shut.

ROSEMARY Roland, I told you you could go.

P.A. You might as well talk to D.N.A.

ROBIN What's that?

P.A. Doubt, Nature, Art.

ROSEMARY Art, Nature, Decay. You've got the order wrong.

ROLAND I had to use my arts to prosper the crabapple before it became an apple fit to eat; fit to be turned into natural manure.

P.A. As Confucius said, 'ground in the mortar of the mind'.

ROBIN My Latin master taught me Livy's parable of the members of the body; he never taught me what the parable meant, any more than Livy taught anybody its meaning.

P.A. What does Coma Berenices mean? It is hung in the sky large enough to be seen, yet its meaning is only in part visible to the astronomer—not the part visible to the poet—though once I knew an astronomer who saw both. Millions have had the wit to be terrified by comets.

ROBIN I understood that psycho-analysts were supposed to make profound interpretations.

(*General murmur of agreement with sarcastic overtones*)

P.A. No more than astronomers viewing Coma Berenices are supposed to 'see' a country far beyond the star. It is common sense to see nothing in Coma Berenices. You assume I am talking ordinary conversational English—nothing profound. Why then do you sound aggrieved? I had a patient who was a good mimic and used to sound just like a man engaging in a conversation. But it became clear that he couldn't understand a thing he or I said. Changes occurred when I interpreted his 'remarks' in light of Kleinian theories—notably those grouped together as *derived* from projective interpretation—

ROLAND Are you talking English now?

ROSEMARY Get out!

ROLAND Gladly.

MAN Shall I shoot?

ROSEMARY No. It's interesting. I don't use P.A.'s language, nor that of Priest. I use Alice.

P.A. I would say it is what anatomists and physiologists and possibly Freudian psycho-analysts would call 'sex'.

ROBIN I thought you would call yourself a Freudian psycho-analyst. Or are you a Kleinian?

P.A. I can recognize and would like to acknowledge my debt to Freud and to Melanie Klein, but they might be affronted by such attribution. I would acknowledge my debt to others, but I am aware that many would think such an acknowledgment more a liability than an asset; they would not wish to be thought my mental forebears. Nor do *I* wish to wear the plumage of the peacock when my true colours should be the feathers of the sparrow.

ROBIN Not even Lesbia's?

P.A. Your interjection sums up the dilemma beautifully.

ROSEMARY I don't know what you are talking about.

P.A. It would not become you to assume the garb of Andromache.

PRIEST What did Queen Mary whisper when she did not dare, in audible English, tell her admiring throngs to cheer?

ROBIN Something she had learned from her nautical husband I believe. Don't you want us to cheer?

P.A. No; cheers are interpreted.

ROBIN Always?

P.A. I interpret such evidence as my senses and my insight provide, but I am not impelled to make it public. In the practice of psycho-analysis I accept tacitly an obligation to try to make my analysand aware of what his insight and 'out'sight tell.

ROBIN Why?

P.A. Because I accept him, provisionally, as needing to hear what his senses have to say.

ROBIN Do you think *we* want to hear what you have to say?

P.A. Occasionally people want to hear something to confirm what they know—be that good or ill. They only rarely want to hear the truth—be it welcome or not. Fewer still wish to know what it will cost. But the psycho-analyst is expected to meet their needs.

ROBIN Is he any worse off than anyone else?

P.A. Probably better off—for those few hours he is given the chance to convey the truth.

ROBIN How do you know they want it?

P.A. I don't. I draw attention only to what the man or woman *seems* to me to want. If they think my comment illuminating they can continue in their way, or decide to change course. It is their choice.

ROSEMARY What do I want?

P.A. As far as I have had an opportunity to judge, a mate who could provide you with the means to gratify your desires.

ROSEMARY Love?

P.A. I do not recognize the need for that word to describe your relationship with anyone.

ROSEMARY Andromache?

P.A. No. Alice may fulfil the part since Roland declined to be her Hector.

MORIARTY Wouldn't you be Hector to Alice's Andromache?

P.A. I have not the courage necessary for the part.

ALICE You sadden me, but I think you are right.

WATSON How can you tell? I have known some ordinary people who behaved with extraordinary courage.

P.A. I know what you mean. I have even had courage attributed to me. But I remember no occasion on which I was not a coward at heart. Even in my prosaically unheroic role of psycho-analyst I always fear to give an interpretation.

ROBIN For fear of being murdered?

P.A. That is usually a remote contingency.

ROBIN But it exists?

P.A. As well as other possibilities. To confirm the accusation sometimes made against analysts that they do not attach importance to the environmental factors, I find that any rational explanation that is 'reasonably' proffered has only ephemeral effect. Environmental factors leave virtually no lasting lesson in the recipient's mind—no trace.

ROBIN Then what does have a lasting effect?

P.A. Anything which stimulates, mobilizes, creates feelings belonging to the love ↔ hate spectrum.

ROBIN I don't know what you mean—it sounds like jargon. I find it difficult to see what differentiates your statement from other jargonese statements.

P.A. You are right—and I don't know what to do about this difficulty when I am 'talking about' psycho-analysis. If I were practising psycho-analysis with you I could try to demonstrate an emotional experience you were having and say, 'What you are *now* feeling is what I call "hate", or "love", or some subdivision between the two'. *Here* I can elaborate what you have called 'jargon' by this rather long-winded story—'construction', as Freud might have called it—

ROBIN 'Might have called it'—there you go again. You're so cautious. Why don't you say right out what you mean?

P.A. Because it would not be the truth I wanted to convey.

ROBIN You make me think psycho-analysis must be very difficult if you can't talk plain English.

P.A. You are right; psycho-analysis *is* very difficult: so is plain English. If I could talk it, it would not be 'talking' what I want to 'say'.

ROBIN I give up.

SHERLOCK If I were able to play my violin, and you could listen to it, the problem would be settled in no time.

P.A. *If* you could play it . . . *if* I could listen to it . . . *if* it would be settled in no time . . . *then* we should pass on to another problem.

ROSEMARY Alice! Put out my evening dress. No, no, not that one. Wait; I want you to dress me.

ALICE Yes, Ma'am.

P.A. (*to Priest*) She has got her where she wants her—beneath her feet.

PRIEST And now—she doesn't want it.

P.A. I'm not so sure; I think she does. What was Shub-ad like?

PRIEST The Queen? Not at all a bad sort. She was quite upset at the King's death.

P.A. That's where you came in with your little beaker and large store of fairy tales; and, in due course, the British Museum.

PRIEST Don't forget the University of Pennsylvania and its large store of dollars. And Freud—don't forget Freud and that load of science beneath which is buried God and Art and Wisdom itself.

P.A. Death, you say, shall have no dominion.

PRIEST No I don't; that is not my view of death. Thoughts live until they find a thinker who gives them birth—and so brings death into the world and all our woe.

P.A. From your vertex is may *seem* so, but that depends on standing on the giddy precipice of 'seeming'.

PRIEST You resort to visual imagery to make your empty thoughts look full.

P.A. I agree it does make them seem full, but I think these formulations have content. I am talking about 'something' and I think it would be worth having respect for 'seeming'. I doubt the equivocation of the fiend that lies like truth.

ROSEMARY Bed time. Alice, have you put out my things? I expect my visitor about midnight. Let him in and then go to bed.

ALICE Yes, Ma'am.

SIXTEEN

Rosemary is greeting Man. Alice stands respectfully aside, takes his hat and coat, and is dismissed.

MAN Still got your maid, I see.

ROSEMARY I have made up my mind to dismiss her.

MAN I thought you would find her somewhat insolent.

ROSEMARY No, it's not that. She weighs heavily—dependent—as if she looks to me for help. (*Laughs*)

MAN I love it when you laugh like that; there is a fascinating music in it.

ROSEMARY That's what Alice says. I think I find her fascination very agreeable—more now than I used to in the old days.

MAN I don't like her—or Roland. I don't know why you shelter them; I feel they are both dangerous.

ROSEMARY I think *he* is.

MAN You would be wise to let me shoot him—or have him shot.

ROSEMARY Well, perhaps I will. But not here please. I hate violence. Alice is going to have a baby.

MAN Does she love the father?

ROSEMARY Love? I shouldn't think so—you know what these

poor people are. When she has had the baby we can get rid of her. It will be a good reason for dismissing her.

MAN Roland is the man I suppose.

ROSEMARY Heavens, no! She hates him. But let's talk about something interesting.

MAN Have you decided when we are to marry?

(*It becomes dark and their voices fade out. When it grows light Rosemary is alone*)

ROSEMARY Marry? It's an idea. I wonder what the laws are now. Of course I could always poison him when I've done with him. Tom could easily be blamed and I don't suppose anyone will be bothered to find out. But . . . shall I have established my position? I expect so; I'm not a damned fool like Alice or Roland. Sometimes I wonder . . . these people must have been some good once. Suppose the brat's a boy—she might take to him. . . . It's quite an amusing situation viewed from my position. How different the same vista is if one's position changes! I used to hate Alice—only a year since—now I almost like her. I was most solicitous when I asked if she was going to have a baby. Very different when she—blast her impudence!—was suggesting to me that Tom was 'a nice boy'. As if she cared! I feel sorry for her. She's in a hole—Tom couldn't give a damn; Roland hates her and is going to be shot . . . which reminds me to tell Man he can shoot him when he likes. I'm not sure though that I have much time. He has changed from his 'gentlemanly' ways recently. I don't put murder beyond his programme. Who's there? I'll shoot! What, no one? My nerve must be going. Where's my torch. (*Rings the bell. After a minute Alice appears*)

ALICE You rang for me?

ROSEMARY Of course, who else? I thought I had better tell you, so that you can find another job, that I won't be able to keep you after the next two weeks.

ALICE Another job? There aren't any. Anyhow, I don't want to leave.

ROSEMARY I'm sorry, but Man was talking it over with me and won't hear of you staying. He seems to have taken a dislike to you and . . . well, what can I do? I shall miss you of course, but perhaps it will be much better to make a break.

ALICE Do you mean you trust *him*?

ROSEMARY No, of course not. Did you trust Roland—with me I mean? Or did you think I led him on? I wouldn't have trusted him an inch. I never understood how a girl with any sense married him.

ALICE I was young—and in love.

ROSEMARY My Mum warned me that if ever I was such a damned fool as to fall in love she'd chuck me out of the house. 'Do what you like, Rosie', she said, 'but don't come telling me you've fallen in love'. I'm telling you the same. I'm surprised you didn't learn it at your school. Now—you may go.

ALICE Is that all for the night . . . Ma'am?

ROSEMARY Go! (*Alice obeys*) Extraordinary! Fancy thinking I would be in love with Man—or her! She hasn't learned that love makes clear thinking impossible. I am sorry to think how I hated her; I never guessed I would be her boss. Not till that day when I was holding her wrists and she couldn't make me go. Still, I shan't make the mistake of letting *her* get up again. She's down—for keeps. I can't waste time on her—I have enough to do to keep Man in his place. It's asking for trouble to let him get the upper hand. No pregnancies—I can make him think it's his fault he can't make me pregnant. I shall be *terribly* upset of course—I mustn't overdo it or he'll persevere—terribly upset; but I shall be very brave about it. Yes—then he will have to keep in my good books. I shall forgive him, tell him not to mind. I shall keep giving him sly digs to remind him what a misfortune it has been—for Alice. It certainly will be a misfortune for her if I can arrange it. It is amusing, but not amusing enough. If only I could make her feel humiliated; but she gets too much pleasure out of it, as if it were a game she had volunteered to play, damn her! After she's had a dose of real starvation perhaps she'll have to come back to some job in my house. But she may be successful now she's rid of that man Roland—what a horrible idea!

It's so dark and cold, I hope I'm not going to need a man. I don't need Roland—never did. But if Alice thought she did, *I* might have thought so had I gone to *her* school. What a fate! Yet, now I *am* going to her school—the school for bosses. I must be going weak in the head; if I go on like this I shall 'fall in love'—with Man.

P.A. No, you are only falling in love with being seduced.

ROSEMARY You again? So you think I am being seduced?

P.A. No, I think you are in love with seduction. You made Alice fall in love with being seduced. She was starved and you were starved, so it was hardly surprising that you were both vulnerable—susceptible to the allurement of physical sex, she perhaps more than you, because in her 'bin', as you call it, she was starved of physical sex in a way which you couldn't experience in your slum. Neither of you knows the first thing about love.

ROSEMARY Excuse me, I do. I know a lot more about it than you do. I know what you and Roland and Robin and that boy thought they were teaching me. I learnt that their love was not worth much.

P.A. Yes, you may have learnt what 'worthless' love is, but that isn't love. In the catalogue it may go for love, as Shakespeare's murderers went for 'men'. No doubt your collection of predators go for 'lovers'; your love may be of much the same predatory kind. You haven't said or done anything *I* call love.

ROSEMARY You are a stickler for good English. How do *you* define 'love'?

P.A. I don't. The word as I've heard it here is constantly conjoined with a number of characteristics, phrases, emotions, experiences, but that is only a part of verbal activity. 'Love', in so far as it relates to the past, is a ghost of a memory; as to the future it is a hope casting its shadow before. 'The thing itself'—

ROSEMARY Yes, I hoped you would get to it in time—

P.A. I must disappoint you. As a psycho-analyst I cannot aspire to success where the Saints, Philosophers, Artists of every kind have not succeeded.

ROSEMARY You can try.

P.A. I know what you mean, but it is not a domain in which 'effort' is applicable. I know "tis not in mortals to command success' may be true of Love; but it is part of being.

ROSEMARY Do you think mankind will ever achieve it?

P.A. It has nothing to do with Past, Present or Future. 'It' has been, is, and will be. Psycho-analysis, or preaching, or painting, or music are not 'it'—they are 'about' it.

ROSEMARY I am tired and it is already day. Sometimes I see things too clearly, but . . . oh, he has disappeared! I must have dreamt him. But it doesn't feel as if I have slept at all. My eyes hurt as if I had been up all night at a party. (*short laugh, instantaneously terminated*) Why laugh? What's the joke? Belly—what are you laughing at? What's so funny? (*sleeps*)

* * *

(*Roland and Robin talking—no one else is apparent*)

ROLAND Only two of us; it's not enough. If that bloody psychoanalyst could be relied on—

ROBIN You've said lots of times that you wouldn't trust him an inch.

ROLAND I wasn't thinking of trusting him. I said *if* he could be relied on . . . he could hold one end of a rope for two minutes. One minute would be enough *if* he could be relied on.

ROBIN What are you afraid he would do?

ROLAND Do? Nothing—but even that is not certain.

ROBIN Well then?

ROLAND Talk when he shouldn't. He could be useful *if* he could be relied on just to shout, 'lie!', once—at the right time.

ROBIN It sounds simple.

ROLAND It is. Instead of which, he is sure to want to know why.

ROBIN He isn't as bad as that.

ROLAND He is *quite* as bad as that. Take it from me, people who ask, 'why?' are no bloody use at all. They set out to do things, become absorbed in what they are curious about, and forget what they meant to do in the first place. Give them a job, expect them to do it—and get let down for your pains.

ROBIN What do you propose to do about Rosemary?

ROLAND Nothing. She's no damn good—only a skivvy with the mind of a skivvy.

ROBIN You ignore the fact that this 'skivvy' is the mistress of the house, and the mistress of the house is her skivvy. That is not her lowest point—yet. She has further to go; so has Rosemary.

ROLAND She has got her hooks into that bastard, Man. She has even persuaded him to get mixed up with this 'talking shop'. *That* is a sign that he is on his way out, mark my words.

ROBIN He may be, but Rosemary is not as impressed with the social summit as you think.

ROLAND She is only interested in beautiful clothes because she can use them to feel how beautiful she is.

ROBIN But she will survive and we shall not. She will get someone's semen—

ROLAND Someone's syphilis or gonorrhoea.

ROBIN That's not the kind of fool she is. You may be, but she isn't. Did you ever succeed in making love to her? No—and never will. I bet she took good care you would never get into her. Aren't I right?

ROLAND Only because I was worried about Alice.

ROBIN You are hopeless.

ROLAND Dammit! That's the second time today that someone has said that to me.

ROBIN Was Rosemary the other one? Don't tell me; I bet she was. Even if she didn't say it, that was what she meant in language louder than any words.

ROLAND (*white with rage*) I'll teach the whole damn lot of you! (*A shot is heard, soft and muffled. Roland falls dead*)

ROSEMARY (*to Man*) Darling! You shouldn't have done that. You've quite upset me! He really—

MAN I'm so sorry; I thought you wouldn't mind.

ROSEMARY Of *course* I mind. Poor Alice. She'll blame me for not having saved him.

MAN Do you mind about her? Was she fond of him? Don't let it spoil our evening. I love you, I love you.

ROSEMARY It's no good. Can't you see I am very upset? I can't take it as if it's nothing. You must give me time.

PRIEST (*turns Roland's body with his toe as if to reassure himself who it is*) I'll get Tom to clear him—it—'him', I mean—away.

ROSEMARY (*whimpers and pushes Man's hands away*) How awful! I wish it hadn't happened.

MAN (*disconcerted, releases her*) I thought you wanted—

ROSEMARY How dare you suggest such a thing! You can't love me to talk like that.

ROBIN Is he dead?

P.A. Quite.

PRIEST Quite dead. Well, well . . . his troubles are over.

ROBIN (*furious*) I thought you believed in a future life.

PRIEST Oh no. Quite a mistaken idea. Lots of people who have not studied the teachings of the Church make that mistake.

ROBIN Then what the hell do you believe in?

PRIEST Well, Hell.

P.A. Hell, like Heaven, is within you.

MORIARTY (*sniggering*) Ridiculous! Can't you see he's dead? What's all the fuss about? A perfectly simple murder—no problem. But you make it a fountain of lies, prevarications and self-deceptions.

WATSON What about you? Haven't you caused endless controversy—you and your demise at Reichenbach?

MORIARTY Doyle may have been a bungler, but nobody can say there are no real crooks in the real world. One of these days *my* human followers will achieve power even if they don't acknowledge their indebtedness to a 'figment of the imagination'. Where's your army, navy and police force? Man has just put a bullet through one English Gentleman and is in a fair way to make a servant into a 'lady'. I think her lack of principle shows great promise. She's even now preparing reasons for throwing Man over with no more compunction than she has for Alice. She's not guilty—

ROSEMARY If you weren't a figment of the imagination I would ring your bloody neck.

MORIARTY If you are not careful you will become evil 'incarnate' and find your neck more wrung than bloody. Look what's happened to your late boss's husband. If he had stuck to agriculture he might not be mutton now!

P.A. I see you are a Platonist.

MORIARTY Never heard of such an animal.

PRIEST Plato said that every man should stick to his last and then the 'world' would become a heaven on earth; so far, hell holds its own.

MORIARTY I always thought he was a philosopher—he must have had more sense—

P.A. Sense, like cheerfulness, keeps breaking in—as Dr Johnson said.

ROSEMARY Is anyone going to remove that object?

ALICE I've told Tom; he's coming. I am upset. After all, I was married to him once.

ROSEMARY I've seen you and Roland together, even though you thought it was just a 'skivvy's-eye view'; it was never what *I* call love.

ALICE You have gone too far, Rosemary. You—

ROSEMARY *You* have gone too far; *I* am the boss now. Tell Tom to hurry up *and* be quick about it. I want *that* removed. And you and Tom can go and find another job.

MAN Can I help?

ROSEMARY No; I have had enough of your help!

MAN I'm sorry. You may want . . .

ROSEMARY When I want it I can ask. Just now I am upset. You are too rough.

PRIEST & P.A. Can I help?

ROSEMARY No, go away. You don't know what a woman is.

P.A. That's true.

PRIEST I have met them before. She reminds me of Sarah and Hagar her servant. They gave Abram a rough passage.

TOM You wanted me?

ROSEMARY Clear that away.

TOM Oh God—it's the master isn't it?

ROSEMARY Fool! Now *he* is upset. Yes, it's Mister Roland—take it away Tom—he's dead.

TOM However did it happen?

MAN I shot him. Bury him in the fields somewhere.

TOM But that's murder!

MAN Go and bury it away from the house. No, *not* in the garden; in the graveyard if you like, but be quick about it.

TOM I'll get a barrow—but it doesn't seem right.

ROSEMARY Take him with you *now*.

TOM I was only going to fetch a barrow.

ROSEMARY No! Take it out!

(Tom, menaced by Man still fingering the automatic, shoulders the body with distaste and goes out. The automatic is not lost on Rosemary who turns disdainfully on him)

ROSEMARY Put that gun away. (*he hesitates*) I said, put that gun down. (*angrily*) Give it to me! (*He goes out in a rage—without surrendering the gun*)

(*Darkness falls—the scene is blotted out*)

SEVENTEEN

ROSEMARY (*at first only faintly discernible—by herself*) What a day! (*A shattered ghost of a beggar woman slowly becomes apparent. Rosemary sees her and is startled*) Who are you? How did you get here? (*There is no response but the figure is increasingly menacing*) Get out! (*The figure slowly raises its hands as if it might clutch her*) You won't frighten me with those tricks. Apparitions are not new to me. What do you want?

APPARITION I am glad you decided to be civil—without being terrified. It wouldn't do if you screamed.

ROSEMARY (*scornfully*) I am not easily terrified; not even though I thought my mind was going.

APPARITION It is. I have come to warn you. I am a friend of yours.

ROSEMARY Andromache? Lady Macbeth? Hecuba? These are friends I have seen before. I know you; you were fooled that day by the priest—at Ur. He turned up today too. I have a lot of friends.

APPARITION Dreams, apparitions, hallucinations may indeed be friends of yours—if you dare to admit the acquaintance. So far you have at least permitted yourself to admit my existence. You may be right to think that I am both the herald of impending disaster and a sign of that disaster.

ROSEMARY Aren't things bad enough without *your* arrival?

APPARITION I disturb your slumbers; you feel I am a symptom of a 'mind diseased'. Freud tried to turn these dreams to good account: you are not obliged to follow his example.

ROSEMARY The only Freud I ever heard of was a psycho-analyst.

APPARITION I don't mind what you call him—or me. You have been warned. Don't let me disturb your sleep—sleep well. (*disappears*)

ROSEMARY Gone! I must have indigestion.

P.A. Mental indigestion perhaps.

ROSEMARY Oh God—now you've turned up.

P.A. No, not God; only myself. I heard talking and came to see what it was. These are curious times, or I wouldn't have departed from the conventions of ordinary good manners. I have not come to get into bed with you—I heard what you told Roland when he came in to see you. Do you want me to go? I see you have a visitor.

ROSEMARY What! Another? Oh, I see—it's Priest isn't it? A full house!

PRIEST I heard voices so I came in because these are not ordinary times—

P.A. I have already explained the reason.

PRIEST Poor woman! The same experience as Hagar—oh, I forgot; you don't read the Bible or believe in God or anything so stupid do you?

P.A. Not quite as you do, but enough to have read that story in Genesis. Tell me more.

APPARITION (*re-appears*) You should not believe what either of these gentlemen has to say; they are no more reliable than Hosea. He thought himself superior too although he did 'admit' that God had told him to marry a whore. Hagar was contemptuous because she could conceive and Sarah could not. Oh, you've turned up, have you?

ROSEMARY Not another!

SCHOOLBOY Sorry! I heard voices and you know these are not ordinary times so—

P.A. Say no more. We *all* thought we heard voices and we *all* thought these were not ordinary times.

SCHOOLBOY We met before, Rosemary. I came to say I was sorry I was so rude.

ROSEMARY I remember . . . you thought I was a skivvy and you were too high-class to go out with me and visit my Mum. In fact, from your point of view—'vertex', P.A. would call it—she wasn't quite 'top drawer'. She was a whore.

APPARITION If any of you are going to survive this 'unusual' situation you will owe it to Rosemary's Mum.

P.A. Scientists think that things and people should be called by their right names.

SCHOOLBOY Yes! I remember what fun we had in my school. 'Please, sir', we used to say in Bible class, 'what is harlotry?' I used to love Bible class; it was the only bright thing on Sundays. 'When you grow up and know as much as I do', some old fool used to say. I hadn't the cheek to say, 'If only you were as young as I and knew as much about "harlotry" as I do, you would not be blushing beetroot red'.

ROSEMARY No one blushes now. What happened to you since those days when you dared—but not quite—to be seen out with a skivvy?

SCHOOLBOY I got killed—being 'heroic', you know.

ROSEMARY I was afraid you might. Shot? Or getting a dose of clap?

WATSON Or syphilis and G.P.I?

ROSEMARY Oh, my God! All day and now all night as well.

PRIEST If you believed in God you wouldn't be so surprised about 'all day and all night as well'.

P.A. Or 'all Science and all Religion'.

ROSEMARY Why leave out 'Beauty and Art'? I felt the night was bad enough without bringing in God.

P.A. All of us feel that that tiny 'increment' of an 'increment' of an 'increment' of one third of human knowledge is more than we can stand. But what happened to Schoolboy? Sunk under the weight of Knowledge? Destroyed by the skivvy's Beauty? Overwhelmed by Venus or her disease? Or mathematics?

SCHOOLBOY At school I wrote some articles for the magazine labelled 'Sex on the Games Field'—a long and pretty accurate account of the biology master's lesson on the reproductive process of dandelions, both sexual and vegetative. I had an imaginary interview with the groundsman whom I asked about sex. He replied, 'I know nothing about sex, but them perky dandelions will certainly be the death of me'. Anyway, funny or not, that *was* the death of me. It was the title that did it, even though there had been a lot about Richard Coeur de Lion. The Head asked for me to be removed. My poor mother was broken-hearted; my dear Dad was furious but secretly thought it funny. In the end, as I was due to go into the army, they let me stay to the end of term; that was more respectable and it was hoped I would get bumped off, so all were satisfied—except my Mum. Even she was cheered up because when I *was* finally bumped off my C.O. said I was a good officer—which I wasn't—and that I had been put in for a posthumous V.C. Luckily she died before the British Army and all its honours were no longer of any interest to anyone.

P.A. And did you have a future life?

SCHOOLBOY In a way, yes. I turned up in her dreams sometimes to say, 'Hullo Mum', and smile just as I used to. She would smile too and when she awoke her cheeks were wet with tears.

P.A. Did that upset you?

SCHOOLBOY Before I died it did, because I was afraid of what would happen if I were killed. I thought even my Dad might be upset.

ROSEMARY So you died a hero's death—that was something.

SCHOOLBOY I'm afraid not. You were right about me—I was too gutless to go out with you. A young friend of mine was killed in the war and that, though I didn't know it, was the end of me too. I never recovered; my courage and chivalry and hope were dead.

PRIEST What are you doing here then?

SCHOOLBOY I told you—I thought I heard voices and as these are not usual times I thought I had better come in.

P.A. Just curiosity?

PRIEST Fear of annihilation, 'everlasting death', perhaps?

P.A. Hallucinations?

SCHOOLBOY *If* they are hallucinations; but are the facts any better?

MORIARTY Facts, however terrible, are not so terrible as thoughts.

ROSEMARY Moriarty is a figment of imagination; Man is not. I prefer figments of imagination.

P.A. Figments of imagination have a way of becoming real. Robin is alive; Roland is not; Man killed him. The chocolate bar killed, or overlaid, suspicion; the real Luger disguised with the figment of his imagination killed Roland. Both were effective in their context. What mattered was the use which Man made of his capacity to talk.

ROSEMARY This *is* a vivid dream. I don't know if I have called out or not . . . There's no one here. I almost wish I were in the sunlight that Sunday long, so long ago . . . I can't get up—it's too dark and too early. I haven't had a wink of sleep. Is the daylight any better? How am I to handle this murderous thug if he is what he calls 'in love' with me? Is that Alice sobbing? No; it's the wind. How quiet it is! There's that noise again—my face is wet with tears. Shall I go and see what it is, or ring for Alice? There was a time when I would have loved to get her under my feet, yet now that I have I am scared out of my life! Let her weep . . . but she's keeping me awake. These awful people—they are bad enough without dreaming about them. At last it's getting light again. I used to hate having to get her tea. It was a nice life—for them. And now? Has Man got a boss? . . . That boy made me laugh about his scripture lessons! I wonder what happened to him. I dreamt he was dead—killed in the war . . . 'Pack up your troubles in your old kit bag . . .' . . . the band sounded so grand. Where are they now? . . . Perhaps I have been hard on Alice . . . (*sleeps*)

EIGHTEEN

R*osemary awakes. It is broad daylight.*

ROSEMARY Nobody here? What's happened? What an awful night—I feel quite worn out. (*rings for Alice; nobody comes; at last she gets up*) Has she run away? Have they all run away? Perhaps Man and his thugs have been here and arrested the whole lot. In that case how did they miss me? Man may have told them to leave me—for him. He doesn't love me, not after what I said to him yesterday . . . was it yesterday? I don't even know what day it was. That young boy . . . ah, it's coming back to me—said he's been killed in the war . . . must be crazy . . . or did I dream it? That was no dream. What was it then? Alice! Alice!! Alice!!! . . . I'm screaming! Mad—and no one to talk to. Mad! And alone. This place gives me the creeps. It's haunted. I am haunted—hag-ridden they call it. Are those guns? No, trucks on the road. They are driving at me—through me—into my head—drumming in my ears! Cassandra, help me, help! Alice! Oh, there you are. Where have you been? I've fallen out of bed; must have had a stroke. Where's the doctor? No, I don't want a psycho-analyst—I'm ill. I need a doctor I say. No, *not* a mind doctor. I must get up or I'll go out of my mind.

ALICE Did you call, Ma'am?

ROSEMARY Oh shut up! Don't talk that 'Ma'am' nonsense to me.

ALICE I'm sorry. I thought you liked it.

ROSEMARY *You* liked it. *You* led me on. How could you put up with that nonsense? I *hated* being your skivvy and I hated you. Now you seem . . . I suppose it serves me right!

ALICE What serves you right? I was sure you liked it.

ROSEMARY I must be mad. How do I come to be mistress of the house? What has happened? What . . . (*begins to be hysterical and Alice becomes angry and frightened*)

ALICE Calm yourself! What's the matter?

ROSEMARY Nothing. I want to get up. I must have had . . . had . . . a nightmare. It was very vivid.

ALICE What did you dream?

ROSEMARY (*Uncertain of the facts and afraid of saying something which might betray her, she plays for time and hopes Alice will say or do something which will give her a lead*) I had better sit in a chair. I feel so queer.

ALICE Here, sit down. Do you want a cushion? There's someone at the door—

ROSEMARY (*suppressing a scream with difficulty*) Don't let him in. That awful man!

ALICE It's only Tom. He won't come in.

ROSEMARY Are you sure it's not . . .

ALICE It's only Tom.

ROSEMARY (*relieved that she has not given herself away, but wanting someone from whom she could get help without making it clear what she is thinking*) Oh, he's quite harmless—quite a nice man really.

ALICE What do you want, Tom? Just wait a minute.

TOM Only came to say the job is finished.

ALICE Thank you—nothing else? I'm busy just now.

TOM Will that be all, Miss? (*goes off talking to himself*) She's a cool hand. Doesn't care what she tells me to do. They are all crazy.

It beats me what has happened to the missus. And Rosemary! She was so dressed up she looked quite the lady. Must see what has happened to Curly. I could have asked the master about her, but now he's gone there's no one to ask except that German bastard and he's no good. Come on Curly lass—what's ailing you? Quite off your feed? (*He approaches her udders but the cow lashes out at him*) Whoa there! I'm not going to hurt you. I wish the master was here to talk to you instead of me. Cows or women—they are all the same—lash out because they think they'll get hurt. The master would have said, 'Cowherds and robbers are all the same—to cows'. Poor Curly!

(*Fade out. Priest and P.A. are seen together*)

PRIEST I had a queer dream last night—I suppose you would call it that.

P.A. How could I call it that? It wasn't my dream.

PRIEST To me all dreams are 'queer' so I thought you would call it that.

P.A. One of your prophets, Isaiah, who was the kind of person to whom you religious people pay attention—forgive me if I don't know what your brand of religion is—

PRIEST (*bows slightly*) I am flattered. May I congratulate you on your discriminatory integrity in not having 'labelled' me with a particular 'brand' of religion.

P.A. Let us leave out the introductory courtesies. I was referring to Isaiah who describes his contact with the Lord in matter-of-fact terms, precisely dated. Of course, we cannot know what happened, but we may have opinions. My object is not to discuss that past experience but to illustrate the unlimited possibilities when you say, 'a queer dream'; possibilities which are limited in this discussion only by my ignorance. The *experience* is not 'limited' by 'finite' considerations of our capacity, though our 'discussion' of it is.

PRIEST I dreamed of an explosion of vast, tremendous and majestic proportions. It was terrifying. It was black as night; not night that I might understand in the solar system, but dark night of the soul—

P.A. As described by Saint John of the Cross perhaps?

PRIEST I am not Saint John of the Cross, nor yet Isaiah; that itself contributes to the sense of queerness that it should be *my* dream.

P.A. I am familiar with reports of terrifying experiences described in terms of varying inadequacy—as you have just been doing. We are both aware of the awe-ful experience. Many are not; they fear 'going mad', some indescribable disaster, 'break-down'; they may express themselves by bringing about disaster. We psycho-analysts think you do not know what a dream is; the dream itself is a pictorial representation, verbally expressed, of what happened. What actually happened when you 'dreamed' we do not know. All of us are intolerant of the unknown and strive instantaneously to feel it is explicable, familiar—as 'explosion' is to you and me. The event itself is suspect *because* it is explicable in terms of physics, chemistry, psycho-analysis, or other *pre*-conceived experience. The 'conception' is an event which has become 'conceivable'; the 'conceivable' it has become is no longer the genetic experience. Pre-conception, conception, birth—what a shock it must have been to know that a woman has a baby! How absurd to suppose that it could have any connection with intercourse! I have found those who think it ridiculous that a woman could initiate an idea or have a thought worthy of consideration.

PRIEST Women are indeed very jealous and envious of other women. In an obstetric ward I have known the havoc created by the envy of unmarried nursing staff for mothers and expectant mothers. A doctor friend told me that an obstetric surgeon must be vigilant to see that he does not allow a nurse, sister or matron to usurp his function of seeing fair play. You are not suggesting that it is only men who are hostile to the creative woman?

P.A. Certainly not. Jealousy and envy are elements which do not conform to physiological and anatomical characteristics; the personality, or mind, does not have physical bounds which can be delineated by appeal to our physical form. Where we differ is not with regard to the corporeal and physical, but in your postulating God to fill in the conceptual gap.

PRIEST I do not think we would be likely to mind a conceptual gap; I am willing to agree to the validity of a 'conceptual' or 'theoretical' gap for purposes of discussion. I maintain that the 'concept' of God is matched by a reality of which the concept is but a shadowy and feeble reflection such as human beings fabricate within the limits of their finite minds. The 'Father of an Infinite Majesty' is a feeble verbalization intended to represent the ineffable and infinite by whatever experiential elements, memories, desires, hopes and fears are within our capacity.

P.A. I can see that. But why drag in Something More—God?

PRIEST I don't; those things which are 'dragged in', as you say, are flattening representations; two-dimensional substitutes for the non-dimensional which misrepresent more than they illuminate.

P.A. 'There plant eyes', as Milton said about the inner world.

PRIEST Milton's tragedy was Paradise Lost and—with due acknowledgement of his greatness—I do not think he was right in supposing that he ever Regained it. Blake saw that Milton was great enough to be able to depict his loss, but not great enough to find the loss of which he was aware.

P.A. I feel you are ignoring the fact—

PRIEST Excuse me, but I claim 'experience', as you'd call it, at least as old as Lilith and beyond, whereas your 'science' is a recent and already macilent growth.

P.A. At least a few thousand years I would—

PRIEST 'A thousand ages in Thy sight are like an evening gone; . . . They fly forgotten as a dream dies at the opening day.'

P.A. Which brings us back to your 'queer dream'. Don't you think our discussion may have thrown light on the multitudinous possibilities corresponding to your 'queer' dream?

PRIEST Just what I was about to remark. Our different, diverging and apparently contradictory views may 'appear' in the 'queer' domain to be more real than they are.

P.A. 'Litora, litoribus contraria.'

PRIEST Virgil was not meaning our debate.

P.A. But his phrase throws forward into the future besides illuminating the past.

PRIEST Where do you suppose that reality originates—only from the genes, the chromosomes, DNA, the double helix?

P.A. I don't know.

PRIEST That's the wisest admission you have made.

P.A. I could not aspire to a scientific inquiry without that basic admission.

PRIEST I could not aspire to God without a similar admission.

P.A. My objection to your people is that they claim an omniscient and omnipotent God.

PRIEST We aspire to a god made in our own image—that is well known; but because we keep company with people that have certain views I don't think we should be debited with those views.

P.A. It is part of my work to point out that all of us are victims of just that experience. Like it or not, of such is the kingdom of men.

PRIEST I don't quarrel with that.

P.A. We have come a long way from your queer dream without, I fear, penetrating the problem. Don't hold it against me or against those who, like me, aspire to know.

PRIEST I don't—so long as you do not claim that 'to aspire' is the same as 'to achieve'. At our stage of development that is arrogant. Let us agree to discourage the idea that we have arrived at the destination.

P.A. If *we* don't, some fact will—perhaps the explosion of which you dreamed. I observe that we are not alone; we can continue later. Good morning, Ma'am; I hope you are well.

ROSEMARY Thank you—very well. Where's Alice? I told her to be here.

ALICE Here, Ma'am.

ROSEMARY Sit down all of you. You two (*addressing Priest and P.A.*) have arrived at an agreement. I am glad—

PRIEST It is more apparent than real.

P.A. We have arrived at the same fence at the same time and that gives an illusion of agreement liable to obscure the fact that we are on different sides of the fence.

ROSEMARY Fence? What fence?

PRIEST Alas! It is invisible, impalpable, insensible . . .

P.A. Nearly inexpressible but for our borrowings from disciplines not our own.

ROSEMARY Then you are in agreement in 'acquisition'.

P.A. No. He steals or borrows from me: I do the same from him.

We both resent each other and even ourselves as we have to collude with each other. Collusion, robbery, theft—what do we not owe to them!

PRIEST Bigotry, ignorance, intolerance—how much science owes to them!

P.A. How firm the foundations on which the Church must build!

PRIEST How persistently the scientists rob us of faith! How unsleeping must be our resistance to their attacks!

ALICE A plague on both your houses and may they soon perish.

ROSEMARY Hold your tongue, Alice!

MAN Shall I shoot her?

ROSEMARY Certainly not—you are too crude. She could be trained to do something useful, like dressing my hair. You may do it now, Alice, but I shall have to send you out of the room if you interrupt.

ALICE Sorry, Ma'am. I thought you objected—

ROSEMARY Don't think. Get on with my hair. And smarten that uniform I gave you.

P.A. Your left-off clothing—mental and physical. Allowing her to participate in intellectual discussion has worn thin the servant's clothing which you left her.

ROSEMARY Mind your own business.

PRIEST She has grown in insolence instead of profiting by the example you set her. Her frame of mind lacks servility. General Violence, who used to command the Armed Forces, saw to it that the troops conformed to religious truth. When that is relaxed military discipline becomes corrupt.

P.A. The mind is ill-disciplined when released from philosophical discipline. When you tried to substitute religious discipline, the executive branch, the Church, had to devote years to the planning of the City of God. Long before it was completed, even while the plans were being elaborated, it was discovered that it was being erected in the wrong places.

PRIEST True. Those who later became known as the psychoanalysts, the Romantics, got hold of it in—of all places—the unconscious; there, amongst its poisonous marshes and gases, the ruins of that wonderful structure were painfully put together to form a romantic ruin ready for the Inauguration—of arguments and controversies about its beauties.

P.A. Are you 'borrowing' or 'stealing'? I seem to have heard something like this about Port Royal.

PRIEST 'Psycho-analysis', like 'Port Royal', is a phrase which may be 'beautifying' something as foul and smelly as 'pourris'. Milton beautified the debate in Hell.

P.A. Farmers acknowledge their debt to 'manure'. Lord Acton horrified his contemporaries by saying that many a beautiful lady owed her safety to whores and whoredom.

PRIEST Men don't like that idea. Hosea owed his wife to the realm of harlotry. When 'Gomer first at Heaven's command' arose from out the azure main . . . Which azure? Heaven? Pornography?—some language is 'blue'.

ROSEMARY That will do, Alice—how does my hair look?

ALICE Beautiful, Ma'am.

ROSEMARY It's a waste of time as far as these two fools are concerned. Science and Knowledge seem unaware of Beauty. I think you have made my already 'beautiful' hair apparent. You certainly had a long and expensive training before you became fit to be my maid; even now you have much to learn. I know I am beautiful; now you have to say I am whether you like it or not. It used to be rather fun when Roland, although a booby, acknowledged my beauty; I never thought you would have to admit it too. (*Lowers her voice*) My trigger-happy admirer who thinks I bow to his gun will be in trouble if I am not very much mistaken. How? Oh, I have my means—not least his belief that I am in love with him and terrified of his friends.

ALICE Aren't you, Ma'am?

ROSEMARY Of course I am, but I don't allow myself to be stupefied by love or terror. That's the advantage of being intelligent enough to turn one's 'education' to good account. I learnt a lot when I was young and could see how to manage the wealthy and powerful and lust-crazed blackguards who came for my Mum. Even now I have nightmares when I wake up sweating with fear. Mind you, (*looking down at Alice's feet*) I wouldn't be in your shoes. How are they, by the way? You gave me them as part of my uniform when I came into service with you. How times have changed! They suit you—I hope you look after them. What are those men talking about? The moment they notice us they shut up. Let's listen . . .

P.A. 'Worship', you say; I would prefer to use some less emotional term.

PRIEST The word is not emotional. It means exactly what I intend it to mean when I am, as at present, talking about God. I avoid using it in contexts such as 'worshipping' Man or our mistress here. If I did I would feel guilty of blasphemy or, at the least, flattering speech.

P.A. Who or what were you speaking of when you used it just now?

PRIEST God, as I have said. I would not consider my 'queer' dream as just a dream with a qualifying adjective.

P.A. Effusions of the unconscious—

PRIEST 'Unconscious'—what's that?

P.A. 'God'—what's that?

PRIEST I realize you think I know as little about God as you do, and perhaps I know even less about the unconscious, but I meant it seriously when I asked you about the unconscious. Do you know more about it than the usual theories of Freud and Melanie Klein and the rest? Do you know the extent to which qualified psychoanalysts are unconscious of reality, even the realities of psychoanalysis? Those I have seen individually and at their congresses appear to me only to be capable of grasping that narrow range of phenomena which fall, so to speak, within the rational band of the spectrum. Unless you can formulate your 'discoveries' within the range of rational, articulate speech you are not satisfied that you 'know'.

P.A. That is probably so; since we try to conform to the conventions commonly accepted by scientists as 'scientific', our formulations are vulnerable to the criticism that they are only rational statements—common sense. Even so, they are challenged as being unsupported by evidence. We are criticised both for being platitudinous *and* incomprehensible—'mad', as it is vulgarly called.

PRIEST I wonder if you have considered 'scientists', as you call them.

P.A. May I ask if you have considered Christian Scientists?

PRIEST Yes indeed, as I have also considered Christian Philosophers. I do not exclude consideration of any phenomenon, but we must consider how much time is available for 'consideration' between birth and death.

P.A. One of my objections to your school of thought is that it appears to encourage a belief in unlimited times such as life after death.

PRIEST Unfortunately we are debited with the views—usually mistaken—that people have about what we teach.

P.A. You yourself appear to debit me with views about psycho-analysis which I do not hold; it would be a part of my task if you were an analysand to elucidate your assumptions so that you could contrast and compare them with any other ideas you might entertain. In this respect I think our activity is different from yours. *You* aspire to tell others how and what to think: *We* aspire only to show what people think—the rest is their choice.

PRIEST Fair enough; I have no quarrel with that. But I have a quarrel with psycho-analysts who talk as if they are subject to no such weakness.

P.A. Fair enough—I reciprocate. We object to that kind of psycho-analyst. I would hope not to be of their number.

PRIEST It sounds ideal.

P.A. It is, but we are aware of the difference between the real and ideal. A few people have existed who have done more to help others to discriminate between the real and ideal than we have.

PRIEST I don't wish to deny you the credit for it; religion also has played an important part in fostering that awareness.

P.A. Scandals of the Church and scandalous behaviour of its devotees could, I suppose, be said to have taught people to discriminate, but that is hardly a virtue of religious activity, or an activity of which religions should claim to be proud.

PRIEST Scandals of psycho-analysis are not different. All should stand in penitential awe before the throne of our Maker.

P.A. You are talking of matters which are known to me only by repute. A psycho-analysis affords an opportunity to compare and acknowledge superiority when seen.

PRIEST It contrast painfully with analysis as I know it.

P.A. Reality often involves pain when brought near the ideal, whether scientific or asesthetic. I am usually sensitive to this pain; I hope to be sufficiently tolerant of it to avoid recourse to 'holier' (more scientific, more artistic, more wealthy, more aristocratic) 'than thou'.

PRIEST In aspiration we seem to be not so far apart—'so far'.

ROSEMARY *How* they talk!

ALICE Yes, don't they.

P.A. I see the ladies are listening. Perhaps it is rather rude not to include them.

PRIEST Or 'superior'?

P.A. People of different sex find it easier to resolve their anatomical and physiological differences than their differences in outlook. After all, the physical can be subjected to tactile and visual and olfactory investigation and resolution.

PRIEST Dogs can be observed using their olfactory inheritance for that purpose.

P.A. True; but that path of solution is easily followed and its destination soon reached. Believing, as I do, that there is a mind—

PRIEST And as I do, a soul and a spirit—

P.A. —the mental differences present goals and problems which are far more difficult.

PRIEST Wasn't it Napoleon—who could hardly be said to be religiously inclined—who compared the physical to the spiritual, the material to the moral, very much in favour of the spiritual?

P.A. No, Emerson—nothing like such an impressive witness.

PRIEST In any case the idea expressed is important, not who said it.

P.A. Emerson certainly claimed great power and importance for ideas.

MORIARTY So did Anatole France who claimed high prestige for the supremacy and power of bigotry and ignorance.

P.A. In *Thaïs* I think.

MORIARTY But where did the idea come from—France or the imagination?

P.A. *His* imagination—the unconscious.

PRIEST *If* unconscious you cannot be consciously aware of its origin, the generator.

P.A. I don't deny the possibility of some generator force any more than I would deny either the force of, or the search for, the Quasars of which we hear so much.

ROSEMARY (*to Alice*) They both ignore the force or presence of yourself and myself.

ALICE P.A. seemed to admit surreptitiously that 'the ladies' were here.

ROSEMARY Fucking idiot!

ALICE Probably both idiocy and fucking, but that is not the same as admitting the presence of you and me.

ROSEMARY True. He's busy getting a pedestal for me to get onto, or a servile function to fulfil. You should see what goes on in the psycho-analytical dovecote when feminine intuition obtrudes. Watch them.

ALICE I know—'celibacy of the clergy' and 'professional integrity', they call it.

ROSEMARY Impotent bastards!

ALICE Put that way it doesn't sound so grand. Look out! Here's your boy friend.

MAN (*bows coldly to Rosemary, ignores Alice*) I have come with news for you. I think the rest may fade out.

(*The scene becomes dark*)

NINETEEN

It is light again. Man and Rosemary are alone. She is attractively and expensively dressed.

MAN I have come to let you know that I have decided, after long and careful consideration, to make you my wife.

ROSEMARY I am amazed.

MAN I thought you might be, but I have gone into the matter most carefully; I have not only had good reports of you but from my own personal observation I have concluded that you are satisfactory and will therefore be married to me at the beginning of next month.

ROSEMARY (*furious but not speechless*) If you kneel at my feet and bring your face conveniently near to me I shall condescend to give you the hardest smack on the jaw you or anyone else has had.

MAN Rosemary, don't, I beg of you, do anything so foolish. You know I don't waste words—by the way, did you see to it that Tom disposed of that silly English fellow?

ROSEMARY Are you daring to threaten me? Who do you think—

MAN Oh come; don't waste words. So far from threatening you

I have told you we are to marry and the details are being arranged. Threats and love and all those sorts of things are all right amongst the vulgar. Surely you can see it is out of place here?

ROSEMARY Indeed? And is sex also only for the vulgar?

MAN That is nothing to do with us. Of course I shall use you for sexual purposes—I have gone into that and you will do, but don't imagine that I am talking the silly juvenile nonsense of animals like P.A. I got over that *many* years ago.

ROSEMARY Love too?

MAN Don't be silly. I have arranged and that is enough.

ROSEMARY Blast your damned impudence!

MAN I have some other matters to arrange. You will be sent for in half an hour. All your possessions will be packed. I take it you want to keep your maid; she will be sent for likewise. Now, good-bye. (*He goes out*)

ROSEMARY Alice!

ALICE What's he going to do?

ROSEMARY It is what *I* am going to do, believe me. If I cannot deal with him I am much mistaken. Bring me the automatic—fully loaded.

ALICE Yes, Ma'am.

(*Rosemary sits brooding in silence. Alice returns*)

ALICE It's gone! Everything has been taken away!

(*Fade out. Man and Priest are alone together when it becomes light*)

MAN I have sent for you to let you know my arrangements. As you are doubtless aware these meetings have served their purpose—

PRIEST They were indeed becoming unruly. I thought that Rosemary no longer had the disciplinary hold she used to have.

MAN No, no—she never had. Just a sexual grasp on her maid and that is of no consequence. A little re-organization will sort it out. I shall confer authority on Rosemary to enable her to keep order when I have married her.

PRIEST Congratulations.

MAN Congratulations? I don't think I understand—oh yes, of course. She was a fairly obvious choice from what I have seen of her ability to make the best of such facilities as were available to her.

She might not be able to live up to increased power and prestige—that does sometimes happen. I am not unhopeful. However, I shall not waste time on the past. I want you to be a religious overseer. You must not be obsessed with the past; it is your weakness. You must adjust to the present and future. I give you the chance; if you don't succeed it will be sad—you will be dispensed with.

PRIEST Like Roland you mean. Are you threatening me?

MAN *That* is an example of your obsession with the past. I don't threaten; I state a fact. You wear the Past as if it were a decoration. It has no importance, though its debris can still be seen and felt impinging on the present. I'll arrange for that kind of rubbish to be looked after so that it can be swept up and discarded.

PRIEST How will you dispense with the debris of 1054?

MAN It would take too long to explain. It's an example of the way visual trash hangs around; there is nothing to see, but that trivial little explosion continues and some people devote time and generations of lives to sweeping up detritus. Now it is being collected into books which soon no one will read—and that, for the time, will be that.

PRIEST For the time?—so you do think it has a future.

MAN That is what I am saying; the past *is* past; it is of no consequence except as debris for collection and disposal. I shall appoint you—

PRIEST I see; as an authority like a—

MAN No, no, no. Not like an anything. There you go again—obsessed with the past and with being 'just like' the past, or a man, or a bishop. You are like a child saying, 'Look—aren't I exactly like a grown up!' The result—no chance of 'becoming' anything, the mind so stuffed full with 'memories' there is room for nothing more. You must clear your mind of cant.

PRIEST That has been said before.

MAN Still harping on the past—'before'. You see what I mean? I can't waste time. Meet here in half an hour.

PRIEST The same half hour? Half an hour from Now? That means that we shall not meet together.

MAN Yes, it will be the same. Every half hour will be different from every other half hour—your half hour, Rosemary's half hour—but 'the Time' will be the same.

PRIEST Roland too? He's dead you know.

MAN I know—I shot him. Now he's dead I have an important job for him.

PRIEST How can he do a job if he is dead? He can't do anything.

MAN That is his qualification. *You* would be able to do almost anything if only you'd shut up thinking you are important and trying to 'look like' an important person.

PRIEST Yet you tell me to take an important post.

MAN You may not be as incorrigible as you sound. Here! In half an hour. *(disappears)*

PRIEST Where's my watch? Gone. Of all the impossible orders from the most impossible of men! As it is Rosemary's half hour and Roland's half hour, it will have to be *my* half hour. What a meeting it will be! If I ran my diocese like that . . .

(*It slowly blacks out and grows light again, revealing Man alone with P.A.*)

MAN You will have to do a different job. This arrangement of your mistress's has become redundant.

P.A. I thought you would find that. You should not have shot Roland.

MAN (*opening his eyes wide*) It was essential that he should be shot to become available for my purposes.

P.A. He is dead.

MAN That is the first essential. I require him—

P.A. You'd better be quick—Tom has buried him and he must be discomposed.

MAN You are a prisoner to reality, buried in 'facts'. It is inevitable that you should have a prejudiced view.

P.A. My view is scientific.

MAN That's what I mean. Scientific outlook; limited outlook, obscured by facts. *You* are scientific; your religion also. But enough of this—I want you as the leader of a department of Truth.

P.A. That is what I have always meant by Science.

MAN Not as far as my observation goes. You are devoted to the *idea* that you are devoted to Truth—

P.A. What truth can I be devoted to if it is not truth as I see it?

MAN Your dilemma is indeed painful; *your* pain, not mine.

P.A. You sound as if you don't care.

MAN I don't. In half an hour—here! (*disappears*)

P.A. (*soliloquizing*) 'In half an hour. Here.' Where is here and what clock do I use? The law of the excluded middle. . . . I thought there could be some alternative to an extreme course; physically I know of no alternative to presenting myself—being or not being. That is, *if* I am right in assuming that the vertex is topographical. Suppose it is typographical—I could be one type or another . . . so many occasions in my life where I have found out what 'it' meant. Which 'it'? Do I choose to be or not to be? That fellow Shakespeare put words to the emotional problem that is still not solved. Has Priest the right idea that this life is a time of testing for a future? Suppose there is no future—I think it unlikely that there is an existence which I shall have to lead, and therefore be prepared for, *after* the next half hour. I shall have to consider a law of the excluded beginning. Logically this means that from the physiological vertex any object would be a figment of imagination. Not even that; if it excluded a beginning it would also exclude imagination which is necessary for its 'figment' to exist. The law of an 'excluded end' would seem to be tacitly believed by artists and, in fact, human beings in general. I am supposing that 'classical' logic is the only kind of logic. But suppose reality does not obey any of the laws laid down by the human animal—not even the 'logic' to which not only human thought, but also the universe *not* included in human thought, is supposed to conform. Is there an ultra or infra logic which does not fall within the spectrum of human logic, the logical spectrum analogous to the visual portion of the spectrum of electro-magnetic waves? 'Geocentral time' is up—'half an hour' is over. Is it geotemporal or sidero-temporal? Galactic-temporal or ultra-temporal? I shall call it Quasi-scientific time, measured in quasi hours. When I want to indicate something of which I *know* nothing but of which I want to talk or even think, it clothes itself with a meaning and I lose my nothing, my alpha or beta element. My variable becomes a constant.

Wake up? Go to hell! Oh, all right—time to get up? Quasi hell? It is the lark that sings so out of tune? Hear it not, Duncan. The wild ass can stamp o'er his head but Bahram's sleep cannot be broken; that great hunter shall sleep no more and therefore Cawdor shall sleep no more, Aeneas shall sleep no more . . . Palinurus! . . . I'm not a damned Dormouse . . . then don't twinkle like a bright and steadfast Star! The war was over last July—it says so in John Bull. We won! Officially! Oh, come in Equivocator . . . that's good news. Gos-spel! Oh, it's Man. Why did *you* act it out? Why did I *only* dream it? Which is worse—that you cannot wake me up, or that you only act it? Is it the sleeper only who poisons his dreams with his mental excrement? Or he who cannot dream of destroying the world but has to transform his dream into a bomb that poisons us with his atomic debris? 'In half an hour' this thug says he expects my answer, and I fool with pretty intellectual Quasar time. I am honest; I think; I am concerned with quasi morals. There is no special science but science. Yes, but I do not know which science, which truth. 'Couvre-toi de flannelle' is less impressive than 'Couvre-toi de gloire', but that kind of glory is comfortable after its kind; so is 'flannelle'. 'Oh my, I don't want to die, I want to go home', we used to sing. *That* was true; we hoped that the ugly reality would not penetrate the joke armour-plate. The armour-plate of a tank was penetrable; we were bewitched, bemused, 'probability'-dazzled cowards. 'Probably' we would not be killed; 'probably' we would survive to inhabit a new heaven and a new earth—'après la guerre'. I did not know I loved life so much. I survived to foot the bill; fight a war and spend the rest of life paying the bill for all those shells and tanks and bullets and the state of mind used to provide an armour more impenetrable than 'gloire' or 'flannelle'. 'Ante Agamemnona multi' . . . I remember, am still penetrated by the memory of brave men whose name did not 'live for evermore'. 'With whatsoever emphasis of passionate love repeated' the echo of their name is faint at last, 'soft as old sorrow, bright as old renown'; it fades and dies. Why do I mind this grizzly, victorious lout? It is not death I fear, but the shame of knowing a few, only a few, of the multitudinous shabby failures. There goes the bell again! Telephone? Alarm? Come in Equivocator—the anarchs of the world of Après la Guerre Fini. From that warfare there is no release—après la guerre fini. Come Phorbas! Come, come. As torrents in summer suddenly rise, though the sky is still cloudless . . . Mene huic confidere monstro? Not bloody likely! Ecce deus . . . ecce homo . . . take your choice. Sleep or wake—'you pays your money and you takes your choice'. Oh! It's you is it?

MAN No. Go away—and send Alice.

(*P.A. fades out*)

(*Alice appears*)

ALICE You want me—sir?

MAN Yes. Pack your mistress's things and meet me here in half an hour.

ALICE Is she going away? Where to?

MAN Mind your business. Be here in half an hour—I can give you your orders then. *You* have nothing to pack. Go!

ALICE But . . .

(*Fade out. Alice alone in the darkness begins to cry out, her calls becoming more terrified, wilder, angrier and more animal-like*)

ALICE Rosamund . . . Roseamund . . . Rosie! Rose . . . Herose! Here-rhose! Heeee . . . rose from the dead!

VOICE *Stop it!* (*silence; then the savage, wilder howls begin again—now unmistakably animal*)

ROSEMARY Hush! Oh hush! What's the matter?

ROBIN It's Roland—that is his howl. I would know it anywhere. He's calling his mate—there it is again! That's Alice—tigerish, but that's her, I know. (*The bloodcurdling duet becomes distant, blends with a storm and stops with a sudden decrescendo*)

* * *

ROSEMARY (*in full daylight, alone*) I can't stand this bloody place.

MAN The priest is ready to unite the happy pair.

ROSEMARY Don't I have any say in the matter?

MAN None. Bow your head modestly as if in prayer; follow me exactly.

ROSEMARY But . . . (*she is struggling to protest but he hushes her peremptorily*)

PRIEST'S VOICE (*droning as if in religious incantation of congregational prayer*) England-have-won-the-toss-and-have-chosen-to-bat. Ah-men. Ah-setting-the-field-as-if-for-a-fast-bowler. Ah-wonder-who-it-will-be. In-heaven-as-it-is-on-earth-because-there-is-no-turf-on-the-pitch-which-is-worn-and-will-almost-certainly-crumble-long-before-the-day. Dies illa, dies irae, calamitas et miseriae.

MAN *(whispers, hoarse with excitement)* Keep your head down! Don't watch—pretend you can't hear a thing. England are coming in to bat. I think it's Kitchener and . . . Kipling! No, it's . . .

PRIEST'S VOICE . . . the weary at rest. Rudyard has ceased from Kipling. He has started his run to the wicket. From outside the main entrance . . . Here he comes and is just going round the bend! Look out! He's using an atomic bomb instead of a ball, and . . . Here is a list of the Glorious dead who batted into the third day after all and have come direct out of the computer, the Holy Boast of our civilization. Quid nunc? These are they who come out of great fibrillation and here endeth the Christo-semitic era and beginneth the post-fissile quasi-epoch. I only am escaped alone to tell thee. What a marvellous day it is! Clear, silent, desolate. There is nothing to see but these gigantic boulders; I stand on top of one and look towards the horizon, a hard brilliant line that separates this brilliant desolation from utter blackness which is absolute—not so cold, so unfriendly as the googly. There is no sound; the silence is as absolute as the vision when there is no beholder. No sight, no sound, no feel of primrose sward, no sun rejecteth no beholder; absolute negation, no affirmation. What's yet to come is still unsure. Man is a discarded experiment like the mammals, like the saurians, like fire, like sparks that fly upward, like troubles when there is no mind to experience them.

MAN I thought we were done-for that time, but it was a dud after all. Now then, are we all present and correct? Read the roll, Sergeant Major, and reply, 'adsum', all of you—that is, if you are here. No cheating, no lying, no delusions, illusions or hypochondriacal hallucinations. Where *is* the Sergeant Major?

ALL We are all minors here now, sir.

MAN Oh yes, of course; quite right. What, *you* here?

PRIEST'S GHOST No, sir. I'm the ghost of the Boast you knew.

MAN Will *you* be acting Miner major? Call the roll!

PRIEST'S GHOST The Roll will be called up yonder in the Heavenly Kingdom.

P.A.'S GHOST What Time Scale?

PRIEST'S GHOST Sidereal Time of course; at Zero Infinite.

P.A.'S GHOST I don't understand.

MAN No one has asked you to. Is Widdecum here?

VOICE No, I'm his uncle—

MAN Uncle Tom Cobley? Pleased to meet—

ALL No, you damn' fool.

MAN I'll have you all bombed if you are impudent.

CROWD (*chanting*) We are immortal. We are evil. When man dies his Evil lives after him. His Evil is immortal.

ALL SOULS For though the body dies the soul shall live for ever.

CROWD (*chanting*) Arse 'oles inspire.

MAN *Very* funny: I'll have you bombed!

ALL SOULS What! No cakes and ale?

MAN You're dead—shut up!

ALL SOULS Our name is forgotten for evermore, but we have not happened yet and we shall live after you when you are dead and gone.

MAN My evil shall live after me. Where's that mistress of mine roaming? Come here!

ALICE Surely you aren't going to obey him.

ROSEMARY Didn't they even teach evil in your holy school? Not even scandal?

ALICE We only read the school for scandal, but we didn't really practise it.

ROSEMARY At *my* school we practised it. Yes—I am going with Man. And mind your own bloody business.

ALICE You aren't in love with him!

ROSEMARY Of course not; I wouldn't let anyone put those blinkers on *me*. Roland couldn't teach you anything—*he* went to a Public School. You'll catch a spirochaete in your next job I shouldn't wonder. And tiny little spirochaetes with their soft inaudible mouths will eat away that brain of yours; they are delicate feeders—

ALICE Are you going to give me to the troops for my livelihood?

ROSEMARY Why not? I gave my mother; that's why she tried to bring me up properly, but thanks to Original Sin I never got taken in. I was tough. Love this murderous blackguard? I should say so! You watch—he's coming now. If you keep your head down you will see the lovelight soften my eyes and dissolve his common sense; it has not softened *my* brain. *Watch*—and pray if you like. Hulloh, *dar*ling! Oh, it's you is it?

P.A. I heard you say, 'watch'—

PRIEST —and 'pray'—

P.A. & PRIEST So I came.

ROSEMARY So long as you don't join in I don't mind.

P.A. & PRIEST You're not going to give yourself to that brute! He's an enemy!

ROSEMARY He won didn't he?

P.A. He and his never stuck to the rules of war.

ROSEMARY The rules of war! What do *you* know about war? You mean *your* rules. Leg-before-wicket, swing together, the halter is round your neck! What Rules—Britannia? The Waves? Even Canute knew better than that!

MYCROFT No, no child—microwaves.

ROSEMARY And who may they be? Scientific bunkum. What do *you* know about the waves emitted by my feet when I chose to make them twinkle, twinkle on the hard, hard slum pavements of my street? I have seen the natural, unspoilt louts and blackguards of my slum follow my heels, threads of invisible steel hooking their eyes and dragging them helpless at my feet till I chose to release them. Love! You don't know what it is—none of you.

P.A. Your beliefs are expressions of great confidence in your powers; how you come to such 'beliefs' and what evidence has convinced you that they are 'facts' I don't know.

ROSEMARY I *do* know—and your doubts do not impress me.

P.A. You think I doubt the truth of your impressions. I am saying that you have not told me what evidential support there is for those beliefs.

ROSEMARY I feel it; I know it.

P.A. Your feelings are one kind of evidence. But don't make the mistake of acting as if you had a different sort of evidence. Alice *feels* you love her, but the feeling leads her to suppose facts. She thinks she can depend on you; she can't. If she cannot depend on herself she would be unwise to depend on anyone else.

ROSEMARY Me, for example.

P.A. For example, yes.

ROSEMARY I agree. My principles would not allow me to think

otherwise; the same principle which would not allow either loving or being loved by Man. I depend on my hooks—

P.A. And on his eyes to provide you with 'material' into which you can insert those same 'hooks'. In other terms—my psycho-analytic terms—sex.

ROSEMARY (*yawning*) How interesting.

P.A. Not in the least. Usually sex interest has died by puberty, leaving only a mental vestige which cannot be relied on any more than you could rely on your vestigial tail to support you if you tried to hang by it from the branch of a tree.

ALICE How ridiculous!

P.A. I gave a ridiculous example to illustrate a ridiculous dependence.

SHERLOCK I thought the whole of psycho-analysis depended on sex.

P.A. In the practice of psycho-analysis I depend on ideas.

ALICE If *that* is not hanging by a vestigial tail I would like to know what is.

P.A. Man, as a thinking animal, has reached the end of the road.

SHERLOCK What road?

P.A. The road which is taken by all experiments that have to be discarded.

MYCROFT Aristarchus had to discard his heliocentric theories.

P.A. No, he died before the instrument makers caught up with him. After they had made telescopes and mathematical theories, which later were recognized as mental instruments, Copernicus found Aristarchus and his theories were right.

MAN No he didn't. It was a German who used a telescope to discover the satellites of Jupiter but was denied the credit.

ROSEMARY Darling, how clever you are! Come and sit by me.

MAN Later. Where's that priest? Get on with the roll-call.

PRIEST Irene Adler

REPLY —and grey mare

PRIEST Tom Pierce

REPLY —the grey mare is mine

PRIEST Robin

REPLY —it is not; it's that Coventry woman

PRIEST Moriarty

REPLY —she's a whoore

PRIEST Miners

REPLY —it's hers

PRIEST Roland

REPLY —it's not

PRIEST All souls

REPLY —it's hers

MAN Whoore or no whoore, Missus Brune will now sing a song.

ALICE

'It's sung to the moon by a love-lorn loon
Who died for the love of a lady.'

ROSEMARY Alice, don't be sentimental. By the way—how's Tom?

ALICE I know nothing about him.

ROSEMARY (*slyly*) Alice, Alice! I'm shocked. Didn't you once tell me he was a very 'suitable' man? Oh well, love dies alas! Tell Man he may sit near me—if he dares.

ALICE He's just coming over—don't look.

P.A. 'Taught by the heavenly muse to venture down the dark descent and up to re-ascend though hard and rare.' I wonder . . . she may be tough enough and so may he, but he is no Horace to survive the storms of Pyrra, and she is quite as tough as Horace's golden-haired lass.

MAN (*solicitously*) How are you dear? Not feeling nervous?

ROSEMARY I don't think (*looking adoringly at him*) I should ever feel nervous with you by my side.

ALICE He shot him, the bastard!

ROSEMARY Which bastard are you referring to dear?

MAN You shouldn't be so familiar with your maid. I love you for it, but it is dangerous to encourage the lower classes. Servants must serve, not aspire.

ROSEMARY Darling, I shall remember that—always. Alice, go and see Tom.

ALICE Yes, Ma'am.

MAN That's better. You should get rid of her.

ROSEMARY I would miss her here; she has been with me so long I almost think of her as part of the place.

MAN I know, but she should know her place *in* this place.

ROSEMARY How wise you are! I always remind her of her rightful place in the house if she ever shows signs of forgetting it. I hope you will remind me—I am sure you will—of *my* place in the house if I ever show signs of forgetting it. When is our wedding?

MAN When you like. I have told them they must all be ready waiting, including the priest.

ROSEMARY Oh, is it to be a real Church wedding? How thrilling!

MAN Well . . . yes. A modern Church wedding. Not the old-fashioned kind. We start with a roll-call to see that they are all present and correct.

ROSEMARY I don't see anyone yet; there were one or two but they have disappeared. Oh, of course dear—how clever of you to arrange for us to have a little quiet time together first!

MAN Where is everyone? Many hours have passed and yet there are a mere handful of people—I told them to be here for the wedding in half an hour.

ROSEMARY Alice—go and fetch them and be quick about it. And bring Roland.

ALICE He's dead.

ROSEMARY So what? I knew he was dead years ago. Fetch his ghost. You can weep for him if you like but that won't bring him back to life. It may flush him out of your eyes.

MAN Call the roll!

ALL SOULS (*in raucous unison*)

Shall we gather at the river?
The river that flows through Paradise.

P.A.

When the roll is called up yonder
I'll be there.

THE DUCHESS Wrong! It should be:

The Happy gate that leads to Ware
Love is like sunshine in the Air.

ROBIN Wrong:

Love is like sunshine in the bier.
Oh drink to me only through your tears
And I'll not ask for beer.

ALICE Wrong: Colonel left in the Knuts Harding, D.S.O.

GULL Left tight, left right—Halt! Left turn!

TOM Well, what brought you to enlist my man? Private Harding, D.S.O., reduced to the ranks for being sober and orderly in your sobriety.

GULL Pardon me sir . . . related to the Duchess.

TOM Oh, that's different . . . promoted to the vice-president of Licensed States of America.

HARDING To *be* vice-president or the *state* of vice-president?

TOM No, no—

GULL Left turn! Quick march! Left right left right. Dis-miss! Sentenced to All the Known States of Psycho-analysis for Eternity.

HARDING My sentence is more than I can bear. Born and bred in a state of sin, entangled in the barb of frivolity, alcohol and fraternity, I shall rejoice in joholity Evermore.

THE DUKE OF SHEHOL My *dear* Colonel! My *very* dear Colonel! I envy you with all my heart. Can I offer you a port? No? I apologize—you are allowed nothing but champagne. In heaven I don't need it for the port is any in a storm.

HARDING There is nothing like champagne. It is either shampain or it . . . isn't. The middle excluded again—

THE DUKE OF SHEHOL Poor fellow! Excluded for ever. These Extremists! I myself am bred extremely—no middle—too sexual. I regret it, I really do. I would give anything to be in your place. Or nearly everything . . . not my halo of course.

MAN What chaos! Tell them to stop it—at once, Rosemary!

ROSEMARY (*rouging her lips*) Alice—tell them to stop it. (*Redoubled noise*)

TOM Man is condemned to live on the fruits of Victory. Here—for the term of his natural life, amongst the English in everlasting freedom.

MAN My prize is more than I can wear.

ROBIN Lucky swine—I always wanted my hair long. This din is fearful.

ROSEMARY (*shouting, almost screaming to make herself heard*) I do so love that hymn, 'Shall we gather at the river'. It used to make me giggle to see the country bumpkins exchanging sly jokes—nothing sly about this though!

MAN (*pushing his fingers into his ears to prevent being deafened*) No.

PRIEST Partners find their ghosts for the Resurrection Blues!

MATHEMATICIAN It is absurd to exclude the middle.

P.A. You might as well say there is either a noise or there is no noise. It only means that either the listener can hear or he can't. It tells something about the personality that hears or does not hear; nothing about the environment of the personality. If I cannot see a tumour because I have no X-ray negative, or cannot interpret the negative, that doesn't mean there is no tumour because it is excluded.

ROSEMARY Thank you, thank you, darling, for . . .

MAN For what?

ROSEMARY This wonderful party. It is lovely; so gay, so happy! Everyone is enjoying it marvellously.

PRIEST All ghosts take the partner who stops in front of them when the music starts—stops I mean.

MATHEMATICIAN It can't do both; it stops, or it does not.

P.A. It is heard, or it is not. Like the music of the spheres—thanks to radio astronomy it is audible to ordinary people who think it is noise or interference.

ROBIN Or denial, or defence, or Kleinian rubbish, or psycho-analysis.

P.A. Some can listen to it and transform it—Mozart, Leonardo, Praxiteles, Bach—

ROBIN Or the Beatles, or Rossini—

MATHEMATICIAN Or Riemann, or Aristarchus.

P.A. You are admitting that the significance of the excluded middle is the excluded 'exclusion', the excluded 'person' or 'thing'.

MAN Nothing is excluded here. Is this your ideal?

P.A. No, not mine, but I don't therefore exclude its existence.

MAN But surely you can see—or hear—from this outrageous rabble, that you cannot allow *everything*? Something must be excluded—or do you British like this muddle? This isn't a marriage—it's a riot.

ROSEMARY *Darling*—it's lovely. 'Lap me in soft Lydian airs' is all right for Alice, but what has it brought her to? Send her to me at once to do the 'lapping' for me.

ALICE Tell Man he must go; this is no place for him without his guns and armour.

(*Rosemary signals to Man to go*)

MAN Go? Why, what has happened?

PRIEST Time for the Resurrection Blues. The Dead will fall in on the right while the Roll is called. Spirits rejoin their partners later for the dance of death.

SPIRIT (*recognizing a friend*) If thou beest he? But oh, how fallen! Quantum mutatus ab illo Hectore . . .

ACHILLES . . . and he walked stiffly into the shadows.

ROBIN What a crowd! All the best people—too highbrow for me.

ROLAND I'm surprised you think so. These are not that kind—

ROBIN The bands have started to play. There is . . . I'm sorry, I have quite forgotten your name. You look more beautiful than ever. May I?

(*The pair dance slowly away into the distance*)

ALICE Who are they?

ROLAND Do you still not know? It is your party.

ALICE No, it is Rosemary's.

ROSEMARY No, it is Time Past's party.

PRIEST *That* is P.A.'s party.

P.A. No, my party is not times past. Always the mistake of thinking the past is owned by psycho-analysis; the past is owned by Regret. Regret is a guest at a psycho-analytic party but is not the host; nor is psycho-analysis the domain of Regret. Regret is so vain that it is regarded as important and treated with deference in religion.

PRIEST Centuries have passed since all was vanity, and Vain Regret took the place of God.

ROLAND Why can't you make up your mind?

ROSEMARY Typically masculine! Men are always making up their minds, yet they think they can look down on women for making up their faces. I don't know of any woman who makes up her mind to be such a mess as the mind is when a man has finished making it up. The years men spend on psycho-analysis and education and religion! All as futile as eye-shadow! They end up each time worse than the last.

ROLAND What would you have us do?

ROSEMARY No idea. I let my mind make me up. I suppose you think I haven't a mind?

ROLAND I always thought you have one of the most acute minds—

ROSEMARY Oh, don't be such a fool! Have enough respect for your intelligence and mine not to descend to flattery. The band has started a new tune—oh, I love this; let's join in.

SOPRANOS

Sum-mer suns are glow-ing over land and sea,
Hap-py light is flow-ing for you but not for me.

ALTOS

The bells of Hell go ting-a-ling-a-ling
Far over land and see
The loud, uplifted, alcoholim go single-im-a-ling
For new but not faugh mer-ley.

TENORS

Oh death where is thy sting-ai-ling
Oh grève thy vick-tau-rhee?

ROLAND Where's the grammarian? At his funeral?

ROBIN Don't let that Boche hear you—he is hostile to Arians.

PRIEST This band is lovely—that is the great advantage of being tone deaf.

ROLAND And colour blind. If you could distinguish colours you would not be able to see me because my kind of visibility does not lie within the spectrum of human ocular vision.

PRIEST I have never been interested in human ocularity except as a blinker used for excluding the 'ghost' that one doesn't want to see. Now and then some fool like Arjuna, or Socrates, or Dante, or Meister Eckhart, or Juan Yeepes y Alvarez—

ROLAND Who on earth is Yeepes Yip-i-addy-i-ay-i-ay?

PRIEST He is not on earth.

ROSEMARY What on earth are you two talking about?

PRIEST The Kingdom of Heaven is not 'on earth' and nor is the place that chap from Hippotades was in when Augustine wrote the City of God. Plato knew that; Socrates was not so wise.

ROBIN '. . . as if of hemlock I had drunk', said Keats.

PRIEST He should have tried peyote; the Aztecs knew better.

SHERLOCK Even they had to wait till the Supreme Court recognized the Native American Church—

PRIEST Which recognized the Holy Spanish Church of Cortes, the Holy Catholic Church. As I was saying, Plato did not lack wisdom to the point of drinking hemlock.

SHERLOCK Nor, I gather, did you take the draught you offered the Court assembled in the Death Pit at Ur.

PRIEST There is no evidence.

SHERLOCK *That* is the evidence. My business is facts and I have to respect all kinds of evidence including negative evidence—

P.A. Which you have to interpret. I interpret—do not dispense—facts.

SHERLOCK I do not argue against your vertex. I only argue against the favouritism you show for one fact rather than another, and one vertex rather than another.

PRIEST So do I. God is not mocked, but you behave as if you do not have to bother with God because you cannot be confronted with a particular category of a fact. Isn't this music hellish?

P.A. You give a perfect example of applying a religious category appropriate to religious categories of localization.

PRIEST I do not. Like you, I have to use topographical terminology to describe categories and locations when I am discussing, as here, a subject which has no known locality. One prophet said, 'The Kingdom of Heaven is within you'.

ROLAND Psycho-analysts deprecate these Kleinian statements.

ROBIN Good lord! Don't say you have psycho-analysts in Heaven.

ROLAND You rush to conclusions. I didn't say I was in Heaven—or Hell. I did say I was dead.

ROSEMARY I never regarded physical death as a necessary qualification for being dead.

PRIEST The classics are dead.

P.A. It has become a sign that a person or theory is dead when it is called a 'classic'. Classic Art, Classic Religion, Classic Science are states of those activities and people when they have reached the stage where no one regards them save as objects. This music—

PRIEST Not music yet, surely? Should there not be some structure, some sign of mental discipline about it?

P.A. If that is what you think, should there not also be some discipline to which religion conforms? In psycho-analysis, though we do support the idea of 'freedom', we also preserve a mental discipline—a rigorous one.

ROBIN Where is the line between licence and freedom?

PRIEST There has always been discipline in religion. Dogma is a succinct statement of religious law. Terms like 'dogmatic' are employed in an undisciplined manner by those who use dogma as a pejorative comment on a scientific statement. We are familiar, from personal experience, with 'life-preserving' religious experience, but we do not and cannot impose that fact on others who have no such experience.

ROLAND The band is playing a jazzed-up version of 'For though the Body dies the Soul shall live for ever'. Do you call that blasphemous?

PRIEST No; it gives a sombre note to a boringly hilarious evening.

ROBIN Aren't you being intolerant of hilarity?

PRIEST I think it would be boring without that tincture of solemnity which the reminder of death gives.

ROBIN Why? What is solemn about death?

P.A. Nothing; but people think so if they suppose they are doing something for the last time. I suppose one would think it doubly solemn if it were felt to be the first. Women have more reason than men to fear death as they know they can die in giving birth.

ROSEMARY Reason has nothing to do with it. If it had, many people would fear pregnancy who don't.

P.A. You mean they do not consciously express it.

ROSEMARY 'The unconscious'! Were you afraid Man was going to kill you, Roland?

ROLAND I meant to kill *him* before he could kill me. I was sure that I should not be left to live for long if I was successful.

ROSEMARY Were you afraid of a future life?

ROLAND No. This 'future life' is no worse than many times I have lived through—periods which were 'future' before they had occurred. The whole of my life had been future at some time. I hope *this* is going to come to an end; once is enough. What does P.A. say?—if this infernal music leaves him able to think.

P.A. 'Infernal music', you call it; are you using the term 'infernal' as pejorative? Or topographical, that is, music appropriate to the region our priestly friend calls Hell?

PRIEST 'Hell' is not a term of religious topology.

CHOIRMASTER Now—All toes only. Starting at page 2, piu, piu poco animato. 'The more we are together.' One, two . . . The more we are together, together, together—no, no! All toes together—poco sostenuto; the froth-blowers' anthem.

BIG TOE I can't find the place.

CHOIRMASTER You are not supposed to—this is not a solo item. This is All toes. You wait for the double bass to come in. Page 3 opens with a crashing bore marking your entry.

ALL TOES Entry? I thought it was the exit.

CHOIRMASTER All toes—exeunt—the entry is through the mouth. T'other end of the anatomy if you want The Way Out. Aut, aut, aut-ishoo! sneezes only!

ROSEMARY Oh, The Blue Danube! What a beautiful tune, I used to think. I once overhead a beautiful young man talking to a beautiful young girl; those two beauties were flushed with grievance because the dance, which glittered like Heaven to me, was 'so *bor*ing!'. 'So *bor*ing!' they repeated over again. I went up to my attic and prayed God to make me good.

MAN Whatever did you do that for? *I* should have killed them. Perhaps you thought that if you were a good girl God would let you go to dances too. So you shall; I will take you.

ROSEMARY This dance frightens me. I think we are dead.

MORIARTY So you are—as only human beings can be. Requiescat in pace—as if they had ever done anything but bore all figments of imagination as they read us without comprehension. I used occasionally to appear in their dreams. That man Roland used to come alive sometimes, enough to shriek with terror and wake some of his fellows. Why, Rosemary, what's the matter? You look quite faint. Just as I thought you were almost interesting. Catch her you dolt!

MAN Here's a chair. Where's your maid?

ROSEMARY I'm all right—it's hot in here, isn't it? I think I would like to sit down.

MORIARTY Sit down?—just as she was coming to life. They think they are going to break down if there is a chance of hatching out: Conan Doyle cracked up when he felt his shell of sanity was breaking. What a tough prison of sanity they grow at any sign of reality! Newton had to support his fragile shell by being Master of the Mint—just like any blathering Big Business construct. To be like everyone else—'sanity', they call it!

MAN (*to Rosemary*) Are you better, dear?

MORIARTY No, you fool—far worse. She is finding her way back to the slavery of mistresshood.

ROSEMARY What's that? I'm hearing voices.

MAN Of course; the room is full of people talking. Shall I tell them to go?

MORIARTY I thought only fragilities like Macbeth had to break up the party. She has no more stamina than the usual day-dream—probably less because she is a desire of Alice's; what P.A. would call a 'sexual' desire.

PRIEST Queer what a hullabulloo was made when Freud decided that some desires could be particularized as sexual. We had recognized the obscurant qualities of Desire years ago. Even Arjuna was unable to tolerate the desire which he almost succeeded in satisfying.

ROBIN 'Desire' is a name given an impulse when it is wished to obscure a precise feeling by generalizing the particular.

PRIEST I didn't know you had a philosophical bent.

ROBIN I haven't. All I wanted was to live in peace and quiet and run my farm. Then a farm worker desired to blow his brains out and did so. Filthy mess he made, too—made worse by coroners and psychiatrists and psycho-analysts, and now invading Germans.

SHERLOCK How do you know 'they' are to blame? If 'they'

had not noticed 'the mess', do you suggest someone else would not have done so?

P.A. I think all the explanations, by all the different specialists of all the different specialities, including my own, are 'rationalizations', that is, 'reasonable' explanations—scavenging.

PRIEST And are correspondingly suspect. When no reason is available, reason itself is called in to show that the unwelcome but observed facts conform to the limits of the human mind and to laws made by the human dictator.

P.A. Logic is set apart in the human pantheon as if thinking can be judged as being in accordance with 'logic'; which is as convincing and ridiculous as all the other standards that have ever been set up for awe, veneration, adoration.

MAN Liberty, Equality, Fraternity—set them up and forget them. Load them with honour and they can be sunk without a trace. Some crack-pot poet or philosopher or saint is bound to give rein to his insatiable curiosity and unearth the forgotten god from his mound of worthless adoration.

PRIEST The god comes to life and upheaves the dead rubbish beneath which he lies buried. The autistic wisdom begins to hatch out of its shell, however stony, unyielding and safe the prison provided to contain the explosion.

ASTRONOMER The cataclysmic explosion can be felt in the periphery of the galaxy. Who is ready—someone always is—to darken council with his knowledge, his reason, his logic to prove that these stupendous upheavals, ineffable explosions are comprehensible and therefore don't exist?

P.A. And that the trivial, miniscule, undiscernible births are biological events which are analogically, and therefore really comparable to, relativistic protons in the physical world.

ASTRONOMER Why 'therefore'?

P.A. Because 'analogy' is a word, and a word is a symptom of mental activity—a fragment of theory.

ASTRONOMER That does not mean that there is a realization that approximates to the theory.

P.A. I agree. There is no 'evidence' of any link between the theory and the realization to which it is supposed to correspond. I am not sure that I need to suppose 'direction' in the way theories of causation presuppose, in this instance, that a 'big bang' set off an 'expanding universe', or that the violent expansion of the universe continues to cause 'perturbations' in the sensitive receiver we call the human central nervous system. If the human CNS is capable of sensitive receptivity of a high order then it may betray events of great power though we remain ignorant of the genesis.

ASTRONOMER What do you mean by 'ignorant'?

P.A. I mean that an event might be powerful enough to stimulate the parasympathetic, but not powerful enough to cause the parasympathetic in its turn to stimulate the cortex. I have to use these anatomical terms to speak about the mind; they are in fact meaningless or inaccurate unless the recipient of these communications can tolerate their reception. Students of the heavens had to become sensitive to the evidence of heliocentric phenomena and tolerant of what their receptors conveyed before they could achieve comprehension.

PRIEST *You* use language of science and language of religion, but if I use it you claim that I am being unscientific. 'Heaven' is a word which should be used with due respect for its history as part of religious thinking.

P.A. You also should use these terms with respect for the scientific truths to which they relate. 'The Kingdom of Heaven is within you', was a statement made by one religious thinker, and should be respected no matter what the 'vertex' of the thinker. Such statements not only give coherence to past conjunctions, but also display conjunctions and coherences which were not suspected at the first adumbration. 'Man's inner world' is a succinct statement recently made, drawing attention to conjunctions of what we would call a similar kind of domain of mental phenomena.

MAN Shall I shoot him?

ROSEMARY Not yet—though I can hardly bear it. Does this waltz go on for ever?

MAN Only till we are totally exhausted.

ROSEMARY The din is getting worse and worse. It penetrates me; it will burst my ear drums. Funny to think . . .

MAN Why do you stop? What were you going to say? I see your maid is dancing with that fellow Roland.

ROSEMARY I thought you had done for him when you shot him.

She dances well—I wonder where she learnt. I think one of her remote forebears must have been of good family. She has grace . . . I feel I am going to faint . . .

MAN I'll call your maid—you there! Come and help your mistress.

ROSEMARY I feel awful; I can't even faint.

MAN You have to be tough; you are dancing as well as ever. I felt upset when I first killed a man and saw how surprised he looked. He never realized he had been killed. Shooting isn't at all bad when you get used to the shock.

ROSEMARY It's a 'shock' to dance with someone—as if you didn't realize you would be 'danced with'. I suppose P.A. would say it was 'sexual'. Priest would say it was religious, like Saint Paul being 'converted'.

MAN Saint Paul was a Jew; he said he was a Roman citizen.

ROSEMARY A Christian, surely? If this waltz goes on I shall die; I'm utterly exhausted.

MAN Your feet are dancing all right.

ROSEMARY They are dancing *me*; I don't mean it to happen. Look at Alice—she doesn't mean it any more than I do.

P.A. Death is not a disease any more than birth. Disease is constantly conjoined to both; so is life—and human beings are liable to think one causes the other.

PRIEST Only because scientists have replaced God by cause.

P.A. I have heard religious addicts talk of a First Cause. Whether scientists or priests, they are restricted by the human mind which clings to ideas such as god; the variable is substituted by a constant and then venerated as Constant.

PRIEST That could be rewarding to a mathematician.

P.A. But I don't see the advantage of substituting God for god, although I can see the value, in some circumstances, for substituting 'G' for 'g'.

PRIEST It is only a sign to denote something to which it is wished to draw attention. No one suggests 'G' should be venerated; we think there is some thing which is worthy of veneration.

P.A. I include the human mind as something worthy of respect.

PRIEST Respect is not veneration.

P.A. You are talking about vocabulary. But I do not discuss

grammar, although I am familiar with the supposition that I only play with jargon. In fact I recognize a reality beyond the word 'veneration'; similarly there is a realization that approximates to the word 'respect'. If 'respect' could be measured against a spectrum it would show a different wave-length from that of 'veneration'. I do not venerate this music, but I do respect the noise that makes it difficult to think.

PRIEST

'Be shellèd eyes with double dark
And find the uncreated light.'

P.A. 'I blind myself artifically', said Freud when he wished to investigate some dark phenomenon of the human mind.

PRIEST

'Shape nothing lips, be lovely dumb
It is the shut, the curfew sent
From there where all surrenders come
Which only make you eloquent.'

Not grammatical—but excused as poetry.

P.A. I do not 'excuse' my silence but when I want to hear my patients I have to be silent. I listen too for more than is said.

PRIEST More than the words?

P.A. Yes, but not only more sound. I listen for something in addition to the sound or the well-known meanings of the words which may not be what is heard by the physiological, sensory apparatus.

PRIEST What is that?

P.A. That is what I expect to find out by being aware.

PRIEST I likewise advocate awareness. I object to the fact that you exclude certain categories of sense and so distort the evidence on which wisdom must rest.

P.A. Yet you quoted Hopkins with approval. Is that not selecting, and therefore undermining the basis for wisdom?

PRIEST No. I assume that more than enough sensual evidence is available for physical needs, but, like the noise here, too much to obviate the screening and marking of evidence needed for spiritual life.

P.A. How do you know what is needed and what is dispensable? I think something must be relevant to psycho-analysis, but if I claimed to be studying or worshipping God I would find it difficult to claim relevance. Even in the limited sphere of human personality it is hard to suppose I can exercise my capacity for discrimination effectively.

PRIEST Yet all psycho-analysis seems to stress certain alleged phenomena as worthy of more attention than others.

P.A. True; but our aims are related only to the practice of psycho-analysis. I may be wrong in thinking that religion relates to something assumed to be far more extensive, 'all-embracing', whereas psycho-analysis relates only to the human mind. That, I think, is more than enough.

PRIEST But—enough for what?

P.A. Studying and helping the development of the human mind. You, like Man, are engaged on tasks which appear to require decisions on whether a human being should retain his life or not.

PRIEST So are doctors. You psycho-analysts are concerned with no less than the life and death of the mind—does that include the spirit?

P.A. Not if I understand what you mean by 'the spirit'. What a man does with his mind is no more the job of an analyst than restoring a broken leg—which is then used in pursuit of robbery or murder—is to do with the use to which the patient is going to make of that leg.

PRIEST Or that saxophonist is going to make of his emphesematous lung. It is deafening—do you advocate listening to his playing?

P.A. If he were coming to me for analysis and it was the most direct way of his keeping me informed—yes. If he is concerned to make noises or weave patterns of sound, I do not consider it any part of my profession.

ROSEMARY Only if he deafens you?

ROBIN Or if it is a ritual? Or a religious pattern?

ROLAND A requiem for the dead—me, for example?

P.A. None of those. If he is deafening you, you could call for the protection of the police. If it is a ritual, I suppose it would be the job of the priest. If, instead of a saxophone, he were weaving a requiem with a lethal weapon, I would consider it the concern of the armed forces.

ROLAND A fat lot of use that would be in this country.

P.A. It would depend on whether I had the sanction of the appropriate authority. I would not psycho-analyse anyone unless I had sanction—permission. In this country the armed forces have been disarmed by superior forces, so I could not call on them to intervene against anyone choosing to make a pattern with a gun.

ROLAND Suppose he wanted a psycho-analysis with a gun?

P.A. I have had the experience.

ROLAND I'd like to see *you* analysing a gun!

P.A. I would not analyse any inanimate object, but I would try to analyse the man *behind* the gun—

ROLAND And suppose he replied with bullets!

P.A. I would hope to have made many interpretations before he had been forced to make his meaning clear with a gun. The interpretations would have to have been such that they seem to have been worth hearing.

MAN I am glad you don't think you can analyse the gun. I often think it's the only defence we have against you people. I have known psycho-analysts who could not be prevented from outraging common sense.

P.A. Common sense can resort to common arms; by the time a nation has been reduced to armed force it is too late.

MAN We had no choice. What were you doing to allow things to come to such a pass? I don't remember any psycho-analytic appeal to redress grievances.

P.A. We are concerned to redress a particular form of grievance, but it takes time for us to gain ability sufficient to make a rewarding contribution.

MAN From what I have seen and heard, that is likely to take several centuries or even millenia.

P.A. Who knows? Change is often catastrophic. Bernard Shaw said it was only politicians who believe in change which is so gradual that no one detects it.

MAN Or it takes place so quickly that it is unobserved.

P.A. Or senses are so dulled or rudimentary that great changes are unobserved. A fetus is not likely to know it is growing.

ALICE Can a fetus commit murder or suicide?

P.A. A fetal idea can kill itself or be killed, and that is not a metaphor *only*. Metaphors can be the ghosts of ideas waiting to be born, and not only, as Berkeley said to Halley, 'ghosts of departed quantities'.

BANDMASTER (*ringing a bell and using a loud-hailer*) Time, ghosts! Time! Time to be departed. All change! Out increments! Out! Fall in by your Rights! Quick . . . march! Dead . . . fall in! By your coffins . . . Quick . . . dead! Quick . . . dead! Loves me . . . loves me . . . not. All change at Purgatory!

MAN What's this?

LEADER OF CELESTIAL CHOIR All change, you bastards! All change!

MAN This is a dismal hole.

ROSEMARY Why have we got out here?

MAN We had to. Arrived. All change.

ROSEMARY All change? Surely not; where are the others? Where is that bloody maid of mine?

MAN You told her to get lost.

ROSEMARY Did I? She *would* obey if she knew I didn't mean it. If this is Purgatory I don't think much of it; I thought Purgatory was religious.

MAN No, the religious place is a dogma; this is scientific.

TOM What is this gloomy hole? Why are you looking about in that curious way?

P.A. They are having an occulo-gyric crisis in unison.

PRIEST In harmony would be better. You can mow them down more easily. I can hear the stutter of the Lewis guns even now.

ROBIN I can't. The damn thing has stopped again. You fool! Don't wrench it like that. It's *not* a number one. I suppose it's the only stoppage for which you know the cure. How quiet it is here! Not a sound . . . Yet I see old ghosts look in on the battle. I say, you chaps, it's awfully good of you to look in on me like that! It is so quiet it might be a morgue. I vote we have a group discussion. Do we have a vote here?

P.A. Of course; you can have as many ineffective votes as you wish. Effective votes to the left; all others to the right—so they can cancel out properly.

MAN That is nonsense.

P.A. No, it is Non Sense.

MAN It sounds mad to me.

P.A. You have forgotten all changed here, and what was nonsense has become Non Sense. The Laws of Nature are now the Laws of Un-Reason. This is the post Big Bang Era.

ALICE What was the Big Bang? I don't remember it.

MORIARTY It has not been discovered yet. The scientists, when they have caught up with the technique, will have to engage on a journey of autismological discovery. Of course archaeology has changed too and has to relate to a spiritual science or spiritual curiosity. Priest may know who his successor will be—some young, inquisitive, post-bang dinosaur. I don't know who is taking over from me yet—no child of Irene and myself.

SHERLOCK So that is what happened to Irene Adler!

MORIARTY Really, Holmes! Didn't you know that? We didn't marry in church, but we married. The Big Bang separated us.

SHERLOCK For the time, I suppose?

MORIARTY No, there is no Time as you used to know it. I never set much store by it—or any other figments of Reality.

ROSEMARY I must say that you have a very high opinion of yourself when you are only the ghost of a figment of reality.

MORIARTY You forget that you are only a figment of imagination of a figment of the imagination of a lie after death. I have never been a figment of reality, and change presents none of the difficulties you seem to be having. As for P.A., I would hate to try to analyse *his* status. He was real to start with and has devoted himself to the reality of other realities even more banal than himself.

ALICE You are being rude.

SHERLOCK If you had been rude to Rosemary you might have done better.

MORIARTY I don't understand your scale of measurement.

ALICE Nor do I.

SHERLOCK It is the same as the scale against which I measure your distance from Roland. Your score, by that scale, was better with Rosemary than it was with Roland.

TOM What a dismal hole this is.

ALICE You said that before. How long do we have to wait here?

MYCROFT There is no time for figments of imagination, dear lady. You haven't forgotten real life yet.

ALICE I wish I could; that would be Heaven.

BANDMASTER That's the next stop. First Class passengers only. Supplementary tickets from Saint Peter.

P.A. I trust that the saint has no prejudice against psychoanalysis.

SHERLOCK You don't have to go first class. After all, I don't.

P.A. In my experience it was easier to appreciate both heaven and hell when in contact with them.

ROBIN What Heaven and Hell? I always understood them to be topological terms.

PRIEST No, religious.

PHYSICIST No, figments of imagination.

P.A. No, what I call definitory hypotheses depending on the vertex.

ROSEMARY My! You haven't changed a bit!

P.A. It certainly sounds as if I were lacking in mental flexibility. That is what I suspected about being dead. I never anticipated the possibility of experience after death; either I am not dead, or I shall have to revise my views.

PRIEST Let me recommend the less dogmatic approach, not least because you may be unfamiliar with dogma and its uses.

P.A. I have usually considered dogma to be the analogue of the so-called 'laws of nature'.

PRIEST I believe it to be a formulation of the 'thing itself'.

P.A. You claim, with the mystics, that you have direct experience of God. I should have thought your organization would have considered that heretical; a psychiatrist would suspect megalomania.

PRIEST There are opinions which question the claim of any human animal to aspire to such experience. Dante only claims such direct experience as a mortal being can have.

MYCROFT Do you find your Deity more convincingly real then myself or Falstaff?

PRIEST I had never heard of you till recently, and Falstaff is only credible as a human is credit-worthy. My experience of God is ineffable, whereas the credibility of human beings and their various representations and creators only *remind* me of God.

P.A. I do not understand, still less know, the experience of which you speak. Does Man remind you of God?

PRIEST His violence and murderous propensities are reminiscent at many removes of the violence of God. A great religious poet once said, 'The Heavens declare the glory of God'; if that is taken to include the violence of the heavens I would say that that came nearer to 'God' corresponding to my experience. 'Who shall abide the day of His coming' is a phrase which expresses *my* feelings of awe and dread which seem to be more appropriate to the God I know than to more agreeable ones.

ROSEMARY Don't you believe in a loving God?

PRIEST Yes; but I do not recognize the feeling you seem to be experiencing when you describe it as 'love'.

P.A. It is notorious that you and your organizations are opposed to sex and even teach sex as if it were opposed to God.

PRIEST It is notorious that it is notorious, although even a superficial knowledge of what we teach would make it clear that we do not.

P.A. Are not your clergy supposed to be celibate?

PRIEST We consider that sexual occupations are not compatible with the work to which clergy are supposed to devote themselves. Psycho-analysts and physicians are not supposed to practise sex with their patients.

P.A. That is not the same as commending or even advocating total abstinence.

PRIEST You enjoin total alcoholic abstinence.

P.A. I don't, but I can and do see characters with whom such totality might be wise. I might hope that in the course of the experience of psycho-analysis the individual would become able to have an opinion of his own and that those options would be more an asset than a liability. But *my* preferences, if I let them obtrude, may be *his* bane, so I do not consider formulation of such ideas to the patient as part of the psycho-analyst's function.

PRIEST But you are suggesting it by being a psycho-analyst.

P.A. I am sometimes asked if I advise psycho-analysis; I incur hostility because I say it is no part of advice I am qualified to give. I agree that merely being what I am suggests something to the patient, but I think it my duty to demonstrate to him that impulse of which he is often unaware.

PRIEST Has not Jung said this?

P.A. He said he agreed with Freud's description of the transference; he talked also of archetypes and a collective unconscious. I don't see why he should not call the Oedipus figure an archetype if he wants to, or say that an equivalent of the Oedipus figure exists in every human being. But I do not see any need to augment Freud's facts and theory; if I saw a better way of demonstration I would not hesitate to use it. The postulate of a collective unconscious seems to me to be unnecessary. I would not say that because two people see a mountain, *that* is evidence of a 'collective eye'; it is simpler to say both people have eyes that function in a similar manner. I would not use an expression which might risk an increase in ambiguity—which is bad enough at best.

TOM I'm bored.

ROBIN Oh shut up! We all are.

PRIEST 'Collective boredom'? Hullo! Who is this?

ROSEMARY ? ! ! !

ALICE Awful-looking specimen.

ROSEMARY Specimen of what?

TOM Reminds me of someone.

ROBIN Don't say it's a bore!

P.A. I hardly recognized him—it's my ghost.

ROBIN I thought so.

GHOST OF P.A. I died at English Farm and I've been working through Purgatory since. I feared I might become like P.A.

ROSEMARY *I* don't think you're a bore; you look rather interesting.

GHOST OF P.A. No, I'm cold. How the wind whistles through me! If only I could be clothed with flesh and blood—that would warm my old bones.

P.A. It wouldn't. I have taken mine off to be a figment of imagination.

GHOST OF AUSER Aren't you . . .?

P.A. No, I'm P.A.

GHOST OF AUSER You reminded me of—ah, there you are! I thought I might find you here.

GHOST OF P.A. When you knew me I was a ghost of myself—at Berles aux Bois. I loved you, but I couldn't save you.

GHOST OF AUSER Never mind, old boy. You were wonderful! Sorry I lost my tank, but there were a lot of them and they shot me through the heart. What's this dismal hole? Seems to be some sort of Transit Camp.

PRIEST That's what *you*'d call it. Some people think they are Stations of the Cross.

GHOST OF AUSER (*cheerfully*) Really? I thought that was a Roman Catholic idea.

PRIEST No—they borrowed the name from a Jew. It's named after him.

GHOST OF AUSER What's that queer get-up you are wearing? Fatigue dress?

PRIEST You might call it that.

GHOST OF AUSER (*to P.A. and Ghost of P.A.*) Well, how's things? How have you been getting on? It's jolly nice seeing you again—I hope you are glad to see me too.

P.A. I am indeed—but truth to tell I've always been afraid of meeting you.

GHOST OF AUSER Afraid of meeting me—whatever for? You were one of the bravest men I ever met! I wanted to get a V.C.—one better than you.

GHOST OF P.A. You only saw me wearing my Hero dress. I was afraid you'd see me—as I saw poor Gates.

GHOST OF AUSER Ah yes, I heard about that—broke down or something didn't he?

P.A. No, poor chap, he went sane long before the war was over; he couldn't bear the truth *and* being in a minority of one at the same time. It was pitiful—lying there in a ditch blubbing. He took to drink; even that couldn't save him from reality. It used to get him by the throat and blind him.

PRIEST I tried him on a stiff dose of religion but he had never been inoculated.

P.A. 'Religio Medici. T.d.s. as ordered'—but no one ordered it. I doubt it would have saved him anyway.

ROSEMARY Quantum mutatus ab illo Hectore qui redit exuvias indutus Achilli.

PRIEST I'd forgotten you knew Hector.

ROSEMARY He was a friend of my friend Paris.

ROLAND I remember it was said you were the party that burned the topless towers of Ilium.

ROSEMARY Yes—now it's the topless style of Saint Francisco. I no more launched a thousand ships than the London Scottish sank the Emden.

GHOST OF AUSER I heard that joke—I thought it rather funny. Like the surrender of the gunners of the Territorial Division to the artillery of the 7th Division when their guns fired too short because of worn barrels. You are very good-looking.

ROSEMARY Thanks! So I'm told—or used to be when I was younger. Luckily I was reconciled to having an ugly soul—more serviceable. It has to be tough, like the sole of a boot. Alice, give me my shoes. There, you see how pretty they are? But the life and soul even of a party shoe has to depend on the life *and* sole of a . . . You're not attending. Where have you gone?

GHOST OF AUSER Sorry, I thought I saw a friend. I thought he had been killed at Ypres.

ROSEMARY Ypres? Never heard of it—unless you mean Wipers.

GHOST OF AUSER (*vaguely*) Yes, I suppose so. I was never there of course—before my time.

GHOST OF P.A. Even now he is as bright as old renown. No one ever heard of him, but *I* knew what we had lost when that brave, cheerful lad was found lying there—dead.

GHOST OF AUSER Old man Horace was wrong for once. I was not at all 'sweet'—dead or alive.

P.A. Ask my ghost what spectacle was presented by those of us who lived to grow old.

GHOST OF P.A. Do you think I was any better *before* English Farm?

P.A. On consideration—no; nor after. The actions of the just—the generous man—stay just; the mean man stays mean. Whatever the dress in which we clothe our 'selves' the structure lives longer than the character we hang upon it—the 'glories' of our blood and state.

GHOST OF AUSER I wanted to ask you—did we win?

(*A long, long silence*)

TWENTY

ROLAND You've been crying.

ALICE And God shall wipe away all tears from . . .

ROLAND Come, wake up!

ALICE It would be nice if there were a God.

ROLAND Perhaps—if He were an improvement on the ones who have won adulation, the famous ones of old.

ALICE That reminds me of the dream I had last night. Terrible! I can't remember it, but I know it went on all night.

ROLAND 'In the silence of the sleep time, when you set your fancies free'—a song we had at school. I think the fancies were supposed to go somewhere . . . I forget.

ALICE 'Music, when soft voices die, vibrates in the memory.' I can't remember who wrote it—

ROLAND It doesn't matter.

ALICE Do you think there is a life after death?

ROLAND I hope not.

ALICE I feel depressed.

ROLAND You were crying in your sleep.

ALICE (*wiping away her tears*) I don't think that's crying—not weeping 'boo-hoo', but crying 'peep-bo'.

ROLAND I've got to go to Munden this morning—

ALICE I dreamt something about Munden, I think . . .

ROLAND Poor Robin's cowman's suicide upset you.

ALICE (*shuddering*) *That* wasn't a dream! Perhaps Shakespeare and Homer were right; it would be awful if we dreamt we were alive when we died.

ROLAND Who knows? These poet crackpots often had something.

ALICE If they had discipline, even the discipline of versification—

ROLAND Farming for me! I'm off to Munden. Goodbye; sweet dreams.

ALICE No, no! Don't let me go to sleep again. Rosemary! Rosemary!

BOOK 3

THE DAWN OF OBLIVION

Q *Can you give me . . . oh it's you is it?*
A *Alas! yes.*
Q *I don't see why you say 'Alas!' I don't mind meeting you! Why . . .*
A *I thought you were going to ask what it's about.*
Q *Oh no. I read the last one.*
A *Splendid! Did you like it?*
Q *No. Is this as bad?*
A *Worse.*
Q *How interesting: I must get it.*
A *I said 'worse'.*
Q *That's what made me want it—I don't see how it could be.*

ONE

EM-MATURE This book is a psycho-embryonic attempt to write an embryo-scientific account of a journey from birth to death overwhelmed by pre-mature knowledge, experience, glory and self-intoxicating self-satisfaction. I was spared any knowledge of the courtship of my sperm with my ovum, but many years later was given to understand that my ancestors had a long and disreputable history extending to the day when an ancestral sperm, swimming characteristically against the current, lodged in a fallopian tube to lie in wait for an unknown ovum. The history of my ovum appears to be virtually non-existent. My sperm impetuously penetrated a Graafian follicle before my ovum had time itself to escape penetration. I cannot vouch for the truth of these tales which became know to me through scientific hear-say many years later. I admit responsibility for what I have experienced, but not for the distortions of scientific sense. I acknowledge dependence on sensible and experienced transcriptions; I cannot promise communication of pure non-sense without the contamination by sense. I shall not repeat my apology for having to borrow the language of experience and reason despite its inadequacy.

My earliest experiences were of something touching what I later heard was 'me'. The changes in pressure in the fluid surrounding me varied from what Me called pleasure to what Me called pain. My optic and auditory pits at the age of three or four somites received sound and light, dark and silent, not usually increasing beyond nice and nasty, but sometimes making Me feel more inanimate than animate.

PRE-MATURE Get on with it—when were you born?

EM-MATURE Don't hurry; I was coming to that.

EIGHT YEARS You always are, but do not arrive.

EM When I was only three somites old—

TWENTY-FOUR YEARS That's not an age.

EM Don't talk about matters you don't understand. If you had some respect for your fore-bears—

EIGHT YEARS You've spelled it wrong.

EM When I spell it, it is right; when you spell it, it is wrong.

EIGHT YEARS That is not how it seems to me, looking at it from my side of the barrier.

LEONARD Shut up both of you and look at this drawing.

EIGHT YEARS Not bad—what is it?

EM I see a great light.

TWENTY-FOUR YEARS Open your eyes and you will see it is darkness of the womb.

MILTON The formless infinite—the void.

EM The light is too intense.

TWELVE YEARS 'it is eye. Be not afraid. And 'e did 'it 'is eye. And Em was afraid. Ha, ha, ha!

EM What a dreadful oscillation of pressure!

THIRTY YEARS Who is talking words you don't understand now?

EM Caught in a web of whirling waters.

LEONARD Hair! Water! If you only looked you would 'see-what-I-mean', but—

FORTY YEARS No—only hair, water, words—

FORTY-TWO YEARS No; if you listened you would only hear 'repetition compulsion' psycho-ese.

P.A. Psycho-analysis?

EM Stop! Stop! I can't bear it. I am blinded, deafened!

KRISHNA I told you so; wait till you are Arjuna.

EM It's quieter now. Gametes quarrelling. Post-natals at it again. Give me Silence. 'Shape nothing lips.' 'Be shellèd eyes.' Stoma—you at the other end—keep closed. 'A sealed tube'? That can't be right. Suck! What?

FOUR SOMITES Come on, wake up! Think!

TWENTY MONTHS Think? You can't think! You haven't even got a central nervous system.

EM You're a fool. Even Four Somites had the sense to want to suck. I admit—

TERM You didn't. You made a fuss about being woken by me and my young co-hairs.

TWENTY MONTHS I sucked an erection.

TERM You made a fuss when my erection wanted me to suck it.

TWENTY MONTHS Rubbish! I objected to being fobbed off with a thumb. No milk, no amniotic fluid—nothing! Le Néant, the Void, the Infinite! Too late—here's Eighteen.

EIGHTEEN YEARS 'There will be too much of me in the coming by and by.'

INFANCY Now shut up, all of you. I'm senior here. Since you can't suck my nipple or penis and have a grouse about my thumb, I have arranged to suck a nipple.

SOMITES We don't want a nipple! We want an erection!

EM I don't want your borrowed erection. It nearly squeezed me to death and drowned me. Luckily I had the intelligence—wisdom—to become erect myself. I may borrow a case or sheath as an exo-skeleton temporarily, but—

TERM No, don't! If you borrow an exo-skeleton you will never get out of it. I swallowed the erection and now it is part of *Me*. It's my endo-skeleton. *I* am an erection. *I* am independent.

EIGHTEEN YEARS Hark at it! What conceit! What pride!

TWENTY-FOUR YEARS If it weren't for pride and conceit you would still be grovelling about on your belly. You owe Term a debt.

EM I may be grovelling around a bit, but if I don't bite the woman's heel, call me *Serpent*!

EIGHTEEN If I don't bruise your head, call me *Heel*!

ALL I don't know what you are talking about.

P.A. You think it's *about* something. It has already been said by Shakespeare—'It is a tale told by an idiot, signifying nothing.'

TWELVE YEARS Shakespeare? I haven't done Shakespeare yet.

P.A. Soon you will have *done* Shakespeare, and when you have realized he is the greatest man who ever lived you will be *done* too—and you won't recover. Shakespeare has been so well *done* he has never recovered either.

EM I shall be so well and truly born I suppose I shall never recover either. It is terrible to dream I may become like Term one day. If only I could be sure to be told by an idiot I would be reconciled to being *Nothing*, but—

EIGHTEEN YEARS You will be well and truly educated; never able to draw out again. I look like being educated by one of those solidified nightmares on the Ypres Canal.

EM Long before my time or yours when I crawled in that primaeval slime I was a nightmare and did as nightmares do in nightmare land. Then I was taught and learned to call it 'only a nightmare'.

EIGHTEEN YEARS It took me a hell of a night time to learn I was wide awake.

TWENTY-ONE YEARS I nearly learned that Peter Pan had been our Commander in Chief, but sweet peace came and put me to sleep again and taught me it was 'only' a dream. P.A. turned up and untaught me it was 'only' real.

P.A. I did not. I thought you might learn something if you could have some respect for Somite Three and the others, Peter and Pan. You seemed to think they were 'ugly' and 'nasty'.

TWENTY-ONE Weren't they?

P.A. It's a matter of taste. After all, you have taste buds—why not respect them and what they tell you?

TWENTY-ONE I did not like the taste of a nine-inch Howitzer.

TWENTY-FOUR Nonsense; you thought you would be killed and feared penetrating the barrier between life and death. It was Somite Three who thought an erection was a 9.2 How.

EM I don't know when the amniotic pressure made my optic pits hurt; the stars were so brilliant, I kicked out.

SOMITE EIGHTEEN Nonsense! Even I don't know where my feet are; you are getting beyond yourself.

TERM You had to depend on your fetal membranes to get beyond yourself when you had no feet.

EM Your fetal membranes, as you call them, are a nuisance as it is impossible to break through them. I cannot reach you because of them. Who or What are you?

TERM I knew till you butted in. I am *mind* and my mental membranes make me able to reach far beyond my feet. How and What and Who used to help.

EM Now you have muddled me. I shall be *body*; for ever I shall gird at your mind.

MIND Hullo! Where have you sprung from?

BODY What—you again? I am Body; you can call me Soma if you like. Who are you?

MIND Call me Psyche—Psyche-Soma.

BODY Soma-Psyche.

MIND We must be related.

BODY Never—not if I can help it.

MIND Oh, come. Not as bad as that, is it?

BODY Worse. You got us into this air. Luckily I brought some liquid with me. What are you doing?

MIND Nothing; it must be my phrenes, that diaphragm going up and down. I'm breathing in air—fluid, not liquid. What did you bring that wet stuff for? Beautiful odour.

BODY You could not know about the odour if I had not the liquid to hold your atoms with. Typical of Mind—all words and no content. Where did you find them?

MIND Borrowed from the future—you are borrowing them from me; do you get them through the diaphragm?

BODY *They* penetrate *it*. But the meaning does not get through. Where did you get your pains from?

MIND Borrowed—from the past. The meaning does not get through the barrier though. Funny—the meaning does not get through whether it is from you to me, or from me to you.

BODY It is the meaning of pain that I am sending to you; the words get through—which I have not sent—but the meaning is lost.

MIND What is that amusing little affair sticking out? I like it. It has a mind of its own—just like me.

BODY It's just like me—has a body of its own. That's why it is so erect. Your mind—no evidence for it at all.

MIND Don't be ridiculous. I suffer anxiety as much as you have pain. In fact I have pain about which you know nothing. I suffered intensely when we were rejected. I asked you to call me Psyche and promised to call you Soma.

SOMA All right Psyche; I don't admit that there is any such person other than a figment of my digestion.

PSYCHE Who are you talking to then?

SOMA I'm talking to myself and the sound is reflected back by one of my fetal membranes.

PSYCHE Your feetal membranes! Ha, ha! Very good! Is that your pun or mine?

SOMA It's the only language you understand.

PSYCHE It's the only language you hear. All you talk is pain.

SOMA All you respect is pain or lack of it. The only time I can get anything over to you is pain-talk from the hills.

PSYCHE Plain talk through your stoma. Excuse me if I borrow to talk to this idiotic nipple a moment—there! An erection at once!

SOMA Thanks to my liquid evacuations. Who is that?

PSYCHE I bit it.

SOMA It had just bitten me. Bite it again! That's *me*—not *it*.

PSYCHE It can't be. I put my foot in it—was it your stoma? You have confused me again. Pain, Feet—all mixed up. Why can't you take your choice?

SOMA I do. If you had any respect for my 'feelings' and did what I feel you, you wouldn't be in this mess.

PSYCHE I am in this mess because I was squeezed into it. Who is responsible—your feelings or your ideas? All that has me is yours—amniotic fluid, light, smell, taste, noise, I'm wrapped up in it. Look out! I am getting absorbed!

SOMA I'll pi you out when I've absorbed you. All piss, shit, and pi-ety. You can idea-lize it—get a good price for it no doubt. Bless me—I'm getting absorbed too. Help!

PSYCHE That's what comes of penetrating in or out. I'm confused.

SOMA That's what comes of not penetrating—you break up or down.

BOY Let's leave them to it. Boys and girls—

TWO

GIRL
Golden boys and girls all must
Like chimney sweepers come to dust.

BOY We are not dandelions. I'm bored. Let's play in the garden.

GIRL No, that's kiddish.

BOY It's not. What's kiddish about it?

GIRL Oh nothing—it's silly. Silly boring old garden. Jennifer is coming.

BOY *Her!* How awful. She's a slob.

GIRL She's not. You shouldn't say awful things like that. I'll tell Ma!

BOY Sneak! It's not awful; you're a sneak.

GIRL I shall tell Ma you called her a sneak!

BOY Oh, you liar—I didn't say anything of the sort.

GIRL You did! What did you say then?

BOY I didn't call her what you said.

GIRL Jennifer's my best friend. She says boys are awful. I'll tell Ma you made me cry.

BOY Sneak!

GIRL I don't sneak. She will see my eyes are red and she will ask you what you have been doing to make me cry. I shan't tell her and then you'll catch it! You know she doesn't like it if you make me cry. She'll tell Dad and he'll be furious.

BOY Oh! You are a . . . are a . . . little beast!

GIRL Now I *shall* tell Ma! I wasn't going to say anything till you started calling me those awful names.

BOY Cyril knows what a sneak you are. (*Girl puts out her tongue at him.*) Ooh! That's awful! You know Ma said you should *never* do that. If you tell Ma I shall tell her you put your tongue out at me. I'm going to play the piano.

GIRL No!

BOY Why not? It's only my exercises. You know I have to do them every day.

GIRL I'll tell Ma you wouldn't play with me.

BOY It was *you* said you wouldn't play.

GIRL Only because you call me names. And why aren't you doing your exercises? Ma told you to do them first thing after breakfast.

MOTHER (*both children fall into a sulk as she enters*) Why don't you two play in the garden? It's such a lovely morning.

BOY Don't want to.

GIRL (*brightly*) I'm waiting for Jennifer.

MOTHER That's good, but why don't you play in the garden till she comes?

BOY (*to himself*) Well, why don't I? Anyhow, I don't. Girls always want to play. Jennifer isn't a bad kid if only she didn't team up with my horrible sister. I hate girls—you always get the worst of it.

GIRL (*to herself*) I don't want to play in the garden. Why did I say I want to? Jennifer hates it too. I wish she would hurry up. She's better than a boy anyway. I suppose . . . *if* there was a decent boy—unlike my horrible brother . . . he lies face down on the floor and wiggles. Told me to try it because it was lovely. Humbug—nothing to it.

MOTHER (*to boy*) Not going?

BOY (*crossly*) Oh, all right.

(*He and Girl go out.*)

P.A. They don't really hate each other—'they' all hate learning—it makes them develop—swell up.

CONTAINER It distends me.

MOTHER Let's see now . . . what have I forgotten? Reminds me of something. Helen perhaps . . . or my mother when I said I had forgotten to say my prayers before cleaning my teeth—luckily she used to forget to ask if I had cleaned my teeth. I remember her sweet, gentle voice. 'Child of the Devil, child of the Devil; go and say them and ask his forgiveness.' I did not dare to reply. 'What! Ask the Devil for forgiveness?—for not praying to him?' She would not have allowed such pert—what is the phrase now?—answers. I suppose we are more enlightened now. And more comfortable perhaps. Will these two look back nostalgically on their present freedom? And guiltily, as I do now, wonder what mistakes *they* are making? What of the children of our imperial family—did the great ones of our time bring them up wrongly? Pakistan? Amin? Indira? Bangladesh? Does God sometimes think He made a mistake to allow the human animal to reproduce . . . or do the viruses roam freely already seeking some cadaver of the vanished races? They shall inherit—our nebula? Or our earth? Well?

GIRL Mummy, Jenny has a super idea—can we go skating? She says the ice is super. She says it is fabulous. Oh, thanks awfully. Of course we will take him. Can I have some money? And could I buy some skates? Dad won't mind—in fact he said he wished I would learn to skate.

MOTHER Yes, I heard him. And I remember your answer. 'Oh no! It's so *boring*. Need I go?' Do you remem. . . .

BOY That's a long time ago. Besides—

GIRL We shall be terribly careful.

MOTHER (*to herself*) Is it déjà vu? Why is it so familiar? (*aloud*) No, I'm very sorry, but you can ask your father when he gets home tonight.

GIRL Oh, Mummy! That's too late. Jenny wants us to go with her *now*! Tomorrow she can't come.

BOY I said it would be no good asking.

MOTHER There—I was sure you wouldn't ask for anything so silly.

GIRL But he has! He wants to go—don't you?

MOTHER (*laughing*) I expect you put him up to it. No; I'm sorry Jenny—another day perhaps. Now run along to the garden.

GIRL But it's so boring.

(*Mother goes out*)

BOY Let's have an otter hunt.

JENNY What's that?

BOY Well, *you* catch Tibs because Tibs doesn't know you—she won't come to us. Then I'll get one of those really large pots from the gardener—his shed I mean, because he would never let us have one. Then while you stroke Tibs I shall put the pot on her and—

JENNY Won't that be terribly cruel? Our cat would hate it.

BOY Oh, Tibs won't mind. Anyway it's only for a moment and then—

GIRL I shall get a croquet mallet and—

BOY Smash it down on the pot and that sets Tibs off to a good start and we have to catch her before she gets up a tree. You have to be jolly quick though.

JENNY While you're chasing Tibs the gardener will be chasing you.

GIRL Oh no—he doesn't mind—he won't know anyhow. He'll only tell Dad when he finds out, and Dad is sure to think it couldn't be us and will beat my brother.

BOY Thanks awfully! Jenny, get Tibs—she was asleep on the wall just now. Come on—we'll break in and she will break out. Do her good—she's always sleeping!

TIBS (*soliloquizing*) It is nice to stretch in the sun. Not that there is much. When there is, that B'yrrh-Lady sends those damned children out into it. Why couldn't she keep them in her womb? Can't blame her if she chucks the devils out *at once*. No wonder the sun becomes darkened. There's one of them. Oh child, get out of the way and let me feel the warmth. Oh, it's you is it Jenny? As bad as the rest if I knew you better. Still—'tickley-tums' if you must make that ridiculous noise instead of purring. If she could talk a sensible language like mine she could hear the difference between a purr and a growl. Now she has to hold me in her arms! Oh dear! Oh dear! But I wouldn't give her kittens anyway. Ah! Here come the little devils. They must think I'm a fool if I don't know what they are up to—Jenny as bad as the rest. I am scared inside this pot I admit. I can't help running—all four of me. Stupid oafs! Woops! Up the tree and claws out. Lucky for them I didn't get my claws into *them* instead of the tree. Nice and warm again; and there they go, little . . . little . . . anyhow I can lick my paws in peace. The hell hounds always behave like a fetus—omnipotent, as old as God and as all-knowing, impossible to teach. In fact they remind me of Grandma who tried to shoo Grandpa's hat off the chair because she couldn't tell the difference between a hat and a cat. These devils can't tell the difference between a flowerpot and a pregnant pot. 'What a pot!', the Boy said to his aunt. In fact it was the only scientific observation he had made, but his Mummy said it was rude. That's what she said to the Girl when she used to stand in front of her 'betters' and say, 'Lavatory, lavatory, lavatory', to find out their reaction. A cat may not look at a psychiatrist without being called a 'Reaction-type'. My sperm-mate, Tom, who lives in the looney bin, tells me they all start in a looney bin and all return to it after a brief spell of making a hell on earth so they won't miss what they have left before they go back to it. It really is enough to make a girl laugh. In the childhood of the race, at least the Egyptians respected animal containers for their content. Blockheads all—I suppose it is understandable that they want to keep their blocks and consult them. The only time we understand and meet is digestion time and that language penetrates—in both directions—the barrier of sense; the sense that is born then is common. Even so, some aristo-c-rat or psychophilo is sure to pounce on it and give us all pollutocracy. Muscle-stretching time—ah! Wait till the Great Cat Ra catches them.

MOTHER Did you have a nice time?

BOY Not bad; is there any cake? Oh, supper—I don't want supper. Can't I have cake? Jenny can run! Can she come tomorrow?

MOTHER If her parents let her. Did you race each other?

BOY Not exactly.

GIRL She's not *your* friend anyway. She's coming to see me.

BOY Anyway I don't like her—she's soppy. Can Cyril come?

GIRL Cyril! *He* is soppy if you like. Do you know what Jenny told me? She said—

MOTHER Please, please! No more quarrelling tonight.

BOY Here's—I wasn't quarrelling—Tibs. Can I give her her milk? Please!

GIRL No. It's my turn. Tibs doesn't like you. Mummy, he chased Tibs till Tibs had to run up the tree.

BOY Ooh, what a whopper! I never did and Tibs loves me—don't you Tibs? What's that tapping the window?!

TIBS (*soliloquizing and licking her whiskers*) The tree and I understand each other—though he is rather rooted in the past.

TREE (*soliloquizing*) I live on earth and water, and even my leaves and branches when they break out feed and feed on air.

TIBS That's what I breathe and smell.

MOTHER Bed!

BOY Gd-ni . . . (*sleeps*) Tibs, you are a spoiled cat. No, it's no good you saying you are a *Tiger*. If you are a tiger you are really a spoiled tiger—a cat that has been spoiled and has turned into a pussy cat. Cyril laughs when he says 'pussy'. He says it's a gross word. Now don't you turn into a gross cat Tibs. That's German. I hope I'm not getting afraid of an unspoiled great Kat. Tiger . . . Tiger . . . we learnt in school—burning bright. Please sir! Its eyes sir—what dread hands question mark and what dread feet? A stop sir? Yes sir, a proper pause. If the wine don't get you the women must. It rhymes with dust.

GIRL Shut up and go to sleep.

BOY I am asleep. *You* shut up. Where's Tibs?

GIRL Never mind—she likes sleeping on my bed. Where's Cyril? I don't care. I don't like him.

* * *

BOY Come on! There are guns in the field behind Prime's Field.

CYRIL Where? Can we get near them? Look! Soldiers! Hundreds of them.

BOY Let's watch. We'll go to the guns later. Look! There are more—thousands—Leicesters, the North Midland Division. They are moving in. There goes the bell for Prep. What a bore! I want to watch. Won't it be awful if the war is over.

CYRIL I know. I really feel sorry for the Germans. They are sure to get licked. Can't we join up?

BOY No. They'll turn us down for being too young.

CYRIL Well, I'm eighteen, so I can join at the end of term. You look it.

BOY I know. A woman gave me a white feather because I hadn't joined up. I felt a terrible fool.

CYRIL Good Lord! What cheek! What did you say?

BOY I didn't say anything. I felt such a fool.

CYRIL You ought to have smacked her face.

BOY I couldn't. I felt I ought to have joined up myself. I feel such a fool wearing a school cap. A woman made my father feel a fool. 'But your boy is wearing a school cap!', she said. I should feel such a fool going to a recruiting station. I feel a fool *not* going.

CYRIL Take your cap off. I know—get a bowler hat—they'll never know.

BOY That's what Miss Tommy said. She looked so smart. She looked me up and down—I knew she thought I was a soft idiot. 'I thought you were captain of school!', she said. Well, I couldn't answer that. I couldn't tell her I felt a fool. You know Tartarin de Tarascon? I thought that was funny when his conscience tells him, 'Couvre-toi de gloire' and someone says, 'Couvre-toi de flannelle!' I feel a fool either way. You are lucky to be joining up. I wish I had *been* captain and left. Here's Prep started. We'll talk after Lights Out. (*Sleeps*)

THREE

SOMITE THIRTY Get back into the Amniotic Fluid.

TERM Get out into the sun! Glory! The fields are bathed in light. Moonlight! Don't lie snoozing in bed.

SOMITE THIRTY Keep warm in bed. Your King and Country want you—you stay in bed.

BOY (*stirring uneasily*) What? Lucky devil—he will win a V.C. What did you say—flannel?

TERM Oh get lost! I can't lie here all night.

BOY Sit Jessica. The moonlight sleeps on the bank. . . . That awful Repetition—I shall have to learn it first thing.

CYRIL Sh, sh, you're making an awful row. Go to sleep.

TWENTY-FOUR YEARS Lights out and stop talking now please—

SEVENTY YEARS That's better. If only one could rely on their always going to sleep.

SEVENTY-FIVE YEARS Unfortunately they never do. Sometimes they all speak at once and it is a perfect Bedlam.

P.A. I think it might some day be possible for them all to be awake and carry on a fairly disciplined debate.

ROBIN I doubt it. I sometimes think it saves my sanity that most of them are usually asleep. It's bad enough when it's only two or three talking at once.

ROLAND That's only because they all talk a different language.

MAN I shot you so you would lie down and stay down—and out. And silent. Your friend Robin too—years ago. I don't want any ghostly voices around. Anyone would think it wasn't bad enough with religious nonsense inventing a future life and angel voices to add to the tumult.

ROBIN I can't see that's any worse than P.A. and his crowd inventing minds and characters and psycho-somatic disturbances.

ROLAND Doctors are as bad—new diseases and expensive new cures and specialists to go with them.

MORIARTY As one who has waged war against religious nonsense much longer than—

P.A. Oh, come—you are a creature of fiction yourself!

SHERLOCK HOLMES But *not* religious fiction. Scientific fiction is entirely superior.

DEVIL I am religious, but I certainly do not consider that I am fictitious. I do not of course hold with the ridiculous theatrical costumes in which I am supposed to appear in gardens of Eden and such primitive landscapes. In fact, I have always been most punctilious about my dress. I defy anyone to say they have ever seen me in anything but unobtrusive clothes, quietly and beautifully cut, and manners to which no real lady or gentleman could possibly take exception. Excuse me—you were about to say?

P.A. I confess I had supposed you inhabited the unconscious.

ALICE At my school we certainly were taught that the Devil existed, but none of us believed it was true.

DEVIL My dear lady—I hardly know how to apologize for my lack of perspicacity. I remember your school very well. I frequently gave away the yearly prizes and used to address you at the close of a ceremony which I was vain enough to regard as a particularly pleasing annual tribute to my services. Very charming, if I may say so, you all looked. Your Headmistresses—I knew all of them very well—were gratifyingly deferential. I even donated a fund for a prize to the most promising pupil—for the promises which were most unlikely to be kept. It carried a scholarship—a university scholarship—for Moral Philosophy. No, no thanks—I never touch sherry. I find it induces a somewhat genuine geniality.

ROLAND Now I understand why your face is so familiar—at our Prize-giving Days! You were responsible for all our sexual troubles I suppose?

DEVIL Certainly not. Sex, like sherry, often produces perfectly genuine feelings of love and affection. I relied on various religious teachers and moralists to inflame moral hatred for those harmless and agreeable practices—

SOMA My department.

DEVIL Quite so; as my friend P.A. was saying—

P.A. Excuse me: *not* your friend. I do not even believe in you.

DEVIL You amaze me. I would have thought by this time the facts would have compelled you to catch up with Priest—he at least believes in me.

P.A. I do not waste time believing facts or anything I *know*. I save my credulity for what I do *not* know.

DEVIL Like God?

P.A. Certainly. Both you and God I leave to Priest and his religious department.

ROLAND But . . . I suppose you would say you do not believe in men and women because they are facts which you know.

P.A. Certainly—I know some men and some women. I know they have minds as well as bodies.

SOMITE THIRTY Somitically speaking I know a lot that I cannot make clear to you but that is factual enough to me. I have to borrow articulate speech from Soma.

SOMA My difficulty exactly. I cannot make anything clear to Psyche unless I borrow a bellyache or headache or respiratory distress from somitic vocabulary for any of these post-natal structures. I believe in mind and personality as there is no evidence whatever for anything but Body. And when I manage to make somebody aware of a bellyache the probability is that they immediately drag in a 'cure'. As for my message, God knows—

DEVIL God knows! Is Soma also among the religious?

ROSEMARY You know that as well as I do. Some of the healthier and most well-nourished bellies I know are to be found amongst the religious. The Celibates look particularly pregnant.

ROLAND I know women who look pregnant. Sometimes they are.

P.A. I *know* pregnant silences—I don't have to believe in them. Seventy-five was speaking of all talking at once as a bedlam.

PRIEST Milton spoke of Pandemonium.

DEVIL That was before Reason took the chairmanship.

P.A. And Bedlam—only because Reason was such a bad Chairman. The so-called *laws* of logic were a prescription for Chaos. They left no living space at all for vitality. Even today it would be still-born if it had not found refuge in what Alice would call craziness or—

DOCTOR Manic-depressive psychosis, or hysteria, or schizophrenia, etcetera, etcetera, etcetera—and quite right too.

P.A. Or the Royal College of Physicians, or the Royal College of Surgeons.

DOCTOR Or the International Psycho-Analytic Association, or the Church.

DEVIL

'Go it Justice, go it Percy,
Go it Eustace, go it Mercy.'

I love to hear it—it's music to my ears! All dead—and all so lively.

P.A. All Institutes are dead and therefore conform, like all inanimate objects, to laws and bye-laws which are comprehensible within the limits of human understanding. However, as they are composed of people and individuals who are liable to develop, the Institution begins to yield to pressure.

TERM So did my uterus; I had had enough of it—the fear of having my life squeezed out of me compelled me to compel *it* to yield to my counter-pressure.

ALICE And nearly lost me my life. When you did squeeze

out—or I squeezed you out—I remained alive, but I often asked myself whether the life with which I was left was worth living.

ROSEMARY Poor old thing—get me my shawl. You make quite a good skivvy even if I feel the draught sometimes. Better a shawl—which I can discard—than a mistress that I can't.

P.A. Better a science you can discard than a religion you cannot. I have no more difficulty with a scientific theory than an insect has with the form it bursts out of. Some of us, I admit, have ideas like exo-skeletons.

DOCTOR Or brains like alimentary canals emitting facts where ideas might be hoped for. Or even 'flights of ideas' when thoughts, articulate thoughts, were necessary.

P.A. I think the problem is pressing when the 'articulations' are so rigid that the individual does not think, but has a psychical osteo-arthritis—to borrow some of my medical friend's terminology.

DEVIL Or, to borrow a perspicuous phrase from my priestly friend, a spiritual bigotry where tolerance should be.

ALICE Or licence where laws should rule.

ROSEMARY Alice, you have ideas beyond your station in life. I shall have to get rid of you if you interrupt with Socratic ideas.

ALICE I thought that this was a practical world—like Aristotle said.

ROSEMARY For goodness sake speak English—not like a skivvy. Socrates! Aristotle! We shall be having Kant or Descartes next.

PRIEST Pascal was very intelligent even though he had not the sense to avoid mathematical indecencies.

DEVIL Mathematics! As bad as music. Pythagoras might have caused great trouble by making a ritual to serve to marry the two. Luckily nobody had the wit to understand him.

P.A. The carapace was too rigid to allow for the development of that marriage. Desargues helped and drew a pretty little picture which many a mind ogled in an inviting way.

DEVIL Pascal—though not one of my favourites—did well till the Church had him under control.

P.A. If the psychiatrists had got hold of him they would have had him in a strait jacket of the pattern that they themselves wear. Nowadays we would confine him in one of our theoretical constructs.

DEVIL Really! I admire your perspicacity. So many of you seem to find it impossible to know a constricting construct when you are faced by one.

SOMA Not even when it's all round them. I have known oscillations, transmitted in a liquid medium, become unrecognizable when transmitted in air—a mere change of fluid!

SOMITE THIRTY I have known post-natals unable to learn because they are unable to be curious, having lost their sense of smell—the only really effective mode of exercising curiosity as any animal knows, except these domesticated, educated, cultivated creatures that have 'forgotten'.

ROLAND You sound like Gilbert and Sullivan.

SOMITE THIRTY Never heard of them.

ALICE Can't bear the stuff. Bach and Mozart for me.

DEVIL I am sure P.A. will recognize the warring musical sects as psycho-analytic theories in a new costume. How Dryden would have laughed!

P.A. He did, does and will do in future, I am sure. It is not quite so amusing to people like me, who are still conscious, awake and aware of the medium which surrounds us, as it is to God and the Devil. By the way, how should I address you? Your Satanic Majesty? Your Id-iocy?

DEVIL (*bowing politely*) Take your choice. I am not fussy as they are in The Other Place. Bigotry and Intolerance are simply the medium in which I flourish. We weave it into a thin veil on to which our demonstrations are projected for identification.

P.A. My God! You are not a Kleinian, are you?

DEVIL You are not by any chance addressing me, are you? Are you one of the people whose God is the Devil? I do not cultivate theories; theories are a symptom of gregarious animals when they function as members of a group. I am special, individual, a victim of disapproval.

MAN Poor devil; it must be very trying, but rather agreeable. At least you appear to thrive.

DEVIL I had to fight for my right to be curious. I had to overcome my morals.

SOMITE THIRTY *You* had to? My sense of smell, my only guide and provider, was of short range in the water on which I relied and had my being. I passed it on to Soma.

SOMA I turned it to good account when I found myself in a gaseous fluid; it was a shock at first. Some never learned how to smell their way through all that gas to food.

THIRTY YEARS I admit that even when my nose led me to discover a durian I was scared to eat it.

SOMA Still, I got through that intellectual—or was it moral?—barrier to what P.A. would no doubt call your mind. Let me acknowledge my debt to gastro-intestinal greed—

DEVIL And, I hope, to my powers of seduction.

SEVENTY-FIVE YEARS Don't you think Somite, Soma and you youngsters owe something to what I have been doing all my life—besides growing older. To me it seems as if I owed and still keep on owing something to all of you.

SOMITE THREE That's the first time I have heard you admit that you still owe me something.

SEVENTY-FIVE YEARS I think it is probably the first time I have got through to you. Even now I can't imagine how anything I say is sufficiently perspicuous to make the journey from here to my fish-like origin, although I have often had 'echoes' of messages from my gills to my conscious mind.

FOURTEEN YEARS Your *what*? Never heard of it.

SEVENTY-FIVE YEARS That is more than I can say for you. I have lost my capacity for shame, thanks largely to being perpetually bombarded with memories of my past association with you.

FIFTY YEARS Oh, I wouldn't say that. After all, you and P.A. between you kept Fourteen awake with your probings. Why can't you let the past sleep in peace?

PRIEST I don't think a little guilt and remorse does anyone any harm.

P.A. A little perhaps, but not the quantities with which you and your friends pollute old age.

TWENTY-ONE TEARS Pollute old age! *I* had plenty to regret, plenty to mourn. I thought I would never survive the shame of having lived beyond my friends who were dead by the end of August 8th.

ROBIN I remember—that was the famous victory, the break-through—Ludendorff's 'black day for the German Army'.

ROLAND I remember that. A marvellous sight as you and I looked back along the Amiens-Roye road in the bright sunlight and saw it crowded with the reserves.

TWENTY-ONE YEARS Too late, blast them, too late! Years too late! They should have been there on November 20th—Cambrai—in 1917.

FIFTY YEARS The staff had to learn their job. That victory would have been the biggest disaster ever, had the reserves been there to get through—and be captured.

P.A. Now we know what we did not know then, that our Governors had not learned their job. At least the army learned; the civilians never did.

TWENTY-ONE YEARS Nor have you since.

FIFTY YEARS Well, why didn't you?

TWENTY-ONE YEARS I tried. But Oxford, good food, marvellous colleges, the incredible excitment of Iffly Road crowded with us all going to see the Varsity play Newport, seduced us. 'How will it seem to you forty years on?'

SIXTY-ONE YEARS I think you were seduced into forgetting. Perhaps it was better than those poor chaps of whose death we spoke in whispers—unable to stand Parson's Pleasure, the Parks bathed in sunlight, Magdalen Tower and Great Tom rolling out the curfew. The war they survived; it was the peace that finished them off. Even now I remember a little rat of a man—Mons Star and a few more meaningless baubles—'Oo yer shuvvin'? 'urryin' to a war?' The heavy, uneducated sarcasm of the under-privileged still smarting at his lack of appreciation, his inglorious, undistinguished nothingness. It should have been me, but I had been so pampered, so praised that I almost—not quite—believed the luxury deserved.

P.A. It may have saved your life more than once. Ultimately

your unbelief rescued you from *that* quagmire—sunk without a trace in your own exudate of complacency.

TWENTY-THREE YEARS I reached a very low ebb. I was so nasty that not even my parents could preserve the illusion intact. I suppose you think it was psycho-analysis?

P.A. I think it helped. Luckily it was not the only source of Truth.

TWENTY-THREE YEARS What else?

P.A. The world you live in—that is, if you read it and not only books.

NINETEEN YEARS I was not reading books. I had forgotten most of those I had read.

TWENTY YEARS I had almost forgotten to read—certainly forgotten how to understand what I read. I wonder if I knew that printed words had a meaning.

FOURTEEN YEARS I thought *Paradise Lost* had a meaning.

FIFTY YEARS You must have been pretty bright in those days.

FOURTEEN YEARS I can't be rude enough to say I think you stupid; or untruthful enough to say I think you clever or wise.

SIXTY YEARS I do not remember Fourteen as clever or polite.

FOURTEEN YEARS I do not remember anyone thinking anything about me except perhaps that I was unprepossessing and gauche. Possibly not my mother, but I didn't count her.

FIFTY YEARS Why didn't you count your mother?

FOURTEEN YEARS Mothers always think that sort of thing.

SIXTY YEARS Do they? I have seen some that do not. Perhaps they disguise their true feelings, but I don't think so.

EIGHTEEN YEARS Weren't you pleased when you were decorated for war service?

TWENTY-THREE YEARS Too late! Besides, I knew too much. I remember Lord Helpus, as we called him, saying to Twenty, 'I always tell my son John that if you see a man with more than two rows of ribbons he is tolerably certain to be a waster'.

TWENTY YEARS I remember. I only had one solitary ribbon which I was afraid I would have to prove—I knew I could not. 'Coward! Coward!' my thumping heart would tell me. At Anvin when I felt the air trembling and throbbing against my ears . . . a bombardment? Twenty and more miles away? I felt no better when that old hand Trapper said, 'It's only a trench raid'. I thought it must be all Hell let loose.

TWENTY-THREE YEARS You were both right—it *was* only a raid and it *was* all Hell let loose.

TWENTY YEARS My pounding heart—surely, I thought, Lord Helpus and the others can hear it?

HEART You heard it—why did you not pay attention to what I was trying to knock into your thick phrenes?

TWENTY YEARS My mind was making such a row—screaming 'Patriotism! Apache! Brigand!' I couldn't hear myself—I suppose it was me?—thinking.

THIRTY YEARS Too much anatomy and physiology to listen to your guts.

SOMITE THIRTY-TWO I could have told you that more than two rows of teeth meant you could be certain that you were a shark, greedy and in love with your food.

FIFTEEN YEARS Couvre-toi de flannelle!

TWENTY-THREE YEARS Couvre-toi de plumes blanches.

EIGHTEEN YEARS Those bloody girls in Kingsway!

TWENTY YEARS They gave me one in March 1918 when I was on leave.

SEVENTY-FIVE YEARS I remember—wasn't it after you had been to the investiture?

TWENTY-YEARS Yes; but that time I knew they were quite right. I was going back to the Front in an hour or so when I had changed back into uniform. 'But', said the almoner, 'Isn't your boy wearing the cap of a famous regiment?'

HEART If the cap fits—wear it. Let you and your damn silly mind go back to the Front, but why drag me in? I didn't enlist 'for the duration.' I was furious when you told me to stop thumping.

SEVENTY-FIVE YEARS You were always thumping—if not with fury, then with fear. Later it was love. Rabbits always 'thump'; it's like trying to interpret a motor car horn—it tells you nothing and leaves you to imagine something is going to happen to someone, somewhere, sometime.

HEART If only you listened to me and learnt my language—why, even your cardiologist told you that!

TWENTY-FIVE YEARS Too late! Too late!

SEVENTY-FIVE YEARS You are as bad as the Brain-fever bird—remember?

SIX YEARS Very well—funny your knowing. 'Brain-fever, brain-fever, brain-fever' it used to sing.

SEVENTY-SEVEN YEARS Ah yes, cuculus varius, you mean.

TWENTY YEARS Do I? You're as bad as our Army Intelligence Officer. When I came out of the Third Battle of Ypres and hardly knew whether I was alive or dreaming, he asked me if I had noticed when the alluvial changed to the cretaceous. I couldn't even laugh. Like all staff officers he thought how stupid we combatant officers were.

HEART So you were.

'So
We go
To face a foreign foe.'

Quite appropriate to a musical like 'White Horse Inn'. You would have done better in a musical—in the audience. Leave fighting to the soldiers—not schoolboys.

EIGHTEEN YEARS You should have seen Kitchener's piercing eyes following you around.

TWENTY YEARS You should have heard what Curzon said about Kitchener. My parents did.

TWENTY-THREE YEARS You should have heard what the soldiers heard Curzon say about the common Tommies in the bath house. 'Why, their skins are quite white!'

TWENTY YEARS I saw them before they had washed the 'alluvial' off. They weren't pretty even when their faces were as white as the cretaceous. And the cold . . .!

TWENTY-THREE YEARS And the warmth! Those nits! Do you remember an inn, Miranda? Do you remember an inn?

TWENTY YEARS No; she was doing war work—handing out white feathers!

THIRTY YEARS Oh, for heaven's sake! Can't you give it a rest?

EIGHTEEN YEARS It didn't—

TWENTY YEARS And doesn't—

TWENTY-THREE YEARS Give me a rest.

THIRTY YEARS Well, put a sock in it.

TWENTY YEARS Luckily we couldn't have fires and couldn't be warm enough for the little devils to feed. But the cold, the blue cold and the dangerous cretaceous view! When I opened my tin of bully beef I found a huge chunk of gristle that filled half the tin. Aghast that my day's rations had gone, 'Fray Bentos never did that to us', I said. 'You can't expect a vast wealthy American firm to bother about us', said Shorty. I admired the icy cretaceous in front. If that sniper fires I hope it will be a good shot through the forehead and out at the back with the brains which are such a useless chunk. Poor Edwards—I hope he didn't know anything about it. I hope it was only I who saw the mess bulge out and interrupt our conversation. He didn't even finish the sentence. 'Can I retire now sir?' 'Where's your tank? You're no bloody use to me without it.' But that was at the 'grand canyon'—no release from Villers Pluich. There was no one to ask anyway. That damned decoration! Why couldn't they give me something useful—like guts?

THIRTY YEARS Are you talking in your sleep? What's the matter with you—shell shock?

TWENTY YEARS No, sir; yessir, I mean ter say, y'know. Not really. I'm all right. Tell me, Eighteen, have I any soft bloody brain stuff behind my right ear?

EIGHTEEN YEARS No. Shut up. How do you expect me to fight if you talk like that? I want a V.C.—not a V. Pluich.

TWENTY YEARS It's cold; I wish it wasn't so cold. What about a nice cosy group session?

THIRTY YEARS It's a pity that Twenty can't make up his mind that he will survive the war, or *has* survived being born.

FORTY YEARS How could he possibly know unless you leaked it back to Twenty-two and told him to pass it on to Twenty-one to pass it on to Eighteen?

TWENTY YEARS I couldn't pass it on to Eighteen—he was so busy thinking he was going to win the V.C. or some such damned nonsense. Besides, I knew I would be far more likely to get a hole drilled in my head—if not then, in the next few months. Had I known I would soon be at that ruddy Salient again I think I would have arranged for one of those nice Boches to drill a hole through my skull and let me out like the Lossiemouth captain's brains. I had neither brains nor guts from then till August 8th 1918.

EIGHTEEN YEARS Nonsense. I was so terrified that I would run away I could hardly think of anything else. If Twenty had told me I could not run away—even if I tried—I would have felt much better.

TWENTY YEARS If I had known what I know now I would not have dared to tell you. I wished I could feel as enthusiastic as you seemed to be.

EIGHTEEN YEARS You were afraid that you would want to seem as brave as I hoped to appear to be.

TWENTY-ONE YEARS Twenty did, and was so busy 'seeming' to be brave that it nearly killed me. If you had had more sense you would have got a soft job at the War Office, but *now* look what you have done—I have to go into action at that terrible place Sequhart.

TWENTY-TWO YEARS What was wrong with Sequhart? I remember your telling me how beautiful it looked with the sun rising behind the slender spire and how you took those two crew members back because they were too gassed to walk. You remember? You described it so vividly it brought tears to me eyes. Such bravery! Such self-sacrificing compassion for those two poor chaps!

TWENTY-ONE YEARS Shut up! I was scared out of my wits and you know it. I do not see that that is any reason for being so very un-funny about me. If I had known you would be sitting knocking back brandies in an Oxford club, being facetious, I would have . . . I would. . . .

TWENTY-TWO YEARS No you wouldn't; and you would not have had the gall to be claiming 'compassion for your men'—you make me sick.

TWENTY YEARS So you do me. I think you're a nasty bastard.

TWENTY-TWO YEARS I can hardly disagree. Still, I didn't do so badly in view of recent fighting.

TWENTY-FIVE YEARS You did. You just cribbed that idea out of your testimonial from that Oxford don who thought he had better be kind to an ex-gallant officer.

FORTY YEARS Ex-officer and ex-gallant. The ex-es have it. I declare the ex-es elected unanimously.

TWENTY-FIVE YEARS Oh my God—not really? Is there no future?

ALICE 'And from that warfare there is no release.'

FOUR

FORTY YEARS What's that? What did you say?

ALICE Oh nothing, nothing. It was Rosemary.

ROSEMARY I agree—nothing! Nothing at all. I was just interested in your debate. Do go on.

TWENTY-FIVE YEARS I have forgotten what I was saying. These women butted—I mean—'said' something.

ROSEMARY Ah—these women! Always our fault!

ALICE I see your 'gallantry' remains unimpaired.

TWENTY YEARS Where would you have been if we had not fought?

MAN And won. Don't forget you won too!

ROLAND We did our best, you sneering lout.

MAN A girl friend of mine taught me how to sneer. She said she had learned it from an English soldier who threw his cigarette butts on the ground to see smoke-crazed German women fight for them in the dust.

ALICE Gallant as always.

ROSEMARY Alice and I keep our butts for—

ROBIN Please, please! Don't be vulgar.

EIGHTEEN YEARS I used to think my old school was marvellous.

TWENTY-FIVE YEARS I had almost forgotten how quaint you were. 'The distant tape and the runner beside.' How it brings it back to me! But 'Où sont les neiges d'antan?' They don't come back—only slush.

EIGHTEEN YEARS 'His own name over all!' It is too sad to think about.

P.A. That is a common fallacy, though it is a habit to which a psycho-analytic intercourse seems prone. But that is not the aim which the analyst pursues.

FORTY YEARS What is his aim?

P.A. That depends on a great many factors, notably on whether he has a disposition compatible with the work he does, his age and experience—

FORTY YEARS Are you referring to his training?

P.A. In part. I do not mean to restrict it to his analytic training, or even to his university, school or home training. All those are important; but I have in mind the need to distinguish between experience of knowledge imparted by others and knowledge derived from the analyst's ability to turn what his senses tell him into nourishment.

FORTY YEARS I don't think I understand.

P.A. As an example of what I mean, I take your last statement. In so far as you *do* understand, I suspect the 'thing' you understand will contribute to your growth. In so far as you *don't* understand, I suspect that it cannot and does not lead to growth.

FORTY YEARS You are very cautious; why do you say you 'suspect' that it does or does not? Or am I being pedantic?

P.A. Not at all. I *try* to be precise and therefore 'suspect'. I cannot *know* because even if I do not understand I may be able to turn that fact to good account by learning that there are some things which I do not understand; whereas if I were an intolerant man I would dismiss the experience before I had time to learn from it.

ROLAND Then I can't have learned much from war, because if I had gone through all this palaver before I pressed the button of my machine gun—well, I wouldn't have 'gone through all this palaver'; I would have been shot like your Lossiemouth captain before I had thought a single word.

P.A. That is why you went through a machine gun course at Grantham so that you could automatically press the button in a crisis *without* going through all this palaver. But you must sometimes have waited, when your patrols were out, to see if it was friend or foe. That would be knowledge acquired, and for it to be 'automatically' available you must have made it your own.

ROBIN I vouch for it—Roland did a lot of 'swotting' on that course.

P.A. Well then—you must have gone through the palaver beforehand. You must be capable of going through it at *some* time. If you had got drunk instead, you would have been unable to press the button when you were 'sober' and under fire.

ROSEMARY How extremely interesting. What is the button?

P.A. I am sorry—we are boring you.

ROSEMARY You are not sorry; nor am I bored. But—

ROBIN But what? Or is that a secret between you and Alice?

P.A. If it is, I might suggest a psycho-analytic interpretation. But this is not a psycho-analytic occasion and therefore the minimum conditions for a verbal, audible interpretation don't exist.

ROBIN Something sexual, I bet.

P.A. A sexual situation affords the conditions for a sexual interpretation, an analytical situation affords an opportunity for a psycho-analytic interpretation.

ALICE What *is* a psycho-analytic interpretation?

P.A. It must be perspicacious and perspicuous. That is—

ROLAND These long words!

P.A. —an expression of a scientifically accurate insight which is phrased in a language comprehensible by the listener. It must be believed to be true by the analyst, and his formulation should be in terms that would penetrate the barriers of the listener's incomprehension.

ALICE Oh, I know—that would get through my thick feminine skull.

ROSEMARY Well, I *don't* know!

P.A. You both give an example of the difficulty I am talking about. Alice, hostile, 'thinks' I am an obtuse male; Rosemary 'remembers' my learnedness. Both—feelings, and ideas remembered—produce an obscurity.

SOMITE TWENTY-FOUR I've got a stomach ache.

ALICE At last—something I *do* understand; I have the advantage of knowing pregnancy.

FOURTEEN YEARS Neither of you knows how painful it is to have an idea.

TWENTY-TWO YEARS You? I didn't know you ever had an idea.

FOURTEEN YEARS I and my friend Thirteen have had ideas—even religious ones.

PRIEST I remember; Thirteen's god was the school swimming captain, and Fourteen used to believe in the school rugger captain.

FIFTEEN YEARS I was—still am—most impressed by Ruskin. Poor Ruskin—I didn't know then what a hell he lived in.

DEVIL Nothing to do with me; must have been your god. He kicked people about, but I didn't.

SIXTEEN YEARS I can't imagine your kicking anything about; you always wore morning dress.

DEVIL You cribbed that idea from Beerbohm.

FORTY YEARS Did he? I had forgotten he read about poor Soames.

SIXTEEN YEARS I read a great deal; I also played hard.

PRIEST And prayed hard.

SIXTEEN YEARS I may even have done that, but no answering god replied and I gave it up. The devil wasn't much use either.

SEVENTY YEARS Poor devil! Blamed for everything—but perhaps he, like the rest of us, had to learn. There are plausible grounds for believing that he exists. He and his trainees—

DEVIL Always ready to learn from Adam and Eve.

SIXTEEN YEARS Seventy owes something to me; his body is in good order considering that he still totters around.

SEVENTY YEARS Sixteen is not one of my favourite characters.

SOMITE TWENTY-FOUR Nor mine; such an ugly character!

ALICE Oh, poor soul—not as bad as you make out, surely?

SOMITE TWENTY-FOUR You are prejudiced. If I had known I would grow a soul I would have remained a fetus.

TWENTY-FIVE YEARS If I had known I had such an ugly somitic ancestor I would not have tried to cultivate a soul.

EIGHTEEN YEARS I don't think I knew your somitic friend, but I had my suspicions and thought a soul would be an asset, not an excrescence.

TWENTY-FIVE YEARS We all make mistakes. Knowing what I know now I would certainly not choose to be intelligent. Wise perhaps, but *not* intelligent.

SEVENTY YEARS That's something you can pat yourself on the back about. I cannot honestly say I feel wise.

TWENTY-FIVE YEARS Perhaps your honesty is overdeveloped—more pathological than benign.

SEVENTY YEARS No, I don't think so. In real life it gets worn off as fast as it grows.

FORTY YEARS You are too personal, Twenty-five. You've learnt that from P.A. He is always being personal.

FIFTY YEARS Not personal—specific.

P.A. I have great respect for the individual. Do you think that is wrong?

FIFTY YEARS No, but it is not in keeping with the growth of the Herd. I can see P.A. will be in serious trouble if the Herd develops faster than he does.

P.A. If the development of the Herd is incompatible with that of the individual, either the individual will perish, or the Herd will be destroyed by the individual who is not allowed to fulfil himself.

PRIEST Surely it depends on whether the Herd develops an intolerance to the individual or the individual to the Herd.

P.A. Some of us think that the development of the individual needs careful supervision.

PRIEST Of course; we are all agreed about that. The disagreement arises when the agreement is to be translated into action. The executive has to decide *what* is to be taught, *what* is to be believed, *what* is to be painted, or musically or aesthetically created.

DOCTOR Or whether the mother or the baby is to live. 'Do not strive officiously to keep alive' is what I was taught.

ROLAND Am I being 'officious' if I strive to keep myself alive?

ROBIN Or cowardly? Or suicidal not to?

P.A. Whether it is better to take arms against a sea of troubles. . . .

PRIEST Who or what decides?

P.A. It appears to be the individual that decides whether to preserve life.

PHYSICIST Nowadays, thanks to us, *one* individual appears to be able to decide whether he *and* people 'not him' are to live or die.

P.A. It appears—to us—to be the case. But is what appears to 'us' to be regarded as identical with fact? Priest and others seem to think that we psycho-analysts claim to know. I regard any thing I 'know' as transitive theory—a theory 'on the way' to knowledge, but not *knowledge*. It is merely a 'resting place', a 'pause' where I can be temporarily free to be aware of my condition, however precarious that condition is.

PRIEST John Bunyan described that state in a number of pictorially vivid phrases.

SCHREBER So did I.

ROLAND Whoever is that?

P.A. Oh, only a poor devil of a paranoiac.

ROBIN A what? Crazy, you mean?

P.A. I suppose I do, though I think Freud suspected that what Schreber wrote was worthy of attention. I slipped into the prevalent mental slough. One cannot avoid instinctively conforming to the quagmire—whatever its defects—in which one has survived so far. Bunyan tried to scramble out; so did Schreber. Both thought that Valiant for Truth, though they did not call him that, would help. Schreber, I suppose, thought he would be safe if he was a judge or a psychiatrist.

PRIEST Or psycho-analyst? Heaven? Or the 'Law'?

ROBIN 'To be'? Or 'not to be'? Shakespeare, like Bunyan, said it. Extraordinary how these old buffers wrote it all down. Of course they can't have known what they were talking about.

ROSEMARY 'Of course.' Like women they would not know. I at least had the intelligence not to have children because I had some respect for the pain in my belly. And some respect for my belly. So had you Alice.

ALICE (*deeply distressed*) No, no, no! Would God I had died for thee oh Absalom my son—

ROLAND That was said by a father.

ALICE I thought I was marrying a father. But a father would have known that I might lay down my life for a son and that he might have to lay down his married life for a daughter. Hopeless, hopeless, hopeless.

ROLAND I am sorry—I know it's no good, but I *am* sorry. It was not my fault I survived the war.

MAN You thought you were winning.

ROLAND You thought you had won. But you did not.

DEVIL Allow me to settle it for you. I can't bear to see you quarrelling. I have a nice chain reaction here which one of my scientific friends will gladly teach you to realize. Temporarily, however, I must limit your freedom by using the reaction to chain you. It is only temporary and then—pouff—it will all be over without even a whimper. No one will even hear a bang.

ROBIN I'm afraid.

ROLAND I don't like this theatrical pose.

ROSEMARY It is so seductive, so intelligent.

ROLAND You bloody women.

DEVIL Don't quarrel—tell me when you are ready and I will do what I can do for you.

PRIEST Or just 'do for us'.

DEVIL (*bows himself out*) At your service. . . .

ROBIN For God's sake don't exasperate him.

ROLAND For God's sake don't worship him.

ALICE I thought you did—especially when you professed to 'worship' me.

ROLAND I have not forgotten; I was scared of bloody women. Even the first man I saw spread-eagled in the shell hole we shared was not bloody—only faintly green parchment stretched over bones.

P.A. The sight impressed you, lying with him on the brickdust stained earth—that insalubrious place, the ghost of Wieltje village.

MAN Our 9.2 Howitzers dealt with that.

P.A. So I understand. As for Roland, I thought you had shot him several times.

ROSEMARY No one can deal with Roland. I tried to dissuade Man from trying.

ALICE He did for me.

ROLAND I died for you; but you thought I was being sentimental.

ROBIN I liked you, but you always thought I was too much of a coward to be allowed to share your body. All the same, if I hadn't made you duck—more than once I may say—you would not be alive today.

ROLAND Thank you—for nothing.

ALICE You only saved his corpse and sent it back for me.

ROLAND Not so much honouring thee but giving it a hope that there it might not withered be. Alas, I was no rosy wreath.

P.A. I remember a woman whose man came back to her after long years of war when she had prayed to God to bring him back safe. But his leg had been amputated so she quit. He thought she would love him as a wounded hero.

ALICE How like a man! If she had had a baby by him *he* would have quit her; if he blushed, which I doubt, he blushed unseen.

P.A. I know a man who was always a deathly white. He was so ashamed that people would see his blushes that he killed himself.

ROLAND Another of your bloody silly stories.

P.A. No, only a fact. I haven't the imagination to invent a story like that. Alice reminds me of a man who didn't blush, but was seen to blush by himself. I did not find out why because, as I say, he killed himself—more efficiently than Man's efforts with Roland.

ROLAND Sometimes I think these debates amongst ourselves are most menacing because they are so private—the same family. Why can't we get together? Not only are we all the same human family, though artificially split by man's art into individuals, groups, nations, but—

ROBIN According to Priest not 'artificially', but by God's command linguistically, religiously, aesthetically and in every this-that way for building a ramp which would—

ROLAND Enable them to storm Heaven and the throne of Heaven's King.

ROSEMARY How bizarre!

ALICE Even Man thinks that by murder, contrived by the instrument of masses of disciplined murderers, men would reach the throne of Heaven. Victory! with a capital V.

P.A. Wee, capital wee-wee.

ROLAND Ghastly pun—even for you.

P.A. What is a ghastly pun for me may be the first step in a new language.

ROBIN What's fun for you is death to me, as Toad is said to have remarked. What is your new language? It reminds me of puns, as the ideograms of Chinese were 'articulated', though articulating was not the correct method of cohering those elements.

P.A. You mean not correct in accordance with the scheme of the inventors of the ideogrammatic signs. But the articulations, though 'false', enabled Fenollosa to enable Ezra Pound to enable future generations to further the knowledge achieved. Artificial or God-made, these divisions into individuals, into seconds, years, millenia, make it extremely difficult to form a meaningful junction between one ideogram, individual (person, race, nation) and the next. There is a screen, a caesura, a resistant material between one particle and the next.

ALICE Unless some person paints on a piece of glass, like Picasso, so that it can be seen from both sides of the screen—both sides of the resistance.

ROBIN Which 'like a dome of many-coloured glass stains the white radiance of eternity' so that we—minute individual particles that we are—may discern what we think is a meaningful pattern projected against the glass. I agree with Roland—'Why can't we get together?'

P.A. No reason—in so far as we know that the same person created all of our characters and we should therefore be free to get together and write a single book sired by 'us'.

ROBIN If it's a book, it has to be split into pages, chapters and so forth. I don't want to lose my identity, swallowed by all you crowd.

ROLAND You wouldn't. How do you know that our being swallowed up in a group—which would mean all of us—would not be indistinguishable from perfect freedom? It would be our fulfilment.

ROBIN How do you know it would end in a Pauline freedom? If I had a Shakespearean vocabulary it would be very helpful. Victor Hugo had an enormous vocabulary and was able verbally to paint a visual image of rose petals scattered by the wind over the surface of a pool of water, like an Armada dispersed by the storm. According to Heredia, Anthony saw, in the pools of Cleopatra's eyes, a fleet in flight. All that has been dealt with—not so overtly as in the undergraduate dining club known as *The Shakespeare,* but just as effectively—by the glorious memorial tomb of Shakespearean Scholarship. Now no one dreams of Shakespeare and I could not mobilize even four thousand words with which to express what I want to communicate. If Shakespeare could not survive—

ROLAND Or Pythagoras, buried under his triangle—

P.A. Or Freud buried under his oedipal triangle, or Melanie Klein under a mass of evacuated identifications—

ALICE Or a mass of Kleinian Theories treated to 'introjective projections', or even what *I* say interpreted, diagnosed, relegated to the lavatory bowl as psychotic distortions by virtue of the neologisms of psychiatry. Time that antiquates antiquity; the neo-news allowed to calcify in the realms of oblivion until the mental archaeologists scrape the arteries free of their horny integuments and display the dead jargons of the past to be admired, re-diagnosed, re-interpreted and re-interred.

P.A. James Joyce tried to break out of the mental ossifications in which his tender shoots of animation were enclosed by the Clongowesian wrappings of Roman Catholicized semitic Zeus.

PRIEST Zeus was a juvenile vulgarian anyway. Truth always has to break out of the wrappings of the latest Enthusiast who wants to bring his pet mummy to life.

P.A. And in doing so dresses it up in the latest fashions of embalming technique. 'Mother' becomes 'Mummy', God borrows the costume of Old Nick, and his son is tricked out, swaddled in his grave clothes. But man only destroys man because he has not yet discovered that minute, ineffable particle which transforms the inanimate and makes it perceptible, distinguishable, noteworthy, because it is alive. 'Though the body dies' the virus shall live for ever. The present is already concealed in Oblivion. Whose finger is on the button?

ALICE My clitoris is passed by unnoticed by your mouth, 'blinded', 'glutted' by your penitential penis. What you don't know is knowledge; once you know it, and once it is known by you, you are too full of knowledge to be able to be curious.

ROSEMARY Even if his alimentary canal can learn no more he opens his eyes wide to take in what his belly can't. Then his eyes are so stuffed with Beauty that he cannot see me. Not even Homer had the wit to see that Helen of Troy was not just an ecto-dermal proliferation.

ALICE They are all the same. I have known no person, clothed in the trappings of the woman's body, that was not imprisoned by those same trappings and unable to break through them to meet her . . . her . . . why, I used to think I could talk, but this same capacity for articulate speech is more an opaque screen than a link which enables me to communicate with something not me.

P.A. Perhaps you could project your ideas on to your resistance; then someone not-you could read the trace left on the resistance.

ROBIN You mean she might use the delay to think some sense before she opens her mouth again?

P.A. No, I don't. I think it might help *you* if you could use the hindering obstacle to think; but from what I know of you it is far more likely that you would fill the silence with just such a damn silly remark as you just made.

MAN Shall I shoot him?

ROSEMARY No. (*to Alice*) Man is a dear, but he has such a one-track mind. Useful enough for bullets, penes and other guided missiles, but no good without either a single track or a guide.

ALICE The boy scouts and the girl guides—as we used to say at school.

ROSEMARY I didn't know you were such a dirty-minded lot at your school.

ALICE Oh yes, we knew quite a lot. Of course we had to hide it from the staff.

VOICE Of course.

FIVE

ALICE What was that? Did you hear it?

ROSEMARY No—I hope you aren't hallucinating or I shall have to get rid of you.

P.A. I should be careful what you do with your voice. Here—suck one of these psycho-analytic pills—slowly. Just let it dissolve in your mind. You've swallowed it! You shouldn't have done that. It won't do you any harm—just a bit of heart ache. But it will spread through your system and be excreted harmlessly by your mind—like cinnamon, or whisky. It was probably the Future casting its shadow before; sometimes it is disguised as the Past casting its memory forward.

ROSEMARY Thank you; I am most grateful. Do you know what gratitude is?

ROBIN 'A lively expectation of benefits to come.'

ALICE You are cynical. What is guilt then?

P.A. Ah yes!—the Cynics.

ROBIN No, she asked about guilt. Guilt is 'a lively apprehension of rewards to be inflicted'.

P.A. For being able to laugh at dirty jokes in school—like, 'It is I. Come forth! And 'e came fifth—and 'e did 'it 'is eye'.

ALICE Oh my God!

ROSEMARY Isn't it awful? Now it has become respectable and is called Psycho-analysis. It hardly makes one anxious to follow Roland's suggestion and become unified.

ROBIN If we could come together we could still preserve our identity—like the hills on a map in which all the same levels could be joined by a contour—

P.A. All right if we could link Somite Three here with all the other Somite Threes. Of course, the auditory and optic pits would have to put up with being linked.

DOCTOR The post-natals may want to keep their distance from the pre-natals—and vice versa. We must assume that the pre-natal crowd can adjust to a change from a liquid environment to a gaseous one, the olfactory elements easing the change by bringing mucus with them so they go on functioning even after birth.

P.A. Some of these post-natal people complain of too much fluid. They call it 'catarrh' or 'influenza' and rush off to someone to 'cure' them. You must be familiar with that demand.

DOCTOR Yes indeed, but I would hesitate to tell them they were complaining of too much cure—being drowned in cure.

P.A. Your somitic friends would complain of being immersed in your intellectual, cerebral evacuations—a rarefied, abstract ocean of theory in which they could not taste or smell. If somites could write, the book would be 'On the Interpretation of Reality' and the theories would all be what we call dreams. We complain both of the unpleasant warmth of psycho-analysis *and* its arid abstractions.

DOCTOR Poor old body; poor old mind. It is hardly surprising that they do not get on well together and look down on each other, especially if we remember that one is derived from the other. In fact they may derive from a biological atomic plutonium breeder.

P.A. If it is true that living matter derives from the heat engendered by the reaction of oxygen with protoplasm, then I can see that brain substance might derive from the 'decay' of involuntary muscle, and the mind likewise from the energy released by the degeneration of athletic ability.

DOCTOR I knew some intelligent, 'brainy' people who played games for Oxford; they seemed to remain brainy *and* athletic.

P.A. Fortunate people! If only one could see how they did it one might solve the problem of how to produce more energy than beef. I would think I was in reality becoming a psycho-analyst if I could *become* more energetic by *being* more energetic. It might enable others to start that reaction. Melanie Klein seemed to do that for psycho-analysis.

BION What! You don't mean to say you are a Kleinian?

P.A. You remind me of Sir Andrew Aguecheek—'And if I thought he were a puritan I would . . .!' Your excellent reason, sir?

BION I thought you would appreciate an experience which we could share together.

P.A. That reminds me—we were talking about linking the different 'levels' of mind as contours portray a mountain on a flat surface. How would you contrive to link your third somite with me? Rosemary was saying that when she was Helen of Troy—

DOCTOR Yes, I heard her—poor paranoiac! She must be as mad as a coot.

P.A. —nobody wanted progenitors whose ancestors were less than ectoderm. But she would be insulted if I said she *looked* like an embryo of thirty somites, or that she had a character like that.

SEVEN-WEEKS EMBRYO If I had thought I would turn out like Helen of Troy I would have drowned myself in amniotic fluid. Luckily Six Weeks appreciated the difference and passed it on to his mesonephros. No wonder Rosemary was tired of people who could only see the progeny of her ectoderm. I'm not sure I want to be jammed up with Six Weeks though.

P.A. Beauty is in the eye of the ectoderm—as soon as the shell has developed it wants to become permanent. No wonder we are all insects at heart—just as well some of us developed an endo-skeleton.

ROLAND What is wonderful about that? I have always had a spine and even my penis was often erect, but I can't see that I am better for it.

DOCTOR You would if your lack of spine got you into a prisoner of war camp or a flabby penis had kept you out of marriage.

ALICE I never discouraged an erection of nipple, clitoris or penis.

P.A. Hmmmm . . . nor do I, though I see plenty who do. Sexual maturity is often thought to be the end of the journey when in fact it is another beginning.

DOCTOR What more is there besides sexual maturity?

P.A. Terms like 'sexual maturity' ought to be used precisely for physical maturity as in adolescence. By being allowed to spread, it disguises the absence of passionate love that is not only physical or mental, but a development of the fusion of both.

ROSEMARY Sounds interesting.

P.A. It is intended to. If you are right about it the sound may travel through the liquid medium and reach the auditory apparatus within you.

ALICE What about the pits?

P.A. Whether it is the pressure of sound waves which are sub-sonic or infra-visual they could reach the auditory and optic pits. Unfortunately, Doctor may be so blinded by his psychiatric training that he would not interpret them correctly when they bounce back to his mind. So many won't see or listen because they say they are visual or auditory hallucinations, or chemically generated feelings of pugnacity, or fear born of the adrenals—as if that made them unworthy of attention. Freud listened to and quoted his great teacher Charcot. If others did likewise they would repeat their observations, however compulsively repetitive they seemed to be, until a pattern became discernible in the chaos of chance. Look at your facts. Respect them even if you do not like them. The mists may clear and reveal a pattern which is so disagreeable—

PRIEST Or so blindingly brilliant, as Arjuna and others found—

P.A. Or so deep a void, so black, so astronomical a hole that you regret the price you have to pay.

VOICE What price is that?

ALICE What echo was that?

ROSEMARY It makes me shudder.

DOCTOR It bounces back from the hole and its sides.

P.A. We probably learn the price too late.

ALICE Too late for what?

P.A. For us to mend our course. Too 'late' or 'early' as measured against a scale of time which is relevant only to our ephemeral existence, not the millenia of millenia needed to plumb the nearest confines of reality.

ALICE Shall we get together?

SOMITE THREE Delighted—but let me remind you that the rest of you have spent all your energies trying to get rid of me. Were it not for my persistence—

GERM PLASM *Your* persistence! *Mine,* you mean.

SOMITE THREE I nourished you and provided the conditions for your survival.

ALL (ANTE-NATAL) SOULS Had it not been for our parental care and your capacity to make the best of it, which we learnt from you, none of the post-natal crowd would exist.

ALL (POST-NATAL) SOULS Let us agree that there are certain basic fundamentals of character and environment—Choice and Chance, as Yeats put it—which cannot be extinguished without our own extinction.

SOMITE THREE All I say is—

SEVEN WEEKS All we say is—

P.A. All I say is, do not forget what we owe to all of us—though I do not find a belly-ache or strabismus helpful.

ALL (ANTE-NATAL) SOULS We do not find it helpful to have to choose 'pains' as our only method of drawing attention to our existence. We do not find Depression or Paranoia helpful to our struggles.

P.A. If I may speak for All Post-Natal Souls, we don't find it helpful to have to be depressed or mad before we get attention.

ROLAND I suppose germ cells had to go on proliferating though I can't see why they should carry it so far as to give birth to a mind. Still, now it has happened I'm all in favour of making the best of a bad job.

ROSEMARY It sounds sensible—though I'm not sure what the *best* is.

ALICE Is anyone? Or is it just *more* cells till there is no room for even the cells to generate.

MAN With co-operation from the rest of us I think I could arrange to have the button pressed.

ROSEMARY I am afraid. I think Post-Natal Souls may get together and a mind will be generated.

ROBIN Like maggots in the warmth of a rotting dung heap. What does—

P.A. I think it is too late to stop a mind developing. The only question is, how to make the best of it. I gather it would be as well for it not to obtrude into notice too much. What does Priest think?

PRIEST Shall we form a small committee—P.A., Robin, Rosemary, Alice and one other.

ALICE Good idea. I suggest we include Priest as he has a truly extensive experience. The others would contribute on occasions when their special gifts would be illuminating.

ROBIN We can speak for others who are not committee members; I know Twenty has a good deal to say.

P.A. Ought we to co-opt him?

ROBIN No, I think I could put it in more uninhibited—if P.A. will excuse me—terms; perhaps more mellow language.

P.A. Right—let's start. I remember how I felt when I was Twenty-one. We had just been ordered up the Line; I was terrified. I did not like the prospect at all. The orders were that we must not allow the enemy any rest, but carry on the pursuit now he had been beaten and a great gap torn in his lines by our victory on August 8th. Unfortunately I had been decorated for gallantry. Twenty-one knew I was terrified and hadn't the courage to get the doc. to invalid me out. I knew I had not the courage for 'heroic' deeds. Besides, I had 'flu; my runner was given a bottle of phyz. to dose me with. No one knew what I was suffering from so it was called p.u.o.—pyrexia of unknown origin. I hoped my death would be painless and sudden. The infantryman by my side had a hole in his belly. We looked at him coldly. 'He's a gonner—why waste time looking at him? Come on—zero hour.' I scrambled out of the trench and started walking forward. I inhibited—as I learned to call it later—any whisper of fact to burst through my p.u.o. A grey-haired man with his legs worn round his neck like a scarf wanted me to 'help' him. It was annoying to be expected to disentangle his neckwear. Besides, I was busy. '*No*—stretcher bearers coming!' I knew they weren't; only regimental stretcher bearers help. Why did I tell him that? I had been taught—disciplined—so that in just such a crisis I would not have an unfamiliar, unthought-out problem to solve in inadequate conditions for its solution. As a doctor I now understand; as an influenza-sodden tank officer, 'S.B.'s coming!' I lied. 'Kamerad kaput!', yelled the little Boche as he ran towards me, his bottom wiggling furiously as he tried not to fall. I could tell the hideously disarticulated old Tommy to go to Hell—'S.B.'s coming'—but I allowed the horrible little Boche to drag me to his cubby hole. No discipline—I knew he would murder me. I entered; in the dark another Boche with his legs wrapped round his neck for scarfwear. 'Kaput?' He dragged me to touch—'Kaput?' I did. 'Yes, kaput.' He burst into tears. I told myself, 'Now—damn fool—get *out.*' Only then I snapped out—out of the hole, out into the air, out into the sense to carry my Smith and Wesson where I had been taught to carry it.

PRIEST You would not have felt any better if you had been a parson. I remember our pink-faced, jolly, card-playing padre and how scornful you were—you and that red-faced, non-conformist private—because he would not come up and bury the dead. Poor Smith! He was so rigorous mortis that we could not force his arms into our grave; we were in a hurry too.

P.A. He preferred bridge with the colonel in H.Q. mess.

ROLAND Oh, don't be so hypocritical—so would you if you had been able to play bridge and hadn't been commanding a tank.

P.A. True. I was not scared—I was nothing. I thought I would be court-martialled. I was surprised that I told such an articulate, coherent story that I couldn't detect a chink of falsehood in it—and my men were so grateful and so full of admiration. I was amazed that I could not believe a word of it. All lies and so completely factual that even now—

ROLAND Well, what happened?

P.A. I caught up with my leading tank. I knew the long-range naval guns must get us. 'Get out!' I told them, 'and walk behind till it gets hit'. I set the controls at full speed and got out myself. It raced—for those days—ahead so we could hardly stumble up with it. And then—*then*!—the full horror came on me. Fool! What had I done? As I scrambled and tripped in my drunken influenza to catch up with the tank, in the shadow of which I had ordered my crew to remain sheltered, my ice-cold reality revealed a *fact*: The tank, in perfect order, with guns, ammunition and its 175 horse-power engines, was delivered into the hands of the enemy. Alone, I alone, had done this thing! My pyrexia left to rejoin its unknown origin.

PRIEST How did you get in—by beating your hands on the cold steel doors?

P.A. I was in; I did get in. A high-velocity shell struck; without thought I shot out of the hatch as the flames of petrol swathed the steel carcass. Are you hurt, sir? No—fell on my arse. Are you all right, sir? Of course! Why? Home—quick!

PRIEST Do you really remember this? It sounds most unlikely—but I cannot claim to attach so much importance to what you scientists call facts.

ROLAND Both Robin and I regard facts as facts. If I did not remember to sow corn and harvest 'facts', the crew you 'saved' would not have anything to eat. Nor would the rooks be blown cawing across the evening sky.

ROBIN I remember P.A. and his doctor friend as boys driving Curley to Munden when she did not want to be separated from her calf. Poor unintelligent animal! No one had told her about 'Separation Anxiety', but she knew all about the way *not* to Munden.

P.A. My twelve-year-old hadn't heard of 'separation anxiety' either, but 'remembered' not to be separated from my intelligently disciplined 175 horse-power acquired $\begin{Bmatrix}\text{conscious}\\\text{conscience}\end{Bmatrix}$ Even now I have to risk being heard by some damned psychiatric neologism-shooter.

ROBIN You speak with bitterness that I more usually hear conjoined with evacuation of hatred. In fact, if you hated psycho-analysts I would not be surprised to hear what I heard you say. As it is, I am almost shocked.

ROLAND If you were twelve years old I would not be surprised to hear that Curley had not arrived at Munden. I am shocked that as a psycho-analyst you are angry that your 'meaning' has not been driven into what you think is the right verbal pen.

P.A. I know, and have reason to fear that the 'pen' into which it has entered will imprison both me and my meaning—inescapably. You think this is all talk and that talk is nothing. I know—though I cannot prove—it is *not*.

ALICE I knew that my baby's noise wasn't all babel; it sounded 'just like' talk; it was not.

P.A. It was a precursor, a prelude to talk perhaps, but now we do not know. We do not know if this conversation is 'just like' talk, a 'prelude' to talk, the thing-in-itself, fact, real. It may be 'It', what our lives have been leading up to.

ROLAND Curley was a good beast. She not only yielded milk for her calf, she produced manure—just what was needed to germinate the wheat. Manure—an essential condition.

ROBIN There is a lot to be said in favour of your tractors, but if I had to choose between the smell of manure and the smell of petrol fumes, I prefer manure.

P.A. Just as well that you did. But you didn't like the smell of my hate which was as out of place in our discussion as you think the smell of fumes is for wheat germ. Maybe that is only because neither you nor I know for *what* the fumes are an 'essential' condition.

ROBIN Surely you do not suggest air pollution is good for us?

P.A. I do not. You, I am sure, do not suggest manure is the ideal floor covering for social discussion. But who could predict that cow dung would one day nourish our social intercourse? Socrates pointed out that 'talk', like 'painting', is not good, not bad, but ambiguous. His talk was interpreted—diagnosed—as corrupting the youth. Death, 'they' said, would cure the spread of those corrupt ideas. His body, as we know, turned to physical corruption. But what of his ideas? Plato caused them to be repeated.

ROBIN When Thirteen and I got together they excited us. Our admiration grew so that—

P.A. His ideas were buried beneath a memorial so deep they could not be heard. It is hard to determine the extent to which an idea survives, deteriorates or develops although apparently we can compare our present ideas with ideas we once had. The words in which we dress ideas disguise, as readily as they display, the meaning to which we aspire. Call ourselves what we will, whether Bacon, Truth, Poet, Newton or Bach, we all disappear. But ideas do not 'appear'; that is an attribute of 'things'.

ROBIN 'Ideas' are 'things'; maybe we have to review our ideas about ideas.

P.A. The germ cell has its 'minimum conditions'.

ROLAND The existing vocabulary of words or ideas needs augmentation. Institutions wear out; like things, they are inanimate and obey the laws of all inanimate objects; they are *not* alive. *Members* of 'institutions' are people; they may not subordinate their developmental qualities to the framework, the structure.

P.A. An idea, it seems, has to submit to the structure if it is to be communicated. You spoke of Plato's ideas, but they had to fall within the discipline of verbal artistry and could not be communicated—

PRIEST —till a soldier captured Constantinople and released the ideas imprisoned within; a soldier had to become operative. Even then a medi-aeval priest had to translate those ideas.

P.A. Erasmus had to break through a cultural prison wall at least as limiting as a wheat germ cell, or a pharaoh's tomb. Tutankhamun's ideas were enclosed within the preservative shells of Thebes.

PRIEST But before we blame the shell for the death of the idea we should acknowledge the 'preservative' function. We should not condemn the helical structure of the DNA molecule.

P.A. Nor need we glorify the structure and lose sight of our ignorance of that which differentiates the animate from the apparently identical inanimate.

PRIEST Socrates recognized God—the insensible, inhuman,

a-biological God; God that does not obey the laws which he should obey to be comprehensible to the human All-Highest Complacency.

ALICE If I admit that I don't know what you are talking about I am confident that I shall be offered more words—disciplines, well-ordered artefacts—like 'love' and 'concern'.

ROSEMARY Or a disorderly, undisciplined, sexual 'love' reminiscent of a baby's love of food. There is nothing between. If, for want of anything to love or by which I could be loved, I find some transient experience on the way to it, like Alice—

ALICE Some psycho-analyst, psychiatrist, man, is sure to 'know' I am having a 'homosexual experience'.

P.A. So you are. That does not mean that you are not having an experience of which the homosexual component is a part. A letter of the alphabet might as well be treated as if it were indistinguishable from the whole of *Paradise Lost.* Yet a psycho-analytical interpretation is often taken as a whole of psycho-analysis.

PRIEST If I say a 'marriage' is a miraculous ritual it is believed a 'miracle' is the whole of religion; I know a 'miracle' is only a transient episode on a human soul's journey to factual Truth. I call it 'God' because it is less misleading than to call it 'Scientific' Truth—that is only truth modified to lie within man's comprehension.

ROLAND I am no poet or painter or musician; I hesitate to claim more than moderate adequacy as a farmer. But I was regarded as responsible—I had to be, though I knew I was not a chemist or meteorologist. I admired the great storm clouds when they towered above the fields of golden corn. 'Robin', I used to say, 'we shall have to use the scythes when this storm has laid the corn flat.'

ALICE I used to hate you all when you and your guns surrounded the last of the narrowing field to kill the cowering beasties as they tried to escape.

ROSEMARY Oh why? That's when we had a good meat meal.

ROBIN Pity they recovered from myxomatosis. What did your god think about that?

PRIEST It was not my function to tell God what to think. If I were a rabbit I would use my rabbity intelligence to use my god-given legs to run. As I am a man I use my teeth.

P.A. After a few hundred years of culinary experience no doubt; even that you left Alice to acquire, who in turn left it to Rosemary.

ALICE So—I retained my place on the top of the pinnacle of which Rosemary was the base. Priest and P.A. pushed me off to leave room for themselves. Well, I do not envy you your eminence.

P.A. You may not envy the kind of eminence which stimulates my envy, but you nevertheless have feelings of envy. The fact that I may not be able to define feelings, either yours, mine or those of others which are neither yours nor mine, does not mean that they do not, did not, or may not in future exist. They may at some stage become so obtrusive that it is possible to attach a name to them.

ROBIN Although I have been aware of the pressure of what I can now call sexual or envious feelings, I would have been outraged had I been told that I was sexual or envious.

ROLAND What other people can verbalize about my feelings, especially if I can't, is particularly exasperating.

P.A. That is one component of the practice of psycho-analysis which is constant even if not constantly perceived. Guilty feelings are unwelcome and even in infants easily evoked. It is difficult to give an interpretation which is distinguished from a moral accusation.

ROLAND Surely this is a defect of psycho-analysis?

P.A. Certainly; but when I agree, you and others are therefore liable to assume that it is psycho-analysis only that suffers from that weakness, whereas I believe that this is a fundamental experience. It is this fundamental experience that underlies Plato's dialogue between Socrates and Phaedrus which is being revived here—a few hundred years later—in this discussion.

ALICE Do men agree with the dismissal of Xanthippe? Do you consider the presence of myself and Rosemary an excrescence? Is our sexual equipment the only worthwhile contribution to the discussion? Or are we tolerated rather than welcomed as servants? Often it is called 'love' when what is meant is that we serve your lust.

ROLAND Robin and I have often discussed this. I have never felt that sex should be abolished; even when I have been aware of what a damned nuisance those impulses are I have not felt easy at their facile dismissal. 'Perverse', 'homosexual', 'lustful'—I am sure P.A. can supply a great number of denigratory expressions, all of the highest scientific respectability.

P.A. I thought Alice was expressing contempt both for the being who requires his or her sexual urge to be fulfilled and for the person, male or female, who 'serves' to fulfil them—whore, pimp, womanizer, homosexual—especially when money is clearly in close attendance.

ROBIN I do not like to think I would need to resort to a prostitute, or that a woman was 'prostituting' her beauty or her gifts. Nor would I like the man who seemed to be using his money or his looks to seduce women.

P.A. What is involved is a capacity for judgement and discrimination. That is something primitive and fundamental, sophisticated and a part of highly developed society. Fish smell a difference between the noxious or dangerous, and the development-nourishing 'thing'. So does the amphibian. So does the animal that lives, like man, in a gaseous fluid.

ROBIN Are you seriously suggesting that we are like fish, frogs, reptiles?

P.A. I am quite serious, but this is not a scientific discussion; I am speculating with the freedom of a social talk. I confine scientific speculation to scientific meetings; here I claim freedom from the discipline imposed by scientific thought.

ROBIN But it sounds to me as if you were discussing scientific matters.

P.A. That is one of the problems of verbal communication. Speech is ambiguous; its ambiguity is the more dangerous for being disguised by its apparent precision.

ROBIN You mean that psycho-analysis, as most of us always have suspected, is couched in apparently scientific terms, but is in fact jargon?

P.A. I think the criticism is just, but I fear to make the

admission as it is usually assumed that I am conceding superior 'truth' to other disciplines.

ALICE Disciplines! That is not a word which spontaneously springs to my mind when I think of psycho-analysis or psycho-analysts. They seem to me to claim the merits of unobstructed emotions, be they sex or rage or what they are pleased to call love.

ROLAND The ones I meet usually seem to be a depressed and anxious—not to mention 'dull'—lot.

P.A. We have the right to feel.

ROLAND Last night I dreamed a dream—

SIX

ROBIN How truly Bunyanesque of you!

ROLAND Don't be a bloody cunt. Do you want me to tell you the dream or not?

P.A. Do go on—

ALICE Well, really! Are we supposed to listen to language like that? It is not even sexual—as P.A. would agree.

ROLAND All right, Xanthippe, darling. Socrates' complaint is comprehensible if we are not allowed to discuss naturally and spontaneously.

ALICE I have no objection at all, but surely it is not necessary to talk like that. Yes, I know—you are going to say 'like what?', but I shan't repeat such . . . such . . . language, though you are trying to make me use the words. You know very well what I mean, but I have to think of Rosemary. I am sure she agrees.

ROSEMARY Oh yes, Ma'am, I do. My mum was very particular how she brought me up. When I asked her what she and her gentleman were doing—I had come into the room innocently because Patricia our dog was barking so loud—Trixie we used to call him because it sounded less girlish if you see what I mean—

him being a dog and not a bitch if you will excuse the expression, Ma'am—

ROBIN Oh God-all-fucking-mighty—do get on, will you.

ALICE There you go again—is it necessary to be blasphemous to make yourself clear?

P.A. He is speaking rhapsodically—not with social or scientific precision.

ROLAND Robin will agree with me that he is being no more blasphemous than I am when I say 'bloody cunt'; bloody is only a quick way of saying 'by Our Lady'—which is sacred. Go on, Rosemary, for Christ sake.

ROBIN Oh Cripes!

ROLAND 'Schoolboy' for Christ. Anyhow, *please* get on.

ALICE Now he has become sufficiently civilized to say 'please', go on, Rosemary.

ROSEMARY Oh yes, Ma'am—my mum was always most particular and wore a crucifix all the time because she told me I should never forget Our Lord, especially when the gentlemen came to see us. That was how I found out that she *only* had high-class gentlemen like lords to see her though my friend Faith—she was called that out of Faith, Hope and Charity—

ALICE I won't ask you two what you are thinking because I can see it in your faces.

ROBIN There must be something wrong with the small muscles of our faces, Roland.

ROLAND 'Myasthenia gravis' no doubt. But Rosemary's story is so exciting I can hardly wait to hear.

ALICE Then why don't you two fucking bastards shut up and let her get on? Can't you control your face muscles? See—I can talk that stuff as well as you can.

ROLAND I am sure P.A. knew you always could.

ALICE Go on, Rosemary—don't take any notice of the ugly faces they make.

ROSEMARY That's what my mum always used to say to me. 'Rosemary', she says, 'don't you take any notice of what people say. You may as well be killed for a Lion as a Cockroach'—now what was I saying?—forgotten—oh yes, Faith and me used to have many a laugh about the gentlemen my mum knew and we used to watch and laugh till one day Trixie flew at the gentleman because he thought he was being cruel to my mum. I was frightened because my mum was so pale and she told me that if it hadn't been for Trixie the gentleman would have beaten her to death with a leather stick he had.

ROLAND P.A. would call it 'pure phantasy'.

P.A. Not only phantasy, but phantasy certainly.

ROBIN Do you mean you don't believe it happened?

P.A. I mean that I do not doubt it was a real phantasy and a real fact—in so far as I am capable of knowing what a fact is and of respecting the factualness of a fact, however 'realized'. Phantasies sometimes burst through into articulate words when the individual is 'off his guard', as when he is asleep; they break out also when the individual is conscious and fully awake. Sometimes they break 'in' to articulate speech, conventionally acceptable art or music, and sometimes into conventionally acceptable 'behaviour'—in this instance unacceptable muscular action. Sometimes the 'acceptable convention' has to stretch, alter, to accommodate the thing that 'breaks through'; sometimes the 'conventionally acceptable' crushes the 'outbreaking impulse'. Usually it is a compromise between the two. Just now Alice allowed her ears and lips to be degraded by 'bloody cunt' and 'fucking bastard'; the rest of us have had to allow ourselves to be limited by being polite and saying 'please'.

ROSEMARY —the gentleman had to run away.

ALICE He was lucky. Or was he?

P.A. This language, which clearly we all know though we have forgotten it, are forgetting it, and hope in future to forget it, makes an unrecognized—an unrecognized archaic and still vital—contribution to our intercourse.

ROLAND And was once, is now, and in future will continue to become more and more refined—or should I say 'refained'?—into a virtually meaningless 'prettiness' or meaningful ugliness.

ROBIN Like a pretty man, boy, girl or woman—nothing deeper than the skin.

P.A. Or more disturbing than a dermatitis if our scrutiny went beyond appearance to the underlying reality.

ALICE Or more disturbing than blasphemy and sex if we

allowed our scrutiny to go beyond spirochaetes, mummification and the beauty parlour. Helen of Troy, Cleopatra, are more than mere shadows of the past; they could be the shadow cast before by the Future we do not know.

P.A. Out of the rotting syphilitic remains of human flesh—

ALICE How elegantly, how poetically, you express it!

P.A. —may the warmth engendered by the decay give rise to a new form of life.

ROBIN Like cockroaches from dirt and neglect, or compost out of a silo.

ROLAND Who or what is to take the place of the silo?

P.A. The effect would be similar if the human race had to expand on a world too small for it—the 'pressure' would increase. With our individual birth the mother's womb would be the silo in which pressure built up till the child burst forth or the mother got sick of carrying such a load of amniotic fluid, fetus, meconium and junk. But now it is the Birth of Mind. 'Mary McSweeney confined in Mount Joy'—'The Birth of a Nation', as some wag scrawled on the wall beneath the slogan about Mary McSweeney.

ALICE I remember that old chestnut. At the time I had no doubt that the 'joke' was typically one that could be seen by a man.

ROBIN I thought it was quite witty. Mary must have done something to precipitate incarceration. It cannot be a man only who initiates a pregnancy.

ALICE Blame. Blame. Blame.

P.A. Blame, or I would rather call it Guilt, is one of the fundamentals, one of the basic assumptions, as fundamental as the sacred 'bloody' and the non-sexual 'cunt'—it is neither masculine nor feminine. I don't want to know your birthday because I am sure you will tell me a date which does *not* outrage ideas of genital intercourse, midwifery, surgery. What I want to know is, when was your character or personality born? Did changes of pressure on your optic pits cause you to become luminosity-aware?

ROBIN It certainly seemed to me that Alice and Rosemary showed distinct signs of being aware of the words 'bloody cunt'.

ALICE I understand that when the police came to restore order at one of the Ivy League schools, these great big tough he-men retired in disorder when greeted by the innocent shouts of 'Mother Fuckers'.

ROLAND It would seem to bear out P.A.'s suggestion that these archaic terms hide or disguise or preserve some powerful germ of vital development in a way that is not true of 'bloody vagina'. Yet a vagina is a real and important canal. So is a penis.

ROBIN Hide or conceal, you say. You might as well say a breast or penis or clitoris 'hides' an erection. But there is no such thing as an 'erection'; it is an invisible state made manifest by 'erectile' tissue.

ALICE Any mother knows that, even if she had never suckled a baby; or father, even if he had never nourished a penis. But why is it that so few men and women are at ease with an erection?

P.A. Some deficiency in our mental growth. The infant potentially is a parent; the parent potentially is, but is not capable of becoming, an infant. In that way it sounds as if developmental processes are directional in one direction only. It seems to me we need to develop a capacity to use a screen, a resistance, a caesura, as Picasso could use a plate of glass. Look on *this* side and see a delineation of a psycho-somatic disorder; look on *this* side and see a soma-psychosis.

ROBIN You remind me of the early days of studentship when a small black cat used to appear in our courtyard, do its evacuations, cover them up neatly and disappear. It was called Melanie Klein—Melanie because it was black, Klein because it was little, and Melanie Klein because it had no inhibitions. Today one could compare a tiny germ of Rhodesia with the independent Rhodesia; then it was tiny, white and inhibited; what it is today I do not know. But tomorrow Africa may be black, huge and uninhibited.

ALICE I do not see what this has to do with our discussion.

P.A. Perhaps this is a constant feature of the present. It is difficult even under discipline to know our past history, impossible to perceive the present while we experience it, and only vaguely as through a glass darkly to perceive the future which casts its shadow before.

ROLAND Not only the group but the individual, not only the individual but the group also.

P.A. I remember that song which we all disliked so much that we did not sing it. 'Rule Britannia! Britannia rule the waves. Britons never, never, never shall be . . .' skivvies? Butlers?

ROBIN No; as Alice would say, only 'civil servants'. Say please, please. '*Good dog!*'—as the clever pet was put through its trick. 'Die for your country', and he would lie on his back; the biscuit casting its shadow before was too much; his tail wagged phrenetically.

P.A. Britannia was a repulsive old dame even when clothed in masculine garb. Wider still and wider were her boundaries set, till at last the weight of greedy spoils became too much to carry on her poor feet and she rebelled against crushing them into the cosmetically beautiful, but inappropriate to old age, shoes of youth.

ROLAND I remember your sister trying on your mother's shoes and shuffling around saying, 'Aren't I just like Mummy!'

P.A. I remember. Do you think groups, and the individuals, pursue an helical progress?

ROBIN I think there is a pictorial similarity.

P.A. Pressure on the optic pits; demands on visual acuity aided by telescopes and microscopes till the poor old cerebral hemispheres sink under the load of spoils won for them by curiosity. As the schoolboy joke of contextual examinations had it: 'Who said, "My punishment is more than I can bear"? Answer—"Agag, when he was hacked in pieces,"' It is not the prize that counts, but the running for it.

ROLAND That may be all very well for rabbits and tortoises, but you try telling that to a real rabbit or a real tortoise.

ROBIN Have you tried? You might ask a plant what it thinks of herbivores. Human animals are both carnivorous and herbivorous—greedy beasts.

P.A. We talk as if there were some force or power which creates an almost infinite variety of animate and inanimate objects. When we are talking about *us*—as we are here—there is an advantage in talking in this way. An inescapable fact is that we tend to wonder, and tend at the same time to refrain from wondering, if it is true or not; that is to say, if the image that we bring will find a real image there. We shall have to consider what a *real* image is, but for the moment I suppose that my image of myself is real. If I meet a Not-me which nevetheless reminds me of Me, then I am likely to wonder what this object is. If it is a nice object, then, Narcissus-like, I have the pleasure of discovering what a nice person I am. If I do not like this Not-me, then I do not like its reminding me of Me; I am outraged; I do not like looking-glasses, sheets of water, novels, psycho-analysis—

ROBIN 'Sheets of water' you say. Would you include sheets of amniotic fluid?

P.A. Certainly—any liquid. I would go further and suggest that sheets of reflective fluid of any kind become objects of dislike.

ALICE You mean the fluid does not have to be liquid but can, as at birth, be changed to a gaseous fluid?

P.A. Quite so. But, liquid or gaseous, the fluid can be constantly changing from calm reflecting state to turbulence.

ALICE When I took my astronomical course we were familiar with conditions for observation.

P.A. Right. It is commonplace for obstetricians to find a fetus is sucking its thumb. Presumably the fetus has an ideal opportunity for 'observing' its thumb.

ROLAND Presumably? May I ask who presumes?

P.A. We may all ask or not as we choose. 'La réponse est le malheur de la question.'

ROSEMARY Please translate.

P.A. I understand it to mean that the question's misfortune is that it is liable to be answered. Your curiosity and that of Trixie was aroused by your mother and her gentleman. In so far as it made you question 'gentle-manliness', its misfortune was that it was answered. You have never quite recovered from wanting, and fearing, to experience a similar 'gentle'ness.

ALICE Oh, nonsense! You are putting ideas into her head.

Now she's spawned off all the bits and pieces which are so small that it is impossible to see how they could cohere even if the environment were right—which it isn't. But your idea would make her try it. You are corrupting her youth.

P.A. I hope you are wrong and that I am right. It seems to me that it is as well for her to be aware that unobserved beneath the calm and mirror-like surface of her character which makes it easier for you to see your reflection as her lovable mistress, there are storms that rage. One of the advantages of the 'real' Mediterranean is that Homer, Virgil, even you and I, can see reflected in it something which, however calm or turbulent, reminds us of ourselves.

ROBIN You sound as if you wanted to teach us to 'semanticide'.

P.A. Alas; language—though I try to speak it articulately, precisely and to the point—is, as used by me, a distorted, distorting and turbulent reflecting surface.

ROLAND Our army ditty was:

Ashes to ashes and dust to dust
If the wine don't get you then the women must.

P.A. In fact it is both.

ROLAND Both? How do you mean?

P.A. I suppose the simplest way I could explain it would be by falling back on Desargues's theorem.

ROBIN Good God! You aren't serious, are you? Even in the mathematical Tripos I found Desargues and Conics impossible.

ROLAND Conics are chronic.

ALICE Punning is a very low form of life.

P.A. Life fundamentally is really 'low life'—cock-roaches, and 'bloody cunt' and swimming in a sea of amniotic fluid and meconium, and now psycho-analysis. Even the fetus is involved with *non-fetus*. One cone intersects another cone. Here the eyes of each of us can be described as sweeping out an area of space more or less cone-shaped. But these cones intersect other cones whose focal origin is different. These points of intersection could be pictorially depicted by resorting to geometrical figures. That is an over-simplification which, as Robin said, is complex enough to make any further description redundant. However, I do not see why the universe in which we live should oblige us by being comprehensible to us mere human beings. This is true of our own bodies and minds in which we have to live. Even if we don't trouble with the 'universe', the *not-us,* we find that merely trying to know who 'I' am involves an intolerable amount of discovery of what we have never been able to tolerate and which, as likely as not, we are right not to tolerate.

ROLAND You remind me—Britannia reminds me—of the mother who on her death-bed collected her children because she wished to confess that she had never loved her husband, their father, and had been constantly unfaithful and promiscuous. The eldest, recovering first from this stupefying information, announced, 'Well, I don't know about you other bastards, but I'm going to the movies', and they all fucked off.

ALICE Very amusing. I regret that my facial muscles do not express my entertainment.

ROBIN I expect you are not perceiving how amused you are at being not-amused.

ALICE Though I said it was 'very amusing', I did not expect you to believe I meant just that.

P.A. Though you do not call it psycho-analysis, you interpret naturally and expect others to interpret your behaviour, including the language you talk. These diagnoses, interpretations, are intrusions, outrages perhaps, on your privacy—our privacy.

ALICE If you are right, that seems to me to be one more reason for behaving in a reasonably civil manner.

P.A. Certainly. But in reality, as far as I am capable of perceiving reality or truth, the more I am aware that reality is not civilized or reasonable or considerate of our feelings or ideas. This applies to you and me; we are not polite, civilized, considerate *only*. So, in so far as we achieve 'civilized' character, our capacity for lying, murdering, robbing, being in *rude health,* 'fusts in us unused', as Milton put it.

ALICE Milton certainly did not mean what you say he meant.

P.A. I am ready to believe that Milton did not mean to mean that. It requires, at least, considerable training to achieve any idea now of what Milton meant—or Nietzsche, or Newton, or any other great figure of the past. In the present we do not have to bother because there are not perceived to be any great figures. In fact we are learning to regard them as figments of our imaginations.

ROLAND I remember the fashion for 'Father Figures'; the mental landscape was such that one could not see one's genetic father, the air was so thick with Father Figures.

ROBIN I smell a Father Figure; I see him in the Air; I will nip him in the Bud.

ROLAND Call me Buddy—so much more friendly.

P.A. Technical terms are not safe from de-value-ation; hence my resort to spelling out the word in a hope that the return to that childhood learning difficulty might re-inforce my communication. Must we keep our technical terms in constant repair? The bloody cunt which is *not* anything to do with anatomical sex, not masculine, not feminine, not haematology, not religion but could be said to be sacred, has nevertheless an almost universal—western at least—comprehensibility. It made Alice angry; even articulate. It degrades the user almost as much as the recipient.

ALICE Then why use it?

P.A. I am not advocating or deprecating its use. Since it is there it seems wise to acknowledge or respect its presence as one should respect any other fact, whether we like it or not.

ROBIN I can see Alice's point—why go out of your way to look for the unpleasant?

P.A. If it were only a matter of pleasant or unpleasant that would depend on the character or person, and on his or her likes or dislikes. I suggest it also involves *is* or *is not*. If it *is*, then the individual should respect the *is-ness* or *is-not-ness* of it. You think these 'things' are so rare that it is perverse to go out of our way to find them. I say they are so universal that it is perverse to make great mental detours to avoid being aware.

ROBIN But who uses language like that?

P.A. I do, for one. So do you. So does Alice.

ALICE I beg your pardon—I don't.

P.A. But you said 'fucking bastard' a little while back; you reacted as to the manner born to Roland saying 'bloody cunt'. If it were a foreign language I would say you must have been born to it, lived it, loved it as your very own favourite language. I agree with you that you spoke to it as if you had forgotten it and didn't want to be reminded of it.

ALICE Only because you chose to drag it up into the conversation first.

P.A. Like the police, asked to intervene in the Ivy League dispute. Like Robin—equally ignorant. But the fact that you are and wish to remain ignore-ant is your affair. Robin, did you never march through a village of innocent, clean English men and women singing—

'When we go out with noise and shout
We'll be buggered if we'll be buggered about,
We won't be buggered about!'

ROBIN Oh, the army!

P.A. Or your very select private Public School.

SEVEN

ROBIN The army and school—that was a long time ago.

P.A. Then, no doubt, you'd have said it would be a long time before you would grow up and use the awful language those great big authorities—starting with your parents—used. But if as a baby you had not been so angry and inarticulate, *that* is the 'cuntish' language you would have talked. In fact I do not believe there has ever been a time when your mental turbulence did not surface gems of this obscene 'water'—amniotic fluid, social freedom—call it what you will. What language does Alice spontaneously use when the alarm clock wakes her and she wants to sleep some more?

ALICE I admit your point. I still wonder what good it does to talk such language or about it.

P.A. Though forgotten, the archaic thing lives and contributes its vitality to an otherwise sterile talk. I remember a dignified board meeting at which the chairman started a long and highly involved address urging members to 'be more circumspect because so much offence was caused by . . . er . . . er . . .'. 'Oh, Christ—Bish been saying 'fuck' again?' The chairman inclined his head in shamed acknowledgement that the surmise was correct. The contrast of the 'civil' communication with the direct primitive phrase was most impressive; the primitive tapped reserves of vitality spread through the somnolent, but well-behaved group.

ALICE I am glad you acknowledge that the group, however somnolent, was well-behaved. I do not think this discussion would be improved by our free exchange of terms like 'fuck' and 'buggery', 'bastard' and . . . and . . .

P.A. We will spare you the embarrassment of demonstrating your familiarity with the vocabulary. But I do not want us to lose sight of this almost universally comprehended speech. It hardly requires translation. I can see that the speeches in the United Nations Assembly might well be enlivened if the 'freedom' was extended to include freedom to choose, without limitation, *how* to express as well as what matter to express.

ALICE I should prefer a civilized and decorous assembly.

ROLAND So would I, but the 'fundamental basic thing' would not oblige by being confined within the rules of debate. Those rules may be all right if our object were to achieve the politeness of polite conversation. But this is not the object of a United Nations Assembly, and I don't think it is the object of this discussion. I wonder if P.A. could enlighten us about the object, not simply of psycho-analytic debates, institutions, 'scientific' papers, but of psycho-analysis itself.

P.A. I would if I could but I am not sure that there is any adequate way of doing this, short of experiencing psycho-analysis itself.

ALICE Do you use terms like 'fuck' and 'buggery'?

P.A. Sometimes; it depends on what I want to communicate and what I think the listener capable of hearing. A child of ten or twelve would be likely to snigger if he heard me use one of these terms. If I asked, 'Why do you snigger?', I don't think he could answer, but from my experience I would expect the response to be unmistakable signs of guilt. 'Guilt' is fundamental, basic, sharing the primitive qualities which Freud attributes to the id. If the id could speak, that is the language I would expect it to use.

ROBIN How does this apply to the practice of analysis? I take it you do not talk to the id, because that is only a theoretical term.

P.A. Even theories and theoretical terms are supposed to remind us of a reality. I have no doubt that one 'talks to' an experienced person; the matter of psycho-analysis is such that analyst and analysand cannot afford to neglect the total sophisticated capacities of which both are capable. The psycho-analyst has a lifetime of experience, including the experience of technical psycho-analytic training; the analysand, even if only a young child, has a considerable body of experience to fall back on. It is certain that the psycho-analysis will fail if the analysand does not respect the knowledge, character and wisdom of the analyst—and vice versa.

ROBIN Doesn't that presuppose some mutual acquaintance with each other? I thought it was important that the analyst should not know the analysand.

P.A. There is substance in the idea, but the idea must be modified by common sense; applied in extreme degree it would mean that psycho-analysis could only be carried out between two people who had neither race, nationality, language nor culture in common. The other extreme would mean that the two knew each other so well that there was no topic which could be discussed profitably. In practice some rough rules can be formulated; close blood relations who know each other well, or husband and wife, would probably not find the psycho-analytic interchange rewarding.

ROBIN I listened to some married friends who were both enthusiastic psycho-analysts, and I felt that if I had to listen to them 'analysing' each other for long I would go mad. If *that* is what analysis does for you, heaven save me from it!

P.A. I sympathize with your dismay. But psycho-analysis does nothing for anyone, any more than do morphia or strychnine or human speech. Most people can turn these facilities to good account, but there are many pairs who would use them and other components of the universe in which we live in ways which you and I might not applaud. Loeb and Leopold appear to have used their chances—even the chance which could be used for homosexual love—for purposes of committing the 'perfect' murder. In the upshot it was *not* perfect although they appear to have been gifted and living in a universe which afforded ample opportunity. The institution of marriage is supposed to offer the legal conditions for a hetero-sexual pair to fulfil themselves. Whether they choose to utilize those conditions for mutual psycho-analysis, mutual masturbation or mutual anything else, is their affair. One, or other, or both may wish to avail themselves of the institute of divorce to 'correct' the prior decision to marry. But what choice they make is their own private affair. The fact that you or I would not decide to live as they do is a matter of no importance whatever—except to you or me.

ROLAND But do you never give any help?

ROBIN Suppose they come to you for help.

P.A. Naturally I should hope that I was the sort of character who would want to help them; but I would like to have the discipline to confine my efforts within the limits of my capacity.

ROBIN It sounds like, 'Find out what you can do and do a little less'.

ROLAND You could hardly advocate '. . . and do a little more'.

P.A. I think there is something to be said for differentiating *knowledge* and *wisdom*—at least for purposes of this discussion. Then I would say that whatever *knowledge* each of us has must be augmented by *wisdom*. However intelligent, the chance of survival is decreased if the character cannot rely on being wise.

ALICE Is it not also true that the wise person's chance of survival depends on intelligence?

P.A. Certainly. Part of the problem is that intelligence, as a capacity for collecting knowledge, needs to be distinguished, isolated—defined for purposes of this discussion—from wisdom. In real life the problem cannot be solved as simply as it can be conversationally. 'Acts' do not arrive clearly labelled. Projected acts are not like a medicine in a bottle.

ALICE Do you remember Prince André in *War and Peace* feeling in the course of a discussion as if an inner voice said, 'That is sooth; accept it'.

ROBIN Yes, it impressed me when I read it.

ALICE Did you ever read *War and Peace,* Rosemary?

ROSEMARY Oh no. I saw it, but it was too thick and learned for the likes of me. Mum always used to say, 'Now don't you go and read those trashy novels', so I never did. Not that I thought a big book like that was trashy.

ROLAND 'Another of those damn thick, square books, Mr Gibbon? Scribble, scribble, scribble!' Upstairs and downstairs and in My Lady's chamber. There I met an old man who wouldn't say his prayers—so—

P.A. These nursery rhymes say a lot. Some analysts study them; so do children, and they understand them. Or, rather, the archaic chord is struck and vitality is released. If we could strike the chord, the vibrations thus initiated could penetrate the barriers which at present act as obscuring screens—the need is for screens sufficiently resistant to catch and display the meaning without destroying it by denial or 'acceptance'—'No' or 'Yes, I know'. I want to display not a psycho-somatic disturbance only, but also the soma-psychotic disturbance that is there; those who wish to see, do.

ROLAND Do you suggest that the old man should say his prayers?

P.A. I knew a young man who would not say his prayers because he was sure that he would be laughed at for being 'converted' out of fear of going into battle.

ROBIN I was. But I had also come to have such a contempt for the act of praying—as I had been taught to practise it and seen it practised—that it would outrage any respect that I had for myself if I did it.

ROLAND Do you think there is any kind of prayer that is not an outrage on one's common sense? Obviously the athletic 'knees bend' exercise could not satisfy any person of integrity. What does P.A. think?

P.A. It is not my department. I have ideas about it like any other man, but I would not like it supposed that because I set up as an expert on psycho-analysis my expertise extended to religion and other disciplines—painting, music, literature.

PRIEST Is that not somewhat cowardly?

P.A. You and others might think so but I do not. Even in my

own limited field I am not unfamiliar with a cowardly shrinking from expressing a truth that I know will be unwelcome. One takes flight into doubt—'"What is truth?" said jesting Pilate'; Bacon himself did not wait for an answer because he knew he might be killed if he did. Physical death is a hard price to pay—especially for those of us who, from training and observation, believe in the obliteration of the body. I believe also in the obliteration of one's respect for the truth; it is not simply by physical methods—alcohol, for example—that one can destroy one's capacity for discerning or proclaiming the Truth.

PRIEST I believe in moral, religious death. Truth can be nourished; it can be allowed to die of neglect or be poisoned by seductions, cowardice too often repeated. But Truth is robust; 'facts' cannot be killed even if we do not know what they are. The fragile human respect for the truth cannot be as easily disposed of as often appears.

P.A. I hope you are right. I cannot, however, say that my knowledge of myself or others provides me with food for hope. Religion itself gives evidence of the great force of power, bigotry, ignorance; and psycho-analysis is shot through with error and the defects of us humans who try to practise it.

PRIEST You are being extremely self-contradictory in claiming that it is a science *and* is true. It must have a point of reference outside itself. You cannot believe in Truth any more than you can 'believe in God'. God is—

ROLAND —or is not.

P.A. No. 'God is, or is not' is only a human formulation in conformity with human principles of thinking. It has nothing to do with the reality. The only 'reality' we *know about* is the various hopes, dreams, phantasies, memories and desires which are a part of us. The other reality exists, *is*, whether we like it or not. A child may want to punish a table for hurting him when he suffers a contusion. But he may desire to punish himself for 'suffering' a contusion. He may ultimately be compelled to believe that, in addition to these facts, there is a table that is neither good nor bad, like it or not, forgive it or punish it. We may decide to punish our god, punish ourselves for believing in 'it' or 'him' or 'her'. It will not affect the reality which will continue to be real no matter how unsearchable, un-knowable, beyond the grasp of human capacity its is/not is. After all, we do not know much about the world we live on, or the minds we are.

ALICE I thought you psycho-analysts were supposed to have discovered all about us.

ROBIN Supposed? By whom? I do not 'suppose' I know either myself or my husband—

ALICE I didn't know you were married! May I congratulate you!

ROBIN *I* do not know whether you are 'married' or 'divorced'; in so far as those two words derive from the Institute of a state, they tell me nothing about the true relationship between you and your husband. But although I have no sensuous experience of it I yet believe there is some reality underlying these words 'marriage' and 'divorce' beyond the meaning I know.

P.A. You say you have 'no sensuous experience', but is it not possible that while you have 'forgotten' the experience it has not, as it were, forgotten you?

ROBIN I don't know what you mean.

P.A. That is relatively rational and may be more acceptable than saying you have 'forgotten' being married and 'forgotten' what *you* meant; perhaps that you never knew what you meant. Some of these thoughts may now be difficult to entertain or formulate because you fear the reception they would get by the recipient; you might discover there was no recipient, or that there was one whose receptivity you feared. It is easier to feel there is an initiator *and* a recipient, and that there is some screen (caesura?) between. That is possible if you believe it is between you and 'me'—a 'not-you' and 'you'. This is less alarming than believing you are now both the initiator and the receptor.

ROBIN Why?

ALICE Every question is liable to suffer from the existence of a potential answer which will kill it. The misfortune, the weakness of curiosity is the answer that will destroy finally curiosity itself.

P.A. 'Yes I know'—how lethal is that response! The wish to start exploration or discovery is destroyed. That response, made to yourself, crushes your curiosity or makes it take refuge out of sight, out of mind, out of social contact. The 'Yes I know' surface, the lifeless society, is all that is left.

ROLAND That was true of 'intellectual' culture in the school to which I was sent to 'learn'. In my time hobbies meant surreptitious sex: education meant answers to questions which no one had asked. Law and Order meant find out what they are up to and tell them not to. Sex meant widespread illegality—which did not exist. Hypocrisy meant religion.

PRIEST It sounds frightful.

ROLAND It was.

P.A. Forsan et haec olim meminisse juvabit. We did not believe it; now I know it is true.

ROLAND Tu Marcellus eris. Date manibus lilia plenis. . . . I did not know I ever learnt it. Had I known that it was all about that same wicked business of loving a man or a boy—'sex', in short—I might have learnt it; but then perhaps I should not have remembered it. Education is a damned rum thing.

ROBIN . . . per varios casus, per tot discrimina rerum.

PRIEST

> 'What hours, O what black hours we have spent
> This night! what sights you, heart, saw; ways you went! . . .'

ALICE Time for supper and bed.

ROLAND All right, Martha.

ROBIN Or is it Xanthippe?

ALICE You would be the first to grumble if some of the ways I went had not led to the market.

P.A. Perhaps we all have to be busy with many things.

ROLAND The many things are all different.

ROBIN Why don't we meet more often?

P.A. Because we don't want to. This is true when our forgotten fishy, amphibian, terranean selves all meet in the same body at the same time—not consecutively or dispersed in space, but here and now in the same body. Draw the blinds. Where shall we make the splits and insert the inhibitions so that we may choose? When the universe in which we live clearly demonstrates the immense variety which chance—

PRIEST Or God—

P.A. I find it more adequate to say 'chance'—spreads before us, *we* have to choose. We choose to be responsible for our actions though we may not deliberate the problem. Choice, however, involves splitting the discriminated objects from each other.

ALICE Do we start as infinitesimal fragments, which cohere, or are we, as P.A. implies, a whole that is fragmented?

ROLAND Do you think we choose whether to be a fish or not?

P.A. No! I feel it more compatible with reality, as I know it, to say I have no say in the matter. The illusion of conscious purpose gives cause for belief—on inadequate grounds—in God, but I would resist any attempt to prevent Priest believing it, provided he didn't want to prevent me from choosing science.

PRIEST Could we agree that both of us support a search for truth, but our paths often appear to separate?

P.A. Lack of choice means that each of us still retains his fishy qualities.

ROBIN Fish out of water.

P.A. Not quite. When we abandon our liquid environment for a gaseous one we take our liquid with us. Like fish, we can still smell by cause of the mucus preserved in our respiratory passages by the glands that maintain our watery medium although we have moved into a gaseous one.

ROBIN I don't see what we are to do about it, or what it has to do with us.

P.A. You would if you caught what is called 'a cold'; or if your tears began to flow. The liquid environment which we take with us or manufacture inside is useful for making it possible to see or smell, or even to provide for the germ plasm which we produce when we transfer to a gaseous medium like air. But if it is overproductive then the mucus makes us feel we are about to drown; we can't smell, we can't see for tears, we can't find a repository for the superfluity of seminal or ovarian fluids.

ROBIN If all these generations of our human development are repeated in each individual, I can see it might also apply to the mind or psyche.

P.A. It is sometimes illuminating to think so.

ROLAND We could borrow from the cartographers and imagine that here we are aware of two dimensions and portray two only. Thus a mountainous district can be represented on a flat surface by contour lines. We 'read' the map; we 'read' the person.

ROBIN What are the elements which our supposititious 'contours' link? It would appear to be uninformative to link the same heights—physical tallness—with the character of the person. I do not imagine that the character displays patterns corresponding to the height.

ROLAND How tall was Shakespeare when he wrote *Hamlet*?

P.A. The question demonstrates the process though it does not—if it could be answered—illuminate a matter of consequence.

ROSEMARY We had to read Lamb's *Tales from Shakespeare*—terrible stuff. It put me off Shakespeare for ever—and Lamb. I thought the story of Roast Pig really silly.

ROBIN Perhaps we could join together, contour, all the ages or heights at which you thought Lamb silly.

P.A. She probably wouldn't remember.

ROSEMARY I remember I never thought him anything else.

ROLAND I wonder what Alice would think—but she has gone to bed.

P.A. We could say we know where she, geographically speaking, has gone.

ROBIN How would you speak if not geographically?

ROLAND I would like a rational answer.

P.A. Rational answers might all be placed on the same contour, but 'rational' means answers that conform to the rules of human thought. Suppose the universe in which we live does not oblige us by conforming to the limitations which are imposed by what is comprehensible to man. We do not expect a child to comprehend all of even the little which we are able to communicate. The wisest of us may be children in comparison with what the solar system alone can communicate—in so far as we know its language.

ROLAND That has been so often observed that it is a commonplace.

ROBIN True; nonetheless we may forget the meaning of the commonplace if it is a fact which we prefer to disregard.

ROLAND Is there any merit in contemplating a fact about which we can do nothing?

P.A. We may not be able to do anything about the fact, but we can do something about ourselves. Particularly we may be able to moderate our conceit of ourselves and our wisdom—our self-inflicted omniscience.

ROLAND Admitting our 'omniscience'—I am not sure that I do, for all that psycho-analysts tell us—can we do anything about it if it is our nature?

P.A. It is matter of opinion; you may not agree with my view that it 'does something' to the person who allows his attention to be drawn to a fact of his personality.

ROLAND I can't say that I have paid much attention although I remember plenty of beaks at school who tried to impress upon me the many unpleasant aspects of my behaviour.

P.A. I can't say anything about the episodes of which you speak, but I gather they were not psycho-analytic sessions.

ROLAND What is there so special about psycho-analytical sessions?

P.A. I doubt I could explain that without your submitting to an analysis. But I can say something about why you should *not* think it special. We use ordinary conversational English and it tends to give an impression that we are as care-less about what we say and how we say it as in any ordinary conversation. In fact we try to speak with care, precision and respect for the person we address. This is not so easy as you might imagine. It is not just a problem of vocabulary or English grammar—it never is a problem of 'just' or 'only' that which is being consciously and intentionally expressed. The important and significant thing is that which we are meaning and intending to transform into action.

ROBIN What are we immediately intending to translate into action here? I am not aware of anything except wanting to follow Alice's example and go to bed—

ROLAND Agreed. Everyone agreed? Let's go then.

EIGHT

P.A. When we were last together we 'solved' the problem of translating thoughts into action by going to bed. That was a precise solution of a precisely defined . . . what? It was apparently 'defined' by being terminated. But that act defined it—in the sense of ending the discussion. It occurred to me later that we were behaving as if we had become aware of human speech, as a child might become aware that grownups are not merely making noises with their mouths, but are communicating with each other or engaging in some prelude to communication. Such an 'event', now used as a free association, can be reviewed in the light of increased experience. The 're-view' can itself be turned to good account.

ROLAND I see what you mean. My complaint is that it does not seem to me that the review is turning our experience to good account.

ROBIN If your discovery, unwelcome though it may be, leads us to reconsider the wisdom of continuing the activity—in this instance, discussion—surely that is a gain.

ROLAND Maybe; maybe not.

P.A. Exactly—maybe; maybe not. That is a risk we have to take. It is the price that we pay for being responsible human beings exercising our freedom to choose. We may choose wrong. I am haunted by the memory of the young officer who, admiring me for what he considered to be my bravery, refused to surrender and was, inevitably, killed. His enemies had no choice except to kill.

ROBIN I remember a young fellow who *did* surrender. It seemed to me he was in a hopeless position and was right to surrender. He never recovered from the discovery that he saved his life rather than die for his country. I knew him when he was a charming young man—little more than a boy—but after his surrender his capacity for gaiety was . . . well, I can only describe it as 'dead'. He never recovered; he became more and more depressed, introspective and withdrawn till finally he could not stand it and killed himself.

ROSEMARY One of my friends, not very good-looking, couldn't bear to think she would never find anyone to marry her when she wanted a baby so badly. She had an illegitimate baby and no one would speak to her.

ALICE The moral superiority of humans in the mass is wonderful to observe. As long as it is morally superior it does not matter how cruel the morally superior person is.

P.A. Cruelty is a very early form of love. The baby bites the nipple and proceeds to bite all the food it loves. It would soon find that the food would 'bite it back' again if it did not chew it; but it may be too afraid to chew it. Wrong either way.

ROLAND Gastro-morality; intestinal revenge; or if those fail there can always be the haemorrhoids that stand ready to prevent the export.

P.A. It had never occurred to me that the customs authorities were sociological haemorrhoids, but I see what you mean. Now you mention it, it seems clear that as far as speech and discussion is concerned there are many obstacles to passing wind if it carries ideas in the way that speech does.

ROLAND 'Sermons in stones' is an eloquent way of describing how even geological fact might convey a moral idea—metaphorically of course.

ROBIN Metaphorically my foot! Clearly you haven't been in a stone-chucking mob—no 'metaphors' about that, I assure you!

ALICE No metaphor about childbirth either. To 'express' a child from one's insides without the proper licence can be Death to one's repute even if physical death has been escaped. The converse is not true; a properly attested moral Birth can kill a woman in spite of the licence.

P.A. Are you talking about legal licence or licentiousness? It seems to me that the moral system, individual and social, requires overhaul but I do not think the old authorities are the ones to do the overhauling.

ALICE Who then is to do it? Psycho-analysts?

P.A. Psycho-analysts are trained to do psycho-analysis only—a considerable undertaking. I would not feel qualified by my training to do more than that although like surgeons, engineers and other citizens, I am expected to carry my civil obligations as well as my professional ones. But I deprecate the idea that my expertise extends beyond that of psycho-analyst; it is hard enough trying to be an 'expert' in one's own profession. Yet we are constantly expected to be expert far beyond our professional domain and are regarded with contempt if we fail to live up to expectations which we strive not to arouse.

ALICE Then—as I said—who is to do the overhauling?

P.A. Whoever did it would have to bring to the task—

ROBIN Psycho-analysis?

ROLAND Kleinian theory?

P.A. —as much devotion to their work as most psycho-analysts display in theirs.

ALICE The ones I know are devoted more to making a handsome income than relieving the suffering of their patients.

P.A. It is a matter of opinion. I can say only what I require to provide good shelter, food and education.

ROLAND As you say—it is a matter of opinion. Who decides what is 'good'?

P.A. I do, of course. You can hardly expect me to choose something less than good. Indeed I should wonder why anyone coming to me for analysis had a philosophy of losing, and why, if they had such a philosophy, they would choose me to help them lose.

ROBIN Yet the boy I spoke of did not surrender when the alternative was clearly death. Perhaps you think it was not clear—that he chose it under some misapprehension.

P.A. Such devotion was, and still is, beyond my capacity. In situations of great danger I always had a belief that I would probably survive. Had I realized—been compelled by some dreadful wound to realize—that such a belief was nonsense, I would have dodged the danger. Nobody told me—nor would I have understood them if they had—that war service would change utterly my capacity to enjoy life. Are we, even today, prepared to tell our children, or our children's children, what price they would have to pay if they served their fellows? Are we to tell them not to do it, that it might cost them too much? What would it cost them if they did *not* serve their fellow men? Socrates chose not to run away after his sentence by the court of fellow Athenians. When remonstrated with, he said it was his free choice. For *that* freedom he paid the price knowingly.

ROLAND Did he believe in survival after death?

ROBIN As Horace pointed out, many brave men had died before Agamemnon without any Homer to confer on them the immortality of verse.

ROLAND What sort of immortality is that—schoolboys complaining about their Greek preparation?

ROBIN 'Immortality', like psycho-analysis, is often mental 'flannelle' to make people's consciences sleep in the cosy warmth of self-adulation.

P.A. It does not last for long. With the best will in the world the authorities wanted returned soldier undergraduates to be comfortable. Haig wished ex-servicemen to be looked after. How was it to be done?

ALICE And the women? Or don't they matter? What should I tell my daughters—and their daughters—about childbirth?

ROBIN Tell them? Something—not nothing. At least tell them to respect their bodies and bodily urges and demands, and to respect their minds and characters. Then they would not think that any old lecher would do as mate for themselves or father for their children. Conversely, they should not suppose that any old whore would do, Hosea-like, as wife or mother.

P.A. The problem is not solved by choosing intellectual monsters for the parenthood of 'souls'. This discussion is appropriate if we are concerned only with discussion; it must not become a substitute for psycho-analysis.

ROLAND Isn't that exactly what the danger is here and now? How do we know that all this isn't a substitute for not doing anything? Unless of course discussing is itself doing something.

ALICE I suppose it is doing something when Parliament 'just' talks. It is not true, I hope, that the 'talk' finds no reflection in the bills that are passed, or that the bills that are passed are simply invented by the Parliamentary stationers. The ones I have seen might as well have been written in a foreign language for all the sense they made.

ROBIN The sense they make is decided by the courts of law that have to interpret them, and the various authorities who are supposed to translate them into action. After all, isn't Parliament just a 'talking shop'?

P.A. It is possible. The price of freedom is constant vigilance. This is true of psycho-analysis; the individual is not analysed, 'cured', so that he can then go to sleep for the rest of his life. If that were all that occurred one could regard it as an exercise in 'good resolutions'.

ALICE Psycho-analysts I know have wonderful intentions and make many 'good resolutions' to put them into practice, but I cannot say I am impressed with the lives they lead as good examples of a fine philosophy finely practised.

P.A. I cannot say anything about other analysts; I do not even know if the 'analysts' of whom you talk are people who have been analysed. I know something of myself and can see how I conform to civilized behaviour. I hope that the failures I see will in time lead to something less sterile than 'remorse' and good resolutions.

ALICE I know I certainly have it frequently brought home to me that I do not conform to the behaviour I regard as desirable or even decent.

P.A. The hope is that psycho-analysis brings into view

thoughts and actions and feelings of which the individual may not be aware and so cannot control. If he can be aware of them he may, or may not, decide—albeit unconsciously—to change them.

ALICE I don't see how that differs from what has been done by parents, teachers, saints, philosophers, for countless generations of prophets of one kind and another.

P.A. What I said—and I cannot say it any better—is a description which could apply to many time-honoured procedures. You would be right to assume from my description that there is no particular reason to attribute any primacy to a psycho-analytic approach. That is why most people do not put themselves to the expense in time and money to go to a psycho-analyst. The 'real psycho-analysis' to which we aspire is at best only a reaching out towards that 'real psycho-analysis'. But it is 'real' enough to make people aware that there is 'something' beyond the feeble efforts of psycho-analyst and analysand. I think it optimistic to suppose that we do more than scratch the surface in our struggles to achieve it.

ROBIN It reminds me of all the religious talk I have heard about God and Christ and Heaven and Hell. I have tried honestly to believe, but now—after countless failures to find any reality corresponding to what my teachers have taught me, countless 'backslidings' as they called it but, as I now know, unwelcome discoveries that there was nothing in the place that should house my goal, my prize—I lack the freshness, vitality and naïvety to start off on the psycho-analytic scramble for 'cure', 'heaven', 'success' or the up-to-date name for 'wild goose'. As far as I am concerned, amongst all the competing 'cures' which my betters offer as superior alternatives, 'stone dead hath no fellow'.

ALICE That sounds depressing.

ROBIN I don't find it so; it is a relief not to have to carry this burden of credulity.

ROLAND You seemed eager enough to find out who had won the Calcutta Cup.

ROBIN It gave me pleasure to hear about these athletic triumphs; I am glad I no longer have to care whether 'England' had won or not.

ROLAND What about war? Do you not mind whether the country wins or loses?

ROBIN Of course. I have been trained to believe horrific stories about the consequences of defeat. Ought I to be able to tell, from what I know of the world in which I live, whether 'you won' or 'I won' or 'they won'? Perhaps I should include '*it* won' as one of the possibilities? In the world of power fashions the latest in patriotic wear is a rearrangement of red, white and blue in a pattern of stars and stripes; I am as unimpressed by 'capital' in a tasteful design of red hammers and sickles.

ALICE I wonder what Helen of Troy or Cleopatra would think of these fashions.

ROBIN They weren't fools. We could do with a woman with some guts today.

ALICE That is all very well, but do you suppose that any woman would be allowed to clear up the mess, leaving no place to wallow in?

ROLAND It doesn't matter whether it is a man or woman—the condition for breeding animate objects is the warmth generated by decay. If decay did not betray its presence by its stink, no ovipositor could find a suitable source of warmth.

ROBIN The ovipositor would have to have a nose.

P.A. Certainly; humans find it difficult to recognize and reconcile an evil smell with creative activity, whether it is producing children, blow-flies or ideas. There are both good and bad bad smells. A cheese can be fermented and that, to me, is unbearable, but the cheese is good. So are durians.

ROBIN I can see that—if you are dealing with nosing out physical food—but we are concerned with mental food. How do you recognize the counterpart of a bad smell when in fact there is no sensuous smell?

P.A. We shall have to revise our views about sensuous experience or about the nature of metaphors, or both. Obscene language may be accompanied by a bad smell which we are too 'civilized' to notice.

ROBIN Perhaps I should try one or two on my red setter bitch. She has a good nose. Ought I to whisper it, or shout it, or say it in an enticing manner?

P.A. It is an idea. I suppose you should express your obscene word in an obscene manner. I suspect there are few truly obscene words—words of which the sound is internationally recognized.

ROBIN They have the same smell, awake or asleep, American or Chinese, dog or human. One's skin could have a different odour if one were in an emotional state in which obscenity only would be adequate.

P.A. The state of mind would have to be genuine; then our noses would satisfy our curiosity.

ALICE If any one of us were to utter a carefully pre-conceived obscenity that would not be a test of sincerity.

ROLAND Lend me your bitch and see what happens when my alarm goes off in the morning. I utter a silent obscenity when that clock suddenly shoots me out of profound sleep. What do you think it would prove?

P.A. Nothing; ultimately I would hope to find out whether there was some physically recognizable as well as verbally recognizable underlying reality which we are investigating, not just a vast mare's nest of thinking about thinking about thinking, which same 'thinking' did not exist but was a symptom of glandular activity.

ROLAND Does the adrenal gland start us thinking, or our thinking start the gland secreting?

ROBIN Why not so of other glands? The most obvious would be the sexual. Does the girl look pretty because a gland is operating, or is the gland operating because the eyes have seen a pretty girl?

ROLAND Does it matter which is first anyhow?

P.A. Direction matters, at least in situations of life and death. Suppose it is a carcinogenic germ that is betraying its presence by some thought pattern: That could help to initiate an appropriate reaction before it was too late, depending on whether thought or germ was the origin.

ALICE Do you suggest that a fear of cancer means there is incipient cancer? Clearly not.

P.A. 'Clearly not', as you say. It might—but only if it were part of a pattern of thought. Even if it were, the pattern might indicate a cancer in a precise part of the body—the breast. The *pattern* of thought would matter—not the component parts of the pattern. The facts do not cease to exist because they are used by the analyst. The free associations might be valid analytically, but dangerous if obscuring the facts. Psycho-analysis is only applying the principle of making the best of a bad job; the bad job remains bad, even if it is turned to good account.

ROLAND You said, if 'thinking' turned out to be a by-product of glandular activity it would be a mare's nest. Why should one deny the reality of thinking, or refrain from turning *that* to good account even if glands originated ideas?

P.A. I did not mean to suggest it was a 'mere' product of glandular activity. It does not surprise me if I betrayed such hostility to thought or its lowly glandular origin. I am too familiar with that kind of intolerance to suppose that I am free of it. I, like my fellow brothers and sisters, aspire to a messianic superiority to my fallible origins. Hatred of our origins seems to be inseparable from any advance.

ALICE Perhaps especially when we owe a debt to the origins from which we rise to 'higher things'. How beastly we are!

ROLAND And were. But how admirable we shall shortly become! It would seem to be an advantage if we could find out the conditions propitious to real progress.

P.A. Or if we knew the direction in which we were progressing. I sometimes doubt it.

ROBIN I thought you psycho-analysts had no doubt about it. You talk as if you were certain at least about your own 'progress' because you have been analysed.

P.A. 'Certainty' is a part of life as is 'uncertainty'. We cannot avoid either; they are opposite poles of the same feeling. I do not know what name to give the 'same feeling'—that is, the feeling of which they are opposite poles. Perhaps if I were a poet or philosopher I could. It does not help that I am thought to be a psycho-analyst because that is my profession.

ALICE There may be a confusion because of the ambiguity of language—if your 'profession' is psycho-analysis, it is assumed that you 'profess' that you are one who professes or claims to be proficient.

P.A. That is true; I have to claim proficiency because I fear that if I do not someone even less proficient will take my place. In courting, if the man or woman did not 'profess' ability to be a husband or wife, what do you suppose would happen? Mankind would be denuded of all but the paranoid braggarts; Hell and Heaven filled with self-destroyed melancholics. 'Weep! Weep for Adonis.'

ALICE Or, 'Adore, adore with me my Helen-ly Beauty'. I prefer 'Venite adoremus Dominum'.

ROLAND If you cannot believe in a religious solution I at least cannot 'believe' in *facts*. Facts do not offer an outlet for a religious impulse—only for scientific curiosity.

P.A. Might they not be the same? The religious people I know certainly think they are concerned with the Truth and nothing but the truth. It is often difficult to retain a sense of awe in the face of what we are more likely to think of as humdrum daily trivialities rather than facts which deserve to be treated with respect.

ROLAND 'With respect' I could manage, but not 'with awe'.

ALICE I would have thought that 'awe' is more appropriately left to people who are religious.

P.A. I agree that we should respect the language we use and be careful not to debase it.

ROBIN Is there any fact which you know and regard with 'awe'?

P.A. Certainly—I know awe inspired by the light curtains of the Aurora, mountains—

ROLAND Not people?

ROBIN Do you make a distinction between individuals—precise, particular men and women—and their 'minds'?

P.A. Sometimes that distinction is relevant. Increasingly I am aware that there is something more than that which presents itself to my senses—sound, sight, hearing, touch. I have feelings that are aroused by something that I do not smell or touch or hear or see. My perceptions are not fine enough—blunted by the constant battering of sensuous reality. I shall not live long enough to reach *those* facts except in rudimentary degree.

ALICE If it is rudimentary, perhaps it is something you could and did experience when you yourself were a rudimentary character—in the womb.

P.A. Were you aware in pregnancy of a 'character' in your body?

ALICE Emphatically. One kick in the belly is not the same as another.

ROBIN I should be interested to know what P.A. thinks of maternal intuition. Do you think that paternally gifted psycho-analysts would be capable of such fine discriminations?

P.A. I am a prey to my prejudices. There may be contributions which paternal genes confer and others which derive from both parents.

ROLAND You seem to suggest that as a psycho-analyst you are compacted of the best of both sexes.

P.A. Would it were true. I hope that that desire does not obscure my inheritance of weaknesses. I have noticed a prejudice in favour of my patients and a related desire to share their excellencies.

ROBIN Counter-transference?

P.A. Do not forget that 'counter-transference' is by definition unconscious; it follows that I do not know the nature, in reality, of my counter-transference. I know theoretically, but that is only knowing *about* counter-transference—that is not knowing the 'thing itself'.

ROBIN Presumably, knowing 'about' counter-transference is helpful. Isn't it inevitable that one learns much of which one has no direct experience? I learn about a trip to the moon, but shall certainly not experience it. It must have some value unless we are to believe that the process of education is unrealistic.

ROLAND I had a lot to learn about machine guns.

P.A. So had I; indeed I was taught and learned a lot which

seems to me to be indistinguishable from what it has become fashionable to call 'brain washing', 'shell shock'; the fashions in nomenclature alter, but the reality does not.

ROBIN Do you think that 'education', 'brain washing', 'shell shock' are the same?

P.A. I do not say they are the same, but in some contexts it may be important to recognize the 'fundamental' meaning of what is said. When I was young I was taught that 'patriotism' and 'courage' were important. I believed that 'Your King and Country want you' was true—as did many thousands of others. When the more sensitive and less robust of my companions learned that the enemy did not want them, they 'broke down', became 'shell shocked'. As time passed it became clear that I had only to go into action often enough and I would be dead. But my 'brain washing' school, training, resisted—and were sufficiently robust to withstand, with the help of a little flattering decoration or so—the increasing assaults of reality. 'Couvre-toi de flannelle' became more audible than the seductive whispers of 'glory'.

ALICE You decry glory, but is there not some reality in that?

ROBIN I was impressed by the regimental motto, 'Quo Fas et Gloria Ducunt'.

ROLAND I still am. 'Ubique', likewise, has that appeal of mystery and invitation.

P.A. I don't deny it. In a world at peace I am glad to be left with some reminiscence, some luminosity that penetrates the shadow and the darkness. However ignorant of ideas to come, the idea of glory withstood my cowardice. But just as it would be impossible to explain to anyone who had not been in action what it would be like to be a combatant soldier or a regimental stretcher bearer, so is it impossible to describe to anyone who has not been a practising psycho-analyst what it is to experience real psycho-analysis.

ROLAND Surely you do not seriously mean that an analytic session is comparable with going into action?

P.A. Comparable, yes. Imminent death is not expected, although there is that possibility. That does not weigh the anxiety—fear in a low key. One shrinks from giving the unwelcome interpretation.

ROLAND Is it not just fear that the patient is going to be angry at being criticized?

P.A. I don't think so; the patient may be angry at a critical comment, perhaps even murderously angry, but I do not think that possibility consciously deters.

ROBIN Is it some unconscious fear—the counter-transference of which you spoke?

P.A. It is. Though one is not 'conscious' of it—to obviate that is one reason why we think analysts must themselves be analysed—there is an inherent fear of giving an interpretation. If a psycho-analyst is doing proper analysis then he is engaged on an activity that is indistinguishable from that of an animal that investigates what it is afraid of—it smells danger. An analyst is not doing his job if he investigates something because it is pleasurable or profitable. Patients do not come because they anticipate some agreeable imminent event; they come because they are ill at ease. The analyst must share the danger and has, therefore, to share the 'smell' of the danger. If the hair at the back of your neck becomes erect, your primitive, archaic senses indicate the presence of the danger. It is your job to be curious about that danger—not cowardly, not irresponsible.

ROLAND You must think highly of yourself if you are such a paragon.

P.A. I am trying to describe the job—not my fitness or otherwise for it. I have enough respect for the psycho-analyst's task to tell the difference between this social chat about psycho-analysis—or even a technical discussion of it—and the practice of psycho-analysis. Anyone who is not afraid when he is engaged on psycho-analysis is either not doing his job or is unfitted for it.

ROBIN An airman or seaman who is not afraid of the elements, afraid of the sea and the skies, is unfit to navigate. The line between fear and cowardice is faint.

P.A. Quite so. I would add, the line between daring and stupidity is similarly faint.

ROLAND How would you define it?

P.A. I would not. In practice, where to draw the line depends on the facts, including the facts of one's personality, with which one judges—the total capacity. Definition is only a matter of theory—useful for discussion and communication of ideas. In practice one does not rely on anything so ambiguous as verbal formulation.

ALICE I am always relying on verbal formulation. I have to tell grocers and butchers and fishmongers and others what I want. Rosemary and I understand each other, so there is no difficulty.

P.A. I can see that for your practical purposes it is adequate, but it may lead to misunderstandings in psycho-analysis.

ALICE There are plenty of those I assure you. Most people know I mean what I say.

ROLAND You are lucky. You would be surprised how few people on the farm do understand that. I suppose one should be surprised that there are some who do.

P.A. In analysis it is more complex. Although I have been engaged on this work for many years I am still far from refining my vocabulary and syntax to a point at which I can satisfy myself that I have said 'what I mean'. There is the added problem of perspicuity because I depend on the analysand's capacity for comprehension to augment my inability to be perspicuous. Ideally, knowing what I have to communicate I could refine my vocabulary to a point where the words available are few, yet adequate to communicate fundamentals.

ROBIN Can you give an example?

P.A. If I wish to point to a primitive archaic feature of the analysand's behaviour I have to decide whether to say 'defecate', or 'shit', or 'urinate', or 'make water', or 'piss', or 'wet yourself'. A child might be able to grasp the last expression, but not 'urinate'. A lady, unfamiliar with me or the freedom of medical terminology, might be outraged if I said 'piss'. You may remember the boy I once mentioned who could not say he had a belly-ache because he thought 'belly' was rude. He said 'body-ache'.

ROLAND Surely that is an extreme example of idiotic priggishness.

ALICE I suppose you are usually dealing with extreme

instances, but it must be pretty clear that you have a very disturbed patient.

P.A. True. Anyone who finds time and money to go to an analyst cannot be doing so unless he is aware of his disturbance. But he may not be aware of the 'disturbance' which is 'disturbing' him. The boy who had a body-ache had consciously clothed the impolite nakedness of his spontaneous speech, but he had 'clothed' it so adequately that he could not himself penetrate the 'civil' language to the 'meaning' that underlay what he was saying.

ROBIN Applying what you said just now—what 'smell' were you aware of and what was the danger you smelled?

P.A. The immediate danger was that he would take flight if I said 'belly', or asked him if he had recently had a proper shit. What language? Constipated? But he was also afraid. What I needed to be able to 'smell' was which danger *both* shared. The danger of the tiger and the deer which approached close.

ROBIN The tiger could not have feared that it would be eaten by the deer.

P.A. Your instance is a good example of my problem. I could diagrammatize it thus—

Tiger	Something is going to be eaten up Something is going to run away and leave nothing to eat	Deer

That describes a shared fear. Out of that shared odour—in the boy let us call it an 'odour of sanctity'—the analyst must find a way of formulating it to himself and then reformulating it in a way 'comprehensible', 'digestible' to the boy.

ALICE I see what you mean; it doesn't seem particularly frightening. Is that the only fear that an analyst has to contend with in the course of his practice? No doubt you have other examples of which you know but we do not.

P.A. Plenty. There are the more extreme instances of danger—as with the armed or murderously disposed patient—but even in the 'harmless' instance I have given, the boy was afraid that the psycho-analyst would tell his parents and other authorities about his 'private' sins which he feared would be exposed by the analyst—in the role of criminal investigator. A disturbed boy, or a boy in one of his disturbed moments, can tell his parents that he 'hates' the analyst and thereby arouse fear and distrust in them. Or he may accuse the analyst of having made sexual advances, or even of having assaulted him sexually.

ALICE Isn't that somewhat unlikely, especially in the instance of a well-known analyst?

P.A. There is no such thing as a 'well-known analyst'; an analyst is one who at one stage of fashion is famous, at another infamous; the barrier between 'famous' and 'infamous' is as slight as the verbal 'in'. It is unimportant—except to the psycho-analyst who cannot afford to be unaware that it is a 'built-in' part of his profession.

ALICE I think you are being a bit paranoid.

P.A. What is 'a bit paranoid' for you either is, or is not, 'paranoid' for me. If paranoid, the psycho-analyst needs to 'smell' the danger as well as know as much as his training and psychiatric textbooks can tell him. He and his family are in danger.

ROBIN I knew a man who maintained he could smell a rattle-snake in its venomous state. Jim Corbett had an uncanny flair for hunting out a man-eating tiger. I thought that was the intuition of a natural hunter.

P.A. We think it important to be able to transform these 'natural instincts' into conscious and rational thought without destroying the natural capacities. Usually the training we all undergo in the process of becoming civilized does destroy, or dangerously cover up, our 'animal' inheritance.

ALICE I have known many, who have been trained to be clever and polite civilized beings, who seemed incapable of wisdom or common-sense. I knew a man with a training at the 'best' school and university who was an unspeakable cad and bigot.

ROBIN I knew a man, with a similar background, who was unable to behave in a way appropriate to a comfortable home. There was nothing wrong with his intelligence.

P.A. It sounds as if you were not impressed with knowledge acquired in the course of organized training. Nor am I; that is one reason why it seems to me that it is a matter of urgency to develop psycho-analysis or something better.

ROBIN Do you think analysis is, or will develop into, something better? It is the same race, with its inherent weaknesses, that has to develop this 'something better'.

P.A. Its weaknesses—and strengths. I do not feel optimistic; or so pessimistic as to give up the attempt. So far I have been more inclined to persist than to give it up; so far it has seemed that the positive part of my experience outweighs the negative.

ROLAND Postive–negative . . . how do you establish that polarity?

ROBIN The question which has worried me—how do we determine direction?

P.A. It is apparently crucial; I suspect there is no absolute answer within the grasp of our capacity, but relatively we assume that the sense of progress towards the decay and degeneration of our capacities acts as an unconscious orientation. Most people seem to believe that our uncontrollable journey to the grave gives us a base-line on which to work and to which our standards are referable.

ALICE Most, but not all. Religious people often think that 'though the body dies the soul shall live for ever'.

ROBIN It's a nice idea.

ROLAND 'Nice' you call it? I think it perfectly horrible—one life is enough. I do my best to maintain my life and that of my family, but that has provided me with enough pain and anxiety to get on with.

ALICE What does P.A. say? Do you believe in religion and a future life?

P.A. I have no doubt of the 'fact' of religion as a part, perhaps an unalienable part, of human character. I have even seen a mouse assume what looked like an attitude of religious beseeching when being tortured by a cat that had caught it. Is that a religious impulse? Or is it an attitude we have learned, from animals, to take when in a hopeless situation—

ROBIN —in the presence of cruel but playful God Cat. If God exists I would have no difficulty in believing that one of his attributes was devouring cruelty.

ALICE A belief of very respectable antiquity; because human beings have considered human sacrifice to be acceptable to God, therefore God is like that. Why not God the fountain of compassion that feeds the surgeon and physician? Maybe even psychoanalysts could drink at that source.

P.A. I do not think we could tolerate our work—painful as it often is for both us and our patients—without compassion. I see no reason for postulating an external source, independent of man, from which compassion flows.

ROBIN

'As without sound or struggle
The stars unhurrying march,
Where Allah's finger points them
Through yonder purple arch . . .'

ROLAND 'Le silence éternel de ces éspaces infinis m'effraie.' The vast universe of Absolute Cold does not call to my mind anything so warm as human love. Give me my fellow men and women every time.

ALICE I agree. But, but . . . the Nazi concentration camps? Were they the unaided creation of men?

ROBIN You are not suggesting they prove the existence of God?

ALICE I am prepared to consider them evidence of a devil or Satan. I am not capable of considering the theology of a Satan, but as far as I depend on my private capacity I find much that is more comprehensible if there is a God *and* a Devil, and men and women who are inspired by both. After all, if the outward manifestations are the product of man, there could be some Power, incomprehensible by man's feeble equipment, which is responsible for the created world and for its being created in accordance with a Divine pattern. The fact that we have not yet discerned that pattern, that no great human scientists have claimed to have seen it, does not convince me that there is no such pattern.

P.A. I do not deny the possibility; my prejudice in favour of a scientific or 'factual' approach has not led me to any mystical experience. Perhaps one day in my room I might experience such an illumination. Even so I should expect it to have an endopsychic origin.

ROLAND 'Endo-psychic'! Pardon me, but that is only one of the technical terms which darken counsel rather than throw a beam through the realms of darkness and brutish ignorance in which we labour to exist.

P.A. I am sorry to have used a term which disturbs your understanding of what I am trying to convey. Technical terms in fact save a lot of time in conversation between colleagues who are familiar with the language of which they are part.

ALICE Do colleagues understand the language? Sometimes the conversations in which they participate seem to become an interchange of jargon which floats off the underlying meaning; it becomes a mental slough like a skin that no longer relates to its parent snake.

P.A. If that is what I was guilty of I apologize; we are open to that criticism and its counterpart—that we are talking a language which is universally comprehended and universally recognized as obscene. 'Bloody cunt' for example.

ALICE Do we really need that example?

P.A. Probably not; you certainly understood what I said. The danger that is never far from erupting is the hostility to 'jargon' when we try to use language precisely, when we try to be perspicuous, or when we use everyday speech with which we are all familiar. The latter vocabulary and syntax is so debased, so devalued that it is like coin whose denomination can no longer be deciphered.

ROBIN Yet you talk.

P.A. Poor as it is and poorly though we use it, verbal communication is one of the latest and most astonishing discoveries. It is only a few thousand years old. So it is probably wise to confine ourselves to verbal methods when we attempt something so ambitious as mental maintenance or repair. It is a great improvement on physical violence.

ROLAND I am not sure that I agree. 'Faire entrer la sagesse par le cul' still has its advocates.

ROBIN So it has, as we have good reason to know. Witness Nazi Germany.

ALICE There is a danger that our concentration on Nazi Germany will distract us from observing its development elsewhere.

P.A. Bigotry and ignorance are two well-developed and ancient characteristics of the human being. In psycho-analysis, and in those who practise it, it shows up with startling freshness and vigour. I trust that our ability to detect will not become so jaded, our taste for it so surfeited, that we cease to be aware of it.

ALICE I am not jaded or surfeited, but perhaps we had better continue our discussion after a night's rest; a pause for digestion.

NINE

ALICE You say you have never had direct experience of a mysterious event; do you mean by that that you have not been in a room at the time when someone, not you, was under the influence of a mystical force?

P.A. I have had no evidence that either I or the other was passing through such an experience. I only remember two or three occasions when an analysand of mine actually claimed a mystical origin for the event. I have been more impressed when the individual was *not* consciously making such a claim.

ROBIN Why? Surely 'unconscious' claims are far more open to mis-interpretation.

P.A. Agreed—I do not wish to decry the events of which I know nothing. But I have been compelled to notice that 'fashions' in beliefs, in theories, in varieties of psycho-analysis and in psycho-analysts, are as plentiful as fashions in cosmetics. I suspect that the fundamental source of fashion, whether in people, religions, 'scientific' theories or holiday resorts is, or ought to be, one goal of our curiosity. As individuals we cannot hope to do more than reach some outlying, peripheral goal and please ourselves by claiming that it is ultimate truth; or alternatively fall into despair at discovering our insignificance.

ROLAND Most people with any common sense know that.

P.A. 'Most people with any common sense' are, in my experience, very few people indeed. Common sense is only rarely in fashion. 'Real' common sense, in contrast to cosmetic common sense, tells too many uncomfortable things. 'Eyes that have seen colossal storms and terraqueous convulsions' are not likely to be sought after if they reveal danger and the emotional state appropriate to it.

ROLAND Don't you think that psycho-analysis itself glorifies the importance of a man's thoughts and feelings as a way of being deaf and blind to facts?

P.A. Yes; it can be used, chosen as a method of 'not choosing', inhibiting awareness of facts which we do not like and cannot do anything about. The danger of such use is that it blinds us to facts about which we might be able to do something if we had not decided to look the other way. Equally we may prefer to look outwards, to turn away from the spectacle of facts of our own character. *We* are devoted to the assistance of those who choose to look inwards. As a private individual it is necessary for me to be as much aware as possible of the universe in which I live; professionally I need to be aware of what I profess to be aware of—the character which the analysand 'is', not simply what he 'is like'.

ALICE Most of those I know to be going for analysis are unimportant; sometimes I think their going to a psycho-analyst is about all they have to boast about. Yet when they have finished they boast of having been to such-and-such an analyst of whom I have never even heard. The only ones I know by name are Freud and Jung and Adler.

ROBIN And two of them were not psycho-analysts—according to Freud.

ROLAND I would hate to go to a psycho-analyst—

P.A. And would hate it still more if you got there. 'Insignificance' is not a discovery which anyone wants to make about himself and his affairs.

ALICE Do you include his analyst in the 'affairs' of which he discovers the insignificance?

P.A. It is part of the reality to which human beings should not be blind. Whether that discovery is achieved or not depends on the two engaged in the psycho-analytic research; they may prefer to discontinue the search before such culmination. Discovery is only transitory—on the way to another discovery.

ROLAND It sounds unrewarding. I was once told the meaning of the phrase 'virtue is its own reward'; I remember thinking it sounded like an elaborate practical, not-kind 'joke'. The reward of analysis appears to be—analysis.

P.A. All science, art and religion may come together, cohere, to expose a 'coherence' which is not in accordance with the predisposition of man. I do not see why he should not be another of Nature's discarded experiments.

ALICE You speak as if you 'personified' Nature.

P.A. I do, because it simplifies the communication of what I wish to communicate. It helps in talking to you and other friends with whom I wish to communicate, and who may also wish to communicate with me. This is not intended to mean that there is, in Rupert Brooke's phrase, a fishy god, 'squamous, omnipotent and kind', some Fate of whom we are the chosen children. This god of our fishy existence—assuming the embryologists are correct—may have wanted to turn me and my fellow fish into amphibians and finally to transform us into mammals.

ROLAND Finally? Why finally? This conversation, carried on by the indulgence of the very gas which has supported our existence may be a prelude to yet another transformation into the gas we use and abuse: 'spirit' or 'soul' we call it. Grandiose to the last. Homo sapiens!

ROBIN You are bitter about this harmless conceit.

ALICE I have seen much of this conceit, but I don't regard it as 'harmless'.

(*All fall silent. After a thoughtful pause of a minute or two . . .*)

P.A. 'Sceptre and Crown
Must tumble down
And in the grave
Be equal made.'

ROBIN I didn't know you read the poets.

P.A. People frequently assume that I am devoid either of culture or of technical equipment—or both.

ROLAND You sound hardly used.

P.A. No; it is part of the analyst's profession to be familiar with the real world, whereas laymen think they can afford to be deaf and blind to these unpleasing components of real life.

ROLAND What solution do you suggest? Psycho-analysis seems to be available only for the wealthy, and even so only to confirm those analysands and their analysts in the belief that the world of riches is the best of all possible worlds.

P.A. I think this is the best of all possible worlds because I know of no other world that is possible. That is not the same as thinking, like Pangloss, that there is no way in which we could strive to improve it. We consider the attempt to improve humans both worth while and urgent. I know no analyst who regards psycho-analysis with complacency, but unfortunately our discontent and the internal discussions and disagreements are easily mis-interpreted to express a belief that some body or institution is better. It is not my belief, but I *am* a critic.

ALICE I wish I didn't so often have evidence of the bigotry and bad temper of psycho-analysts.

P.A. So do I—I have plenty of opportunity to observe my own. And I have good reason to be familiar with the tension to which the practising psycho-analyst is exposed. It is understood that the work of doctors and surgeons must be responsible, arduous and trying, but it is not clear that psycho-analysts are exposed to the same stresses.

ROBIN You will admit that the lay public have difficulty in seeing what hardship there is in having a comfortable home, good food, an office which is easily and inexpensively maintained, and a not inconsiderable income.

P.A. I do not blame the public. It is foolish to nurse grievances about having to live in the same world as our patients. My impression is that my colleagues and I show considerable tolerance of characteristics of which we must necessarily be aware. A surgeon does not think a cancer pretty, or a physician admire a chancre's purity; still less does he think it necessary to contract the disease—though Hunter was over-bold in his exploration of spirochaetes. A psycho-analyst is expected to be sensitive to psycho-neurotic or psychotic suffering.

ROBIN Don't we all suffer these pains?

P.A. In a sense, yes. The experience of a physician who observes suffering about which he can do nothing is similar to that of the psycho-analyst who knows how intense is the mental pain of a neurosis but can do nothing because his intervention would be resented as officious and self-interested.

ROLAND Wouldn't that diminish with the experience of the efficacy of psycho-analysis?

P.A. Probably—as it does when a general practitioner is known to be very skilful. But the psycho-analyst cannot fall back on a long history of therapeutic success. In physical medicine the triumphs are lost in the un-observed, unspectacular jungles of Public Health—pure water, pure air, untainted food. Who gives a thought to the solitary with his microscope, or the crank who deprecates smoking in a food market or other public place?

ROLAND If you want the doctor to be honoured he should also be recognized as the source of the knowledge that enables the addict to inject his veins with heroin.

P.A. I did not mean to be advocating honours. Perhaps, if I were to do so, I should also advocate 'dishonours', statues erected to the Marquis de Sade for his services to cruelty.

ROLAND Are you then opposed to 'honours'?

P.A. 'Honours', as part of institutional organization, is not a matter on which I am qualified to speak. I do not remember anything in the course of my experience with small groups which provided me with material for interpretation. Even a social conjecture becomes hazardous if, when I am speculating or privately discussing a few speculative phantasies, it is assumed that it carries the force of a scientifically derived formulation. But I *would* be prepared to express an opinion in a psycho-analysis and to be held responsible for what I said. In that context there is evidence that a patient must respect himself. If this sounds too obvious I can only regret that I have to use words which have become debased and for which there is little respect. Here it is easier to see that we must respect each other. I knew a successful and wealthy farmer who had great and justified respect for a drunken and illiterate cowherd when he spoke of any matters relating to cattle. 'Honour thy father and thy mother' is an injunction which lacks validity unless the father and mother are worthy of respect. The general principle has to be worth applying in a precise instance. The individual is always a particular instance to himself; whether he can respect himself is a matter which *he* must decide. I do not know if this bears on the question you ask, but I think it is related to it. There are good grounds for supposing that the character of a group would be revealed by the individual people or activities or achievements it chose to honour + or −.

ROBIN By 'honour + or −' I suppose you mean honour or dishonour.

P.A. Yes. Part of the ambiguity and uncertainty of psycho-analytic interpretation is that we have to speak spontaneously and cannot at such short notice express ourselves with precision. However accurate we may try to be, there is the ambiguity of imprecision of the language we use.

ROLAND You should cultivate the precision of mathematics.

P.A. I doubt whether we can do much in the realm of mathematics—unless you consider the introduction of plus and minus signs as a 'mathematical enlargement'. We have to forge our instruments while engaged in the work for which we need them. Rosemary is very quiet.

ROSEMARY I'm sorry I haven't much to say, but I was listening.

ROLAND A flattering thought; I hope it is worth listening to.

ROSEMARY Oh yes—though I don't always understand in spite of trying.

ALICE Rosemary and I spend so much of our lives in mundane activities that we cannot spare time for erudite books. If a house has to be kept liveable it is women who have to do so.

How much respect do you think is paid to the minutiae to which we devote ourselves?

ROLAND Probably not much; isn't that true of all necessary but unspectacular activities? After all, we cannot erect monuments to all the heroes and heroines who have invented cheese. I love Camembert but I don't say grace to its creator. Perhaps I ought.

ROBIN Is that why some have a poly-gratitudinous all-purpose ritual—to ward off the evil eye that watches the scales recording our greed? No one seems to regard mental greed as reprehensible—people speak with admiration of the 'omnivorous reader'. What does P.A. think of that?

ALICE I would like to ask P.A. why there is no book on mental dietetics.

P.A. The principle is recognized though not formulated. We do not consider that children should be allowed access to every book; it is thought that some form of regulation is required to produce and maintain mental health—

ROBIN And freedom—see *Areopagitica.*

P.A. As a general principle the personality must be stimulated so that curiosity is aroused but not surfeited; if desire is too easily satisfied there is a loss of mental vigour. The danger of mental indigestion must be watched.

ROBIN I understand your metaphors, but can you give me a concrete example?

ROLAND Would you regard childhood masturbation as a surfeit?

P.A. It can be—later it would be lascivious or pornographic stories, or pictures or films. But what is pornographic for one man may not be so for another, even at the same age. One man can sit facing another and be sexually stimulated by his vision reinforced by imagination; he has a homosexual experience which cannot be prevented by any physical obstruction. He may thus have a facile sexual life which outwardly arouses no censure. A similar experience, but heterosexual, can be equally mentally debilitating. It is as if the mind itself required some difficulty, some obstruction in order to function in a health-evoking manner. The diet must not be too easily digestible for physical health. Freud considered that analysis should be conducted in an atmosphere of deprivation.

ALICE Oh, Freud! You people seem to believe that no one ever thought before Freud. Any *woman* knows that it does not do to give children everything they want, but you should hear the row when you try to introduce moderation—

P.A. I can still hear the yells and reverberations—all disguised in terms that might be used by an articulate cat while it licked the stolen cream from its whiskers. I am sure you would not maintain that cats are only male.

ALICE Or that only women are catty or tigerish? I do not.

ROLAND You sound a little ruffled yourself.

ALICE I am getting tired of the blameless innocent.

P.A. Sometimes the weary unite and . . . there is a Massacre of the Innocents. Then we start all over again to grow more Innocents and more teeth and claws to match.

ROLAND Nowadays we are growing more and better psychoanalysts to produce better minds to turn out bigger and more efficient bombs—

ROBIN And more and more breeder reactors to keep up the supply of fissile material.

ROSEMARY Isn't Nature wonderful!

P.A. I remember an old man who had retired, but liked to pride himself on his youthful, up-to-date vision. His eyes used to twinkle as he waggled his snowy beard. 'We live in stirring times!' he used to say. 'We live in stirring times.' 'What stirring times?' said an irreverent nephew. But by this time he had gone to sleep.

ROLAND And the moral of that is?

P.A. I don't know; I only fear that whatever Freud or Melanie Klein or Alice may say, the temptation to release a BIG BANG may be greater than the rewards of depriving ourselves of that pleasure.

ROBIN Litora litoribus contraria;

'Bring your sticks of chewing gum
  and sit upon the floor
And we'll tell you Bible stories
  you have never heard before.'

P.A. Pleasure, particularly sexual pleasure, is one of the earliest pleasing events to be appreciated. Thanks to Freud it is not difficult to detect the existence of that pleasure.

ROLAND Surely that is general. I have always regarded Freud's discovery as somewhat naïve and over-rated.

P.A. Freud himself was astonished that something so commonplace should create such a furore—but it did. Today, the theories of psycho-analysis have to be formulated in tired language and it is thought that the *meaning* of Freud's formulations is correspondingly tired. Illnesses don't become tired, and mental pain is as fresh and lively as ever it was. People who complain of mental pain are regarded as being as unreasonable as an ancient Egyptian would have been had he complained about what *we* diagnose as syphilis. Mental pain is regarded, even today, as a fuss about nothing. *Theories* are discussed—rarely the pain the sufferer inflicts or embodies. I remember being called to see a German prisoner of war who complained of pains in his wrists which had been caused, he said, by the British who chained his hands together when he surrendered at Narvik. A German naval officer captured at the same time was called to interpret. I could do nothing because the officer, instead of translating, made use of the opportunity to express his contempt for the man and for the British for resorting to such barbarous tricks. I did not respond to his own self-hate for surrendering either to us or, as I began later to suspect, to the Nazis.

ROLAND What made you think that about the Nazis? I should have thought it most unlikely.

P.A. I did not in fact have any evidence of the kind that I would consider necessary had I been psycho-analysing him. I am citing it as a specific example of a general principle which I had formulated for myself. In the practice of psycho-analysis I always aim for specific evidence for the scientific facts which I am interpreting. But an accumulation of such experiences leads me to discern a pattern underlying all the examples. This pattern I then try to formulate. No doubt if I were a painter I would try to transfer my discovery to a canvas; if a musician, to a musical score.

ALICE Do you mean the black marks on paper or the sounds which an orchestral instrument might produce?

P.A. Since I am speaking of the underlying, fundamental reality I imagine it would be the sound. I cannot know because I am not a musician; nor am I a painter. In those performed arts I am only capable of reception. When I aspire, as here, to be the transmitter I have to fall back on articulate speech. It is not because I am good at it, but because I am 'less bad' at it than I am at other methods of communication. It is not lost on me that Alice might again ask, 'Do you mean the black marks on paper, or the noises people make with their vocal chords when they speak?' I mean to use all my resources of language. I think there is a better chance for someone to interpret my spoken words correctly than to interpret the black marks on paper correctly. In both instances the fate of the meaning which I wish to convey is dependent on me—on my ability to communicate—*and* on the existence of a receiver.

ALICE So it depends on 'transmitter' and 'receiver'.

P.A. The Nazi officer was not a good transitory link in the chain—the episode afforded him an opportunity to communicate what *he* wanted to communicate. From his point of view—vertex—*I* was not a good transitory link, but the best available. It was that or nothing. Earlier he would have been able to augment his verbal apparatus with guns; disarmed, he had the spoken word.

ALICE And such gestures and tones of voice and facial contortions as he could command. I had not the slightest doubt when Robert was a baby that he could understand what I said and could make himself clear. What sets me against psycho-analysts is that they seem to have to resort to an enormous quantity of jargon in order either to conceal their ignorance, or to express a minute particle of common sense which any woman would know.

P.A. Not any woman, alas! Nor any man. As for the profession of psychiatry or psycho-analysis, it is no different from any other in that it has to be practised by human beings. I cannot transform myself into a person fit to be a psycho-analyst but, to be fair to myself and my colleagues, I know of no other occupation where such unceasing efforts are made to become fit for the job we do. Unless we submit to the discipline we cannot call ourselves psycho-analysts.

ROLAND Can't this be done without an apparatus which is so costly in time and money?

P.A. No; mental pain requires careful handling. So does physical pain—although we usually regard a headache, or stomach ache, or abrasion as unworthy of the attention of a trained surgeon or physician.

ALICE What about your hypochondriacs?

ROBIN Yes; you seem to me to encourage some of the most tiresome people on earth. Aren't you encouraging such behaviour and profiting by its encouragement to make a living?

P.A. It is not our intention. Our difficulties are contributed to by the debasement and devaluation of our technical terms—'paranoid' and 'narcissistic', for example. We have to use such language as is available and it may seem that we use it in the way that it is used in social intercourse.

ROLAND You make it sound as if psycho-analysts are all professors of English. That is not the impression I get when I read—which is not often, thank God—their books and papers.

ROBIN }
ALICE } 'Amen' to that.

P.A. 'And so say all of us.' We are not professors of English—though no doubt we would all be the better for it if we were. In practice we need a restricted capacity for English for accurate use in a limited area of experience.

ROLAND I do not understand in what sense you use 'area'. Do you mean an epoch of time, or geographical space, or part of the anatomy, or . . .?

P.A. You point my difficulty. It is assumed that the character or personality corresponds to the physical boundaries which we can see and touch, but that does not seem a wise assumption—if there is in reality such an entity as a mind or character. For example, if one of us went out of the room and spoke, we would recognize that it was . . .

ROBIN Oh surely! We should only recognize the sound and interpret that to be evidence of an individual, not a 'character'.

P.A. Perhaps. But I think that I would soon learn to distinguish between a recording, however faithful, and the real thing. I do not believe a baby would be unaware of the distinction if it listened to a recording of the mother's voice, even if the mother were physically present and appearing to be speaking to it.

ROLAND Hasn't that test been carried out?

P.A. I should not be impressed if it were; I do not believe that a mother, being requested to act the part of a mother to her child while a record of her voice was being played, would not betray her deception. I suspect that the baby would react to that sense of falseness in the mother.

ROLAND But this is pure conjecture! Is there no scientific proof?

P.A. It is conjecture; but I am not sure that it is 'pure' conjecture any more than I consider 'pure' truth to be available to mere human beings like ourselves. Psycho-analysts have to be cautious about their claims of scientific truth. The nearest that the psycho-analytic couple comes to a 'fact' is when one or the other has a feeling. Communicating that fact to some other person is a task which has baffled scientists, saints, poets and philosophers as long as the race has existed. 'Nymphs and shepherds weep no more', 'Weep you no more, sad fountains'—could there be any statements more simple, any grammar or vocabulary less obscure? Yet those words have had a powerful effect on generations of people.

ROBIN 'Mummy, what does "a bloody fucker" mean?'—that is a simple question too, words and grammar. But it likewise has been know to create an emotional state in the 'Mummy' to whom it is communicated. Perhaps Alice could throw some light on the problem.

ALICE I admit that just now when the words were uttered they created a momentary flutter; in fact I immediately wondered if you were right to say them in front of Rosemary.

ROLAND I have known the reciprocal of that when something shocking has *not* been said. On one occasion the authorities in war did not divulge facts which might have saved many lives; they did not wish the enemy to know that his secrets were no longer secret. I suppose that we who survive would be willing to concede that those who died did not die in vain. But I wonder what the dead would say if they knew.

P.A. Going into action in war I knew I might lose my life. I don't think I mobilized my patriotism; I simply succeeded in believing that I would probably *not* be killed.

ROLAND That seems to me to be not divulging facts, even to yourself, for fear of what use you might make of them.

P.A. That is true. A decision involves choosing a particular set of ideas, inhibiting another.

ROBIN I thought 'inhibition' was a technical term for a pathological process.

P.A. Certain terms are chosen for technical use in discussion, but reality does not obey the rules of grammar or psycho-analysis. Our apparatus of thinking may have served us in good stead so far, but 'so far' only means as far as the limited range of our perceptions. André Green has pointed out that in the limited sphere of our chosen subject our intuition may be 'un oeil en trop'; we are able to grasp a meaning so unwelcome that we cannot tolerate what our own perceptions reveal.

ROBIN I remember the depictions in the caves of Elephantine being considered by my parents to be too gross for my innocent eyes to observe.

ALICE Was it you who asked your mother what 'bloody fucker' meant?

ROBIN No—I was so 'innocent' that I was hardly fit to survive in the strange world of the 'bloody little sods' of my prep school.

ALICE Rosemary, do you object to this sort of language as much as I do?

ROSEMARY My mum was most particular that I should *not* hear and see what the gentlemen who came to see her behaved like.

ROBIN So you must be quite used to the behaviour of 'ladies and gentlemen'—your 'betters', in fact?

ROSEMARY My mother was 'pertikler' how I was brought up; of course I learnt it from my friends who used to tease me because they said my mum was a 'whoore', as they called it. One day in class, when the teacher told me to read the end of a poem, the children began to whisper, louder and louder, 'Rosemary's a whoore, Rosemary's a whoore', till at last the teacher said, 'Whoore or no whoore, Rosemary will now read the end of the ninth book of *Paradise Lost*'. I remember it clearly because I was dreaming of the words, 'Paradise the blest'—something about 'blest communion, fellowship divine'. I didn't know what the words meant, but they made me cry and everyone thought I was crying because my mother was a whore, but I wasn't.

ROLAND Poor kid. What did you do?

ROSEMARY Oh, I didn't mind. I told the boy next to me that I'd knock his block off if I caught him after school; that shut them up because they knew I could fight. I was a terrible kid.

ALICE Worse than the 'gentlemen' who came to see your mum I expect. Do you blush, Roland?

ROLAND No; by the time I could go a-whoring I was so scared of spirochaetes and gonococci that I didn't dare. It is one occasion on which my cowardliness paid off. I expect P.A. must know something though.

P.A. Yes—though I too must plead guilty to cowardice as far as practice is concerned. I have plenty of second-hand, hear-say experience, and some experience of dealing with people who think that a psycho-analyst is a second-class citizen hardly worthy of common courtesy or respect. If he knows what he is talking about he is thought to be beneath consideration; or beneath consideration because he does not know what he is talking about. I don't think we are any worse off than anyone else, but we are supposed to be able to tolerate facts, however disagreeable. On the whole we get used to the low regard in which we are held. After all, not everyone would treat Rosemary as a human being or a social equal.

ROBIN In Russia perhaps, or the U.S.A.

ROLAND Is the culture of a country more than skin deep?

P.A. Any culture, civilization or temporarily exposed characteristic of persons or peoples is subject to penetration and displacement by the unexpected. They say animals are aware of the imminence of an earthquake. Humans are sensitive to the imminence of an emotional upheaval.

ALICE You mean people who are afraid they are going mad, or going to have a breakdown?

ROLAND Break up, down, in, out, or through?

P.A. Yes, though I was thinking of being subject, as human animals, to a cosmic upheaval. We probably would not be consciously, scientifically conceptually aware of it for some centuries. Until we are able to discern some such pattern we cannot 'test' it by submitting it to related forms of validation.

ROLAND Since none of us lives for centuries, a store, exposed to scrutiny, would be required to reveal a pattern.

P.A. I suppose so—unless there is some unknown form of communication between discrete individuals. Even if individual humans are separated by Time, Space, Deity—to borrow Alexander's formulation—this barrier is penetrable by forces whose understanding is beyond the range of our logical, rational modes of thought.

ALICE Such as . . .?

P.A. Speculative imagination, speculative reason. André Green has pointed out that there may be something about the dramatic art 'form' which is perspicuous. That might make communication possible through the barrier. I was thinking of something which I cannot support in any way that I regard as scientific unless we suppose that science develops from a germ of phantasy. Suppose the results of a colossal cosmic explosion—as for example the explosion which is visibly evident to us as the Crab Nebula—could now be reaching us in a way that affected the DNA molecule. That could exert an influence on the germ plasm of the entire human race; from that, the outbreak of many generations of humans all irritated into violent, murderous activity.

ROLAND Science fiction surely.

ALICE So he said, But what of it? Isn't it more reasonable to suppose some explanation like the wide dissemination of violence by film, press and television?

P.A. Much simpler—much more rational too. That is my point; a rational explanation is always welcome especially in contrast to no explanation at all, or a confession of ignorance. The fact that it is more acceptable to our insignificant little minds does not mean that an unwelcome fact would just go away because we did not like it.

ROBIN Somewhere Freud describes a paramnesia as being a secondary elaboration intended to take the place of something forgotten.

P.A. Or something that has never been known—the gap where a fact ought to be but isn't.

ROLAND Yes; but is there any evidence for a mind at all? It has no colour, smell, or any other sensuous component. Why should not the whole of psycho-analysis be just a vast, towering Babel of paramnesias to fill the gap where our ignorance ought to be?

P.A. I do not think Freud or any psycho-analyst would welcome such an extension; it is typical of the devaluation to which the language we use is subjected. I am prepared to entertain the possibility that the cloud-capp'd tow'rs of human imaginative structures may disappear like the insubstantial vision of a dream. I do not have any difficulty in thinking that the human race itself might disappear in a puff of smoke. Suppose the sun were to flicker as a prelude to its disintegration, would any human survive? This world is only a grain of cosmic dust and our sun an ordinary star—so the astronomers tell us. We know of no other world to which we could fly as a new home.

ROBIN On the other hand it would be extraordinary if amongst the many millions of solar systems there were not some other accident similar to that which produced 'homo sapiens'.

ROLAND A fat lot of use that would be to us.

P.A. In the meantime we should remain true to our nature and endeavour to make the best of ourselves.

ROLAND Is P.A. also among the moralists? I thought you people prided yourselves on being above that.

P.A. I am not aware that we pride ourselves or deprecate ourselves on account of our being ordinary members of the human race. Like my fellows I would be gratified if I discovered that I was in some way excellent; in fact I have found no evidence of my 'excellence' as a psycho-analyst.

ALICE Your colleagues think highly of you.

P.A. Some do, luckily; I am not unappreciative of the fact, but it tells me more of the generosity and affection of my colleagues than of *my* merits. I think we could discuss something of greater interest than me and my qualities and defects.

ROBIN Doesn't your working day consist in discussing the qualities and defects of others?

P.A. I try to demonstrate the qualities of the individual. Whether they are assets or liabilities he can then decide for himself.

ROLAND I thought you were supposed to cure them.

ROBIN So did I.

P.A. 'Cure' is a word which, like 'illness' or 'disease', is borrowed from physicians and surgeons to account for our activities in a comprehensible manner.

ROLAND I hope you will not murder the language by introducing monstrosities like 'anti-bodies'.

ROBIN That was one of Quiller-Couch's aversions, but I do not see why. Quiller-Couch was hampered by his admiration for the translators of King James's Bible and did not recover from the fact that medical science was not written by men of literary genius at the height of English culture. I think James Strachey's achievement in translating Freud may yet come to be valued at its worth.

ALICE Is the matter he translated to be thought of as comparable in value to the matter of the Bible? Perhaps we should discuss it with Priest when he returns. He's been away a long time but I understand he is coming back in time for our next meeting.

ROLAND Oh my . . . good.

ALICE You don't sound pleased; what is the matter?

ROLAND I'm glad he's coming, but I don't want to be involved with God and the rest of that pious stuff.

ROBIN To do him credit he does not try converting us; to be fair to P.A. he doesn't try to convert us to psycho-analysis either.

TEN

ALICE (*to Priest*) It is very pleasant to welcome you back to our group. I hope your trip was successful.

PRIEST It was; I am glad to be back and to find you all looking so well. How's the debate been progressing?

ROBIN Well; though I don't think we made any discoveries. We were wondering whether you could re-light the flame which seems to have grown dim to near extinction. How was your conference?

PRIEST Much like others I have known—in fact I suspect my experience has not been so different from yours. Your account could be transferred to the religious conference without verbal alterations—insignificant, but not in the eyes of God.

ROBIN Why drag in God? We have no evidence of his existence.

PRIEST True. But the fact that we cannot prove that God exists may be a matter of importance only to our self-admiring selves. 'Self-yeast of spirit a dull dough sours', as the poet says. 'But, swollen with wind and the rank mist they draw . . .', as an earlier poet said.

ROLAND You do not mention that the two you quote were of opposing sects.

PRIEST Of opposing sects, yes; but at one in agreeing there is a God.

ROLAND Between them there is not *one* god but two. In fact there seem to be as many gods as there are people to believe in them.

P.A. I agree, but that is only saying that different individuals have different ideas about whom they are addressing and in what manner they should communicate their approach.

PRIEST That does not prove there is no God.

ALICE I think the discussion pointless. Some people have an experience which they cannot explain in any way comparable to that in which they describe other experiences. The sense of contact with God is not similar to other contacts.

P.A. You are, here and now, making just that comparison. That could be because when you speak of 'contact with God' you are using 'contact' metaphorically; when you speak of contact with air or water or Tom Smith you do not mean it to be supposed that it is a metaphorical contact. I have not had such an experience and therefore find no necessity for any explanation. Freud had a good deal to say about the psycho-analysis of religion; he seemed to think there was no need to seek any other than a psycho-analytical explanation.

ROBIN In other words, he did not believe in God.

P.A. That could be one conclusion. I do not know if he had any other views.

PRIEST Whether he had or not, I cannot see that any one man's views, however impressive, can be regarded as relevant to someone who is not Freud. Freud spoke of a psycho-analysis of religion; if I had time I could write a book about the religion of psycho-analysis.

P.A. Could you give us a rough idea of what your book would contain?

PRIEST I think I could write an introductory volume or two about the many 'religions' that have existed, been discarded for another, been in turn replaced as more in conformity with the needs of its time. For all its apparatus of erudition I see Psycho-analysis as yet one more religion—not the True Religion—destined to flourish for its day and then be heard no more.

P.A. Why categorize it as a religion? Most of us try to be scientific; this is tantamount to claiming only one standard—the Truth. It is not incompatible with the religious stress on truth, but that does not make it a religion.

PRIEST The fact that people who have claimed to be God-fearing show little respect for the truth does not make all religion false, or God only a fiction spawned by a fevered imagination. Is that not more likely to be true of psycho-analysis? After all, who are the originators in psycho-analysis? Is it not generated by neurotics and worse?

P.A. I think it likely, but the revolt against neurosis and psychosis is also generated from amongst these same people. If you gather together a group of neurotics, psychotics, hypochondriacs and other disturbed people they soon rebel against themselves and their troubles.

ROBIN Is that any more than what people do who want to escape the consequences of a mistaken choice?

P.A. I think so. I doubt if individuals make a choice; they cannot know what the 'choice' is. The first requisite of a choice is that the person making it knows what the alternatives are from which he or she is to choose. But assuming that they have had a choice and made the wrong one, ought we not to attempt to correct it? If the belief in an almighty spirit is mistaken, if experience leads us to suppose that there is no such spirit, we should cease behaving as if there were.

PRIEST I agree. But does your experience support the idea that people give it any serious thought? From what I see of psycho-analysts they do not know what religion is; they simply transfer their allegiance from one indisciplined, desire-ridden system of emotions and ideas to another. I have heard psycho-analysts discussing; their discussion itself betrays all the characteristics which I have recognized as pathognomic of religion of a primitive, undisciplined, intellectually unstructured kind. They argue heatedly, adducing national, racial, aesthetic and other emotionally coloured motivations in support of their particular brand of activity.

P.A. I would not deny that we do all these things, but we do in fact continue to question ourselves and our motives in a disciplined manner. We may not succeed; neither do we give up the attempt.

PRIEST I hate to appear to sit in judgement but I have to judge, to appraise such evidence as I have as it touches my private life and my responsibility for my own thoughts and actions. You have as many sects of psycho-analysts as there are in any religion I know. You have as many psycho-analytic 'saints' with their individual following of devotees.

P.A. We are human and show all the weaknesses of that biological category. We do not cease to worship and adore because adoration and worship are basic, fundamental and therefore unalterable, inalienable characteristics; we try to allow for that fact.

PRIEST Ought you not then to make room for the capacity to worship and adore—even to depend on something worthy of dependence, adoration and worship? Otherwise such capacities either 'fust in us unused', or become debased by the object worshipped.

P.A. True. The individual who adores a particular nation, or drug—such as alcohol—may be debased by that fact and unable to release himself from a loyalty which has become debasing and dangerous. Loyalties that are health-giving and growth-fostering at one stage become a barrier when the individual cannot transcend them. The barrier can be anything from the limitations imposed by our animal nature, to something temporary that has become hardened, calcified, rigid—I borrow the terms from medical descriptions of arterial degeneration; there is reason to suppose some spiritual counterpart, some unwillingness to entertain new ideas, which is inseparable from advancing physical age.

ROBIN Cannot the 'religion' of psycho-analysis, or the investigation of psycho-analysis by theologians, teach psycho-analysts something valuable, as the psycho-analysis of religion could teach theologians something valuable for theology? Why should there be any difficulty?

P.A. There *is* a difficulty; the very efficacy of teaching is a matter for caution because we do not know what those taught will learn. Children often learn to emulate their parents' faults. Even the good intentions of parents and teachers can be nullified by that fact.

PRIEST What man professes is not so important as what man is.

ALICE Whatever facets we observe, it is those facets, temporarily obscured, which exert such influence—perhaps because men deliberately hide from scrutiny what they wish to do.

PRIEST I would rather men learnt that God was the observer from whom nothing is hidden than that they only have to hide from their confessor or psycho-analyst.

P.A. That is one reason why I would avoid being trapped into being a 'good analyst' who does not require to be correctly informed. It must often lead some religious aspirant to hate and rebel against an all-seeing God, or even human being, whose business it is, like the police, to find out.

PRIEST A parent does need to be loving, but that does not mean he has to be a fool or believe in God as an expression of his folly. We do not recruit fools for our work, or choose fools to be God's servants by virtue of their folly.

P.A. We don't choose psychopaths to be candidates for psychoanalysis.

ALICE We do not knowingly choose fools for husbands or to be the parents of our children. The trouble in real life is to know how to choose from what chance offers us—only men.

ROSEMARY No, Ma'am—only males. We hope they will turn into men. I would rather be your servant, Ma'am, than risk a boy friend who might never become a man. They are all pretty free if it is a matter of messing about with us—no one wants to change.

PRIEST That is so; men are similar to women, and women to men. That is the problem stated in terms—correct terms—of biological sex. We try to show people there is more to passionate love than simply the activity—contact—between genitalia.

ROBIN Does anyone believe that sex is only physical contact between genitalia? I have been a farmer nearly all my life and have never believed such nonsense. You would have to be someone really intelligent—like a psycho-analyst—to think something so divorced from reality.

P.A. I agree. It requires intelligence and the resources of an educational system at full stretch to produce a real fool. I have had experiences which could be understood as genuine endeavour; no fool, no *real* fool, could be the product of effortless pleasurable exercise. I have known people who think that effortless pleasurable activity must be the height of bliss. Do you, Robin, think that only a psycho-analyst could achieve this?

ALICE I'm sure Robin does not think that.

P.A. Exaggeration, all exaggeration, is analogous to the use of a mental microscope which makes visible what otherwise would remain unobserved.

ROBIN It is no exaggeration. I don't want to be rude to P.A. but I have seen experts of all sorts—architects, soldiers, sailors, statesmen—and though it took me years before I broke through the crust of training, by which I learned to revere my superiors and their wisdom, I did achieve my freedom.

P.A. I congratulate you on your felicity. I still find it easier to suppose that farmers and doctors and artists and others on whom I depend are wise.

ROLAND Should you be 'finding it easier', or are you being sarcastic? Rosemary, Alice, Robin and I are all wiser now than we were. It is a mistake—however natural—to be a creature of habit, to slip into these well-worn grooves of thinking. *You* should have had no difficulty in maintaining a disciplined 'way'.

P.A. Nevertheless I have difficulty. I am not exempt from the failings of my fellow men. I do not plead guilty to your complaint that I was being sarcastic—although I am not debarred from the freedom to be sarcastic or hostile. When I am professionally engaged I do my best to refrain from thoughts and feelings which are irrelevant to my work. That does not mean I am obliged to be incapable of anger.

ROBIN You seem disturbed. I think Roland must have penetrated your adamantine calm.

P.A. Not adamantine: I expect to be treated with civility even though I pursue a profession which is disliked—

ROLAND —because it claims the right, on technical grounds, to say hurtful things.

P.A. I claim the right to say things that are correct psycho-analysis though they are hurtful. A surgeon uses a scalpel, but cutting into flesh is not done because of the pain it inflicts. A sadist may be a surgeon, but that is not the same as being a surgeon in order to conceal a forbidden pleasure. I might have to demonstrate that a patient was gaining surreptitious pleasure from the survival—active survival—of an emotionally charged idea that I was a father inflicting corporal punishment.

ROBIN Don't you use the expression 'Father figure'?

P.A. I should of course use it if I felt it expressed something I wished to say and the person to whom I said it understood what I meant.

ROBIN Can you give me an example?

P.A. I had a patient who was educated and cultivated. Yet he ejaculated 'God' with great emphasis in a context which made it clear that he was feeling angry and resentful towards me.

PRIEST How do you know he was not simply using the noise—'god'—as a swear word? I would say he was uttering the name of God in vain.

P.A. That is assuming that there is a God.

PRIEST It is an assumption based on many years of experience.

P.A. Yes; but in the practice of my profession I have to consider the nature of the experience which you describe as lasting through years. I have to consider whether the 'experience' was not prompted by some events within your body and mind. The fact of a father and the fact of a mother are both impressive. You can say it is only a theory, but I should have thought it would occur to any parent that the theory could be plausibly regarded as compatible with known facts.

PRIEST Plausibly, yes. But why do you regard 'plausibility' as significant? An adult's conjecture about his views when he was an infant is called a scientific fact, but not when the discussion is of a 'religious' fact. You say the psycho-analyst—a real psycho-analyst—is a compassionate man or woman only concerned to be helpful even as he reminds the patient of a bad or cruel father or mother.

P.A. You go further than we do when you claim that there is in fact a 'guardian angel'.

PRIEST You go further than I do when you say there is a compassionate man or woman who is only concerned to be helpful. Tell me—have you ever known one? *I* do not say there is a sincere, compassionate, God-fearing, God-loving priest. I do not wish to denigrate any surgeon, physician, psycho-analyst, artist or other; nor do I want to endorse the claims of anyone who expects me to take such a figure at its reputed value. It is a less ridiculous claim when I say I have evidence of guardian angels who save us fallible creatures from our folly if we let them, and if it is in accordance with God's plan.

P.A. There are many 'ifs' in your discourse.

PRIEST Are there less in any other?

P.A. Yes, because only by comparison and discrimination shall we refine and discipline our unruly selves.

PRIEST I do not want to obstruct your aim, yet I am not unaware of the narrowness of your view.

P.A. When are blinkers a hindrance, not a help, to the horse?

PRIEST The horse's rider no doubt would be prepared to argue that he has improved the breed of horse. I think God has improved mankind—

P.A. Men have improved the race of gods, but they have not improved their methods of choosing their gods or of expressing devotion to the chosen one. When I say 'improved' I admit thinking in conformity with a scale of 'better' and 'worse'.

PRIEST So I noticed. Can you give any idea of the nature of that standard?

P.A. Not really; I suppose I would regard 'progress' as good if it were associated with what I regard as further development. Devotees of religion often do not appear to develop any increase in mental ability.

PRIEST Do you suggest that in this respect religious people are any worse than scientists or artists or musicians?

ROSEMARY Men and women always do just as they please,

and find an explanation afterwards. Sometimes it is difficult because they haven't enough money, or the police stop it—

P.A. Or they haven't the physical health, or there is not time, or—as psycho-analysts think—there are unknown or unrecognized elements in their character which contribute obstacles to the fulfilment of their conscious aims even though there is no hindrance in the known universe of not-self. There are facts which I would like to demonstrate to you, but I cannot because I have not the experience and the training which are essential. Even if I had, you would have to be able to understand the 'language' I used.

ROBIN Well, what's the trouble?

P.A. You think you speak English and can therefore understand a Shakespeare play: I think the Shakespeare play would have to be competently produced and acted. An Englishman has to learn English.

ROBIN Poor Shakespeare! What a time he must have had to be able to write the world's most marvellous plays and have no one to help him put them over but a crowd of ranting ham actors.

ALICE Yet they did it. The Elizabethan crowd saw, and kept on going to see, plays in Elizabethan England.

PRIEST Does P.A. still believe in progress? Does he think that the world has 'progressed' positively, increasing the chance of development?

P.A. I could ask the same question of you. So far I still feel able to say 'Yes'—just. How long I shall continue to be able to nurse my capacity for hope before black despair and depression swallow me in everlasting night I do not know. I cannot fall back on your belief in a life after death, although I *can* entertain the hypothesis, fantasy, fairy-story, that a fetus has a pre-natal existence. I am not in a position to argue with an opponent who says that these fanciful 'theories' have no place in a scientific discipline.

PRIEST Then what hinders? If you cannot exclude the possibility that there is a fetal mentality suitable to a watery, fluid environment, then why deny an after-life?—a post-gaseous-fluid existence?

P.A. It is a fact of my nature, to which I have become accustomed, to believe that when I die I shall cease to exist.

PRIEST I do not deny that; I see no reason to believe that the creature that conforms to that same creature's 'laws' of nature, logic, science, will continue to exist in accordance with those same laws, any more than I believe that the post-natal creature conforms to such 'laws' that the fetus 'regards' as reasonable. The fetus could 'believe' that a baby was a 'fabulous monster'.

P.A. I have had patients who are on bad terms with whatever they feel they have become; they are on bad terms with human beings who remind them of themselves. One of the difficulties of psycho-analysing such patients is that they do not want to be reminded of 'ordinary' behaviour—theirs or anyone else's.

ALICE Has this anything to do with real life?

P.A. It has a great deal to do with real life. Amongst the many and frequent dangers of psycho-analysis none is more dangerous than the experience of the coming together of the pre-natal and the post-natal personalities. It can be easily appreciated that the danger is associated with anything whatever—psycho-analysis, music, painting, mathematics—which could remind those two personalities of their continued and continuing 'contact' with each other in the same body and mind.

ROLAND You make it sound most dramatic.

P.A. It would require a drama of Shakespearean quality to portray the reality.

ROLAND Shakespeare must be responsible for many murders and suicides.

P.A. He said, 'Upon the King! let us our lives, our souls, our debts, our careful wives, Our children, and our sins lay on the King!' Shakespeare, doctors, and lesser fry like psycho-analysts, have been accused of inventing, 'creating' the diseases of which we would have our fellows be aware—*Be-ware!*

ROBIN Be ware! How certain this sound alarms! The alarm is dealt with as a substitute for, not a prelude to, action. If your belly aches tell it not to belly-ache!

ROLAND If your mind tells you not to bore the un-offending

world with your private cares, go to a psycho-analyst and enlist his support against such old-fashioned ideas!

P.A. Psycho-analysts do not advocate indiscriminate broadcasting, but discriminating, meaningful, and consciously directed discussion. A parliament cannot achieve its highest function if it chooses caterwauling rather than debate. Why didn't Bion go on with groups?

BION I had more pressing problems which could be adequately dealt with only by psycho-analysis—or something better; particularly the problem, which P.A. had been discussing, of the relationship of the highly equipped fetus with its own and its parents' 'parental' qualities.

ROLAND The fetus's parental quality! That sounds wonderful.

BION I was afraid it would arouse someone's contempt. The crackling of thorns under a pot is more serious when it becomes the crackling of radio-interference, or the marriage of divorced nuclear elements. Not that I would or can deny you your fun.

ROLAND I'm sorry if you felt I was making fun of you, but I do find it somewhat exasperating when people take themselves so seriously. I think you have an inflated view of your importance.

BION I regret that I give such an unfortunate impression. I should be less than sincere if I said you are only a source of innocent merriment. There are times when I find your supposedly sane and balanced outlook, your fascinating sense of humour, difficult to tolerate.

ALICE I don't wish to take sides, but 'peace! you English fools'.

ELEVEN

ALICE Surely it should be possible to discuss reasonably.

BION It is also possible—as we have reason to know—to resort to arms. The disastrous meeting I have been imagining as taking place between a potentially gifted fetal mind and its divorced but equally gifted post-natal self also occurs when two or more groups of individuals meet. The history of the relationship between French and English, German and British, and now Black and White races looks likely to end in mutual annihilation, not mutual beneficient stimulation.

ROLAND What is the ground for disagreement—colour? sex? prosperity?

ROBIN Father and son? Guardian and ward? Exploiter and exploitee? Mother and daughter?

P.A. The possibilities are endless. Once the problem obtrudes there is no end to explanations—*rational* explanations, though I would not like to say how a 'rational' explanation is distinguishable from a rationalization.

ROBIN You are as bad as the Intuitionist mathematicians who seem to disparage logic.

P.A. The Intuitionists would say that logical and intuitionist mathematics can exist happily with one another provided the logicians admit the reality of another approach. Quantum mechanicians do not deny the existence of wave motion.

ROBIN Is there an analogy in the relationship between group analysis and psycho-analysis proper?

P.A. It is a seductive possibility. Detailed psycho-analytic scrutiny reveals movements, up and down, of the individual particles composing a group; the 'up and down' movement would give an illusion of waves, as when the sea is compared visually with the drops of water in it. Visual images penetrate deeply in the way that a capacity for sight extends the range of the infant; it is not limited to what it can grasp or touch. Mobility does not extend as far as the eye can reach.

ROBIN What about the range of visual images in geometry? That was extended by algebraic, not visual pictures of lines and circles.

ROLAND Desargues extended the grasp of mathematics even though his diagram was visual.

ROBIN The development of projective geometry which followed was not visual.

P.A. The person concerned with conic section falls back on the operation of an inner eye. Psycho-analytically individuals still seem to rely on the existence of a diaphragm analogous to that separating the lungs from the digestive canal. There is a survival of that mentality in the 'division' which is made between pre-natal and post-natal—as if *birth* were of great significance—

PRIEST And death which, as I have remarked before, you also speak of as if it were obvious to anyone except possibly stupid people like priests. We are assumed to deny death because we are afraid of it. It seems to me to be a naïve example of psycho-analytical misinterpretation and ignorance of religious teaching and experience.

P.A. It is not naïvety that is limited to psycho-analysis. I would not defend myself against such a charge, but the tone you employ when you formulate your observation invites a response which becomes either an admission of guilt or an aggressive repudiation.

ROLAND Admission of guilt? You don't say what crime.

P.A. I am not bringing the accusation. I am merely trying to draw attention to the way in which a feeling of guilt is evoked or created; it is basic, fundamental. The crime—rational, logical—and the feeling of guilt are natural partners. It is a matter to which justice, morals, intellectual ingenuity can be devoted for so long as anyone can spare the time and energy.

ROLAND The psycho-analytical view is an invitation to create a lawless and undisciplined world.

P.A. There is no 'psycho-analytical' view. But there are people who can use psycho-analytical theories to support any activity they choose. That is why we try to train people who are not only able, but who also wish to help, not hinder, the individual.

ROLAND Individual burglars, robbers, murderers as well?

P.A. The occupation or the philosophy of individuals is not usually—in the culture with which I am acquainted—believed to be the concern of doctors or surgeons; they are usually expected to confine themselves to medicine and surgery. I have an idea of how I ought to run my own life, but what I consider to be appropriate for me has nothing to do with an individual 'not-me'. I choose to train people I wish to help, but my ambition is not psycho-analysis—it is me.

PRIEST I could not watch a child putting its hand into a fire to grasp a live coal. If I saw adult behaviour likely to have similarly evil consequences I would intervene.

ALICE Anyone would.

P.A. These are hypothetical situations and the problems posed can be solved logically. In real life problems appear in a form which is not susceptible to solution theoretically; you have to act or refrain from acting. These discussions are important not in themselves, but because they promote readiness. Psycho-analysis is a kind of action which is a *prelude* to action. In the individual a nerve impulse is a prelude to action; it is not a thought. 'Tell me', a neurologist will say, 'if you feel anything when I touch your foot'. I do not need to ask such a question because I can see for myself if the patient feels anything when I touch his sensory apparatus with an idea, or a grimace, or a tone of voice. That is one reason why a psycho-analysis is not a social conversation or vice versa; the behaviour of a psycho-analyst conversing in a psycho-analysis is *not* the same as the behaviour of a psycho-analyst conversing at a dinner party. Confusion occurs because that important distinction is not observed.

ROBIN You spoke one day about articulate speech being indistinguishable from splitting. I don't understand your meaning when you say that speech at a dinner party is not the same as psycho-analysis.

P.A. If I say that it is a hot but rather muggy day, that articulated statement consists of bringing together a number of ideas—of heat, daylight, humidity, feeling—that have been split apart. Splitting is a convenience when prelude to an articulate sentence. But weather remains weather—a totality, not a mass of discrete particles. An individual angry with the weather might wish to attack it and split it into minute fragments. That, I would say, was an expression of impotent (and therefore omnipotent) rage. Atoms of hydrogen, oxygen, carbon and the rest are consequent on scientific observation—primitive splitting transformed to sophisticated use.

ROLAND How does it help a patient to be told that?

P.A. You are making the mistake about which I was just talking. This conversation is *not* a psycho-analysis; it is a social discussion *about* psycho-analysis. What I said to Robin was not psycho-analysing him. If I used the same words to a patient the circumstances would be different. I would have to ask myself the question Roland has just put to me—what would be the good, if any, of saying it to the patient?

ROLAND I often hear that a psycho-analyst tells a patient that 'when he was a child . . .', or 'when he was an infant . . .', such an event took place. There seems to be no evidence to support those statements and nothing that the analysand can do about some event reputed to have taken place in the past.

P.A. I agree that the 'past' is past and nothing can be done about it. All that can be 'done' is whatever can be done in the present and about the current consequences of some action which was taken in the past. What is *done* in psycho-analysis is 'done' by means of articulate speech in the present. In surgery we don't say, 'You once had a tail like a monkey'; we say, 'There is a malformation in the lower part of your spine; I think it would be worth your while allowing me to operate. I think you will find that we can make you comfortable and that when you have convalesced from the operation you won't have your present complaint any longer.' I am not concerned to say that something or other happened 'in infancy', or 'before you were born', and so on ad infinitum. That might be relevant if I were teaching psychological embryology, or psychological archaeology or history. Psycho-analysis, in practice, is more closely analogous to surgery, but it is only an analogy.

ROBIN You seem to me to come near to making reassuring, even flattering, comments about what most of us regard as a disastrous state of affairs—what we call being mad or insane. Don't you regard psychosis as serious?

P.A. Of course I do; I regard all states of mind as worthy of study. The seriousness of the state is not improved by its being untreated or misnamed. All descriptive terms—asleep, awake, sane—need to be kept in constant repair. Relatives and doctors allow their hopes to be stimulated by the facts of surgery, medicine, psycho-analysis, to an optimism indistinguishable from being carefree or careless. That is a misfortune as great as depression or despair amounting to passivity and negligence.

ROLAND There is no substitute for common sense.

P.A. Substitutes for common sense are legion; people turn to any course of action which offers an alternative to common sense. They become devoted to psycho-analysis because they think the theories are a romantic and seductive escape from common sense; they become devoted to individual analysis when analysis common to the sense of a group would be preferable. The fact that infants—perhaps even fetuses—display 'common sense' is most unwelcome.

ROLAND Oh come! Can you really give an example of an infant that shows common sense?

P.A. Let me start with something which I think you may

even have observed for yourself; it has fascinated me and I have still found no adequate explanation. A baby, almost newborn, has a pot placed against its posterior by a mother who hopes it will defecate into the pot rather than its nappies. Its face is immediately suffused with expressions of intense concentration and determination, and there!—to the mother's delight—lies a modest but adequate contribution to the pot.

ROLAND There must be a simple explanation.

P.A. I agree; but I have not found out what it is. Any amount of 'interpretations' but—which is correct? With regard to the fetus I have no difficulty in supposing that at some stage two or more senses are in common—for example smell and hearing. Why should that not be a prototype of an experience which later becomes known as 'common sense'?

ALICE How do you link high intelligence, or a gifted personality, with something so disastrous as psychosis, insanity and even delinquency? That seems very peculiar—and most disturbing.

P.A. I do not find it difficult to do, but that very fact increases my hesitation about doing so. I do not wish anyone to seize on what, as far as I am concerned, are mere fancies and conjectures as if they were facts.

ALICE But don't you think you can rely on us to be fairly reasonable?

P.A. 'Fairly' reasonable, yes; but my experience is not the same as yours, and what I regard as 'fair' may not correspond to your idea. I am used to finding that what I say is regarded as strange, incomprehensible, fantastic. After a time what I say is regarded as obvious, commonplace, not worthy of remark. Later still I discover that the formerly incomprehensible comment has become an established creation of the listener which *I* have plagiarized.

ROLAND You sound ill-treated.

P.A. I do not agree that I display grievance. The reality of the world often provokes feelings of grievance; people cannot reconcile themselves to the facts which they cannot deny and do not like.

ALICE What has that to do with the fetus?

P.A. A fetus might take a dislike to its experiences including awareness of them. As a result of her experiences with infants a theory was formulated by Melanie Klein which became known later as 'projective identification'. She did *not* attribute it to fetuses.

ROLAND Then why complicate the theory by supposing an even earlier existence of the mental mechanism? Isn't it a fact that this Kleinian theory is already questioned by many psycho-analysts?

P.A. If it were simply a matter of saying 'ditto, ditto to Mrs Klein, only earlier still' I would agree that there would be every reason for dismissing both the Kleinian theory and its supposed 'improvement' as probably ridiculous and not worth the expenditure of time and effort involved in their consideration. Many analysts repudiate Klein's extension of psycho-analysis as elaborated by Freud. I found it difficult to understand Klein's theory and practice though—perhaps because—I was being analysed by Melanie Klein herself. But after great difficulty I began to feel there was truth in the interpretations she gave and that they brought illumination to many experiences, mine and others, which had previously been incomprehensible, discrete and unrelated. Metaphorically, light began to dawn and then, with increasing momentum, all was clear.

ALICE Did you remain convinced by further experience?

P.A. Yes—and no. One of the painful, alarming features of continued experience was the fact that I had certain patients with whom I employed interpretations based on my previous experience with Melanie Klein, and though I felt that I employed them correctly and could not fault myself, none of the good results that I anticipated occurred.

ROBIN In other words the objections raised by contemporary psycho-analytic colleagues to Kleinian theories were being supported by your own experience of futility?

P.A. That was indeed one of my anxieties and one I did not feel disposed to ignore.

ROLAND But you must have ignored it. Did you not feel you had a vested interest in continuing to support psycho-analysis, Kleinian or otherwise?

P.A. I was aware that I would be likely to cherish my preconceptions. Every now and then something would occur that convinced me I would be foolish to abandon my ideas as if they were clearly wrong. In fact it was clear that they were not always wrong. So—it became a problem of discrimination.

ROLAND What led you to persist?

P.A. Partly a chance recapitulation of Freud's description of the impression created on him by Charcot's insistence on continued observation of facts—unexplained facts—until a pattern began to emerge; partly his admission that the 'trauma of birth' might afford a plausible but misleading reason for believing that there was this caesura between natal and pre-natal. There were other impressive 'caesuras'—for example, between conscious and unconscious—which might be similarly misleading. Melanie Klein's interpretations began to have a vaguely but truly illuminating quality. It was as if, literally as well as metaphorically, light began to grow, night was replaced by dawn. I was aware, with a new comprehension, of the passage of Milton's invocation to light at the commencement of the Third Book of *Paradise Lost*. I re-read the whole of *Paradise Lost* in a way which I had not previously done, although I had always been devoted to Milton. This was true likewise of Virgil's *Aeneid*—though it involved much painful regret for the way in which I had wasted and hated the privilege of being taught by certain schoolmasters whose devotion had but a sorry response from me. Let me now praise men who ought to have been famous. For my own pleasure I write their names: E. A. Knight, F. S. Sutton, Charles Mellows. Later came the debt to my friends whom I will not name lest it cause embarrassment.

ROBIN I appreciate the point, but I would like to know more about the 'illumination'.

P.A. Had you not better ask yourself to whom you owe such illumination as has saved your journey from being plunged in everlasting night or, worse still, in the blaze of everlasting certainty and good fortune?

PRIEST May I introduce a note of pity for the unfortunates who have been plunged in the everlasting gloom and self-satisfaction of scientific knowledge—a fate which has deterred many from the joys of devotion to God and respect for His truth.

ALICE Surely scientists devote themselves in all modesty to the truth. Even women have been known to wish to bear children in whom a love of truth can germinate; we are not only ambitious to be sexually satisfied.

ROSEMARY Most of the men my mother knew behaved as if that was the only thing in life.

ROLAND Good God!

PRIEST Poor God! Can you imagine what it would be like to be worshipped by men and women? Even Socrates is said to have been tried and condemned to death by his betters. Some of you may remember the story of the Garden of Gethsemane.

ROLAND God Almighty first planted a garden and, indeed, said Bacon, it is the purest of all pleasures.

P.A. One of the purest of human pleasures appears to be the pleasure of cruelty. Could Priest enlighten us about this?

PRIEST Perhaps I can do so by reminding you of a religious doctrine of the Immaculate Conception; that is in contrast to 'human pleasures'. It seems to me that psycho-analysts' discoveries may be something which has been known to the Church for a long time.

P.A. Psycho-analysts who respect the truth have done and still try to do just that—respect the truth. But we do not put it in the terms you use.

PRIEST But what you say and the way you say it matter. For this reason the Catholic Church is particular about what it says and how it says it. We are often accused of narrow-mindedness and bigotry for being particular and not co-operating with people who believe themselves to be our allies.

P.A. We have been deflected from our problem, namely, to account for facts that lead us to think that existing theories are inadequate but too true to be discarded without loss. Maybe it is significant that the discussion that obtrudes centres on ownership, on who created or owned the idea.

PRIEST Or rather, who owned the owner—God or man? But let us debate the idea further tomorrow.

TWELVE

PRIEST What is the psycho-analytic view of original sin? Do you deny there is such a thing.

P.A. I hesitate to say I believe or disbelieve in something reported as a fact by someone else. I have been convinced that certain observations could be most easily explained if there were such a thing as original guilt.

ALICE You have often said this; I have no doubt about it.

P.A. A most unwelcome feeling—even to an infant. As I became aware of good psycho-analysis, even by myself, 'faulty psycho-analysis' was inadequate explanation, so I cast around for some pattern other than our failings. Considering the great intelligence shown by some analysands, it was absurd to suppose that the intelligence sprang into being merely at the fact of physical birth. Surely, I thought, the offspring of gifted and intelligent parents might be as likely to be intelligent as much and as often as the offspring of stupid or handicapped parents might be expected to be stupid. In other words, the fetus must have inherent characteristics which sooner or later become apparent. If the fetus subsequently becomes an intelligent or wise or gifted man or woman, why should it not, as it approaches full term, show prototypes of the sort of behaviour expected of children and adults? It occurred to me that a fetus might hear noises, see sights, smell odours, in a watery fluid such as the amniotic fluid and meconium. The significance of this did not become apparent at once, but I felt that past experiences with patients would have been less obscure if I had dared to imagine that the emotions displayed might be pre-natal. They were often expressed in a manner which differed from commonly accepted modes of expression.

ALICE How did that differ from any other person?

P.A. That is what I asked myself. I wondered whether the highly endowed fetus might employ the mechanisms which psycho-analysis had made familiar in the treatment of children and adults, even before birth, precociously. Such a precociously developed fetus could try to rid itself both of the senses when they became sensitive to changes of pressure in the watery medium, and of the feelings, 'emotions' of sub-thalamic intensity; it might be prey to experiences unmodified in the way we expect them to be by the 'higher' centres. Then comes the 'trauma of birth'.

ALICE I have some difficulty about the expression 'trauma'. Whose experience is traumatic? The mother might find it so, although even the unmarried girl must have a good idea that the prospect of giving birth would be frightening. Is the baby supposed to find it a traumatic experience? Or the father? Most people must be aware that the birth of a child is likely to be dangerous—one of the few experiences which bring home the fact that issues of life and death are never far away.

P.A. At the moment I want to be oblivious of these manifold considerations so as to concentrate on 'hypo-theory'. I am supposing that the gifted child has tried, even when a fetus, to be without 'feelings' or 'sensations'. It cannot get rid of its inborn, inherent genealogical inheritance; it can possibly get rid of what used to be called 'acquired characteristics', what I have called phenomenes—phenomena as contrasted with genotypes. So it remains the gifted, inherently gifted, person. Since this is so, it is able to learn what is expected of it, how to be what Mother or

Father, or both, want. It learns the difference between what Father and Mother call right and wrong, what will one day be called The MacNaughton Rules. All this, however, is split off from its fundament, its base, its real self. So there you have a civilized, apparently well-adjusted moral being; its armoury of accomplishments is daily augmented in the way that a really intelligent animal learns to augment its repertoire of parlour tricks. 'Die for your country', the fond dog-lover says to her pet who obediently lies down on its back and wags its tail. In due course the young patriot learns to die for his country but may get killed in the process—unless one of these powerful but anaemic emotions breaks through the caesura and causes the young man to have 'shell-shock', or to have his brain washed according to the fashion prevalent in the culture current. His intelligence hardly need cause a ripple in the depths of his personality even though engaged on what would be a difficult task of maintaining his shell-shocked, brain-washed personality in good repair if he had to do it with the conscious skill of an actor playing a part.

BION In the meantime—if I may join in the discussion—his premature personality continues its life in uneasy proximity with his post-mature lodger in the same physical soma. Sometimes the psycho-somatic partner demonstrates his soulful qualities; sometimes his soma-psychotic demands acknowledgment and recognition of his physical and psychotic gifts. I describe the situation in naïvely pictorial terms. There are other descriptions, but most of them have been impregnated with pejorative connotations.

ALICE Such as 'hypochondria'?

BION Yes; or 'crazy', or 'insane', or 'difficult', or 'tiresome'.

ROSEMARY My mum used to say her boy-friend was always belly-aching about something.

P.A. Such creatures cannot have any respect for their bodies unless they become medically, physically ill.

BION Or outstandingly athletically gifted.

ROLAND You don't mean to suggest that our Olympic athletes are all hypochondriacs?

P.A. I'm sure he does not—any more than you think that all

those athletes are confined to Olympus. But you can see that it is quite respectable to be massaged before or after taking part in a race or other athletic contest.

ROSEMARY I took service once with a lady who regularly had her face massaged.

P.A. I am sure she was a perfect lady.

ALICE I knew her—she was an absolute bitch! I don't know how Rosemary ever put up with her.

BION I get the idea—thanks to the bi-lingual description achieved by Alice and Rosemary co-operating to describe the . . . the . . . er

ALICE } Bitch.
ROSEMARY } Lady.

BION Your happy combination and the clarification you achieve by your joint efforts encourages me to draw attention to another union not unlike the one I was describing between our two enemies Soma and Psyche. Sometimes the two characters do not share the same body; each contributes a real physical and imaginary component. They tend to be over-simply described as 'homosexual', or 'heterosexual', or 'married', or 'in partnership'. In those situations in which the disguise—the conventional costume—excites psychiatric attention, they are liable to be described as participating in a *folie-à-deux*. If they excite the attention of the Board of Trade they may become known as a famous business venture, although the dividing line—caesura?—between that and a bankruptcy, or criminal association, or un-happy-marriage, may not be so easy to determine in close investigation as it is in a purely literary or grammatical scrutiny. Words and articulate speech are wonderful inventions—still in their infancy.

ROLAND Yet you psycho-analysts talk as if you were learned people.

P.A. True; and that often leads the cognoscenti—amongst whose prophetic community perhaps I should include Roland—to suppose that we know nothing whatever.

PRIEST It is often assumed that theologians, priests, prophets—as P.A.'s intonation just suggested—also know nothing, that God is a figment of the imagination. There is truth in the criticism because the gods that most people believe in *are* figments created by such imaginative capacity as is available.

P.A. Some religions could be described as *folies-à-deux*; that is, relationships between the individual and a god created by the individual. These realities are often fundamentally real, but are made to appear unreal by verbal dependence on splitting as the basis of articulate speech. For example, we speak of 'religious melancholia'. A poor labourer I knew was in a state of profound depression because he *believed* that the cow on which he depended to earn a living had tuberculosis.

BION Who or what had tuberculosis? His cow? His wife? Or daughter? Or the society he had to serve? These questions cannot be investigated here—only in contact with the patient.

P.A. There is always the risk the investigator will catch the complaint—a risk he may not want to run. The analogy in the mental sphere of activity is the psychiatrist's fear that he himself will 'catch the complaint'—or find he has already caught it—if he allows himself to have a close contact.

BION In the relationship I have been describing—pre-natal ↔ post-natal—the individual often behaves as if his wisdom and intelligence would be contaminated if he allowed himself to recognize that his body thought; conversely, that his physique would suffer if he allowed his body to know what his mind thought.

ALICE The bloom on the cheeks of men or women can show that the pair in love are suffused by a reality which cannot be gainsaid.

BION Many wise people would not want to believe that the suffusion on the faces of the pair might be traced to a fetus in contact with the walls of the uterus. I see no reason to deny that the fetus—the germ plasm itself for that matter—could be affected by the loving relationship between the parents. Could not the blush on the bridal cheeks be communicated by a corresponding blush on the walls of the uterus and vice versa?

ROBIN So what?

P.A. 'So what' indeed. I was taught the Laws of Mendelian Inheritance, but not the laws of phenomene inheritance. Yet the child might inherit a passionate love which seemingly could only be acquired.

ROLAND What would obstetricians and gynaecologists think about these ideas? I suppose Priest would say that the Church had preached these matters for generations—even before there was a Christian church.

P.A. I don't suppose that medical science would be satisfied with anything less than the kind of documentary evidence that X-ray films provide—in time no doubt it will be forthcoming. The demand for it now—at this stage of human endeavour—might be more likely to stifle than encourage investigation. Psycho-analytic conjecture can be dismissed as too fanciful, but it is possible that a psycho-analyst might reconcile one of his analysands to respect what his body was trying to tell him and even persuade his body to have some respect for his mind. There has never been much anxiety to attribute an important function to the brain substance.

ROBIN I should have thought there must have been sufficient suspicion of it to encourage the vogue for decapitation—at least of one's enemies.

BION In war, public or private, no one thinks of anatomy or physiology but about hurting the opponent without getting hurt oneself. The relationship between man and woman which results in a pregnancy is emotionally significant; the feelings, absent or aroused, have powerful physical accompaniments. I see nothing inherently unlikely in these being communicated to the fetus. The only problem is whether, and at what point, these events could communicate conflicting ideas and feelings in a child or adult; whether there is evidence that the conflicts were being worked out in a domain which may not be known to us—yet.

ROLAND What if they are? How does that effect a 'talking cure'—as psycho-analysis is sometimes called?

P.A. The problem has been raised before in our discussions—what language must we talk to the body? I think we must talk our own native language, ordinary articulate conscious speech, as correctly as we can. The speaker must also be free of the need to silence his body. If he is talking, the conversation must not be interrupted by the need to silence his hands, or his feet, or his facial muscles, or his eyes. For that matter he has to be free to talk even without fear of what lies his tongue may communicate. I have known analysands who could talk perfectly but who were nevertheless disturbed by the thought that they would stammer; that one of the 'two' people present would be the mouthpiece of a third even though invisible and inaudible.

BION To borrow from the embryologists, the analysand, though physically correctly formed, fears the intervention, in the tasks of his ears and eyes, of an over-active supposedly archaically surviving system of auditory or optic pits.

P.A. They might be regarded as prematurely active; in adulthood the causes of suspicion are variously, rationally described; in essence something excites comment because it is inappropriate. Hence the 'consciously' dubbed 'stammer'. In short: A and B meet, but fear the presence of x, y, z, a, b, c. . . . 'Friends, Romans, countrymen, lend me your ears . . .', but the rest of you lay off and do *not* borrow my sense apparatus—

BION —or mind; it may know too much. 'Vulgar Errors', or, as an old farm-hand said to his employer, 'To tell you the ghastly truth, Mister. . . .'

ROLAND How can you make these matters clear to the sufferer in his anxiety state or insanity?

P.A. Or his unconquerable self-satisfaction; or equally unconquerable rectitude—

PRIEST —or scientific training, or mathematical flair.

BION Great is the Truth and shall prevail—when none cares if it prevail or not.

MORIARITY My old friend Iago said to me as I went over the Reichenbach Falls, 'Don't worry—Sherlock Holmes will be sure to recover when Conan Doyle discovers on what side his bread is buttered'. 'But, Iago my friend, don't you realize our frightful predicament? We are due to be dashed in pieces on these frightful rocks at any moment. Indeed, I think we are overdue at the bottom now.' Don't worry. Falstaff is still alive, but where are all the Figments of Imagination who used to strut around patting themselves on their Reality? Careful now, how you dash yourself to pieces on those rocks of reality. There! Well done—you could hardly have done better if you were the Devil himself.

THIRTEEN

PRIEST Really, this is hopeless. I wanted to have a serious talk about right and wrong, and we are interrupted by these rowdy street urchins.

BION I remember those terrible, never-ending half-hours called 'Search the Scriptures'.

MORIARTY You were a very naughty little boy, forever thinking about trash like Sherlock Holmes instead of the . . . er . . . er . . . ranks of . . .

BION I know—'prowl and prowl around'. We used to sing it 'ppp'. Terribly exciting! And *then* 'fff', 'Christians up and smite them'. I loved that bit. Was it Midian or Gideon? I forget.

MORIARTY There! Didn't I tell you? You should have learnt your scripture.

BION What *did* happen at the Reichenbach Falls?

MORIARTY I got dashed to bits, but we were all reunited again and went to Heaven.

BION How awful!

MORIARTY Yes. For a few aeons I was in reserve as a Solar Myth.

SEXTON Myth Whybrow.

MORIARTY No, you fool. You were her Favourite; don't you remember?

SEXTON Oh yes. I died of appendicitis, didn't I?

BION Yes; perfectly simple case.

PRIEST I suppose you disguised it as a Figment of Imagination.

MORIARITY 'Scientists' always do. Anyone with any sense knows that Figments of Imagination are the hereditary Rulers of Intellectual Life. Everything starts as a figment of imagination; it is the intellectual counterpart of what biologists call the germ plasm, or what Bion chooses to call a phenomene. We figments of imagination are *not* dependent on sexual reproduction. People ought to take the advice, 'Shut up! Give your arse a chance'. But do they? No! They go to see a doctor who is only interested in his training and not in a body—which will probably tell him something he doesn't want to hear. It is worse still with a split or fragmented mind—and the rocks that cause all the trouble.

ALICE From what I have heard, the complacency and ignorance of psycho-analysts makes it difficult for them to take any adequate steps to perfect either themselves or psycho-analysis.

P.A. A danger lies in the belief that psycho-analysis is a novel approach to a newly discovered danger. If psycho-analysts had an overall view of the history of the human spirit, they would appreciate the length of that history of murder, failure, envy and deceit.

MORIARTY I at least, like my master the Devil, advocate civility and kindness and a decent evening dress. What is the big novelty about rudeness and dirt and hair all over the body?

P.A. You practise so well what you preach that you almost seduce me—I nearly said 'persuade' me—but in reality nothing is so simple that it can be disposed of as if it were a matter of personal cleanliness. Honesty can be regarded as devoting oneself to speaking the truth. But we have to depend on our senses to keep us correctly informed and to teach our children the truth—assuming that they want to know it. Although Moriarty is a figment of the imagination—

MORIARTY So is your god.

P.A. I haven't one. I am not opposed to the idea, but nor do I favour it—I am impartial.

MORIARTY I was about to congratulate you on your impartiality when you took the words out of my mouth.

ALICE Sarcastic fool—devil, I mean.

MORIARTY Do you? Or are you just meaning to be rude? What did she mean, P.A.?

P.A. I think she is afraid of being fascinated by you. *I* was, and I bet Bion was too during his 'Search the Scriptures'; so was Conan Doyle.

ALICE Conan Doyle was only a writer and Moriarty a figment of his imagination.

P.A. Exactly; but you are afraid that if Moriarty fascinated you, you might become a writer of detective fiction; or even influence a baby inside you to 'get born' so that it might be a criminal who fascinated you—indeed *the* criminal that fascinated you.

ROBIN Is that what Bion means by phenomenes?

BION I think it convenient to have such a term. This episode to which you refer could be an example; if Alice was fascinated by a well-behaved, civil crook, that idea could be propagated and influence the growth or development of the 'character' inside her.

ROLAND You are being very fanciful!

BION Fancy? Or fact? Just fancy, if there was something about ideas which might make them 'generative'! The transmission of ideas may not follow the biological laws of sex, or the Mendelian laws of inheritance. Alice may fear—to resort to biological analogy and metaphor—the movement of a 'phenomene' in her mind. When an 'idea' is created, there is, in addition to the actual creation, a series of reactions to the created idea.

PRIEST Gerard Manley Hopkins strove to express an awareness both of a sense of being ideationally or artistically pregnant, and of the reaction, the counter-actions, to that activity. He believed this applied whatever role he played. He might identify himself with the poet that he himself was, or with the priest who hated and feared the fetus, or the poet who feared the priestly fetus. He seemed to be well aware of murderous envy which is born when the envied idea or person is born. Where? Who knows? The only certain thing is, *somewhere*.

P.A. You talk about envy in a way that I would expect to hear from one of my colleagues—or even from one of your colleagues predicting the birth of the Messiah. I do not restrict these expectations of a messiah or of envy and hatred to any profession. I am familiar with expectations, even announcements, of the existence of a saviour. Sometimes it is a military saviour; sometimes a scientist who is going to make the world safe for mental defectives of one kind or another. Heaven will presumably then consist of boobies and a number of angel nurses who will save the boobies from liquidation.

MORIARTY That Great and Good Man Adolph Hitler has not been assessed at his true value.

ALICE You are a swine. I don't like saying so, and hitherto I have been saved the necessity by the fact that you are a figment of the imagination.

P.A. I think you may in future have to have a great deal of respect for figments of imagination and take them seriously. I could draw up a considerable list of Saviours of the Nation; for example, Hindenburg, Sir John French, Henry V.

ALICE But surely some of them were good men? Or do you want to suggest that none was?

P.A. I understand your unease. Mine is perhaps even greater because I am convinced that all the men and women I have ever known have some good in them. Conversely, probably all had some bad. Let me say at once that I am aware of the utter banality of that conclusion, but that this is one reason why I do not wish to regard it as a *conclusion*. I am sometimes consoled by the possibility that the goodness, the capacity for love and concern for our fellows may be a greater force than hate.

ROLAND Possibly. But don't you think it pathetic that when Science and its brood of astronomers leads unmistakably to the discovery of our insignificance in contrast with these gigantic forces—novae, super novae, black holes and the rest—someone is sure to apply a mental first-aid dressing and hurl us back into the downy comfort of ignorance. Doesn't that depress you?

P.A. No. Down serves the fledgling; mental down preserves us, however praise- or blameworthy we may be. The fact that the blackness and absolute cold lies beyond the charming blue of a summer sky does not make the blue less lovely to me. The vast incomprehensibility of the Absolute surrounding me is not so biting as a tooth-ache. I have not begun to cope with the fear of tooth-ache, whereas God and Devil do not even make my flesh creep.

MORIARTY Splendid! Splendid! Allow me to congratulate you on your perspicacity and courage. *Carpe diem* say I. A good ghoulish murder is worth all the rest of Priest's high-falutin' nonsense—as any reader of the more sensational parts of a newspaper knows. Even Priest knows better than to cut all the spicier bits of the Bible from Sunday reading. 'Search the Scriptures' indeed! Why *not*? Instead of that you humbugs search the quotations! No wonder life—real life—doesn't seem worth living. You priests and doctors, and now psycho-analysts, would have made some pretty vile sadistic monsters if you had not been so afraid of your imaginations and the figments to which they would have given birth.

PRIEST Do you suppose we don't know that?

P.A. We advocate knowledge of what we are really like—in so far as we can. But we do not thereby close the options. On the contrary; the options that are there, whether we like them or not, remain open. The patient, who may not have had the knowledge, cannot be regarded as making a truly moral judgement—as he can if he re-views his opportunities when more mature. We do not even know what our nature—bodily, mental, spiritual—is capable of doing. We can hardly, therefore, regard ourselves as responsible in any true sense.

ROBIN Real human beings are usually so difficult to believe in that we have to be introduced to them, gently, by the medium of the figments of imaginative genius.

P.A. Even so, we do not want to be reminded of our selves.

PRIEST We may want to remind *others* of something they would rather forget; they fear they might not be able to survive the shock of the reminder. Hell is feared—by some.

P.A. I know people who do not need to be told that the kingdom of Hell is within them.

ROLAND If they do not need to be told, what do you psycho-analysts tell them?

P.A. What *they* tell *me* may remind me of something relevant to what they are saying which is not clear to them.

ALICE Suppose, while I am pregnant, I have some disturbing news. Would this affect the fetus?

P.A. It would surprise me if it did not. I do not restrict 'news' to information conveyed to the mother by relatives or books or newspapers. Suppose you had been brought up in ignorance of the physical facts of sex either by the folly of your authorities, or through your unwillingness to learn; then you became aware of being pregnant. The information, from the fetus or your body, might be unwelcome—'bad news'. The waves of pressure communicated through the amniotic fluid would form a different pattern from those usual in a mother pregnant with a fetus she wanted from a man by whom she wanted it. The fact that there is no demonstrable communication between mother and fetus as clear as that between mother and baby is not an adequate reason for asserting that there isn't one. I expect unbelievers to state the 'facts' on which their 'unbelief' rests.

ROLAND The facts on which *my* unbelief rests are the multitudinous and multiform theories of psycho-analysis itself. I do not become more confident in a doctor's ability the greater the number of theories he expresses about a pain in my thumb. I prefer him to hold his tongue until he is able to tell me precisely what to do about it. When a psycho-analyst produces more and more erudite explanations about why I believe or think as I do the more impatient I feel.

P.A. Then go to another psycho-analyst or doctor. I do not believe that you or Alice are asking me questions for nothing; *why* you are asking these questions is no business of mine—though I may have my suspicions.

ALICE Would you tell me what to do?

P.A. If I thought there was anything you could *do*—in the sense that you mean it—I would advise you to go to someone who *does* things. Experience has taught me that there are many things which need to have something *done* about them; they first need to be discussed. The fact that the British believe in *parliamentary* government is evidence that this has at least been unconsciously recognized. It is absurd to condemn those who believe that 'discussion' is a way of doing things; 'talk' is not a substitute for action.

ROBIN But you don't think it is disastrous when action, say, war, is required and people prefer to talk in the hope that the problem will go away or be solved if they talk long enough?

P.A. Yes, but it is just as serious if people, rather than face the pains and frustrations of talk, fall back on murder or war as a substitute for discussion, Similarly, the individual may feel that drugs or self-murder are preferable to the tedious discipline of analysis; they are seductively shorter.

ROLAND It is sometimes seductively less painful to talk than to undergo a physical operation.

P.A. Seductive possibilities, concealed in the wide range of options available, will ultimately compel the growth of a capacity for discrimination—or catastrophe.

ROBIN Why catastrophe?

P.A. Because unless the human animal learns to become expert in discrimination, he will be in imminent danger of the *wrong* choice.

ALICE Nuclear war, for example.

P.A. There are no labels attached to most options; there is no substitute for the growth of wisdom. Wisdom or oblivion—take your choice. From that warfare there is no release.

A *I see you turn to the last page as you always used to do.*

Q *Of course. Last time you told me how much it had cost you to publish. Did you find it interesting? How was America—North and South?*

A *Marvellous; a nice change from the Third Battle of Wipers.*

Q *Lots more since then. And more to come—which reminds me; I must rush; I have a date to meet Fate.*

A *Bye-bye—happy holocaust!*

. . . & EPILOGUE

. . . FUGUE

. . . DONA ES REQUIEM

. . . MANY

All my life I have been imprisoned, frustrated, dogged by common-sense, reason, memories, desires and—greatest bug-bear of all—understanding and being understood. This is an attempt to express my rebellion, to say 'Good-bye' to all that. It is my wish, I now realize doomed to failure, to write a book unspoiled by any tincture of common-sense, reason, etc. (see above). So although I would write, 'Abandon Hope all ye who expect to find any facts—scientific, aesthetic or religious—in this book', I cannot claim to have succeeded. All these will, I fear, be seen to have left their traces, vestiges, ghosts hidden within these words; even sanity, like 'cheerfulness', will creep in. However successful my attempt, there would always be the risk that the book 'became' acceptable, respectable, honoured and unread. 'Why write then?' you may ask. To prevent someone who KNOWS from filling the empty space—but I fear I am being 'reasonable', that great Ape. Wishing you all a Happy Lunacy and a Relativistic Fission. . . .

A Key

Compiled by
W. R. Bion and F. Bion

Chapter numbers are preceded by I, II or III, indicating:

Book I	The Dream
Book II	The Past Presented
Book III	The Dawn of Oblivion

AVE . . .

F *Are you there?*

W *You have woke me too soon, I must—*

F *Oh, do get a move on—we shall never finish this index at this rate—three pages an hour! It's endless—*

W *It's very hard work—and whenever am I going to get any writing done?*

F *This* is *writing*—and *a necessary part of the trilogy.*

W *I hate having to examine my own vomit.*

F *All right—let me know when you have a free hour and the inclination—*

W *I never have. Let's get on with it—*

F *I can arrange my schedule to suit you—*

W *For Christ's sake let's get the ruddy thing done now!*

F *It's no good trying to do it if you are in a bad temper. I shall do some gardening.*

A

there are any absentees; an English public (i.e. private) school custom. II.19

adulation as a method of silencing the generator of unwelcome trains of thought. II.1

Aeneas hero of the ILIAD. I.13

Aesthetic as universal linguistic. II.1, II.2

aesthetic mathematical formulation as analogue of poetic creation. II.1

Agamemnon and religion. II.9
husband of *Clytemnestra*; murdered by his wife. II.11
see Horace, ODE TO LOLLIUS. I.11, I.13; II.3, II.19

Aguecheek, Sir Andrew *Shakespeare,* TWELFTH NIGHT. III.5

Alexander SPACE, TIME, DEITY. I.38; III.9

algebraic deductive systems. I.28
geometry, and development of projective geometry. III.14

Alice 'a fabulous monster', ALICE IN WONDERLAND. I.PRO
and bad night. I.PRO
and *Lewis Carroll.* II.7
and *Rosemary,* symbols of master and mistress; cf. arbitrium. I.15
dreams of imperial honour and maid *Rosemary.* I.1
wealthy background. I.3
wish to help *Rosemary.* I.2

alimentary canal bad night and dream. I.PRO
and telescopic view. I.PRO

alimentary canals brains like. III.3

ali-metric word invented to describe hunger as making the passage of time explicit. II.14

Allah Akbar [*see* **God, Godhead**]. I.38

all-alone [*see* **dependent**]. II.16

All change! call used on British railways to warn passengers that they have arrived at a railway junction where it is necessary to mount another train. II.19

all-conquering Implicit in the idea, expressed by *Rosemary* referring to the chocolate bar which has intimidated the rest of the group, is the psychological experience of the all-conquering dominance of sight *vis-à-vis* the other senses. I.39

Allen war reminiscence; dream or breakthrough of imperfectly verbalized feelings. I.12

All-mighty omnipotence as mental archaism still active. I.9

α ref. *Bion,* THE GRID. I.13

α **and** *β* [*see also* **'trick'**]. I.39

Alpha a communicable shorthand for something which is not, and is not like, but is becoming [*see* **Beta**]. I.14

Alps as minor preparation for Himalayas. II.1

All Souls an Oxford college founded as a memorial to British dead in the battle of Agincourt in 1415. I.27

'All's right with the world' state of optimism described by *Browning* in PIPPA PASSES; also as a sarcastic comment on the optimism of German philosophy by *Voltaire* through *Pangloss* in CANDIDE. II.1

All toes pun linking dancing with singing (altos). II.19

Amiens-Roye road road running in the direction of the advance of the First French and Fourth British Armies on 8 August 1918. II.2

amplifier mechanical means used to magnify a sound which might otherwise be unnoticed; used metaphorically. I.43

anachronism The ordinary calendar or other measure of time is good enough for conversation but not adequate for psycho-analysis. I.34

anal eroticism seems to me to cover an activity which is pre-verbal. There is gynaecological evidence for the evacuation by the fetus of meconium. It provokes in my mind the possibility that evacuation could be one of the earliest active functions of the physical body. This being so, it may be the counterpart of a primordial 'thinking'. This primitive activity, to which *Melanie Klein* appears to relate what she was aware of, is matched by my own experience. Evacuation could thus be indistinguishable from 'blotting out', i.e. making opaque, an area of the mind. I.40

analogue link between two objects which are usually specified. Here the emphasis is on the link and not on the two objects to which it is 'moored'. I.44

analogy as link between two objects, not the objects. I.16; II.2

anarchs ref. *Shelley*, HELLAS. I.34; II.1

Anatole France quotation from LA REINE PEDAUQUE. II.4

angels common to many religions. Is it a pointer to a basic reality, or a cover for 'nothingness'? I.26

angry Anger is one of the emotions that is so obtrusive that it can be given a recognizable name in any individual life. Its detection can often be used to arouse guilt in the angry person. II.20

angstrom units used in measurement of light waves. I.34

animate contrasted with *inanimate* for which there is no adequate definition. I.30

answers popular journal of that name typical of the facile search for substitutes for truth. II.1

anus as analogical link. I.16

anxiety Herodic, and infanticide. I.10

Apparition spoken of by *Rosemary* as personified in poetry and fiction. II.17

apparitions and hallucinations, claimed to have a health-preservative function if acknowledged by the person who experiences them. II.17

Arab Lady described by *Yeats* as lying with *Solomon*. II.2

archetype term used by *Jung*. II.19

AREOPAGITICA *Milton*, SPEECH FOR THE LIBERTY OF UNLICENSED PRINTING. III.9

arf childhood version of 'Our Father . . .', THE LORD'S PRAYER. I.11, I.12, I.13, I.16

Aristarchus thinker who contributed to train of thought that led to modern astronomy [*see* **Palomar** and **Jodrell Bank**]. II.3, II.19

his helicocentric hypotheses used as models of the mind. I.30

aristocrat In fact the murderer was an ordinary businessman who had never been known to depart from respectability. The assault he made could not be described in terms of 'human conduct'; it is typical of an accredited fact which would not be believed if reported in a work of fiction. II.10

Aristotle and a practical world. III.3

Arjuna criticizes, and criticized by, God. I.17

quoted by BAGHAVAD GITA. I.16, I.34; II.20

presumption of [*see* **uncertainty principle**]. I.43

arrogance expressed by music or anatomical posture. I.17

arsenic poison discredited in use for murder because of its capacity for preserving the evidence of the crime. II.14

arse 'oles One school caused a Protestant hymn to be unusable by pronouncing 'Our souls' in an irreligious manner. I.15; II.19

artefacts used in the sense of facts whose source, origin and creator is a human mind. It could be debated whether it is equally applicable to animals other than human. II.2

articulate articulated language contrasted with hieroglyphic. I.43

'articulate' communication dominant method of, between the self and the self. I.43

articulation as a method of putting words together to construct an 'architectonic'; this is analogous to the use of materials in architecture to construct a building. I.38

artificial Analysis is artificial, but is an attempt to approach a basic reality. II.9

artisan as 'respect-worthy'. I.30

artist differentiated from scientific detection. I.20

artistic Whether a scientist or a painter, composer, the person to whom this book is addressed is assumed to be driven by an urge to the truth. I cannot conceive of a drive to untruth as being separable from what is evil. II.7

art nouveau Art has never been new, although the current method of communication conforms to changing fashions. The thing itself—painting, sculpture, mathematics etc.—is unchanging even though its method of communication changes. II.9.

asses a reference to *Omar Khayyam,* RUBAIYAT: 'The wild ass stamps o'er his head', *Fitzgerald* translation. I.PRO

asthma relationship to personality. I.22

astronomers their discoveries are unlikely at present to cause panic. Any scientific work is liable to be resented if it exposes human beings to dread. II.5

Athanasian Creed exact, elaborate Catholic statement of the Trinity and the Incarnation, no longer believed to be by Saint Athanasius. I.39

athletic dominance an early form of dominance fairly easily established in the rivalry of games [*see* **pits**]. II.1

Attlee, Clement British prime minister succeeding *Winston Churchill* after World War II. II.1

audiences *P.A.* draws attention to the fact that a communication is dependent on there being a receptor. II.11

auditory apparatus comprehensive term used to describe everything from auditory pits to ears and their accompanying sensory extension, and finally to mechanical aids, including radio. I.26

August 8 August 1918, Battle of Amiens, described by *Ludendorff* as 'a black day for the German Army'. It was delivered by the

B

cerned in the survival of terms like 'rhinencephalon'. These 'survivals' should be regarded with respect by psycho-analysts concerned with patients who are sensitive about their noses and their watery productions. Even physiologically there are traces in the 'extra-cellular fluid' unpolluted by salt and other chemicals, as are the oceans. Only psycho-analytical observation is likely to unveil the relationship between post-natal and pre-natal mentation. II.1

representing the physiological source of what at a later stage could be expressed verbally; ref. *Gray,* ELEGY WRITTEN IN A COUNTRY CHURCHYARD. II.4

blushing invisible yet intolerable [*see* **self-murder, suicide**]. I.11

body-ache [*see* **blush**]. II.1

books as the repository of metal activity that is irrelevant to the present and the future. II.19

bomb atomic. I.14, I.23

bored This word is often used for a feeling which is unmistakable, but which is nevertheless difficult to analyse. The emotion itself is ambiguous and complex. Like 'love', it is often facetiously or carelessly used, but the analyst cannot afford to ignore the reality which transcends both words. I.42

borogroves *Lewis Carroll,* THROUGH THE LOOKING GLASS. II.14

boundary physical, used as anatomy of metal boundaries. I.17

bounds physical boundaries, to be distinguished from mental. II.18

brain convolutions of. I.30

damage and genesis in war. I.21

brains like alimentary canals. III.3

brain washing fashions in nomenclature. III.8

Braughing House social significance contrasted with brutal helplessness. I.6

brave supposed to have a basis in reality; frequently emphasized by honours and decorations intended to give substance and reality to what otherwise might pass unnoticed—if it exists. I.32

bravery cover for cowardice. I.14

Bray, Vicar of well-known English song about a character notorious for changes of opinion according to self interest. II.12

break-down Words borrowed from special direction are often combined and liable to lose their significance in combination.

C

represented throughout by a line thus: memory/desire. This indicates that a change is taking place when the thing represented by the two words is a dynamic change from the one state of mind to the other without showing the direction of the change. As in the example, memory relates to the past state; desire is the present or future state. Day-dream/dream: in this context day-dream/ is a different state of mind from /dream. That is to say, the 'state of mind' when asleep and dreaming differs from the 'state of mind' when fully conscious. In short, the 'state of mind' is the transcendent significance.

used as a screen on which can be projected the explicit/implicit. I.35

Cain name used to brand a quality of mind. I.17

Campbell, Roy English poet, 1901–1957. II.14

Cambrai 20 November 1917; a battle in which tanks were used to effect a surprise on the German army. The surprise was so successful that the British, like the Germans, almost failed to recover. I.32

canals of Mars. I.41

cancer an example of unwillingness to make discoveries. I.22

cannibal and blackguard, used anachronistically. I.34

and mental cannibalism. I.35

cannibalism and blood drinking; ritualistic, imaginary or factual? I.27

primordial, self-devouring. I.26

capacity development of awareness. I.22

Cap'n 'art tha sleepin' there below?' *Newbolt,* DRAKES'S DRUM. Compare *Palinurus*. I.9, I.21

Carnarvon, Lord and *Howard Carter*; their combined efforts led to the discovery of the tomb of Tutankhamun. II.10

Carroll, Lewis Not only is there a devaluation and debasement of words which could still have a useful value, but this could also apply to entertaining and valuable stories such as ALICE IN WONDERLAND. They can suffer by being regarded as children's books hardly worthy of adult attention until they reach a point where they become the victims of 'psycho-analytic' interpretation. The vogue for prestigious, scientific erudition can undermine the original value without adding any illumination whatsoever. II.7

carte blanche used as a metaphor for freedom of thought. II.4

D

dandelions sexual and vegetative reproduction. II.17
Dante and direct experience of the mortal being. II.19
daring and stupidity. III.8
darkness not to be considered negatively as an absence of light, but as a function of light. I.39
dawn The reference is to a popular theory about sleep. It is also supposed to be the time when the individual passing from a state of sleep to a state of wakefulness is assailed by irrational and frightening thoughts and feelings. II.10
'day of his coming'; dies illa, dies irae. II.14, II.19
daylight associated with safety. Darkness is regarded as safer if 'heavenly'. I.13
dead quite; cf. the religious view of the life after death. II.16
Roland presumed to have suffered physiological death. II.16
unconscious equated with somatic pattern. I.14
used to describe a language no longer in everyday use. II.19
deafening The threshold of sound varies enormously according to the individual. In psycho-analysis the analysand may talk in such a way that the analyst's interpretations appear to be lost. Therefore the analyst needs to adhere to the volume of sound which he is able to maintain during his day's work; engagement in a shouting match does not help. II.19
death and freedom. I.8
as the price which may be paid for decisions made by men or women. I.38
assumed and threatened. I.3
like birth, always exciting comment. II.19
quoted for its prominent role in the minds of the living. II.15
death pit Cadavers ultimately provide a record for archaeologists to interpret scientifically. I.27
of Ur. I.8; II.8
debris remnants of ideas acquired that are no longer of service. II.19
decapitation as an example of violent separation. This is similar to the splitting involved in 'evacuation' of projective identification; it is also related to *Freud's* and *Breuer's* tentative trial of catharsis. II.2
decay warmth generated by, as a condition for breeding. III.8
deception and lying. I.10
decision involves choosing and inhibiting. III.9

Duncan character in *Shakespeare's* MACBETH. II.19
dust galactic, thought to obscure the galactic centre from earth inhabitants. II.2
Duty Sense of, *Priest's* reply to 'sense or non-sense'? II.4
dwarfs white, likened to compact objects in mental space. I.8

E

eclogue a pastoral poem. *P.A.* refers to *Virgil's* Fourth, and discussion follows. II.11
Edmund representing an astronomical vertex. II.1
education educated love indistinguishable from shop-soiled. I.8
Egyptians and animal containers; reference to the deification of the cat. III.2
ejaculation an ambiguous word biologically often referring to sudden evacuation of anything from 'sensuous phenomena' to the function of disruption of a train of thought. The source of such intrusion is likened to destroying a painting. I.40
elaboration of instruments to reveal facts. I.22
electron microscope, and radio telescope as instruments to aid observation. I.30
elements constant conjunction of. I.21
Elephantine caves, on the island of Elephanta near Bombay, in which various aspects of Siva are depicted by carvings from solid rock. III.9
Ellis, Havelock contributed to the knowledge of *Krafft-Ebing's* PSYCHOPATHIA SEXUALIS and of *Freud* who was scarcely known in England before 1918. II.10
Elizabeth of Bohemia the transience of fame typified when applied to beautiful women. II.2
Elohistic code conflict between two streams of thought [*see* **Priestly code**]. II.1
embryonic sense related to non-sensuous thought. I.11
Empire empery founded on violence. I.38
emotions pre-natal, displayed by patients in analysis. III.12
Emerson as a philosopher. II.18
end used as if it were a sense organ. I.24
English inadequate for psycho-analysis. I.24
P.A. is referring to conversational English and the belief of

F

G

Gomer concubine of the prophet *Hosea*. II.18

good girl rewarded by the prospect of jollity. II.19

goodness The attempt to focus on the goodness of God contributes to blindness to the qualities of the world in which we live. II.9

good report sarcastic reference to a school aspiration. II.10

googly cricket term describing a particularly deceptive spin imparted to the ball by the bowler. II.19

grammar system of rules. I.20

Great is the Truth originally, 'For great is truth and shall prevail', *Thomas Brooks,* THE CROWN AND GLORY OF CHRISTIANITY. III.12

greed mental. III.9

greedy soul [*see* **glittering prizes**]. II.3

Greeks used to represent the educational model. I.17

Green, André his book, UN OEIL EN TROP. III.9
 perspicuous nature of the dramatic art form pointed out. III.9

Griffiths, D. W. producer of spectacular films. I.23

grin [*see* **Cheshire Cat**]. I.14

gross words cunt and prick. I.16
 discussed. III.6, III.7
 guilty response to. III.7
 language of the id. III.7
 primitive reserves of vitality tapped. III.7
 universally comprehended. III.6, III.7

group as a vertex from which observations can be made similar to a 'macroscopic' examination. This is contrasted with psycho-analysis of the 'individual' which, in its detail, resembles a 'microscopic' scrutiny. I.38
 term borrowed from mathematics. The implications of the problem seen from a mathematical vertex have been described by *Ignacio Matte Blanco* in THE UNCONSCIOUS AS INFINITE SETS. That exploration can be so difficult as to be forbidding; it is evocative and rewarding. The difficulty is not different from that confronting anyone who embarks on the discipline of a psycho-analysis [*see* **set theory**]. I.42

group analysis and psycho-analysis; possible relationship discussed. III.11

groups Disciplined groups, such as armies and their leaders, can in certain circumstances succumb to the pressure of intense and

H

J

Jodrell Bank the site of a radio telescope in England. II.1
JOHN BULL a disreputable journal published by *Horatio Bottomley*; notorious amongst the troops in World War I in a song parodying its prognostications. II.19
joke cruel. I.16
kind and loving. I.11
journey end of; part of a bawdy song sung by the troops in World War I. II.2
Joyce, James compared with sculptors in stone, *Michelangelo* and *Moore*. I.11
his illuminating use of 'idées mères'. I.41, I.43
Jung nomenclature of, contrasted with *Freud's*. II.19
juvenile nonsense the contemptuous reference to psycho-analytic theory and outlook contrasted with the new version of old male dominance. II.19

K

K minus and plus, assume a linear model for conveying lack or otherwise of experience. I.33, I.34
Kant 'concepts without intuition are empty . . .', CRITIQUE OF PURE REASON. I.8, I.39, I.40, I.41
'thing-in-itself', CRITIQUE OF PURE REASON. I.PRO
Karno sarcastic reference by the men of Kitchener's Army, sung to the tune of the hymn, THE CHURCH'S ONE FOUNDATION. II.2
Keats 'Beauty is truth, truth beauty', ODE ON A GRECIAN URN. II.12
used the term 'negative capability' in a letter to his brother. I.43
Kenner, Hugh [*see* ***Ruskin***]. II.2
kicking off a ludicrous ritual, often observed, in which the wife of some highly-decorated authority initiates a regimental event. I.23
killed in action. I.22
killing and war. I.17
Kingdom of Heaven; used from historically early times to describe the existence of internal objects. II.19
Kipling, Rudyard parody of *Horace's* ODES. I.17
was obsessed by a school friend whom he described as 'Stalky'. II.19

L

Lesbia *see* poems by *Catullus*. II.15

L'Estrade the police detective in the MEMOIRS OF SHERLOCK HOLMES. I.28

Lethe the river of forgetfulness in Hades, used as a soporific drug by the god *Somnus*. I.28

Leviathan aquatic monster, described in the BOOK OF JOB, OLD TESTAMENT. I.9

liar *Rosemary's* disillusion leads her to assume that there is nothing but illusions deliberately created. To what extent the human being is capable of assessing what is a fact has always been a matter of doubt, but psycho-analysis helps to expose the doubtful nature of many 'facts' assumed to be true. Dis-illusionment is frequently accompanied by the unpleasant emotion of disillusionment; there needs to be a method by which dis-illusionment could be differentiated from disillusionment. Words are therefore of great importance to clear thinking, but they need to be correctly attached to the 'real' thing. II.7

liars heroic; quoted as a parody of *Horace's* ODE TO LOLLIUS. I.28

lie simulation of truth. I.11

lies and deceptions. I.28

Lies indistinguishable from Truth. I.11

Light Heavenly, described by *Milton* in PARADISE LOST, BOOK III. II.5, II.12

Lilith Jewish female demon. The reference here is to the legend of *Lilith* as the wife of Adam. It is worth comparing to the story told by *Colette* (and the opera by Ravel), L'ENFANT ET LES SORTILÈGES. II.18

representative of primordial thought. I.17

limits What are the borders which have temporarily to be established as the confines within which a discussion is to take place? I.42

linear co-ordinates use of, in the formulation of narrative. I.39

link Sometimes the word is used to express the conventional function and is then coloured by the context in which it is used, e.g. *Alice* married *Roland*. At others it has to be interpreted in the context of all that has been told the analyst. At other times the interpretation depends upon the context, which the analyst can see for himself, in the conversation; at others, it has to be interpreted in the context of the analysand's hopes, expectations and forebodings. I.41

loyalty to truth, as the aim of and criterion for validation of the products. II.12

£.s.d. and L.S.D. The pun as a compact free association, dispersed as in these pages, is assumed to have a meaning when 'interpreted'. I.29

Ludendorff supposed to be the strategical mind governing *Hindenburg*. II.7

lunar illustration as an example of the problem of the differentiation of unthinking obedience from disciplined thought. I.30

Luria, Isaac sixteenth-century Jewish cabalist and mystic. II.2

lust-crazed lust as conducive to the destruction of clear thought. II.18

M

M31 Andromeda nebula, used to exemplify. I.43; II.1, II.2

macroscopic used to contrast 'the general' from 'the specific'. I.41
vertex [*see* **microscopic**]. I.29

mad loosely used to express a state of mind that is feared. II.18

mademoiselle part of a soldiers' song of World War I. II.4

Maginot a line of fortification on which France depended for its safety. I.14

MAID OF THE MOUNTAIN stage musical. I.17

♀ In what way does this symbol differ from the word 'male'? This is typical of the problem confronting the analyst where he has to consider that what he hears said by the analysand should be interpreted in a psycho-analytically correct manner. Usually it is safe to assume that the patient is aware of the conscious meaning of what he says, his problem being to know what is the 'over-interpretation' that requires to be discussed. But in practice it matters whether it is 'over', 'under', 'ironic', 'punning' etc. [*see also* ♂]. I.41

Mammon and God. I.8

Man a character made prominent by *Rosemary* analogous to an inanimate object made prominent by the invitation to discuss. *passim*
his scorn of English hypocrisy. I.24
memoirs of. I.28

N

O

P

in Greece by the Arabs. Psycho-analysis today is carrying on from origins which were philosophical, religious and even athletic. II.16

plausible theories and fictitious constructions. I.37

play the playing of games as a prelude to making the thing 'played at' explicit; 'real' as a description of the quality of a thought or idea which has been made explicit by transformation into action. I.36

playing The practice of psycho-analysis has given a new dimension to the understanding of the play of children. The ability to 'understand' has to be extended to cover the significance and meaning of adult 'games'. The ability to regard psycho-analysis as one of these adult 'games' can aid in the comprehension of what is going on when two people are engaged in what is nowadays known as psycho-analysis. II.7

pleasure, sensuous ignorance of. I.3

+ mathematical symbol borrowed for purposes of indicating 'the couple' which is the biological unit in the case of living objects which depend on mating for genesis. I.43

PNS/CNS peripheral nervous system/central nervous system [*see* **phrenes**]. I.36

poetry a disciplined method of communication in the shortest possible terms known to the serious thinkers. II.1

Poincaré and mathematical beauty. I.28

THE FOUNDATIONS OF SCIENCE. I.21

'poison gas' [*see* **flatus**]. I.26

Poisson distribution statistical concept. I.39, I.40

Poisson's Law remains of archaic survival of 'embryological mentality' likened to. I.8

poles of confusion, as represented by the printed page. I.19

police The patient who resorts to violence forces the analyst to seek auxiliary aid; the consequent disruption of the conditions of his work has to be allowed for. II.19

polymorphous-perverse psychiatric technical term. II.14

Pontius Pilate a famous handwasher, now enshrined in literature. I.27

Pooter, Mister a fictitious character in THE DIARY OF A NOBODY by *George Grossman*. I.20

Popsy nickname for an officer training cadet. II.4

precise contrasted with 'conversational' speech. I.42

preconception a word that might be useful to describe something not yet conceived; also a mind of a creature before conception. II.14

pre-conception The word 'conception' is often ambiguous; the context has to be relied upon to resolve the ambiguity. II.18

premonitions related to omnipotence. I.11

pre-natal and post-natal personalities; their coming together is a danger in psycho-analysis. III.10, III.11

pre-natal ↔ post-natal two-way relationship. III.12

present unobserved. I.4

pretend the ability to stimulate belief in the pretender's experience. I.24

pretty prettiness as a weapon used to humiliate. I.24

prick as a gross word. I.16

prides companies of lions etc. I.27

Priestly Code detectable in the OLD TESTAMENT. In the 51ST PSALM there are signs which may indicate the struggle between two states of mind. In psycho-analysis these usually appear as conflicts between the profession pursued for the sake of gain and the more God-oriented motives. II.1, II.2

priests of Ur. I.28

primal scene cruel version. I.4

Prime's Field schoolboy reminiscence. III.2

Prince the name of a cart-horse; boyhood reminiscence. II.4

prize a sarcastic reference to the alleged freedom of life in England. II.19

probability all theories of, are inseparable from an awareness of improbability. II.7

Procrustean In Greek mythology *Procrustes* was a highwayman who forced passers-by to fit one of two beds by cruel methods. I.9

profits financial, of psycho-analysis. I.27

progress and direction. III.8
  conditions propitious to. III.8

projection 'algebraic projective geometry' as a soothing term. I.20
  shadows unprojected. I.8

projective identification presumed to imply domains of thought not at the time explicit. I.37
  resentment at being the receiver. I.18

psycho-analysts and doctors and surgeons, exposed to comparable stresses. III.9

psycho-analytic investigation and teaching, compared with problems of the religious. II.18

psycho-analytical conversation and social conversation; important distinction. III.11

psycho-analytical experience untoward effect of. I.24

psycho-analytical theories possible use of, to support any activity. III.11

Psycho-flim-flam contemptuous reference to psycho-analysis. It is a typical hostile comment on an activity likely to disturb existing modes of thought. II.4

psycho-somatic and soma-psychotic, partners in the same physical soma. III.7, III.12

Public School in England open to 'all' if wealthy enough. I.15

Puckeridge a Hertfordshire village near Standon on the Road from Bishops Stortford to the North. II.4

pulsations rhythmic marching beat. I.23

punning typical of a state of mind. II.4; III.6

Purgatory used as a time or place for discarding meaningless accretions. II.14

pussy and grin. I.14

Pyrrha a character in *Horace's* FIFTH ODE on very unsentimental views of men. I.31; II.19

Pythagoras theorem of. I.30

Q

Q.E.D. quod erat demonstrandum; used to signalize the conclusion of the discussion. I.28

quackery derived from an animal noise, now contrasted with truth. I.14

quack-quack German machine-guns were superior by virtue of their slow rate of fire. The sound was believed to be more like the quacking of a duck than the nervous chattering of the Lewis gun. II.4

quanta not suitable to replace wave mechanics. I.39

quantity increase transformed from quantity to quality. I.21, I.22 loudness often contrasted with 'the still small voice'. I.42

+, zero, −: too much, just right, too little. I.14
quantum a discrete particle. I.28
quarters servants'; parts of a house reserved for 'inferiors'. II.7
Queen Mary sometimes known for her 'unqueenly' characteristics. II.15
Quee-Quegg a character in MOBY DICK by *Herman Melville*. I.19
Quentin modern disguise for the name of a soldier who 'broke down' and never recovered. II.6
questionnaire as a method of revealing a pattern. I.22
'Quo Fas et Gloria Ducunt' 'Where duty and glory lead', regimental motto. II.4; III.8
Quoodle 'bright smell of a stone'; incorrect quotation of 'The brave smell of a stone,' *G. K. Chesterton,* THE SONG OF QUOODLE. I.28
'even the smell of roses is not what man supposes, And goodness only knowses the Noselessness of Man'. *G. K. Chesterton,* THE SONG OF QUOODLE. This is an example of 'concretion' [*see* **concrescence**]. I.14
quoth parody of *Poe's* poem, THE RAVEN: 'Quoth the Raven, "Nevermore".' II.6

R

rack reference to *Shakespeare's* description in THE TEMPEST of the ephemeral nature of man's imagination. II.3
radiant term borrowed from mathematics. I.42
radiographers inaccurate without computer aid. I.28
rage *Alice's* loss of self control. I.3
and pleasure. I.20
ragged colloquial for 'teased'. I.15
ram caught in a thicket; an archaeological find at Ur of the Chaldees. I.8
random the supposition that chance might have 'laws' of its own and that 'logic' as it is known is a symptom of the limitations of the human mind and not a quality of *absolute* law. II.3
rape as cruel love. I.8
rational conforming to rules of human thought. III.7
rational explanation more acceptable than ignorance. III.9
rationalization as logical 'cause'. I.8

Resurrection Blues an alleged dance corresponding to the dancing movements of a fetus before birth. II.19

revelation term often used in a religious context, e.g. REVELATIONS OF ST. JOHN, and the APOCRYPHA. II.11

revenge of past degradation. I.4

reversed perspective and vectors to indicate the direction of the 'reverse'. I.35

In psycho-analysis the analyst's observation must be acute enough to discriminate between metaphors and reversals of perspective. I.33, I.43

R.F. and punning associations. I.8

rhapsodically cf. scientifically precise. III.6

rhythm distinguished from pulsation by its timing. I.23

Rib the small river; a reminiscence of happy days, with the miseries of the muddy trickle of a beck in the Battle of Ypres remaining. II.4

Richthofen celebrated German airman. When he was killed the British dropped a wreath over the German lines. This was a dangerous action, as when a German airman, dropping mail from British war prisoners and carrying a mark indicating that he was not on a combat mission which was not seen by the anti-aircraft gunners, was shot down. I.33

ridiculous a description which can be used to undermine any claim to scientific truth. II.19

Riemann and *Lobachevsky*. I.14

rigour of thought, dependent on destructive criticism. I.20

Rimbaud a French poet whose creative verse was written in a period of mental distress; considered by some people to be insane. He emerged from this into a period of physical travel and did not return to his poetic creations. II.2

ritual and sacramental death, equated with health. I.29

rivalry related to victory, success, triumph and failure—all expressed linearly from plus to minus; dependent on quality of emotion and amount of emotion, but without a scale of measurement. I.37

river 'shall we gather at the ...'; from a revivalist, nonconformist hymn. II.19

road the end of the ..., on a supposed journey to reach certainty. II.19

roaring associated with swelling. If psycho-analysis makes it pos-

with script read from left to right. In psycho-analysis the emergence of that kind of thinking can pass unobserved. II.3

Royal Court impossibility of unearthing archaeologically an archaic state of mind. I.28

ruck and reel *G. M. Hopkins,* THE HABIT OF PERFECTION. I.9

rudimentary brain, possibly related to rudimentary personality. I.18

Ruin Among the Lovers; distorted reference to LOVE AMONG THE RUINS by *George Meredith.* II.14

rules of war; contemptuous reference to war as a game played according to the rules of chivalry. II.19

Ruskin deflected from his true vocation by *Rose la Touche.* II.1
his elucidation of *Milton's* metaphoric communications. II.1
his interpretation of LYCIDAS compared with *Kenner's* interpretation of *Shakespeare.* II.2
on 'reading' without thinking the thought through. II.3
stressed the artist's loyalty to truth. II.1

S

Sade *Alice* and *Rosemary* similar to *Sade v. Masoch.* I.8
Marquis de; his services to cruelty. III.9

Sade* versus *Masoch suggested as a wrestling match by an analysand. I.22

sadism and mocking. I.4

sado- *Rosemary* interrupts *P.A.* before he can articulate a psycho-analytic concept; she expresses indifference for the psycho-analytic approach and for 'thought' as contrasted with material action. II.7

safety dominance of. I.7

Sagittarius supposed direction of galactic centre. II.1

Sahagun, Bernardino sixteenth-century Franciscan missionary in Mexico; on the use of divine attributes for the purposes of ordinary human beings. I.30

'Sail on!' quotation from *Longfellow,* THE BUILDING OF THE SHIP; used in an interchange between *Franklin Roosevelt* and *Winston Churchill.* II.1

tive or obscuring effect on human feelings. II.15
relationship to smoke drums and real life. I.PRO

screens obscuring. III.7
resistant. III.7

sculpture its tangible qualities shown to be extended by what is seen; the difference elaborated between the pattern made by 'light' and the pattern made by the shadow. *Myself* discusses this and its similarity to 'rests' as distinguished from the musical notes. I.39

Search the Scriptures reminiscence of school task set for Sundays. III.13

'seasons return' *Milton,* PARADISE LOST, BOOK III. II.14

Second Army British. The general officer commanding in World War I was famous for his respect for his troops. II.6

SECOND THOUGHTS collected psycho-analytic papers. I.16

secrets *P.A.'s* reference to secrets is a summary of a theory that in psycho-analytic practice thoughts and ideas are made overt, the implicit is made explicit. Whether such a state of affairs is possible and how it could come about might be debated by considering that Euclidean geometry, though different from algebraic projective geometry, nevertheless 'implies' algebraic projective geometry which becomes explicit after *Descartes*. The reader might also consider the ideals of psycho-analysis; the aims of *President Wilson* with regard to international covenants being openly arrived at; and the present-day debate of the scientific exposure of secrets which some think should have been kept unavailable to potential enemies. II.8

seduction in love with. II.16
word used as one extreme of a linear progression from sexual love to sexual hate. I.43

See punning use. II.1

seeing an instance of the psychotic ability to transfer impressions of hearing to impressions of sight. I.26

seepage of the content of one idea into another idea. I.16

self-control lack of. I.3

self-destruction its counterpart in ideas and feelings. I.14

self-murder Psycho-analytic work has revealed—although it has long been a common-place observation—that the patient can, by a series of minute steps, achieve the destruction of all that makes life worth living without resorting to the destruction of life itself by murder or self-murder. II.8

'Self-yeast of spirit . . .' *Gerard Manley Hopkins,* POEM 67, (untitled, 4th edition, Oxford University Press). III.10

semantic term applicable to discussion of articulate speech, but often, as with 'logic', spoken of as if applicable to cosmic space. II.4

semen as accompanied with venereal disease. II.16

sense ambiguity of 'sense'. I.21

sensual scale of sensuous experience; the problem of stating in scalar terms 'where' the 'diaphragm' separating conscious from unconscious is to be located when there is no scale. I.13

sensuous impressions [*see* **desires**]. II.9

sentence reference to an old school-masterly joke about a student's description of *Agag's* punishment when he was hewn in pieces. II.19

sentential calculus psychologists' exploration. II.1

'sermons in stones' *Shakespeare,* AS YOU LIKE IT. III.8

Serpent OLD TESTAMENT, GENESIS III.15. III.1

set theory The mathematical theories have recently been worked on in a very suggestive and disciplined manner by *Ignacio Matte Blanco.* This sophisticated approach appears to illuminate many of the events and episodes with which I am familiar when using psycho-analysis to investigate the personality. This is particularly illuminating with regard to thoughts and ideas which have never been conscious, e.g. vestigial remains of what appear to be primordial 'thinking' even before birth. If this conjecture is correct it may open up a revision of the relationship between 'states of mind' when awake, conscious and rational, and 'states of mind' when asleep; in particular, reports made by a fully conscious and alert being about what he says is a dream and, conversely, the relationship between the 'sleeper' or unborn personality and facts (so-called by the scientists) which make themselves felt by the fetus, and possibly the embryo, in the womb. I.38, I.39

Seven pillars *T. E. Lawrence,* SEVEN PILLARS OF WISDOM. II.10

Seventh Division The gun barrels of their artillery were worn through constant firing without replacement. II.19

sex 'all sex'. At the present phase in which 'psycho-analysis' is part of a vogue, though possibly the 'fashion' is declining, the

splitting and articulate speech. III.11

spoils of war. Primitively, sexual freedom was regarded as the reward for victory; quoted by *Rosemary* as one of the primitive rewards of power, financial or social. II.15

Sport 'a Good Sport', an expression used of athletes; also used to parody the facile optimism of some Christian attitudes to troops at war. It did much to bring all religion into contempt. II.5

spy The suspicion of psycho-analysis, attributed to *Roland,* is in fact easily evoked no matter how 'officially' it may be recognized. Like any other human activity, it can be put to malevolent, as well as benevolent, use. In practice it would seem that there is no satisfactory aim other than demonstration of what is true. This can be obscured by an analyst wanting to be 'helpful'. II.14

spying usually used to express an evil branch of curiosity. In real life investigation is indistinguishable from the purpose for which it is carried out. II.8

'square one' term borrowed from games in which a checkered board is used to describe the starting point, e.g. snakes and ladders. I.44

stammer provoked by shock at reaction to death. I.22

standards impressions of the human being may be difficult or impossible to validate. II.9

starvation both literally and metaphorically conducive to seduction. II.16

stegosaurus heavily armoured dinosaur. I.18, I.32
the saurians as a stage in animal development. I.14

Sterne, Laurence his method of verbal communication; ref. SENTIMENTAL JOURNEY [*see* **concrescence**]. I.14

stickler one who is a pedant. In psycho-analysis the pedantic use of a word emphasizes its grammatical importance to the exclusion of its essence. II.16

stockings, black at one time almost a uniform of the 'inferiors'. II.7

Stokes a South African in the days when it was still possible for such a man to fight against oppression. II.6

stone and stick; inanimate objects used by the animate. I.29

stops and dashes space-fillers, substitutes for true thought or action. I.7

T

tangent measurements of, dependent on the pictorial image of a triangle. II.1

tarpaulin jump into; a reference to a 'funny' story. I.15

tea and cooling off, in contrast to an emotionally powerful evocative reminiscence. II.1

tears of fear and rage. I.3

teeth somatic and metaphorical. I.14

telescope [*see* **microscope**]. I.13

telescope, radio as an auxiliary to the senses. I.30

television an apparatus for facilitating long-range scrutiny. I.24

Tenochtitlan ancient city of Mexico, now Mexico City. *Priest* makes a sarcastic reference to the triumphs of modern science. II.8

Teotihuacan the site of the Aztec pyramids. II.4

terror of combatant individual [*see* **groups, panic, thalamus**]. I.24

Thaïs Athenian courtesan, 4th century BC, said to have been the mistress of *Alexander the Great* and later the mistress of the king of Egypt. I.8, I.17

Thalamus used for any proto-types of thought. I.14

thalamus anatomically close to the optic chiasma and in this book supposed to have a psycho-analytic counterpart in 'feelings' [*see* **phrenes**]. I.37

There are some forms of terror which can be observed in psycho-analysis which have their origin in the developing thalamus and its 'non-myelinated nervous connections'. This, of course, is an 'imaginative conjecture' which may take years to confirm scientifically. It is likely to be denied by those who claim that the infant or embryo cannot display primordial mental symptoms on the grounds that myelinated nervous tissue does not exist in these early embryological states [*see* **adrenals, theorizing**]. I.42

theocratic society [*see* **democratic society**]. II.2

theorizing an attempt to evolve 'scientific' knowledge. In the practice of psycho-analysis the analyst has to pass through an experience of 'rational conjecture' and 'imaginative conjecture' before he can reach a point where he is able to formulate a 'theory' of what is taking place. All these stages are vulnerable to 'scientific' assessment. The whole discussion between *Myself, Bion* and *Sherlock Holmes* is an 'imaginative conjecture'. I.42

Tiger 'Tyger! Tyger! burning bright . . .', *William Blake,* SONGS OF EXPERIENCE. III.2

Time, the [*see* **watch**]. II.19

Time! a call used in English public houses to indicate the closure of the premises. II.19

time concept of, as a means of 'measuring' the otherwise immeasurable 'space'. I.16

the passage of, as affecting all expressions of human thought. II.3

the passage of, necessary condition for the confirmation or refutation of a hypothesis. I.38

times, ordinary contrasted with 'novel experiences'. II.17

timidity and fear of discovery; courage is required for the initiation of a train of thought. II.3

Tom and impotent, violent and unloving sexuality. I.17

tomb robber and the death pit at Ur. I.8

tomb robbers and archaeologists. I.27, I.28

Tonks This conversation took place between the two artists, *Tonks* and *Sargent.* I.33

tool depending on the function of the user. I.14

invisible, embryo as. I.10

said of a traitor who can betray either enemy or friend, or both. II.14

tools and tool-making. I.9

topless towers *Christopher Marlowe,* FAUSTUS. I.8

tower of Babel, as a symbol of confusion, OLD TESTAMENT, GENESIS XI. I.8, I.26

trail 'There's a long, long trail awinding . . .'; a song popular with the British Army in World War I. II.6

training It is a commonplace that loving parents like to have their children correctly trained. Since we cannot foretell the future we do not know for what we need to be trained, or for what to train the child. We, therefore, fall back on memories of the past and assumptions about the future. Memory and desire can be seductively useful and as misleading as seductions are. II.7

traitor one who does not conform or subscribe to the prevailing culture. II.7

transference *Freud's* term borrowed to stress transience. II.2

transformation as one process of development. I.20

U

V

W

watch and pray: a reference to religious and scientific activities combined. II.19

mechanism regarded as an inadequate aid to measuring the dimension of time. II.19

water sheets of, as reflective fluid. III.6

drawn by *Leonardo da Vinci,* equated with turbulence. I.11

Watson character in *Sherlock Holmes* stories by *Conan Doyle*; superior in commonsense action, logically inferior. I.20

wave theory contrasted with quanta. I.28

way out expression used by *Roland* to indicate deterioration. II.16

wealth ordinarily supposed to be measured in monetary terms, but often used where no such scale exists. The scale, whether cowrie shells or gold coins, is misleading. I.37

wedding marking the start of a deteriorating relationship. I.22

'Weep for Adonis' *Shelley,* ADONAIS. The model for this poem was LAMENT FOR ADONIS, attributed to *Bion,* Greek bucolic poet, circa second century BC. III.8

'Weep you no more, sad fountains' sixteenth century, anonymous; set to music by *John Dowland.* III.9

Wembley the sports ground on which the Final of the Association Football Cup is played in England. I.22, I.23, I.27

West Front a reference to the idle use of heavy artillery. II.6

'What hours, O what black hours . . .' *Gerard Manley Hopkins,* POEM 67 (4th edition, Oxford University Press). III.7

'what's Dunton' punning reference to *Theodore Watts-Dunton,* poet and critic, benefactor to *Swinburne.* I.29

wheels of God distorted version of 'Though the mills of God grind slowly, yet they grind exceeding small', from the SINNGEDICHTE of *Friedrich von Logau,* translated by *Longfellow* under the title, RETRIBUTION. I.17

whirlwind God answering *Job.* I.28

White Queen *Lewis Carroll,* ALICE IN WONDERLAND. I.21

whoore dialectical pronunciation of 'whore'. II.19

whore commercial love. I.5

quotation of a remark heard at Plymouth. I.17

why a fundamental question; perhaps one of the earliest, after 'what?', of which the personality is aware. II.16

Why-bro a reminiscence of schooldays and a punning reference to curiosity and its inhibition. I.11

X

Y

Z

. . . ATQUE VALE

W *Are you there?*

F *Don't interrupt me—I'm trying to finish this index.*

W *I wondered what you had been doing these last few months.*

F *Well, since you went off on an extended trip I thought I'd better have a go at completing the job we started so long ago.*

W *We were aiming high, weren't we? An index, glossary, notes, a book in itself, the definitive volume that would illuminate the obscurities—*

F *I only hope it can stand up to scrutiny in its final form. By the way, I'm going to call it 'A Key'.*

W *What is it supposed to open?*

F *A few small chinks perhaps. Anyway, it's refreshingly short. Have you any suggestions?*

W *How about 'The Long Week-end'?*

F *Have you forgotten? That's supposed to be the title of your autobiography.*

W *More words, words, words—how do you stand it? Excuse me, I must get back to my cubby-hole.*

F *Sweet dreams.*

For Product Safety Concerns and Information please contact our EU representative GPSR@taylorandfrancis.com
Taylor & Francis Verlag GmbH, Kaufingerstraße 24, 80331 München, Germany

www.ingramcontent.com/pod-product-compliance
Lightning Source LLC
LaVergne TN
LVHW021001300926
849160LV00007B/217
9780946439799